Relations, Locations, Positions

Relations, Locations, Positions

Composition Theory for Writing Teachers

Edited by

PETER VANDENBERG
DePaul University

SUE HUM
University of Texas at San Antonio

JENNIFER CLARY-LEMON
Arizona State University

National Council of Teachers of English
1111 W. Kenyon Road, Urbana, Illinois 61801-1096

Manuscript Editor: Lisa McAvoy
Staff Editor: Bonny Graham
Interior Design: Jenny Jensen Greenleaf
Cover Design: Frank P. Cucciarre, Blink Concept & Design, Inc.

NCTE Stock Number: 24003

It is the policy of NCTE in its journals and other publications to provide a forum for the open discussion of ideas concerning the content and the teaching of English and the language arts. Publicity accorded to any particular point of view does not imply endorsement by the Executive Committee, the Board of Directors, or the membership at large, except in announcements of policy, where such endorsement is clearly specified.

Every effort has been made to provide current URLs and e-mail addresses, but because of the rapidly changing nature of the Web, some sites and addresses may no longer be accessible.

Library of Congress Cataloging-in-Publication Data

Relations, locations, positions : composition theory for writing teachers / edited by Peter Vandenberg, Sue Hum, Jennifer Clary-Lemon.
p. cm.
Includes bibliographical references and index.
ISBN 0-8141-2400-3 (pbk.)
1. English language—Rhetoric—Study and teaching (Higher) 2. Report writing—Study and teaching (Higher) 3. English language—Rhetoric—Study and teaching—Social aspects. I. Vandenberg, Peter. II. Hum, Sue. III. Clary-Lemon, Jennifer.
PE1404.R387 2006
808'.0420711—dc22
2005034174

For R. M., Pauline, and Karen

For Kim Choy, Poh Sim, Carl, and Stefanos

For Chris

Permission Acknowledgments

"What Is Literacy?" by James Paul Gee. Originally published in *Teaching and Learning* 2 (1987), pp. 3–11. Reprinted with permission of the author.

"The Ideology of Literacy: A Bakhtinian Perspective" by Charles Schuster. Reprinted by permission of the Modern Language Association of America from *The Right to Literacy*, edited by Andrea A. Lunsford, Helene Moglen, and James Slevin. Copyright © 1990 by MLA.

"What's 'New' in New Literacy Studies? Critical Approaches to Literacy in Theory and Practice" by Brian Street. From *Current Issues in Comparative Education* 5.2 (2003). May 12, 2003. http://www.tc.columbia.edu/cice/articles/bs152.htm. Reprinted with permission.

"The Intellectual Work of 'Mixed' Forms of Academic Discourses" by Patricia Bizzell. Reprinted by permission from *Alt/Dis: Alternative Discourses and the Academy* edited by Christopher Schroeder, Helen Fox, and Patricia Bizzell. Copyright © 2002 by Boynton/Cook Publishers, Inc. Published by Boynton/Cook Publishers, Inc., a division of Reed Elsevier, Inc., Portsmouth, NH. All rights reserved.

"Generalizing about Genre: New Conceptions of an Old Concept" by Amy J. Devitt. From *College Composition and Communication* 44 (1993), pp. 573–86. Copyright © 1993 by the National Council of Teachers of English. Reprinted with the permission of NCTE.

"Sites of Invention: Genre and the Enactment of First-Year Writing" by Anis Bawarshi. Originally published as Chapter 5 of *Genre and the Invention of the Writer: Reconsidering the Place of Invention in Composition*. Copyright © 2003. Utah State University Press. Reprinted by permission.

"Genre and Identity: Individuals, Institutions, and Ideology" by Anthony Paré. From *The Rhetoric and Ideology of Genre* edited by Richard Coe, Lorelei Lingard, and Tatiana Teslenko. Copyright © 2002 by Hampton Press. Used by permission of Hampton Press.

"The Ecology of Writing" by Marilyn M. Cooper. From *College English* 48 (1986), pp. 364–75. Copyright © 1986 by the National Council of Teachers of English. Reprinted with the permission of NCTE.

"Location, Location, Location: The 'Real' (E)states of Being, Writing, and Thinking in Composition" by Johnathon Mauk. From *College English* 65.4 (2003), pp. 368–88. Copyright © 2003 by the National Council of Teachers of English. Reprinted with the permission of NCTE.

"Composition's Imagined Geographies: The Politics of Space in the Frontier, City, and Cyberspace" by Nedra Reynolds. From *College Composition and Communication* 50 (1998), pp. 12–35. Copyright © 1998 by the National Council of Teachers of English. Reprinted with the permission of NCTE.

"Breaking Ground in Ecocomposition: Exploring Relationships between Discourse and Environment" by Sidney I. Dobrin and Christian R. Weisser. From *College English* 64.5 (2002), pp. 566–89. Copyright © 2002 by the National Council of Teachers of English. Reprinted with the permission of NCTE.

"Constructing Disciplinary Space: The Borders, Boundaries, and Zones of English" by Daniel Mahala and Jody Swilky. From *JAC* 23.4 (2003), pp. 765–97. Reprinted with permission.

"Bodysigns: A Biorhetoric for Change" by Kristie Fleckenstein. From *JAC* 21 (2002), pp. 761–90. Reprinted and excerpted with permission.

"The Subject Is Discourse" by John Clifford. Reprinted by permission of the Modern Language Association of America from *Contending with Words: Composition and Rhetoric in a Postmodern Age*. Copyright © 1991 by MLA.

"Class Dismissed" by Mary Soliday. From *College English* 61.6 (1999), pp. 731–41. Copyright © 1999 by the National Council of Teachers of English. Reprinted with the permission of NCTE.

"History in the Spaces Left: African American Presence and Narratives of Composition Studies" by Jacqueline Jones Royster and Jean C. Williams. From *College Composition and Communication* 50.4 (1999), pp. 563–84. Copyright © 1999 by the National Council of Teachers of English. Reprinted with the permission of NCTE.

"Articulating Authentic Chineseness: The Politics of Reading Race and Ethnicity Aesthetically" by Sue Hum. From *Readerly/Writerly Texts*

9.1-2 (Spring/Summer & Fall/Winter 2001), pp. 61–82. Reprinted with permission.

"Local Pedagogies and Race: Interrogating White Safety in the Rural College Classroom" by Amy E. Winans. From *College English* 67.3 (2005), pp. 253–73. Copyright © 2005 by the National Council of Teachers of English. Reprinted with the permission of NCTE.

"Becoming Visible: Lessons in Disability" by Brenda Jo Brueggemann, Linda Feldmeier White, Patricia A. Dunn, Barbara A. Heifferon, and Johnson Cheu. From *College Composition and Communication* 52.3 (2001), pp. 368–98. Copyright © 2001 by the National Council of Teachers of English. Reprinted with the permission of NCTE.

"Taming Multiculturalism: The Will to Literacy in Composition Studies" by Peter Vandenberg. From *JAC* 19.4 (1999), pp. 547–68. Reprinted with permission.

Contents

ACKNOWLEDGMENTS

The coeditors are indebted to the wonderful team at NCTE whose care and support made this project possible. We especially thank Kurt Austin, who recognized potential in our proposal and helped us turn it into a book through consistent, generous guidance. To Bonny Graham, our expert production editor, whose patience and goodwill are endless, and to our copyeditor, Lisa McAvoy, we are very grateful.

Sue Hum wishes to acknowledge the support of Dean Dan Gelo of the College of Liberal and Fine Arts at the University of Texas at San Antonio; Bernadette Andrea, Chair of the Department of English, Classics and Philosophy; Rebecca Smith, her research assistant; and Kristie Fleckenstein and Carlos Salinas, her colleagues.

Critical Introduction

PETER VANDENBERG, SUE HUM, AND JENNIFER CLARY-LEMON

When we teach composition," Donald Murray wrote in 1972, "we are not teaching a product, we are teaching a process" (11). Murray's use of the first-person pronoun in 1972 may have been more wishful thinking than fact, but now, well into the first decade of the twenty-first century, few would argue with Murray's declaration. The bestselling composition textbooks, rhetorics, readers, and handbooks all reflect what Maxine Hairston, in 1982, declared a "paradigm shift" in writing about and teaching college writing—a change in focus from product to circumstances of production. The editors of the book you are holding assume that most individuals who are now preparing to teach college writing at all levels have some experience with writing-as-process. Perhaps in your own experience as a student you engaged self-consciously in prewriting exercises, traded early drafts of writing assignments with classmates, revised your writing after a conference with a teacher, and came to think of "editing" as a writing task separate from "composing." Indeed, some students who have learned to write in the past thirty years may well think of "process" as it is described in one well-known anthology of composition theory—as "the given" in discussions about the teaching of writing (Villanueva 1).

Without question, the *process movement*, which gained prominence when composition researchers began asking what writers actually do *as* they write, is responsible for constructing around the teaching of writing a vigorous and expansive academic discipline. Informed by, or consistent with, classical rhetoric's canons of invention, arrangement, and style, process-based composition teaching is largely responsible for the rediscovery of rhetoric as an intellectual pursuit within English departments. In their landmark 1970 book, *Rhetoric: Discovery and Change*, Richard E. Young, Alton Becker, and Kenneth Pike fuse rhetoric and process together in the activity of the writer: "[T]he discipline of rhetoric is primarily concerned with the control of a process. Mastering rhetoric means not only mastering a theory of how and why one communicates, but mastering the process of communication as well" (9). The rewards of the process movement, for both teaching and research in composing, as Gary A. Olson has acknowledged, have been many: "It emphasized that the activities involved in the act of writing are typically recursive rather than linear; that writing is first and foremost a social activity; that the act of writing can be a means of learning and discovery" (7).

While "process" has dominated the scholarship of composition studies for some three decades, what it can or should mean for writing research and pedagogy has been under critique for nearly as long. In the early to mid-1980s, process-based writing pedagogies began facing persistent criticism for staying "too close to the text" (Odell qtd. in Reither 142). More than twenty years ago, James Reither pointed to a "tendency in composition studies to think of writing as a process which begins with an impulse to put words on paper," a tendency that leads Reither to wonder if "our thinking is not severely limited by a concept of process that explains only the cognitive processes that occur as people write" (622). It is significant that some of the process movement's most influential proponents have been instrumental in this criticism. Already in 1982, Janet Emig, author of the groundbreaking book, *Composing Processes of Twelfth Graders*, called into question the theory and methodology of early process research. In retrospect, it is apparent that the empirical methodology of early process researchers—the effort to "control variables," approximate laboratory conditions, and pursue "objectivity" and the replication of results—tended to occlude crucial elements of context. Sondra Perl, who published the influential process-based essay "Understanding Composing" (1980), is the editor of *Landmark Essays: On Writing Process*; she points out in the introduction, "Writing Process: A Shining Moment," that by the late 1980s "the scene of writing is more often understood not as a room in which a writer is isolated and alone, but as a room in which many voices reside, those that both shape the writer and to which he or she responds in return" (xvi).

This attention to writer-in-context, often referred to as composition's "social turn," inflected composition scholarship with questions about the nature of knowledge (Bizzell; Bruffee), the relationship of writing to communal interaction (Bartholomae; Nystrand), and the larger societal functions of writing instruction, including its potential to assimilate students into unacknowledged relations of unequal power (Berlin; Trimbur). Although much of this research emerged as part of an uncamouflaged frontal attack on the scientistic assumptions driving early writing-process experiments (Connors, Afterword), there remained a good deal of apparent congruence between writing-process *pedagogies* and the idea that knowledge is socially constructed. A commitment to the notion that writing is always the product of a dialogue with self and others—a process—came to animate a particular conception of writing process; the "social turn" seemed to underscore the value of prewriting, drafting, and revising by encouraging students to do these activities together.

In practice, however, there is no necessary connection between a social view of knowledge and a collaborative pedagogy. By 1990, Richard Fulkerson was encouraged to declare that a "full theory of composition" necessitated a conscious awareness that a teacher's goals (axiology), belief in the nature of knowledge (epistemology), classroom practice (pedagogy), and sense of what students ought to do to achieve the teacher's ends (procedure) must be understood as distinct formulations so as to ensure their unity. A given teacher may encourage students to engage with each other in a collaborative, seemingly process-driven pedagogy; the teacher might do so, however, in the most formulaic of fashions, driven not by a belief in the social construction of knowledge, but by a desire that students assimilate each other to a rigid demand for surface correctness. When such a teacher declares that "process works," nearly everything remains to be explained about what is happening in his or her classroom. As one of the reviewers for this book astutely notes, "[w]hen scholars object to 'process,' they are usually objecting to . . . empirical research, expressive individualism, unstated assumptions of a universalized writing subject, or universalized standards for academic writing." Fulkerson's important article demonstrates that the critique of writing as a process had reached a level of disciplinary maturity in composition's published scholarship more than fifteen years ago.

More recently, the sort of research that continues to address the complexity and multiplicity that Fulkerson and our reviewer speak to has begun to coalesce under the rubric *postprocess*. The term is shot through with controversy, and as Lee-Ann Kastman Breuch points out, its prominence is unfortunate in that "the broader implications of postprocess theory have very little to do with process" (120). Breuch seems to use the term *process* here to refer to the now common recognition that any text is, in its final form, the product of physical activity and cognitive processes in which a reader recursively engages. This point can be taken as axiomatic in postprocess theory. Like most postprocess theorists we know, we see nothing dangerous or troublesome about a process pedagogy per se. We expect that your education as a composition teacher-scholar will include explicit consideration of the process movement and how theories of process may inform the teaching of writing. Indeed, you will encounter references to writing processes throughout this book. We hope you will come to see *postprocess* not as a term that signals a flashpoint between opposed scholarly camps, but rather as a sign of a healthy, evolving disciplinary discourse—one that is increasingly responsive to the world of symbolic representation it hopes to explain and influence. We have no interest in rejecting or overturning process pedagogy, but in continuing the inquiry *beyond process*, an effort that was in motion within composition well before most of our undergraduate students were learning to write.

Beyond Process

"The ways in which writing gets produced," Joseph Petraglia writes, "are characterized by an almost impenetrable web of cultural practices, social interactions, power differentials, and discursive conventions governing the production of text" (54). Petraglia, like other contributors to Thomas Kent's influential collection *Post-Process Theory: Beyond the Writing Process Paradigm*, speaks to the multiple, overlapping layers of context that constitute scenes of writing. The most obvious commonality among scenes of writing may be, most significantly, difference. Any theory of writing—whether grounded in matters of surface correctness or prewriting, drafting, and revision—can be limiting if it is "justified as a distillation of the practices in which all 'good' writers engage" (Pullman 23) and then "reduced to rote repetition or pedantry" (Couture 30). We believe, as does Breuch, that more focused attention to contexts in which individuals' writing processes function might reveal "philosophical principles" capable of guiding teaching practice in increasingly complex times.

Peter Vandenberg's essay "Taming Multiculturalism" (included in this volume) demonstrates that when a writing pedagogy is yoked to a universalized, amorphous conception of "good writing," matters of context are subordinated to procedures designed to ensure conformity to that conception of "good writing." The risks are at least twofold; such a pedagogy (1) promotes a universal response to infinitely disparate rhetorical circumstances, allowing students to infer that a standard procedure should yield uniformly positive results independent of an immediate context or the expectations of readers in a given context; and (2) can erase a broad range of differences that students bring to the writing classroom, diminishing alternative ways of thinking, acting, and communicating in the world.

Given the changing realities of the writing classroom, this second risk is particularly troubling. James A. Banks shows that the use of two "infusion" approaches—developed in response to increasing diversity—tends to highlight diversity even as these approaches erase or assimilate differences (30). Using a "contributions" approach, teachers "colorize" their syllabi with texts written by minority writers and consider the influence of minority-culture elements such as heroes, rituals, beliefs, celebrations, food, and "costumes." All the while, these cultural differences are located in or limited by their "native" environments, remaining on the margins even as they contribute to mainstream culture. Similarly, the "additive" approach assimilates issues of diversity into the existing educational framework by simply appending multicultural concepts, themes, and perspectives while maintaining the current (and, some might argue, discriminatory) curricular structure. Thus, while process pedagogies seem amenable to explorations of difference, they routinely homogenize these inclusions under the universalized rubric of "good writing."

If we are to do more than promote one set of discursive practices as *the* way to write or one procedure as *the* writing process, we must continue to open ourselves—and open our undergraduate students—to the rich implications of context. The need for writing pedagogies that resist a monolithic conception of "good writing" and respond to wide differences may seem largely academic, the province of *theory*. But those of you who are preparing today to teach writing will work in classrooms very different than those of the 1970s, when process theory emerged. Projections of striking demographic change in college enrollments suggest the need for a more robust, democratic, and inclusive model of literacy instruction.

Contemporary composition scholars appear to anticipate recent college enrollment projections when they advocate pedagogies that range beyond the individual writer's procedures or a one-size-fits-all definition of "good writing." Indeed, the National Center for Education Statistics reports an increase in minority-student college enrollments and an estimated 20 percent share for minorities earning Bachelor of Arts degrees in recent years, thus making the student population in college composition classrooms increasingly diverse ("Condition"). Border states such as California, Texas, and New York—because of their disproportionate share of immigrants from around the world—have seen the most significant racial and ethnic change in college classrooms. Yet even states that are perceived to be more demographically homogeneous have experienced a steady evolution. Already in 1999, Connecticut's Department of Higher Education reported a 3.2 percent growth in minority enrollment, the fifteenth consecutive year of such growth ("Connecticut"). And teaching writing will become only more complicated as student populations become more heterogeneous. In "Economics, Demography, and the Future of Higher Education Policy," a report commissioned by the Educational Testing Service (ETS),

Anthony Carnevale and Richard Fry project that college-age racial and ethnic minorities will increase by 40 percent in the United States over the next dozen years; by 2016, college enrollments will increase by 2.6 million, and minority students will make up 80 percent of this increase ("Boom"). Some states that already teach the largest contingent of college students will experience the most significant change. A San Diego–area newspaper assessing the import of the ETS study for California finds parallels with Texas, where "[b]y 2020, whites will also be a minority in colleges and universities" (Contreras). As student populations are increasingly characterized by variety and difference, pedagogies that avoid attention to context become increasingly less relevant.

The process movement has been powerfully important to the teaching of college writing, yet we will have to continue building on the earliest critiques of the process movement by considering *process* in relation to *context*. To move "beyond process" is not to denigrate or replace the value of process theory, but to promote the idea that *writing* stands for a radically complex network of phenomena: no single unifying theory can provide teachers of writing with all they need to know; no generalized process can prepare students for the manifold writing contexts they will go on to occupy.

Twenty years ago, composition scholars could presume a dominant consensual belief that preparing students to meet the demands of college writing should be our primary concern (Bartholomae). Today, no such consensus exists (Fulkerson, "Summary"). Rhetoric and composition has expanded well beyond the focus of the first-year writing class to embrace Writing Across the Curriculum, professional writing, and even major programs in writing (Corbett; Connors, Afterword). Increasingly, those who speak at national conferences and write for professional journals and essay collections are more likely to advance pedagogies grounded in an "understanding of how diverse reading, writing, and discourse activities function in disparate temporal, spatial, social, cultural, political, economic, racial, sexual, and gendered contexts" (Goggin 185).

Engaging Context

"Collecting" scholarship that reflects an enterprise as expansive and diverse as the one Goggin describes is a project fraught with pitfalls. First, we cannot hope to provide enough essays here to capture the richness and complexity of theoretical positions that extend beyond writers' processes. Composition studies is an interdisciplinary formation that draws on and informs scholarship across the university; we recognize that the introduction to composition theory that this book constructs will present a limited view on that expansiveness. While we might like to hand you a larger book, we could never hope to give you one that would settle all debates. Our choices will inevitably imply a rationale of selection and division; however, we want you to see this sorting process—and the naming of categories bound up with it—to reflect what it means to engage with a theoretical, scholarly discourse. As I. A. Richards explains in *How to Read a Page*, those words that are relied upon most to make meaning in crucial circumstances are typically characterized by a "'systematic ambiguity,' the capability to 'say very different, sometimes even contradictory, things to different readers.' Such words, Richards declared, 'are the servants of too many interests to keep to single, clearly defined jobs'" (qtd. in Heilker and Vandenberg 2). Such is the case with the terms we use to demarcate the three sections of this book—**relations, locations,** and **positions.**

An effective encounter with this book will lead not to a rigid internalization of the categories we establish here, or the terms we use to define them. Rather, such constructions are formed and reformed through the discussions that scholars have about them, and we expect that questioning the value and limitations of our inevitably artificial boundaries and contingent vocabulary will be part of how this book will be used. We hope that you will see **relations, locations,** and **positions** not as a set of containers for static concepts, but rather as evidence of three convictions, each of which we see as central to meeting the changing demands of teaching college writing.

- Writing occurs through conversations and negotiations with others (**relations**).

- Writing is shaped by material places and intellectual spaces (**locations**).
- Writing reflects the contingency of our beliefs and values, and in so doing composes identity (**positions**).

Collectively, these convictions imply that how composition theory can or should influence instruction may be determined only in specific material circumstances. We hope you will find that a sustained encounter with the varied claims that emerge from these three convictions—which we elaborate below—will help prepare you to weigh alternatives in the particular conditions you go on to find yourself.

Theories of Relation

"I am writing a book which will be read by thousands," Walter Ong writes, feigning impatience with a disruptive visitor, "So please, get out of the room!" (16). Ong's imagined dialogue is meant to highlight the apparent irony of text production—that to *commune* with others through writing demands isolation from them—while asserting the importance of audience in the composing process. Ong's essay has been cited often as a reflection of composition studies' concerns with the needs and function of readers, yet Ong simply heightens the irony by going on to declare the audience "a fiction," an *imagined construct* to which a writer's self-motivated intentions should consistently and systematically appeal.

Ong's goals are no doubt more complex than our retelling of this anecdote reveals, but a commonsensical interpretation is hard to resist, given the dominant view of authorship in which we are steeped. That writing should be understood as an expression of individuality is one of the more durable claims even in composition scholarship. This orientation, no doubt, has a great deal to do with composition's historical origins in departments of English, where the cult of solitary literary genius is often nurtured; however, by no means did it arise there. We need look no further than the concept of intellectual property rights to see the extent to which the broader culture understands literate practice as a privatized activity; the supposition that writing is an intimate, self-possessed enterprise is reinforced by law! The need to shut others out in order to write seems, if nothing else, to confirm the writer as an autonomous agent, and writing as the revelation of introspection and personal intention.

Few would argue that writing comes from writers, but to what extent can writing be labeled a private activity? Theorists interested in carrying writing instruction "beyond process"—those represented throughout *Relations, Locations, Positions*—suggest that composition pedagogies focused on the writer tend to mask or oversimplify the act of composing. Instead, they argue, the individual writer and his or her intentions are already interconnected with other writers, readers, and social institutions in a complex web of *relations. By "theories of relation," we refer to explanations of how reading and writing practices, and the knowledge they produce, both structure and are structured by social interaction.* Theories of relation, taken up in composition studies and presented in this book under the rubrics *literacy, discourse, discourse community,* and *genre*, share a number of broad, interrelated presuppositions:

1. *Writing, like all language practices, is an invariably social activity.* An individual's vocabulary, style, and voice are all themselves an outcome of prior language use. While no one would deny the significance of the individual as a point of synthesis and composition—and the exhaustive range of variation possible—the "raw material" with which any writer works is never generated autonomously.
2. *Writing, like all language practices, is ideological.* It is unavoidably bound up implicitly or explicitly with the advancement of certain values and beliefs and the denunciation of others; writing is therefore an instrument of power.
3. *Writing is constitutive.* It is inextricably interrelated with the creation, organization, and continuing development of contemporary Western society, as well as the formation and evolution of individual identity.

Theories of relation foreground the functions of writing in sustaining, altering, or organizing social action, and in so doing account for the ways in which individuals are connected through literate practices. Because such interaction can be understood as a continual exchange of value claims, theories of relation remain attentive to the ways in which power is conserved, shared, and appropriated through writing and how such exchanges affect individuals. Writing pedagogies influenced by such theories propose that students are best prepared to write in college and beyond when they are encouraged to develop a self-conscious awareness of the complexity of writing and the interrelationships that make individual agency possible. This preparation, then, must surely include an emphasis on the social, cultural, and communal nature of writing.

Generalizations such as these can seem both eminently sensible and disturbingly cloudy; however, as the readings in the Relations section will demonstrate, theories of literacy, discourse, and genre become concrete when analyzed in specific, material-conceptual circumstances. And so a final presupposition of theories of relation is that social, constitutive, value-laden discourse is always *situated activity*—a manifestation of localized circumstances. The importance of location, and the attention to critical and material differences in particular writing contexts, is the focus of this book's second section.

Theories of Location

While theories of relation make clear that writers are always connected within a social matrix of readers and other writers, theories of location remind us that acts of writing are inevitably "situated," that one always writes from some place. "Writers are never nowhere," as Thomas Kent has written (*Post-Process Theory* 3). The perspectives from which writers respond to rhetorical exigencies or filter newly encountered experiences and ideas are considered in composition scholarship as both concrete, material sites and imagined, conceptual spaces. In all cases, theories of location are grounded in the belief that a sense of place or scene is crucial to understanding rhetorical contexts. Such thinking also helps foreground awareness of the possibilities and limitations created by location, how social control or power is "structured" by the design and maintenance of public and institutional space, and how sometimes unequal differences among social actors are naturalized or held "in place." *Responsible discourse, theorists of location argue, depends on a self-conscious awareness of how one is* ***located.***

The living human body is the standard for theories of location in much composition scholarship. Drawing on feminist poet Adrienne Rich's "Notes toward a Politics of Location," many compositionists see the physical body as *the* place where theory is actualized; one's body defines a point of location relative to others, a sense of *where* from which one can act through language. Reflecting on a scholarly tradition marked by a difference-erasing tendency toward abstraction, Rich argues that "[t]o say 'my body' reduces the temptation to grandiose assertions" (215). Moreover, to begin with the corporeal body encourages one to recognize gender, skin color, age, and the mild or debilitating physical effects of one's labor. Such observations can become an inroad to the recognition of privilege and difference, or the value-laden "station" one occupies while engaging others in language. The body can be seen, then, as a register of life in action, a locus of personal experience as a source of knowledge.

It is "not enough to claim the personal and locate ourselves" in rhetorical action, however; like other postprocess theorists of location, Gesa Kirsch and Joy Ritchie maintain that experience and identity—one's location—must be seen as a reflection of discursive interaction (8). By recognizing that meaning is a product of the social, theories of location *place* the body among other language users and in the physical sites they occupy; this situated relationship can be understood to reflect "the materiality of language" (Bleich). These physical sites, however, are never self-evident. How we demarcate space, define its use, and delimit action within it foregrounds *location* as an inseparable combination of the material and the conceptual.

One influential theory of location that foregrounds this material-conceptual understanding of place emerged from literary studies in the work of Mary Louise Pratt. Arguing against orderly, utopian conceptions of "community" used to describe social interaction, Pratt instead proposed the term *contact zone* to identify "social spaces where cultures meet, clash, and grapple with each other, often in contexts of highly asymmetrical relations of power" (34). By suggesting that a contact zone could be reimagined as a "safehouse," in which connections among participants could be reconstituted in terms of trust, understanding, and protection, Pratt demonstrates the interplay between the conceptual and the material in theories of location. Many composition scholars have drawn on Pratt's ideas to emphasize that in any social situation, differences are always present and power is always being enforced and/or contested; notions of the contact zone in composition scholarship tend to foreground connections between specific pedagogical locations and the exercise of power.

The significance of theorizing location for future teachers of writing and rhetoric is profound. Indeed, rhetorical effectiveness in a given location depends on one's interpretation of and attitude toward place, and much public and institutional discourse is engaged—tacitly or otherwise—in endorsing particular ideas about place and the role individuals should play in it (Mauk). Consider a given teacher's classroom, for example. It is not only the instructor's degree and title that define the division between *teacher* and *student*; the architecture of the room and the arrangement and shape of furniture, all of which are serially reinforced in everyone's experience, help define and sustain the *situated identities*, functions, and expectations of all participants. Location-centered inquiries have led to an understanding of ways in which the traditional classroom actually prohibits effective learning, and theories of location are used to elaborate and justify "real-writing," service-learning, and experiential pedagogies that operate outside the material university and thereby refigure associations among participants.

Theories of location have helped redirect the attention of composition scholars as well. Indeed, when seen as a function of location, scholarly writing itself becomes evident as an "institutional practice" (Kent, "Consequences" 159) or mode of labor rather than a disinterested or universalized search for truth. Seen as a situated material-conceptual practice, modes of research can become evident as unintended mechanisms by which unequal relations of power are unwittingly substantiated (Kirsch and Ritchie). The notion that writing "cannot be separated from place, from environment, from nature, or from location" (Dobrin 13) has spawned an area of study unified around metaphors of ecology. If writing is deeply bound up with space, as ecocomposition proposes, then writing instruction cannot remain limited to formalism, process, or a preferred body of grammatical or mechanical skills. The study of writing might inquire into the mediating influences of an array of material and conceptual spaces.

Theories of location, then, are interdependent with theories of relation; it is in material and conceptual spaces that speakers and writers engage each other for the purpose of making and remaking the world in which we live. But as we act through discourse, as individuals and in unison with others, who is it that our words say we are? And since our ways of seeing, and naming, and promoting change inescapably imply other ways of doing so—all that we have come to call *critical difference*—who is it that our words address? Theories of position engage these questions.

Theories of Position

While we use the term *location* in this book to stand for the interdependence or mutual reciprocity between people *in* the material and conceptual spaces they occupy, we use the term *position* to stand for those markers of identity—such as gender, race, class, ableness, sexual orientation, and so on—that are either physically apparent or culturally constructed at a level so basic that they impact social relations in nearly every context we occupy. *Think of positions, then, as the corporeal and cultural* ***differences*** *we carry with us—or that others believe we carry—as we move within and between locations across the sweep of our daily lives.* These differences critically affect the way we frame our experiences and encounters with others, and the way we are framed by others as we enter new contexts.

Crucial to theories of position is the conviction that the influence or effect of all of these differences, regardless of their origins in biology, is primarily the product of language in action. To be born black or white, male or female, rich or poor, ambulatory or disabled has considerably less impact than how these differences are organized or valued/devalued in cultural practice. In a given cultural formation, the relationship between authority and a particular set of characteristics emerges to define status and privilege, and to mark variation as undesirable. The continued acquisition of limited social goods (money, status, power) by those exhibiting the favored characteristics—and the lack of success by those who do not—begins to rationalize the hierarchy until it is understood to reflect a "natural" order, simply "the way things are." This process is enabled by social institutions—including law, religion, and education—that effectively inscribe these idealized cultural norms onto the consciousness of all those who participate; the favored and unfavored alike are made subjects of the social formation. One's relative status in this socially determined hierarchy begins to position or "mark" one in some ways (consider nutrition or the lack of it) even before birth. As one's identity emerges in language use, the relative access to dominant or "powerful secondary discourses" (Gee 5)—and the capacity to function within them or not—begins to impact how one is positioned in relation to other language users.

The positions we might occupy in relation to others are defined by the relative status of the differences we exhibit. It seems clear that those differences that are most distant from the cultural ideal, and most difficult to overcome or displace in an effort to approximate the ideal, are most influential on positionality. How we are positioned by this process and by other social actors and institutions with which we interrelate can define the range of possibilities and limitations we recognize, and thus establish the position from which we view the world.

Positionality is far from immutable, however, and mass education is the best evidence of that fact. The dominant function of government-sponsored education in any culture, some argue, is to reproduce commitment to a culture's social and economic structure across generations (Carnoy). This can be done by denying access to those who demonstrate substantial difference, or by ensuring that those who exhibit particular differences remain degraded by limiting their potential to access discourses of cultural power. The organization, funding, and oversight of public schools by localized districts—a process that effectively handicaps poor, inner-city schools in the competition for money, equipment, and competent teachers—is one way of accomplishing this. A far more insidious route to the maintenance of cultural authority, however, is to use education to colonize critical differences and, thus, alternative positions through processes of assimilation and acculturation (Hum). The teaching of "academic writing" in particular—through the eradication of emotion (West) and the imposition of standardized norms for grammar, organization, register, citation, etc.—reflects a history of improving writing by radically constraining the variety of acceptable conventions. By linking the acquisition of particular "writing skills" to utility, employability, and success in the dominant culture, alternate ways of creating knowledge, naming the world, and claiming a place in it can be displaced at the outset.

Most prominently, theories of position in composition studies underscore the way conventional writing pedagogies promote a white, middle-class, heterosexual subject position that passes for an "objective" or disinterested standard. Such theories encourage writing teachers to recognize their historical institutional role in suppressing difference through the imposition of one set of discursive norms. By engaging differences and encouraging them to the fore, writing teachers can allow students to explore the ways they have been positioned and perhaps position themselves differently. Students may gain some sense of an expanded potential for writing as their teachers become repositioned as learners in relation to them.

Conclusion

Theories of relation, location, and position remind us that as writers we are never alone, that "writing takes place" (Dobrin), and that all forms of symbolic action reflect a way of knowing the world conditioned by how we are positioned in it. In concert, these theories foreground the overriding significance of context in theorizing and teaching writing, and claim that contexts can be generalized or anticipated only by distorting what it means to compose. They encourage us, as teachers and scholars, to resist the systematic and to recognize that no conception of "good writing" emerges outside an implied or interpreted context.

Exploring relations between composition and the many critical discourses that inform it will no doubt lead you, as it has the authors whose work is included in this book, far afield from the college writing classroom. We feel composition studies is best served by scholarship that pursues questions about writing well beyond conventional academic contexts, and we encourage you, as a prospective scholar, to read your way into new conceptual relations, locations, and positions. We recognize, however, that most of you will have come to this book by way of a university course or program that positions you, in varying degrees, as a prospective teacher, and with your professor we share a responsibility to help you find composition theory relevant.

Toward that end, we have asked some of the best teacher-scholars we know to write short, focused pieces that explain the value of contemporary composition theory to their work with students. These scholars offer ways of seeing the essays in this collection in situ; that is, within the contexts and spaces where theory meets practice—the classroom. We know that for most of you, this "location" will perhaps be in the back of your mind all along; it is our hope that these pieces call it to the fore as you create a sense of praxis, or theorized practice, for the spaces, contexts, and communities that you know best. We call these short texts "pedagogical insights," and we hope they will provoke discussion among you and your colleagues as you explore *Relations, Locations, Positions*.

Works Cited

Banks, James A. *An Introduction to Multicultural Education*. 3rd ed. Boston: Allyn and Bacon, 2002.

Bartholomae, David. "Inventing the University." *Journal of Basic Writing* 5 (1986): 4–23.

Berlin, James A. "Rhetoric and Ideology in the Writing Class." *College English* 50 (1988): 477–94.

Bizzell, Patricia. "Cognition, Convention, and Certainty: What We Need to Know about Writing." *Pre/Text: A Journal of Rhetorical Theory* 3.3 (Fall 1982): 213–43.

Bleich, David. *Know and Tell: A Writing Pedagogy of Disclosure, Genre, and Membership*. Portsmouth: Boynton/Cook, 1998.

"Boom in College Enrollment by Minorities Seen." CNN.com. May 24, 2000. http://www.cnn.com/2000/US/05/24/minority.college.students/.

Breuch, Lee-Ann M. Kastman. "Post-Process 'Pedagogy': A Philosophical Exercise." *JAC: A Journal of Composition Theory* 22 (2002): 119–50.

Bruffee, Kenneth. "Collaborative Learning and the 'Conversation of Mankind.'" *College English* 46 (1984): 635–52.

Carnevale, Anthony P., and Richard A. Fry. "Economics, Demography, and the Future of Higher Education Policy." Educational Testing Service. http://www.nga.org/cda/files/HIGHEREDDEMOECON.pdf.

Carnoy, Martin. *Education as Cultural Imperialism*. New York: Longman, 1974.

"Condition of Education: Racial Differences in the Transition to College, The." National Center for Education Statistics. http://nces.ed.gov/pubs99/condition99/indicator-54.html.

"Connecticut College Students—Younger and More Diverse but Still in Short Supply." Board of Governors for Higher Education, Department of Higher Education, State of Connecticut. http://www.ctdhe.org/info/oldnews/newsShortSupply.htm.

Connors, Robert J. Afterword. *Coming of Age: The Advanced Writing Curriculum*. Ed. Linda K. Shamoon, Rebecca Moore Howard, Sandra Jamieson, and Robert A. Schwegler. Portsmouth: Heinemann-Boynton/Cook, 2000. 143–50.

———. "Composition Studies and Science." *College English* 46 (1983): 1–20.

Contreras, Raoul Lowery. "The Coming White Minority." *North County Times* [San Diego] Aug. 2000. http://www.nctimes.net/news/052700/k.html. 15 January 2004.

Corbett, Edward P. J. "The Usefulness of Classical Rhetoric." *College Composition and Communication* 14.3 (1963): 162–4.

Couture, Barbara. "Modeling and Emulating: Rethinking Agency in the Writing Process." Kent, *Postprocess Theory* 30–48.

Dobrin, Sidney I. "Writing Takes Place." *Ecocomposition*. Ed. Christian R. Weisser and Sidney I. Dobrin. Albany: State University of New York P, 2001. 11–25.

Emig, Janet. "Inquiry Paradigms and Writing." *College Composition and Communication* 33 (1982): 64–75.

———. *The Composing Process of Twelfth Graders*. Urbana: NCTE, 1971.

Fulkerson, Richard. "Composition Theory in the Eighties: Axiological Consensus and Paradigmatic Diversity." *College Composition and Communication* 41 (1990): 409–29.

———. "Summary and Critique: Composition at the Turn of the Twenty-First Century." *College Composition and Communication* 56.4 (June 2005): 654–87.

Gee, James Paul. "What Is Literacy?" *Teaching and Learning* 2 (1987): 3–11.

Goggin, Maureen Daly. *Authoring a Discipline: Scholarly Journals and the Post–World War II Emergence of Rhetoric and Composition*. Mahwah, NJ: Erlbaum, 2000.

Hairston, Maxine. "The Winds of Change: Thomas Kuhn and the Revolution in the Teaching of Writing." *College Composition and Communication* 33 (1982): 76–88.

Heilker, Paul, and Peter Vandenberg. Introduction. *Keywords in Composition Studies*. Portsmouth, NH: Boynton/Cook, Heinemann, 1996. 1–8.

Hum, Sue. "'Yes, We Eat Dog Back Home': Contrasting Disciplinary Discourse and Praxis on Diversity." *JAC: Journal of Advanced Composition* 19.4 (Fall 1999): 367–87.

Kent, Thomas. "The Consequences of Theory for the Practice of Writing." *Publishing in Rhetoric and Composition*. Ed. Gary A. Olson and Todd Taylor. Albany: State University of New York P, 1997. 147–62.

———, ed. *Post-Process Theory: Beyond the Writing-Process Paradigm*. Carbondale: Southern Illinois UP, 1999.

Kirsch, Gesa E., and Joy S. Ritchie. "Beyond the Personal: Theorizing a Politics of Location in Composition Research." *College Composition and Communication* 46.1 (1995): 7–29.

Mauk, Johnathon. "Location, Location, Location: The 'Real' (E)states of Being, Writing, and Thinking in Composition." *College English* 65.4 (2003): 368–88.

Murray, Donald. "Teach Writing as a Process Not Product." *The Leaflet* (Nov. 1972): 11–14.

Nystrand, Martin. *What Writers Know: The Language, Process and Structure of Written Discourse.* New York: Academic, 1982.

Olson, Gary A. "Toward a Post-Process Composition: Abandoning the Rhetoric of Assertion." Kent, *Postprocess Theory* 7–15.

Ong, Walter J., S.J. "The Writer's Audience Is Always a Fiction." *PMLA* 90 (Jan. 1975): 9–21.

Perl, Sondra. "Introduction: A Shining Moment." *Landmark Essays on Writing Process.* Ed. Sondra Perl. Davis, CA: Hermagoras, 1994.

———. "Understanding Composing." *College Composition and Communication* 31 (1980): 363–69.

Petraglia, Joseph. "Is There Life after Process? The Role of Social Scientism in a Changing Discipline." Kent, *Postprocess Theory* 49–64.

Pratt, Mary Louise. "Arts of the Contact Zone." *Profession 91.* New York: MLA, 1991. 33–40.

Pullman, George. "Stepping Once Again into the Same Current." Kent, *Postprocess Theory* 16–29.

Reither, James A. "Writing and Knowing: Toward Redefining the Writing Process." *College English* 47 (1985): 620–28.

Rich, Adrienne. "Notes toward a Politics of Location." *Blood, Bread, and Poetry: Selected Prose 1979–1985.* London: Virago, 1987. 210–32.

Trimbur, John. "Consensus and Difference in Collaborative Learning." *College English* 51 (1989): 602–16.

Vandenberg, Peter. "Taming Multiculturalism: The Will to Literacy in Composition Studies." *JAC: Journal of Advanced Composition* 19.4 (1999): 547–68.

Villanueva, Victor. "The Givens in Our Conversations: The Writing Process." *Cross-Talk in Comp Theory.* 2nd ed. Ed. Victor Villanueva. Urbana: NCTE, 2003. 1–2.

West, Thomas R. *Signs of Struggle: The Rhetorical Politics of Cultural Difference.* Albany: State University of New York P, 2002.

Young, Richard Emmerson, Alton L. Becker, and Kenneth Lee Pike. *Rhetoric: Discovery and Change.* New York: Harcourt, 1970.

I

Theories of Relation

By the early 1970s, theories of process began offering a viable alternative to product-centered pedagogies. Following a model of empirical research provided by the social sciences, compositionists such as Janet Emig, Sondra Perl, and Donald Graves designed studies that focused, they believed, on the cognitive activities of individual writers during the composing process. Near the beginning of perhaps the most influential of such studies, Linda Flower and John Hayes ask, "What guides the decisions writers make as they write?" The answer, it was presupposed, could be found by analyzing "distinctive thinking processes" that a writer uses to develop a chain of goals. Although Flower and Hayes were not completely inattentive to matters of context, their study well represents the relationship between process theory and an overriding attention to the author as self-directed agent; "the most important thing about writing goals," they assert, "is that they are *created* by the writer" (365).

Well before *process* became a touchstone in composition textbooks, however, its grounding assumption, that a "writer's own set of self-made goals guide composing" (Flower and Hayes 288), was under heavy scrutiny in rhetoric and composition journals. By the early 1980s, drawing on work in sociolinguistics, philosophy, literary criticism, and the history of science, "inner-directed" theories of composing were being contested from the position that acts of making meaning are "circumscribed by the systematic relations that obtain in the speech community of the writer" (Nystrand 17). The phrase *discourse community* came to represent composition studies' early attempts to widen the scope of disciplinary concern beyond the individual writer to the mediating role of context.

Once a linguistic term used in formal analysis to designate an organized language unit larger than a sentence, *discourse* has evolved to stand for language use "seen as a form of social practice" (Fairclough 7). A *discourse*, David Bartholomae writes, is a "peculiar way of knowing, selecting, evaluating, reporting, concluding, and arguing" (135); shared language acts bind individuals together as participants in a "socially meaningful group or 'social network'" (Gee 3). More than just a sort of lexical glue, however, *discourse* imbues language with a "constitutive" force; theories of discourse argue that shared language practices are ideological, or infused with communal values that they are organized to sustain and defend, and thereby *constitute* in some sense the individuals and groups who use them, and are used by them, as they speak and act. It is discourse, then, as "language in use" that creates and sustains institutions by organizing the identities and practices of individuals who animate them. To wed *discourse* and *community* together tends to emphasize shared purpose or like-mindedness among a group of language users.

Early expressions of such discourse community theory, however, were dogged by charges of ambiguity, irrelevance, and exclusivity. Critics found something "maddening and vague" about the term *community* (Harris) and decidedly abstract (Killingsworth) or ominous (Vandenberg and Morrow) about the term *discourse*; as Patricia Bizzell wrote in 1991, qualifying her earlier enthusiasm ("Cognition"), *discourse community* can be used to represent "an oppressive affirmation of one—and only one—set of discursive practices" ("Marxist Ideas" 59). And many composition teachers—perhaps both anxious about and proud of the stacks of student-essay drafts called for through process pedagogies—continued to ask, but what does all this have to do with *writing*? What do drafting, revising, and editing have to do with "politics"? These questions have persistently marked a divide between composition's historical interest in the participial form of *writing*, "as an unfolding activity of composing," and the less fettered interest in its noun form, which refers "to the material manifestations and consequences of writing as it circulates in the world" (Trimbur 18). Scholarly inquiry into the nature of *literacy* has been fundamental to a growing interest among composition scholars in theories of relations.

Since the late 1970s, literacy scholars have recognized the "preeminent" relationship between individuals and social groups "in determining both what is read and written and what is necessary to reading and writing" (Szwed 16). Influenced heavily by the work of Brazilian educator Paulo Freire, who argued for using literate activity to overcome the dehumanizing effects of illiteracy as an overtly political project, literacy researchers began asking, whose interests and purposes are served by writing instruction? Such questions have redefined *literacy* as an interactive, interpretive, social phenomenon rather than a static skill possessed or deployed by an individual. For example, in "The Ideology of Literacy" (included in this volume), Charles Schuster equates illiteracy directly with social exclusion—the deprivation of politically significant relations. Similarly, James Paul Gee's "What is Literacy?" (also included in this volume) explicitly defines *literacy* in terms of relations within and across social contexts. In "What's 'New' in New Literacy Studies?" (also included in this volume), Brian Street, extending Gee's definition, goes on to say that literacy is always "contested," and is "always rooted in a particular world-view and in a desire for that view of literacy to dominate and to marginalize others."

Given composition's historical connections to rhetoric, few teachers of writing would argue for a disconnect between the activity of writing and the world surrounding the writer; yet how, precisely, notions of discourse, community, literacy, and power relate to text production has not always been clear. Quite recently, however, composition scholars have turned to an expanded and invigorated notion of an old concept, genre, to connect the activity of writing—what process-movement researchers thought of as cognition—to the broader cultural network in which that activity is suspended. "To write," Anis Bawarshi argues, "is to position oneself within genres—to assume and enact certain situated commitments, identities, relations" (14). Mary Jo Reiff positions herself thusly within a specific genre in her Pedagogical Insight essay in this section, "Moving Writers, Shaping Motives, Motivating Critique and Change: A Genre Approach to Teaching Writing." She reflects on the chosen genre of the Pedagogical Insight essay itself, asserting that "the larger cultural context beyond the immediate situation of this Pedagogical Insight essay also helped to generate and organize my response" (158).

While genre theorists do not propose that genre can account for all we need to know about writing, both Amy J. Devitt in "Generalizing about Genre" and Nancy Myers in "Genre as Janus" (included in this volume) see it as a way to dissolve dichotomies (form/content, product/process, individual/society) that trouble the professional discussion about writing instruction. We typically think of a *genre* as a container of sorts, a category for discursive constructs or *texts* that are identified as similar on the basis of recurring formal, stylistic, or structural characteristics. Derived from the Latin word for "kind" or "class," the term *genre,* the Humanities' equivalent of the sciences' *genus*, reflects the classical impulse to group clusters of objects on the basis of evident, although arbitrarily identified, features. As a biologist collects together the lion, leopard, tiger, and panther and calls them "cat," so the literary critic assembles the sonnet, haiku, epic, and lyric and calls them "poem." Dependent as such definitions are on observable commonalities, naming a text a member of a given genre requires that it be understood as a "bounded object"; in other words, thinking in conventional terms about genre encourages us to focus on those attributes that *distinguish* a "thing" from what surrounds it rather than on how that thing might *relate* to other "things."

New conceptions of *genre* continue to define categories of text on the basis of observable similarities; however, genres become important not for what is apparent about a given textual object, but for the way it operates in its larger context. And operation is key, for a genre is most meaningfully understood for the action it performs. Widely understood as the seminal proponent of contemporary genre theory, Carolyn Miller argues that "a rhetorically sound definition of genre must be centered not on the substance or form of discourse but on the action it is used to accomplish" (151). As expected responses to reoccurring rhetorical situations, genres help to organize and stabilize institutional settings in which writers operate.

The social interactions that take place in such institutions are grounded in generic participation; from this perspective, such institutions can be identified as *genre systems.* As Charles

Bazerman explains, genre systems are characterized by the generic involvement of all involved: "each participant makes a recognizable act or move in some recognizable genre, which then may be followed by a certain range of appropriate generic responses by others" (96–97). When actors in a genre system engage in this activity habitually, the written genres themselves orchestrate their interaction and simultaneously reinforce the genre system. In this way, institutions whose purposes are achieved primarily through symbolic production and interpretation—such as schools, professional workplaces, and governing bodies—are largely defined and sustained by the genres they produce. And so, genre theory maintains, are the actors who populate those settings; it is in part through the processes of learning and reproducing situated genres that "education" and contextual identity (as expert, professional, graduate, authority) emerges (see also Russell 1997).

Like "discourses" or "discourse communities," then, genre systems are implicated in the creation and maintenance of stratified power relations. Individual genres necessarily restrict possibilities, and individuals limited by the genres they are allowed to engage or learn can be cut off from authority within genre systems. If enculturation within a genre system turns ways of writing into ways of looking, one's degraded place in relations of power can seem fixed, natural, and even necessary. It is crucial, then, that an ethical theory of genre include a method of analysis that foregrounds an analysis of the function of genre in normalizing oppression and creating control (see Paré in this volume). To avoid simply preparing students for the tacit acceptance of their places within genre systems that they go on to occupy, writing teachers must be able to think of genres also as potential sites of resistance and transformation. In "Sites of Invention: Genre and the Enactment of First-Year Writing" (included in this volume), Anis Bawarshi proposes that individuals carry with them into new situations an "alpha-genre," or "genre identity"—a subject position (see this book's last section) defined elsewhere that can help disrupt the ideological intentions of newly encountered genre systems. While more abstract theories of discourse, discourse community, and even literacy all foreground the dialectical relationship between individual, language, ideology, and social context, genre theory clarifies the role that the activity of writing plays in these relations. It is, therefore, a fertile area of inquiry for those motivated to pursue what it means to write well, beyond answers grounded in form and private introspection.

Embracing the most durable of warrants for writing instruction, teachers who subscribe to theories of relation want their students to succeed in the rhetorical situations they go on to inhabit. They are not convinced, however, that a knowledge of grammar, a context-free conception of "good writing," or the development of a "personal style" is appropriate to that goal. Theories of relation project a pedagogical commitment to writing as a social activity, and state that writing well demands a conception of one's role as a writer in relation to readers, other writers, and the operations of social formations in which they interact. Effective participation, however, is a limited goal if, as theories of relations propose, writers' identities, values, and possibilities for agency are bound up in such relations; students must also develop a self-conscious, critical awareness of how they are suspended in systems of relations so that they might engage in the ongoing process of transforming them.

Works Cited

Bartholomae, David. "Inventing the University." *Journal of Basic Writing* 5 (1986): 4–23.

Bawarshi, Anis. "Sites of Invention: Genre and the Enactment of First-Year Writing." Chapter Five of *Genre and the Invention of the Writer: Reconsidering the Place of Invention in Composition.* Logan, UT: Utah State UP, 2003.

Bazerman, Charles. "Systems of Genres and the Enactment of Social Intentions." *Genre and the New Rhetoric.* Ed. A. Freedman and P. Medway. London: Taylor and Francis, 1994. 79–101.

Bizzell, Patricia. "Cognition, Convention, and Certainty: What We Need to Know about Writing." *PRE/TEXT* 3 (1982): 213–43.

———. "Marxist Ideas in Composition Studies." *Contending with Words*. Ed. Patricia Harkin and John Schilb. New York: MLA, 1991. 52–68.

Devitt, Amy J. "Generalizing about Genre: New Conceptions of an Old Concept." *College Composition and Communication* 44 (1993): 573–86.

Emig, Janet. *The Composing Processes of Twelfth Graders*. Urbana: NCTE, 1971.

Fairclough, Norman. *Critical Discourse Analysis: The Critical Study of Language*. London: Longman, 1995.

Flower, Linda, and John R. Hayes. "A Cognitive Process Theory of Writing." *College Composition and Communication* 32 (1981): 365–87.

Freire, Paulo. *The Politics of Education: Culture, Power, and Liberation*. Trans. Donaldo Macedo. South Hadley: Bergan, 1985.

Gee, James Paul. "What Is Literacy?" *Teaching and Learning* 2 (1987): 3–11.

Harris, Joseph. "The Idea of Community in the Study of Writing." *College Composition and Communication* 40 (February 1989): 11–22.

Killingsworth, M. Jimmie. "Discourse Communities—Local and Global." *Rhetoric Review* 11 (1992): 110–22.

Miller, Carolyn. "Genre as Social Action." *Quarterly Journal of Speech* 70 (1984): 151–67.

Nystrand, Martin. Introduction. *What Writers Know: The Language, Process, and Structure of Written Discourse*. New York: Academic Press, 1982. 1–28.

Paré, Anthony. "Genre and Identity: Individuals, Institutions, and Ideology." *The Rhetoric and Ideology of Genre*. Ed. Richard Coe, Lorelei Lingard, and Tatiana Teslenko. Cresskill, NJ: Hampton, 2002.

Perl, Sondra. "The Composing Processes of Unskilled College Writers." *Research in the Teaching of English* 13 (1979): 317–36.

Russell, David R. "Rethinking Genre in School and Society: An Activity Theory Analysis." *Written Communication* 14 (1997): 504–54.

Schuster, Charles. "The Ideology of Literacy: A Bakhtinian Perspective." *The Right to Literacy*. Ed. Andrea A. Lunsford, Helene Moglen, and James Slevin. New York: MLA, 1990. 225–32.

Szwed, John F. "The Ethnography of Literacy." *The Nature, Development, and Teaching of Written Communication*. Ed. Marcia Farr Whitman. Mahway, NJ: Erlbaum, 1981. 13–23.

Trimbur, John. "Changing the Question: Should Writing Be Studied?" *Composition Studies* 31.1 (2003): 15–24.

Vandenberg, Peter, and Colette Morrow. "*Inter*textuality or *Intra*textuality? Rethinking Discourse Community Pedagogy." *The Writing Instructor* 14 (1994): 17–24.

CHAPTER ONE

What Is Literacy?

JAMES PAUL GEE

It is a piece of folk wisdom that part of what linguists do is define words. In over a decade as a linguist, however, no one, until now, has asked me to define a word. So my first try: what does "literacy" mean? It won't surprise you that we have to define some other words first. So let me begin by giving a technical meaning to an old term which, unfortunately, already has a variety of other meanings. The term is "discourse." I will use the word as a count term ("a discourse," "discourses," "many discourses"), not as a mass term ("discourse," "much discourse"). By "a discourse" I will mean:

> a socially accepted association among ways of using language, of thinking, and of acting that can be used to identify oneself as a member of a socially meaningful group or "social network."

Think of a discourse is an "identity kit" which comes complete with the appropriate costume and instructions on how to act and talk so as to take on a particular role that others will recognize. Let me give an example: Being "trained" as a linguist meant that I learned to speak, think, and act like a linguist, and to recognize others when they do so. Now actually matters are not that simple: the larger discourse of linguistics contains many subdiscourses, different socially accepted ways of being a linguist. But the master discourse is not just the sum of its parts; it is something also over and above them. Every act of speaking, writing, and behaving a linguist does as a linguist is meaningful only against the background of the whole social institution of linguistics. And

From *Teaching and Learning* 2 (1987): 3–11.

that institution is made up of concrete things like people, books, and buildings; abstract things like bodies of knowledge, values, norms, and beliefs; mixtures of concrete and abstract things like universities, journals, and publishers; as well as a shared history and shared stories. Some other examples of discourses: being an American or a Russian, being a man or a woman, being a member of a certain socio-economic class, being a factory worker or a boardroom executive, being a doctor or a hospital patient, being a teacher, an administrator, or a student, being a member of a sewing circle, a club, a street gang, a lunchtime social gathering, or a regular at a local watering hole.

There are a number of important points that one can make about discourses. None of them, for some reason, are very popular with Americans, though they seem to be commonplace in European social theory (Belsey; Eagleton; Jameson; Macdonell; Thompson):

1. Discourses are inherently "ideological." They crucially involve a set of values and viewpoints in terms of which one must speak and act, at least while being in the discourse; otherwise one doesn't count as being in it.

2. Discourses are resistant to internal criticism and self-scrutiny since uttering viewpoints that seriously undermine them defines one as being outside them. The discourse itself defines what counts as acceptable criticism. Of course, one can criticize a particular discourse from the viewpoint of another one (e.g., psychology criticizing linguistics). But what one cannot do is stand outside all discourse and criticize any one or all of them—that would be like trying to repair a jet in flight by stepping outside it.

3. Discourse-defined positions from which to speak and behave are not, however, just defined internal to a discourse, but also as standpoints taken up by the discourse in its relation to other, ultimately opposing, discourses. The discourse of managers in an industry is partly defined as a set of views, norms, and standpoints defined by their opposition to analogous points in the discourse of workers (Macdonell). The discourse we identify with being a feminist is radically changed if all male discourses disappear.

4. Any discourse concerns itself with certain objects and puts forward certain concepts, viewpoints, and values at the expense of

others. In doing so it will marginalize viewpoints and values central to other discourses (Macdonell). In fact, a discourse can call for one to accept values in conflict with other discourses one is a member of, for example, the discourse used in literature departments used to marginalize popular literature and women's writings. Further, women readers of Hemingway, for instance, when acting as "acceptable readers" by the standards of the discourse of literary criticism, might find themselves complicit with values which conflict with those of various other discourses they belong to as women (Culler 43–64).

5. Finally, discourses are intimately related to the distribution of social power and hierarchical structure in society. Control over certain discourses can lead to the acquisition of social goods (money, power, status) in a society. These discourses empower those groups who have the fewest conflicts with their other discourses when they use them. For example, many academic, legalistic, and bureaucratic discourses in our society contain a moral subdiscourse that sees "right" as what is derivable from general abstract principles. This can conflict to a degree with a discourse about morality—one that appears to be more often associated with women than men—in which "wrong" is seen as the disruption of social networks, and "right" as the repair of those networks (Gilligan). Or, to take another example, the discourse of literary criticism was a standard route to success as a professor of literature. Since it conflicted less with the other discourses of white, middle-class men than it did with those of women, men were empowered by it. Women were not, as they were often at cross-purposes when engaging in it. Let us call discourses that lead to social goods in a society "dominant discourses" and let us refer to those groups that have the fewest conflicts when using them as "dominant groups." Obviously these are both matters of degree and change to a certain extent in different contexts.

It is sometimes helpful to say that individuals do not speak and act, but that historically and socially defined discourses speak to each other through individuals. Individuals instantiate, give body to, a discourse every time they act or speak; thus they carry it (and ultimately change it) through time. Americans tend to focus on the individual, and thus often miss the fact that the individual is simply the meeting point of many, sometimes conflicting discourses that are socially and historically defined. The crucial question is: how does one come by the discourses that he or she controls? And here it is necessary, before answering the question, to make an important distinction. It is a distinction that does not exist in nontechnical parlance but nevertheless is important to a linguist: the distinction between "acquisition" and "learning" (Krashen, *Principles* and *Inquiries*; Krashen and Terrell). I will distinguish these two as follows:

Master-Apprentice Relationship

> *Acquisition* is a process of acquiring something subconsciously by exposure to models and a process of trial and error, without a process of formal teaching. It happens in natural settings which are meaningful and functional in the sense that the acquirers know that they need to acquire something in order to function and they in fact want to so function. This is how most people come to control their first language.
>
> *Learning* is a process that involves conscious knowledge gained through teaching, though not necessarily from someone officially designated a teacher. This teaching involves explanation and analysis, that is, breaking down the thing to be learned into its analytic parts. It inherently involves attaining, along with the matter being taught, some degree of meta-knowledge about the matter.

Much of what we come by in life, after our initial enculturation, involves a mixture of acquisition and learning. However, the balance between the two can be quite different in different cases and different at different stages in the process. For instance, I initially learned to drive a car by instruction, but thereafter acquired, rather than learned, most of what I know. Some cultures highly value acquisition and so tend simply to expose children to adults modeling some activity and eventually the child picks it up, picks it up as a gestalt rather than as a series of analytic bits (Heath; Scollon and Scollon). Other cultural groups highly value teaching and thus break down what is to be mastered into sequential steps and analytic parts and engage in explicit explanation. There is an up side and a down side to both that can be expressed as follows: "we are better at what we acquire, but we consciously know more about what we have learned." For most of us, playing a musical instrument, or dancing, or using a second language are skills we attained by some mixture of acquisition and learning. But it is a safe bet that, over the same amount of time, people are better at these activities if acquisition predominated during that time. The point can be made using second language as the example: most people aren't very good at attaining functional use of a second language through formal instruction in a classroom. That's why teaching grammar is not a very good way of getting people to control a language. However, people who have acquired a second language in a natural setting don't thereby make good linguists, and some good linguists can't speak the languages they learned in a classroom. What is said here about second languages is true, I believe, of all of what I will later refer to as "secondary discourses": acquisition is good for performance, learning is good for meta-level knowledge (Scribner and Cole). Acquisition and learning are differential sources of power: acquirers usually beat learners at performance, while learners usually beat acquirers at talking about it, that is, at explication, explanation, analysis, and criticism.

Now what has this got to do with literacy? First, let me point out that it renders the common-sense understanding of literacy very problematic. Take the notion of a "reading class." I don't know if they are still prevalent, but when I was in grammar school we had a special time set aside each day for "reading class" where we would learn to read. Reading is at the very least the ability to interpret print (surely not just the ability to call out the names of letters), but an interpretation of print is just a viewpoint on a set of symbols, and viewpoints are always embedded in a discourse. Thus, while many different discourses use reading, even in opposing ways, and while there could well be classes devoted to these discourses, reading outside such a discourse or class would be truly "in a vacuum," much like our repairman above trying to repair the jet in flight by jumping out the door. Learning to read is always learning some aspect of some discourse.

One can trivialize this insight to a certain degree by trivializing the notion of interpretation (of printed words), until one gets to reading as calling out the names of letters. Analogously, one can deepen the insight by taking successively deeper views of what interpretation means. But there is also the problem that a "reading class" stresses learning and not acquisition. To the extent that reading as both decoding and interpretation is a performance, learning stresses the production of poor performers. If we wanted to stress acquisition we would have to expose children to reading, and this would always be to expose them to a discourse whose name would never be "Reading" (at least until the student went to the university and earned a degree called "Reading"). To the extent that it is important to gain meta-level language skills, reading class as a place of learning rather than of acquisition might facilitate this, but it would hardly be the most effective means. Traditional reading classes like mine encapsulated the commonsense notion of literacy as "the ability to read and write" (intransitively), a notion that is nowhere near as coherent as it at first sounds.

Now I will approach a more positive connection between a viable notion of literacy and the concepts we have dealt with above. All humans, barring serious disorder, get one form of discourse free, so to speak, and this through acquisition. This is our socio-culturally determined way of using our native language in face-to-face communication with intimates (intimates are people with whom we share a great deal of knowledge because of a great deal of contact and similar experiences). This is sometimes referred to as "the oral mode" (Gee, "Units," "Orality"). It is the birthright of every human and comes through primary socialization within the family as this is defined within a given culture. Some small, so-called "primitive," cultures function almost like extended families (though never completely so) in that this type of discourse is usable in a very wide array of social contacts. This is due to the fact that these cultures are small enough to function as a "society of intimates" (Givon). In modern technological and urban societies which function as a "society of strangers," the oral mode is more narrowly useful. Let us refer then to this oral mode, developed in the primary process of enculturation, as the "primary discourse." It is important to realize that even among speakers of English there are socioculturally different primary discourses. For example, lower socio-economic black children use English to make sense of their experience differently than do middle-class children; they have a different primary discourse (Gee, "Narrativization"; Michaels, "Sharing"). And this is not due merely to the fact that they have a different dialect of English. So-called Black Vernacular English is, on structural grounds, only trivially different from Standard English by the norms of linguists accustomed to dialect differences around the world (Labov). Rather, these children use language, behavior, values, and beliefs to give a different shape to their experience.

Beyond the primary discourse, however, are other discourses which crucially involve social institutions beyond the family (or the primary socialization group as defined by the culture), no matter how much they also involve the family. These institutions all require one to communicate with nonintimates (or to treat intimates as if they were not intimates). Let us refer to these as "secondary institutions" (such as schools, workplaces, stores, government offices, businesses, or churches). Discourses beyond the primary discourse are developed in association with and by having access to and practice with these secondary institutions. Thus, we will refer to them as "secondary discourses." These secondary discourses all build on, and extend, the uses of language we acquired as part of our primary discourse, and they are more or less compatible with the primary discourses of different social groups. It is of course a great advantage when the secondary discourse is compatible with your primary one. But all these secondary discourses involve uses of language, whether written or oral or both, that go beyond our primary discourse no matter what group we belong to. Let's call those uses "secondary uses of language." Telling your mother you love her is a primary use of language; telling your teacher you don't have your homework is a secondary use. It can be noted, however, that sometimes people must fall back on their primary uses of language in inappropriate circumstances when they fail to control the requisite secondary use.

Now we can get to what I believe is a useful definition of literacy:

> *Literacy* is control of secondary uses of language (i.e., uses of language in secondary discourses).

Thus, there are as many applications of the word "literacy" as there are secondary discourses, which is many. We can define various types of literacy as follows:

> *Dominant literacy* is control of a secondary use of language used in what I called above a "dominant discourse."
>
> *Powerful literacy* is control of a secondary use of language used in a secondary discourse that can serve as a meta-discourse to critique the primary discourse or other secondary discourses, including dominant discourses.

What do I mean by "control" in the above definitions? I mean some degree of being able to "use," to "function" with, so "control" is a matter of degree. "Mastery" I define as "full and effortless control." In these terms I will state a principle having to do with acquisition which I believe is true:

> Any discourse (primary or secondary) is for most people most of the time only mastered through acquisition, not learning. Thus, literacy is mastered through acquisition, not learning, that is, it requires exposure to models in natural, meaningful, and functional settings, and teaching is not liable to be very successful—it may even initially get in the way. Time spent on learning and not acquisition is time not well spent if the goal is mastery in performance.

There is also a principle having to do with learning that I think true:

> One cannot critique one discourse with another one (which is the only way to seriously criticize and thus change a discourse) unless one has meta-level knowledge in both discourses. And this meta-knowledge is best developed through learning, even when one has to a certain extent already acquired that discourse. Thus, powerful literacy, as defined above, almost always involves learning, and not just acquisition.

The point is that acquisition and learning are means to quite different goals, though in our culture we very often confuse these means and thus don't get what we thought and hoped we would.

Let me just briefly mention some practical connections of the above remarks. Mainstream middle-class children often look as if they are *learning* literacy (of various sorts) in school. But in fact I believe much research shows they are acquiring these literacies through experiences in the home both before and during school, as well as by the opportunities school gives them to practice what they are acquiring (Wells, *Meaning Makers*). The learning they are doing, provided it is tied to good teaching, is giving them not the literacies, but meta-level cognitive and linguistic skills that they can use to critique various discourses throughout their lives. However, we all know that teaching is by no means always that good—though it should be one of our goals to ensure that it is. Children from non-mainstream homes often do not get the opportunities to acquire dominant secondary discourses—including those connected with the school—in their homes, due to their parents' lack of access to these discourses. At school they cannot practice what they haven't yet got and they are exposed mostly to a process of learning and not acquisition. Therefore, little acquisition goes on. They often cannot use this learning-teaching to develop meta-level skills, which require some control of secondary discourses to use in the critical process. Research also shows that many school-based secondary discourses conflict with the values and viewpoints in some non-mainstream children's primary discourses and in other community-based secondary discourses (e.g., stemming from religious institutions) (Cook-Gumperz; Gumperz; Heath).

While the above remarks may all seem rather theoretical, they do in fact lead to some obvious practical suggestions for directions future research and intervention efforts ought to take. As far as I can see some of these are as follows:

1. Settings which focus on acquisition, not learning, should be stressed if the goal is to help non-mainstream children attain mastery of literacies. These are not likely to be traditional classroom settings (let alone my "reading class"), but rather natural and functional environments which may or may not happen to be inside a school.

2. We should realize that teaching and learning are connected with the development of meta-level cognitive and linguistic skills. They will work better if we explicitly realize this and build the realization into our curricula. Further, they must be carefully ordered and integrated with acquisition if they are to have any effect other than obstruction.

3. Mainstream children are actually using much of the classroom teaching-learning not to *learn* but to *acquire*, by practicing developing skills. We should honor this practice effect directly and build on it, rather than leave it as a surreptitious and indirect byproduct of teaching-learning.

4. Learning should enable all children—mainstream and non-mainstream—to critique their primary and secondary discourses, including dominant secondary discourses. This requires exposing children to a variety of alternative primary and secondary discourses (not necessarily so that they acquire them, but so that

they learn about them). It also requires realizing that this is what good teaching and learning are good at. We rarely realize that this is where we fail mainstream children just as much as non-mainstream ones.

5. We must take seriously that no matter how good our schools become, both as environments where acquisition can go on (so involving meaningful and functional settings) and where learning can go on, non-mainstream children will always have more conflicts in using and thus mastering dominant secondary discourses. After all, they conflict more seriously with these children's primary discourse and their community-based secondary discourses, and (by my definitions above) this is precisely what makes them "non-mainstream." This does not mean we should give up. It also does not mean merely that research and intervention efforts must be sensitive to these conflicts, though it certainly does mean this. It also requires, I believe, that we must stress research and intervention aimed at developing a wider and more humane understanding of mastery and its connections to gatekeeping. We must remember that conflicts, while they do very often detract from standard sorts of full mastery, can give rise to new sorts of mastery. This is commonplace in the realm of art. We must make it commonplace in society at large.

Works Cited

Belsey, C. *Critical Practice*. London: Methuen, 1980.

Cook-Gumperz, J., Ed. *The Social Construction of Literacy*. Cambridge: Cambridge UP, 1986.

Culler, J. *On Deconstruction: Theory and Criticism after Structuralism*. Ithaca, N.Y.: Cornell UP, 1982.

Eagleton, T. *Literary Theory: An Introduction*. Minneapolis: U of Minnesota P, 1983.

Gee, J. P. "The Narratization of Experience in the Oral Mode." *Journal of Education* 167 (1985): 9–35.

Gee, J. P. "Units in the Production of Discourse." *Discourse Processes* 9 (1986): 391–422.

Gee, J. P. "Orality and Literacy: From the *Savage Mind* to *Ways with Words*." *TESOL Quarterly* 20 (1986): 719–46.

Gilligan, C. *In Different Voice*. Cambridge: Harvard UP, 1982.

Givon, T. *On Understanding Grammar*. New York: Academic Press, 1979.

Gumperz, J. J., Ed. *Language and Social Identity*. Cambridge; Cambridge UP, 1982.

Heath, S. B. *Ways with Words: Language, Life, and Work in Communities and Classrooms*. Cambridge: Cambridge UP, 1983.

Jameson, F. *The Political Unconscious: Narrative as a Socially Symbolic Act*. Ithaca, N.Y.: Cornell University P, 1981.

Krashen, S. *Principles and Practice in Second Language Acquisition*. Hayward, CA: Alemany, 1982.

Krashen, S. *Inquiries and Insights*. Hayward, CA: Alemany, 1985.

Krashen, S. and Terrell, T. *The Natural Approach: Language Acquisition in the Classroom*. Hayward, CA: Alemany, 1983.

Labov, W. *Language in the Inner City*. Philadelphia: U of Pennsylvania P, 1972.

Macdonell, D. *Theories of Discourse: An Introduction*. Oxford: Basil Blackwell, 1986.

Michaels, S. "'Sharing Time': Children's Narrative Styles and Differential Access to Literacy." *Language in Society* 10 (1981): 423–442.

Michaels, S. "Hearing the Connections in Children's Oral and Written Discourse." *Journal of Education* 167 (1985): 36–56.

Scollon, R. & Scollon, S.B.K. *Narrative, Literacy, and Face in Interethnic Communication*. Norwood, N.J.: Ablex, 1981.

Scribner, S. and Cole, M. *The Psychology of Literacy*. Cambridge: Harvard UP, 1981.

Thompson, J. B. *Studies in the Theory of Ideology*. Berkeley and LA: U of CP, 1984.

Wells, G. "Preschool Literacy-Related Activities and Success in School." *Literacy, Language and Learning*. Ed. D.R. Olson, N. Torrance, and A. Hildyard. Cambridge: Cambridge UP, 1985.

Wells, G. "The Language Experience of Five-Year-Old Children at Home and at School." *The Social Construction of Literacy*. Ed. J. Cook-Gumperz. Cambridge: Cambridge UP, 1986.

Wells, G. *The Meaning Makers: Children Learning Language and Using Language to Learn*. Portsmouth, N.H.: Heinemann, 1986.

Chapter Two

The Ideology of Literacy: A Bakhtinian Perspective

Charles Schuster

Let's begin with a straightforward statement—namely, that all of us engaged with this text are literate. The basis for establishing ourselves as literate, when we cannot even agree what the term *literacy* means, is constituted by our ability to generate and process language, to write and read, to make sense of texts. But literacy also has something to do with intuitive understanding, with shared boundaries of meaning, with making sense of each other through verbal and written interaction—factors that are too often ignored in discussions of literacy. I shall want shortly to return to this notion of socially constituted meaning making, but for now I want to critique two more accepted views of literacy. One holds that literacy is bound by notions of educational praxis; the other argues that literacy is an outcome of intellectual power and training.

Certainly, I would agree that *literacy*, whatever we precisely mean by it, can be promoted through educational and intellectual development. Illiteracy flourishes in the dark; its tumorous growth thrives on neglect, poverty, ignorance, privation. Too little public and private energy and money have been concentrated on this problem, leading to what Jonathan Kozol calls *Illiterate America*. Kozol opens his book with a statistical indictment of illiterate America:

> Twenty-five million American adults cannot read the poison

From *The Right to Literacy*. Ed. Andrea A. Lunsford, Helene Moglen, and James Slevin. New York: MLA, 1990. 225–32.

> warnings on a can of pesticide, a letter from their child's teacher, or the front page of a daily paper. An additional 35 million read only at a level which is less than equal to the full survival needs of our society.
>
> Together, these 60 million people represent more than one third of the entire adult population.
>
> 15% of recent urban high school graduates read at less than 6th grade level.
>
> The U.S. ranks 49th among 158 member nations of the U.N. in its literacy levels.
>
> 47%—that is nearly half—of all black 17-year-olds are functionally illiterate. (4–5)

Kozol's analysis strongly suggests a conspiracy theory of capitalism: he posits an America that maintains illiteracy in order to maintain itself politically, socially, economically. Illiterates are a submissive work force, a neo-slave population in twentieth-century America.

Even if we grant this appalling state of affairs, defining the problem as educational and political does not allow a meaningful solution. That is, if a third of America is illiterate, then apparently what is needed is a massive political and economic mobilization. Through a domestic peace corps, sixty million people could be taught to read and write. End of problem. That this solution oversimplifies is obvious: it addresses the issue in the wrong terms. Illiteracy is not just the ability to read and write; if it were, we could eliminate it through educational outreach, repeated viewings of *Sesame Street*, a proliferation of bookmobiles. *Literacy*, however, does not consist exclusively of the ability to encode and decode written texts, although that is certainly part of its meaning.

Perhaps the problem is not educational deprivation but intellectual limitation; Robert Pattison seems to think so. Pattison defines *literacy* as "a combination of variables—individual and cultural awareness of language and the interplay of this awareness with the means of expression" (7). "Reading and writing," he tells us, "may be parts of literacy but do not constitute the whole" (7). For Pattison, literacy is not just the ability to process words; more important it is the ability to use language critically and intellectually to synthesize judgment and form original perspectives.

Pattison describes three kinds of illiteracy: the illiteracy of "The Wild Boy" (10) who lacks language altogether; the illiteracy of Gracie Allen, who purports to understand words on a purely literal level and thus operates only on the surface of language; and the illiteracy of Agamemnon, who appears to function within a language community but who is in some intellectual and psychological sense "unconscious and egoless" (15). This last kind of illiteracy chiefly concerns Pattison, for it is the most common and can occur "in high places" (17). Agamemnon, according to Pattison, "is a robot, and even though he is a character from an age that had not yet adopted reading and writing, he may more justly be called illiterate because of his insensitivity to speech, thought, and their relation to action" (16). Pattison attributes this insensitivity to a lack of brain development and inadequate educational training.

Pattison's model of illiteracy, however, carries unfortunate implications. His Agamemnon is not really illiterate. His insulting of Chryseis, his naive belief in false dreams, his bumbling actions—all point not so much to a basic illiteracy as to a basic stupidity, just as the persona of Gracie Allen represents, in a comic sense, a basic ingenious stupidity. Pattison works hard to erase this unfortunate characterization by describing language processing in terms of underdeveloped cranial hemispheres, but the inescapable conclusion is that by any outside evaluation Agamemnon and Gracie Allen are—pun intended—dumb. If their brains functioned better—that is, if they were smarter or were made smarter through a growth in critical intelligence—they would become literate.

I propose an alternative model for illiteracy, one that develops a social-constructionist view derived from the work of the Russian critic Mikhail Bakhtin. As a starting point, I nominate a different model for the illiterate—not the Wild Boy or Gracie Allen or Agamemnon but another player in the tragedy of the Trojan War, Cassandra.

Cassandra, of course, speaks language. She is beautiful, intelligent, thoughtful. From Apollo she learned the gift of prophecy but, because she refused the god's amorous advances, she is cursed by him so that her prophecies are never believed. Cassandra foretells the Greek invasion and warns against the Trojan horse, all to no avail. Thus Cassandra speaks to the Trojan hierarchy, but they cannot hear her. Articulate and prescient, Cassandra is struck dumb through the very act of speaking. The more she reveals her incisive predictions and native intelligence through language, the stupider she becomes, or, at least, the more stupid she is perceived to be by Priam, Hector, Paris, and the other Trojan leaders. For Cassandra, meaning becomes meaninglessness. Her ultimate rape by Ajax and her murder at the hands of Aegisthus underscore her powerlessness, her role as a victim of forces beyond her control.

Kozol's illiterates might be able to learn how to read and write if we funded libraries, night schools, and community centers. Agamemnon might be able to learn how to be smarter through a long and painstaking education. Gracie Allen and even the Wild Boy of Aveyron might be able to learn language use in some fashion with intensive tutelage. They are potentially educable. Cassandra's situation, however, is hopeless. She cannot learn anything that will allow her to communicate what she knows, what she feels to be certain. She is doomed to a solipsistic existence, despite the power of language that she possesses. Because of Apollo's curse, Cassandra no longer functions within a community of utterance. Her speech genres exist in some separate sphere of meaning and, thus, no longer intersect with those around her. In a sense, only by being struck dumb could she ever hope to become a functioning, literate member of Greek society. Her literacy is and always will be illiteracy.

Cassandra's predicament mirrors that of many individuals as well as whole classes in American society—intelligent, knowledgeable, informed individuals who cannot participate interactively in meaning making through language. We label these people "illiterate." From a Bakhtinian point of view, illiterates today are cursed not by Apollo but by dominant cultures within society to endure a state of alienation wherein speaking, listening, reading, and writing become meaningless activities. In the view that I am promoting here, literacy is the power to be able to make oneself heard and felt, to signify. Literacy is the way in which we make ourselves meaningful not only to others but through others to ourselves.

For Bakhtin and V. N. Vološinov, a key member of his circle, language is not just a social construct; on the contrary, language constructs us socially. Vološinov states, "It is not experience that organizes expression, but the other way around—*expression organizes experience.* Expression is what first gives experience its form and specificity of direction" (*Marxism* 85). In this view, language is primal. All that we see, do, and experience—all that we are—is filtered and organized through language; it permeates all our ideas, actions, and basic understandings of the world around us. If we grant this epistemological view of language, illiterate people are not just marginalized; they are excluded from understanding themselves and their place in the world. They lack much of the power necessary to organize experience, to make themselves both heard and understood in society at large.

To state this is to overstate the matter—but only slightly. Illiterate people are not completely absent from the dominant culture and society, although Ralph Ellison has shown us how invisible many of them are. That they are not completely absent is a result of the ways in which their illiteracy is defined. The illiterates I am describing—mainly poor whites, blacks, and Hispanics, economic and social outcasts—are not illiterate within their own cultures. In their communities, they possess the power to speak and be heard and often the power to write and be read. Once they move outside those communities, however, their particular brand of illiteracy becomes felt. Literate at home, they become illiterate at work, illiterate in society at large. They are Dr. Jekyll and Mr. Hyde, only in this case the dark transformation is not located within the individual but is imposed from outside by a dominant society that defines them as other.

Language, after all, is the ligature that binds person to person, individual to culture, human to the world of humanity. It is the connective that binds *I* to *you* because language is always addressed to the other. As Vološinov reminds us:

> The *word is oriented toward an addressee*, toward *who* that addressee might be . . . *the word is a two-sided act.* It is determined equally by *whose* word it is and *for whom* it is meant. As word, it is precisely *the product of the reciprocal relationship between speaker and listener, addresser and addressee.* Each and every

> word expresses the "one" in relation to the "other." . . . A word is a bridge thrown between myself and another. If one end of the bridge depends on me, then the other depends on my addressee. A word is territory shared by both addresser and addressee, by the speaker and his interlocutor. (*Marxism* 85–86)

This concept of "addressivity" is a central one to Bakhtinian theory. Language does not exist in isolation; it is always addressed to a listener who is another user of language. As we speak or write, we are always addressing the other who is simultaneously responding to us—otherwise words would, quite literally, fail us. Every meaningful use of language simultaneously engages both self and other: we speak and conceive of ourselves as being listened to; we write, and the reader is created within the written word, within ourselves. An addressee enters into the territory of the utterance—shaping it, giving it evaluative accents, permeating it with an appropriate tone and style, forming it from within. Words are shared archipelagoes of social interaction, linked beneath the surface by history, by shared values, by mutual responsiveness. For Bakhtin, this idea of responsiveness is crucial:

> The listener and his response are regularly taken into account when it comes to everyday dialogue and rhetoric, but every other sort of discourse as well is oriented toward an understanding that is "responsive." . . . Responsive understanding is a fundamental force, one that participates in the formulation of discourse, and it is moreover an *active* understanding, one that discourse senses as resistance or support enriching the discourse. (*Dialogic Imagination* 281)

This active responsiveness is precisely what is missing for those branded as illiterate. Through acts of social, political, and economic exclusion by the dominant culture, they have been denied genuine listeners, denied response on the part of those whom they are purportedly addressing. Like Cassandra, they use language with no effect. In view of their powerlessness to be understood, their inability to influence or signify, it should come as no surprise that they both define themselves and are defined by others as illiterate. Indeed, they are illiterate.

This is not to say that they cannot speak or write words, sentences, phrases. For Bakhtin, there is a crucial difference between a word as it appears in a dictionary or in a sentence and a word as it appears in an utterance. A word in a dictionary is not a word at all but a mirage, having the appearance of a word but no body or spirit. Likewise, the sentence, as opposed to "the utterance," is a grammatical unit, a typesetter's convention. Sentences, like individual words, are neutral, grammatical categories. They contain words, but "like the word, [the sentence] has no author. Like the word, it belongs to *nobody*" (Bakhtin, *Speech Genres* 84). Thus the sentence "has no capacity to determine directly the responsive position of the other speaker, that is, it cannot evoke a response" (*Speech Genres* 74).

The actual word exists in an interactive medium—spoken or written. "Verbal discourse" says Vološinov, "is the skeleton that takes on living flesh only in the process of creative perception—consequently, only in the process of living social communication" ("Discourse" 109). In his notes from 1970–71, Bakhtin states:

> Everything that pertains to me enters my consciousness, beginning with my name, from the external world through the mouths of others (my mother, and so forth), with their intonation, in their emotional and value-assigning tonality. I realize myself initially through others: from them I receive words, forms, and tonalities. . . . Just as the body is formed initially in the mother's womb (body), a person's consciousness awakens wrapped in another's consciousness. *(Speech Genres* 138)

This quality of social interaction, of shared consciousness, is what distinguishes an utterance from a sentence (see also Stacey, esp. 62–71). An utterance necessarily exists within a social setting. An utterance creates and completes a meaning that is oriented toward another individual or socially constructed reality. *Utterance* is the term Bakhtin chooses to describe language that conveys meaning, that creates expression. Sentences are inert; utterances are interactive, intertextual, transformative.

Let me be deconstructive for a moment and consider how I wrote this essay. After several tedious false starts, some lasting as long as three and one half pages, I was stuck. I had not yet found a way to conceive of this essay. What I did was apply the method that I have elsewhere termed "situational sequencing"—that is, I placed myself within a context of readers who shared my interest in literacy. I imagined this essay being read and responded to by literacy specialists. I had no specific idea what it meant to write to literacy specialists. Although unsure, I assumed that I could engage in a communicative utterance, that they and I would share certain speech conventions, verbal routines, political and disciplinary values.

In imagining my audience, I also imagined myself interacting with them. I thus created an addressee toward whom my utterance oriented itself—a voiceless addressee, it is true, but one who read attentively, sympathetically, questioningly, thoughtfully, empathetically. This constructed addressee was, for me, enabling: it allowed me to choose words that were framed within utterances, not sentences, for those words were engaged responsively with a reader even before I wrote them. If my language was not so engaged, then my utterances would have undergone an ontological shift back to sentences—which is precisely what I had before—sentences that contained meaning but that were not aware of themselves within this mirrored network of responsiveness and addressivity of utterance and speech genre. Ultimately, were I to speak to literacy specialists more often, I would not have to engage in the artificial step of constructing a situation for my discourse; that situation, that ideological state of multiple rejoinder, would operate as a formative principle in my language. This shared context of mutual responsiveness is what is lacking among those we characterize as illiterate: other than their own politico-racial-socioeconomic class, they have no audience, no ability to construct one, and, thus, they cannot operate from a position of mutual responsiveness. No matter how much they try, they cannot conceive of themselves as participating in the literacy event of writing and reading this essay, because they lack the prior experience of creating responsive addressees beyond their own social class structure.

Given this problem, illiterate people inevitably engage in mock conversation when their words are directed to the dominant society that surrounds them. As mock speakers, they use words and sentences that are directed toward mock listeners. Utterance is impossible, for speaker and listener do not exist within the same ideological plane, the same social purview. Illiteracy is an outcome of this isolation, for, as Bakhtin informs us, "addressivity, the quality of turning to someone, is a constitutive feature of the utterance; without it the utterance does not and cannot exist" (*Speech Genres* 99). Illiterate people are embedded within a language use that won't allow them to transform sentences into utterances that reach beyond their own communities. For them the condition is existentially insufferable: since their language cannot be directed toward an other, it is impossible for them to constitute a self. They possess a self only within the ghettoized communities that they seek to escape; and, once they escape those communities, they have no self at all.

Bakhtin's discussion of utterance and addressivity should be considered within the context of his analysis of speech genres, which he describes as socially defined and accepted conventions that organize forms of utterance. Anecdotes, letters, formal and informal greetings, business memorandums, the romantic novel—these are speech genres. Not only do we create these speech genres as we speak and write, but they also create us, for they establish the accepted forms that shape our utterances. These speech genres represent forms accreted over time by society, naturalized through social usage. Moreover, speech genres take on particularized definition within specific speech communities. Thus the speech genres within the business community are not identical to those within the academic community or to those used by black teenagers or young, male, blue collar workers. Not sharing in the values of the dominant culture, not participating in meaningful linguistic exchange with that culture, illiterate people find themselves on the margins of the dominant-culture speech genres. Excluded from engaging in meaning making in society, they can choose either to violate speech genres as an act of verbal rebellion or imitate them without hope of succeeding at communication.

If I offer a dire picture of illiteracy, it is because the situation is dire. The only opportunity I see for eliminating illiteracy in America is social transformation in which persons discover a means to engage one another meaningfully through language—not as antagonists, not on the basis of class differences, not through racism or sexism or commodification but through a shared identification of self with other. To be effective, this ideological alteration must be initiated largely by the dominant classes within society, for only they have the power to create speaking subjects out of individuals currently considered illiterate. Bakhtin tells us that "understanding is imbued with response," that the act of understanding requires that "the listener becomes the speaker" (*Speech Genres* 68). For Bakhtin, the concept of addressivity merges with the concept of alterity: the more there is of the other, the more there is of the self, but only if the other can be addressed and held in genuine relation to the self. The condition of human otherness, of alien people and alien words, does not just threaten the self—it constitutes the self. Viewed in this way, literacy is, as it should be, an essential act of community. Unless we can become a literate society, we are no society at all, for in losing the other, what we really lose is ourselves.

Works Cited

Bakhtin, Mikhail M. *The Dialogic Imagination: Four Essays*. Ed. Michael Holquist. Trans. Caryl Emerson and Michael Holquist. Austin: Texas UP, 1981.

———. *Speech Genres and Other Late Essays*. Trans. Vern W. McGee. Austin: Texas UP, 1986.

Kozol, Jonathan. *Illiterate America*. Garden City: Anchor-Doubleday, 1985.

Pattison, Robert. *On Literacy*. Oxford: Oxford UP, 1982.

Schuster, Charles. "Situational Sequencing." *Writing Instructor* 3 (1984): 177–84.

Stacey, Michelle. "Profiles: At Play in the Language (Allen Walker Read)." *New Yorker* 4 Sept. 1989: 51–74.

Vološinov, V. N. "Discourse in Life and Discourse in Art (Concerning Sociological Poetics)." App. 1. *Freudianism: A Critical Sketch*. By Vološinov. Trans. I. R. Titunik. Ed. in collaboration with Neal H. Bruss. 1976. Bloomington: Indiana UP, 1987. 93–116.

———. *Marxism and the Philosophy of Language*. Trans. Ladislav Matejka and I. R. Titunik. Cambridge: Harvard UP, 1973.

Chapter Three

What's "New" in New Literacy Studies? Critical Approaches to Literacy in Theory and Practice

Brian Street

The Context and Background

A rich vein of articles and books has recently addressed some critical issues in the field of New Literacy Studies, both in terms of theoretical perspectives and of their implications in educational and policy contexts. I address some of these critiques as a way of both updating NLS and of addressing its implications for practice.

What has come to be termed the "New Literacy Studies" (NLS) (Gee, *Social*; Street, *Social*) represents a new tradition in considering the nature of literacy, focusing not so much on acquisition of skills, as in dominant approaches, but rather on what it means to think of literacy as a social practice (Street, *Literacy*). This entails the recognition of multiple literacies, varying according to time and space, but also contested in relations of power. NLS, then, takes nothing for granted with respect to literacy and the social practices with which it becomes associated, problematizing what counts as literacy at any time and place and asking "whose literacies" are dominant and whose are marginalized or resistant.

To address these issues ethnographically, literacy researchers have constructed a conceptual apparatus that both coins some

---

From *Current Issues in Comparative Education* 5.2 (12 May 2003) <http://www.tc.columbia.edu/cice/articles/bs152.htm>.

new terms and gives new meanings to some old ones. My own work, for instance, begins with the notion of multiple literacies, which makes a distinction between "autonomous" and "ideological" models of literacy (Street, *Literacy*) and develops a distinction between literacy events and literacy practices (Street, "Literacy"). The standard view in many fields, from schooling to development programs, works from the assumption that literacy in itself—autonomously—will have effects on other social and cognitive practices. Introducing literacy to poor, "illiterate" people, villages, urban youth, etc. will have the effect of enhancing their cognitive skills, improving their economic prospects, making them better citizens, regardless of the social and economic conditions that accounted for their "illiteracy" in the first place. I refer to this as an "autonomous" model of literacy. The model, I suggest, disguises the cultural and ideological assumptions that underpin it so that it can then be presented as though they are neutral and universal and that literacy as such will have these benign effects. Research in NLS challenges this view and suggests that in practice literacy varies from one context to another and from one culture to another and so, therefore, do the effects of the different literacies in different conditions. The autonomous approach is simply imposing western conceptions of literacy on to other cultures or within a country those of one class or cultural group onto others.

The alternative, ideological model of literacy, offers a more culturally sensitive view of literacy practices as they vary from one context to another. This model starts from different premises than the autonomous model—it posits instead that literacy is a social practice, not simply a technical and neutral skill; that it is always embedded in socially constructed epistemological principles. It is about knowledge: the ways in which people address reading and writing are themselves rooted in conceptions of knowledge, identity, and being. It is also always embedded in social practices, such as those of a particular job market or a particular educational context and the effects of learning that particular literacy will be dependent on those particular contexts. Literacy, in this sense, is always contested, both its meanings and its practices, hence particular versions of it are always "ideological"[;] they are always rooted in a particular world-view and in a desire for that view of literacy to dominate and to marginalize others (Gee, *Social*; Besnier and Street). The argument about social literacies (Street, *Social*) suggests that engaging with literacy is always a social act even from the outset. The ways in which teachers or facilitators and their students interact is already a social practice that affects the nature of the literacy being learned and the ideas about literacy held by the participants, especially the new learners and their position in relations of power. It is not valid to suggest that "literacy" can be "given" neutrally and then its "social" effects only experienced afterwards.

It follows from this distinction that researchers in NLS employing an "ideological" model of literacy would find it problematic to simply use the term *literacy* as their unit or object of study. *Literacy* comes already loaded with ideological and policy pre-suppositions that make it hard to do ethnographic studies of the variety of literacies across contexts. So we have found it helpful to develop alternative terms. I have developed a working distinction between "literacy events" and "literacy practices" (Street, "Literacy") that I suggest is helpful for both research and in teaching situations. David Barton notes that the term *literacy events* derived from the sociolinguistic idea of speech events ("Literacy"). It was first used in relation to literacy by Alonzo Anderson et al., who defined it as an occasion during which a person "attempts to comprehend graphic signs" (59). Shirley Brice Heath further characterized a "literacy event" as "any occasion in which a piece of writing is integral to the nature of the participants' interactions and their interpretative processes" (93). I have employed the phrase "literacy practices" as a means of focusing upon "social practices and conceptions of reading and writing" (Street, *Literacy* 1), although I later elaborated the term to take into account both "events" in Heath's sense and of the social models of literacy that participants bring to bear upon those events and that give meaning to them (Street, "Literacy"). Barton and Roz Ivanic, in an introduction to their edited volume, *Writing in the Community*, attempted to clarify these debates about literacy events and literacy practices, and in a later collaborative study of everyday literacies in Lancaster, England, Barton and Mary Hamilton begin their account with further refinements of the two phrases. Mike Baynham entitled his book *Literacy Practices: Investigating Literacy in Social Contexts*. Similarly Martin Prinsloo and Mignonne Breier's volume, *The Social Uses of Literacy*, a series of case studies of literacy in South Africa, used the concept of "events," but then extended it to "practices," by describing the everyday uses and meanings of literacy amongst, for instance, urban taxi drivers, struggle activists in settlements, rural workers using diagrams to build carts, and those involved in providing election materials for mainly non-literate voters. The concept of literacy practices in these and other contexts not only attempts to handle the events and the patterns of activity around literacy events, but to link them to something broader of a cultural and social kind.

Recently, I have further elaborated the distinction with respect to work on literacies and multilingualism, in an important edited volume by Marilyn Martin-Jones and Kathryn Jones. As part of that broadening, for instance, I noted that we bring to a literacy event concepts and social models regarding what the nature of the event is and what makes it work, and what gives it meaning. *Literacy practices*, then, refers to the broader cultural conception of particular ways of thinking about and doing reading and writing in cultural contexts. A key issue, at both a methodological and an empirical level, is how we can characterize the shift from observing literacy events to conceptualizing literacy practices.

A wealth of "ethnographies of literacy" has emerged, deploying and developing these and other key concepts in a variety of international contexts, including the U.K. (Barton and Hamilton); the U.S.A. (Collins, Heath); South Africa (Prinsloo and Breier); Iran (Street); India (Mukherjee and Vasanta); Mexico (Kalman); South America (Aikman); and multiple development contexts (Street, *Literacy*). The strength and significance of the approach and the considerable literature it has generated is attested by a recent spate of critical accounts that have addressed some of the problems raised by it both in general theoretical terms and, more specifically, for practice in educational contexts. I firstly summarize some of the theoretical critiques and then turn to the applications to policy and practice that they entail.

Theoretical Concerns

In terms of theory, Deborah Brandt and Katie Clinton have recently commented on "the limits of the local" apparent in many NLS studies. They argue that NLS ought to be more prepared to take account of the relatively "autonomous" features of literacy without succumbing to the autonomous model with its well documented flaws. This would involve, for instance, recognizing the extent to which literacy does often come to "local" situations from outside and brings with it both skills and meanings that are larger than the emic perspective favored by NLS. Whilst acknowledging the value of the social practice approach, they:

> wonder if the new paradigm sometimes veers too far in a reactive direction, exaggerating the power of local contexts to set or reveal the forms and meanings that literacy takes. Literacy practices are not typically invented by their practitioners. Nor are they independently chosen or sustained by them. Literacy in use more often than not serves multiple interests, incorporating individual agents and their locales into larger enterprises that play out away from the immediate scene. (1)

They also point out the important and powerful role of consolidating technologies that can destabilize the functions, uses, values and meanings of literacy anywhere. These technologies generally originate outside of the local context; they cannot be understood simply in terms of local practices. Whilst the field has learned much from the recent turn to "local literacies," they fear that "something [might] be lost when we ascribe to local contexts responses to pressures that originate in distant decisions, especially when seemingly local appropriations of literacy may in fact be culminations of literate designs originating elsewhere" (2).

I would agree with most of Brandt and Clinton's characterization here of the relationship between the local and the "distant" and indeed it is the focus on this relationship, rather than on one or other of the sites, that characterizes the best of NLS. Brandt and Clinton's account provides a helpful way of characterizing the local/global debate in which literacy practices play a central role. But, I would want to distinguish between agreeing with their caveat about overemphasizing "the local" and labeling the "distant" as more "autonomous." The "distant" literacies to which Brandt and Clinton refer are also always ideological and to term them autonomous might be to concede too much to their neutralist claims.

Brandt and Clinton's concern with the overemphasis on the local in some NLS accounts, their recognition that for many people the literacies they engage with come from elsewhere and are not self-invented, and that there is more going on in a local literacy than "just local practice," are all important caveats to deter NLS from over emphasizing or romanticizing the local, as it has been accused of doing (see the response by Street to McCabe in Prinsloo and Breier). But this important debate can be continued without resorting to terming "distant" literacies as "autonomous"—as Brandt and Clinton imply in their attempt to address certain "autonomous" aspects of literacy without appealing to the "autonomous model" of literacy. The features of distant literacies are actually no more autonomous than those of local literacies, or indeed than any literacy practices: their distantness, their relative power over local literacies and their "non-invented" character as far as local users are concerned, do not make them "autonomous," only "distant," "new," or hegemonic. To study such processes we need a framework and conceptual tools that can characterize the relation between local and "distant." The question raised in the early NLS work concerning how we can characterize the shift from observing literacy events to conceptualizing literacy practices does, I think, provide both a methodological and empirical way of dealing with this relation and thereby taking account of Brandt and Clinton's concern with the "limits of the local."

NLS practitioners might also take issue with the apparent suggestion that distant literacies come to local contexts with their force and meaning intact. As Kulick and Stroud indicated a decade ago in their study of new literacy practices brought by missionaries to New Guinea, local peoples more often "take hold" of these new practices and adapt them to local circumstances. The result of local-global encounters around literacy is always a new hybrid rather than a single essentialized version of either. It is these hybrid literacy practices that NLS focuses upon rather than either romanticizing the local or conceding the dominant privileging of the supposed "global." As we shall see when we discuss practical applications of NLS across educational contexts, it is the recognition of this hybridity that lies at the heart of an NLS approach to literacy acquisition regarding the relationship between local literacy practices and those of the school.

James Collins and Richard K. Blot are similarly concerned that, whilst NLS has generated a powerful series of ethnographies of literacy, there is a danger of simply piling up more descriptions of local literacies without addressing general questions of both theory and practice. In exploring why dominant stereotypes regarding literacy are so flawed, such as the notions of a great divide between oral and literate, and the now challenged assumptions of the autonomous model, they invoke NLS, but then want to take account of its limitations and to extend beyond them:

> Such understanding also has a more general intellectual value for it forces us to explore why historical and ethnographic cases are necessary but insufficient for rethinking inherited viewpoints . . . although ethnographic scholarship has demonstrated the pluralities of literacies, their context-boundness, it still has also to account for general tendencies that hold across diverse case studies. (7–8).

They argue, then, for "a way out of the universalist/particularist impasse," which had troubled Brandt as we saw above, "by attending closely to issues of text, power and identity." These are issues that are at the heart of current developments in NLS, from Lesley Bartlett and Dorothy Holland's concern with identities in practice (see below), to my own attention to literacy and power in the ideological model, and Maybin's refinement of Bakhtin's "intertextuality" with respect to literacy practices. Writing in *Situated Literacies*, Maybin also links NLS to wider strands of social-critical work, offering a way of linking Foucauldian notions of Discourse, Bakhtinian notions of intertextuality and work in Critical Discourse Analysis with the recognition from NLS of "the articulation of different discourses [as] centrally and dynamically interwoven in people's everyday literacy activities." James Paul Gee, in the same *Situated Literacies* volume, also located the "situated" approach to literacies in relation to broader movements towards a "social turn" which he saw as a challenge to behaviorism and individualism—a challenge which NLS has also pursued. Hilary Janks, located in South Africa, likewise links literacy studies to broader social theory, invoking the concepts of "Domination, Access, Diversity and Design" as a means of synthesizing the various strands of critical literacy education. Peter Freebody, writing from Australia, but like Janks taking a broad theoretical and international view, likewise writes of the relationship between NLS and "critical literacy," an approach to the acquisition and use of reading and writing in educational contexts that takes account of relations of power and domination.

Bartlett and Holland likewise link NLS to broader social theory. They propose an expanded conception of the space of literacy practices, drawing upon innovations in the cultural school of psychology, sociocultural history and social practice theory. In locating literacy theory within these broader debates in social theory, they build, especially, on the concern of Pierre Bourdieu to characterize the relationship between social structures (history brought to the present in institutions) and "habitus" (history brought to the present in person) and suggest ways in which NLS can adapt this approach: "Bourdieu's theory suggests that we can analyze literacy events with an eye to the ways in which historical and social forces have shaped a person's linguistic habitus and thus impinges upon that person's actions in the moment" (6).

However, they argue that Bourdieu's theory is itself "limited by his tendency to underplay the importance of culturally produced narratives, images and other artifacts in modifying habitus" (x). It is here that they suggest ways of extending both Bourdieu and literacy studies by putting them together with other key concepts in their work: "We propose to strengthen a theoretical approach to literacy studies by specifying the space of literacy practice, examining in particular the locally operant figured world of literacy, identities in practice, and artifacts" (6).

Applying their concept of "figured worlds"—"a socially produced and culturally constructed realm of interpretation"—to literacy practices, they suggest that "a figured world of literacy might include 'functional illiterates,' 'good readers' and 'illiterates,' any of which might be invoked, animated, contested and enacted through artifacts, activities and identities in practice"

(6). In the world of schooled literacy in particular, scholars have noted the tendency to invoke and deploy such figurings and identities to characterize children and their attainment—Holland and Bartlett enable us to see such characterizations as themselves part of what we should be taking into account when we try to understand literacy practices in context: we should be wary of taking them at face value, a skepticism that will prove useful as we move towards applying social literacy theory to education in general and schooling in particular.

Pahl ("Ephemera" and "Habitus") has built upon Holland and Bartlett's use of *habitus* in relation to figured worlds in order to help her describe the multi-modal practices of young children at home in her research on London families. Drawing also upon Gunther Kress and Theo van Leeuwen for *multi-modality* and Street ("Literacy"; *Social*) for *literacy practices,* she describes the ways in which young children take from and adapt family narratives as they do drawings, create three-dimensional objects, and write graffiti on walls. The work of figuring these family worlds is done through a combination of oral, visual and written artifacts through which over time key themes—such as a family's connection with the railways in India or with a farm in Wales—become sedimented and persistent. Through these narratives, embedded in material and linguistic form, the identity of family members is constructed and adapted over time. Again, there is a pedagogic message regarding how schools might recognize and build upon such home practices, but there is also an important theoretical contribution to NLS, namely that Pahl shows how any account of literacy practices needs to be contextualized within other communicative modes. Also, like Bartlett and Holland and Collins, she develops a sophisticated analysis of how such practices relate to concepts of textuality, figured worlds, identity, and power.

Another update and extension of NLS is to be found in Nancy Hornberger's edited volume, in which authors attempt to apply her conception of the "continua of biliteracy" to actual uses of reading and writing in different multilingual settings: *biliteracy* is defined as "any and all instances in which communication occurs in two (or more) languages in or around writing" and is described in terms of four nested sets of intersecting continua characterizing the contexts, media, content, and development of biliteracy. A number of the authors, as in the Martin-Jones and Jones book, draw out the links of NLS to such multilingual settings.

Applications to Education

The next stage of work in this area is to move beyond these theoretical critiques and to develop positive proposals for interventions in teaching, curriculum, measurement criteria, and teacher education in both the formal and informal sectors, based upon these principles. It will be at this stage that the theoretical perspectives brought together in the "New Literacy Studies" will face their sternest test: that of their practical applications to mainstream education. Glynda Hull and Katherine Schultz have been amongst the first researchers to directly apply insights from NLS to educational practice and policy. They build upon the foundational descriptions of out-of-school literacy events and practices developed within NLS, to return the gaze back to the relations between in and out of school, so that NLS is not seen simply as "anti school" or interested only in small scale or "local" literacies of resistance. They especially want to use the understandings of children's emerging experiences with literacy in their own cultural milieus to address broader educational questions about learning of literacy and of switching between the literacy practices required in different contexts. They

> are troubled by a tendency . . . to build and reify a great divide between in school and out of school and that sometimes this dichotomy relegates all good things to out-of-school contexts and everything repressive to school. Sometimes it dismisses the engagement of children with non-school learning as merely frivolous or remedial or incidental. (3)

In contrast to this approach and drawing strongly on work in NLS, they argue for "overlap or complementarity or perhaps a respectful division of labor." They cite Dewey's argument that there is much we can learn about successful pedagogies and curricula by foregrounding the relationship between formal education and ordinary life. "From the standpoint of the child" Dewey observed, "the great waste in the school comes from his inability to utilize the experiences he gets outside of the school in any complete and free way within the school itself; while on the other hand, he is unable to apply in daily life what he is learning in school" (76–78).

But how are we to know about the experiences of the child outside of school? Many teachers express anxiety that the children in their classes may come from a wide variety of backgrounds and it is impossible to know them all. Hull and Schultz respond by invoking the work of researchers "who have made important contributions to understanding literacy learning through ethnographic or field-based studies in homes, community organizations and after-school programs" (14). Their edited volume consists of accounts of such research in a variety of settings. They are aware of the criticism of such approaches that might overemphasize the "local" or even "romanticize out-of-school contexts" and aim instead to "acknowledge the complexities, tensions and opportunities" that are found there. Nor is their aim to provide an exhaustive account of such contexts—teachers are right to argue that this cannot all be covered. Instead, they aim to provide us all, but especially those responsible for the education of children, with understanding of the principles underlying such variation and with help in listening to and appreciating what it is that children bring from home and community experience. Indeed, the book consists of both articles about such experience and comments by teachers and teacher educators on their significance for learning. Here, then, NLS meets educational practice in ways that begin to fulfill the potential of the approach, but through dialogue rather than simply an imposition of researchers' agendas on educators.

In Australia, the work of Peter Freebody and Allan Luke provides powerful examples of the application of new theoretical perspectives on literacy, including NLS, to education, especially work on curriculum and assessment in Queensland (Luke and Carrington; Luke and Freebody).

In my recent *Literacies Across Educational Contexts*, a number of authors from a variety of international contexts likewise take on this challenge and attempt to follow through such practical applications of the NLS approach. As with Hull and Schultz's work, the authors are conscious of the links between theoretical debate and the work of teachers in school addressing literacy issues. The collection of case studies ranges from formal education, including elementary, secondary and higher education and informal sectors such as community associations, international development programs and workplace literacies. Across these educational contexts, the authors are concerned not just to apply the general principles of NLS but with offering practical critiques of its application that force us to refine the original conceptualization: the volume, then, is intended to be not a static "application" of theory to practice, but a dynamic dialogue between the two. In attempting to work through the implications of these approaches for different sectors of education, the authors find limitations and problems in some NLS approaches—such as the "limits of the local" in educational as well as theoretical terms—that require them to go back to the underpinning conceptual apparatus. Theory as well as practice is subject to the critical perspective being adopted there and researchers and practitioners will have to either adapt or even reject parts of NLS as it engages with such new tasks.

Such a challenge is raised by current research by Baker, Street and Tomlin, who apply literacy theory to the understanding of numeracy practices in and out of school. Numeracy even more than literacy has been seen as a "universal," "context free" set of skills that can be imparted across the board, irrespective of children's background experiences and prior cultural knowledge. Recent approaches to "situated learning," when allied to those from situated literacy, suggest that such a "banking" model of education, as Paulo Freire termed it, is inappropriate especially in the multilingual, multicultural situations that characterize contemporary hybrid cultural contexts. The question that Street and Baker address is how far such a culturally-sensitive approach can be applied to numeracy education: can we talk of multiple numeracies and of numeracy events and practices as we do of literacy? Can we build upon cultural knowledge of number, measurement, approximation, etc. in the way that Hull and Schultz and those in the *Literacies Across the Curriculum* volume believe we can do for cultural knowledge of literacies, scripts, languages? Again, the questions being raised by NLS, when applied to new fields such as this will lead to critiques not only of current educational practice but also of the theoretical framework itself. As with the critiques by Brandt, Collins, etc., NLS will be forced to adapt and change—the validity and value of its original insights and their applications to practice will be tested according to whether they can meet this challenge.

In an international context the application of NLS to both schooling and adult literacy has likewise raised new questions and faced new problems contingent on the nature of the particular context. The aim of such "applications" has not been to simply impose a pre-given template onto local work in the field but to enter a dialogue (see my *Literacy and Development: Ethnographic Perspectives* for detailed examples). A telling case of such work is the Community Literacies Project in Nepal, supported by the U.K.'s Department for International Development (DFID) and based in Kathmandu. CLPN provides a resource for supporting local literacy initiatives, be they women working in credit groups, Forestry User Groups, or people setting up wall newspapers and local broadcasting. Such organizations come to CLPN for support when their members need to enhance their literacy but instead of sending them to sit in formal classes—to be "infantilized," treated like their children with desks, grade levels, and demeaning assessments—the CLPN team attempt to work with them in the local context and to build upon what they already know as a way of developing what else they want to know—to create better forms for the credit group, to read and write minutes for the Forestry Users Group, to makes tape recordings for broadcast.

However, as with other "applications" of NLS (see Rogers, and Street, *Literacy*), the local context generates its own new problems that force us to rethink and adapt the initial conceptualization. In this case, as in many development contexts, the problem arises as to whether there is a conflict between theory and policy on one hand and the local and the needs of scale faced by administrators on the other. The more those ethnographers explain the "complexity" of literacy practices, the more policy makers find it impossible to design programs that can take account of all that complexity. The more ethnographers demonstrate that literacy does not necessarily have the effects that the rhetoric has suggested—improved health, cognition, empowerment—the harder does it become for policymakers to persuade funders to support literacy programs. The more ethnographers focus on specific local contexts, the harder does it seem to "upscale" their projects to take account of the large numbers of people seen to be in need. So how can contemporary literacy projects bridge this apparent divide between policy and research in general and in particular between large scale needs and micro ethnographic approaches?

The Community Literacies Project in Nepal aims to do precisely this. Based on a spirit of engagement between theory and practice, academic and applied concerns, it aims to make a contribution at the interface, clarifying conceptual issues, and enhancing knowledge on the one hand and aiding policy making and program building on the other (Rogers). The participants approach the issues in a spirit of reflective and critical inquiry, less concerned to advocate particular approaches, methodologies, and theories than to extend current thinking and thereby facilitate informed local practice. Anna Robinson-Pant's book about Nepal—"*Why Eat Green Cucumbers at the Time of Dying?" Exploring the Link between Women's Literacy and Development*—which won the Unesco Literacy Prize, provides some of the answers to the worries about ethnography that some literacy campaigners might express. "Why eat green cucumbers at the time of dying?"—why take on the luxury of new literacy practices when your communicative repertoire seems already sufficient? Because, says Robinson-Pant, "learning to read—like eating cucumber in rural areas—is both a luxury and a challenge when you are old" (indeed, at any age) (1). Taking on reading, new readings, and new literacy practices, broadening the communicative repertoire, and challenging dominant epistemologies are continuing processes, not a one-off shift from "illiteracy" to "literacy," from dark to light, as the early approaches to literacy work would have it. There are always new things to experience and learning and life can always be enhanced—even at the time of dying!

Policy Issues

Despite the willingness of DFID to fund such imaginative approaches to literacy work overseas, in the U.K. itself as in the U.S.A., the qualitative and ethnographic work that characterizes NLS and underpins such an approach is currently out of fashion in higher policy circles. A recent important political development in the validating and funding of research in education in general and literacy in particular has been the demand that such research conform to "scientific" standards. Key words in this approach include "Systematic Reviews," "Rigor," and "Evidence-Based Policies." In both the U.K. and U.S.A., governments and their agencies are insisting that funding will only be permitted on the basis that programs and the research on which they are based can be proven to be "scientific." A number of commissions and panels have reviewed research on literacy in this light, e.g., the National Academy of Science report "Preventing Reading Difficulties in Young Children" (Snow, Burns, Griffin); the National Reading Panel set up by the National Institute of Child Health and Human Development (NRP, 2000); and the U.S. Department of Education's (ED) newly formed Institute of Education Sciences' plan to evaluate research as part of its web-based What Works Clearinghouse project. For instance, the Clearinghouse, founded in August 2002, aims to become a trusted, one-stop source of scientifically proven teaching practices for educators, policy makers, and the public. It will contain systematically evaluated research to help educators more easily identify scientifically proven teaching methods as required by the No Child Left Behind Act of 2001 (NCLB).

Academic researchers, including those active in the field of literacy, are playing a leading role in these developments. For instance, in the U.S.A. Robert Slavin, the founder of "Success for All," argued in a recent paper in *Educational Researcher* that: "the use of randomized experiments that transformed medicine, agriculture and technology in the 20th century is now beginning to affect educational policy" (18). He concludes from a survey of such research that "a focus on rigorous experiments evaluating replicable programs and practices is essential to build confidence in educational research among policymakers and educators" (19). In particular, this approach suggests ways in which what is known from experimental studies of literacy acquisition can be built into programs and policies for early schooling. In the U.K., the Evidence for Policy and Practice Information Coordinating Centre (EPPI-Centre) has been established at the Institute for Education in London to conduct "systematic reviews" of research in designated fields and the English National Literacy Strategy was justified on similar grounds, although the use of "systematic reviews," etc., was less well developed at the initial stages. Researchers summarizing the research base for the National Literacy Strategy have since claimed that we now "know what works" in teaching initial literacy and that the task is simply to apply this in schooling (Beard, Harrison).

Critiques of these approaches have come from a number of well-known qualitative researchers in the literacy field (Gee, *Social*; Coles; Goodman; Hamersley; Erickson and Gutierrez). A special issue of *Educational Researcher* (Vol. 31, no. 8, Nov 2002) was devoted to the question of "Scientific Research in Education" and a special edition of the *Journal of Teacher Education* was devoted to teacher preparation research (*Journal of Teacher Education* 53: May–Jun 2002). In the U.K. the *British Educational Research Journal* likewise published a number of articles on Systematic Reviews in its Nov 2001 issue (Vol. 27, No. 5). Martyn Hamersley, for instance, writing in that issue, links the trend to "systematic reviews" to a resurgence of positivist epistemology as an alternative to "narrative" ("subjective," qualitative, interpretive?) reviews. Hamersley comments: "What is curious about the dual (both doing research and producing research reviews) application of the positivist model to the task of reviewing is that it takes little or no account of the considerable amount of criticism that has been made of that model since at least the middle of the twentieth century" (545). Adam Lefstein (2003) provides a helpful survey of much of this literature, invoking the philosophical terms *techne* and *phronesis* to analyze the difference between "scientific technical rationality" and "practical reason" as they are applied to education and specifically to the U.K. Literacy Strategy.

In the U.S., likewise, qualitative researchers in the literacy field have addressed both the wider epistemological assumptions underpinning the "scientific" move and the specific issues regarding acquisition of reading that are often the focus of such approaches. Ken Goodman has set up an email network that circulates details of new initiatives, e.g., the What Works Clearinghouse project, and offers scathing critiques. Joanne Larson's wittily titled *Literacy as Snake Oil* has a number of sharp criticisms of the way the Reading Panels have been set up, run and then invoked for policy purposes. The authors demonstrate some of the problems with the "scientific" approach—its inability to engage with the nuances of cultural meanings, the variation in uses of literacy across contexts and the problems already highlighted with the autonomous model of literacy—and attempt to construct more meaningful solutions. Similarly, critics in a special issue of *Educational Researcher* berate the U.S. Dept of Education initiatives for "confusing the methods of science with the process of science" (Berliner). Frederick Erickson and Kris Gutierrez, for example, critique the NRC Committee for taking "an evidence-based social engineering approach to educational improvement" and argue for replacing the "'white coat' notion of science . . . with a more complicated and realistic view of what actual scientists do" (qtd. in Lefstein).

All of this has considerable importance for literacy work, both in terms of the kind of research that can get funded, the kinds of procedures for reviewing research that are considered legitimate and the policy effects of that research which does get through the sieve. The wider political and ideological context of such research is itself part of what counts as engaging with literacy in theory and practice.

Conclusion

The effects of these critical engagements with social theory, educational applications and policy is that New Literacy Studies is now going through a productive period of intense debate that firstly establishes and consolidates many of the earlier insights and empirical work and secondly builds a more robust and perhaps less insular field of study. A major contribution arising from the work cited here has been the attempt to appeal beyond the specific interests of ethnographers interested in the "local" in order to engage with both educationalists interested in literacy acquisition and use across educational contexts, both formal and informal, and with policy makers more generally. That practical engagement, however, will still need to be rooted in sound theoretical and conceptual understanding if the teaching and studying of literacy are to avoid being simply tokens for other interests. We still, then, need to analyze and contest what counts as "literacy" (and numeracy); what literacy events and practices mean to users in different cultural and social contexts—the original inspiration for NLS—but also what are the "limits of the local"; and, as the writers cited here indicate, how literacy relates to more general issues of social theory regarding textuality, figured worlds, identity, and power.

Works Cited

Aikman, Sheila. *Intercultural Education and Literacy: An Ethnographic Study of Indigenous Knowledge and Learning in the Peruvian Amazon*. Amsterdam: Benjamins, 1999.

Anderson, Alonzo B., William H. Teale, and Elette Estrada. "Low-Income Children's Preschool Literacy Experiences: Some Naturalistic Observations." *The Quarterly Newsletter of the Laboratory of Comparative Human Cognition* 2 (1980): 59–65.

Baker, D. A., B. Street, and A. Tomlin. "Math as Social: Understanding Relationships Between Home and School Numeracy Practices." Submitted to *FLM*. 2002.

Bartlett, Lesley, and Dorothy Holland. "Theorizing the Space of Literacy Practices." *Ways of Knowing* 2 (2002): 10–22.

Barton, David. *Literacy: An Introduction to the Ecology of Written Language*. Oxford: Blackwell, 1994.

Barton, David, and Mary Hamilton. *Local Literacies: Reading and Writing in One Community*. London: Routledge, 1998.

Barton, David, Mary Hamilton, and Roz Ivanic. *Situated Literacies: Reading and Writing in Context*. London: Routledge, 2000.

Barton, David, and Roz Ivanic. *Writing in the Community*. Newbury Park, CA: Sage, 1991.

Baynham, Mike. *Literacy Practices: Investigating Literacy in Social Contexts*. London: Routledge, 1995.

Baynham, Mike, and Dave Baker. "'Practice' in Literacy and Numeracy Research: Multiple Perspectives." *Ways of Knowing* 2 (2002): 1–9.

Baynham, Mike, and Martin Prinsloo. "New Directions in Literacy Research." *Language and Education* 3/4 (2001): 92–104.

Beard, Roger. "Research and the National Literacy Strategy." *Oxford Review of Education* 26 (2000): 421–36.

Berliner, David C. "Educational Research: The Hardest Science of All." *Educational Researcher* 31 (2002): 18–20.

Besnier, Niko, and Brian Street. "Aspects of Literacy." *Encyclopedia of Anthropology*. Ed. Tim Ingold. London: Routledge, 1994. 527–562.

Brandt, Deborah. *Literacy in American Lives*. Cambridge: Cambridge UP, 2001.

Brandt, Deborah, and Katie Clinton. "Limits of the Local: Expanding Perspectives on Literacy as a Social Practice." *Journal of Literacy Research* 34 (2002): 337–356.

Coles, Gerald. "Reading Research and Skills-Emphasis Instruction: Forcing 'Facts' to Fit an Explanation." *Literacy as Snake Oil: Beyond the Quick Fix*. Ed. Joanne Larson. New York: Peter Lang, 2001. 27–44.

Collins, James. "Literacy and Literacies." *Annual Review of Anthropology* 24 (1995): 75–93.

Collins, James, and Richard K. Blot. *Literacy and Literacies: Texts, Power, and Identity*. Cambridge: Cambridge UP, 2003.

Erickson, Frederick, and Kris Gutierrez. "Culture, Rigor, and Science in Educational Research." *Educational Researcher* 31 (2002): 21–24.

Freebody, Peter. "Critical Literacy." *Multidisciplinary Perspectives on Literacy Research*. Ed. Richard Beach, Judith Green, and Timothy Shanahan. Cresskill, NJ: Hampton Press, 2005.

Gee, James Paul. "The New Literacy Studies: From 'Socially Situated' to the Work of the Social." *Situated Literacies: Reading and Writ-*

ing in Context. Ed. David Barton, Mary Hamilton, and Roz Ivanic. London: Routledge, 2000. 180–196.

———. "Orality and Literacy: From *The Savage Mind* to *Ways with Words*." *Social Linguistics and Literacy: Ideology in Discourses*. London: Falmer, 1990.

———. "Reading Language Abilities and Semiotic Resources: Beyond Limited Perspectives on Reading." *Literacy as Snake Oil: Beyond the Quick Fix*. Ed. Joanne Larson. New York: Peter Lang, 2001. 7–26.

———. *Social Linguistics: Ideology in Discourses*. London: Falmer, 1990.

Hammersly, Martyn. "On 'Systematic' Reviews of Research Literatures: A'Narrative' Response to Evans and Benefield." *British Educational Research Journal* 27 (2001): 543–554.

Harrison, C. *The National Strategy for English at Key Stage 3: Roots and Research*. Department for Education and Skills. London: HMSO, 2002.

Heath, Shirley Brice. *Ways with Words: Language, Life and Work in Communities and Classrooms*. Cambridge: Cambridge UP, 1983.

Hornberger, Nancy H. *Continua of Biliteracy: An Ecological Framework for Educational Policy, Research, and Practice in Multilingual Settings*. Clevedon, UK: Multilingual Matters, 2003.

Hull, Glynda A., and Katherine Schultz. "Literacy and Learning Out of School: A Review of Theory and Research." *Review of Educational Research* 71 (2001): 575–611.

———. *School's Out: Bridging Out-Of-School Literacies with Classroom Practice*. New York: Teachers College, 2002.

Janks, Hilary. "Domination, Access, Diversity and Design: A Synthesis for Critical Literacy Education." *Educational Review* 52 (2000): 175–186.

Kalman, Judy. *Writing on the Plaza: Mediated Literacy Practices Among Scribes and Clients in Mexico City*. Cresskill, NJ: Hampton, 1999.

Kress, Gunther, and Theo van Leeuwen. *Multimodal Discourse: The Modes and Media of Contemporary Communication*. London: Arnold, 2001.

Kulick, Don, and Christopher Stroud. "Conceptions and Uses of Literacy in a Papua New Guinean Village." *Cross-Cultural Approaches to Literacy*. Ed. Brian Street. Cambridge: Cambridge UP, 1993. 30–61.

Lefstein, Adam. "Teaching and Reading between Technical Rationality and Practical Reason in the National Literacy Strategy." Paper for discussion in RWLL, King's College London. 2003.

Luke, Allan, and Victoria Carrington. "Globalisation, Literacy, Curriculum Practice." *Language and Literacy in Action*. Ed. Roz Fisher, Maureen Lewis, and Greg Brooks. London: Routledge/Falmer, 2002.

Luke, Allan, and Peter Freebody. "Reading as a Social Practice." *Constructing Critical Literacies*. Ed. Sandy Muspratt, Allan Luke, and Peter Freebody. New York: Hampton, 2002.

Martin-Jones, Marilyn, and Kathryn Jones, eds. *Multilingual Literacies: Comparative Perspectives on Research and Practice*. Amsterdam: Benjamins, 2000.

Maybin, Janet. *Language and Literacy in Social Practice*. Open UP, 1993.

———. "The New Literacy Studies: Context, Intertextuality, and Discourse." *Situated Literacies: Reading and Writing in Context*. Ed. David Barton, Mary Hamilton, and Roz Ivanic. London: Routledge, 2000. 197–209.

Mukherjee, Aditi, Duggirala Vasanta, eds. *Practice and Research in Literacy*. Delhi and London: Sage, 2003.

Prinsloo, Martin, and Mignonne Breier. *The Social Uses of Literacy*. London: Benjamins, 1996.

Pahl, Kate. "Ephemera, Mess and Miscellaneous Piles: Texts and Practices in Families." *Journal of Early Childhood Literacy* 2 (2002): 145–166.

———. "Habitus and the Home: Texts and Practices in Families." *Ways of Knowing* 2 (2002): 45–53.

Robinson-Pant, Anna. *"Why Eat Green Cucumber at the Time of Dying?": Exploring the Link Between Adult Literacy and Development*. Hamburg: Unesco: 2001.

Rogers, Alan. *Adults Learning for Development*. London: Cassell, 1992.

———. *Using Literacy: A New Approach to Post Literacy Materials*. London: ODA, 1994.

Slavin, Robert E. "Evidence-Based Education Policies: Transforming Educational Practice and Research." *Educational Researcher* 31 (2002): 15–21.

Snow, Catherine E., Susan Burns, and Peg Griffin, eds. *Preventing Reading Difficulties in Young Children*. Committee on the Prevention of Reading Difficulties in Young Children. Washington, DC: National Academy, 1998.

Street, Brian. "Literacy Events and Literacy Practices." *Multilingual Literacies: Comparative Perspectives on Research and Practice*. Ed. Marilyn Martin-Jones and Kathryn Jones. Amsterdam: Benjamins, 2000. 17–29.

———. *Literacy in Theory and Practice*. Cambridge: Cambridge UP, 1984.

———. "Literacy Practices and Literacy Myths." *The Written World: Studies in Literate Thought and Action*. Ed. Roger Saljo. New York: Springer-Verlag, 1988. 59–72.

———. *Social Literacies*. London: Longman, 1995.

Street, Brian, ed. *Literacy and Development: Ethnographic Perspectives*. London: Routledge, 2001.

———. *Literacies Across Educational Contexts*. Philadelphia: Caslon, 2005.

Chapter Four

The Intellectual Work of "Mixed" Forms of Academic Discourses

Patricia Bizzell

To identify alternative forms of academic discourse, we need to have some sense of what a "standard" or non-alternative academic discourse, sometimes called traditional academic discourse, might be. A primary way to define academic discourse is to see it as the language of a community—hence the phrase, academic discourse community. I think it is possible to speak of the academic community's language-using practices as conventionalized; that is, there are certain customary ways of doing things. The way one employs these language-using conventions (with familiarity, grace, or tentative bravado, for example) establishes one's place within the community: people of higher status use language (within the shared conventions) differently than do people of lower status. Following these language-using conventions shapes participants' way of looking at the world—their worldview—including notions of what's real, normal, natural, good, and true. The people in the group use the shared language to work together on some shared project in the world—something they are trying to do together.

Because academic discourse is the language of a human community, it can never be absolutely fixed in form. It changes over time, and at any given time multiple versions of it are in use. In this sense, "alternative" forms of academic discourse have always been knocking around the academy. Nevertheless, because academic discourse is the language of a community, at any given

From *Alt/Dis*. Ed. Christopher Schroeder, Helen Fox, and Patricia Bizzell. Portsmouth, NH: Boynton/Cook, 2002. 1–10.

time its most standard or widely accepted features reflect the cultural preferences of the most powerful people in the community. Until relatively recently, these people in the academic community have usually been male, European American, and middle or upper class. Hence it is possible to say that traditional academic discourses generally share certain features.

For one thing, such discourses employ a grapholect, the most formal and ultra-correct form of the participants' native language, treating as "errors" usages that would be unproblematic in casual conversation. Also, traditional academic genres shape whole pieces of writing, such as the lab report, the reflective journal, the critical essay, the research paper, and so on. Finally, the ones in power in the traditional academic community create discourses that embody a typical worldview. This worldview speaks through an academic persona who is objective, trying to prevent any emotions or prejudices from influencing the ideas in the writing. The persona is skeptical, responding with doubt and questions to any claim that something is true or good or beautiful. Not surprisingly, the persona is argumentative, favoring debate, believing that if we are going to find out whether something is true or good or beautiful, the only way we will do that is by arguing for opposing views of it, to see who wins. In this view, only debate can produce knowledge. Knowledge is not immediately available to experience, nor is it revealed from transcendent sources. Additionally, the persona is extremely precise, exacting, rigorous—if debate is going to generate knowledge, all participants must use language carefully, demonstrate their knowledge of earlier scholarly work, argue logically and fairly, use sound evidence, and so on.

The academic community is changing, however, and becoming more diverse—more people of color, more women, more people from the lower social classes, more people whose native language is not English or not the so-called Standard English (not all of these groups are mutually exclusive). Gaining access to higher education for these diverse groups has certainly not been easy, of course, and as they brought with them diverse discourses from their various home communities, gaining acceptance for these discourses, too, is an ongoing struggle. Yet, slowly but surely, previously nonacademic discourses are blending with traditional academic discourses to form the new "mixed" forms. These new discourses are still academic, in that they are doing the intellectual work of the academy—rigorous, reflective scholarship. We find these discourses appearing in articles in top-rank academic journals and in books from prestigious academic presses. But they have combined elements of other ways of using language, admitting personal experience as evidence, for example, or employing cultural allusions or language variants that do not match the cultural capital of the dominant white male group. After all, in how many communities is it considered appropriate to critically question everything one's interlocutor says, picking apart the other person's statements and even her or his grammar and word choice, while keeping one's own emotions and investments in the topic carefully hidden?

I want to emphasize that I see these mixed forms not simply as more comfortable or more congenial—they would not be gaining currency if comfort was all they provided, because the powerful people in the academic community are still, to a large extent, middle- and upper-class white men who would have no stake in allowing discourse forms that were alien to them. Rather, I think these new, alternative or mixed discourse forms are gaining ground because they allow their practitioners to do intellectual work in ways they could not if confined to traditional academic discourse. That is why these discourses can be found in so many academic disciplines today. These new discourses enable scholarship to take account of new variables, to explore new methods, and to communicate findings in new venues, including broader reading publics than the academic. I attempted to sketch the contrasts between old and new academic discourses in "Hybrid Academic Discourses: What, Why, How" (Bizzell, "Hybrid").

These new forms of academic discourse probably should not be termed *hybrid,* however, a correction I attempted to explain in "Basic Writing and the Issue of Correctness" (Bizzell, "Basic"). For one thing, this concept relies on a reified notion of academic discourse that obscures institutional dynamics of power. Earlier in this essay I provided a brief taxonomy of the traits of traditional academic discourse in order to conceptualize the hybridization of discourse from two distinct "parents." As I also noted, however, I would not want to suggest that traditional academic discourse was a fixed and unchanging entity until very recently. This is certainly not the case, and one does not need to go back very far to discover that fact.

Moreover, research by Michelle Hall Kells among English-Spanish bilinguals shows why it is dangerous to imply that academic discourse has not changed much over time. Such a presentation tends to give academic discourse an air of superiority that all too readily plays into linguistic minority students' tendency to see the academy's formal language as "more logical" or "purer" than their home dialects—"dialect misconceptions" that lead to "linguistic shame," as Kells describes it, which impedes learning and school success (137). It might be more accurate to say that what has remained constant is the privileged social position of whatever currently counts as academic discourse.

Furthermore, the term *hybrid* is at once too abstract and too concrete. It is borrowed from postcolonial theory, and the problems with its abstraction are well analyzed in Deepika Bahri's work on applications of postcolonial theory to composition studies. I was attracted to the term *hybrid* because it upsets the dichotomy established in my earlier work between academic discourse and students' home discourses, and thus implies that discursive and cultural boundaries are more blurred and, perhaps because of that blurring, more easily crossed than had been thought in so-called current-traditional, error hunting writing instruction. But Bahri points out:

> If the concept of hybridity is useful in undoing binaries and approaching the complexities of transnationalism, as many would find in composition studies, I would warn that it also tends to avoid the question of location because it suggests a zone of nowhere-ness, and a people afloat in a weightless ether, of ahistoricity. . . . The scores of underclass immigrants in Anglo-America and illegal border-crossers not only cannot "make themselves comfortable" with the same ease that other postcolonials have but also know that a border-crossing can be dangerous and potentially fatal. The deeply racial and class segregated nature of our cities, moreover, should also alert us to the intransigent borders within, rather than invoking the more glamorous cultural borders that metropolitan postcolonial celebrities [such as Homi Bhabha and Salmon Rushdie] invoke. (39)

It would be a mistake to imply that the "mixing" in alternative academic discourses can go on easily, naturally, or without political opposition from the powers that be.

At the same time as the concept of hybrid gets in trouble for being too abstract, however, it can also be critiqued for being too concrete. Hybrid, after all, is a biological metaphor, as in such statements as, the mule is a hybrid of the donkey and the horse. Using a biological metaphor for discourse risks essentializing people's language use. Thus, for example, while Black English Vernacular is deeply significant to many people of African descent, deeply rooted in their sense of their individual and collective identities, its linguistic features are not genetically determined, and people of African descent may well be able to use and to enjoy using other dialects of English. There is a larger problem here, as well, and that is the nature of the variant forms that are coming into academic discourse. The biological metaphor of hybridity implies that what mixes in the new forms, as I noted earlier, are two distinct "parents," that is, distinct, well-defined, and culturally independent linguistic and discursive practices. It is not at all clear that this is the case, however.

In short, we must not ignore the profound cultural mixing that has already occurred in the United States. Even students who are the first members of their families or their communities to attend college come with already mixed linguistic and discursive resources, as Scott Lyons explains in discussing the narratives of American Indian students:

> To my mixedblood mind, the stories of Indian students are clearly *heteroglossia*—produced against, within, and in tandem with the grand narratives of contemporary American life and culture . . . . There is a European in every Indian and an Indian in every "white"—each relationship positioned differently—and the two are not together by choice. It is this kind of *contact heteroglossia* that has been repressed by educators and theorists for centuries, and that Indian students not only know, but also use daily—we can all learn from them in this respect. (88–89)

Lyons argues forcefully for the need for Indian students to use Indian discursive resources in their college writing, but at the same time, he shows how very difficult it would be to tease out the Indian strands in academic writing that nevertheless may be clearly recognized as "non-traditional," variant, or new.

Moreover, Lyons points in passing to another important aspect of mixing that many of us have experienced in our classrooms today, and that is the *contact heteroglossia*, to use his term, that can be seen in the writing of European American students. Basic writing teachers know that it is a mistake to expect traditional academic discourse from all the students who appear racially white or who self-identify as white. Experimentation with new discourse forms certainly cannot be attributed to any essentialized linguistic heritage in the case of these students. Yes, increased access has happened, and a wide range of published scholarship employs new forms of academic discourse, as I have noted, but it is misleading to imply that new forms have emerged simply to make new students and scholars feel more comfortable. The new forms are being used by everyone, not only by students and scholars from underrepresented social groups, and the reason is not far to seek: as noted previously, they make possible new forms of intellectual work.

The best evidence I can present for the compelling nature of this new intellectual work is to find examples of powerful white male scholars who are employing alternative discourses, possibly at some risk to themselves, because they cannot do what they want to do in their scholarship any other way. Especially persuasive might be examples drawn from elsewhere than English studies, a field that has been experimenting with alternative discourses for some time, particularly in the work of feminist theorists and scholars in composition and rhetoric. Accordingly, I offer an example from *The Journal of American History*, the official scholarly publication of the Organization of American Historians.

A long meditation by Joel Williamson, a very senior and eminent scholar, leads off the March 1997 issue. Williamson attempts to explore how his own personal background has affected his scholarship, and thus to make a point about historiography in general. Williamson is interested in trying to understand why he, a southerner "born and bred" (1228) as he describes himself, took so long to realize that lynching and other racially motivated forms of violence were important factors in black-white relations in the South. His meditation is triggered by the Clarence Thomas confirmation hearings, in which Thomas clinched his own defense by accusing his critics of perpetrating a "high-tech lynching." Thomas' use of this metaphor spurs Williamson to examine how knowledge of lynching and understanding of its cultural significance are variably distributed according to race. Williamson argues not only that white people are ignorant on the subject of racial violence, but that they are willfully so—that there is a deliberate forgetting or erasure going on, and that it has affected even the practice of research in American history, even the research done by scholars such as himself, whose focus has been race relations. Williamson has published an important book on lynching and racial violence, and yet, in this essay, he indicts himself for the unconscionably slow growth of his own awareness of the importance of this topic and for the blind spots that he knows exist in his vision even today. He concludes by noting that a major blind spot has to do with the sexual politics of lynching, and he calls for a new vision of southern history that deals more frankly with gender as well as with race.

Scholars in composition and rhetoric may find nothing surprising in Williamson's meditations other than that 1997 seems rather late for the discipline of history to be examining the personal roots of its scholarly agendas, compared to what has gone on in our field, in the work of Helen Fox, Keith Gilyard, Mike Rose, and Victor Villanueva, to name a few examples. But David Thelen, editor of the journal when Williamson's essay appeared, finds Williamson's experiment so challenging that he takes the very unusual course of printing Williamson's essay as he submitted it, along with six referees' reports as they submitted them—nothing edited for publication. Evidently Thelen is so anxious about publishing the Williamson piece that he must invite the journal readers to scrutinize the evidence on which he made the decision to print. Ongoing anxiety is evinced, too, in Thelen's decision to commission a seventh response to Williamson's piece from a woman who is a scholar of women's history, once he noticed that Williamson's six referees, all male, were none of them scholars of women's history. She is the only one of the reviewers who knew she was writing for publication.

What interests me about this now rather notorious fracas is that the reviewers, all but one, clearly address themselves to the issue of whether the historiographical insights provided by Williamson's essay are worth struggling with his alternative discourse form. Five end up voting in the affirmative, though there is ample evidence that the form disturbs them. A principal concern seems to be the nonlinear structure of the essay, familiar to writing teachers from what we call the personal essay, but not the traditional structure of academic argument. Williamson's reviewers react to this structure by finding it hard to connect the themes he broaches. Steven M. Stowe notes "two strands" of thought in the essay that "do not always adhere": "the author plays with one and then the other, then both, but shifting and spinning them in ways that are not always clear" (1264–65). David Levering Lewis finds "three themes" in the essay that "are insufficiently explored, and their putative interconnectedness is either strained or fallacious" (1261). David W. Blight condemns "a cacophony of themes and subthemes, plots and subplots" in Williamson's essay—he counts no less than eight (1255).

The reviewers also notice the personal style of Williamson's essay, his use of autobiographical examples and his willingness to reveal his emotions. Lewis, the most negative of the seven reviewers, is repulsed by this style; he says, "the tone of the piece borders on self- promotion written in mighty florid prose" and he finds some passages "embarrassing" (1261). The majority of the reviewers, however, seem to react more like Edward L. Ayers, who, although "embarrassed to admit how much I like this essay," feels that it is "revealing without being self-indulgent," and he is "pulled along by this essay's momentum, by its revelations and emotional power" (1254). Stowe characterizes the essay as "a kind of heart of darkness journey" that "seeks out something horrible at the center of things" (1264; a perhaps unintentionally ironic reference, given the well-known controversy in literary studies over the racism of Conrad's story—does Stowe enact with this reference another sort of the willful blindness Williamson condemns?). Stowe asserts that "the most powerful parts of this paper are when the author speaks most personally about his struggle to understand" (1266). George M. Frederickson states the dilemma for the male readers most clearly:

> It is a highly personal, partially autobiographical statement that lacks the objective tone and scholarly apparatus of the normal *JAH* article. It is, *however,* intelligent, incisive, and full of interest for anyone concerned with southern history. . . . Should the *JAH* publish this kind of piece? It would be a new departure, I think . . . but my view is that essays of this kind, if they possess the authority and quality found here, deserve a place in the *Journal.* . . . The personalized, confessional mode does not seem to me objectionable when used in historiographic essays that involve the author's own work. In fact, a good argument could be made that such disclosure is not only appropriate but highly desirable. (1257-58, emphasis added)

It is interesting that Jacquelyn Dowd Hall, the woman invited to compose a seventh response to Williamson's piece, does not seem to be bothered in the slightest by the mode of discourse the male reviewers found so complicated, although she takes exception to Williamson's preference for military metaphors. Perhaps as a feminist historian, she has encountered alternative discourse forms often enough—unlike the male reviewers—to be comfortable with them.

In spite of some reviewers' struggles with Williamson's alternative discourse, most found much to value in the intellectual work he accomplishes, as Frederickson hints when he notes that "such disclosure is not only appropriate but highly desirable" (1258). Here is how some of the other reviewers articulate what they find of value in Williamson's piece:

> Hall praises the analysis Williamson provides, however unconventionally, of what she calls the "symbiosis between cultural amnesia and historiographical neglect" and its impact on southern history (1268).

> Blight calls Williamson a "wise provocateur" who "has much to say about the cycles of historiographical discovery and decline"; Blight finds "stimulating" Williamson's call at the end of the piece for "a fuller embrace of gender—a new men's and a new women's history of the South" (1256; is there a pun intended here?).

> Stowe provides perhaps the most detail about what Williamson contributes. He notes that Williamson illuminates the ways that

> "the historiography of southern race relations in the past thirty to forty years divides into three overlapping vistas," dealing with slavery, segregation, and lynching, and that Williamson helpfully points out "how dim and limited the last one is" and asks "Why do we not know how to write about lynching?" (1265) Stowe believes that Williamson's valuable answer to this question is that historians need to do more self-searching work of the kind Williamson does in this essay. In other words, Stowe sees the essay as exemplifying a new kind of history writing that addresses the critical problems to which it calls attention, or as Stowe puts it, "the author suggests that historians look, not just in a different direction, but to a different dimension of experience for the next step in the history of the races" (1266).

It would seem, then, that for five of Williamson's seven readers, the alternative mode of discourse enables valuable, even uniquely valuable, intellectual work.

Two of the original six referees, however, recommended against publication, and most vehemently. But their objections do not seem to focus primarily on the use of an alternative discourse. Before I discuss them, however, I want to mention that Williamson's essay, and all seven responses, were accompanied by photos of the authors. No other articles in this issue of the *Journal of American History* are accompanied by photos of the authors, so evidently it is not this journal's usual practice. Are these photos included to let us know that the two negative reviewers, David Levering Lewis and Robin D. G. Kelley, are African American, without having to tell us? Racial identity is not always evident from photographs, but I wonder.

Although Lewis, as noted previously, makes clear that he does not like Williamson's alternative discourse, he condemns Williamson's entire body of work in southern history. Lewis's review is by far the longest of the seven and ranges over many issues only tangential to the Williamson essay he is reviewing. Not knowing the field of American history, I can only guess that in this review, a long-standing scholarly rivalry reemerges. Certainly Williamson's discursive experiment did nothing to win over an old adversary. I have to wonder, though, whether, since Lewis is African American, his rancor was motivated at least in part by some of the objections Kelley raises.

Kelley does not seem to be bothered by Williamson's alternative mode of discourse, either. At any rate, he does not say anything about it. His chief objection is that Williamson talks about his own problems of what Hall calls "cultural amnesia and historiographical neglect" as if they beset American historians universally. Kelley does not say in so many words that black historians have no problem with amnesia where lynching is concerned, but he devotes much of his review to citing works on racial violence that Williamson has neglected to mention, at least some of them, I know, by African American historians. Kelley argues forcefully that Williamson's portrait of a forgetful profession can only hold through the use of a prejudicially defined "we" that most ironically, the work of historians who clearly have not suffered from Williamson's own debilities.

Yet, I don't think Kelley's strictures destroy my point about Williamson's essay doing valuable intellectual work. Rather, Kelley prompts me to ask, valuable intellectual work for whom? In this case, it seems that Williamson's willingness to dig deep within himself and reveal the emotional underpinnings of his work is most valuable for other white male historians. Their reviews answer the emotion in his piece, bespeaking their embarrassment, explicitly in Ayers, and at the same time, expressing gratitude for Williamson's intensity, most notably in Stowe. Perhaps the white male readers are assisted in identifying with Williamson because, as Hall notes, he tends to couch his emotional disclosures in military metaphors—scholars rush to combat, hold the high ground, look over the battlefield, etc. Perhaps Kelley and Lewis, on the other hand, are left cold by this essay, and Hall tempers her enthusiasm, because historians of color and white women historians do not need so much assistance in exploring the emotional roots of their scholarly agendas.

I want to make clear that I do not mean to devalue Williamson's contribution by suggesting that his alternative intellectual work is not equally valuable for everyone. On the contrary, Kelley helps me make the point that a diversity of intellectual approaches is exactly what we need. That is why, as I have argued, alternative forms of academic discourse are emerging. The academy collectively has finally grasped the point of the old fable about the blind men and the elephant. One gets a hold of the elephant's ear and says, "The elephant, I find, is very like a fan!" Another gets a hold of the elephant's trunk and says, "No, the elephant is very like a snake!" A third grabs the leg and says, "No! Very like a tree!" And so on. If we want to see the whole beast, we should be welcoming, not resisting, the advent of diverse forms of academic discourse, and encouraging our students to bring all their discursive resources to bear on the intellectual challenges of the academic disciplines.

Works Cited

Bahri, Deepika. "Terms of Engagement: Postcolonialism, Transnationalism, and Composition Studies." *JAC: A Journal* of *Composition Theory* 18 (1998): 29–44.

Bizzell, Patricia. "Hybrid Academic Discourses: What, Why, How." *Composition Studies* 27 (1999): 7–21.

———. "Basic Writing and the Issue of Correctness, or, What to Do with 'Mixed' Forms of Academic Discourse." *Journal of Basic Writing* 19 (2000): 4–12.

Kells, Michelle Hall. "Leveling the Linguistic Playing Field in First-Year Composition." *Attending to the Margins: Writing, Researching, and Teaching on the Front Lines.* Ed. Michelle Hall Kells and Valerie Balester. Portsmouth, NH. Heinemann-Boynton/Cook, 1999.

Lyons, Scott. "A Captivity Narrative: Indians, Mixedbloods, and 'White' Academe." *Outbursts in Academe: Multiculturalism and Other Sources of Conflict.* Ed. Kathleen Dixon. Portsmouth, NH: Heinemann-Boynton/Cook, 1998. 87–108.

Williamson, Joel. "Wounds Not Scars: Lynching, the National Conscience, and the American Historian." *The Journal of American History* 83 (1997): 1221–53; preceded by David Thelen, "What We See and Can't See in the Past: An Introduction," 1217–20, and followed by referees' reports by Edward L. Ayers, David W. Blight, George M. Frederickson, Robin D. G. Kelley, David Levering Lewis, and Steven M. Stowe, with "A Later Comment" by Jacquelyn Dowd Hall, 1254–72.

Chapter Five

Generalizing about Genre: New Conceptions of an Old Concept

Amy J. Devitt

Our field has become riddled with dichotomies that threaten to undermine our holistic understanding of writing. Form and content (and the related form and function, text and context), product and process, individual and society—these dichotomies too often define our research affiliations, our pedagogies, and our theories. If we are to understand writing as a unified act, as a complex whole, we must find ways to overcome these dichotomies. Recent conceptions of genre as a dynamic and semiotic construct illustrate how to unify form and content, place text within context, balance process and product, and acknowledge the role of both the individual and the social. This reconception of genre may even lead us to a unified theory of writing.

The most recent understandings of genre derive from the work of several significant theorists working with different agendas and from different fields: from literature (M. M. Bakhtin, Tzvetan Todorov, Jacques Derrida), linguistics (M. A. K. Halliday, John Swales), and rhetoric (Carolyn Miller, Kathleen Jamieson). However, this work has not yet widely influenced how most scholars and teachers of writing view genre. Our reconception will require releasing old notions of genre as form and text type and embracing new notions of genre as dynamic patterning of human experience, as one of the concepts that enable us to construct our writing world. Basically, the new conception of genre shifts the focus from effects (formal features, text classifications) to sources of those effects. To accommodate our desires for a

From *College Composition and Communication* 44 (1993): 573–86.

reunified view of writing, we must shift our thinking about genre from a formal classification system to a rhetorical and essentially semiotic social construct. This article will explain the new conception of genre that is developing and will suggest some effects of this new conception on our thinking about writing.[1]

The Conventional Conception of Genre

The common understanding of genre among too many composition scholars and teachers today is that genre is a relatively trivial concept, a classification system deriving from literary criticism that names types of texts according to their forms. Viewed in this way, genre is not only a rather trivial concept but also a potentially destructive one, one that conflicts, with our best understandings of how writing, writers, and readers work, one that encourages the dichotomies in our field.

Treating genre as form requires dividing form from content, with genre as the form into which content is put; but we have largely rejected this container model of meaning in favor of a more integrated notion of how meaning is made: "Form and content in discourse are one," as Bakhtin writes ("Discourse" 259). Similarly, treating genre as form and text type requires binding genre to a product perspective, without effect on writing processes or, worse yet, inhibiting those processes. As a product-based concept, in fact, this view of genre seems to have more to do with reading than with writing (as attested to by the frequency of genre interpretations among literary critics). Finally, a formal view of genre exaggerates one of the most troubling current dichotomies, that between the individual and the group or society. It makes genre a normalizing and static concept, a set of forms that constrain the individual; genuine writers can distinguish themselves only by breaking out of those generic constraints, by substituting an individual genius for society's bonds.

Though this conventional conception of genre contradicts our best knowledge of how writing works, it has a long history and is not so easily discarded. Formalisms in general have sustained much of the work in linguistics, rhetoric, and literature in the past, the fields out of which genre theories have developed. Not surprisingly, then, most genre theories in the past have been concerned with classification and form, with describing the formal features of a particular genre, describing the embodiment of a genre in a particular work, or delineating a genre system, a set of classifications of (primarily literary) texts. The emphasis on classification can be traced back to the followers of Aristotle, who turned his initial treatment in the *Poetics* of the epic, tragedy, and comedy into an infinitely modifiable classification scheme. The rhetorical division of discourse into epideictic, judicial, and deliberative can be seen as a similar classification system, one still in use by some today. Other writers propose broader or narrower schemes of text types: literature and nonliterature; narrative and nonnarrative; narrative, exposition, argument, description; the lyric, the sonnet; the Petrarchan sonnet. Whether called genres, subgenres, or modes, whether comprehensive or selective, whether generally accepted or disputed, these systems for classifying texts focus attention on static products.

The efforts spent on devising a classification scheme may be time well spent for some purposes: for supporting or elaborating an interpretation of literature (that literature's import is its effect on readers, for example, or that all literature tells stories), or, to use Anne Freadman's examples (106), for developing a filing system, a library classification system, or disciplinary divisions within a university. For our purposes, perhaps it is enough to agree with Todorov that "We do not know just how many types of discourse there are, but we shall readily agree that there are more than one" (9). Or, along with Miller, perhaps we can accept that "the number of genres current in any society is indeterminate and depends upon the complexity and diversity of the society" (163). Understanding genre requires understanding more than just classification schemes; it requires understanding the origins of the patterns on which those classifications are based. As I. R. Titunik comments in summarizing P. M. Medvedev's ideas about genre, "Genre is not that which is determined and defined by the components of a literary work or by sets of literary works, but that which, in effect, determines and defines them" (175).

Once our attention shifts to the origins of genres, it also shifts away from their formal features. Traditional genre study has meant study of the textual features that mark a genre: the meter, the layout, the organization, the level of diction, and so on. Where literary criticism has delineated its invocation to the muse and its fourteen-line sonnet, composition has delineated its five-paragraph theme, the inverted-triangle introductory paragraph, the division into purpose, methods, results, and discussion of the lab report, and the you-attitude in the business letter. Certainly, such formal features are the physical markings of a genre, its traces, and hence may be quite revealing. In merging form and content, we do not wish to discard the significance of form in genre (see Coe, "Apology"). But those formal traces do not *define* or *constitute* the genre (see Freadman 114). Historical changes in generic forms argue against equating genre with form; note the formal changes in what we call a poem, for example, or in the familiar letter. The forms may change but the generic label stays the same. Distinguishing definitive from insignificant forms has proven troublesome, perhaps possible only after the fact. More importantly, equating genre with form is tenable only within the container model of meaning. By integrating form and content within situation and context, recent work in genre theory makes genre an essential player in the making of meaning.

To begin seeing how much more than classification or textual form genre comprehends, consider what we know when, *as readers*, we recognize the genre of a text. Based on our identification of genre, we make assumptions not only about the form but also about the text's purposes, its subject matter, its writer, and its expected reader. If I open an envelope and recognize a sales letter in my hand, I understand that a company will make a pitch for its product and want me to buy it. Once I recognize that genre, I will throw the letter away or scan it for the product it is selling. If, in a different scenario, I open an envelope and find a letter from a friend, I understand immediately a different set of purposes and a different relationship between writer and reader, and I respond/read accordingly. What I understand about each of these letters and what I reflect in my response to them is much more than a set of formal features or textual conventions. Our theory of genre, therefore, must allow us to see behind particular classifications (which change as our purposes change) and forms (which trace but do not constitute genre). Genre entails purposes, participants, and themes, so understanding genre entails understanding a rhetorical and semiotic situation and a social context.

New Conceptions of Genre

To develop our new genre theory, we begin with rhetorical situation and expand it to encompass a semiotic situation and social context. One major strain of recent genre theory which connects genre to purposes, participants, and themes derives from the notion of genre as response to recurring rhetorical situation. In particular, Miller defines genres as "typified rhetorical actions based in recurrent situations" (159). Although potentially deriving from Aristotle or Burke, the connection of genre to rhetorical situation has been most frequently drawn from the 1968 work of Lloyd Bitzer. In his elaborate exploration of rhetorical situation, Bitzer refers to what happens when situations recur:

> Due to either the nature of things or convention, or both, some situations recur. . . . From day to day, year to year, comparable situations occur, prompting comparable responses; hence rhetorical forms are born and a special vocabulary, grammar, and style are established. . . . The situation recurs and, because we experience situations and the rhetorical response to them, a form of discourse is not only established but comes to have a power of its own—the tradition itself tends to function as a constraint upon any new response in the form. (13)

Genres develop, then, because they respond appropriately to situations that writers encounter repeatedly. In principle, that is, writers first respond in fitting ways and hence similarly to recurring situations; then, the similarities among those appropriate responses become established as generic conventions. In practice, of course, genres already exist and hence already constrain responses to situations. Genre's efficiency and appropriateness appear clearly in a relatively fixed genre like the lab report: its particular purposes and reader's needs can best be met by its formal features—such as a quick statement of purpose or separate methods and results sections. If all writers of lab reports use these forms, then all lab reports will respond in some appropriate ways to the needs of their situation. Even a more loosely defined genre reveals the appropriateness of generic conventions to situation. The opening of a letter to a friend, for example, just like all our everyday greetings, signals affection and maintains contact, whether the standard "Hi! How are you?" or a more original nod to the relationship. The features that genres develop respond appropriately to their situations.

If each writing problem were to require a completely new assessment of how to respond, writing would be slowed considerably. But once we recognize a recurring situation, a situation that we or others have responded to in the past, our response to that situation can be guided by past responses. Genre, thus, depends heavily on the intertextuality of discourse. As Bakhtin points out in his important essay on speech genres, a speaker "is not, after all, the first speaker, the one who disturbs the eternal silence of the universe" (69). The fact that others have responded to similar situations in the past in similar ways—the fact that genres exist—enables us to respond more easily and more appropriately ourselves. Knowing the genre, therefore, means knowing such things as appropriate subject matter, level of detail, tone, and approach as well as the usual layout and organization. Knowing the genre means knowing not only, or even most of all, how to conform to generic conventions but also how to respond appropriately to a given situation.

This straightforward connection of genre to recurring situation begins but does not complete our understanding of genre's origins, for recent theory has expanded the notion of situation. Bitzer's definition of the rhetorical situation has come under attack (see, for example, Vatz; Consigny), and his requirement of a narrowly defined rhetorical exigence as a main component of situation has been troublesome for more wide-ranging composition theory. Based on a fuller range of language behavior, B. Malinowski's concepts of context of situation and context of culture have been developed by M. A. K. Halliday and others (see, especially, Halliday and Hasan), and this conception offers perhaps the best contemporary understanding of situation. Specifically, as Halliday defines it, situation consists of a field (roughly, what is happening), a tenor (who is involved), and a mode (what role language is playing) (31–35). Those components of situation determine what Halliday calls "register," essentially the linguistic equivalent to what I and many of his followers, including Hasan, have called "genre." Like so many other important concepts in Halliday's system, register/genre is a semantic as well as functional concept. He defines it as "the configuration of semantic resources that the member of a culture typically associates with a situation type. It is the meaning potential that is accessible in a given social context" (111). Halliday's definition associates genre/register with situation type and the making of meaning, the most important elements of our reconception of genre so far. It keeps genre as a semantic and functional concept.

Even with a more comprehensive definition of situation, one problem remains with our treatment of genre as response to recurring situation: where does the "situation" come from? In light of recent nonfoundational philosophy and social construction, I would suggest that our construction of genre is what helps us to construct a situation. Genre not only responds to but also constructs recurring situation.

Context, often seen as the larger frame of situation, has long been a troubling concept for linguists and rhetoricians because, among other reasons, it is difficult to specify what context includes. Not everything about the surrounding environment (the temperature, what is happening in the next block) is relevant for the language use being considered, and some things outside the surrounding environment (potential readers, previous texts) are relevant. The concepts of context of situation and context of culture were devised in part to deal with this problem of framing. Yet, if the context of situation is not a physical fact of the surrounding environment, as it clearly is not, where does it come from? Today's answer would be that writers and readers construct it. Halliday and Hasan come close to this perspective when they write, "Any piece of text, long or short, spoken or written, will carry with it indications of its context. . . . This means that we reconstruct from the text certain aspects of the situation, certain features of the field, the tenor, and the mode. Given the text, we construct the situation from it" (38). In fact, the situation may exist only as writers and readers construct it. As Miller writes, "Situations are social constructs that are the result not of 'perception,' but of 'definition'" (156), or what Halliday would call semiotic structures. Even more clearly, the recurrence of situation cannot be a material fact but rather what Miller calls "an intersubjective phenomenon, a social occurrence" (156).

We do not construct the situation directly through the text, however; rather, we reach the situation through the genre. Since genre responds to recurring situation, a text's reflection of genre indirectly reflects situation. Thus the act of constructing the genre—of creating or perceiving the formal traces of a genre—is also the act of constructing the situation. As discussed earlier, when we as readers recognize the genre of a particular text, we recognize, through the genre, its situation. Like readers, writers also construct situation by constructing genre. A writer faced with a writing task confronts multiple contexts and must define a specific context in relation to that task (teachers tells writers to "figure out who your audience is" or "state your purpose"). By selecting a genre to write in, or by beginning to write within a genre, the writer has selected the situation entailed in that genre. The assignment may ask for a letter to the editor, but the writer who begins with an inverted-triangle introduction is still writing for the teacher.

Writers and readers may, of course, mix genres and situations and may use genres badly. Consider, for example, what happens when writers or readers match genre and situation differently. A writer may try to vary the *situation*—say by treating the audience as a friend in a formal scholarly article—but the readers will likely note a change in the *genre* (either noting a flawed text that violates the genre or concluding that the writer is changing the genre). Similarly, a writer who shifts genre in the middle of a text causes confusion for the reader, not because the reader cannot label the genre but because the reader cannot be sure of the writer's purpose or the reader's role—cannot be sure of the *situation*. For a final example, a reader who "misreads" a text's genre—who reads "A Modest Proposal" as a serious proposal, say—most significantly misreads the situation as well. Genre and situation are so linked as to be inseparable, but it is genre that determines situation as well as situation that determines genre.

If genre not only responds to but also constructs recurring situation, then genre must be a dynamic rather than static concept. Genres *construct* and *respond* to situation; they are *actions* (see Miller). As our constructions of situations change and new situations begin to recur, genres change and new genres develop. Since situation is inherently a social as well as rhetorical concept, genres change with society, as Gunther Kress explains:

> If genre is entirely imbricated in other social processes, it follows that unless we view society itself as static, then neither social structures, social processes, nor therefore genres are static. Genres are dynamic, responding to the dynamics of other parts of social systems. Hence genres change historically; hence new genres emerge over time, and hence, too, what appears as "the same" generic form at one level has recognizably distinct forms in differing social groups. (42)

Dynamic genres are also fluid rather than rigid, are possible responses that writers choose and even combine to suit their situations. "The wealth and diversity of speech genres are boundless," Bakhtin writes, "because the various possibilities of human activity are inexhaustible, and because each sphere of activity contains an entire repertoire of speech genres that differentiate and grow as the particular sphere develops and becomes more complex" ("Problem" 60). The connection to social spheres and groups has led some to tie genre to the constructions of a discourse community, a promising connection developed most fruitfully by John Swales in his 1990 book on genre. Whether through discourse communities or some other social frame, genre must respond dynamically to human behavior and social changes.

One concern that has been raised in the past is that genre can become deterministic. Especially for such a social view of genre as this, some worry that the individual writer no longer matters. The split between the individual and society, however, is another false dichotomy that our new conception of genre can help to resolve. Denigrating genre became popular with the glorification of the individual, a romantic strain in literary criticism that considers genre and previous texts as constraints, as something that great writers must transcend, as producing anxiety for the writer. Yet an opposing trend has seen the inherent intertextuality of all writing, has discerned that T. S. Eliot's "historical sense" enriches rather than constrains the individual writer. Writers work creatively within the frame of past texts and given genres just as they work within the frame of a given language.

It is indeed true that "the single utterance, with all its individuality and creativity, can in no way be regarded as a *completely free combination* of forms of language" (Bakhtin, "Problem" 81). Genres are existing and somewhat normative constructs, some more rigid than others, but so too are all language forms. All language constrains the individual to the extent that language is an existing set of forms; however, as Bakhtin points out, "Speech genres are much more changeable, flexible, and plastic than language forms are" ("Problems" 80). Language and genre constrain but do not eliminate the individual writer. As constituents of society, individuals create language and create genre. Being part of society enables individuals to change society, and hence to change genres, for genres, as Volosinov/Bakhtin writes, "exhibits an extraordinary sensitivity to all fluctuations in the social atmosphere" (20). Individuals may, of course, combine different genres or may "violate" the norms of an existing genre, thereby confirming that genre's existence and potentially changing it. (See discussions in Todorov, Derrida, and Freadman.) Working within existing genres as well, individuals choose and create: even the most rigid genre requires some choices, and the more common genres contain substantial flexibility within their bounds. Ultimately, as Frances Christie writes in her article "Genres as Choice," "Capacity to recognize, interpret and write genres is capacity to exercise choice" (32). Individuals choose within linguistic and generic conventions, and they create and recreate the society that those conventions reflect. Although genre thus is a social concept and construct, it also clarifies the nature of individual choices. Again, genre proves the dichotomy false. In sum, genre is a dynamic response to and construction of recurring situation, one that changes historically and in different social groups, that adapts and grows as the social context changes.

This new conception of genre has managed to overcome several dichotomies in our understanding of language use and writing. In reuniting genre and situation, it reunites text and context, each constructing and responding to the other in a semiotic interchange. Form and function are both inherent in genre, as are form and content. Miller explains that genre semiotically fuses the syntactic, semantic, and pragmatic. Sigmund Ongstad has genre fusing the form, content, and function. Genre is both the product and the process that creates it. Genre is what Bakhtin calls "the *whole* of the utterance" ("Problem" 60), a unity and a unifier.

This new conception of genre helps us to see how individual writers and individual texts work, then, by removing us one level from the individual and particular. Genre is an abstraction or generality once removed from the concrete or particular. Not as abstract as Saussurian notions of *langue* or language system, genre mediates between *langue* and *parole*, between the language and the utterance. Not as removed as situation, genre mediates between text and context. Not as general as meaning, genre mediates between form and content. Genre is patterns and relationships, essentially semiotic ones that are constructed when writers and groups of writers identify different writing tasks as being similar. Genre constructs and responds to recurring situation, becoming visible through perceived patterns in the syntactic, semantic, and pragmatic features of particular texts. Genre is truly, therefore, a maker of meaning.

Implications

So what does such a reconception of genre do for us as composition scholars and teachers? For our scholarship, a new conception of genre might fill some significant gaps in our existing theories of writing.[2] We have already seen how genre can help us to reintegrate several dichotomies in our view of writing. Most particular to genre theory might be the better reintegration of form with content and of text with context, the former a longstanding marriage we still struggle to explain to others, the latter a more recent split whose divorce we are just beginning to contest. Can we speak of context apart from text? Contexts are always textualized. Through genre we can speak of both, as do many scholars who study particular genres in particular communities (such as Bazerman and Myers, in their studies of the experimental article in science and articles in biology, respectively). Studies of particular genres and of particular genre sets (as, for example, the research-process genres in Swales, or the genre sets of tax accountants in Devitt, "Intertextuality") can reveal a great deal about the communities which construct and use those genres, and studies of particular texts within those genres can reveal a great deal about the choices writers make.

The reintegration of product and process that this new genre theory enables can clarify the value of studying products or texts, but it also can contribute to our understanding of process and text-making. Some of the longstanding (and often unspoken) questions about writing processes can be addressed through considering genre's role. Two such questions will illustrate: Where do writers' goals come from? How do writers know what to change when they are revising? One of the classic articles on writing processes, Linda Flower and John Hayes's 1981 article "A Cognitive Process Theory of Writing," might have had a different emphasis had a better understanding of genre been well shared when it was written. Flower and Hayes concentrated in part on how writers generate and regenerate goals. In one paragraph, they acknowledge a small role for genre:

> but we should not forget that many writing goals are well-learned, standard ones stored in memory. For example, we would expect many writers to draw automatically on those goals associated with writing in general, such as, "interest the reader," or "start with an introduction," or on goals associated with a given genre, such as making a jingle rhyme. These goals will often be so basic that they won't even be consciously considered or expressed. And the more experienced the writer the greater this repertory of semiautomatic plans and goals will be. (381)

With our new conception of genre, we would agree that "well-learned, standard" goals are "so basic that they won't even be consciously considered or expressed," and that more experienced writers will be well-stocked with "semiautomatic plans and goals." However, rather than being uninteresting because unconscious and rather than being trivial ("such as making a jingle rhyme"), these "basic" and "well-learned" generic goals may be the stuff of which all writing goals (at least partly) are made.

Bakhtin ("Problem"), for example, describes "primary" speech genres, which are the culturally established building blocks of more complex "secondary" genres, most written genres being secondary genres. To understand the situational and social constructs behind such primary and secondary genres may be to understand more deeply the goals that writers have and the forces at work in their generation and regeneration. Understanding writing processes, then, must include understanding generic goals: what they are—the historical, community, and rhetorical forces that shape them—how writers learn them, and how writers use them.

Similarly, a better understanding of genre may help us understand better how writers know when and what to revise. As an important part of revision, scholars have described the perception of dissonance, between intention and text or between intention and execution (see, for example, Sommers; and Flower and Hayes). But James Reither asserts that "Composition studies does not seriously attend . . . to the knowing without which cognitive dissonance is impossible" (142). A large part of that "knowing" must be knowing genres. How, Flower and her coauthors ask, "can we say that a writer detects a dissonance or a failed comparison between text and intention when the second side of the equation, an 'ideal' or 'correct' or intended text doesn't exist—when there is no template to 'match' the current text against?" (27). Genre might provide at least part of that template, might provide at least part of the writer's notion of the ideal text. If a writer has chosen to write a particular genre, then the writer has chosen a template, a situation and an appropriate reflection of that situation in sets of forms.[3] In revising, a writer may check the situation and forms of the evolving text against those of the chosen genre: where there is a mismatch, there is dissonance. Genre by no means solves the problem of determining why writers revise what they do; but without genre a complete solution to the problem is impossible.

As these brief discussions of goals and dissonance illustrate, studies of writing processes and cognitive perspectives on writing must take genre into account. In fact, researchers most interested in the cognition of individual writers can make essential contributions to genre theory by studying how writers learn and use a variety of genres. The creation, transmission, and modification of genres can be studied further by those most interested in social and rhetorical perspectives on writing.

As mentioned earlier, many scholars studying nonacademic discourse have used genre as a variable, even as a controlling concept for understanding the community. In my study of tax accountants' writing ("Intertextuality"), for example, understanding the group's values, assumptions, and beliefs is enhanced by understanding the set of genres they use, their appropriate situations and formal traits, and what those genres mean to them. Swales develops the fullest and most complex treatment of genre's relationship to discourse communities in his important book *Genre Analysis*. His significant work embedding genre in discourse communities can be extended and developed by others, if we can resolve such discourse-community issues as the nature of the community, overlapping communities, and writers participating in multiple communities. In fact, the same kind of semiotic interchange that is so useful for understanding genre may help us to understand discourse community. Just as genres construct situations and situations construct genres, discourse may construct communities and communities construct discourse. Thus, rather than looking at human membership to define community, perhaps discourse membership—that is, genre sets—can better define the nature and constitution of a discourse community, just as the community better defines the nature of the discourse.

As someone who has been working on understanding genre for many years, I, of course, see the potential benefits of genre in virtually every article or book I read on composition theory and teaching. Studies of the relationship between reading and writing need to acknowledge that genre connects readers and writers, both their products and their processes, and need to investigate how their interpretations of genre vary (or do not). Research on assessment and on assignments needs to consider the power of differing generic demands to influence results. Judith A. Langer, for example, found that "genre distinctions were stronger than grade distinctions in their effects on student writing (167). Researchers of basic writing need to go beyond the forms of academic genres to see their situational constructs, with ideologies and roles that may pose conflicts for some basic writers. A study of Athabaskans, a group of Alaskan Indians, discussed by Michael B. Prince, found that learning to write a new genre "implied cultural and personal values that conflicted with pre-existing patterns of thought and behavior" (741). Christie goes so far as to assert that "Those who fail in schools are those who fail to master the genres of schooling: the ways of structuring and of dealing with experience which schools value in varying ways" ("Language" 24).

Although it may be premature to outline full programs, many powerful revolutions in our teaching might develop from a better understanding of genre. Teachers of writing need to discover how to teach novices the situations and forms of the genres they will need without undermining the wholeness of a genre. Aviva Freedman's research suggests that some novices may learn to write particular genres without explicit instruction, even ignoring explicit feedback. Richard M. Coe, on the other hand, argues for making all such models conscious "so that we may use them critically instead of habitually" ("Rhetoric" 11). Research needs to be done to discover the most effective techniques of translating our better genre theory into better writing instruction and thence into practice.

Even as we await more substantial knowledge of how novices can best learn and use genres, we can use the new conception of genre to improve our teaching, especially our diagnosis and treatment of students' problems. Since the genre constructs the situation, students will not be able to respond appropriately to assigned situations unless they know the appropriate genre. What we often diagnose as ignorance of a situation or inability to imagine themselves in another situation may in fact be ignorance of a genre or inability to write a genre they have not sufficiently read: they may feel great love but be unable to write a love sonnet. Conversely, since genre and situation are mutually constructive, what we diagnose as inability to write a particular genre may in fact be unfamiliarity with the genre's situation: students may know the genre of letters to the editor in a superficial way, but if they have never felt the need to write such a letter—if they have never experienced the situation—they may be incapable of writing one that appropriately responds to that situation. When we create assignments and as we evaluate responses to them, we must consider both their situational and generic demands.

Once we acknowledge genre as more than a formal constraint on writers but rather an essential component of making meaning, we might find it influencing other notions that we teach. Prewriting and revising processes probably differ for different genres, since those genres represent different situations, including constraints. Certainly, teaching students how to define their audiences and purposes would change under a new notion of genre since it would be clear that selecting a genre would automatically narrow the possibilities for audience and purpose; conversely, wanting to address a particular audience and purpose constrains one's choice of genre. Newly conceived genres should, of course, serve the final death notice to the modes as a classification system. Even usage standards might be most clearly explained through genre, as sets of language forms that are a small part of the larger conventions of some genres deriving from particular situations. Depending on our individual theories of writing and teaching, we may still value originality above all, or self-expression, or clarity, or correctness; but we may no longer ignore the fact that genre operates as a force on our students as they try to meet our expectations.

In spite of what my genre-colored glasses show me, genre may not be the answer to all of our dilemmas in composition theory and teaching. But only by ignoring what writers themselves recognize can we ignore the significance of genre. This new theory of genre reveals and explains the centrality of genre to writing, its importance to understanding how writers and writing work. It also suggests how we might develop an integrated, unified theory of writing. With a unified theory of genre, we can reintegrate text and context, form and content, process and product, reading and writing, individual and social. In the end, genre's ability to capture both form and situation, both constraint and choice, may capture the essence of writing as well.

Notes

1. This article was supported in part by the University of Kansas general research allocation #3629-0038. I would like to thank those who gave me many helpful comments on an earlier draft of this article: Richard Coe, Aviva Freedman, James Hartman, Michael Johnson, Pat McQueeney, and the anonymous readers for *CCC*.

2. See Devitt, "Genre" for a discussion of the implications of a new genre theory for the study of language.

3. The notion of genre as template might be indebted to schemata theory and script theory. These theories, as rich as they are for understanding the complexities of human conventions, may have been a necessary precursor to this understanding of generic conventions.

Works Cited

Bakhtin, M. M. "Discourse in the Novel." *The Dialogic Imagination: Four Essays by M. M. Bakhtin*. Ed. Michael Holquist. Trans. Caryl Emerson and Michael Holquist. Austin and London: U of Texas P, 1981. 259–422.

———. "The Problem of Speech Genres." *Speech Genres and Other Late Essays*. Ed. Caryl Emerson and Michael Holquist. Trans. Vern W. McGee. Austin: U of Texas P, 1986. 60–102.

Bazerman, Charles. *Shaping Written Knowledge: The Genre and Activity of the Experimental Article in Science*. Madison: U of Wisconsin P, 1988.

Bitzer, Lloyd F. "The Rhetorical Situation." *Philosophy and Rhetoric* 1 (Winter 1968): 1–14.

Campbell, Karlyn Kohrs, and Kathleen Hall Jamieson, eds. *Form and Genre: Shaping Rhetorical Action*. Falls Church: Speech Communication Association, 1978.

Christie, Frances. "Genres as Choice." Reid 22–34.

———. "Language and Schooling." *Language, Schooling, and Society*. Ed. Stephen N. Tchudi. Upper Montclair, NJ: Boynton/Cook, 1984. 21–40.

Coe, Richard M. "An Apology for Form; or, Who Took the Form Out of the Process?" *College English* 49 (1987): 13–28.

———. "Rhetoric 2001." *Freshman English News* 3.1 (1974): 1–13.

Consigny, Scott. "Rhetoric and Its Situations." *Philosophy and Rhetoric* 7 (1974): 175–86.

Derrida, Jacques. "The Law of Genre." Trans. Avital Ronell. *Critical Inquiry* 7 (1980): 55–82.

Devitt, Amy J. "Genre as Textual Variable: Some Historical Evidence from Scots and American English." *American Speech* 64 (1989): 291–303.

———. "Intertextuality in Tax Accounting: Generic, Referential, and Functional." *Textual Dynamics of the Professions: Historical and Contemporary Studies of Writing in Professional Communities.* Ed. Charles Bazerman and James Paradis. Madison: U of Wisconsin P, 1991. 336–57.

Flower, Linda, and John R. Hayes. "A Cognitive Process Theory of Writing." *College Composition and Communication* 32 (1981): 365–87.

Flower, Linda, *et al.* "Detection, Diagnosis, and the Strategies of Revision." *College Composition and Communication* 37 (1986): 16–55.

Freadman, Anne. "Anyone for Tennis?" Reid 91–124.

Freedman, Aviva. "Learning to Write Again: Discipline-Specific Writing at University." *Carleton Papers in Applied Language Studies* 4 (1987): 95–115.

Halliday, M. A. K. *Language* as *Social Semiotic: The Social Interpretation of Language and Meaning.* London: Arnold, 1978.

Halliday, M. A. K., and Ruqaiya Hasan. *Language, Context, and Text: Aspects of Language in a Social-Semiotic Perspective.* 2nd ed. Oxford: Oxford UP, 1989.

Jamieson, Kathleen. "Antecedent Genre as Rhetorical Constraint." *Quarterly Journal of Speech* 61 (1975): 406–15.

Kress, Gunther. "Genre in a Social Theory of Language: A Reply to John Dixon." Reid 35–45.

Langer, Judith A. "Children's Sense of Genre: A Study of Performance on Parallel Reading and Writing Tasks." *Written Communication* 2 (1985): 157–87.

Malinowski, B. "The Problem of Meaning in Primitive Languages." Supplement I. *The Meaning of Meaning: A Study of the Influence of Language upon Thought and of the Science of Symbolism*. C. K. Ogden and I. A. Richards. 10th ed. New York: Harcourt and London: Routledge, 1952. 296–336.

Miller, Carolyn R. "Genre As Social Action." *Quarterly Journal of Speech* 70 (May 1984): 151–67.

Myers, Greg. *Writing Biology: Texts in the Social Construction of Scientific Knowledge*. Madison: U of Wisconsin P, 1990.

Ongstad, Sigmund. "The Definition of Genre and the Didactics of Genre." Rethinking Genre Colloquium. Ottawa, April 1992.

Prince, Michael B. "Literacy and Genre: Toward a Pedagogy of Mediation." *College English* 51 (1989): 730–49.

Reid, Ian, ed. *The Place of Genre in Learning: Current Debates*. Deakin University: Centre for Studies in Literary Education, 1987.

Reither, James A. "Writing and Knowing: Toward Redefining the Writing Process." *College English* 47 (Oct. 1985): 620–28. Rpt. in *The Writing Teachers' Sourcebook*. Ed. Gary Tate and Edward P. J. Corbett. 2nd ed. New York: Oxford UP, 1988. 140–48.

Sommers, Nancy. "Revision Strategies of Student Writers and Experienced Adult Writers." *College Composition and Communication* 31 (1980): 378–88.

Swales, John M. *Genre Analysis: English in Academic and Research Settings*. Cambridge: Cambridge UP, 1990.

Titunik, I. R. "The Formal Method and the Sociological Method (M. M. Baxtin, P. N. Medvedev, V. N. Volosinov) in Russian Theory and Study of Literature." Volosinov [Bakhtin] 175–200.

Todorov, Tzvetan. *Genres in Discourse*. Trans. Catherine Porter. Cambridge: Cambridge UP, 1990.

Van, Richard. "The Myth of the Rhetorical Situation." *Philosophy and Rhetoric* 6 (1973): 154–61.

Volosinov, V. N. [M. M. Bakhtin]. *Marxism and the Philosophy of Language*. Trans. Ladislav Matejka and I. R. Titunik. Cambridge and London: Harvard UP, 1986.

CHAPTER SIX

Sites of Invention: Genre and the Enactment of First-Year Writing

ANIS BAWARSHI

> *Genres themselves form part of the discursive context to which rhetors respond in their writing and, as such, shape and enable the writing; it is in this way that form is generative.*
>
> AVIVA FREEDMAN, "Situating Genre"

> *We need to be aware not only that genres are socially constructed but also that they are socially constitutive—in other words, that we both create and are created by the genres in which we work.*
>
> THOMAS HELSCHER, "The Subject of Genre"

> *[A genre's discursive features] are united within the relatively stable discursive "type" to offer us a form within which we can locate ourselves as writers—that is, a form which serves as a guide to invention, arrangement, and stylistic choices in the act of writing.*
>
> JAMES F. SLEVIN "Genre Theory, Academic Discourse, and Writing in the Disciplines"

Reflecting on the concept of invention in the classical rhetorical tradition, Jim Corder writes that "*inventio,* by its nature, calls for openness to the accumulated resources of the world

---

This essay appeared in slightly different form in *Genre and the Invention of the Writer* by Anis S. Bawarshi. Logan: Utah State UP, 2003. 112–44.

a speaker lives in, to its landscapes, its information, its ways of thinking and feeling. . . . *Inventio* is the world the speaker lives in" (109). Similarly, Sharon Crowley writes that "invention reminds rhetors of their location within a cultural milieu that determines what can and cannot be said or heard" (*Methodical* 168). Invention takes *place*, which is why classical rhetoricians recommended the topoi or commonplaces as the sites in which rhetors could locate the available means of persuasion for any given situation. As heuristics for invention, the topoi were thus rhetorical habitats—"language-constituted regions" (Farrell 116) and "resources, seats, places, or haunts" (Lauer, "Topics" 724)—which framed communal knowledge and provided rhetors with shared methods of inquiry for navigating and participating in rhetorical situations. Invention, as such, was not so much an act of turning inward as it was an act of locating oneself socially, a way of participating in the shared desires, values, and meanings already existing in the world. As Scott Consigny explains, the topoi were both "the *instrument* with which the rhetor thinks and the *realm* in and about which he thinks" (65; my emphasis). The topoi helped rhetors locate themselves and participate within common situations.

In much the same way, genres are also instruments and realms—habits and habitats. Genres are the conceptual realms within which individuals recognize and experience situations at the same time as they are the rhetorical instruments by and through which individuals participate within and enact situations. The Patient Medical History Form, for example, not only conceptually frames the way the individual recognizes the situation of the doctor's office; it also helps position the individual into the figure of "patient" by providing him or her with the rhetorical habits for acting in this situation. Likewise, George Washington "invents" the first state of the union address by rhetorically situating himself within the conceptual realm of an antecedent genre, the "king's speech," which provides him not only with a way of recognizing the situation he is in, but also a way of rhetorically acting within it. And similarly, D. H. Lawrence is motivated to invent his autobiography differently as he perceives and enacts it within different genres. As such, why individuals are motivated to act and how they do so depends on the genres they are using.

These genres serve as the typified and situated topoi within which individuals acquire, negotiate, and articulate desires, commitments, and methods of inquiry to help them act in a given situation, thereby inventing not only certain lines of argument (logos), but also certain subjectivities (ethos—think of the subject position Washington assumes when he writes the "king's speech) and certain ways of relating to others (pathos—think of the relation Washington sets up between himself and Congress, and, as a result, how Congress reacts to Washington).[1] Conceived thus, invention does not involve an introspective turn so much as it involves the process by which individuals locate themselves within and devise ways of rhetorically acting in various situations. In this way, invention is a process that is inseparable from genre since genre coordinates both how individuals recognize a situation as requiring certain actions and how they rhetorically act within it.

Genres, thus, are localized, textured sites of invention, the situated topoi in which communicants locate themselves conceptually *before* and rhetorically *as* they communicate. To begin to write is to locate oneself within these genres, to become habituated by their typified rhetorical conventions to recognize and enact situated desires, relations, practices, and subjectivities in certain ways. I will now consider one such genre-constituted environment within which teacher and students "invent" various situated practices, relations, and subjectivities as they (re)locate themselves from one genre-situated topoi to the next: the first-year writing course.

In *Modern Dogma and the Rhetoric of Assent*, Wayne Booth speculates on a theory of interaction and self-formation similar to the one I have been proposing in my discussion of genre and agency. "What happens," he wonders, "if we choose to begin with our knowledge that we are essentially creatures made in symbolic interchange, *created in the process of sharing intentions*, values, meanings? . . . What happens if we think of ourselves as essentially participants in a field or process or mode of being persons together?" (134, my emphasis). In this chapter, I will examine the first-year writing course from the perspective of Booth's question, describing and analyzing the first-year writing course as an activity system coordinated by a constellation of genres, each of which constitutes its own topoi within which teachers and students assume and enact a complex set of desires, relations, subjectivities, and practices. By investigating how teachers and students make their way through these genres, we can observe the complex relations and repositioning that teachers and students negotiate as they participate within and between genred discursive spaces. Invention takes place within and between these genred spaces, as one genre creates the timing and opportunity for another. When they write their essays, for example, students are expected to perform a discursive transaction in which they recontextualize the desires embedded in the writing prompt as their own self-sponsored desires in their essays. Invention takes place at this intersection between the acquisition and articulation of desire. By analyzing the syllabus, writing prompt, and student essay as genred sites of invention, I hope to shed light on how students and teachers reposition themselves as participants within these topoi at the same time as they enact the activity system we call the first-year writing course.

The First-Year Writing Course and Its Genres

Elsewhere I have discussed how a site of activity (for example, a physician's office) is coordinated by a variety of genres, referred to as "genre sets" (Devitt, "Intertextuality") or "genre systems" (Bazerman, "Systems"), each genre within the set or system constituting its own site of action within which communicants instantiate and reproduce situated desires, practices, relations, and subjectivities. Within a site of activity, thus, we will encounter a constellation of related, even conflicting situations, organized and generated by various genres. David Russell, adapting Vygotsky's concept of activity theory to genre theory, has described this constellation of situations that make up an environment as an "activity system," which he defines as "any ongoing, object-directed, historically conditioned, dialectically structured, tool-mediated human interaction" ("Rethinking" 510). Examples of activity systems range from a family, to a religious organization, to a supermarket, to an advocacy group. As Russell defines it, an activity system resembles what Giddens calls "structure." Like structure, an activity system is constituted by a dialectic of agents or subjects, motives or social needs, and mediational means or tools (what Giddens refers to as "structura-tional properties"). Each element of the dialectic is constantly engaged in supporting the other, so that, for instance, agents enact motives using tools which in turn reproduce the motives that require agents to use these tools and so on. As Russell explains, "activity systems are not static, Parsonian social forces. Rather, they are dynamic systems constantly re-created through micro-level interactions" (512). In their situated, micro-level activities and interactions, discursively and ideologically embodied as genres, participants in an activity system are at work "operationalizing" and, in turn, reproducing the ideological and material conditions that make up the activity system within which they interact. Each genre enables individuals to enact a different situated activity within an activity system. Together, the various genres coordinate and synchronize the ways individuals define, interact within, and enact an activity system.

Russell's description of an activity system helps us conceptualize both how genres interact within a system of activity and how they help make that system possible by enabling individuals to participate within and in turn reproduce its related actions. The genres that constellate an activity system do not only organize and generate participants' activities within the system, however. They also, as Russell describes, link one activity system to another through the shared use of genres ("Rethinking"; "Kindness"). Participants in one activity system, for instance, use some genres to communicate with participants in other activity systems, thereby forming intra- and intergenre system relations. By applying the concept of activity system to school settings, especially to the interactions among micro-level disciplinary and administrative activity systems that together form the macro-level activity system of the university, Russell provides us with a model for analyzing the first-year writing course as one activity system within a larger activity system (the English department), within an even larger activity system (the College of Liberal Arts and Sciences), within an even larger activity system (the university), and so on. The constellation of genres within each of these related systems operationalizes the situated actions of participants within that system in order "to create stabilized-for-now structures of social action and identity" (Russell, "Rethinking" 514). The genres that coordinate each of the micro-level activity systems within a macro-level activity system function interactively as a series of uptakes, with one genre creating an opportunity for another, as in the example of the Department of Defense, in which requests for proposals generate funding proposals, which generate contracts, which generate reports and experimental articles, and so on (520). At the same time, not everyone involved in an activity system is or needs to be engaged in all its genres. As Russell explains, "in a typical school, for example, the teacher writes the assignments; the students write the responses in classroom genres. The administrators write the grade form; the teachers fill it out. The parents and/or the government officials write the checks; the administrators write the receipts and the transcripts and report to regents" (520). In this scenario, the various participants (teachers, students, parents, administrators) are all involved in micro-level activity systems which interact in close proximity to one another and which together comprise the macro-level activity system called a school. In what follows, I will focus on one particular micro-level activity system within a college or university: the first-year writing course.

Like other college or university courses, the first-year writing (FYW) course takes place, for the most part, in a physical setting, a material, institutionalized site most often situated within a building on campus.[2] It is a place a teacher and students can physically enter and leave. But as in the case of the physician's office, the classroom is not only a material site; it is also a discursive site, one mediated and reproduced by the various genres its participants use to perform the desires, positions, relations, and activities that enact it. For example, one of the first ways that a classroom becomes a FYW course (or any other course for that matter) is through the genre of the syllabus, which, as I will describe shortly, organizes and generates the classroom as a textured site of action which locates teacher and students within a set of desires, commitments, relations, and subject positions. At the same time, the syllabus also manages the set of genres that will enable its users to enact these desires, relations, and subjectivities. In this way, the syllabus and its related FYW course genres orient teachers and students in a discursive and ideological scene of writing which locates them in various, sometimes simultaneous and conflicting positions of articulation. The choices teachers and students make in this scene emerge from, against, and in relation to these positions. As such, "the classroom is always invented, always constructed, always a matter of genre" (Bazerman, "Where" 26). When we only identify students as writers in the writing classroom, then, we are ignoring the extent to which teachers (as well as those who administer writing programs) are also writers of and in the writing classroom—writers of the genres that organize and generate them and their students within a dynamic, multitextured site of action. The FYW course, thus, is a site where writing is already at work to make writing possible. Seen in this light, the FYW course is not as artificial as some critics make it out to be. It may be artificial when, chameleon-like, it tries to mimic public, professional, or disciplinary settings, or when it tries to imagine a "real" external audience for student writing. But the classroom in its own right is a dynamic, textured site of action mediated by a range of complex written and spoken genres that constitute student-teacher positions, relations, and practices.[3] As they reposition themselves within and between these genres, teachers and students acquire, negotiate, and articulate different desires, which inform the choices they make as participants in the FYW course.

The set of written genres that coordinates the FYW course includes, but is not limited to, the course description, the syllabus, the course home page, student home pages, the grade book, the classroom discussion list, assignment prompts, student essays, the teacher's margin and end comments in response to student essays, peer workshop instructions, student journals or logs, peer review sheets, and student evaluations of the class. These "classroom genres" (Christie, "Curriculum"; Russell, "Rethinking") constitute the various typified and situated topoi within which students and teacher recognize and enact their situated practices, relations, and subjectivities. I will now examine three of these classroom genres, the syllabus, the assignment prompt, and the student essay, in order to analyze how writers reposition and articulate themselves within these sites of invention. By doing so, I hope to demonstrate the extent to which, when they invent, writers locate themselves in a complex, multilayered set of discursive relations, so that by the time students begin to write their essays they do so in relation to the syllabus, the writing assignment, and the various other genres that have already located them and their teachers in an ideological and discursive system of activity.

The Syllabus

In many ways, the syllabus is the master classroom genre, in relation to which all other classroom genres, including the assignment prompt and the student essay, are "occluded" (Swales, "Occluded"). According to Swales, occluded genres are genres that operate behind the scenes and often out of more public sight, yet play a critical role in operationalizing the commitments and goals of the dominant genre, in this case, the syllabus. As such, the syllabus plays a major role in establishing the ideological and discursive environment of the course, generating *and* enforcing the subsequent relations, subject positions, and practices teacher and students will perform during the course. In some ways, the syllabus, like the architecture students' sketchbooks described in the previous chapter, functions as what Giltrow calls a "metagenre," an "atmosphere surrounding genres" (195) that sanctions and regulates their use within an activity system. It is not surprising, thus, that the syllabus is traditionally the first document students encounter upon entering the classroom. Immediately, the syllabus begins to transform the physical setting of the classroom into the discursive and ideological site of action in which students, teacher, and their work will assume certain significance and value. That is, within the syllabus, to paraphrase Giddens, the desires that inform the structure of the course become textually available to the students and teacher who then take up these desires as intentions to act. No doubt, the syllabus is a coercive genre, in the same way that all genres are coercive to some degree or another. It establishes the situated rules of conduct students and teacher will be expected to meet, including penalties for disobeying them. But even more than that, the syllabus also establishes a set of social relations and subjectivities that students and teacher have available to them in the course.

It is curious that, as significant a genre as it is, the syllabus has received so little critical attention (Baecker 61). In fact, to the extent that it is discussed at all, the syllabus is mostly described in "how to" guidebooks for novice teachers. For instance, both Erika Lindemann's *A Rhetoric for Writing Teachers* and Robert Connors and Cheryl Glenn's *The St. Martin's Guide to Teaching Writing* describe the syllabus in terms of its formal conventions, listing them in the order they most often appear: descriptive information such as course name and number, office hours, classroom location, significant phone numbers; textbook information; course description and objectives; course policy, including attendance policy, participation expectations, policy regarding late work, etc.; course requirements, including kinds and sequence of exams and writing assignments; grading procedures; any other university or departmental statements; and then a course calendar or schedule of assignments. In addition to presenting these conventions, Lindemann and Connors and Glenn also describe the purpose of the syllabus, acknowledging its contractual as well as pedagogical nature. Lindemann, for example, cites Joseph Ryan's explanation of the informational and pedagogical purposes of the syllabus:

> Students in the course use the syllabus to determine what it is they are to learn (course content), in what sense they are to learn it (behavioral objectives), when the material will be taught (schedule), how it will be taught (instructional procedures), when they will be required to demonstrate their learning (exam dates), and exactly how their learning will be assessed (evaluation) and their grade determined. (256–57)

In this sense, Lindemann claims that "syllabuses are intended primarily as information for students" (256).

Connors and Glenn, however, recognize the more political function of the syllabus. For them, "the syllabus, for all intents and purposes, is a contract between teacher and students. It states the responsibilities of the teacher and the students as well as the standards for the course" (10). The syllabus, then, informs the students and the teacher, protecting both from potential misunderstanding. It also informs the "structure of the class" by developing "a set of expectations and intentions for composition courses" (10–11). In other words, the syllabus establishes the course goals and assumptions as well as the means of enacting these goals and assumptions—both the structure of the course and the rhetorical means of instantiating that structure as situated practices. As Connors and Glenn remind teachers, the syllabus is "the first written expression of your personality that you will present to your students" (10).

Neither Lindemann nor Connors and Glenn, however, go on to analyze exactly how the syllabus locates teachers and students within this position of articulation or how it frames the discursive and ideological site of action in which teacher and students engage in coordinated commitments, relations, subjectivities, and practices. What effect, for instance, does the contractual nature of the syllabus have on the teacher-student relationship? What positions does the syllabus assign to students and teacher, and how do these positions get enacted and reproduced in the various situations and activities that constitute the FYW course? An analysis of the typified rhetorical features of the syllabus, especially its use of pronouns, future tense verbs, and abstract nominalizations, helps us begin to answer some of these questions.[4]

One of the more obvious characteristics of the syllabus is the way it positions students and teachers within situated subjectivities and relations. The student is frequently addressed as "you" ("This course will focus on introducing *you* to . . ."), as "students" ("*Students* will learn . . ." or "The goal of this course is to introduce *students* to . . ."), and as "we" ("*We* will focus on learning . . .") quite often interchangeably throughout the syllabus but at times even within the same section. For example, one teacher addresses her students in the "Course Objectives" section as follows: "Over the course of the semester, *you* will develop specific writing strategies which will help *you* adapt *your* writing skills to different contexts and audiences. Also, *we* will discuss how to approach and analyze the arguments of other writers, and how to either adapt or refute their views in *your* writing." This interchange between "you" and "we" on the pronoun level reflects a larger tension many teachers face when writing a syllabus: between establishing solidarity with students and demarcating lines of authority (Baecker 61). This tension is especially heightened in FYW courses which tend to be taught mostly by inexperienced teachers, most often graduate students who are themselves struggling with the tension between being teachers and students. Diann Baecker, drawing on Mühlhäusler and Harré's work on pronouns and social identity, applies this tension within pronouns to the social relations they make possible in the syllabus. Pronouns such as "you" and, in particular, "we" not only create social distinctions among communicants; they also "blur the distinction between power and solidarity and, in fact, allow power to be expressed as solidarity" (Baecker 58).

It is perhaps this desire to mask power as solidarity that most characterizes the syllabus, a desire that teachers, as the writers of the syllabus, acquire, negotiate, and articulate. Positioned within this desire, the teacher tries to maintain the contractual nature of the syllabus while also invoking a sense of community. On the one hand, the teacher has to make explicit what the students will have to do to fulfill the course requirements, including the consequences for not doing so. On the other hand, the teacher also has to create a sense of community with the students so they can feel responsible for the work of learning. This balance is difficult, and, as we saw in the above example, many teachers will awkwardly fluctuate between "you" and "we" in order to maintain it. The following excerpt from another syllabus also reveals this fluctuation:

> The goals of the course are two-fold. During the initial part of the semester, *we* will focus on learning to read critically—that is, how to analyze the writing of others. The skills that *you* will acquire while learning how to read an argument closely . . . will be the foundation for the writing *you* will do for the rest of the course. *Our* second objective . . .

This "we"/"you" tension reflects the balance the teacher is attempting to create between community and complicity. As Baecker explains, citing Mühlhäusler and Harré, "*we* is a rhetorical device that allows the speaker(s) to distance themselves from whatever is being said, thus making it more palatable because it appears to come from the group as a whole rather than from a particular individual" (59). The "we" construction tries to minimize the teacher's power implicit in the "you" construction by making it appear as though the students are more than merely passive recipients of the teacher's dictates; instead, they have ostensibly acquiesced consensually to the policies and activities described in the syllabus. The teacher, then, uses "you" and "we" in order to position students as subjects, so that without knowing it, they seem to have agreed to the conditions that they will be held accountable for. In this way, the syllabus is an effective contract, incorporating the student as other ("you") into the classroom community ("we") at the same time as it distinguishes the individual student from the collective. What the "you"/"we" construction seems to suggest is that "*we* as a class will encounter, be exposed to, and learn the following things, but *you* as a student are responsible for whether or not you succeed. *You* will do the work and be responsible for it, but *we* all agree what the work will be."

In her research, Baecker finds that "you" is by far the most common pronoun employed in syllabi (60), a finding supported by my own analysis. This "you," coupled with the occasional "we," the second most common pronoun, works as a hailing gesture, interpellating the individual who walks into the classroom as a student subject, one who then becomes part of the collective "we" that will operationalize this activity system we call the FYW course. As Mühlhäusler and Harré explain, it is "largely through pronouns and functionally equivalent indexing devices that responsibility for actions is taken by actors and assigned to them by others" (89). When a teacher identifies the student as "you," he or she is marking the student as the "other," the one on whom the work of the class will be performed: "You will encounter," "You will develop," "You will learn." But who exactly prescribes the action? Passive constructions such as the following are typical of the syllabus: "During the semester, *you* will be required to participate in class discussions," "*You* will be allowed a week to make your corrections." But who will be doing the requiring and the allowing? The teacher?

Not really. As much as the syllabus locates students within positions of articulation, it also positions the teacher within a position of articulation. The teacher's agency is seldom explicitly asserted through the first person singular; Baecker finds that "I" comprises an average of 24 percent of total pronoun usage per syllabus (60). More often, teachers mask their agency by using "we." Yet this "we" implicates the teacher into the collective identity of the goals, resources, materials, and policies of the course so that the teacher as agent of the syllabus becomes also an agent on behalf of the syllabus. The syllabus, in short, constructs its writer, the teacher, as an abstract nominalization in which the doer becomes the thing done. This is in part the genred subjectivity the teacher assumes when he or she writes the syllabus. For example, writers of syllabi rely on abstract nominalizations and nominal clauses to depict themselves as though they were the events and actions that they describe. Take, for instance, these typical examples: "Missing classes will negatively affect your participation grade," "Good class attendance will help you earn a good grade," "Acceptable excuses for missing a class include . . . ," "Each late appearance will be counted as an absence," "Guidance from texts constitutes another important component," "Writing is a process," "Conferences give us a chance to discuss the course and the assignments," "Plagiarism will not be tolerated." In these examples, we find objects, events, and actions that are incapable of acting by themselves treated as if they in fact are performing the actions. When a verb that conveys action in a sentence is transformed into a noun, we have the effect that somehow the action is performing itself—is its own subject, as in "missing classes" or "attendance." Rather than being the identifiable agents of the syllabus they write, teachers become part of the action they expect students to perform. This way, students come to see teachers less as prescribers of actions and more as guiding, observing, and evaluating student actions. As such, activities become substitutes for the agents who perform them, activities that teachers recognize and value and students subsequently enact.

The syllabus, therefore, is not merely informative; it is also, as all genres are, a site of action that produces subjects who desire to act in certain ideological and discursive ways. It establishes the habitat within which students and teachers rhetorically enact their situated relations, subjectivities, and activities. Both the teacher and the students become habituated by the genre of the syllabus into the abstract nouns that they will eventually perform. It is here, perhaps, that the syllabus's contractual nature is most evident, as it transforms the individuals involved into the sum of their actions, so that they can be described, quantified, and evaluated. No wonder, then, that the most dominant verb form used in the syllabus is the future tense, which indicates both permission and obligation, a sense that the activities and behaviors (the two become one in the syllabus) outlined in the syllabus are possible and binding. To be sure, the overwhelming number of future tense verbs present in the syllabus ("you will learn," "we will encounter") indicate that it is a genre that anticipates or predicts future action. Yet the discursive and ideological conditions it initially constitutes are already at work from day 1 to insure that these future actions will be realized.

The syllabus, in short, maintains and elicits the desires it helps its users fulfill. When a teacher writes the syllabus, he or she is not only communicating his or her desires for the course, but is also acquiring, negotiating, and articulating the desires already embedded in the syllabus. These desires constitute the exigencies to which the teacher rhetorically responds in the syllabus. For example, the contractual nature of the syllabus, especially the way it objectifies agency by constituting actors as actions which can then be more easily quantified and measured, is socio-rhetorically realized by such typified conventions as the "we"/"you" pronoun constructions, the abstract nominalizations, and the auxiliary "will" formations. By using these rhetorical conventions, the teacher internalizes the syllabus's institutional desires and enacts them as his or her intentions, intentions that he or she will expect students to respect and abide by. The teacher's intentions, therefore, are generated and organized rhetorically by the generic conventions of the syllabus. Teachers invent their classes, themselves, as well as their students by locating themselves within the situated topoi of the syllabus, which functions both as the rhetorical instrument and the conceptual realm in which the FYW course is recognized and enacted. Indeed, the syllabus, as Connors and Glenn warn teachers, *is* "the first expression of your personality," but the syllabus does not so much convey this a priori personality as it informs it.

The syllabus, then, helps establish the FYW course as a system of activity and also helps coordinate how its participants manage their way through and perform the various genres that operationalize this system, each of which constitutes its own site of invention within which teachers and students assume and enact a complex set of textured actions, relations, and subjectivities. Within this scene of writing, one such genre, the assignment (or writing) prompt, plays a critical role in constituting the teacher and student positions that shape and enable student writing.

The Writing Prompt

While it does receive scholarly attention, mainly in handbooks for writing teachers such as Lindemann's and Connors and Glenn's (see also Murray and James Williams), the writing prompt remains treated as essentially a transparent text, one that facilitates "communication between teacher and student" (Reiff and Middleton 263). As a genre, it is mainly treated as one more prewriting heuristic, helping or "prompting" student writers to discover something to write about. As Connors and Glenn describe it, "a good assignment . . . must be many things. Ideally, it should help students practice specific stylistic and organizational skills. It should also furnish enough data to give students an idea of where to start, and it should evoke a response that is the product of discovering more about those data. It should encourage students to do their best writing and should give the teacher her best chance to help" (58). Indeed, the most obvious purpose of the writing prompt is to do just that, prompt student writing by creating the occasion and the means for writing.

To treat the writing prompt merely as a conduit for communicating a subject matter from the teacher to the student, a way of "giving" students something to write about, however, is to overlook the extent to which the prompt situates student writers within a genred site of action in which students acquire and negotiate desires, subjectivities, commitments, and relations before they begin to write. The writing prompt not only *moves* the student writer to action; it also *cues* the student writer to enact a certain kind of action. This is why David Bartholomae insists that it is *within* the writing prompt that student writing begins, not *after* the prompt. The prompt, like any other genre, organizes and generates the conditions within which individuals perform their activities. As such, we cannot simply locate the beginning of student writing in student writers and their texts. We must also locate these beginnings in the teachers' prompts, which constitute the situated topoi that the student writers enter into and participate within. As Bartholomae notes, a well-crafted assignment "presents not just a subject, but a way of imagining a subject as a subject, a discourse one can enter, and not as a thing that carries with it experiences or ideas that can be communicated" ("Writing Assignments" 306). This means that the prompt does not precede student writing by only presenting the student with a subject for further inquiry, a subject a student simply "takes up" in his or her writing, although that certainly is part of its purpose. More significantly, the prompt is a precondition for the existence of student writing, a means of habituating the students into the subject as well as the subjectivity they are being asked to explore so that they can then "invent" themselves and their subject matter within it.

As situated topoi, writing prompts are both rhetorical instruments and conceptual realms—habits and habitats. They conceptually locate students within a situation and provide them with the rhetorical means for acting within it. We notice examples of this in assignments that ask students to write "literacy narratives," narratives about their experiences with and attitudes relating to the acquisition of literacy. Teachers who assign them usually presume that these narratives give students the opportunity to access and reflect on their literacy experiences in ways that are transformative and empowering, ways that describe the challenges and rewards of acquiring literacy. What these assignments overlook, however, is that literacy narratives, like all genres, are not merely communicative tools; they actually reflect and reinscribe desires and assumptions about the inherent value and power of literacy. Students who are asked to write literacy narratives come up against a set of cultural expectations—embedded as part of the genre—about the transformative power of literacy as a necessary tool for success and achievement. Kirk Branch, for instance, describes how students in his reading and writing class at Rainier Community Learning Center struggled to invent themselves within the assumptions of these narratives. Aware of the social motives rhetorically embedded within these narratives, Branch explains, students wrote them as much to describe their experiences with literacy as to convince themselves and others of the transforming power of literacy. For example, commenting on one such student narrative, titled "Rosie's Story," Branch concludes,

> "Rosie's Story" *writes itself* into a positive crescendo, a wave of enthusiasm which tries to drown out the self-doubt she reveals earlier. "Rosie's Story" does not suggest an unbridled confidence in the power of literacy to solve her problems, but by the end of the piece she drops the provisional "maybes" and "shoulds" and encourages herself to maintain her momentum: "Just keep it up." Her story, then, reads as an attempt to quash her self-doubt and to reassert the potential of literacy in her own life. (220; my emphasis)

In the end, it seems, the power of genre and the ideology it compels writers to sustain and articulate wins out. Rosie does not seem to be expressing some inherent intention as she writes this narrative. Rather, she seems to be locating herself within the desires embedded within the literacy narrative, desires that inform how she recognizes and performs herself in the situation of the reading and writing class. To claim, then, that her narrative begins *with* and *in* her is to overlook the extent to which she herself is being written by the genre she is writing.

We notice a remarkable example of how genres shape our perceptions and actions when Lee, a student in Branch's class, writes in his literacy narrative: "Furthermore Mr. Kirk gives us our assignments and he has always wanted us to do our best. He said, 'If you hadn't improved your English, you wouldn't have got a good job.' Therefore I worry about my English all the time" (Branch 221). "Does it matter," Branch wonders afterwards, "that I never said this to Lee?" (221) Apparently, Branch does not have to say it; Lee's assumption about literacy as a necessary tool for success is already rhetorically embedded in the genre of the literacy narrative as understood by the student, an assumption that

Lee internalizes as his intention and enacts as his narrative when he writes this genre. It is within the situated topoi of the genre that Lee "invents" his narrative.

Often, teachers of writing overlook the socializing function of their writing prompts and consequently locate the beginnings of student writing too simply in the students rather than in the prompts themselves. What these teachers overlook—and writing teacher guides are no exception—is that students first have to situate and "invent" themselves in our prompts before they can assume the position of student writer. In fact, as we will discuss momentarily, it is the prompt that tacitly invokes the position that student writers are asked to assume when they write, so that students read their way into the position of writer via our prompts. Given this, it is perhaps more than a little ironic that most guides to writing effective assignment prompts emphasize the importance of specifying an audience *in* the prompt while more or less ignoring the students as audience *of* the prompt. As one of her five heuristics for designing writing assignments, for instance, Lindemann includes the following: "*For whom are students writing?* Who is the audience? Do students have enough information to assume a role with respect to the audience? Is the role meaningful?" (215). Here, the student is perceived only as potential writer to the audience we construct in the prompt. But what about the student as audience to the teacher's prompt, the position that the student first assumes before he or she begins to write? The assumption seems to be that the student exists a priori as a writer who has only to follow the instructions of the teacher's prompt rather than as a reader who is first invoked or interpellated into the position of writer by the teacher's prompt. This process of interpellation involves a moment of tacit recognition, in which the student first becomes aware of the position assigned to him or her and is consequently moved to act out that position as a writer.

The prompt is a genre whose explicit function is to make another genre, the student essay, possible. Within the FYW course activity system, it helps to create a timeliness and an opportunity for student writing in what Yates and Orlikowski, following Bazerman, refer to as "kairotic coordination" (110). In coordinating this interaction, the writing prompt functions to transform its writer (the teacher) and its readers (the students) into a reader (the teacher) and writers (the students). It positions the students and teacher into two simultaneous roles: the students as readers and writers, the teacher as writer and reader. First of all, the prompt rhetorically positions the teacher as both a writer and a reader. As he or she writes the prompt, the teacher positions him or herself as reader for the student text that the prompt will eventually make possible. The challenge that the prompt creates for the teacher is how to create the conditions that will allow students to recognize him or her not as the writer of the prompt, but as the eventual reader of their writing. That is, the teacher has to find a way to negotiate a double subject position, a subject subject, one who is doing the action (the subject as writer) and one on whom the action is done (the subject as reader). One way the teacher manages this double position is through a series of typified rhetorical moves and statements. For example, the following phrases are typical of prompts: "You should be sure to consider," "You probably realize by now that," "As you have probably guessed," "As you all know."[5] These are loaded phrases, because they not only offer suggestions the teacher-writer is giving to the student-readers; they also offer hints about what the teacher-writer will be expecting as a teacher-reader. When the teacher writes, "You probably realize by now that one effective way to support YOUR evaluation of those reviews is to offer examples from them in the way of quotes," he is telling the students something about him as an audience. He is basically saying, "Look, I care about using quotes to support evaluation, so if you want to write an effective evaluation for me, use quotes." Writing "one effective way" allows the teacher-writer to covertly express what he cares about as a reader. The next example is even more covert—and clever. After describing the assignment to the students, the teacher writes:

> To do this, *you should be able* to explain why the scene is central to the story's plot, what issues are being dealt with, and how or why the characters change. *The trick here* is to employ as many specific details from the story as possible. *You have the responsibility* to explain to your audience why you made the decision you did. (my emphasis)

The teacher who begins this prompt as a writer describing the assignment to the students as readers here begins to emerge as a reader to the students as writers. "You should be able to" is a subtle, or perhaps not so subtle, way of letting students know what he as a teacher-reader expects from their writing. "The trick here" is even more effective, because it allows the teacher to enact the role of reader while seeming to be an objective observer giving helpful advice. In fact, however, there is no "trick" involved here, just a calculated rhetorical way for the teacher to let students know that he as a reader cares a great deal about the use of specific details. The only "trick" at work here is how the teacher creates the illusion that the writer addressing them is not the same person as the reader who will be reading their writing. It is this rhetorical sleight of hand that the prompt makes possible.

The prompt, therefore, allows the teacher to occupy two subject positions at once: writer/coach and reader/evaluator. As a result, and at the same time, the prompt also constitutes the students as readers and writers. The students are prompted into position or invoked as writers by the prompt, within which they read and invent themselves. Indeed, every prompt has inscribed within it a subject position for students to assume in order to carry out the assignment. In FYW prompts, these roles can be quite elaborate, asking students to pretend that "you have just been hired as a student research assistant by a congressperson in your home state" or "you have been asked by *Rolling Stone* to write a critique of one of the following films." The prompts do not stop here, however. They go on to specify to students how they should enact these roles, as in the following example, in which the teacher asks students to pretend that they are congressional aides:

> You must not explain what you "think" about this subject; the congressperson is more interested in the objective consideration of the issues themselves. And *of course*, you shouldn't recommend whether or not your employer should support the bill; *you are, after all, only an aide*. (my emphasis)

Words such as "of course," "obviously," "after all," "remember," and "certainly" all typically appear in prompts. Their function is to establish shared assumptions; however, we have to question just how shared these assumptions really are. How shared, for example, is the "of course" in the above example? Does the student-writer share this knowledge about congresspersons or is this a subtle way in which the prompt writer coerces complicity? The fact that the teacher-writer goes to the trouble of mentioning it suggests that perhaps the knowledge is not so obvious, that, in fact, "of course," "certainly," and "as we all know" are rhetorical means of presenting new information in the guise of old information (Pelkowski 7). If this is the case, then what we are witnessing is the prompt at work constituting the students as writers who assent to the ideology presented in the prompt, just as we saw in the case of the literacy narratives.

To a great extent, students have to accept the position(s) made available to them in the prompt if they are to carry out the assignment successfully. As all genres do, the prompt invites an uptake commensurate with its ideology, just as we saw in the example of the first state of the union address in which George Washington's choice of the "king's speech" prompted an appropriate congressional reply mirroring the echoing speeches of Parliament. While there is room for resistance, for students to refuse to accept the shared assumptions the prompt makes available to them, Pelkowski reminds us that "the power structure of the university denies students the ability to offer alternative interpretations of prompts. . . . Rather, an alternative interpretation of the assignment is not seen as such, but as a 'failure to respond to the assignment' (the F paper is often characterized in this way in statements of grading criteria)" (16). The writing prompt, in short, functions as a site of invention in which teacher and student create the conditions in which they will eventually interact as reader and writer.

The Student Essay

The very coercion masked as complicity that we observe in the syllabus and writing prompt is also at work when students begin to write their essays. This time, though, rather than being objects of this discursive move, students are expected to become its agents. In this way, students learn to enact the desires they acquire as participants within the FYW course and its system of genres. For example, one of the tricks teachers often expect students to perform in their writing involves recontextualizing the desires embedded in the writing prompt as their own self-generated desires. That is, students are expected to situate their writing within the writing prompt without acknowledging its presence explicitly in their writing so that it appears as though their writing created its own exigency, that somehow their writing is self-prompted. This rhetorical sleight of hand appears most visibly in the introductions of student essays, because it is there that students are asked to create the opportunity and timing for their essays in relation to the opportunity and timing as defined by the writing prompt. Experienced student writers know that they must negotiate this transaction between genres and do so with relative ease. Less experienced student writers, however, sometimes fail to recognize that the prompt and essay are related but separate genres, and their essays can frustrate teachers by citing the prompt explicitly in a way that shatters the illusion of self-sufficiency we desire students to create in their writing. In what follows, I will look at several examples of student essays to examine to what extent and how students negotiate this difficult transaction between genres as they function as agents on behalf of the prompt and agents of their own writing.

Yates and Orlikowski's work on the function of chronos and kairos in communicative interaction can help us interrogate the relation between the writing prompt and the student essay. They describe how genre systems choreograph interactions among participants and activities chronologically (by way of measurable, quantifiable, "objective" time) and kairotically (by way of constructing a sense of timeliness and opportunity in specific situations) within communities (108–10). In terms of chronos, the writing prompt assigns a specific time sequence for the production of the student essay, often delimiting what is due at what time and when. In this way, the writing prompt defines a chronological relationship between itself and the student essay. At the same time, however, the writing prompt also establishes the kairos for the student essay by providing it with a timeliness and an opportunity. In this way, the writing prompt defines a recognizable moment that authorizes the student essay's raison d'Être.

Participating within this kairotic relationship between two genres, the student must, on the one hand, recognize the opportunity defined for him or her in the prompt and, on the other hand, reappropriate that opportunity as his or her own in the essay. Carolyn Miller describes this interaction as "the dynamic interplay between . . . opportunity as discerned and opportunity as defined" (312). Engaged in this interplay, the student writer must discern the opportunity granted by the prompt while writing an essay that seemingly defines its own opportunity. As such, the student writer needs to achieve and demonstrate a certain amount of generic dexterity, functioning within a genre system while masking its interplay. I will now look at some examples of how student writers negotiate this discursive transaction.

The following examples, from a FYW course, are all written in response to the same writing prompt. The students had read and discussed Clifford Geertz's "Deep Play: Notes on the Balinese Cockfight," had been assigned to take on the "role of 'cultural anthropologist' or 'ethnographer,'" had conducted some field observations, and were then prompted to write, "in the vein of Geertz in 'Deep Play,'" a

> claim-driven essay about the "focused gathering" [a term that Geertz uses] you observed. Your essay should be focused on and centered around what you find to be most significant and worth writing about in terms of the "focused gathering" you observed . . . . Some issues you might want to attend to include: How does the event define the community taking part in it? What does the event express about the beliefs of the community? What does the event say about the larger society?

Not only does the prompt assign students a subjectivity (the role of cultural anthropologist), but it also grants them an opportunity to transform their observations into an argument. In taking up this opportunity, the students perform a range of transactions between their essays and the writing prompt. Below, I will describe a sample of these transactions, starting with essays in which the writing prompt figures prominently (so that the coercion is visible) and concluding with essays in which the writing prompt is recontextualized as the student's own self-generated opportunity.

In those examples where students fail to enact the desired relationship between the prompt and the essay, the writing prompt figures explicitly in their essays, fracturing the illusion of autonomy that the essay, although prompted, tries to maintain. In the most obvious cases, such as the following, the student narrates explicitly the process of the essay's production:

> In my last literary endeavor [ostensibly referring to an earlier draft of the essay] I focused on one facet of the baseball game that I had gone to see. This time I am going to try to bring a few more topics to the table and focus on one thing in particular that I feel is significant.[6]

In this excerpt, the student appears to be narrating the prompt's instructions (stated as "be focused on and centered around what you find to be most significant") as he fulfills them. That is, he is telling us what he has been asked to do from one stage of the assignment sequence to the next as he does it, thereby making the coercion visible, as in the words, "This time I am going to try to . . ." Purposefully or not, the student in this case fails to perform the desired uptake between the prompt and his essay so that the prompt essentially speaks through him.

In a similar but less explicit way, the next essay also fails to reappropriate the prompt's defined opportunity as its own, so that the essay remains overly reliant on the prompt. The essay begins:

> Cultural events are focused gatherings that give observers insights to that certain culture. Geertz observes the Balinese culture and gains insights on how significant cockfighting is to the Balinese: including issues of disquieting and the symbolic meaning behind the cockfights. My observations at a bubble tea shop in the International District also have similarities with Geertz's observations of the Balinese cockfight on the cultural aspect.

The phrases "cultural events" and "focused gatherings" locate the language of the prompt in the essay, but the first sentence simply rewords the language of the prompt rather than recontextualizing it as part of the essay's own constructed exigency. The question that would likely come to most teachers' minds, even though they already know the answer, would be, "So what? Why do we need to know this?" Similarly, in the second sentence, the only way to understand the relevance of the transition into Geertz is to know the prompt, which makes that connection. By the time the student describes her own observations in the third sentence, too much of the prompt's background knowledge is assumed, so that, for the logic of these opening sentences to work, a reader needs the prompt as context, yet this is the very relationship that the prompt and essay wish to downplay.

Compare the opening sentences of the above essay to the opening sentences of the following essay:

> When you want to know more about a certain society or culture what is the first thing that you need to do? You need to make and analyze detailed observations of that particular society or culture in its natural environment. From there you should be able to come up with a rough idea of "why" that particular culture or society operates the way it does. That's exactly what Clifford Geertz did. He went to Bali to study the Balinese culture as an observer.

As in the earlier example, this excerpt borrows the language of the prompt, but rather than rewording that language, it reappropriates it. This time, the reader meets Geertz on the essay's terms, after the student has provided a context for why Geertz would have done what he did. The same exigency that motivated Geertz becomes the student's exigency for writing his essay. Crude as it might be, the question that begins the essay performs the sleight of hand I described earlier, in which the student recontextualizes the question the prompt asks of him and asks it of his readers as if this is the question *he* desires to ask. In this way, the student becomes an agent of the agency at work on him. The student, however, seems unable or unwilling to sustain this uptake, for in the very next paragraph, he fractures the illusion he has begun to create. He writes:

> A couple of weeks ago I decided to go visit some friends in Long Beach Washington. Since it was something different from the norm of people in my class analyzing concerts and baseball games

> I decided to do my paper on Long Beach. I didn't have to look far for a cultural event to observe because the little ocean-side town was having a parade. . . . I pretty much took the Geertz approach and just tried to figure out what was going on.

Here, the student not only slips out of his assigned role as a "cultural anthropologist" by acknowledging his position as a student, along with other students writing a paper for class, but he also makes visible the coercion that prompted his essay when he writes that it did not take him long to find a cultural event to observe. Suddenly, he identifies himself as someone who has been prompted to find an event. At the same time, although he does refer to Geertz in the previous paragraph, the student's statement, "I pretty much took the Geertz approach," appears to be addressed to a reader who knows more than what the student has already explained about Geertz. That is, the statement imagines a reader who is familiar with the prompt that directed the student to take the Geertz approach in the first place. After all, the prompt asks students to write an essay "in the vein of Geertz."

In the previous example, we witness a student who begins to negotiate but does not quite sustain the complex interplay between the genred discursive spaces of the writing prompt and the student essay. In the next couple of examples, we observe students who manage this discursive transaction by recontextualizing the desires embedded in the prompt as their own seemingly self-prompted desires to write.

The following student begins her essay by describing the activities and interactions that typically occur at her church, thereby performing her role as a cultural anthropologist. Her third paragraph, which follows two paragraphs of observations, marks a transition. She writes:

> What purpose does all this serve? Geertz states in Deep Play: Notes on the Balinese Cockfight, "the cockfight is a means of expression." (Geertz 420) In much the same way the Inn [the name of the church] is the same thing. It is a gathering for college aged people to express their faith in God.

By asking, "What purpose does all this serve?" this student asks the question that the prompt asks of her. In so doing, she makes it appear as though the inquiry that follows stems from her own curiosity. In the context of this appropriation, Geertz is not so much a figure she inherits from the prompt as he is a figure she invokes to create an opportunity for her essay to analyze the significance of the Inn. The student recontextualizes the opportunity as well as the authority from the discursive space of the prompt to the discursive space of the essay.

The next student performs a similar uptake, and does so with greater elegance. The student begins her essay by describing underground hip-hop music and the function it serves for its listeners, and then poses the question: "Is music created from culture, or is culture created from music?" The second paragraph begins to compare hip-hop to symphonies. The student writes:

> On a different note, a symphonic band concert creates a congregation of different status people uniting to listen to a type of music they all enjoy. "Erving Goffman has called *this* a type of 'focused gathering'—a set of persons engrossed in a common flow of activity and relating to one another in terms of that flow" (Geertz 405). This type of "focused gathering" is an example of music created from culture. "Focused gatherings" provide different emotions according to preference. The flocking of similar interests in the form of "focused gatherings" makes up a culture. Similar values are shared to create one group of equals producing music for the same reason." (my emphasis)

By posing the question, "Is music created from culture, or is culture created from music?" the student creates an opportunity for her essay rather than inheriting that opportunity from the prompt. This is the question the *student* is asking. In the above excerpt, the student does not rely on the prompt's authority to justify the claim that "a symphonic band concert creates a congregation of different status people uniting to listen to a type of music they all enjoy." Instead, she appropriates the authority the prompt grants her to assert this claim. Only in the context of her authority does Geertz then figure into the essay. Notice how cleverly the student uses the quotation from Geertz to make it appear as though his description of a "focused gathering" was meant to define her focused gathering, the symphonic band concert. The determiner "this" no longer modifies the cockfight as Geertz meant it to;

instead, it refers back to the concert, which is the student's subject of inquiry. In a way, this move creates the impression that the student found Geertz rather than having been assigned to use Geertz. There is very little evidence of prompting here.

In the remainder of the above excerpt, the student appears to perform what Fuller and Lee have described as an interiorized uptake, in which the student becomes positioned, through her interaction with the writing prompt, as a desiring subject who speaks from that subjectivity (222). In this case, the student internalizes the authority embedded in the prompt as her own authority in statements such as, "The flocking of similar interests in the form of 'focused gatherings' makes up a culture. Similar values are shared to create one group of equals producing music for the same reason." The student has appropriated the subjectivity assigned to her and now speaks from that position as a "cultural anthropologist." Fuller and Lee refer to this process of negotiation as "textual collusion," a term they use to describe how writers and readers move "around inside relations of power" (215). More so than her peers, this student seems able to negotiate the textured relations between the prompt and the essay, repositioning herself in the interplay between genred spaces so that she becomes an agent of the agency at work on her.

Invention takes place at the intersection between the acquisition and articulation of desire. When teachers assign students a writing prompt, they position students at this intersection so that part of what students do when they invent their essays involves recontextualizing the desires they have acquired as their own self-prompted desires to write. As such, teachers expect students to manage the interplay between coercion and complicity that we saw teachers perform in the syllabus (manifested in the "you" and "we" formations). Not all students, as we see in the above examples, are able to perform this sleight of hand with the same dexterity. And the reason for this, I would argue, has partly to do with the fact that some students do not know that this transaction requires them to move around between two genred sites of action, each with its own situated desires, relations, subjectivities, and practices—in short, its own positions of articulation. When they conflate these two worlds, students not only fracture the illusion of self-sufficiency the essay desires them to maintain, but students also fail to reposition their subjectivity and their subject matter within the discursive and ideological space of the essay. One way teachers can help students reposition themselves within such spheres of agency is to make genres analytically visible to students so that students can participate within and negotiate them more meaningfully and critically. . . .

Summary

Writing involves a process of learning to adapt, ideologically and discursively, to various situations via the genres that coordinate them. Writing is not only a skill, but a way of being and acting in the world in a particular time and place in relation to others. The FYW course bears this out. As an activity system, it is sustained and coordinated by its various genres. Teachers and students assume ways of being and acting in the classroom not only because of its material setting—although that certainly does play a major part (see Reynolds)—but also because of its multitextured sites of action as they are embodied within and between genres. As such, the writing that students do in the FYW course does not just begin with them by virtue of their being (enrolled) in this setting; it begins, rather, in the textured topoi that are already in place, shaping and enabling the writing that students as well as teachers do. As such, the environment of the classroom—or any other environment for that matter, including the doctor's office—is not only an ontological fact, but also a generic fact. It exists largely because we reproduce it in our genres, each of which constitutes a different but related topoi within which students and teacher function, interact, and enact subjectivities and practices. Since we reproduce the FYW course in the ways we articulate it, there is really little that is artificial or arbitrary about it, at least not in the way that Paul Heilker describes the FYW course as being artificial: "Writing teachers need to relocate the *where* of composition instruction outside the academic classroom because the classroom does not and cannot offer students real rhetorical situations in which to understand writing as social action" (71).

Part of my argument in this essay is that the FYW course *is* a "real rhetorical situation," one made up of various scenarios within which students (and their teachers) recognize one another, reposition themselves, interact, and enact their situated practices in complex social and rhetorical frameworks. Once we recognize this, once we acknowledge that the FYW course, like any activity system, is "not a container for actions or texts" but "an ongoing accomplishment" (Russell, "Rethinking" 513), we are on our way to treating the FYW course as a complex and dynamic scene of writing, one in which students can not only learn how to write, but . . . can also learn what it means to write: what writing does and how it positions writers within systems of activity. Participating in the textual dynamics of the FYW course is as "real" a form of social action and interaction as any other textual practice.

As we have observed . . . , genres position their users to perform certain situated activities by generating and organizing certain desires and subjectivities. These desires and subjectivities are embedded within and prompted by genres, which elicit the various, sometimes conflicting, intentions we perform within and between situations. To assume that the writer is the primary locus of invention, then, is to overlook the constitutive power of genre in shaping and enabling how writers recognize and participate in sites of action.

Rather than being defined as the agency of the writer, invention is more a way that writers locate themselves, via genres, within various positions and activities. Invention is thus a process in which writers act as they are acted upon. The Patient Medical History Form is a case in point. So are the examples of George Washington and the first state of the union address, the example of the social workers' assessment report, and the example of the student essay in relation to the assignment prompt. All these examples point to the fact that there is more at work in prompting discourse than simply the writer's private intentions or even, for that matter, the demands of the writer's immediate exigencies. After all, George Washington responded to the exigencies of an unprecedented rhetorical situation not by inventing something new, but by turning to an antecedent genre, the "king's speech," which carried with it a rhetorical form of social action very much at odds with his more immediate exigencies. The available genre, rhetorically embodying social motives so powerful as to override the inspired democratic moment at hand, not only shaped the way Washington recognized and acted within his rhetorical situation, but the way Congress did too.

We notice a similar phenomenon at work in the example of the writing prompt. The writing prompt does not merely provide students with a set of instructions. Rather, it organizes and generates the discursive and ideological conditions which students take up and recontextualize as they write their essays. As such, it habituates students into the subjectivities they are asked to assume as well as enact—the subjectivities required to explore their subjects. By expanding the sphere of agency in which the writer participates, we in composition studies can offer both a richer view of the writer as well as a more comprehensive account of how and why writers makes the choices they do. . . .

Notes

1. It is worth noting here that the word *ethos* in Greek means "a habitual gathering place." Just like rhetorical strategy, then, the persona a rhetor assumes takes place within a place, a habitation or topoi, so that when rhetors invent, they are not only formulating the available means of persuasion, but also the rhetorical persona they need to carry out that rhetorical strategy. As LeFevre explains, "ethos . . . appears in that socially created space, in the 'between,' the point of intersection between speaker or writer and listener or reader" (46). Considered as situated topoi, genres not only shape and enable how communicants recognize and enact social situations; genres also shape and enable how communicants recognize and enact their ethos or subjectivities within these situations.

2. With the increased use of computer technology in education, especially networked classes and distance learning, this claim becomes less generalizable. If anything, though, the emergence of the "virtual classroom" only strengthens my claims about genre and the classroom that follow.

3. It is worth noting that the FYW classroom is no more artificial than Epcot is "artificial" when compared to the "real" Florida. As I dis-

cussed in chapter 4, Epcot is as complex a rhetorical ecosystem as any wilderness-designated area. Both are rhetorical constructions, ways we define, conceptualize, and behave in our environments.

4. For this analysis, I randomly collected fifteen syllabi from colleagues at a research university and from published teaching guides. All the syllabi are from FYW courses, and reflect a balance between experienced and new teachers.

5. The examples I analyze in this section are culled from my examination of fifteen randomly collected writing prompts from experienced and new teachers of FYW at a research university.

6. I reprint this and the following student excerpts as they appear in the students' essays, errors and all.

Works Cited

Baecker, Diann L. "Uncovering the Rhetoric of the Syllabus: The Case of the Missing I." *College Teaching* 46.2 (1998): 58–62.

Bartholomae, David. "Writing Assignments: Where Writing Begins." *Forum: Essays on Theory and Practice in the Teaching of Writing*. Ed. Patricia L. Stock. Portsmouth: Boynton/Cook, 1983. 300–312.

Bazerman, Charles. "Systems of Genres and the Enactment of Social Intentions." Freedman and Medway: 79–101.

Bazerman, Charles. "Where is the Classroom?" Freedman and Medway: 25–30.

Bishop, Wendy, and Hans Ostrom, Eds. *Genre and Writing: Issues, Arguments, Alternatives*. Portsmouth: Boynton/Cook, 1997.

Booth, Wayne. *Modern Dogma and the Rhetoric of Assent*. Chicago: U of Chicago P, 1974.

Branch, Kirk. "From the Margins at the Center: Literacy, Authority, and the Great Divide." *College Composition and Communication* 50.2 (1998): 206–231.

Christie, Frances. "Curriculum Genres: Planning for Effective Teaching." *The Powers of Literacy: A Genre Approach to Teaching Writing*. Ed. Bill Cope and Mary Kalantzis. Pittsburgh: U of Pittsburgh P, 1993. 154–78.

Coe, Richard, Lorelei Lingard, and Tatiana Teslenko, eds. *The Rhetoric and Ideology of Genre*. Cresskill, NJ: Hampton, 2002.

Connors, Robert J., and Cheryl Glenn. *The St. Martin's Guide to Teaching Writing*. 3rd ed. New York: St. Martin's, 1995.

Consigny, Scott. "Rhetoric and Its Situations." Young and Liu: 59–67.

Corder, Jim. "Varieties of Ethical Argument." Young and Liu: 99–133.

Crowley, Sharon. *The Methodical Memory: Invention in Current Traditional Rhetoric*. Carbondale: Southern Illinois UP, 1990.

Devitt, Amy J. "Intertextuality in Tax Accounting: Generic, Referential, and Functional." *Textual Dynamics of the Professions: Historical and Contemporary Studies of Writing in Professional Communities*. Ed. Charles Bazerman and James Paradis. Madison: U of Wisconsin P, 1991. 335–357.

Enos, Theresa, ed. *Encyclopedia of Rhetoric and Composition: Communication from Ancient Times to the Present*. New York: Garland, 1996.

Farrell, Thomas B. "Commonplaces." Enos: 116–117.

Freedman, Aviva. "Situating Genre: A Rejoinder." *Research in the Teaching of English* 27 (1993): 272–281.

Freedman, Aviva, and Peter Medway, eds. *Genre and the New Rhetoric*. Bristol: Taylor and Francis, 1994.

Fuller, Gillian, and Alison Lee. "Assembling a Generic Subject." Coe, Lingard, and Teslenko: 207–224.

Geertz, Clifford. *Local Knowledge*. New York: Basic, 1983.

Giltrow, Janet. "Meta-Genre." Coe, Lingard, and Teslenko: 187–205.

Heilker, Paul. "Rhetoric Made Real: Civil Discourse and Writing Beyond the Curriculum." *Writing the Community*. Ed. Linda Addler-Kassner, Robert Crooks, and Ann Watters. Washington D.C.: American Association for Higher Education, 1997. 71–76.

Helscher, Thomas P. "The Subject of Genre." Bishop and Ostrom: 27–36.

Lauer, Janice M. "Topics." Enos: 724–725.

LeFeve, Karen Burke. *Invention as a Social Act*. Carbondale: Southern Illinois UP, 1987.

Lindemann, Erika. *A Rhetoric for Writing Teachers*. 3rd. ed. New York: Oxford UP, 1995.

Miller, Carolyn R. "Kairos in the Rhetoric of Science." *A Rhetoric of Doing*. Ed. S. P. Witte, N. Nakadato, and R. D. Cherry. Carbondale: Southern Illinois U P, 1992. 310–27.

Mühlhäusler, P., and R. Harré. *Pronouns and People: The Linguistic Construction of Social and Personal Identity*. Oxford: Basil and Blackwell, 1990.

Murray, Donald. *Expecting the Unexpected: Teaching Myself and Others to Read and Write*. Portsmouth: Boynton/Cook, 1989.

Pelkowski, Stephanie. "The Teacher's Audience is Always a Fiction." Unpublished Manuscript.

Reiff, John D., and James E. Middleton. "A Model for Designing and Revising Assignments." *Fforum: Essays on Theory and Practice in the Teaching of Writing*. Ed. Patricia L. Stock. Portsmouth: Boynton/Cook, 1983. 263–68.

Reynolds, Nedra. "Composition's Imagined Geographies: The Politics of Space in the Frontier, City, and Cyberspace." *College Composition and Communication* 50.1 (1998): 12–35.

Russell, David R. "Rethinking Genre in School and Society: An Activity Theory Analysis." *Written Communication* 14.4 (1997): 504–554.

Russell, David R. "The Kind-ness of Genre: An Activity Theory Analysis of High School Teachers' Perceptions of Genre in Portfolio Assessment across the Curriculum." Coe, Lingard, and Teslenko: 225–242.

Slevin, James F. "Genre Theory, Academic Discourse, and Writing in the Disciplines." *Audits of Meaning: A Festschrift in Honor of Anne E. Berthoff*. Ed. Louise Z. Smith. Portsmouth: Boynton/Cook, 1988. 3–16.

Swales, John M. "Occluded Genres in the Academy: The Case of the Submission Letter." *Academic Writing: Intercultural and Textual Issues*. Amsterdam: Benjamins, 1996. 44–58.

Williams, James D. *Preparing to Teach Writing*. Belmont: Wadsworth, 1989.

Yates, JoAnne, and Wanda Orlikowski. "Genres of Organizational Communication: A Structural Approach." *Academy of Management Review* 17 (1992): 299–326.

Young, Richard, and Yameng Liu, eds. *Landmark Essays on Rhetorical Invention*. Davis, CA: Hermagoaras, 1994.

Chapter Seven

Genre and Identity: Individuals, Institutions, and Ideology

Anthony Paré

The personality is strangely composite.

Gramsci 324

. . . each act of writing is a potential struggle because there are competing systems of values and beliefs at work.

Clark and Ivanic 71

As the chapters in this book indicate, the reconception of genre as social action inaugurated by Carolyn Miller's 1984 article offers a rich theoretical ground on which to reunite aspects of rhetorical action that were estranged by previous theoretical perspectives. The expanded notion of genre has allowed theorists and researchers to fuse text and context, product and process, cognition and culture in a single, dynamic concept. In addition, by enlarging the focus of attention in rhetorical inquiry to include the full social and symbolic action of textual practice, the reconception of genre encourages us to consider the complex interconnections among these once-separated aspects of writing.

This chapter explores one particularly promising avenue for genre theory and research: the relationship between language and ideology.[1,2] As habitual practices, genres serve as one of the chief discursive forces in what Fairclough (1995) calls the "naturalization of ideology":

From *The Rhetoric and Ideology of Genre*. Ed. Richard Coe, Lorelei Lingard, and Tatiana Teslenko. Cresskill, NJ: Hampton, 2002. 57–71.

> A particular set of discourse conventions (e.g., for conducting medical consultations, or media interviews, or for writing crime reports in newspapers) implicitly embodies certain ideologies—particular knowledge and beliefs, particular "positions" for the types of social subject that participate in that practice (e.g., doctors, patients, interviewees, newspaper readers), and particular relationships between categories of participants (e.g., between doctors and patients). In so far as conventions become naturalized and commonsensical, so too do these ideological presuppositions. (94)

The automatic, ritual unfolding of genres makes them appear normal, even inevitable; they are simply the way things are done. And their status as historical practice within institutions or disciplines makes them appear immutable and certainly beyond the influence of the transitory individuals who participate in them, and who become implicated in the subtle ideologies they enact. Coe argues that "genres embody attitudes," and adds that "[s]ince those attitudes are built into generic structures, they are sometimes danced without conscious awareness or intent on the part of the individual using the genre" (183). In *Critical Discourse Analysis*, Fairclough makes a similar claim when he argues that "there is a one-to-one relationship" between "ideological formations" (Althusser) and "discursive formations" (Foucault, Pêcheux), and coins the term "ideological-discursive formations" to get at "the inseparability of 'ways of talking' and 'ways of seeing'" (40). He says that "in the process of acquiring the ways of talking which are normatively associated with a [particular] subject position, one necessarily acquires also its ways of seeing, or ideological norms" (39).

This essay explores this ideological action of genre and, in particular, the ways in which genres locate or position individuals within the power relations of institutional activity. For me, as for Green and Lee, "rhetoric is as much concerned with the formation of identities as the construction of texts" (208). The workplace settings considered here are those common to social work. By examining a variety of rhetorical situations within different workplaces, the chapter offers a peek through the chinks that develop when a genre's facade of normalcy is cracked by resistance, inappropriate deployment, unfamiliarity, or critical analysis. Evidence to support the chapter's claims comes from interviews with social work students, educators, and practitioners, as well as from transcripts of supervisory sessions between veteran social workers and their student apprentices.

Seeing through Genre

Institutional genres are successful patterns in local discursive forms and functions. In the institution's evolution of textual practices, they have proven effective and endurable; they have shown themselves capable of adapting to (and influencing) the changing scene. But their persistence is not the result of natural selection so much as human volition: genres are sociorhetorical habits or rituals that "work," that get something done, that achieve desirable ends. Their existence raises a series of questions that lead inexorably to ideology: For whom do they "work"? To what end? Do they "work" equally for all who participate in or are affected by them? According to Gunnarson, Einell, and Nordberg, "[w]e must . . . ask ourselves not only how professional genres have been constructed but also for whom, for what needs and why they have been formed the way they are" (3).

However, that inquiry may prove difficult because, as Fairclough suggests above, discourse conventions may cloak vested interests or imbalances in power. "Ideology," says Berlin, "always brings with it strong social and cultural reinforcement, so that what we take to exist, to have value, and to be possible seems necessary, normal, and inevitable—in the nature of things" (78). Fairclough says it this way: "metaphorically speaking, ideology endeavours to cover its own traces" (*Critical* 44). The result, in Bruce Kidd's earthy and memorable phrase, is that "[i]deology is like B.O., you never smell your own" (250). Unlike B.O., however, others' ideology is also difficult to detect.

Further complicating this camouflaging effect is the fact that ideology, as manifest in institutional practice, is fragmented and conflictual, so that no single, unadulterated ideological perspective prevails entirely. In other words, power is rarely naked and never monolithic: In most institutional contexts, there is a constant struggle for ideological supremacy, with competing visions and values being advanced, challenged, negotiated, and altered. Genres are key institutional sites for such struggles (Schryer). Consequently, it "is quite possible for a social subject to occupy institutional subject positions which are ideologically incompatible, or to occupy a subject position incompatible with his or her overt political or social beliefs and affiliations, without being aware of any contradiction" (Fairclough, *Critical* 42). Or, as Berlin says, "we are constituted by subject formulations and subject positions that do not always square with each other" (62). Just as ideology is masked by convention, so, too, can these contradictions be hidden by the apparent naturalness of daily practice.

But genre's illusion of normalcy may be cracked or exposed at certain moments: when an event occurs that does not match the anticipated, socially construed exigence to which the genre responds; or, in a related situation, when the genre is stretched too wide, and its forms and actions are inappropriate or ill-suited to the occasion (as when textual forms are transported out of the contexts in which they developed); when newcomers first begin to participate in a genre and find it "unnatural" or counter to their own discourse habits and aims (developed in school, for example); when there are shifts in power relations within institutions, so that the values produced by discourse practices no longer favor those with authority to change or influence those practices.

For the past ten years I have taken advantage of these cracks in genre to study the complexities of power in the rhetorical activity of social work, and I have come to agree with Berlin that ideology is "minutely inscribed in the discourse of daily practice, where it emerges as pluralistic and conflicted. A given historical moment displays a wide variety of competing ideologies, and each subject displays permutations of these conflicts" (78). As with other professional discourses, social work genres are most ideologically charged and conflicted in institutional settings—such as hospitals, school systems, and courts of law—where multiple communities of practice create overlapping jurisdictions and activity systems (Dias; Russell), a highly competitive "linguistic marketplace" (Bourdieu), multilayered hierarchies, and complex, articulated genre sets (Devitt) and genre systems (Bazerman). Within such settings, social work texts move beyond disciplinary boundaries into legal contexts, medical charts, psychologists' files, and school records; they serve as well to monitor workers and to justify budget cuts or allocations: invariably, and in countless ways, they influence the worker-client relationship. In this intricate web of rhetorical relations, social workers are powerful and powerless simultaneously, and any single genre is both an act of and a response to authority (Hall, Sarangi, and Slembrouck). And it is most often within the stress of these complex settings that the ideological action of genre can be glimpsed, as the following examples demonstrate.

The Dogs of Genre

Some time ago, I had the extraordinary experience of working with thirteen Inuit social workers in an intensive course in social work writing. The students, all women from arctic Quebec, and all practicing social workers, were enrolled in McGill University's Certificate in Northern Social Work Practice, a course of studies designed, in part, to train the uncredentialed Inuit in the theory and practice of contemporary, "professional" (i.e., southern, urban) social work.[4] Although they carry a full case load and are indispensable to the practice of state-supported social work in the north, the women are called "social assistants" and work under the supervision of nonaboriginal social workers.

The course was meant to help the workers with their recordkeeping tasks. Social workers in the north, like those elsewhere, must write many different types of records, and each text is woven into complex, regular patterns of discourse and action. There are linked and sequenced texts within their own discipline—what Devitt calls genre sets—that track a client's trajectory from initial assessment to discharge summary, and these texts join, overlap, complement, and compete with texts from other disciplines in a complex universe of discourse that Bazerman calls a "genre system." The social work texts are entered as court evidence in abuse cases; they justify forced removal of children from their families; they alert health workers to patients' psychosocial contexts. They share file space with police reports, psychological assessments, medical charts. All their texts contain, and often create, stories of pain, anger, violence, and loss.

Both the workers and their managers were dissatisfied with the women's recordkeeping, but for very different reasons. I was told that the workers needed help with English grammar, spelling, and punctuation so that they could provide more information and more detail in their records. The workers, however, complained that their managers always wanted to know so much about clients. As Katie said, "white people are greedy for other people's problems."

To put them somewhat at ease, I began the course by asking the workers to tell me about something from their own culture: some story, idea, event, or custom that I didn't know about. They wrote about making bannock, sewing sealskin boots, ice fishing, and other traditional activities. Marta wrote a vivid account of using dog hair to trim parkas and mittens. She stood beside my desk as I read it. "This is very good, Marta," I said, "it's so detailed and clear I could almost do it myself using your instructions, but I still have two questions. First, what do you use to trim the hair and, second, how do you hold the dog still?" Marta looked at me for a long moment, took my pen from my hand, and wrote on the bottom of her paper: "It's a dead dog." When the two of us stopped laughing long enough to tell the others what had happened, another worker, Angie, went back to her recipe for *misiraq*—a dip made from beluga whale fat—and added "step number one: shoot a beluga." More laughter and, after talking among themselves in Inuktitut, the workers told me that when a white person's dog goes missing in the north, all the white folks look to see who among the Inuit has a new parka. Apparently, they have good reason to do so.

For all of us, the episode was dramatic evidence of the gap in knowledge and trust that separates cultural groups. I spoke of the need to be generous with detail and explanation when writing as an expert to those less knowledgeable; they spoke of their reluctance to be so open, so revealing. The degree of explicit detail required in documentation—the thorough records that their managers wanted—meant exposing their clients, all of whom were friends, family, or acquaintances, to the white authorities. Most painfully for the workers, records reduced their clients' stories to narratives of failure and textually organized their lives under institutional and cultural categories of dysfunction and deviation. Recordkeeping, said Elisuaq, was like "stealing someone's life."

The workers' dilemma indicates how participation in workplace genres situates writers in relations of power. Obviously, in the case of the Inuit workers, culture and colonization introduced multiple levels of ideological tension, but their struggles with recording exposed something else: The Inuit workers were being forced to employ rhetorical strategies developed in the urban south, where workers and clients live apart and have no relationship outside the interview, the office, or the courtroom. Transporting textual practices to the north meant transporting as well the elements of context and culture that had created and sustained them: the impersonal, detached persona of professional life, the anticipated narratives of southern social work clients, the categories, lifestyles, values, beliefs, and power relations of the urban welfare state. As a result, the Inuit workers were forced into a position between cultures and into the role of professional representatives of the colonial power. As Evelyn, one of the workers, said, I "have to satisfy both distinct cultures: the paper-work culture [white bureaucracy] . . . and my culture, you know, who I am, who [my clients] are, the way we speak, the way we talk." More than any other aspect of their work, writing separated them from their everyday lives, their everyday selves. Most striking to me was the way in which participation in the social work genres pushed the workers toward the detached professional self that was essential for participation in those genres in the south. But, as Evelyn said, "If I become a professional person with my family, I'm not going to have any more family . . . I'm going to push them away."

Genre and the Divided Self

According to Gee, "[d]iscourses are ways of being in the world, or forms of life which integrate words, acts, values, beliefs, attitudes, and social identities, as well as gestures, glances, body positions, and clothes" (127). A discourse, says Gee, is an "identity kit" (127). The Inuit workers' resistance to the distancing role of professional and the ideology it supports is resistance to at least two enforced identities: a nonaboriginal persona imposed and signaled by the use of English, and the detached, professional persona of southern, urban social work.

Although this tension may be most apparent and uncomfortable in cross-cultural settings, such as that experienced by the Inuit workers, where participation in a professional or disciplinary discourse may impose dual identities (at least), entry into any new discourse requires new subject positions, new identities. This was apparent during a workshop I conducted with a group of workers in an urban, state-funded, health and social service agency. The workers were comparing and evaluating two fictional records that I had modeled on actual records produced by the agency. There were certain key differences between the records; for example, one record contained such constructions as "I believe," "I think," and "I recommend," whereas the other had typical passive and self-effacing constructions such as "It is recommended" and "the undersigned believes"—the latter a peculiar and deflected reference to the self commonly found in institutional social work discourse. Inclusion of the self in the text, of course, lays bare the workers' position in power. As usual when I introduce this difference to a group of writers in an institutional setting, there was general agreement that first-person pronouns should not be used in official records, but one senior social worker challenged the others: "Why not," he asked. At first he got the usual answers: too personal, too informal, not professional; but then one worker, grasping beyond clichés, said this: "The 'I' in the record is not the same 'I' that sits at home on the couch, eating a hamburger, and watching T.V."

I think the accumulation of mundane detail in his explanation—home, couch, hamburger, and T.V.—points to a division the Inuit workers were trying to resist, but that many social workers feel they must make between the lived experience of their daily lives—the "I" in the world—and the disembodied experience of institutionalized collective life—the "I" subsumed in the professional role of organizational member, and implicated in a complex and conflicted ideology. As another social worker told me, becoming a professional means "learning to separate yourself. . . . You can't let yourself get emotionally attached or involved with your clients; and there has to be a point where you remove yourself. . . . You have to harden yourself to some degree." Social work ethnographer and practitioner Gerald de Montigny says that social workers must learn "a grammar of expression and a professional form of disembodied presence marked by containment, control, and managed emotionality" (41).

I believe that workers develop this "disembodied presence," in part, to help them reconcile the ideological conflict between their dual and contradictory role as advocate for the client and agent of the state. But similar dissension exists between their role and status as social workers vis à vis other workers in complex institutional structures (Dias, Freedman, Medway, and Paré; Paré). Social work often proceeds in both concert and conflict with more powerful professions, such as law and medicine. In the "linguistic marketplace" (Bourdieu) thus created, social work suffers: "Social work involves a 'defensive discourse,' in which accounts offer rebuttals to potential charges even before they are made" (Hall, Sarangi, and Slembrouck 268). In the following interview excerpt, a hospital social worker explains this tension:

> [D]octors have in their mind one idea, one suggestion for someone, and you have a different idea and the length of time that it takes you to implement your idea might not fall in conjunction with the doctor's. So if the doctor wants a discharge but the patient has nowhere to go, then it becomes time for you to advocate on their behalf. But it becomes also very difficult because you're dealing with a structure, an institutional structure where there are rules and regulations about how long a patient can stay, etc. So it puts pressure on your job. . . . I think you're constantly battling with the structure and I think you're battling with doctors who don't want to agree with the recommendations that you've made if it hinders a patient's medical progress.

In the same hospital, the director of the social service department, told me, "we're constantly being looked at by the administration to justify our establishment. . . . You've got to be able to document who it was that you've seen, and what it is you've done." The individual writer is caught between social work and medicine, between the messy complexity of a client's life and the bottom-line efficiency of budget-conscious administrators. Similar stress exists for a social worker within the juvenile court system, who says that her advisory report "will be totally dissected, usually by two lawyers, a judge, the parents, and the kid; so you have to write this report with shields all around you." The professional persona of institutional genres provides protection within these ideological tensions. It divides the individual's sense of identity, and it allows the workers to manage the ideology of everyday practice and the conflicts between belief and action that result from their multiple subject positions and their location in overlapping and occasionally opposing cultures or communities of practice. The move into the professional persona is an ideological transformation that occurs through participation in workplace genres.

"The text," says de Montigny, "is a mask concealing the embodied speaker who utters this or that claim. Through the text, social workers can promote their claims as though these were the universal wisdom of the profession in general" (64). The role of professional raises the individual newcomer above the fray. In narrative terms, the author becomes narrator rather than actor or character: an observer, not an agent, outside the action, recording events for posterity. It is what Hydén calls "the view from nowhere": "not the perspective of the omnipresent narrator of the nineteenth century novel, but rather a story told by an implicit narrator who is all-embracing and all-knowing. In this way, a specific effect is produced, namely, the impression of objectivity and impersonal professionalism" (259).

Learning Genre, Learning Ideology

How does this occur? How do individuals learn the divided and disembodied persona that allows them to negotiate the contradictions and conflicts of institutional ideology? In the following interview excerpt, a social work student describes his experience during field placement in a hospital setting:

> My first assessment that I wrote. . . I worked closely with my supervisor on and . . . she really reworded a lot of it. And then the child psychiatrist said to me, "I can't sign this!" So it was quite a shock. And he had different expectations in terms of how

> information should be organized than she did. . . . So she was speculating in a way or drawing links throughout the write-up of the assessment. And what the psychiatrist wanted was fact, fact, fact, fact, fact. . . . So he had a couple of categories which she didn't have. . . . I understand where they're both coming from and sometimes I feel like I'm between a rock and a hard place.

Thus positioned, the newcomer may find the lure of "fact" irresistible, especially because psychiatry is a more powerful discourse than social work, one with far greater currency in the hospital's "linguistic marketplace." Even more influential is the discourse of medicine, which strips the institutional narrative down to the minimum and entirely erases the narrator. The student who found himself caught "between a rock and a hard place" experienced a similar division between the ideologies of social work and medicine:

> [The doctor] said to me, "your writing is very literary and you are writing in a medical context." So I think that's part of what it's about, that it's medical and scientific and so in science we want, well, western science is very much like categorization wouldn't you say? So I think that's the justification. Basically what I see I'm learning is how to practice an art, an art of working with people's lives, an art of helping people get unstuck and heal themselves and their families through communication and various other things. But it takes place within a scientific domain. So that you can write up a report as artistic and literary and that doesn't fly. Or you can write it up in a way that looks more scientific and closer to objective.

According to Fairclough, "[w]here contrasting discursive practices are in use in a particular domain or institution, the likelihood is that part of that contrast is ideological" (88). While this newcomer to professional practice was struggling to reconcile the ideology he had developed through his social work education with the dominant ideology of medicine, the hospital's social service department was in the process of shortening and standardizing all of its records, in large part because the doctors and nurses would not read the longer accounts typically produced by social workers. The new "ideological-discursive formations" (Fairclough, *Critical*) thus formed would, in time, turn ways of talking into ways of seeing, and strand the social work writer in a complex web of sometimes competing ideologies.

In the following and final example, a brief excerpt from a tape-recorded session between a social work student (St) and his supervisor (Su), the supervisor gives the student dramatically explicit advice on removing himself from the social work text. The two are revising a text the student has written:

> Su: Now, when we write as social workers in a dossier, we kind of depersonalize it as opposed to taking "I"; and we use "the worker" or "the social worker."...
>
> St: It has to be impersonalized as in "the worker," even if it's you, you have to say "the worker"?
>
> Su: That's right. So you wrote here, "I contacted." You want to see it's coming from the worker, not you as Michael, but you as the worker. So when I'm sometimes in Intake and [working] as the screener, I write in my Intake Notes "the screener inquired about." . . . So it becomes less personal. You begin to put yourself into the role of the worker, not "I, Michael." . . . [I]t's a headset; it's a beginning. And even in your evaluations . . . the same thing: as opposed to "I," it's "worker," and when we do a CTMSP for placement for long-term care, "the worker." So it positions us, I think. It's not me, it's my role; and I'm in the role of a professional doing this job. . . .
>
> St: So in the notes all the "I"s—"I did this, I did that"—should be eliminated; and just "worker" and it has to be like impersonal.
>
> Su: Impersonal yet you're identifying yourself professionally. It's not "I," a regular person going into somebody's dossier, but it's in the capacity of a professional.

This erasure of the self or—more accurately, perhaps—this transformation of the self into a "professional" locates the learner anonymously within the institution's naturalized ideology. It is a transformation realized through participation in workplace genres, a process nicely summarized in this passage from de Montigny:

> Professional consciousness emerges through the intellectual practices required to do organizational work. The semblances of ho-

> mogeneity that mark its production, and ultimately its reification as professional knowledge, are rooted in the mundane socially organized methods used by actual practitioners to make sense, sustain the warrant of claims, and distinguish proper understandings from improper understandings. Documentary production provides a basis for the practical expression and reification of a universalized professional consciousness. A documentary reality provides a space where the impersonal, general, and situationally transcendent standpoint of the profession and the organization can be substituted for the lived standpoints of those who are subject to and subject themselves to its determination. (27–28)

Lemke makes a similar point when he argues that discourses "function to legitimate, naturalize or disguise the inequities they sustain. They function to get us thinking along particular lines, the lines of a common sense, which are not as likely to lead to subversive conclusions as using other discourses might" (13). The routines of genre—their regularity, their durability, their status as historical practice—are collective and conservative forces operating to make sense "common" and to locate individuals in identities and relationships that maintain ideologies and allow them to pass as "sense."

Are we so constrained by institutional discourse that we cannot alter its outcomes or undermine the values and beliefs it promotes? I have seen too many social workers subvert institutional discourse practices to believe that, but it is not easy. The Inuit workers continue to struggle with the "professional" identity demanded by their recording routines, although they have created alternative methods of practice—methods developed within their own cultural and rhetorical traditions. Critical front line social workers in hospitals, agencies, and other institutions learn the words that raise concern among doctors, psychologists, lawyers, and the police. They learn to play the linguistic market, and by subtle rhetorical force can initiate action helpful to their clients. But resistance or subversion is not always easy or possible, especially for the student, the new practitioner, or those who practice social work (or other professions) in the shadow of more powerful disciplines. Learning to participate in workplace genres means learning one's professional location in the power relations of institutional life. Those of us who meet with students or workers might help create the critical consciousness required to undermine that process, but we ourselves will have to work to escape the identities our own discourse compels.

Notes

1. Ideology has been an unstable and highly contested concept since the word *ideology* first appeared in English in 1796 (Williams 153–157). In some contemporary use, *ideology* describes what other people have: those with an agenda; the so-called "politically correct." In this sense, *ideology* suggests ulterior motives and is contrasted with neutrality, impartiality, disinterestedness. Or *ideology* is used as a label for the grand political narratives: capitalism, communism, fascism, liberalism, socialism, conservatism. In this sense, *ideology* is philosophy or political power writ large: the actions of the state, the ruling class, a force from above: this use of the word implies that most of us are either victims or observers of ideology, rather than its agents. Its use in this chapter follows from the work of Gramsci, Althusser, Foucault and, in disciplines concerned with language, Berlin, Faigley, Fairclough (*Discourse*, *Critical*), Gee, and Lemke among others. This use acknowledges what Gramsci calls the "strangely composite" (324) make-up of human personality and belief and views *ideology* as complex, conflictual, and contradictory social practice: as activities in the world that construct and maintain privilege, knowledge, prevailing values, relations of power, and so on. This is ideology as a process, as socially organized activity, as the daily practices of a society's cultural, economic, and political institutions—practices that favor a dominant minority. Moreover, these ideologically influenced practices "interpellate" (Althusser) or constitute individuals as social subjects, locating them in multiple and competing subject positions within institutional life. Such an understanding of ideology helps to explain both the disjunctures between stated beliefs (what one says) and actual activity (what one does) and the unconscious ways in which those disjunctures arise as people, through their participation in socially organized practices, take on the subject positions, the social roles, the values and the visions of the communities they join.

2. Perhaps the most explicit and methodical of recent research attempts to link ideology and language have been made by Norman Fairclough and his colleagues and associates (e.g., Fairclough [see, especially, *Critical* 86–96]; Caldas-Coulthard and Coulthard). These efforts—variously known as "critical discourse analysis," "critical linguistics," and (in pedagogic manifestations) "critical literacies" (e.g., Muspratt, Luke, and Freebody) and "critical language awareness" (e.g., Clark and Ivanic)—

frequently rely on Fairclough's three-levels of analysis: "(a) analysis of text, (b) analysis of processes of text production, consumption, and distribution, and (c) sociocultural analysis of the discursive event (be it an interview, a scientific paper, or a conversation) as a whole" (*Critical* 25). Here, too, genre offers a unifying view of rhetorical action by encouraging a search for significant patterns at each level of the analysis and for cohesive significance that relates those patterns across the levels.

3. Although it is true that genres can enable and even liberate writers, institutional genres serve primarily to conserve and standardize, and usually offer the individual writer little room to improvise. In this chapter I am interested in exploring this constraining force of genre—what Carl Herndl calls "the ideologically coercive effects of institutional and professional discourse," or, "the dark side of the force" (455). From this perspective, workplace genres may be seen as the scripted text and action of institutional dramas: Within their encompassing language and activity, genres place participating individuals in the relatively inflexible roles and relationships required for the enactment of institutional values, beliefs, and attitudes (Paré and Smart). As Fairclough puts it: "Each institution has its own set of speech events, its own differentiated settings and scenes, its cast of participants, and its own norms for their combination—for which members of the cast may participate in which speech events, playing which parts, in which settings, in the pursuit of which topics or goals, for which institutionally recognized purposes" (*Critical* 38). In his analysis of social work records as "institutional narratives," Lars-Christer Hydén points out that "a narrative always excludes another possible story" (261), and it is this exclusionary effect of genre that makes it a useful lens on institutional ideology.

4. To be fair, the southern, white social work educators who have been most involved in McGill's Certificate in Northern Social Work Practice have attempted to bring a cultural and critical perspective to the curriculum and, increasingly, have turned teaching responsibilities over to Inuit graduates, who then conduct the courses in Inuktitut.

Works Cited

Althusser, Louis. "Ideology and Ideological State Apparatuses." *Lenin and Philosophy and Other Essays*. Trans. Ben Brewster. London: New Left Books, 1971. 121–173.

Bazerman, Charles. "Systems of Genres." Freedman and Medway 79–101.

Berlin, James. *Rhetorics, Poetics, and Cultures: Refiguring College English Studies*. Urbana, IL: National Council of Teachers of English, 1996.

Bourdieu, Pierre. *Sociology in Question*. Trans. Richard Nice. London: Sage, 1984.

Caldas-Coulthard, Carmen Rosa, and Malcolm Coulthard, eds. *Texts and Practices: Readings in Critical Discourse Analysis*. London: Routledge, 1996.

Clark, Romy, and Roz Ivanic. *The Politics of Writing*. London: Routledge. 1997.

Coe, Richard. "An Arousing and Fulfilment of Desires: The Rhetoric of Genre in the Process Era—and Beyond." Freedman and Medway 181–190.

de Montigny, Gerard. *Social Working: An Ethnography of Front Line Practice*. Toronto, ON: U of Toronto P, 1995.

Devitt, Amy. J. "Generalizing About Genre: New Conceptions of an Old Concept." *College Composition and Communication* 44 (1993): 573–586.

Dias, Patrick. "Writing Classrooms as Activity Systems." *Transitions: Writing in Academic and Workplace Settings*. Ed. Patrick Dias and Anthony Paré. Cresskill, NJ: Hampton Press, 2000. 11–31.

Dias, Patrick, Aviva Freedman, Peter Medway, and Anthony Paré. *Worlds Apart: Writing and Acting in Academic and Workplace Contexts*. Mahwah, NJ: Erlbaum, 1999.

Faigley, Lester. *Fragments of Rationality: Postmodernism and the Subject of Composition*. Pittsburgh: U of Pittsburgh P, 1992.

Fairclough, Norman. *Critical Discourse Analysis: The Critical Study of Language*. London: Longman, 1995.

———. *Discourse and Social Change*. Cambridge, UK: Polity, 1992.

Freedman, Aviva, and Peter Medway, eds. *Genre and the New Rhetoric*. London: Taylor and Francis, 1994.

Foucault, Michel. *The Archaeology of Knowledge*. Trans. A. M. Sheridan Smith. London: Tavistock, 1972.

Gramsci, Antonio. *Selections from the Prison Notebooks*. Ed. and Trans. Quintin Hoare and Geoffrey Nowell-Smith. New York: International, 1971.

Gee, James Paul. *Social Linguistics and Literacies: Ideology in Discourses.* 2nd ed. London: Falmer, 1996.

Green, Bill, and Alison Lee. "Writing Geography: Literacy, Identity, and Schooling." *Learning and Teaching Genre.* Ed. Aviva Freedman and Peter Medway. Portsmouth, NH: Boynton/Cook Heinemann, 1994. 207–224.

Gunnarson, Britt-Louise, Per Linell, and Bengt Nordberg, eds. *The Construction of Professional Discourse.* New York: Longman, 1997.

Gunnarson, Britt-Louise, Per Linell, and Bengt Nordberg. Introduction. Gunnarson, Linell, and Nordberg 1–12.

Hall, C., Srikant Sarangi, and Stef Slembrouck. "Moral Construction in Social Work Discourse." Gunnarson, Linell, and Nordberg 265–291.

Herndl, Carl. "Tactics and the Quotidian: Resistance and Professional Discourse." *Journal of Advanced Composition* 16 (1996): 455–470.

Hydén, Lars Christer. "The Institutional Narrative as Drama." Gunnarson, Linell, and Nordberg 245–264.

Kidd, Bruce. "Sports and Masculinity." *Beyond Patriarchy: Essays by Men on Pleasure, Power and Change.* Ed. Michael Kaufman. Toronto: Oxford UP, 1987. 250–65.

Lemke, Jay. *Textual Politics: Discourses and Social Dynamics.* London: Falmer, 1995.

Miller, Carolyn. "Genre as Social Action." *Quarterly Journal of Speech* 70 (1984): 151–167.

Muspratt, Sandy, Allan Luke, and Peter Freebody, eds. *Constructing Critical Literacies: Teaching and Learning Textual Practice.* Cresskill, NJ: Hampton, 1997.

Paré, Anthony. "Writing as a Way into Social Work: Genre Sets, Genre Systems, and Distributed Cognition." *Transitions: Writing in Academic and Workplace Settings.* Ed. Patrick Dias and Anthony Paré. Cresskill, NJ: Hampton, 2000.

Paré, Anthony, and Graham Smart. "Observing Genres in Action: Towards a Research Methodology." Freedman and Medway 146–54.

Pêcheux, Michel. *Language, Semiotics, and Ideology.* London: Macmillan, 1982.

Russell, David R. "Rethinking Genre in School and Society: An Activity Theory Analysis." *Written Communication* 14 (1997): 504–554.

Schryer, Catherine. "The Lab vs. The Clinic: Sites of Competing Genres." Freedman and Medway 105–124.

Williams, Raymond. *Keywords: A Vocabulary of Culture and Society.* Hammersmith, UK: Fontana, 1976.

Moving Writers, Shaping Motives, Motivating Critique and Change: A Genre Approach to Teaching Writing

MARY JO REIFF
University of Tennessee

What prompted me to write this essay for this anthology? My "assignment" was to write about the genre of the *Pedagogical Insight* essay. I immediately called on my genre knowledge—my past experience with reading and writing similar texts in similar situations—to orient me to the expectations of this genre. While I am familiar with the genre of "the essay"—and my awareness alerted me to the fact that my piece could be less formal than an article, a piece based more in experience than in research—I was not as familiar with the expectations of this particular genre, a Pedagogical Insight essay. I began, then, with these questions: What are the actions that this genre performs? How will I position myself within this genre—what identity and relations will I assume? In what ways will the genre define and sustain the field's discussions of pedagogy or pedagogical approaches? What are the potential sites of resistance and transformation?

I looked for clues about how the assignment located me within a situation and provided me with the rhetorical means for acting within that situation. From the authors' invitation, I constructed the rhetorical situation that helped motivate and shape my response. The audience was described as "new teachers," and the purpose was "to ground abstract composition theory, as presented by the anthologized articles, in the immediacy of a real classroom context and a real teacher's lived experience." There was a specified length (1,500 words), but within the constraints of audience, purpose, and format, there was also a great deal of choice within this genre, with the authors noting that they "hope for a great diversity in tone, stance, and focus." A sample Pedagogical Insight essay was included in the materials sent—an example of one writer's "appropriate" response.

Writing an effective response would mean conceiving of my role as a writer not only in relation to readers and other writers and their purposes, but also in relation to the social and cultural formations in which they interact. As a result, the larger cultural context beyond the immediate situation of this Pedagogical Insight essay also helped to generate and organize my response. In the materials passed along to help contextualize my response, I was given the proposal (shaped in response to the editors at the National Council of Teachers of English as well as to a secondary audience of contributors and reviewers) that positioned the imagined readers of this anthology, positioned the book intertextually (among "competing texts"), and provided an overview of how the book responds to material conditions and functions epistemologically. My response, then, is situated very purposefully and mediated by various contextual factors, not the least of which is a response to the multiple and related voices included in this section on relations.

Genre in the Classroom (or "How Our Students Can Relate")

Our students are similarly positioned within and by genres. When confronted with a writing assignment, students are suspended within a complex web of relations—from the institutional, disciplinary, and/or course objectives that frame the assignment to the defined roles for writers, their purposes, their subjects, and their conventions for writing. More important, a genre approach allows students to see a writing assignment itself as a social action—a response to the whole disciplinary and institutional context for the assignment, not just a response to the teacher. Students can access and participate effectively in academic situations by identifying the assumptions and expectations regarding subject, their roles as writers (as critics, knowledgeable professionals in the field), the roles of readers (teacher-readers, specialist audiences, implied audiences), and purposes for writing (to describe, analyze, argue, evaluate, etc.) that are embedded in the assignment.

Approaching writing through a contextual genre theory consists of using genre as a lens for accessing, understanding, and writing in various situations and contexts. A genre approach to teaching writing is careful not to treat genres as static forms or systems of classification. Rather, students learn how to recognize genres as rhetorical responses to and reflections of the situations in which they are used; furthermore, students learn how to use genres to intervene in situations. Students begin by (1) collecting samples of a wide range of responses within a particular genre; (2) identifying and describing the larger cultural scene and rhetorical situation from which genre emerges (setting, subject, participants, purposes); (3) identifying and describing the patterns of the genre, including content, structure, format, sentences, and diction; and (4) analyzing genres for what they tell us about situation and making an argumentative or critical claim about what these patterns reveal about the attitudes, values, and actions embedded in the genre.

For example, a prelaw student in my advanced composition class explored the genre activities of the law community by first examining the genre system—the textualized sites such as opinions, wills, deeds, contracts, and briefs—that defines and sustains the legal community. After choosing to focus her study on the genre of case briefs, the student began by collecting samples of constitutional law briefs, discovering that the shared purposes and functions "illustrated the legal community's shared value of commitment to tradition, as well as the need for a standard and convenient form of communicating important and complex legal concepts." Through her study of the repeated rhetorical patterns and social actions of legal briefs, the student gained access to the habits, beliefs, and values of the law community. She not only learned about the genre features of case briefs—such as the technical terminology, rigid format, and formal style—but she also become more aware of how these formal patternings reflected and reinforced the goals of the community. Recognizing that all the briefs follow the same organizational strategy of presenting sections labeled "case information," "facts of the case," "procedural history," "issue," "holding," and "court reasoning," she surmised that "Even the rigid structure of the format [suggests] the community's emphasis on logic and order, which are two esteemed values of the profession." The genre not only reflects the legal community's valuing of logic and order but, as the student discovered, also reinscribes these values by "maintaining a system of communication that relates the scientific and the complex world of law," establishing a relationship, in effect, between scientific, technical precision and the less precise interpretation of law and, as a result, reinforcing the belief that legal cases are unambiguous and clearcut. Furthermore, reflecting on the legal jargon, such as *writ of mandamus*, or the formal language of verbs like *sayeth* and *witnesseth* or words like *hereunder* and *wherewith*, the student makes the following connections among text, contexts, and the ideological effects of genres:

> Legal language is part of a lawyer's professional training, so the habit of "talking like a lawyer" is deeply rooted in the practices of the community. This tells us that lawyers feel compelled to use established jargon to maintain a legitimate status in the eyes of other community members. In addition, formal language is needed to surround legal proceedings with an air of solemnity, and to send the message that any legal proceeding is a significant matter with important consequences.

The writer also notes how this use of legal language reinscribes a power relationship of sorts, separating "insiders" (members of the profession) from "outsiders" (the public) by cultivating a language "that reads like a foreign language to those outside the profession." For students like this one, using genre as a lens for inquiry cultivates a consciousness of the rhetorical strategies used to carry out the social actions of a group or disciplinary community, thus making the complex, multitextured relations of the legal community more tangible and accessible.

Relating and Resisting

Students' critical awareness of how genres work—their understanding of how rhetorical features are connected to social actions—enables them to more effectively critique and resist genres by creating alternatives. For example, a student's critique of the wedding invitation as a genre allowed the discovery of a particular cultural view of women or gender bias in its rhetorical patterns and language (particularly in the references to the bride's parents who "request the honor of your presence"). Embedded in the invitation are cultural assumptions of women as objects or property to be "handed over" from parents to spouse. The textual patternings of the genre, such as references to the parents and the bride as "their daughter" and the omission of the bride's name (while naming the bride's parents and the groom), reinforce what the student describes as a cultural attitude toward marriage that involves a loss of identity for women. Wedding invitations, then, in the student's final analysis, are cultural artifacts that through their repeated use in similar situations—the repeated cultural event of formally announcing marriages—not only reflect but reinscribe gender inequality and unequal distributions of power in relationships (Devitt, Reiff, and Bawarshi).

Classroom genres, too, reflect and enact the social relations of classrooms, and because of the recurring forms of language use of genres, the institutionally sanctioned academic genres might be more easily perpetuated, thus excluding students for whom these genres are less accessible. Brad Peters, in "Genre, Antigenre, and Reinventing the Forms of Conceptualization," describes a college composition course in which students read about the United States invasion of Panama in a book that takes a Panamanian perspective. The students were then told to write an essay exam that followed a particular format moving from a summary of the argument, to the three most compelling points for a Latin American reader, to the three most fallacious points for a Latin American reader, and finally to the student's reaction compared to that of the Latin American reader. One student, Rita, wrote the essay exam from the fictional perspective of her close friend

Maria, a native Latin American, and after completing the rhetorical analysis part of the exam, dropped the persona and took up her own in the form of a letter to Maria. Peters identifies this as an "antigenre" but points out that Rita's response satisfies the social purpose of the genre while reconstituting voice and varying the format of the genre. This demonstrates that even when the writing assignment is fairly prescriptive and students are asked to write a fairly traditional genre, there is room for them to maneuver within (and because of) the constraints of the genre.

Toward Changing Relations and Developing New Textual Relations

One criticism leveled against a genre approach to literacy teaching is that it focuses on analysis and critique of genres, stopping short of having writers use genres to enact change. Genres—as they function to define, critique, and bring about change—can provide rich pedagogical sites, sites for intervention. Bruce McComiskey, for example, pairs academic and public genres—having students write a critical analysis of education followed by a brochure for high school students, or following an analysis of the cultural values of advertisements with letters to advertisers arguing the negative effect on consumers. Genre analysis encourages students to critique sites of intervention, analyzing how such genres enable participation in the process while also limiting intervention. Students identify linguistic and rhetorical patterns and analyze their significance, while simultaneously critiquing the cultural and social values encoded in the genre (what the genre allows users to do and what it does not allow them to do, whose needs are most/least served, how it enables or limits the way its users do their work).

But the final step would be to ask students to produce new genres or genres that encode alternative values for the purpose of intervening. Students could create their own genres that respond to those they analyzed. Or, after interrogating the sites at which change happens, students can more directly intervene in these sites by writing their own alternative genres or "antigenres" in response. I often have my students follow their analysis of genres by inventing and formulating their own generic response or by writing a manual for others on how to write that genre. The idea is that as students critique genres as sites of rhetorical action and cultural production and reproduction, they also see how genres function as motivated social actions, enabling them to enter into the production of alternatives.

Teaching Alternatives (or Coming Full Circle)

As is typical in the genre of the essay, I am going to conclude by returning to my introduction, where I invoked the genre of the Pedagogical Insight essay. This genre seeks to intervene in the theoretical readings in this section on *Relations* by reflecting, according to the authors' goals, "some concrete, practical instantiations of theoretical positions." Ideally this genre will function for new teachers as a "conversation starter" about how teaching writing means teaching relations, and how genre analysis can move teachers beyond teaching academic forms to teaching purposeful rhetorical instruments for social action. By teaching students to interrogate how social groups organize and define kinds of texts and how these genres, in turn, organize and define social relations and practices, teachers can construct assignments that enable students to engage more critically in situated action and to produce alternative ways of interacting.

More important, perhaps, is an understanding of how our own work as teachers is also situated institutionally and organized and generated by genres ranging from textbooks to syllabi to assignments to the end comments we write on papers (see, for instance, Summer Smith's "The Genre of the End Comment" and her research on how our comments on papers both enable and restrict writing choices). From the conversations we have with other teachers about our classroom practices to the syllabi that we write that position us as teachers, define our roles in the classroom, establish relationships between us and our students, and reflect and reinforce the goals of our writing courses, the genres we use are sites of action—sites in which we, as teachers, communicate, enact, and carry out our teaching lives. Just as genres may provide a framework for facilitating both inquiry and intervention for our students, as teachers we can use our understanding of the institutional genres that situate us and our teaching—our understanding of our "teaching assignment"—to prompt us to explore ways we might enter into the production of alternative approaches.

Works Cited

Devitt, Amy, Mary Jo Reiff, and Anis Bawarshi. *Scenes of Writing: Strategies for Composing with Genres*. New York: Longman, 2004.

McComiskey, Bruce. *Teaching Composition as a Social Process*. Logan, UT: Utah State UP, 2000.

Peters, Brad. "Genre, Antigenre, and Reinventing the Forms of Conceptualization." *Genre and Writing: Issues, Arguments, Alternatives*. Portsmouth: Boynton/Cook, 1997.

Smith, Summer. "The Genre of the End Comment: Conventions in Teacher Responses to Student Writing." *College Composition and Communication* 48.2 (1997): 249–68.

Genre as Janus in the Teaching of Writing

NANCY MYERS
University of North Carolina at Greensboro

Janus, the Roman god of gates and doors, is represented as a double-faced head gazing two ways at once. Just like a door, he always sees the interior and exterior, operating as both a closing off and an opening up. I find this image of the double view useful for understanding the paradoxes presented by genre and writing pedagogy, for the Janus figure draws attention to the way in which genres open up options for writing while simultaneously closing them off. In *Writing Genres*, Amy Devitt argues for genre as the "nexus" in the complex rhetorical and social situations from which a text arises: "Genre is a reciprocal dynamic within which individuals' actions construct and are constructed by recurring context of situation, context of culture, and context of genres" (31). Using Devitt's definition, I can view genre as a Janus figure—a metaphor that makes tangible a tension intrinsic to genre between social linguistic norming and unique enactments of individual language use. Genre's double view provides a threshold for seeing the teaching of genre as more than just classifying texts by type, listing traits of specific forms, and transmitting a community's textual abstractions. Moreover, this double view opens students to a richer understanding of genre within its social, cultural, and linguistic complexity, one that enables choice and critique within each enactment.

With this Janus metaphor and this view of genre's contextual complexity comes also the need for teaching genre responsibly, for without an understanding of genre, students do not succeed (see Delpit). However, teaching academic genres as rhetorical forms and grammatical structures is not enough. I need to make visible the double view of genre as both controlling its users and being controlled by them, and I need to contextualize academic genres as only a subset within the larger understanding of the generic communication processes and products, ones that are never static. Devitt argues that to incorporate all of this effectively in my teaching I have to complicate the approaches I take:

> [W]e must teach contextualized genres, situated within their contexts of culture, situation, and other genres. Generic forms must be embedded within their social and rhetorical purposes so that rhetorical understanding can counter the urge toward formula. Genres must be embedded within their social and cultural ideologies so that critical awareness can counter potential ideological effects. Genres must be taught as both constraint and choice so that individual awareness can lead to individual creativity. The teaching of genres, in sum, must develop thoughtfully, critically, and with recognition of the complexity, benefits, and dangers of the concept of genre. (191)

In response to Devitt's charge, I have evolved a heuristic, a series of questions that helps me think about genre on two pedagogical levels: the teaching of specific genres and the genre of course design. Underlying these two pedagogical levels are two discourse sites of paradoxical—Janus faced—tensions that are particularly important for my classroom: grammar/rhetoric and disciplinary writing/individual learning. Across these two sites, genre supplies the double view for a both/and rather than an either/or pedagogy. Both grammar and rhetoric are at play within a text. Both academic and personal knowledge are the objectives. Both the perspectives of understanding genre's features and forms and of analyzing its control and its potential are valued. My heuristic, then, keeps my classroom poised on the threshold between genre as a closing off and genre as an opening up.

To keep from teaching genre as mere regulated parts, formula, or grammar, I ask my students to examine those parts within the rhetorical situation. As we analyze genres and practice their features through composing, we are continually asking, What are the rhetorical means and the grammatical means that account for this genre in this context? The genre heuristic I use with my students asks questions such as, What are the features of a genre? What social and cultural contexts does it work within? What are its constraints rhetorically and grammatically? What other forms are like it? What can be changed and what cannot in both the genre and the situation in order for a text to maintain its genre classification and its effectiveness? For example, across the semester as we examine different genres, we explore who is cited, how exactly, and what authority or credibility issues arise because of that citing. Citation and documentation are grammatical features of genre; how a source is referenced shifts according to genre. Thus, we compare the citation practices of a *Time* article to an academic journal article or of one Web site to another, analyzing issues such as reliability, credibility, and liability. When examining and constructing Web pages or PowerPoint slides, we approach them from a rhetorical stance, asking not just how these genres operate but what their purposes and messages are and how that affects various audiences. Again here, grammar and rhetoric collide when we discuss flashing and flying images and words as adding to that message or detracting from it. Whether analyzing a Web site, a video game, or an essay, genre's double view allows for discussions, analyses, and critiques that identify this tension between rhetorical creation and grammatical limitations. It is this friction between manipulation and regulation, between playfulness and correctness, and between the centrifugal force toward linguistic freedom and centripetal force of standardization that genre allows us to explore.

Since writing courses are institutionally situated, I find questioning my course design through genre's double view useful for understanding my own role in working within, or closing off, and pushing against, or opening up, the traditional discourse values of academe. Issues of correctness and academic expectations are compounded when examining the tension between academic discourse and expressive discourse (see Bartholomae; Elbow). For me, an essential question in exploring the conflict between academic writing and student expression is, What are the aims in teaching and learning about genre?

To keep from teaching academic discourse as a disembodied set of forms or rules learned solely for academic success, I need to find those aspects of me that work within those ideologies and those aspects of me that are foreign to them, valuing and critiquing both. My heuristic approach here continually asks me to readdress and reassess questions such as, What is the role of the writing course for the university? Is its objective to prepare students for the writing expected of their chosen academic disciplines and professions, or is the goal to empower students through personal expression? What knowledge matters, and what genres represent it?

The double view of genre allows me to work toward a balance between the constraints of institutional or societal expectations and the freedom of individual voice (and choice). I directly address these issues in my course design by demonstrating that academic texts are only one part of the genre landscape. I employ a diverse range of texts for analysis, including multigenre texts, such as a zine or Michael Ondaatje's *The Collected Works of Billy the Kid*, and multilingual texts, such as Gloria Anzaldúa's "How to Tame a Wild Tongue" or Umberto Eco's *Baudolino*. This range allows for a regular and systematic exploration into why and how genres operate "within their social and cultural ideologies" (Devitt 191). Moreover, I often include an assignment that looks at how the same information, such as a scientific discovery, is articulated across genres. Regularly my writing assignments ask students to choose their genre based on their purpose, message, and audience. Students have composed and designed texts such as essays, pamphlets, newspaper and magazine articles, children's books, Web sites, one-act plays, songs, poems, letters, board games, zines, and, more recently, animated stories through Macromedia Flash technology. In these situations, I ask them to analyze the features of the genre they choose, to reflect on why that genre is the most appropriate for their goals, and to document how and why they made the decisions they did in the construction of their text. Continually addressing the tensions between individual learning and disciplinary writing, I work to help students see how genres represent the perspectives of those who control them and exclude the perspectives of those who do not.

Genre matters. It both closes off and opens to the powerful discourses of a discipline, an institution, a community. Its tensions between grammar and rhetoric and between disciplinary writing and individual learning are highlighted in my courses through exploration, experimentation, critique, and play. Any text—linguistic, imagistic, musical, kinesthetic—can be examined and revised for how it operates both within and outside of a specific genre, how it demonstrates the constraints of its genre and the freedom of its creator's choices, how it privileges specific perspectives and their inherent logics and excludes others. Understanding genre in its myriad forms within its social and cultural contexts and enacting its features within specific situations make us both part of the world and separate from it, both controlled and controller. M. M. Bakhtin argues that through this conscious knowledge of genres' structures, meaning and uniqueness are possible: "The better our command of genres, the more freely we employ them, the more fully and clearly we reveal our own individuality in them (where this is possible and necessary), the more flexibly and precisely we reflect the unrepeatable situation of communication—in a word, the more perfectly we implement our free speech plan" (80). Thus, the metaphor of genre, as the two-faced Janus, challenges me to attempt different ways of teaching so that students may experience different ways of knowing, ways of reading, and ways of writing.

Works Cited

Anzaldúa, Gloria. "How to Tame a Wild Tongue." *Borderlands/La Frontera*. San Francisco: Aunt Lute Book, 1987. 53–64.

Bakhtin, M. M. "The Problem of Speech Genres." *Speech Genres and Other Late Essays*. Trans. Vern W. McGee. Austin: U of Texas P, 1986. 60–102.

Bartholomae, David. "Writing with Teachers: A Conversation with Peter Elbow." *College Composition and Communication* 46 (1995): 62–71.

———. "Response." *College Composition and Communication* 46 (1995): 84–87.

Delpit, Lisa. *Other People's Children*. New York: New Press, 1995.

Devitt, Amy J. *Writing Genres*. Carbondale: Southern Illinois UP, 2004.

Eco, Umberto. *Baudolino*. New York: Harcourt, 2000.

Elbow, Peter. "Being a Writer vs. Being an Academic: A Conflict in Goals." *College Composition and Communication* 46 (1995): 72–83.

———. "Response." *College Composition and Communication* 46 (1995): 87–92.

Hicks, Deborah. "Working Through Discourse Genres in School." *Research in the Teaching of English* 31 (1997): 459–85.

Ondaatje, Michael. *The Collected Works of Billy the Kid*. New York: Vintage, 1996.

Purcell, William M. *Ars poetriae: Rhetorical and Grammatical Invention at the Margin of Literacy*. Columbia: U of South Carolina P, 1996.

II

Theories of Location

As we acknowledge in the introduction to this book, the divisions offered between theories of relation, location, and position are somewhat arbitrary. In theorizing about the teaching of writing, the concepts represented by these categories necessarily overlap and inform each other. A theory of genre conversant with the essays in the first section of the book, for example, would depend on the recognition that, as Anis Bawarshi has it, a given genre must be understood as a "*site* of action" (26; our emphasis), and that precisely how one engages a genre is interdependent with the subject positions the genre calls out, resists, or deflects. Our goal in this section of the book, then, is not to sort ideas about location into a distinct class, but to highlight them, so to speak, as they emerge in postprocess theories of writing.

The essays that follow are attentive to how potentially abstract theories of location map out in real social spaces and specific material circumstances. If writing is called out by perceived needs or imperfections in the environment, then all such exigencies are necessarily local, and fitting rhetorical responses must be similarly *situated.* "Situatedness," according to Lee-Ann M. Kastman Breuch, "refers to the ability to respond to specific situations rather than rely on foundational principles or rules" (138). A theory of location is crucial to a complex understanding of writing precisely because written texts so effectively erase the circumstances of their production. We tend to think of the action of producing and interpreting text as interior, and the portability of rhetorical artifacts across space and time helps us forget that both reading and writing are done, quite literally, in place. For these reasons Nedra Reynolds reminds us in "Composition's Imagined Geographies: The Politics of Space in the Frontier, City, and Cyberspace" (included in this volume) that only at his or her own peril can a writing teacher imagine space to be transparent or "innocent" (19). To say that a writer is situated is to account for the ways in which particular social and material conditions influence what is written, or not, and who writes it, or not. Those of us whose authority or expertise is constructed by the specific situations in which we operate—think of the significance of the classroom-as-location in defining any teacher's sway over a large group of eighteen-year-old students—have a fairly pressing obligation to consider the ways in which material space factors in our practices (Ede). "Where writing instruction takes place," Reynolds therefore explains, "has everything to do with *how*" (20).

Some rhetoric and composition scholars reference feminist poet Adrienne Rich's influential 1986 essay on the importance of place, "Notes toward a Politics of Location," in accounting for the emergence of "the local" in conversations about writing instruction. Rich defines an attention to "the material" as a "struggle against the lofty and privileged abstraction" (213). Rich's dissatisfaction with generalization encourages her to focus on perhaps the most obvious manifestation of the material, her own body: "To say 'my body' reduces the temptation to grandiose assertions" (215). Indeed, the value of scholarship is often concomitant with the effectiveness of its separation from "living contexts"; academic editors frequently admonish authors not to "air their dirty laundry" unless they can appear to make it belong to everyone. That standard often results in the quite literal isolation of much situated experience. While Rich is careful to distinguish the differences between saying "my body" and "*the* body," theories of positionality remind us that one's sense of one's *own* body can serve to normalize experience by diminishing difference and alternative views, and thereby distort the most localized experience (Kirsch). Much composition theory, drawing on social epistemologies that deny essential, absolute, or individuated explanations for the nature of things, has tempered attention to the significance of individual bodies and specific places and instead employed spatial metaphors to define collective, discursive action.

One such persistent expression is *discourse community*, a term that had great explanatory power in the mid-1980s when it was used to demonstrate the problem of thinking about writing exclusively in terms of the writer. The term helped popularize the now commonplace understanding that writing is done by and within groups of individuals who are linked together by shared discursive practices. The "descriptive adequacy" (Raforth 141) of the term came into question even before it had achieved full prominence in the field; not only does the concept of *discourse community* fail to account adequately for the function of genre in ordering relationships among participants and for significant differences in positionality among those it otherwise links together, it also tends to deflect attention from the role of material place in dis/joining discursive participants. Reynolds explores other prominent metaphors, such as *frontier, city* and *cyberspace*; calling for "more effort to link material conditions to the activities of particular spaces" (30), she argues that these metaphors function ideologically in composition studies by hiding the local as they highlight broadly imagined groupings. Engaging in a material analysis intended to "understand how built environments actually mediate social interaction" (767), Daniel Mahala and Jody Swilky's "Constructing Disciplinary Space" also investigates the "geographically-inflected language" (766) of recent composition scholarship. Mahala and Swilky's essay (also included in this volume) interrogates the "erasure of place," the occlusion of difference, and the blind eye to power, all of which emerge through the construction of imagined *dis*locations such as "the contact zone" and "the border."

While critiques such as those by Reynolds and Mahala and Swilky caution against the inattention to the local, they do not deliver us back to the notion of a narrowly embodied rhetoric. One's body does indeed create the possibility to distinguish *here* from *there*, but such understandings are always ideations, composites of the material and conceptual (Mauk), reality and our way of naming it. In "Bodysigns" (included in this volume), Kristie Fleckenstein refers to this relationship between the material and semiotic as "biorhetoric," a dialectic or "double lens that is neither the product of language nor the product of materiality but the confluence of both" (770). Fleckenstein's position between essentialism and an extreme version of textuality (the notion that everything is a product of interpretation) marks much contemporary theorizing about location. Establishing the relationship between the linguistic and the material with great concision,

Sidney I. Dobrin argues in "Writing Takes Place" that how we operate within and against the systems in which we find ourselves "is both a matter of discursive maneuvering and a matter of physical, material positioning" (12). Dobrin's project, which he calls "Ecocomposition," is to open composition studies to ecological methodologies, to reframe it as "the study of all the complex interrelationships between the human activity of writing and all of the conditions of the struggle for existence" (13). Ecocomposition, then, is an enterprise firmly committed to what Fleckenstein calls biorhetoric.

For ecocompositionists, "the struggle for existence" (Dobrin 13) is defined by the relationship between language and place, and for writing teachers the primary locus of struggle is the classroom. A site of generalization itself—consider the term *classroom*—the conventional teaching space has been further generalized in theories of location as a scene of alienation and dislocation (Moreno; Mauk). As the site in which the colonial legacy of mass education plays out (Vandenberg, "Taming"), the classroom is a site of material-conceptual dissonance where students and faculty cannot be meaningfully said to "occupy the same 'here' as professors" (Mauk 374). The classroom is a material discursive site distinct from those in which many student identities are formed, and, as Johnathon Mauk points out in "Location, Location, Location" (included in this volume), one very different from where students (and the larger culture) imagine their identities to be headed. The classroom, like other locations that create or endorse unequal relationships between participants, encourages us to be attentive to the relationship between built environments and the exercise of power. Place is a "network of relationships," as Mahala and Swilky write (770), and attitudes that reflect relationships of power and control are routinely designed into classrooms and classroom buildings (McComiskey and Ryan).

As a politicized space, according to Julie Drew, the classroom is "both the location of hegemony and, importantly, the location of the veiling of power" (59). Short of the occasional springtime retreat to the shady spot under the oak tree on the quad—which may only further veil the authority of the teacher, who after all must sanction the trip—writing teachers are hard pressed to resolve the negative implications of the classroom. Drew sees a potential resolution in reimagining students as "travelers" by expanding "the role of place in the pedagogical, and the politics that work within and around identifiable spaces, to include the material realities of movement—of travel—and the multiple spaces within which students reside and learn" (61). While the vast majority of all writing classes will no doubt remain situated in conventional classrooms, a variety of "traveling" pedagogies have emerged in recent years, resituating writing pedagogies off campus. Service learning, community outreach, experiential learning, community literacy, and writing for the public sphere—all of these programmatic initiatives have been designed to resituate students and faculty in nontraditional academic space. Such "hybrid experiences" (Drew 63) are motivated, in part, by the recognition of and responsibility for the spatial segregation that marks current teaching and research practices.

In "Service Learning and Public Discourse," Bruce Herzberg recognizes the tendency to think of the world off campus as a "research site" rather than a "realm of true engagement" (396). Drew argues that our relationships with students are marked by a structured forgetting, that students "are already engaged in various forms of critical thinking and would best be served by an increased understanding of theories and practices of discourse that will help them move more successfully between and among the various spaces they inhabit" (64). And Mauk believes that the answer to student underinvestment and dislocation in college is to find ways to help them "conceive the space outside of the campus, outside of the classroom as academic" (380). Like Mauk, Herzberg promotes the notion of "going public" as a way to bring academic perspective to public exigencies. The discourse of off-campus writing pedagogy promises greater enthusiasm among students, a notion of audience awareness that extends beyond the teacher, a return to the ideal of the public intellectual, and firmer connections between the material realities of students' lives and their college experience (Owens).

Christian Weisser's 2002 book, *Moving beyond Academic Discourse: Composition Studies and the Public Sphere*, forecasts pedagogies of the public sphere as "the next dominant focal point" (qtd. in Owens 458) for composition studies. Yet even as composition studies has begun to underscore pedagogies of the public sphere, Linda Flower points out that this new "impulse" to engage dialogically outside the institution is chugging forward despite institutional practices that are poorly attuned to dialogic action and "ill-equipped to recognize community expertise" (183). Flower's compelling approach is intended to arrive at "transformative understanding[,] . . . a kind of knowledge making that names problems in the world and transforms our representations both of them and of ourselves" (186). Promoting a pedagogy grounded in what she calls "intercultural inquiry," Flower shows how place-based teaching can lead to the same sort of dislocation and apprehension for professors that students experience in the classroom. And depending on the positionality and discursive location of student participants, students' own expectations can be radically disrupted as well.

Location-based teaching expects students to encounter oppositional discourses and work through tensions in hopes of arriving at hybrid positions. "But these out-of-classroom experiences come with an obligation to explore along with students the implications of a service-related education, and these implications often entangle students in tensions between discourses" (Chaden et al. 21). Some of the students identified by Caryn Chaden and her coauthors seemed to approach what James Gee has called "powerful literacy" by traversing discourse boundaries, triangulating across the discourses they encountered, the discourse of the discipline in which they studied, and the discourse of service learning, which they were exposed to through the course. Flower, however, identifies "discourse expectations" as barriers her students were unable to overcome; the methodologies and patterns students had learned for making sense in the classroom proved too normative, evaporating the local knowledge they had learned on site. Flower seems too harsh in declaring this tendency a "revealing failure" of her project (198); the tenacity of classroom learning is, after all, the exigency that calls out the need for situated pedagogies, and a term-long encounter with extraclassroom contexts is likely not going to be a sufficiently transformative experience.

Numerous structured practices will continue to make attention to the local difficult within postsecondary education: the alienating and isolating effects of the classroom; the persistence of the notion that literacy is universal and "autonomous" (Street); the privilege of decontextualized research over "'local' values" in the reward structure of higher education (Vandenberg, "Composing" 26); and a "rootless professoriate" (Mahala and Swilky 771), the product of national labor markets, which ensures that the best and brightest new scholar-teachers will end up working somewhere they know nothing about. However, central to postprocess theories of location is the notion that these problems await resolution by rhetorical action where they exist, in specific material-conceptual spaces. The Pedagogical Insight essays that follow the readings in this section open up to the transformational possibilities of *teaching in place*.

Works Cited

Bawarshi, Anis. *Genre and the Invention of the Writer: Reconsidering the Place of Invention in Composition*. Logan, UT: Utah State UP, 2003.

Breuch, Lee-Ann M. Kastman. "Post-Process 'Pedagogy': A Philosophical Exercise." *JAC: A Journal of Composition Theory* 22.1 (2002): 119–50.

Chaden, Caryn, Roger Graves, David Jolliffe, and Peter Vandenberg. "Confronting Clashing Discourses: Writing the Space between Classroom and Community." *Reflections: A Journal of Writing, Service-Learning, and Community Literacy* 2.2 (Spring 2002): 19–39.

Dobrin, Sidney I. "Writing Takes Place." *Ecocomposition: Theoretical and Pedagogical Approaches*. Ed. Christian R. Weisser and Sidney I. Dobrin. Albany: State University of New York P, 2001. 11–25.

Drew, Julie. "The Politics of Place: Student Travelers and Pedagogical Maps." *Ecocomposition: Theoretical and Pedagogical Approaches*. Ed. Christian R. Weisser and Sidney I. Dobrin. State University of New York P, 2001. 57–68.

Ede, Lisa. "Writing Centers and the Politics of Location: A Response to Terrance Riley and Stephen M. North." *The Writing Center Journal* 16.2 (1996): 111–30.

Flower, Linda. "Intercultural Inquiry and the Transformation of Service." *College English* 65.2 (2002): 181–201.

———. "Talking across Difference: Intercultural Rhetoric and the Search for Situated Knowledge." *College Composition and Communication* 55.1 (2003): 38–68.

Fleckenstein, Kristie. "Bodysigns: A Biorhetoric for Change." *JAC: A Journal of Composition Theory* 21.4: (2001): 761–90.

Gee, James Paul. "What is Literacy?" *Teaching and Learning* 2 (1987): 3–11.

Herzberg, Bruce. "Service Learning and Public Discourse." *JAC: A Journal of Composition Theory* 20 (2000): 391–404.

Kirsch, Gesa E. "Toward an Engaged Rhetoric of Professional Practice." *JAC: A Journal of Composition Theory* 22.2 (2002): 414–21.

Mahala, Daniel, and Jody Swilky. "Constructing Disciplinary Space: the Borders, Boundaries, and Zones of English." *JAC: A Journal of Composition Theory* 23.4 (2003): 765–97.

Mauk, Johnathon. "Location, Location, Location: The 'Real' (E)states of Being, Writing, and Thinking in Composition." *College English* 65.4 (2003): 368–88.

McComiskey, Bruce, and Cynthia Ryan. Introduction. *City Comp: Identities, Spaces, Practices*. Ed. Bruce McComiskey and Cynthia Ryan. Albany: State U of New York P, 2003. 1–20.

Moreno, Renee M. "'The Politics of Location': Text as Opposition." *College Composition and Communication* 54.2 (2002): 222–42.

Owens, Derek. Rev. of *Moving Beyond Academic Discourse: Composition Studies and the Public Sphere*, by Christian R. Weisser. *JAC: A Journal of Composition* Theory 22.2 (2002): 458–63.

Raforth, Bennett A. "The Concept of Discourse Community: Descriptive and Explanatory Adequacy." *A Sense of Audience in Written Communication*. Ed. Gesa Kirsch and Duane H. Roen. Newbury Park: Sage, 1990. 140–52.

Reynolds, Nedra. "Composition's Imagined Geographies: The Politics of Space in the Frontier, City, and Cyberspace." *College Composition and Communication* 50 (1998): 12–35.

Rich, Adrienne. "Notes toward a Politics of Location." *Blood, Bread, and Poetry: Selected Prose 1979–1985*. London: Virago, 1986. 210–32.

Street, Brian. *Literacy in Theory and Practice*. Cambridge: Cambridge UP, 1984.

Vandenberg, Peter. "Composing Composition Studies: Scholarly Publication and the Practice of Discipline." *Under Construction: Working at the Intersections of Composition Theory, Research, and Practice*. Ed. Christine Farris and Chris M. Anson. Logan, UT: Utah State UP, 1998. 19–29.

———. "Taming Multiculturalism: The Will to Literacy in Composition Studies." *JAC: A Journal of Composition Theory* 19.4 (November 1999): 547–68.

Weisser, Christian R. *Moving beyond Academic Discourse: Composition Studies and the Public Sphere*. Carbondale: Southern Illinois UP, 2002.

Chapter Eight

The Ecology of Writing

Marilyn M. Cooper

The idea that writing is a process and that the writing process is a recursive cognitive activity involving certain universal stages (prewriting, writing, revising) seemed quite revolutionary not so many years ago. In 1982, Maxine Hairston hailed "the move to a process-centered theory of teaching writing" as the first sign of a paradigm shift in composition theory (77). But even by then "process, not product" was the slogan of numerous college textbooks, large and small, validated by enclosure within brightly-colored covers with the imprimatur of Harper and Row, Macmillan, Harcourt Brace Jovanovich, Scott, Foresman. So revolution dwindles to dogma. Now, perhaps, the time has come for some assessment of the benefits and limitations of thinking of writing as essentially—and simply—a cognitive process.

Motivation for the paradigm shift in writing theory perhaps came first from writing teachers increasingly disenchanted with red-inking errors, delivering lectures on comma splices or on the two ways to organize a comparison-contrast essay, and reading alienated and alienating essays written from a list of topic sentences or in the five-paragraph format. Reacting against pedagogy that now seemed completely ineffective, we developed methods that required students to concentrate less on form and more on content that required them to think. We decided to talk about ideas rather than forms in the classroom and sent students off to do various kinds of free writing and writing using heuristics in order to find out what they thought about a topic—best of all, we found we didn't have to read any of this essential but

From *College English* 48 (1986): 364–75.

private and exploratory "prewriting." We told students they had primary responsibility for the purpose of their writing: only they could decide what was important to them to write about, only they could tell whether what they intended was actually fulfilled in the writing they produced. We decided to be friendly readers rather than crabby Miss Fidditches; we said things like, "You have lots of ideas," and, with Pirsig's Phaedrus, "You know quality in thought and statement when you see it," instead of "Your essay does not clearly develop a point," and "You have made many usage errors here."

These ideas were in the air—and in print. We developed them in talking with colleagues, in reading the advice of fellow teachers Peter Elbow and Donald Murray. We found further support for them in similar ideas being developed by literary theorists, educational psychologists, and linguists—some of whom were also writing teachers. In literary theory the shift from a New Critical emphasis on the text to a post-structural emphasis on the reader paralleled the shift from product to process in writing theory. As Jonathan Culler and Stanley Fish adapted the nouvelle French notions to American tastes, the complementarity between reading and writing in terms of their both being mental processes became clear. Culler states that readers possess "literary competence," that they make sense of texts by applying various conventions that explain how one is to interpret the cues on the page. Writers, ideally, possess the same literary competence. Fish states that readers are guided by interpretive strategies, that these strategies are constitutive of interpretive communities, and that the strategies originate with writers. Culler's conventions, Fish's strategies, are not present in the text; rather, they are part of the mental equipment of writers and readers, and only by examining this mental equipment can we explain how writers and readers communicate.

In the fields of educational psychology and linguistics, research on how readers process texts also revealed an active reader who used strategies to recreate meaning from the cues on the page. These strategies implied certain expected structures in texts. When adopted by writing teachers, readers' expectations became a new way of explaining "errors" in student writing and a new rationale for instruction on matters of form. George Dillon, expanding David Olson's analysis, attributes much of the incomprehensibility of his students' writing to their inability to shift from the conventions of utterance to the conventions of text, conventions that enjoin explicitness, correctness, novelty, logical consistency, and so forth. Linda Flower and Joseph Williams explain how readers link new information to old information in order to comprehend texts, and they advise students, consequently, to supply context and to clearly mark old and new information in sentence structure.

Gradually, as interest in writing theory increased, a model of writing as a cognitive process was codified, and the unified perspective the model offered in turn allowed us to redefine other vexing problems: the relation between grammar and writing, the function of revision. These were all undoubtedly beneficial changes. But theoretical models even as they stimulate new insights blind us to some aspects of the phenomena we are studying. The problem with the cognitive process model of writing has nothing to do with its specifics: it describes something of what writers do and goes some way toward explaining how writers, texts, and readers are related. But the belief on which it is based—that writing is thinking and, thus, essentially a cognitive process—obscures many aspects of writing we have come to see as not peripheral.

Like all theoretical models, the cognitive process model projects an ideal image, in this case an image of a writer that, transmitted through writing pedagogy, influences our attitudes and the attitudes of our students toward writing. The ideal writer the cognitive process model projects is isolated from the social world, a writer I will call the solitary author. The solitary author works alone, within the privacy of his own mind. He uses free writing exercises and heuristics to find out what he knows about a subject and to find something he wants to say to others; he uses his analytic skills to discover a purpose, to imagine an audience, to decide on strategies, to organize content; and he simulates how his text will be read by reading it over himself, making the final revisions necessary to assure its success when he abandons it to the world of which he is not a part. The isolation of the solitary author from the social world leads him to see ideas and goals as originating primarily within himself and directed at an unknown and largely hostile other. Writing becomes a form of parthenogenesis, the author producing propositional and pragmatic structures, Athena-like, full grown and complete, out of his brow. Thus, the solitary author perceives the functions that writing might serve in limited and abstract terms. All four of the major pedagogical theories James Berlin describes assume that the function of writing is solely cognitive, a matter of discovering the truth and communicating it: the solitary author can express his feelings, pass on information, persuade others to believe as he does, or charm others with his exquisite phrases (cf. Kinneavy's taxonomy of the aims of writing). Finally, the solitary author sees his writing as a goal-directed piece of work, the process of producing a text.

Such images of the solitary author inspire a great deal of what goes on in writing classes today—and more of what is recommended in composition textbooks, especially those that depend on the latest theory. But many classes still escape its tyranny, classes in which students engage in group work, activities such as collaborative brainstorming on a topic, discussions and debates of topics or readings, writers reading their texts aloud to others, writers editing other writers' texts. Some teachers eschew setting writing assignments (even writing assignments that are "rhetorically based") in favor of letting writing emerge from the life-situations of their students, whether this writing takes the form of papers that fulfill requirements for other courses, letters written for employment or business purposes, journals kept as personal records, reports of projects completed or in progress. And in some classes, students even use writing to interact with one another: they write suggestions to their teacher and to other students; they produce class newspapers full of interviews, jokes, personal stories, advice, information.

Such changes in writing pedagogy indicate that the perspective allowed by the dominant model has again become too confining. I suggest that what goes on in these classes signals a growing awareness that language and texts are not simply the means by which individuals discover and communicate information, but are essentially social activities, dependent on social structures and processes not only in their interpretive but also in their constructive phases. I am not, of course, the only—or even the first—

writing theorist to notice this. In 1981, for example, Kenneth Bruffee argued that "writing is not an inherently private act but is a displaced social act we perform in private for the sake of convenience" (745). And, more recently, James A. Reither, summarizing the work of four other prominent theorists, comes to the same conclusions I have as the beginning point of his attempt to redefine the writing process:

> the issues [Larson, Odell, Bizzell, and Gage] raise should lead us to wonder if our thinking is not being severely limited by a concept of process that explains only the cognitive processes that occur as people write. Their questions and observations remind us that writing is not merely a process that occurs within contexts. That is, writing and what writers do during writing cannot be artificially separated from the social-rhetorical situations in which writing gets done, from the conditions that enable writers to do what they do, and from the motives writers have for doing what they do. (621)

The idea that language use is essentially social also underlies much current work in literary theory and sociolinguistics. David Bleich proposes a literature classroom in which students transform their initial responses to a text into communally negotiated and thus valid interpretations: "although the resymbolization of a text is usually a fully private affair, it is always done in reference to some communal effort" (137). Fredric Jameson, perhaps the foremost of the neo-Marxist theorists, argues that interpretation "must take place within three concentric frameworks, which mark a widening out of the sense of the social ground of a text" (75). Among linguists, William Labov is renowned for his demonstrations that the so-called verbal deprivation of children in ghetto schools is an artifact of the means of data collection, face-to-face interviews of black children by white adult investigators, and that "the consistency of certain grammatical rules [of black English vernacular] is a fine-grained index of membership in the street culture" (255). And in *Ways with Words,* a book already nearly as influential as Labov's *Language in the Inner City*, Shirley Brice Heath delineates the complex relationship between children's differential acquisition of reading and the uses of and attitudes toward texts in their home communities.

Just as such research calls for new models of the interpretation of literature language use, so too do the intuitively developed methods we are now beginning to use in writing classes and in literacy programs call for a new model of writing. Describing such a model explicitly will lend coherence to these intuitions by bringing out the assumptions on which they are based, illuminating aspects of writing that we have perceived but dimly heretofore through the gaps in the cognitive process model.

What I would like to propose is an ecological model of writing, whose fundamental tenet is that writing is an activity through which a person is continually engaged with a variety of socially constituted systems. Ecology, the science of natural environments, has been recently mentioned by writing researchers such as Greg Myers, who, in his analysis of the social construction of two biologists' proposals, concludes: "Like ethnologists, we should not only observe and categorize the behavior of individuals, we should also consider the evolution of this behavior in its ecological context" (240). The term *ecological* is not, however, the newest way to say "contextual"; it points up important differences between the model I am proposing and other contextual models such as Kenneth Burke's dramatistic pentad.

Such models, oddly, abstract writing from the social context in much the way that the cognitive process model does; they perceive the context in which a piece of writing is done as unique, unconnected with other situations. Kenneth Burke's is perhaps the best contextual model that is applied to writing; Burke develops a heuristic for interrogating the immediate situation in order to impute motives for individual language acts. The terms of his pentad are conceived of as formal or transcendent, and Burke tellingly labels his description of them a "grammar," a model of "the purely internal relationships which the five terms bear to one another" (xvi). Actual statements about motives utilize these "grammatical resources," but the grammar determines the statements only in a formal sense, much as syntactic rules predict the occurrence of certain structures in sentences. One's perspective, or "philosophy," crucially guides how the terms will be applied, and, since Burke proposes no link between the grammar and the perspective, what perspective is chosen appears to be arbitrary, and, perhaps, trivial: "War may be treated as an Agency, insofar as it is a means to an end; as a collective Act, subdivisible into many individual acts; as a Purpose, in schemes proclaiming a cult of war" (xx). Thus, though the grammar allows one to assign labels to important aspects of a situation, it does not enable one to explain how the situation is causally related to other situations. Burke is perhaps more aware of the limitations of his model than are some of his disciples. The description of linguistic forms the pentad enables is, in his opinion, "preparatory": "the study of linguistic action is but beginning" (319).

In contrast, an ecology of writing encompasses much more than the individual writer and her immediate context. An ecologist explores how writers interact to form systems: all the characteristics of any individual writer or piece of writing both determine and are determined by the characteristics of all the other writers and writings in the systems. An important characteristic of ecological systems is that they are inherently dynamic; though their structures and contents can be specified at a given moment, in real time they are constantly changing, limited only by parameters that are themselves subject to change over longer spans of time. In their critique of sociobiology, R. C. Lewontin et al. describe how such systems operate:

> all organisms—but especially human beings—are not simply the results but are also the causes of their own environments. . . . While it may be true that at some instant the environment poses a problem or challenge to the organism, in the process of response to that challenge the organism alters the terms of its relation to the outer world and recreates the relevant aspects of that world. The relation between organism and environment is not simply one of interaction of internal and external factors, but of a dialectical development of organism and milieu in response to each other. (275)

In place of the static and limited categories of contextual models, the ecological model postulates dynamic interlocking systems which structure the social activity of writing.

The systems are not given, not limitations on writers; instead they are made and remade by writers in the act of writing. It is in this sense that writing changes social reality and not only, as Lloyd Bitzer argues, in response to exigence. A historian writes a letter of appreciation to an anthropologist whose article she has read and connects with a new writer with whom she can exchange ideas and articles. A college president who decides to write a Christmas letter to his faculty creates a new textual form that will affect his other communication and at the same time alters, slightly, the administrative structure of his institution.

Furthermore, the systems are concrete. They are structures that can be investigated, described, altered; they are not postulated mental entities, not generalizations. Every individual writer is necessarily involved in these systems: for each writer and each instance of writing one can specify the domain of ideas activated and supplemented, the purposes that stimulated the writing and that resulted from it, the interactions that took place as part of the writing, the cultural norms and textual forms that enabled and resulted from the writing.

One can abstractly distinguish different systems that operate in writing, just as one can distinguish investment patterns from consumer spending patterns from hiring patterns in a nation's economy. But in the actual activity of writing—as in the economy—the systems are entirely interwoven in their effects and manner of operation. The systems reflect the various ways writers connect with one another through writing: through systems of ideas, of purposes, of interpersonal interactions, of cultural norms, of textual forms.

The system of ideas is the means by which writers comprehend their world, to turn individual experiences and observations into knowledge. From this perspective ideas result from contact, whether face-to-face or mediated through texts. Ideas are also always continuations, as they arise within and modify particular fields of discourse. One does not begin to write about bird behavior, say, without observing birds, talking with other observers, and reading widely in the literature of animal behavior in general. One does not even begin to have ideas about a topic, even a relatively simple one, until a considerable body of already structured observations and experiences has been mastered. Even in writing where the focus is not on the development of knowledge, a writer must connect with the relevant idea system: if one is recommending ways to increase the efficiency of a particular department of a publishing firm, one must understand what the department does and how it fits into the firm as a whole.

The system of purposes is the means by which writers coordinate their actions. Arguments attempt to set agendas; promises attempt to set schedules and relationships. Purposes, like ideas, arise out of interaction, and individual purposes are modified by the larger purposes of groups; in fact, an individual impulse or need only becomes a purpose when it is recognized as such by others. A contributor to a company newspaper writes about his interest in paleontology; his individual purpose is to express himself, to gain attention, purposes we all recognize; but within the context of the company newspaper, his purpose is also to deepen his relationship with other employees.

The system of interpersonal interactions is the means by which writers regulate their access to one another. Two determinants of the nature of a writer's interactions with others are intimacy, a measure of closeness based on any similarity seen to be relevant—kinship, religion, occupation; and power, a measure of the degree to which a writer can control the action of others (for a particularly detailed discussion of these factors, see Brown and Levinson). Writers may play a number of different roles in relation to one another: editor, co-writer, or addressee, for instance. Writers signal how they view their relationship with other writers through conventional forms and strategies, but they can also change their relationship—or even initiate or terminate relationships—through the use of these conventions if others accept the new relationship that is implied.

The system of cultural norms is the means by which writers structure the larger groups of which they are members. One always writes out of a group; the notion of what role a writer takes on in a particular piece of writing derives from this fact. I write here as a member of the writing theory group, and as I write I express the attitudes and institutional arrangements of this group—and I attempt to alter some of them.

The system of textual forms is, obviously, the means by which writers communicate. Textual forms, like language forms in general, are at the same time conservative, repositories of tradition, and revolutionary, instruments of new forms of action. A textual form is a balancing act: conventional enough to be comprehensible and flexible enough to serve the changing purposes of writing. Thus, new forms usually arise by a kind of cross-breeding, or by analogy, as older forms are taken apart and recombined or modified in a wholesale fashion.

The metaphor for writing suggested by the ecological model is that of a web, in which anything that affects one strand of the web vibrates throughout the whole. To reiterate, models are ways of thinking about, or ways of seeing, complex situations. If we look at, for example, a particularly vexed problem in current writing theory, the question of audience, from the perspective of this model, we may be able to reformulate the question in a way that helps us to find new answers. Though I cannot attempt a complete analysis of the concept of audience here, I would like to outline briefly how such an analysis might proceed.

The discussion of how authors should deal with their audience has in recent years focused on the opposition between those who argue that authors must analyze the characteristics of a real audience and those who argue that authors always imagine, or create, their audience in their writing. The opposition, of course, has classical roots: in the *Phaedrus* Plato suggests that the rhetorician classify types of audiences and consider which type of speech best suits each; while, at the other extreme, epideictic rhetoric sometimes took the form of a contest in which speakers imagined an audience. Lisa Ede and Andrea Lunsford characterize "the two central perspectives on audience in composition" as "audience addressed and audience invoked" (156). Douglas Park identifies the conception of audience "as something readily identifiable and external" with Lloyd Bitzer, and the opposite conception of audience as represented to consciousness, or invented, with Walter Ong (248).

I would like to draw attention, however, to what unites both these perspectives: whether the writer is urged to analyze or invent, the audience, the audience is always considered to be a construct in the writer's mind. Park specifies four meanings of audience, then argues that "the last two meanings are obviously the most important for teachers or for anyone interested in forms of discourse": "the set of conceptions or awareness in the writer's consciousness," and "an ideal conception shadowed forth in the way the discourse defines and creates contexts" (250). Park concludes, "Any systematic answers to these important questions will depend upon keeping in constant view the essential abstractness of the concept of audience" (250).

The internalization of the audience, making it into a mental construct often labeled the "general audience," is inescapable within the perspective of the cognitive process model. By focusing our attention on what goes on in an author's mind, it forces us to conceive all significant aspects of writing in terms of mental entities. Even Fred Pfister and Joanne Petrick, often cited as proponents of the idea of real audiences, begin by conceding that for writers the "audience is unseen, a phantom. . . . Students, like all writers, must fictionalize their audience. But they must construct in the imagination an audience that is as nearly a replica as is possible of those many readers who actually exist in the world of reality and who are reading the writer's words" (213-14). Less surprisingly, in her textbook Linda Flower labels one of her "problem-solving strategies for writing" "talk to your reader," but she actually recommends that the writer play both roles in the conversation (73).

Barry Kroll, who breaks down approaches to audience into three perspectives—the rhetorical, the informational, and the social—demonstrates, in his definition of the third perspective, how pervasive the tendency to internalize all aspects of writing is: "writing for readers is, like all human communication, a fundamentally social activity, entailing processes of inferring the thoughts and feelings of the other persons involved in an act of communication" ("Writing for Readers" 179). The redefinition of social activity as a cognitive process is even more striking here in that it is unmarked, mentioned as an afterthought in the gerundive phrase. Kroll goes on to conclude, "From [the social] view, the process of writing for readers inevitably involves social thinking—or 'social cognition'" (182–83). In a more recent discussion of studies of the relation between social-cognitive abilities and writing performance, Kroll more clearly advocates the social-cognitive approach to audience: "It seems reasonable that individuals who can think in more complex ways about how other people think ought to be better writers" ("Social-Cognitive Ability" 304). But, as he also admits, "successful performance (in terms of creating texts that are adapted to readers' needs) may not always reflect social-cognitive competence, because writers probably learn to employ many of the linguistic and rhetorical devices of audience-adapted writing without needing to consider their readers' characteristics, perspectives, or responses" (304).

As should be obvious, the perspective of the ecological model offers a salutary correction of vision on the question of audience. By focusing our attention on the real social context of writing, it enables us to see that writers not only analyze or invent audiences, they, more significantly, communicate with and know their audiences. They learn to employ the devices of audience-adapted writing by handing their texts to colleagues to read and respond to, by revising articles or memos or reports guided by comments from editors or superiors, by reading others' summaries or critiques of their own writing. Just as the ecological model transforms authors (people who have produced texts) into writers (people engaged in writing), it transforms the abstract "general audience" into real readers (for an insightful discussion of the use of "audience" vs. "reader," see Park 249–50).

These real readers do appear in discussions of audience dominated by the cognitive process model, if only in glimpses. Ruth Mitchell and Mary Taylor point out that "the audience not only judges writing, it also motivates it. A writer answers a challenge, consciously or unconsciously. The conscious challenges are assignments, demands for reports, memos, proposals, letters" (250–51). Ede and Lunsford criticize Mitchell and Taylor's model from the familiar cognitive process perspective: "no matter how much feedback writers may receive after they have written something (or in breaks while they write), as they compose writers must rely in large part upon their own vision of the reader, which they create . . . according to their own experiences and expectations" (158). But in their account of the readers of their own article, it is the real readers who are obviously most important: "a small, close-knit seminar group"; each other; Richard Larson, who "responded in writing with questions, criticisms, and suggestions, some of which we had, of course, failed to anticipate"; and readers of *College Composition and Communication,* pictured as "members of our own departments, a diverse group of individuals with widely varying degrees of interest in and knowledge of composition" (167–68). Ede and Lunsford know their readers through real social encounters; the cognitive act of analyzing them or creating them is superfluous. As Park suggests, "as a general rule it is only in highly structured situations or at particular times that writers consciously focus on audience as a discrete entity" (254).

The focus on readers as real social beings opens up new vistas for research on audience and for classroom methods. Questions we might seek answers to include: What kind of interactions do writers and readers engage in? What is the nature of the various roles readers play in the activity of writing? What institutional arrangements encourage writer-reader interaction? How do writers find readers to work with? How do writers and readers develop ideas together? How do writers and readers alter textual forms together?

In the classroom, we can enable our students to see each other as real readers, not as stand-ins for a general audience. Students learn about how to deal with their readers not "by internalizing and generalizing the reactions of a number of specific readers" and thereby developing a "sense of audience" (Kroll, "Writing for Readers" 181), but by developing the habits and skills involved in finding readers and making use of their responses. Students, like all writers, need to find out what kind of readers best help them in the role of editor, how to work with co-writers, how to interpret criticisms, how to enter into dialogue with their addressees.

In contrast, then, to the solitary author projected by the cognitive process model, the ideal image the ecological model projects is of an infinitely extended group of people who interact through writing, who are connected by the various systems that constitute the activity of writing. For these "engaged writers" ideas are not so much fixed constructs to be transferred from one mind to the page and thence to another mind; instead, ideas are out there in the world, a landscape that is always being modified by ongoing human discourse. They "find ideas" in writing because they thus enter the field of discourse, finding in the exchange of language certain structures that they modify to suit their purposes. Nor for them do purposes arise solely out of individual desires, but rather arise out of the interaction between their needs and the needs of the various groups that structure their society. As Dell Hymes says about purposes in speaking, "Ultimately, the functions served . . . must be derived directly from the purposes and needs of human persons engaged in social action, and are what they are: talking [or writing] to seduce, to stay awake, to avoid a war" (70). The various roles people take on in writing also arise out of this social structure: through interacting with others, in writing and speaking, they learn the functions and textual forms of impersonal reporting, effective instruction, irony, story-telling. In the same way they learn the attitudes toward these roles and toward purposes and ideas held by the various groups they interact with, and they come to understand how these interactions are themselves partly structured by institutional procedures and arrangements. These attitudes, procedures, and arrangements make up a system of cultural norms which are, however, neither stable nor uniform throughout a culture. People move from group to group, bringing along with them different complexes of ideas, purposes, and norms, different ways of interacting, different interpersonal roles and textual forms. Writing, thus, is seen to be both constituted by and constitutive of these ever-changing systems, systems through which people relate as complete, social beings, rather than imagining each other as remote images: an author, an audience.

It is important to remember that the image the ecological model projects is again an ideal one. In reality, these systems are often resistant to change and not easily accessible. Whenever ideas are seen as commodities they are not shared; whenever individual and group purposes cannot be negotiated someone is shut out; differences in status, or power, or intimacy curtail interpersonal interactions; cultural institutions and attitudes discourage writing as often as they encourage it; textual forms are just as easily used as barriers to discourse as they are used as means of discourse. A further value of the ecological model is that it can be used to diagnose and analyze such situations, and it encourages us to direct our corrective energies away from the characteristics of the individual writer and toward imbalances in social systems that prevent good writing; one such analysis by my colleague Michael Holzman appeared recently in *CE*.

Writing is one of the activities by which we locate ourselves in the enmeshed systems that make up the social world. It is not simply a way of thinking but more fundamentally a way of acting. As Wilhelm von Humboldt says of language, it "is not work (*ergon*) but activity (*energia*)" (27), an activity through which we become most truly human. By looking at writing ecologically we understand better how important writing is—and just how hard it is to teach.

Works Cited

Barthes, Roland. *S/Z*. 1970. Trans. Richard Miller. New York: Hill, 1974.

Berlin, James. "Contemporary Composition: The Major Pedagogical Theories." *College English* 44 (1982): 765–77.

Bitzer, Lloyd F. "The Rhetorical Situation. " *Philosophy and Rhetoric* 1 (1968): 1–14.

Bleich, David. *Subjective Criticism*. Baltimore: Johns Hopkins UP, 1978.

Brown, Penelope, and Stephen Levinson. "Universals in Language Usage: Politeness Phenomena." *Questions and Politeness: Strategies in Social Interaction*. Ed. Esther N. Goody. Cambridge: Cambridge UP, 1978. 56–289.

Bruffee, Kenneth. "Collaborative Learning. " *College English* 43 (1981): 745–46.

Burke, Kenneth. *A Grammar of Motives*. Berkeley: U of California P, 1969.

Culler, Jonathan. *Structuralist Poetics: Structuralism, Linguistics, and the Study of Literature*. Ithaca, NY: Cornell UP, 1975.

Dillon, George. *Constructing Texts: Elements of a Theory of Composition and Style*. Bloomington: Indiana UP, 1981.

Ede, Lisa, and Andrea Lunsford. "Audience Addressed/Audience Invoked: The Role of Audience in Composition Theory and Pedagogy." *College Composition and Communication* 35 (1984): 155–71.

Fish, Stanley. *Is There a Text in This Class? The Authority of Interpretive Communities.* Cambridge: Harvard UP, 1980.

Flower, Linda. *Problem-Solving Strategies for Writing.* New York: Harcourt, 1981.

Goffman, Erving. *Forms of Talk.* Oxford: Blackwell, 1981.

Hairston, Maxine. "The Winds of Change: Thomas Kuhn and the Revolution in the Teaching of Writing." *College Composition and Communication* 33 (1982): 76–88.

Halliday, M. A. K. *Language as Social Semiotic.* Baltimore: University Park, 1978.

Heath, Shirley Brice. *Ways with Words: Language, Life, and Work in Communities and Classrooms.* Cambridge: Cambridge UP, 1983.

Holzman, Michael. "The Social Context of Literacy Education." *College English* 48 (1986): 27–33.

Humboldt, Wilhelm von. *Linguistic Variability and Intellectual Development.* 1836. Trans. George C. Buck and Frithjof A. Raven. Philadelphia: U of Pennsylvania P, 1971.

Hymes, Dell. "Models of the Interaction of Language and Social Life." *Directions in Sociolinguistics.* Ed. John J. Gumperz and Dell Hymes. New York: Holt, 1972. 35–71.

Jameson, Fredric. *The Political Unconscious: Narrative as a Socially Symbolic Act.* Ithaca, NY: Cornell UP, 1981.

Kinneavy, James. *A Theory of Discourse.* Englewood Cliffs, NJ: Prentice, 1971.

Kroll, Barry M. "Writing for Readers: Three Perspectives on Audience." *College Composition and Communication* 35 (1984): 172–85.

———. "Social-Cognitive Ability and Writing Performance: How Are They Related? " *Written Communication* 2 (1985): 293–305.

Labov, William. *Language in the Inner City: Studies in the Black English Vernacular.* Philadelphia: U of Pennsylvania P, 1972.

Lewontin, R. C., Steven Rose, and Leon J. Kamin. *Not in Our Genes: Biology, Ideology, and Human Nature.* New York: Pantheon Books, 1984.

Mitchell, Ruth, and Mary Taylor. "The Integrating Perspective: An Audience-Response Model for Writing." *College English* 41 (1979): 247–71.

Myers, Greg. "The Social Construction of Two Biologists' Proposals." *Written Communication* 2 (1985): 219–45.

Park, Douglas B. "The Meanings of 'Audience.'" *College English* 44 (1982): 247–57.

Pfister, Fred R., and Joanne F. Petrick. "A Heuristic Model for Creating a Writer's Audience." *College Composition and Communication* 31 (1980): 213–20.

Reddy, Michael J. "The Conduit Metaphor—A Case of Frame Conflict in Our Language about Language." *Metaphor and Thought.* Ed. Andrew Ortony. Cambridge: Cambridge UP, 1979. 284–324.

Reither, James A. "Writing and Knowing: Toward Redefining the Writing Process." *College English* 47 (1985): 620–28.

Williams, Joseph. *Style: Ten Lessons in Clarity and Grace.* Glenview, FL: Scott, 1981.

Chapter Nine

Location, Location, Location: The "Real" (E)states of Being, Writing, and Thinking in Composition

Johnathon Mauk

The banal catch phrase of the real estate industry suggests that the only thing more important than location is . . . well . . . location. But what every real estate agent knows is that location is more than the material, more than the physical orientation of a place. Location involves the imagination. The economy, geology, geography, demographics, aesthetics, and history of a surrounding region, or neighborhood, all figure into the *idea* of a particular place—hence into its value. Landowners, and would-be owners, are not buying and selling mere property, but ideas about the way property works. Essentially, then, the real estate industry focuses on the buying and selling of ideas about place.

While I am not going to suggest that real estate and higher education are completely similar enterprises, I do see a compelling, and somewhat helpful, analogy. Like real estate, higher education is promoting, attempting to get students to buy (into) ideas about place. The ideas have value, and like plots of land, their value is based on an intersection of the material and conceptual, of the real and the imagined. In other words, the value of academia for students depends upon their interpretation or creation of academic space. To buy (into) academia (and its attendant postures, behaviors, and perspectives), students must buy (into) a particular conception of the terrain.

From *College English* 65 (2003): 368–88.

However, the processes of learning academic terrain are far more complicated than the processes of buying a plot of land. Students do not merely buy the terrain of academia as one might buy a new house. As students enter into academic space, they must, at the same time, enter into its making. And succeeding at such a feat requires significant guidance. Students must learn a vast array of cartographic skills which help them gain a sense of location, a sense of *where*. And without those skills, without a sense of location, students (and their teachers) are quite simply lost.

As I illustrate in this essay, significant numbers of college students are lost. They come through colleges without a sense of location, without the cartographic skills necessary for placing themselves in the layers and complexities of academic life, and traditional academic perspectives have not yet detected the degree to which they are influencing the geography. Although the average college student is impossible to profile, a vast number of college students share a common trait: they are unsituated in academic space. Or, put another way, academic space is not an integral part of their intellectual geography. They are first-generation college students; they are commuters; they are part-time community college students; they are "nontraditional" (above twenty-four years old), with jobs and families, and as I will explain later, they are also the traditional residential students. And, collectively, their presence portends change for academic space.

It has become important for teachers in higher education to begin exploring what happens when a college career, traditionally conceived as a time and space of intellectual immersion, and traditionally lived out within a particular kind of geography, is defined by a state of constant movement away from campus. More specifically, we might begin asking the question: What happens to writing pedagogy, and the practices of learning to write, in the absence of traditional university geography? When the discourses of composition studies have "trickled down"[1] from or transferred over to community colleges from universities, but have done so largely without the geographical makeup of traditional universities, what happens to writing pedagogy? What happens to the spaces in which the act of writing is conceived?

Such questions come only when we attend to the geographical shifts presently reanimating academic life and everyday life outside of academia. If such questions are going to be asked, the potential answers are manifold. And in the reality of academic institutions, if teachers do not offer answers, those who are less interested in students' well-being probably will. Therefore, I suggest a rigorous exploration of the changing academic space outside of our offices and off our campuses. Such an exploration will require (or result in) evolving theories about academic space. And it is appropriate for writing theorists and teachers to lead in (or at least promote) this enterprise not only because our field emerges from the study of classical rhetoric (and its focus on situation or *kairos*), but also because of composition's role in academia. In composition courses, perhaps more than any other *place* in the institution, students and academia interface (collide?) for the first time; hence academic space and the nonacademic spaces drift together. And because compositionists witness this spatial collision first hand (some of us even consider it part of the job), we have a unique opportunity to explore what it all means.

In this essay I explore the emerging spatial crises in academia: what might be seen as an increasing disintegration of traditional academic space and the apparent *placelessness* of many new college students. This shift, I believe, calls for a pedagogy and theoretical lens that accounts for and engages the spatial and material conditions that constitute the everyday lives of students. To this end, I propose a heuristic for orienting the acts of teaching and learning writing in increasingly spaced-out college environments: *third space*, a concept borrowed from critical geography, which projects a "real and imagined" realm of intellectual-social action.

Living in [Their] Nowhere Land

> *But how did we get here? And where is "here?"*
> Karen Powers-Stubbs and Jeff Sommers

A few years ago, after taking a full-time position at a community college, I witnessed groups of students, and their composition teachers, struggling for a sense of location. I observed, and participated in, a particular academic space that seemed, on one hand, ill-defined, and on another, highly contested. I saw how students who struggled to gain a sense of location also struggled in the practices of learning to write, and how the metaphysics of location were bound to the metaphysics of composition.

I was at the end of a doctoral program in rhetoric, and took a job at a nearby community college. On my first morning at Gordon Community College,[2] a growing school in a Midwestern city, I noticed something peculiar about the place. Of course, I expected certain changes from the familiar: students would not be filing down the sidewalks from the dorms; the lawns would not be filled with Greek-life announcements or sideshows; the main courtyard would not have an evangelical preacher trying to save passers-by. But what I did not expect at Gordon was isolation and detachment. Rather than groups of students walking or sitting casually, I saw students waiting alone in cars for their classes. They were cut off from one another, sealed up in their own mornings, staring ahead, sipping coffee or Mountain Dew, and listening to their radios.

Before pulling into Gordon that first morning, I had assumed most college students, to some degree, experience a certain college "vibe," an involvement in a climate of student-ness. But at Gordon, students seemed *unsituated* in the institution. They were, somehow, nonoriented, as though student orientation, the official set of processes by which an institution begins to make nonacademic people into students, was not achieving its objective. This is not to say that those offices in charge of such processes were performing inadequately. In fact, as will become apparent, I believe no particular office or department could necessarily oversee the complexities of orienting students into academic space; the processes of such an orientation involve not only the geography of that particular space (or campus) but also the geopolitics of the culture(s) surrounding that space.

The Gordon campus was defined, exclusively, by (full-time) faculty and administration.[3] While the relatively small number of full-time faculty had ample office space to decorate with posters of literary greats, philosophical quotations, and Victorian verse, students had no place to settle—no place to define. They had no dorm rooms, no student lounge (other than vending areas or the main cafeteria), no spirit rock, no mall, no communal lawn or park. In the center of College Hall, full-time writing instructors[4] worked amidst their stylized lamps, fern plants, and framed Yeats musings, while students read their assignments eating a bag of potato chips by the ATM machine. In short, students did not have a place at Gordon, other than classrooms.

And because class attendance tended to be erratic, according to instructors, the classes constantly shifted character and so rarely took on a sense of place. The official rhetoric of the institution further obfuscated any sense of place for the students. In meetings and committees, counselors prompted faculty to make the connection between the students' presents and futures. They suggested that framing assignments within the "someday-this-will-be-important-to-your-career" rhetoric would help make classes relevant to the students. Meanwhile, television and radio commercials for the institution sought to attract students based on their potential future success, on their potential earning power. The students were being prompted elsewhere, to some other teleological point, during their time there and even before they came to campus.

And in compliance with these messages the students seemed appropriately detached. In the classroom, many students seemed like half-realized specters of someone/someplace else. One writing instructor, Lewis, sensed in his students a clear divide between academic life and mainstream everyday living, between "out there" and "in here." This perception echoed in the sentiments of many of the full-time writing instructors. The problem, as they perceived it, was that students' nonacademic lives were in constant tension with academia, intellectually, ideologically, physically, and metaphysically. The consequence of that tension was students' lack of intellectual investment in the courses. Many instructors described their students as uninvolved, uninterested, and unmotivated, and most blamed their students' domestic, workplace, and recreational commitments—those elements that provided centrifugal force away from the academic institution.

The students who constituted first-year composition classes at Gordon ranged from overworked eighteen-year-olds to underpaid middle-aged parents. Regardless of their age or role in life (son, mother, grandparent, laborer, nurse), a large majority of the Gordon students shared an ontology, a state of ongoing and *unsituated* movement through time. They seemed to be racing relentlessly away from the college, away from their own presence there. Each day, the campus, for them, was something to get *through*. They scheduled classes adjacently, stacked as many as possible into short spans of time—often leaving only a few minutes to get across campus for the next class. An individual course, then, only "took up" a certain window of time, and the entire college experience only "took up" a portion of their day. From the perspective of Gordon faculty, the students were controlled by centrifugal forces that prompted them out of traditional academic space, and into an ongoing race through time. (Critical geographers such as David Harvey explain such compression of time as a condition of capitalist society. They suggest that the attempt to squeeze more life into less time eradicates space—or at least makes it seem to disappear.)

It seemed that entire academic programs were based on the idea that students were already bound for the exit. Students in technology (diesel engines, agricultural sciençes, tool and dye) programs, for example, planned on being at Gordon for two years, some even less, and then moving on to jobs within the region. A significant number even had jobs, or higher positions, waiting for them at completion of their degrees. For these students, the meaning of their experience at Gordon, then, was tied to some place other than Gordon. A large cadre of younger, incoming students seeking the first two years of a four-year degree were in a similar situation. They were taking prerequisite and core-requirement courses for the purpose of transferring—taking "higher level" (and in their minds, more important) classes elsewhere. For both groups, then, the meaning of their experience was removed, abstracted, or in the words of geographer Anthony Giddens, *distanciated,* from them and was related to the economics of their job fields, or to the academic standards of some other institution—some other place.

From the perspective of the faculty, it seemed that the Gordon students were everywhere except in the academic institution. It seemed as though they were merely passing through campus to some other destination. As one instructor, Karen, explained, her composition students were steeped in daily goings-on which consistently took priority over writing:

> Almost all our students are parents. I mean, how can I sit here and say, "You have to have this composition done," when somebody's like . . . "My kid was in the hospital." I mean come on. So their lives have other planes that are much bigger than college. And this wasn't the case at [two state universities] where most of my students were eighteen years old, just out of high school . . . still living at home . . . not worrying about rent . . . or children . . . and they could focus more on college.

Like many of the instructors at Gordon, Karen acknowledged academia's marginal place in her students' lives. They were already being pulled away from academia, from the composition class, before they even entered the door. The *other* places, which drew students away from college, the would-be intellectual center of their lives, had already crystallized their identities as mothers, fathers, laborers, managers, business owners, skater punks, farmers, and fulltime slackers—all of which seemed contrary to traditional student subjectivity. Like many of the instructors at Gordon, Karen understood that her students were indifferent to college—or at least, less inspired by learning than she had been as a college student. While sitting in her classroom, Karen's students had somewhere, and someone, else to be. And their inclination to be elsewhere manifested itself in writing assignments:

> They have a hard time finding the time to make [writing] a process. We can say, "Writing is a process" until we're purple, but when people have a full-time job, all these kids, three other classes [. . .] finding time to make it a real process is difficult. They sit down and crank it out the night before because that's all the time they got.

As Karen's rendering of her students suggests, the Gordon Communications/Humanities writing faculty and its students were experiencing a clash of expectations. The traditional wisdom of writing pedagogy seemed useless. For example, process pedagogy, which suggests that students should experience writing as a recursive set of behaviors that evolve into increasingly focused discourse, assumes, at the very least, that students have time to invest themselves in such an act. But students at Gordon did not, often could not, envision themselves engaged in such activity. Their lives, quite often, acted against the possibility of such an idea. Another composition instructor, Zena, put it bluntly: "It is difficult for [students] to understand the nature of a process if that process is broken up because of lack of attendance."

Making All [Their] Nowhere Plans

As a composition instructor, I was uncertain how to address such an ethereal problem. Much of my time as a first-year faculty member at Gordon was spent wondering how to meet students on their own "ground" because they were not, it seemed, invested in the space of traditional academia, nor were they invested in a space perceptible to traditional academic view. Students in both my classes and in those of the instructors I interviewed seemed, for lack of a better term, *where-less*. At the time, my strategy was to create writing space, to construct a material *where* for students in my composition classrooms. I prompted students to write from and about their own material/physical experiences in nonacademic life, abandoned assignments that seemed unrelated to students' material lives, and renounced any prompts and any textbooks that did not correspond with my newfound emphasis. Because I was convinced that students needed to locate themselves, and their writing, within material reality, within the goings-on of their daily lives, any pedagogical strategy that prompted students into a discursive vacuum seemed inherently counterproductive.

However, for instructors like me who are (were) determined to steep students in materiality, to begin "where students are," in the words of John Dewey, the Gordon students offer a valuable lesson: students are not necessarily situated in a single, coherent place. That is, from the traditional academic perspective, which sees only a particular kind of space, and a particular kind of student occupying that space, beginning where students are can sometimes turn into an absurd game of "Where's Waldo?"

The ultimate objective for a pedagogy that begins where students *are* is to lead students where they are *not*: to academia. The idea, it seems, is to take students from somewhere outside of academia and draw them inward. Of course, composition studies has numerous metaphors for such an enterprise: we take students *across the academic threshold*; we guide them *over the academic borderland*; we bring them into *a new frontier*. As Nedra Reynolds argues, such metaphors provide meaning for the work of writing instruction, but those metaphors can, in fact, misdirect our collective attention.

The assumption working throughout most of our metaphors is that academia (and specifically a composition class) is a knowable place—that it is constituted by geographical elements, which would suggest (to a student) that there is a *here* here. However, at Gordon, it seemed as though many of the students were not experiencing the same *here* as instructors—if they were experiencing one at all. Basing pedagogy on *where students are* requires that students are someplace, that even intellectually, they are connected to a material-intellectual *where* which has given rise to their identities, or to their discursive makeup. However, the students at Gordon were not necessarily in one, or from one, particular place—or so it seemed. Instead, they seemed scattered among several places (places which often seemed inherently contradictory to one another, and always in tension with Gordon Community College). The Gordon students were mired in the processes of coming and going; stretched across many places (the college being only one). Beginning a semester where students are also asserts a particular conception of place, one that makes place transparent, readable. It suggests that instructors can see the meaning of students' lives and make assignments that emerge out of that understanding. But the *where* of the Gordon students' lives was elusive, and composition classes felt, to students and instructors, like nowhere lands.

What I am suggesting, then, is that the geography of the Gordon students' lives and of the campus itself have something to do with the complexities of teaching writing in composition courses. In a very literal sense, I am suggesting that the physical geography of an institution, and the human geography which surrounds and constitutes it, have an impact on the topography of composition courses—and ultimately influence the success (or failure) of pedagogical strategies. As Nedra Reynolds explains,

"Place does matter; surroundings do have an effect on learning or attitudes towards learning, and material spaces have a political edge. In short, *where* writing instruction takes place has everything to do with *how*" (20). It seems, then, that any exploration of *how* to teach must also be a thorough exploration of *where*—of the geographical complexities that constitute the materiality and the conceptual elements of place. And because the vast imagined geographies of composition studies do not necessarily serve students (like those at Gordon Community College) or their teachers, "it is time to think smaller and more locally" (Reynolds 30).

Materiality, Body, Writing

Composition studies is increasingly focused on the material of life and language. Kristie Fleckenstein, a composition theorist who borrows from the field of geography, argues that composition studies "need[s] an embodied discourse, one that interprets body as neither a passive *tabula rasa* on which meanings are inscribed nor an inescapable animal that must be subdued before pure knowing can be achieved" (281). The body, she argues, has been consistently removed from view by either the illusion of "transcendent truth [in traditional philosophy] or culturally constituted textuality [in poststructuralist thought]." From both perspectives, the meaning of the body has been, in Fleckenstein's words, "eclipsed." These perspectives eradicate the immediacy of lived experience and remove the meaning of situated/corporal events from the individual. In response to these traditions, she offers the "somatic mind," or a "being-in-a-material-place." Such a conception, she argues, situates knowing within a place (a tangible and experiential place). And what is most significant about Fleckenstein's conception is that body and place become a coupling, a dynamic unity:

> The materiality of the somatic mind is tangible location plus being. [. . .] Both organism and place can only be identified by their immanence within each other; an organism in this place (body, clothing, cultural scene, geographical point) is not the same organism in that place. Who and where (thus, what) are coextensive. (286)

She goes on to explain the nature of this dialectical relationship through time, arguing that since body and place form such an inextricable bond, they evolve together. Individual body and particular location form a context that is mutable, dynamic. The individual *is* the intersection of place and practice, *is* the here and now of the place. That is, the individual experiences immersion within a place and the practices that define it as different from some other place (for example, her home town two hours from campus). These claims also resonate with the work of Michel de Certeau, who focuses inquiry on the individual human body *because it is both location and practice at once.* According to de Certeau, "the opacity of the body in movement, gesticulating, walking, taking its pleasure, is what indefinitely organizes a *here* to an *abroad*, a 'familiarity' in relation to a 'foreignness'" (130). The body, in other words, creates location, a sense of *where.*

Beyond Fleckenstein's valuable contribution, numbers of important voices in rhetorical theory are materializing discourse and carrying out a collective exploration of the physical goings-on of language production. Jack Selzer argues in the introduction of *Rhetorical Bodies* (a collection of essays on the "material situatedness of literate acts") that "language and rhetoric have a persistent material aspect that demands acknowledgment, and material realities often (if not always) contain a rhetorical dimension that deserves attention: for language is not the only medium or material that speaks" (8). Selzer's point is essential to the ongoing transportation of rhetoric—out of the prison-house of language and into the traffic of material-bodily existence. In Celeste Condit's chapter, "The Materiality of Coding: Rhetoric, Genetics, and the Matter of Life," she argues that materiality not only speaks, or communicates, but has a coding process. She uses DNA as a model for illustrating how the material world carries, and delivers, meaning:

> If we thus say that organisms reproduce themselves by motivated motion in the world—specifically by the motivated motion of reproducing a code (that is, their analog-identity), where coding is the repetition of a discrete form in a duality of relational forms—we are also saying that coding and living must be identified as verbs, not nouns. Coding implies a construction, an activity; at-

> oms are not codes, even though their forms occur millions of times in the universe. Thus in thinking about language and life, our focus should not be on codes but on coding. (344)

Her analysis is profoundly significant (to understate the issue) for rhetorical studies, especially in the wake of a poststructuralist reign during which language and materiality existed separately. As Condit argues, poststructuralism, which she characterizes as *ultra-structuralism*, "worked energetically and appropriately to repudiate the notion of 'objectivity' to establish that the object is arbitrary. However, in the process, [ultra-structuralists] have tended *to conflate objectivity with materiality*, and they have thus tended to repudiate, or at least fail to account for, the material component of discursive action" (332). Fleckenstein similarly argues that a "poststructuralist orientation amputates physiology from meaning, crippling its own transformative critique and undermining its potential contribution to transformative pedagogies in composition studies" (283).

Theorists such as Fleckenstein and Condit envision language as part of bodily existence (as a process sparked by material life) and see language itself (not only meaning) emerging out of the material-social world. In this vision of a material world, rhetoricians cannot hope to see the complexities of language production without exploring the life processes that make language possible—and vice versa. Says Condit, while "language can imagine for us something that is not in the material world," language cannot be without beings-in-action. Or, put more succinctly, "if the stomach dies, the brain cannot live" (346).

David R. Russell offers an important trajectory (or twist) to this argument. In "Rethinking Genre in School and Society: An Activity Theory Analysis," Russell, borrowing from Yrjö Engeström's version of Vygotskian cultural-historical activity theory and applying Charles Bazerman's articulation of genre, argues that the study of language should expand to a study of activity systems, which are "ongoing, object-directed, historically conditioned, dialectically structured, tool-mediated, human interaction[s]" (507). Russell says that a focus on language or conversation (in the dialogic model) minimizes, even ignores, the impact of materiality:

> The ongoing social practices in which speaking and writing operate also use a host of nonlinguistic tools: buildings, machines, demarcated physical space, financial resources, data strings, and so on. This can be a particular limitation in studying writing, because writing is used to organize ongoing actions over larger reaches of time and space than does face-to-face conversation, mobilizing material tools in much more regularized and powerful ways. (505)

Understanding the complexities of language-in-use, then, requires an understanding of social actions and systems that prompt and give meaning to those actions. It is not enough to explore the relationship between language and consciousness—or language and identity. We must examine the multiple and competing systems that constitute human identity and interaction.

Theories such as these (Fleckenstein's somatic mind, Condit's coding process, and Russell's conception of activity theory) emphasize a crucial point: that a thorough examination of practice necessarily involves an examination of social space—the material conditions that generate language and the social conditions that give it meaning. Moreover, an examination of materiality, of space, is also an examination of identity. In other words, to understand the problems and nuances of any set of practices, as they are acted out by a particular group of people, we must have some intellectual tools for understanding the spatial-social complexities of those practices—for understanding how material existence and geopolitical location figure into knowing and acting.

Finding Third Space

> *Thus conceived, discourse is not the majestically unfolding manifestation of a thinking, knowing, speaking subject, but, on the contrary [. . .] a space of exteriority in which a network of distinct sites is deployed.*
>
> —Michel Foucault

For modern critical geographers, the study of social behavior is commensurate with the study of social space. To understand the politics of location is to understand the politics of being, say critical geographers. Theorists such as Edward Soja, David Harvey, and Doreen Massey assert that the spatial is inherently social, and the social inherently spatial. Massey says,

> we need to conceptualize space as constructed out of interrelations, as the simultaneous coexistence of social interrelations and interactions at all spatial scales, from the most local level to the most global. [. . .] On the one hand, all social (and indeed physical) phenomena/activities/relations have a spatial form and a relative spatial location: the relations that bind communities, whether they be local societies or worldwide organizations; the relations within an industrial corporation; the debt relations between the South and the North; the relations that result in the popularity in certain European cities of the music from Mali [. . .]. [T]here is no way of getting away from the fact that the social is inexorably also spatial. ("Politics" 155)

What seems most important for geographers such as Massey is that space be conceived as a dynamic entity, constituted and reconstituted by the interrelations of real people and real communities. In this view, space is not simply a template, an objectified and abstracted entity, or even something that is "mappable" outside of the social. (See also Massey's *Space, Place, and Gender.*)

To envision space as an animated social phenomenon, rather than a fixed backdrop of social action, is to see its potential in the transformation of public life. Critical geographers argue that imagining social and political change requires imagining new spaces. According to Edward Soja,

> [s]patiality exists ontologically as a product of a transformative process, but always remains open to further transformation in the contexts of material life. It is never primordially given or permanently fixed [. . .] it is precisely this transformative dynamic, its associated social tensions and contradictions, and its rootedness in active spatial praxis, that has been blocked from critical theoretical consciousness for over the past one hundred years. The spaces that have been seen are illusive ones, blurring our capacity to envision the social dynamics of spatialization. (*Postmodern* 122)

For Soja, the real radical power of space has been concealed from the vision of critical perspectives. And, according to his argument, critical theory needs to conceive new ways to highlight the transformative power of space. To this end, Soja points to Henri Lefebvre's theory of the trialectics of spatiality. Borrowing from Lefebvre's multidimensional understanding of space, Soja suggests that in "third space," "things and thought" are on equal terms—always working and reworking the relationship between consciousness and space. Consciousness, sociality, and space are bound together. And, in that union, these phenomena are generative; they make life what it is. In other words, they are the basis of ontology, or, for Soja, "spatialized ontology" (*Postmodern* 131–37). Third space, then, generates possibilities of acting and of knowing; it associates individuals with others, with particular locations, and with the possibilities of acting therein; it is "the terrain for the generation of counterspaces, spaces of resistance to the dominant order" (67–68).

Soja's notion of third space offers a lens for understanding the intersection of materiality, action, language, and consciousness—where language is both material and produced by material, where action is both social and spatial, where consciousness is body and action. In third space, we can imagine the place created in the collision of materiality and conceptuality. Third space is "the real and the imagined," or, in the terms of language study, the indicative (*what is*) and the subjunctive (*what could be*). But perhaps the most compelling aspect of third space is that it provokes rather immediate notions about practice. Lingering among the theoretical complexities of third space are explicit pronouncements for reflective action, for ongoing revision of and re-acting in particular places.

Practicing Third Space

The problems for the Gordon Community College students and instructors could, of course, be diagnosed in a number of ways. Perhaps because I was a newcomer (and in a new space myself), I found the pedagogical crises attributable to spatial confusion. For me, there was no doubt that the students' nomadic lifestyles (at least as commuter students) clashed with the writerly expectations in the composition classrooms, that the apparent fragmentation of their student-ness worked against the processes of composition.

Without a theory of academic space, and in the midst of such a pedagogical crisis, instructors might be tempted to blame students—to argue that students need to situate themselves within the appropriate writerly space of the composition enterprise. But it is too easy to suggest that the act of writing demands location, and so writers must learn to locate themselves within a particular (academic) place and then generate ideas accordingly. It is too easy to argue that composition students must learn how to invest themselves in traditional academic space—even if they are part of a commuter campus. It is even too easy to claim that composition programs must work to provide a *where* for composition students and situate all writerly activities in the "here and now." And it is too easy to suggest that composition assignments must necessarily integrate the discourses of students' lives and the discourses of academia, that each assignment should be a dynamic intersection of both. Such a totalization, I think, evacuates the complexities of both academia and nonacademic life.

What students do require is a way to make sense of the particular academic space that contextualizes their own writing and thinking. Students need to be placed within assignments, or, put another way, assignments need to create a *material-discursive where*. If we accept the terms of critical geographers, who argue that space and being are coupled (that, in Kristie Fleckenstein's words, "who and where [thus, what] are coextensive") then we must understand the importance of creating a *where* for our students. However, a where need not be traditionally academic—traditionally situated within residential geography. In other words, a locatable writerly consciousness need not be attached to residential consciousness. The problems of dislocation, or being in a writerly nowhere, do not arise from the lack of traditional academic geography. In fact, what seems more reasonable is that traditional academic geography often conceals the need to create a material-discursive place for students.

What must happen for students such as those at Gordon (and maybe for those at more residential places) is a change in the metaphysics of *where*. Students need to conceive the space outside of the campus, outside of the classroom, as academic. And the academic space needs to be conceived as transportable and mutable—as something that is tied to being, rather than to exclusive material surroundings. In other words, what it means to be a student and what it means to be in an academic space need to converge—rather literally. And in that convergence, both entities will be changed. Academic space must extend itself, not merely outward, but in all the directions of being which constitute the lives of students. In composition studies, we need to recognize the spatial complexities that define our students' (and our own) lives, but not in order to vanquish those complexities, to wish them away, but to include them in our understanding of how to write. If what it means to write is synonymous with what it means to write in a particular place, then composition instructors (and the entire field of composition studies) need to become critical geographers—or cartographers, as Patricia Harkin has argued (136). We need to understand what kinds of real and imagined spaces are "out there," beyond academia, what kinds of spaces constitute being "in here" (within the ontological regions of academia), and what kinds of spaces are created at the intersection.

What I am suggesting is a rendering of Soja's third space: the region created by the juncture of "things and thought," where places and thoughts about places are fused, where the two are always reworking each other, and most important here, generating possibility (*Postmodern* 131–37). Academic third space is born of the juncture between academic space and student ontology, the region where academic space is dispersed throughout students' daily lives, a dimension emergent from the generative collision of academic, domestic, and work spatialities. Students, themselves, in an academic third space *are* the intersection of academic and nonacademic spatialities—a *where* defined by their own bodies, their "somatic minds," in Fleckenstein's terms.

In this space, the act of writing must be contextualized by students' academic and nonacademic lives. For example, in a recent first-year composition course, my students were asked to write an argument paper, a standard assignment for first-year college writing courses. They were asked to read a variety of essays on education in America. And in what amounts to standard practice for writing pedagogy, the students then had in-class group discussions about the issues raised in the essays, a necessary step for establishing a rhetorical context for their own positions. But the pre-text did not stop there. Students then carried the discussion with them out of the classroom, into the places that constitute their nonacademic lives. They interviewed at least five people (who consistently share in their daily lives at home, work, and so on) about the issues raised in the essays and class discussions. The information/opinions from these interviews were then reported to the class, and used as part of their arguments—as evidence of opinion. The writing prompt did not simply ask students to "form an opinion" but to argue for or against the validity of others' opinions, to situate their own writing within the views and positions they excavated from everyday life.

Such an assignment, one only slightly more layered than a traditional argument prompt, invites students to see themselves, their own bodies, as the intersection between academia and non-academic life. It provides a conceptual place (a topic) while also prompting students to make meaning out of the people-places that constitute their daily lives. Assignments that provide such conceptual-material space might resemble the following:

- A critique essay assignment prompts students to formally evaluate a short expository text on the nature of work in American culture. In addition to formally analyzing the features of the text, students are prompted to interview people at their places of employment, asking co-workers to respond to claims made in the text. Students are to argue for the validity of the claims made based on the information/opinions drawn from the interviews.
- An investigation or explaining assignment begins with readings on political action. The students are prompted to find the names of city, district, state, and federal officials elected to serve their communities. Then they are prompted to write a brief essay or develop a pamphlet that explains how an average citizen can correspond with government officials. Students then deliver their texts to their neighbors. In a follow-up essay, students explore the significance of their work. They may draw on particular encounters and/or outside texts on civic action.
- Students are prompted to "conjure interest" in a public issue (by initiating discussion among non-classmate peers). They should record their discussions and bring notes/ recordings to class. In groups, students analyze the proceedings of each discussion. The writing assignment asks each student to analyze his or her own discussion by explaining how it reveals/represents/illustrates public interaction or public opinions. They might also be

prompted to share their work with the original discussion participants.

- After reading and analyzing a published text in class, students write questions for and conduct discussion with non-classmate peers. Students use the two discussions (in class and out of class) as material for a paper about perspectives, ideology, or political positions.

For such assignments, the world around the student is not merely something to feed or prompt writing; it is also implicated in the act of language/text production. Also, in such assignments, students are agents of academic work: they are not merely writing about their lives outside of an academic setting, but are using academic tools within their nonacademic lives. Or, as a perspective from third space would suggest, such assignments prompt students beyond the academic/nonacademic dichotomy and enable them to imagine themselves as public intellectuals who bring together the activities of various spaces and systems. Assignments from/in/of third space do not simply steep students in their own local/personal goings-on; rather, they invite students to become intersections of "the real and the imagined," of *what is* and *what could be*, and to produce what John Trimbur calls "socially useful knowledge" (214). Picturing students as agents of academic/intellectual work may help cast writing as a transformative (rather than gymnastic) exercise. If writing situations emerge from material conditions, students may be more apt to associate writing with the political and social. As Joseph Harris explains, "[W]e need to talk about language not simply as a form of expression, but also as a form of action" ("After" 643). This call to action has been resonating since "after Dartmouth," and probably brewing since after Dewey.

If the practice of writing helps to fuse various social spaces of students' lives, college might better serve their needs. Presently, it seems, colleges are getting better at attracting students and worse at meeting their needs. Increasing numbers of students do not return after their first year. A study in *American Demographics* found that "nearly one-third of college freshmen will not enroll for the following year of study," and while retention rates have been declining since 1983, they have dropped even more significantly since the mid-1990s (Cravatta 41). The study also found that persistence rates are lowest at two-year colleges—which may be no surprise for faculty at schools such as Gordon.

Such numbers also point to what Lynn Bloom calls the "virtually absent" subject in academic scholarship: class (655). While academia projects a veneer of middleclass-ness over its students (and its objectives), it fails to address the complexities of those students who are below the powerful but consistently imperceptible line marking the middle class: those who work several jobs while attending classes, those who lack the resources to concentrate (and concentrate on) a college career, those who are drawn to the allure of low-cost (that is, two-year college) education. (See Felski's "Why Academics Don't Study the Lower Middle Class"). While college becomes more of an economic imperative, and its cost continues to grow out of proportion to average American salaries (see Tinberg's interview with Ira Shor), college students will not necessarily be the children of middle-class parents, but will be children and parents alike attempting to enter the middle class. In other words, as some form of college education becomes a requisite component of participating in (rather than struggling beneath) the economy, colleges will attract growing numbers of *non-middle-class* students. What this means for faculty is that growing numbers of lower-middle-class, many first-generation,[5] students will continue to enter and exit their classrooms, and they will be mired in the nonacademic business of working to pay for school. Meanwhile, these students tend to exist outside (or underneath) academia's collective gaze because they are largely transient, and transience does not seem to register on scholarly radar—even though significant numbers (38 percent according to the *Chronicle of Higher Education*) attend two-year colleges[6] and, according to the *Chronicle of Higher Education Almanac 2001–2002*, one-third of all college students are part-time.

Spacing Out: The Impending Dislocation of Composition Studies

Critical geographers teach us that particular college spaces create, and are created by, particular forms of socialization. Like the material space of any institution, college spaces are designed to create particular effects. The buildings constitute beliefs about appropriate practices—and those beliefs, in turn, are maintained by those practices. Dick Hebdige explains how these dynamics work particularly in an academic place:

> [T]he buildings literally reproduce in concrete terms prevailing (ideological) notions about what education is and it is through this process that the educational structure, which can, of course, be altered, is placed beyond question and appears to us as "given" (i.e., as immutable). In this case, the frames of our thinking have been translated into actual bricks and mortar. (Qtd. in Cresswell 17)

The geography of a campus and the architecture of its buildings, then, are projections or products of a prevailing imagination, and in turn, they help to reproduce imagination (assumptions about what is good and bad, what should be done, what can be done, and how things should be carried out). Academic space is not simply a transparent template in which teaching and learning go on; the materiality of a campus (and/or life beyond campus) is inextricable from its sociality.

If we accept the connection between geography and consciousness (even to a limited degree), we should acknowledge the vast numbers of commuter students, who *come to and go away from* colleges as part of their daily, every-other-daily, or weekly routines. Simply by virtue of statistics, we can imagine that the kinds of crises experienced by Gordon students and faculty are rampant. But the situation is far more complicated than the distinctions between residential and commuter campuses. While the distinction sheds some light on the problem of student dislocation, spatial ontology involves more than the academic space itself. Although the geography of campuses (and of coming to and going from campuses) undoubtedly messages certain actions, ideas, and identities into being, the materiality of broader cultural design is inflected into student life.

What current statistics on part-time students do not express is a more elusive issue: growing evasiveness and transience among all college students. A wide range of factors suggests that college students are increasingly removed from traditional academic space. For example, students are increasingly less apt to study in, or even visit, university libraries. According to Scott Carlson, in a recent issue of the *Chronicle of Higher Education*, university libraries are becoming "deserted" as students opt to fetch information from online sources off campus and to study at more fashionable locations such as Barnes and Noble. In response, library deans are redesigning the traditional library space to attract students "back to the physical structures" (A35).

The centrifugal movement away from campus is further prompted by college students' participation in the productive/consumptive practices of the general public, lifestyle trends among post–baby boomer generations that suggest an increasing transience among college students. A recent article in *American Demographics* makes clear the growing trend of working college students: "College enrollment is growing, and so is college tuition. One result is that the number of employed students is growing faster than college enrollment" (B. Miller 26). While college tuition may create more economic imperatives, students seem to be more financially involved than previous student generations. According to another study in *American Demographics*, "Today's college students have more money than their predecessors, and they don't mind parting with it" (Speer 40), and marketers hawking everything from cellular communications to cars are maneuvering for attention. In short, college students are increasingly steeped in the activity systems of nonacademic life. They are more apt to own cars, more apt to own cellular phones. And for growing numbers of young adults, college is part of a twisted path toward independence. In what has been called "boomeranging," numbers of young adults "sample options" such as college, jobs, living situations, and relationships (Riche 26). These post–baby boomers experience college sporadically (on for a semester, off for two, and so on) rather than in one concentrated effort.

Of course, many of the claims based on college student demographics seem contradictory. While some sources point to the increasing numbers of lower-middle-class students, with presumably less money than their predecessors, others depict nouveau bourgeois yuppies. Despite the apparent contradictions, we can be certain that college students are (and will be) increasingly steeped in the activity systems beyond academic life. If the last decade is any indication, the twenty-first-century college student will have many layers. If he or she is not a (single) parent or laborer or manager or supervisor or victim of "downsizing" or first-generation student on the fringes of middle-class life, he or she might well be a car-owner or a cell-phone slinging transient beckoned by the voices of late capitalist enterprise. College students will live in a time/space marked by increasing calls to participate in the rhetorical-economic-material life beyond collegiate space. Such trends need not alarm us. In fact, it seems that we have been waiting for this shift, to be pulled outside of ourselves and into students' social spheres: We have been called on by Joseph Harris "to imagine a different sort of social space where people have reason to come into contact with each other" ("Negotiating" 39), by Richard Miller to understand "the inevitable conflicts that occur between the expectations created by the student's lived experience of the world and the academy's efforts to master that world" (284), and by Kristie Fleckenstein "to live and write in the gaps" (303). In other words, those of us teaching writing in spaces that appear fundamentally different from our own training need not be threatened by the fragmentation or unsituatedness our students embody. Instead, we should attempt to smear ourselves across the new spatialities of student life. And given the present momentum of change in education, in writing environments, and in commuter campuses and the general realization of an increasingly transient ontology among our students, it seems necessary for us to practice in and help articulate such real-and-imagined spaces.

What this means for writing instruction is a vast rethinking of the theory and practices which have grounded the field in its present form. As the nature of space in higher education continues to transform itself (continues to become less and less situated), the most basic assumptions about being a composition student or instructor will become ever-less-fixed. One such assumption about the daily practice of composition is that being "in composition" means being in a classroom—that a composition class is a particular place. (Instructors and students alike say, "I'm going to comp class," or, "I can't wait to get the hell out of comp class.") But what may assist composition students (and instructors) most is recasting the classroom as the place where(ever) the student is carrying out the practices of writing.

As such conceptual changes occur (and I believe they will occur in some fashion), the field (or house) of composition as we know it will change dramatically. The standard tools of daily composition instruction are likely to change, and online courses and virtual spaces are bound to help promote change. Pedagogical tools such as workshops, peer editing, debates, informal discussion, impromptu writing, small group discussion, and conferences (and the perspectives that give them meaning) will increasingly become only particular (and maybe a particularly small) components of writing pedagogy—or their features will be entirely transformed. As the number of commuter students rises throughout higher education, as students with jobs (or with bills and no jobs) hurry into colleges, as new generations of café students locate themselves in coffee shops and bookstores, and as Internet-minded students situate (at least part of) their identities in cyberspace, the traditional classroom may still exist but it will signify something different. It will not be a center or even a solid place. Although the foundations of the buildings may not move, the classrooms students and teachers conjure in their (somatic) minds will. In fact, it seems only fitting that classrooms (and academia in general) come to be seen as places in a continuum of signifiers for intellectual space.

As students become less situated in the classroom, instructors will have to conceive of activities that prompt students into writerly behavior outside of the classroom. Such activities might not resemble the traditional student behavior of situated academic settings. They might prompt students to write an essay with a nonstudent (with a "peer" who is defined as such because of his or her working or social relationship with the student). They might prompt students to discuss or debate with people off campus. They might even be so bold as to have a nonacademic (someone off campus) evaluate students' texts. While workshopping and peer editing may always be valued practices in the composition classroom, instructors will have to prompt students into new kinds of reflection, invention, and planning. These behaviors will fundamentally include all facets of the students' lives.

The implications for such thinking are far-reaching. As the practices of composition pedagogy become increasingly defined by an emerging academic third space, so too will the study of rhetoric. The study of invention, for instance, will involve the study of space and perhaps the analysis of particular places—and the relationships among consciousness, discourse, and place. Perhaps invention, and all writerly acts, will be seen not only as a social act (as Karen Burke LeFevre has taught us) but also a spatial act—one precipitated by, and emergent from, geographies of daily life.

Given the changing cultural conditions that surround academia, the number of commuter students, the rhetoric of higher education advertisements (which call potential students through college rather than to college), and the momentum away from stationary (that is, non-auto-mobile) student life, we can no longer invite students to move into academic space. Instead, academia (its attendant postures and perspectives) must be dispersed (but not packaged) into the material-spatial ontology of everyday life. If we want students to move into academic space, if we want them to buy into the real estate, it is time for academia to embody and become embodied in the new spaces of student life. Or perhaps we should avoid the idea of buying and selling altogether, and, as Robert Haight suggests, "approach the classroom community [. . .] as a climate to be created."

Notes

1. Of course, my use of Reaganomic rhetoric carries a certain hierarchical connotation—that universities are somehow above community colleges and it is this downward slope which carries university pedagogy to more lowly community colleges. While such notions are somewhat distasteful in the field of composition studies, they are supported by the fact that faculty who teach at community colleges come from university graduate programs (where they explore and model the practices of scholarly research) and carry out their professional lives without time or funding for research. Meanwhile, the vast majority of scholarship in the field is blind to, and mute about, community college pedagogy and politics.

2. Institutional and individual names have been changed.

3. Gordon had recently been transformed from a technical college to a community college and it had grown significantly since the change; even while local universities' enrollments were decreasing, Gordon's was increasing. In its development into a comprehensive community college, Gordon's story mirrors Beverly Derden Fatherree's retrospective of Hinds Community College in *Teaching English in the Two-Year College.*

4. Full-time writing instructors made up a small percentage of the entire writing faculty—the department averages about 25 percent full-time. Of course, this implies the large cadre of contingent faculty who were, themselves, unsituated within (by) the institution.

5. According to a study by the Education Resources Institute, first-generation students are more likely to have nonacademic obligations that challenge their success and they report less support from friends and family. That is, they are more likely to be unfamiliar with the geography of academia (see Haworth).

6. The numbers vary widely depending on the source. While the *Chronicle of Higher Education* projects an average 38 percent for the next nine years, the National Center for Education Statistics reports that 47 percent of all college students attended two-year schools in 1999 and projects that 46 percent will attend public two-year schools in 2011 ("Projections").

Works Cited

Bloom, Lynn Z. "Freshman Composition as a Middle-Class Enterprise." *College English* 58 (1996): 654–75.

Carlson, Scott. "The Deserted Library." *Chronicle of Higher Education* 16 Nov. 2001: A35–38.

Chronicle of Higher Education Almanac 2001–2002. 31 Aug. 2001.

Condit, Celeste. "The Materiality of Coding: Rhetoric, Genetics, and the Matter of Life." *Rhetorical Bodies*. Ed. Jack Selzer and Sharon Crowley. Madison: U of Wisconsin P, 1999. 326–56.

Cravatta, Matthew. "Hanging On to Students." *American Demographics* (1997): 41.

Cresswell, Tim. *In Place/Out of Place: Geography, Ideology, and Transgression*. Minneapolis: U of Minnesota P, 1996.

de Certeau, Michel. *The Practice of Everyday Life*. Trans. Steven Rendall. Berkeley: U of California P, 1984.

Durden, William. "Liberal Arts for All, Not Just the Rich." *Chronicle of Higher Education* 19 Oct. 2001: B20.

Fatherree, Beverly Derden. "The More Things Change, the More They Stay the Same." *Teaching English in the Two-Year College* 27 (1999): 41–50.

Felski, Rita. "Why Academics Don't Study the Lower Middle Class." *Chronicle of Higher Education* 25 Jan. 2002: B24.

Fleckenstein, Kristie. "Writing Bodies: Somatic Mind in Composition Studies." *College English* 61 (1999): 281–306.

Foucault, Michel. *The Archaeology of Knowledge* and *The Discourse on Language*. Trans. A. M. Sheridan Smith. New York: Pantheon, 1972.

Giddens, Anthony. *The Constitution of Society: Outline of the Theory of Structuration*. Berkeley: U of California P, 1984.

Haight, Robert. "The Business Metaphor and Two-Year College Writing Instruction." *The Politics of Writing in the Two-Year College*. Ed. Barry Alford and Keith Kroll. Cross Currents. Portsmouth: Boynton, 2001. 74–85.

Harkin, Patricia. "The Postdisciplinary Politics of Lore." *Contending with Words: Composition and Rhetoric in a Postmodern Age*. Ed. Patricia Harkin and John Schilb. New York: MLA, 1991. 124–38.

Harris, Joseph. "After Dartmouth: Growth and Conflict in English." *College English* 53 (1991): 631–46.

———. "Negotiating the Contact Zone." *Journal of Basic Writing* 14 (1995): 27–42.

Harvey, David. *Consciousness and the Urban Experience*. Baltimore: John Hopkins UP, 1985.

Haworth, Karla. "Report Cites Obstacles to College Entrance." *Chronicle of Higher Education* 9 Jan. 1998: A50–51.

Lefebvre, Henri. *Everyday Life in the Modern World*. Trans. Sacha Rabinovitch. London: Penguin-Allen Lane, 1971.

Massey, Doreen. "Politics and Space/Time." *Place and the Politics of Identity*. Ed. Michael Keith and Steven Pile. New York: Routledge, 1993. 141–61.

———. *Space, Place, and Gender*. Minneapolis: U of Minnesota P, 1994.

Miller, Berna. "Waiters, Painters, and Big-Mac Makers." *American Demographics* 19 (1997): 26.

Miller, Richard. "The Nervous System." *College English* 58 (1996): 265–86.

Powers-Stubbs, Karen, and Jeff Sommers. "Where We Are Is Who We Are." *The Politics of Writing in The Two-Year College*. Ed. Barry Alford and Keith Kroll. Cross Currents. Portsmouth: Boynton, 2001. 19–41.

"Projections of Education Statistics to 2011." National Center for Education Statistics. 29 September 2002. http://nces.ed.gov/pubs2001/proj01/chapter2.asp#6.

Reynolds, Nedra. "Composition's Imagined Geographies: The Politics of Space in the Frontier, City, and Cyberspace." *College Composition and Communication* 50 (1998): 12–35.

Riche, Martha Farnsworth. "The Boomerang Age." *American Demographics* 12.5 (1990): 24–27, 30, 52–53.

Russell, David R. "Re-Thinking Genre in School and Society: An Activity Theory Analysis." *Written Communication* 14 (1997): 504–54.

Selzer, Jack. "Habeas Corpus: An Introduction." *Rhetorical Bodies*. Ed. Jack Selzer and Sharon Crowley. Madison: U of Wisconsin P, 1999. 3–15.

Soja, Edward W. *Postmodern Geographies: The Reassertion of Space in Critical Social Theory*. New York: Verso, 1989.

———. *Thirdspace: Journeys to Los Angeles and Other Real-and-Imagined Places*. Oxford: Blackwell, 1998.

Speer, Tibbet L. "College Come-ons." *American Demographics* 20 (1998): 40–45.

Tinberg, Howard. "An Interview with Ira Shor—Part 1." *Teaching English in the Two-Year College* 27 (1999): 51–60.

Trimbur, John. "Composition and the Circulation of Writing." *College Composition and Communication* 52 (2000): 188–219.

CHAPTER TEN

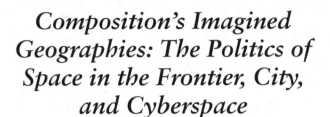

Composition's Imagined Geographies: The Politics of Space in the Frontier, City, and Cyberspace

NEDRA REYNOLDS

> *We must be insistently aware of how space can be made to hide consequences from us, how relations of power and discipline are inscribed into the apparently innocent spatiality of social life, how human geographies become filled with politics and ideology.*
>
> EDWARD W. SOJA (6)

> *It is helpful to remind ourselves that one of the things a university does is alter one's sense of geography.*
>
> MARY N. MUCHIRI ET AL. (178)

In their recent article on "Importing Composition: Teaching and Researching Academic Writing Beyond North America," Mary N. Muchiri and her co-authors challenge our assumptions that composition is "universal" in its uses and applications, and that writing instructors and writing students do not occupy particular geographic locations. Muchiri et al. remind readers that composition is very much a product of North America and of capitalism and illustrate what happens to composition research when it is exported—how it changes in a different, de-localized

From *College Composition and Communication* 50 (1998): 12–35.

context of its origination. "Importing Composition" highlights some of the assumptions that form the basis of U.S. research on academic writing—assumptions that sometimes seem "bizarre" in a new context (176). In our limited notions of geography, we make assumptions about serving the world in our writing classes: "The teacher in New York or Los Angeles may look out over a classroom and think, 'The whole world is here.' It isn't" (195).

In its analysis of contemporary writing instruction—informed by imports and exports, journeys, the local and the global—"Importing Composition" contributes to a geographic study of composition that asks us to confront many of our assumptions about place and space. My purpose here is to extend that contribution by using concepts from postmodern geography to explore how spaces and places are socially produced through discourse and how these constructed spaces can then deny their connections to material reality or mask material conditions.[1] Cultural geography invites us to question the relationships between material conditions and imagined territories, a relationship I identify here as the politics of space, and asks us to attend to the negotiations of power that take place across and within a number of spaces: regional or topographical, domestic or institutional, architectural or electronic, real or imagined. Making a geographic turn enables me to examine the politics of space in composition with three general aims: (1) to interpret some of composition's most enduring spatial metaphors as "imagined geographies" responsible, in part, for composition's disciplinary development and identity; (2) to illustrate the effects of time-space compression on composition's workers; (3) and to argue for a spatial politics of writing instruction that denies transparent space and encourages the study of neglected places where writers work.

Attending to the politics of space can begin with simple observations about where writers and writing instructors work—in a variety of institutional, public, and private spaces (some of them difficult to categorize as either public or private): the academic buildings of our offices, computer labs, and writing centers; the cafeterias, libraries, and classrooms of our campuses; the large conference hotels where we meet to exchange ideas and socialize; the kitchen table, desks, or computer corners in our homes. These actual locations for the work of writing and writing instruction coexist with several metaphorical or imaginary places where we write, study writing, or create theories about writing: webs of meaning, research paradigms, home departments, discourse communities, frontiers, cities, and cyberspaces.

Composition workers have long had to deal with the politics of space, whether this has involved trying to reduce section sizes, find a room to establish a writing center, or stake out disciplinary territory. In carving out areas to call its own, composition has created imagined geographies that hold a number of implications. A writing center, for example, occupies a certain number of square feet in a campus building, but it also occupies an imaginary place where writing is taught, learned, or talked about very differently than in a lecture hall or around a seminar table. Edward Soja, in *Postmodern Geographies: The Reassertion of Space in Critical Social Theory*, defines postmodern geography as the study of the social production of spaces or studying the linkages among space, knowledge, and power (20). The social production of spaces takes place in all discourse arenas, wherever rhetors are "inventing" the boundaries of inquiry, the agendas of research, or the languages of arguments. How have composition theorist-practitioners imagined the spaces of writing, writers, and writing instruction? "Where" have they placed the work of composition studies as a field or discipline, and what implications do these real or imaginary placements hold? After demonstrating the endurance of one of composition's most important imagined geographies, the *frontier,* and the emergence of two more, the *city* and *cyberspace,* I argue that these imaginary places for writing and writing instruction have been rendered benign, or anesthetized by the influence of transparent space; that we have neglected the relationship between material spaces and actual practices; and that we need to attend to the effects of time-space compression on composition's workers.

Spatial Metaphors in the Discourses of Composition Studies

Spatial metaphors have long dominated our written discourse in this field ("field" being one of the first spatial references we can name) because, first, writing itself is spatial, or we cannot very well conceive of writing in ways other than spatial. In "The Limits of Containment: Text-as-Container in Composition Studies," Darsie Bowden asserts that composition "is especially rife with metaphors because composing involves complex cognitive activities . . . that are difficult to talk about and understand" (364). As Bowden's analysis suggests, many of our metaphors in writing and composition studies involve or depend on imaginary conceptions of space. From bound texts to pages to paragraphs, sentences, and words, we read and write in distinctly spatial ways. We read from left to right (in most languages), and we scan pages up and down or rifle through a stack of pages from top to bottom. We are accustomed to margins and borders that frame texts for us and page numbers or arrow icons that mark our place. (How often have you found a remembered passage by its placement on a page, its position in the text?) Academic and professional writers are comfortable with manipulating textual spaces and know that the tasks of organizing and presenting information—with spatial constraints all around—constitute one of a writer's biggest challenges. Techno-revolutions are changing our notions of texts on pages, most of us realize, and the days of container metaphors for texts may be numbered.

Jay David Bolter's *Writing Space: The Computer, Hypertext, and the History of Writing* thoroughly demonstrates that writing specialists would be hard pressed to imagine or explain writing in terms other than spatial. From *topoi* to transitions, we make decisions throughout the writing process based on spatial relationships; for example, where an example goes or what point connects to what claim. To control textual space *well* is to be a good writer; in fact, controlling textual spaces is very much tied to both literacy and power. Chris Anson identifies some commonly-accepted practices that are really about writing teachers' efforts to assert control over textual space—rules about margins and double-spacing, about where the staple or paper clip goes, about where the writer's name and the date belong—all of these practices or rules are about control, which as he points out, might slip away from us in the age of electronic writing.

When created via computer interfaces, texts burst out of their containers, as Cynthia Selfe and Richard Selfe have argued. One of the reasons that word processing has been so revolutionary to writers is that it allows for easier, faster manipulation of space: sentences, chunks, or paragraphs can be deleted or moved in seconds. Because readers orient themselves spatially within printed texts—"How many more pages?"—Bolter explains that spatial disorientation is, in fact, one of the problems or challenges of electronic writing, where "the reader seldom has a sense of where he or she is in the book" (87).

Because writing teachers recognize both the spatial nature of writing and the importance of controlling textual as well as disciplinary space, compositionists have developed a rich repertoire of memorable spatial images and referents, everything from webs of meaning to turf wars. Spatial metaphors have served to establish what composition should be or to lament what composition has become. For example, claims of composition as a discipline have called on the lofty spatial metaphors of paradigms and "domains" (Phelps) or on the more mundane: inside Stephen North's sprawling, junky house of lore resides a group of sad occupants who live in the basement (Miller). Feminist readings of the field have concentrated on the domestic spaces of composition, where underpaid women are assigned primarily chores and housekeeping tasks (Slagle and Rose; Neel). In our discussions of economic and political issues about composition, we refer to heavy courseloads as teaching "in the trenches" because composition occupies the "low" position in the academy, akin to a carnival (Miller).

Generally, as composition has encountered postmodernism, metaphors of inside and outside, margin and center, boundaries and zones have become increasingly familiar, appealing, even comfortable. Mike Rose's *Lives on the Boundary;* Carolyn Ericksen Hill's *Writing on the Margins;* and Mary Louise Pratt's "arts of the contact zone" identify three of the most popular spatial metaphors for discussing issues of difference and diversity or for asserting where the work of composition studies should concentrate. Perhaps the most appealing spatial metaphor right now is Gloria Anzaldúa's "borderlands" (*La Frontera*), where cultures are mixed and mingled and where geographic borders do not hold. Imagining spaces where differences mingle is important to a field characterized by interdisciplinarity and populated with some of the most marginalized members of the academy: per-course instructors, teaching assistants, and first-year students.

Despite composition's affinity for spatial metaphors, and despite rhetoric's attention to spaces for public discourse, there has not yet been a concerted effort to examine composition's geographies, nor have composition scholars typically looked to the disciplinary area of geography studies. Composition and geography have undergone similar changes in recent decades due to the impact of new technologies, and both fields are pursuing a growing interest in spatial theories.[2]

Geographic Literacy: Yet Another Crisis

Geography is, literally or etymologically, *writing the earth,* yet composition studies has not drawn much from it, exploring instead the terrains of history, philosophy, linguistics, and cognitive psychology. The lack of engagement so far between composition and geography is particularly striking in light of the fact that both fields remain so marginalized among academic disciplines and that both have been targeted by media-driven campaigns regarding literacy, composition in the mid-1970s and geography in the mid-1980s.

Like composition studies, geography has experienced the national media attention of a declared "literacy crisis." Approximately a decade after the claims that schoolchildren could not read or write, the media began reporting on survey and test results showing that college students guessed wildly on geography tests and were unable to read a map, identify important countries, or name boundary rivers or mountains.[3] With the collapse of several subjects into "social studies," American students had become geographically illiterate. Surveys confirmed that nearly 70% of all secondary students had no formal course work in geography, and the media were eager to report the most egregious examples of ignorance; for example, the belief that Canada was a state ("Teachers Lament").

In 1985, in response to "deterioration of geographic knowledge," two professional organizations set forth new guidelines for the teaching of geography in elementary and secondary schools, and Congress designated a "National Geography Awareness Week" in 1988 "to combat a widespread ignorance of geography" ("Redoubling"). The National Geographic Society pumped over two million dollars into the D.C. public school system alone, for teacher-training, a high-tech classroom, atlases, maps, and software (Horwitz A8).

Now, just ten years after the nation-wide concern with geographic ignorance, interest in geography is said to be soaring, with a declared "Renaissance" in geographic education (ABC World News). From inflatable globes to such popular programs and games as "Where in the World is Carmen Sandiego?," American schoolchildren have improved test scores. Geography's fortunes are changing because of a new push towards geographic education—complete with corporate sponsorship—and because of near-revolutionary changes in map-making technology (Hitt).

A driving force behind geography's renaissance is economics: the interest in geography aligns sharply with the expansion of multi-national capitalism across the globe. Satellites, cable, NAFTA, and the information superhighway—all of these developments have motivated politicians and educators to argue that American students need to be able to navigate these new horizons for commercialism. Functional illiteracy is bad for the goals of capitalism, and educators recognize the urgency of knowing more about other places and cultures in order to be competitive in the world market. A new urgency about geographic literacy accompanies other signs of the impact of time-space compression, or the belief that the planet is shrinking, with a general speed-up in the pace of everyday life.

Time-Space Compression

> Our daily life, our psychic experience, our cultural languages, are today dominated by categories of space rather than by categories of time.
>
> Fredric Jameson (16)

The huge campaign to remedy the geography literacy crisis gained momentum, in part, by changing conceptions of space in our late-capitalist economy. With technologies that allow the rapid, almost instantaneous, transmission of information and ever-faster modes of transportation, our world is perceived to be "smaller" than it used to be, a phenomenon known as *time-space compression*. First named by Marx as the annihilation of space through time, time-space compression means more time to work and thus more profit (Massey 146; Harvey 293; Soja 126). As spaces seem to shrink, time seems to expand—and the illusion that there is more time would allow capitalists to get more out of workers. "Time-space compression refers to movement and communication across space, to the geographical stretching-out of social relations, and to our experience of all this" (Massey 147). The perception that the earth is shrinking to the size of a "global village"—a perception that benefits the expansion of capitalism—is important to contemporary geography studies and to any examination of the spatial turn in postmodernism.

The general sensations of a shrinking planet—busier, noisier, and more crowded—triggers the temptation to look out over urban classrooms and think "the whole world is here." Other examples of time-space compression include: (1) satellites beaming events "around the globe"; (2) the weird sense of mobility that comes from "surfing the net" or from exchanging e-mail with someone in Johannesburg or Berlin or Seoul; (3) the "really there" feeling enhanced by big-screen televisions or expensive sound systems in theaters; (4) Microsoft's slogan "Where do you want to go today?" and (5) the IBM slogan "solutions for a small planet." Notably, these examples are from business, the media, and technology—forces that have combined to give us an onslaught of everyday images about how small our world is and how easily traversed.

In *The Condition of Postmodernity,* geographer David Harvey claims that the history of capitalism has been characterized by this speed-up in the pace of life. Harvey explains that time-space compression forces us "to alter, sometimes in quite radical ways, how we represent the world to ourselves" (240), the consequences of which "have particular bearing on postmodern ways of thinking, feeling, and doing" (285). These postmodern effects have by now become quite familiar: a dominance of images, where the images themselves become more real than reality: "reality gets created rather than interpreted under conditions of stress and time-space compression" (306). We get the false sense of going somewhere when we log on and having been somewhere after we log off. Through the ability of technology to simulate travel, we think we're "experiencing" a different culture, otherness, or diversity, but we're not even leaving the comfortable (or crowded) confines of our homes or offices.

As technology and capitalism have combined to make time-space compression more common and familiar, one alarming result has been the idea that space is negligible or transparent. This consequence is related to what Jameson identifies as "a new kind of flatness or depthlessness, a new kind of superficiality, . . . perhaps the most supreme formal feature of all the postmodernisms" (9). As space flattens out, time becomes both harder to notice *and* more important; the masking of *time* through the changing boundaries for *space* has consequences for workers, students, women, for all of us. Time-space compression masks the politics of space by producing the illusion that, for example, electronic gadgets can overcome space and create more time. There are distinct dangers in believing that space does not matter, and a number of geographers or spatial theorists have named this threat *transparent space.*

Transparent Space

> Transparent space assumes that the world can be seen as it really is and that there can be unmediated access to the truth of objects it sees; it is a space of mimetic representation.
>
> Alison Blunt and Gillian Rose (5)

It is easy to take space and time for granted because they are such an obvious part of our everyday existence; they become routine because there doesn't seem to be anything we can do about them. However, it is important to challenge the idea of a single and objective sense of time or space, against which we attempt to measure the diversity of human conceptions and perceptions. Time-space compression leads us to believe that space is no big deal, that every divide is smaller than it seems, but feminist and other cultural geographers insist that divides are real, that differences are material and concrete, and that space cannot be treated as transparent or "innocent."

In *Space, Place, and Gender,* Doreen Massey explains that the "usual" explanation for time-space compression is internationalized capitalism, but that such an explanation is "insufficient" for women:

> The degree to which we can move between countries, or walk about the streets at night, or venture out of hotels in foreign cities, is not just influenced by 'capital'. Survey after survey has shown how women's mobility . . . is restricted—in a thousand different ways, from physical violence to being ogled at or made to feel quite simply 'out of place'—not by 'capital,' but by men. (147–48)

Time-space compression is a "high theory" concept that feminist geographers have tried to make more practical and more concerned with the everyday. As Elizabeth Wilson notes, feminists are more interested in policy issues related to space—women's safety, street lighting, or the dearth of public transport—than in theoretical or conceptual considerations (148). Massey and other feminist geographers are working towards notions of space as paradoxical, provisional, contradictory, fragmented. A notion of paradoxical spaces helps feminists to resist "transparent space," which is a particularly dangerous notion for women and other minorities because it denies differences or neglects the politics of space, especially in domestic or everyday environments. Documenting women's relationships to space has resulted in numerous studies of the home or neighborhoods—locales particularly important for women. Whether women find themselves in public space or private homes, real or imagined communities, they often experience those spaces as oppressive (Gillian Rose 143–50). Their experiences and emotions in domestic spaces are so geographically-rooted, they can vary with the floor plan—women can get angry in the kitchen, for example, but not in the bedroom (Blunt and Rose 2).

Even spaces presumed to be safe are often a threat to women. College campuses provide a good example of this image, especially as they are represented in typical media shots (especially recruitment or fundraising videos or photographs). The stately buildings, wide green lawns, and gatherings of people, presumably engaged in collegial exchanges, give the impression of harmonious intellectual activity in a tranquil environment. I spent four years on one of the most attractive college campuses ever to appear in a brochure, Miami University in Oxford, Ohio. The buildings match. Framed in buildings of southern Georgian architecture, red brick with large windows trimmed in the (exact) same shade of creamy yellow, the campus is famous for its gardens and landscaping. The serene appearance, however, masks the politics of space; for example, the numerous "keep off the grass" signs that dot the lush green lawns or the threat to women who dare to walk alone at night.

I began to think more about the politics of space after Jane Marcus visited Miami University and, struck by its wealth and privilege, spoke about the material conditions at her institution, City College, where instructors were lucky to have an office with a desk at all; forget about photocopying, a phone, chalk, or paper. If your walls weren't covered with graffiti and you had a chair, you were truly lucky. Then I read Jonathan Kozol's *Savage Inequalities* with an undergraduate course, a book which details the educational injustices done to students in cold, damp, dark classrooms, with falling plaster and trashy playgrounds. Place does matter; surroundings do have an effect on learning or attitudes towards learning, and material spaces have a political edge. In short, *where* writing instruction takes place has everything to do with *how.* When, for example, open admissions' policies went into effect, writing-center directors found themselves fighting for the most modest of spaces. Hard-won writing centers were often located in basements or tiny rooms, far from the heart of campus activity.

Some composition scholars *have* recognized issues of transparent space. In the February 1996 *CCC,* Ellen Cushman uses photographs and community history to show how "the Approach," a granite walkway leading up the hill to RPI in Troy, NY, illustrates "deeply rooted sociological distances" between the university and the community (8). The Approach is not simply a set of steps and pillars in disrepair—not transparent space—but a symbol of the wide gap between town and gown, a gap that is economic and political. Cushman's material analysis of a physical location resists the notion of transparent space. It is more typical in composition texts, however, to find notions of space that reach beyond the physical confines of classrooms or campuses, to think bigger and wider, to imagine frontiers, cities, and cyberspaces.

Imagined Geographies: Frontier, City, and Cyberspace

In what follows, I offer three extended examples of sites where time-space compression and transparent space have played out in the discourses of composition studies. While I hesitate to make the argument that time-space compression "causes" the creation of these imagined geographies, these three sites offer powerful examples of the social production of spaces in composition. In addition, their features and metaphors illustrate how material conditions can be ignored when a pioneering spirit takes hold.

The Frontier of Basic Writing

As composition workers struggled with the impact of open admissions and the demands of an expanding population, they faced working in crowded, inadequate building space populated by speakers and writers of many languages or dialects, few of them closely resembling traditional academic discourse. The feeling of "foreignness" and claustrophobia led to the construction, in discursive terms, of spaces where their struggles could be enacted. The only space big enough for such a struggle was a *frontier*.

From the first day of Open Admissions at City College, more space was needed for writing instruction. *The New York Times* reported in October of 1970 that tutoring was taking place in coat rooms while classes were being held in former ice skating rinks and supermarkets. At John Jay College, the square feet per student shrunk from 93 in 1969 to 31 the following year. "With lounge space scarce and college cafeterias jammed, many students study, do homework and eat their lunches sitting on corridor floors and stairways," and this crowding was reported in October, before the weather forced all students inside (Buder). Nearly everyone associated with the Open Admissions program has commented on the overcrowded conditions; Adrienne Rich's famous essay on "Teaching Language in Open Admissions" refers to the "overcrowded campus where in winter there is often no place to sit between classes" (60), and she gives another account to Jane Maher: "the overcrowding was acute. In the fall of 1970 we taught in open plywood cubicles set up in Great Hall [where] you could hear the noise from other cubicles; concentration was difficult for the students" (109).

The crowded and otherwise inadequate material conditions at City College led to composition's first imagined geography—and perhaps its most enduring spatial metaphor for arguing composition's legitimacy as a discipline. Mina Shaughnessy's *Errors and Expectations* opens with pointed attention to the local environment and to a very concrete physical space: she sits "alone in [a] worn urban classroom," reading with shock and dismay the folder of "alien" student essays (*vii*). The worn urban classroom, however, is soon replaced by a metaphoric location, larger and more romantic—the frontier: "the territory I am calling basic writing . . . is still very much of a frontier, unmapped, except for . . . a few blazed trails" (4). Instead of concentrating on the worn urban classroom as a site for the study of basic writing, Shaughnessy creates a guide for teachers "heading to [a] pedagogical West" (4). She admits the flaws of her map—"it is certain to have the shortcomings of other frontier maps, with doubtless a few rivers in the wrong place and some trails that end nowhere"—but what is important here is that she does not map the classroom, or the urban college spaces, or the city of New York (4). A concrete physical location, then, is erased by the more powerful American metaphor of the frontier.

Shaughnessy's early reviewers eagerly picked up on this frontier imagery because it allowed inexperienced, tentative, even resistant writing teachers to feel like brave, noble conquerors. Harvey Wiener, for example, describes Shaughnessy's book as the map, compass, and guide for those who dare to venture—or who would be sent—into the "jungle of trial and error" where teachers must "hack branches" through students' tortuous prose (715).

One way to read Shaughnessy's construction of the frontier metaphor is to see it romantically as desire for the open space of the frontier, in reaction to the crowded, chaotic conditions of City University in an Open Admissions system. Shaughnessy was, undoubtedly, surrounded by overwhelming needs and demands, and all of her biographers or reviewers connect her frontier imagery to her regional identity, formed in the Black Hills of South Dakota. For example, Janet Emig writes in her eulogy for Shaughnessy, "Mina could not be understood without understanding that she came from the West" (37). To read Shaughnessy's work through the lens of the Western motif is tempting not only because of her family roots in the West, but also because of the contrast provided by her move to New York City and her major life's work spent in crowded, urban classrooms. Imagining her homeland and her own identity as a strong prairie-dweller gave her a form of escape from the multiple and oppressive institutional structures of City College. In this version, sustaining her practical, perhaps even vocational, emphasis can be draining and frustrating because of the enormity of the task; thus, Shaughnessy looks to the West for energy and a sense of mission.

Others have interpreted Shaughnessy's frontier metaphor through the realities of her workload and the crowded material spaces of City College. Robert Lyons claims that "her frequent allusions to the pioneer role of basic writing teachers and to the 'frontier' experience of such work had more to do with her sense of taxing work loads than with nostalgia for her Western past" (175). Indeed, Shaughnessy worked herself to exhaustion, suffering a brief physical collapse in 1971 (Lyons 175). For teachers in the trenches, hard work defines their experience more accurately than large expanses of hope and possibility.

Metaphors of the frontier result from dominant ideologies of space, place, and landscape in the U.S.: the more the better; own as much as possible; keep trespassers off; if it looks uninhabited, it must be. Canonical in American studies, F. J. Turner's thesis, "The Significance of the Frontier in American History" (1893), claimed that pushing west into the frontier was the most defining aspect of the American spirit, that the social, political, and intellectual development of the U.S. can be traced along the line of Western expansion. Settling the frontier, according to Turner, reenacted the history of social evolution. Turner's thesis, along with more recent studies from literature and film, can help to explain the power of the frontier metaphor in composition studies. As critics have shown, Western films capture the harshness and supposed "emptiness" of the landscape. One cinematic shot of rock and desert puts into place "an entire code of values," especially the lure of "infinite access": "the openness of the space means that domination can take place" . . . . The blankness of the plain implies—without ever stating—that this is a field where a certain kind of mastery is possible" (Tompkins 74–75).

The frontier metaphor appears again and again in the literature of composition studies, often as a way of establishing or confirming composition's disciplinary status. Janice Lauer, for example, in an article which begins by asking, "Is this study a genuine discipline?" reinscribes Shaughnessy's frontier imagery. Lauer traces "the field's pioneer efforts" as it "staked out [the] territory [of writing] for investigation" (21). She characterizes composition's early theorists in "their willingness to take risks, to go beyond the boundaries of their traditional training into foreign domains" (21). According to Lauer, composition's "dappled" character as a discipline holds both advantages and risks: composition can be a "rich field of inquiry" or "a terrain of quicksand":

> The immensity of unexplored land presents a subtle seduction, drawing newcomers by promising not to relegate them to tiny plots in which to work out the arcane implications of already established scholarship. But once committed, some individuals have difficulty finding entries or end up losing their way because the role of pathfinder is challenging and thus ill-suited to everyone. The field's largely unmapped territory, therefore, has rewarded some handsomely but been fatal to others. (25)

To construct composition as a risky venture, not for the fainthearted, as Lauer does, gives composition studies a tough image: if only the fittest can survive, then it must be worthy of the status of a discipline. Joseph Harris has argued that Shaughnessy mistakenly assumed the frontier of basic writing was unoccupied, and the frontier metaphor has problematic colonialist echoes that are fairly obvious (79). Harris also makes the case that the frontier metaphor is actually quite innocuous; it gave teachers of literature a dose of missionary zeal about teaching writing to underprepared students, but also allowed them to imagine that they were not changing but simply extending the reach of the curriculum (80). Naming basic writing a frontier served to mask the politics of space—the real material conditions that crowded students into classrooms with overworked and underpaid teachers.

The frontier metaphor endures because composition's professional development was dependent on sounding "new," bold, untamed and exciting without really changing the politics of space at all. Frontier was an important imaginary space for the early days of open admissions because it seemed to invite "vision," hope, and wide expanses of possibility, but the frontier metaphor was also a reaction against the overwhelming work and responsibility that went along with educating larger, more diverse populations of college writers. Composition's development and growth meant changes in its imagined geographies, and after a brief investment in the geography of "community," composition needed a more powerful and diverse space in which to imagine its work, subjects, and practices—the *city*.

Composition as City: Postmodern and Rhetorical Spaces

As composition grew and developed, different settlements sprang up all across the wide frontier, communities characterized by differences in philosophy, political allegiances, or research methods. Acknowledgment of the diverse communities within composition was one way of demonstrating its legitimacy, but the appeal of the community metaphor soon wore thin, replaced by evocations of the city. Naming composition a city marks a moment of maturity in its history, but there are consequences to any imagined geography, and the politics of space can be either illuminated or disguised by images of the modern city.

As a second generation imagined geography, "community" offered tremendous rhetorical power. As Joseph Harris explicates, the metaphor of community is "both seductive and powerful" and "makes a claim on us that is hard to resist" (99). However, like the notion of frontier, community too often assumed transparent space—where there are clear insiders or outsiders; where differences may not be so welcomed or encouraged; or where the goal of consensus silences productive dissensus (Trimbur 608–10).

Composition scholars were quick to recognize that a warm, fuzzy notion of composition—where like-minded peoples cooperate harmoniously—would not serve the diverse populations of composition dwellers. If the frontier metaphor characterized composition as a tough field, community sounded too "wimpy," and composition continued to need authority or legitimacy within the academy. "Community" was also not geographically loaded enough to be appealing and enduring, not in the ways that frontier and city are geographically expansive and symbolically romantic. In other words, community did not last long as an imagined geography in composition because its spaces were just too limited. An imagined geography big enough to hold composition's ambitions was that of the city. Cities offer diversity of peoples and places, models of cooperation, more sites for public gathering, and more feelings of exhilaration, sometimes a keen sense of "survival of the fittest." A city metaphor seems richer and more exciting; the bustle of a city implies that work is getting done.

Seeing composition as a city also invokes the places where rhetoric flourishes—the agora, marketplace, theater, or coffeehouse. The city, therefore, offers at least two ideologies or dominant sets of images and metaphors: 1) city as an embodiment of postmodernism; 2) city as a reflection of democratic ideals. The material conditions of the city are more "in your face" than those of the frontier, which assumes a blank plain; the politics of space, therefore, seem more obvious in the city or less difficult to identify. Still, notions of the city differ ideologically, and too many views of the city glamorize its appeal.

Contemporary geographers often turn to the city to illustrate their claims about postmodernism. Edward Soja reads Los Angeles as the perfect example of "the dynamics of capitalist spatialization"; LA is *the* capitalist city (191). One view of the city emphasizes simultaneous stimulation and terror, where postmodern subjects feel most keenly a kind of 21st-century panic: the fear of being crowded; that all the space is being taken up; that the planet is overpopulated and toxic. Simultaneously, however, caught between contradictory desires, we also want the excitement and exhilaration of a city. The goal of postmodern city life is not to achieve stable orientation, but to accept disorientation as a way of life.

To invoke a city is, on one hand, to identify composition with postmodernism since crowded urban streets, like busy visual images, are more postmodern. On the other hand, unlike postmodern geographers, Harris and Lester Faigley want to claim the democratic, rhetorical, or public images of the city; for example, the idea that cities revolve around a center (Soja 234–35). In contrast to the frontier, cities have a central location, a "polis," or a "heart" (as in "in the heart of the city"). Thus, the city seems a more appropriate, more invigorating site for the exchange of ideas: there is a central place to meet, an especially appealing notion for rhetorical scholars interested in the gathering places of ancient cultures and in public spheres for communication.[4]

The city seems a more sophisticated image for composition's maturity than that of the frontier because it invites a more paradoxical notion of space and represents a different kind of work. Composition as a city invites more diversity because many different activities can go on simultaneously and, following the logic of traffic lights, no one will cause accidents or pileups; everyone cooperates. To navigate a city requires more experience, skill, or wits than to navigate a small community, and the alienation or anonymity are outweighed by the opportunities or stimulation. The frontier signifies the hard physical labor of sod-busting and planting and harvesting, with a landscape of plains or rolling hills, capped by big skies. The city holds bolder or more complicated signifiers, but corporate work images come to mind: high-rise office buildings, with photocopiers and air conditioning and water coolers, where the politics of space are both enhanced and complicated by modern architecture and technologies.

In representing the city as a place of either postmodern exhilaration or democratic participation, scholars and theorists may be glamorizing the city and overlooking some of the material realities—the same problem that exists with the frontier metaphor. Visitors to cities almost never see the ghettos, for example, and tourists are herded—through promotional materials, transportation routes, and hotel locations—to the most attractive sites. In addition, time-space compression works to make city-dwellers believe that technologies to shrink space have actually resulted in more time. As most commuters will attest, however, "having more time" is not exactly their experience. As cultural geographer Peter Jackson points out, ideologies of city and frontier do not differ all that much: "frontier ideologies are extraordinarily persistent even in the contemporary city, where they reappear as ideologies of 'pioneering' or 'homesteading' in the urban 'wilderness'" (111). Thus, Turner's thesis is once again reinforced—that the pioneering spirit is deeply American, and that American ideologies celebrate pioneering myths.

While the appeal of frontier turns on the American fantasies of space and place (that it is endless; the more the better; that space can be mastered), the appeal of the city turns on busy visual images, heightened adrenaline, movement, and a desire for public space or mutual co-existence with others. As Shaughnessy found out, however, work in the city was just as hard and taxing. Both of these appeals are present in a potent geographic site—*cyberspace*. Cyberspace is an imagined geography where visitors or homesteaders can be simultaneously stimulated and terrified, where order and disorder co-exist, and where the frontier metaphor continues its hold over our collective imagination. Cyberspace and its attendant electronic technologies also offer the most representative example of time-space compression, where space seems to shrink as time seems to expand.

Cyberspace and the New Frontier

> Space is not a scientific object removed from ideology and politics; it has always been political and strategic.
>
> Henri Lefebvre (qtd. in Soja 80)

As electronic writing technologies radicalize the work of our field once again, with an impact probably as large as that of Open Admissions, the pattern repeats itself: in the face of some confusion and an overwhelming sense of responsibility, the frontier beckons. It is tempting to call cyberspace "the new frontier" because it offers a sense of excitement and possibility in the face of otherwise frightening changes, and those influences combine to make cyberspace the latest imagined geography.

The frontier metaphor served well during the Kennedy Administration to justify the space program; now the frontier extends beyond space, into new imaginary territory called cyberspace. Without NASA-level technology and equipment—with only a PC and Internet access—"anyone" can go there, making it far more accessible. It is not difficult to illustrate the dominance of the frontier metaphor in discourses of electronic technologies. A core course in the telecommunications MA at George Mason University is titled "Taming the Electronic Frontier" (Cox). The Electronic Frontier Foundation lobbies to stop legislation limiting the freedom of computer users. Howard Rheingold's *The Virtual Community: Homesteading on the Electronic Frontier* addresses the idea of domesticating space—making a home in unfamiliar territory, staking a claim, naming it ours. Even the moral code of the frontier is reproduced: "The Internet has been like the Wild West before law and order was brought to it" (Vitanza 133). When two hackers meet in the OK corral for a shoot-out, the good guy usually wins (Markoff 121).

Composition, like Star Trek and NASA, is so completely "American," as the Muchiri essay argues, that the temptation to claim a new final frontier is strong and appealing. Despite the attractiveness of naming cyberspace a new frontier, cyberspace is not transparent space, as several scholars have recognized. Emily Jessup says it quite succinctly: "The land of computing is a frontier country, and, as in the development of most frontier countries, there are many more men than women" (336). Women and other disenfranchised groups will have to follow the maps, tracks, and instructional manuals written by the techies, mostly men who got to the colony first. Concerns of colonialism have been addressed by invoking democracy—claims that cyberspace offers more opportunities for voices to be heard, that "anyone" can participate. This view has its critics, too; for example, Mark Poster claims that promotions of Internet news groups and other virtual communities as "nascent public spheres that well renew democracy" are "fundamentally misguided" because they "overlook the profound differences between Internet 'cafes' and the agoras of the past" (135). Cyberspace is not transparent space, and dominant sexual-social politics are reproduced on the Net (Tannen, Bruckman): crimes have been committed in MUDs and MOOs, with rape and death in "the Bungle case" on Lambdamoo (Dibbell).

Granted, much about cyberspace is hugely inviting: chat rooms and emoticons and a "web" of access to information (and to "community"). The notion of the web, familiar to composition through both Janet Emig and Marilyn Cooper, touches on ecological metaphors that many writing teachers found more inviting than other mechanistic metaphors for the writing process. The World Wide Web has the same inviting ecological tenor, and the implication is that strands seem to connect the whole world, stretching across and enveloping many sites. At odds with these "warm and fuzzy" notions of the WWW are some material realities: the whole world is *not* in the Web. Issues of access aside, the metaphor of a web also evokes entrapment. Webs, as any fly knows, can be sticky traps for the negligent or gullible; not all of us are safe in a web. A web has thousands, if not millions, of intersecting strands. What I want to know is, how do I get around in here? And how do I get out when I want to leave? (If it weren't for the "Back" and "Home" icons on the newer Web browsers, I would still be lost in cyberspace!)

A lot of Net users find it hard to leave—not only from confusion but from a sense that virtual spaces are more inviting or attractive. When they devote themselves to screens and keyboards, online participants are removing their actual bodies from physical spaces, and that creates another set of problems for geopolitics. As Stephen Doheny-Farina argues in *The Wired Neighborhood,* participation in online communities removes people from their geophysical communities—the streets and schools, sidewalks and shops that make up a neighborhood. People have understandably turned to virtual communities to fulfill some of their needs not being met by physical communities, but Doheny-Farina critiques claims that the Internet's chat rooms are new public spaces. Admitting his own fascination with MediaMOO, in one chapter, Doheny-Farina shows how the supposedly public spaces are more accurately a maze of private rooms, where one's participation ("socialization") is dependent upon one's technical expertise, including one's skill as a typist (61). Settling upon the analogy of virtual communities being like airport bars, Doheny-Farina admits to the compelling nature of these online enterprises, but repeatedly notes the seduction, even the danger, of ignoring the politics of space in our daily environments.

While I am no expert on computers and writing or electronic technologies, my lack of expertise is precisely the point: Most people aren't, and we are the ones entering frontierland well behind the first settlers. The material spaces have changed but the challenges and responsibilities have not. Much as Shaughnessy sat in her worn urban classroom wondering how to help her stunningly unskilled students through the tangle of academic discourse, I sit in a new, well-equipped computer classroom and wonder how I can guide my students through the maze of electronic writing technologies—or if I should turn my composition classes into Computer Literacy 101, Advanced Word Processing, or Introduction to the Internet. Our field is beginning to feel very keenly the responsibility for educating students about electronic writing technologies, and that creates a new level of anxiety (and stimulation) akin to city life. From my experience at a fairly large state university in the Northeast, most of my first-year students are not computer-literate or computer-comfortable. Their high schools in this and surrounding states did not exactly pass out laptops as students walked through the security terminals. Most literacy workers are more affected by budget constraints than by a technology explosion, so expectations to educate students in electronic discourses and computer technologies—while also helping them to think more critically, write more fluently and persuasively, and edit more carefully—becomes an overwhelming responsibility.

The frontier, city, and cyberspace are three imagined geographies that illustrate how composition's socially-produced spaces have served to give composition vision and a sense of mission but have also served to mask the politics of space. In the concluding section below, I want to turn to more unfamiliar material places that need our attention, especially in their implications for workers and working conditions.

Between Spaces and Practices: Geographic Possibilities for Studying Composition

As this section suggests, time-space compression affects composition's workers on a daily basis, in concrete ways that need our attention. A spatial politics of writing instruction works to deny transparent space and to attend to neglected places, in their material rather than their imaginary forms, where writers and writing teachers work, live, talk, daydream, or doodle. I'm particularly interested in the increased demands on *time* because technologies have shifted *space*, along with the ways in which technology has increased responsibilities and workloads while material spaces for writing instruction continue to crowd or deteriorate. Composition needs to develop ways to study space differently that might close the gap between imagined geographies and material conditions for writing, between the spaces and practices or that might confront the way that time-space compression creates illusions about "more time" and "overcoming" spatial barriers.

First, instead of thinking bigger and wider, as composition has typically done—using large imagined geographies to situate and validate composition studies as a discipline—now it is time to think smaller and more locally. And while there have been plenty of studies of classrooms or writing centers or writing programs, a geographic emphasis would insist on more attention to the connection between spaces and practices, more effort to link the material conditions to the activities of particular spaces, whether those be campuses, classrooms, office, computer labs, distance-learning sites, or hotels.

The material spaces of campuses, schoolyards, and classrooms across the country—especially those in economically-devastated areas—are marked by ceiling tiles falling onto unswept floors, in rooms with graffiti, trash, and no chalk, or no chalkboard. Classrooms are crowded and too hot or too cold, or with badly filtered air. Certain buildings on many campuses are said to be "poison," where a disproportionate number of illnesses develop, including cancer.[5] To neglect these material realities in qualitative studies of writing instruction is to ignore the politics of space, the ways in which our surroundings or location affect the work that is done there. In research studies of all types, there is scant attention to the conditions and context affecting participants and researchers alike: the weather, the room, the amount or quality of space.

To illustrate, the teaching assistant offices at my institution are referred to, variously, as the pit, the rat's nest, or the hole, where the walls are paper-thin dividers; where there's only one phone for roughly 24 instructors; and where occupants last winter had to dodge buckets and trash cans strategically placed to catch rain leaks and falling plaster. Any outsider would immediately recognize the status of the teaching assistants based only on the appearance of their office space. Moving beyond a "thick description," a qualitative study of this space would have to account, in the fullest possible ways, for the material conditions of this office which have everything to do with the work that gets done there. Even newcomers to the academy recognize that the larger or nicer the office, the more senior its occupant, and they don't need a member of a space allocation committee to tell them that.

Perhaps more important than a spatial-politics approach to qualitative research, understanding more about how time-space compression works would enable us to both acknowledge and address working conditions in writing instruction, an issue of the 1990s that will not go away in the new century. Time-space compression creates the illusion that we have "shrunk" space or overcome wide distances; with such a notion comes the conclusion that without travel time, workers can produce more. The capitalist equation—less space equals more time—makes issues of worker exploitation even more complicated for writing instruction.

Issues of working conditions are near the top of the agendas of our professional organizations, with CCCC and MLA having passed or considering resolutions committed to the improvement of the status of non-tenure track faculty in composition studies. Given the complexity of trying to make any concrete or measurable changes, it seems that one way to improve the status of non-tenure-track faculty in composition is to examine closely the spaces in which we ask them to work, the conditions of those spaces, and the assumptions about time and space that control workers' daily environments.

With laptop computers, around-the-clock access, and the option of asynchronous dialogue, the idea that workers can be productive from "anywhere" at "any time" permeates our culture. Composition workers are just now beginning to recognize how new technologies have affected our workdays, as this passage illustrates:

> In theory, email should create more time. But even though readers can chug along at their own paces, individual paces may not always be in sync. . . . [In participating in Portnet, an online discussion], I was desperate for time. Because of my teaching and professional schedule, my email communication had to wait until evening—late evening. My commitment to Portnet faltered somewhat the first time I turned on my computer at eleven o'clock p.m. and discovered more than forty Portnet messages waiting for me. The next night over eighty Portnet messages appeared on the screen. . . . between . . . more than twenty posts from my students . . . and another ten from local colleagues on various matters (Dickson, qtd. in Allen et al. 377).

Questions about working conditions multiply, too, when considering the impact of distance-learning, the latest rage in the competitive world of higher education, especially in areas of the west and Midwest where towns and cities are far apart. Questions should arise for composition programs about how distance-learning changes our ideas about writing instruction and our common practices involving, as just one example, peer response groups (that is, f2f meetings between writers). What happens to classrooms, libraries, "memorial unions," or lecture halls, especially on some already-deteriorating campuses, many built on the cheap in the late 1960s and early 70s? Should colleges invest more in electronic technologies than in buildings that invite gatherings? Some colleges, in an effort to combine community outreach, distance learning, and keen competitiveness, have all but eliminated central campuses. For example, Rio Salado Community College in Tempe, Arizona, "has no campus and educates 34,000 students in places like churches and shopping malls, and, increasingly, at home on their computers" (Applebome 24). What happens, then, to the geopolitical spaces of university campuses, especially in light of Doheny-Farina's concerns?

Despite the growing attention to new spaces for the work of our profession, the material sites for composition extend beyond offices, classrooms, computer labs, or cyberspaces. Many of the debates, discussions and conversations about writing instruction take place in hotels or on conference sites distinguished by huge buildings in the downtown areas of major cities, and these sites are especially prone to being treated as transparent space. With the growth of CCCC in the last 50 years, our meeting sites have had to expand and change to accommodate the growing numbers, and site selection for our annual meetings has become the most highly charged, time-consuming, and hotly-politicized issue of the CCCC Executive Committee in recent years.

First, on a very practical level, CCCC's annual meeting, held in the spring months of every year, requires 35 contiguous meeting rooms and 1,500 sleeping rooms for a four-day gathering of over 3,000 members. Those numbers and needs alone make it difficult to find cities that can serve our membership, and the equation is complicated by the desire to represent fairly or sensitively every diverse constituency within CCCC—to attend to a complicated variety of geographic, economic, and political concerns. While the effort to rotate the locations by region has been in place for years, increasing efforts to accommodate political concerns have made the process of site selection fraught with difficult decisions about "whose" interests count more or which cities have the least offensive laws or statutes. An inept process of site selection was finally challenged after the Executive Committee decided to go to Atlanta for the 1999 convention. Some members of the Gay and Lesbian Caucus announced, in response, that they would boycott that convention, citing in particular their exclusion from the process of selecting convention cities. Since then, the CCCC Officers and Executive Committee have worked to institutionalize the voices and concerns of various caucuses within the organization, making communication across the membership a more integral part of the site selection process (culminating in a recently named "Convention Concerns Committee").

What does it matter where we meet? First, convention sites are tangible examples of the politics of space in composition—where discourses, practices, and people meet in a geopolitical space—and convention hotels and cities also represent some of the neglected places where the work of writing instruction is impacted by geophysical factors. Second, beyond the large concerns about the personal safety of CCCC members, there are many small material realities that affect many things about the success of a conference site. For example, when we are occupied with transportation woes, the cost of a meal in a hotel, or the lack of women's bathroom stalls, time and energy are taken away from conversation about writing, about students, about our programs and ideas. When hotels don't have a central meeting place, or the main lobby is hard to find, or the levels are oddly numbered, members waste time finding each other and sacrifice time talking or listening or engaging.

Imagined geographies have served their purpose in composition's identity-formation and will continue to shape a sense of vision and possibility for writing teachers and researchers. However, the imaginary visions must be more firmly grounded in material conditions: traveling through cyberspace, for example, does require hardware and software, and meeting in hotels does mean that workers must serve and clean up after us.

A spatial politics of writing instruction would not call for a new frontier but for a more paradoxical sense of space to inform our research and practices and to approach the study of the social production of spaces in a field already committed to examining the production of discourse. Most importantly, a spatial politics of writing instruction would resist notions of transparent space that deny the connections to material conditions and would account for the various ways in which time-space compression affects composition's workers.

Acknowledgments

Thanks to those who read, responded, and made me think harder: Kristen Kennedy, Arthur Riss, Nancy Cook, and the two *CCC* reviewers, John Trimbur and Gregory Clark.

Notes

1. Many of the geographers I have been reading have been influenced by Henri Lefebvre and by Foucault's later writings, particularly "Questions on Geography" and "Of Other Spaces." Michel de Certeau's *The Practice of Everyday Life* has been tremendously helpful in thinking about the rhetoric of negotiating space (see esp. "Walking in the City" 91–110) and the connection between spaces and practices. Feminist geographers draw from a range of landscape studies, women's travel writing, and colonialist theories, and urban geographers are likely to frame their work with postmodernist architecture; the fascination with Los Angeles is particularly striking (Jameson; Soja; Harvey). My turn to geography is one response to John Schilb's challenge to rhetoricians: that we should be explaining and illustrating postmodernism for those who cannot (or will not) read Fredric Jameson. In an RSA presentation in May, 1994, Schilb demonstrated this claim through a reading of a Clint Eastwood film, set at the Hotel Bonaventure in Los Angeles.

2. Composition scholarship is increasingly interested in spatial theories and the importance of locations. A quick review of the program for the 1998 CCCC Annual Convention program yields at least a dozen panel or forum titles with such keywords as space, place, landscapes, the politics of space, the public sphere, postmodern geography, or travel. See also Gregory Clark's 1998 *CCC* essay, "Writing as Travel, or Rhetoric on the Road."

3. For example, a 1988 Gallup survey showed that 75% of Americans age 18–24 couldn't locate the Persian Gulf on a world map and 25% couldn't find the Pacific Ocean (Horwitz A8).

4. Most recently, Harris has offered *public* as a better keyword than community. See *A Teaching Subject,* pp. 107–10.

5. The campus building I work in is just plain filthy, one result of severe budget cuts, and the conditions do affect the morale of workers. The state of the bathroom, while it may "bond" the women on my floor, does not exactly promote worker loyalty or productivity.

Works Cited

Allen, Michael, et al. "Portfolios, WAC, Email, and Assessment: An Inquiry on Portnet." *Situating Portfolios*. Ed. Kathleen Blake Yancey and Irwin Weiser. Logan: Utah State UP, 1997. 370–84.

Anson, Chris. "Assigning and Responding to Student Writing." Colgate U, Hamilton, NY, August 1995.

Anzaldúa, Gloria. *Borderlands/La Frontera.* San Francisco: Aunt Lute, 1987.

Applebome, Peter. "Community Colleges At the Crossroads: Which Way Is Up?" *New York Times* 3 August 1997: 4A; 24–26; 30.

Blunt, Alison and Gillian Rose, eds. *Writing Women and Space: Colonial and Postcolonial Geographies.* NY: Guilford, 1994.

Bolter, Jay David. *Writing Space: The Computer, Hypertext, and the History of Writing.* Mahwah: Erlbaum, 1991.

Bowden, Darsie. "The Limits of Containment: Text-as-Container in Composition Studies." *College Composition and Communication* 44 (1993): 364–79.

Bruckman, Amy S. "Gender Swapping on the Internet." Vitanza. 441–47.

Buder, Leonard. "Open-Admissions Policy Taxes City U. Resources." *The New York Times* October 12, 1970: A1 +.

Certeau, Michel de. *The Practice of Everyday Life.* Berkeley: U of California P, 1984.

Clark, Gregory. "Writing as Travel, or Rhetoric on the Road." *College Composition and Communication* 49 (1998): 9–23.

Cooper, Marilyn M. "The Ecology of Writing." *College English* 48 (1986): 364–75.

Cox, Brad. "Taming the Electronic Frontier." http.//gopher.gmu.edu/ bcox/ LRN6372/ 00LRNG572.html.

Cushman, Ellen. "Rhetorician as Agent of Social Change." *College Composition and Communication* 47 (1996): 7–28.

Dibbell, Julian. "A Rape in Cyberspace." Vitanza. 448–65.

Doheny-Farina, Stephen. *The Wired Neighborhood.* New Haven: Yale UP, 1996.

Emig, Janet. "Mina Pendo Shaughnessy." *College Composition and Communication* 30 (1979): 37–8.

Faigley, Lester. *Fragments of Rationality: Postmodernity and the Subject of Composition.* U of Pittsburgh P, 1992.

Harris, Joseph. *A Teaching Subject: Composition Since 1966*. Upper Saddle River: Prentice, 1997.

Harvey, David. *The Condition of Postmodernity: An Enquiry into the Origins of Cultural Change*. Cambridge: Blackwell, 1989.

Hill, Carolyn Ericksen. *Writing From the Margins: Power and Pedagogy for Teachers of Composition*. New York: Oxford UP, 1990.

Hitt, Jack. "Atlas Shrugged: The New Face of Maps." *Lingua Franca* 5.5 (1995): 24–33.

Horwitz, Sari. "No Longer a World Apart: Grant Brings Geography Home to District Students." *Washington Post* 19 March 19 1994: A1; A8.

Jackson, Peter. *Maps of Meaning: An Introduction to Cultural Geography*. New York: Routledge, 1989.

Jameson, Fredric. *Postmodernism, or, The Cultural Logic of Late Capitalism*. Durham: Duke UP, 1991.

Jessup, Emily. "Feminism and Computers in Composition Instruction." *Evolving Perspectives on Computers and Composition Studies: Questions for the 1990s*. Ed. Gail E. Hawisher and Cynthia L. Selfe. Urbana: NCTE, 1991. 336–55.

Kozol, Jonathan. *Savage Inequalities: Children in America's Schools*. New York: Crown, 1991.

Lauer, Janice M. "Composition Studies: A Dappled Discipline." *Rhetoric Review* 3 (1984): 20–29.

Lyons, Robert. "Mina Shaughnessy." *Traditions of Inquiry*. Ed. John Brereton. New York: Oxford UP, 1985. 171–89.

Maher, Jane. *Mina P. Shaughnessy: Her Life and Work*. Urbana: NCTE, 1997.

Markoff, John. "Hacker and Grifter Duel on the Net." Vitanza. 119–21.

Massey, Doreen. *Space, Place, and Gender*. Minneapolis: U of Minnesota P, 1994.

Miller, Susan. *Textual Carnivals: The Politics of Composition*. Southern Illinois UP, 1991.

Muchiri, Mary N., Nshindi G. Mulamba, Greg Myers, and Deoscorous B. Ndoloi. "Importing Composition: Teaching and Researching Academic Writing Beyond North America." *College Composition and Communication* 46 (1995): 175–98.

Nash, Catherine. "Remapping the Body/ Land: New Cartographies of Identity, Gender, and Landscape in Ireland." *Writing Women and Space: Colonial and Postcolonial Geographies.* Ed. Alison Blunt and Gillian Rose. 227–50.

Neel, Jasper. "The Degradation of Rhetoric; Or, Dressing Like a Gentleman, Speaking Like a Scholar." *Rhetoric, Sophistry, Pragmatism.* Ed. Steven Mailloux. New York: Cambridge UP, 1995. 61–81.

North, Stephen M. *The Making of Knowledge in Composition: Portrait of an Emerging Field.* Upper Montclair: Boynton, 1987.

Phelps, Louise Wetherbee. "The Domain of Composition." *Rhetoric Review* 4 (1986): 182–95.

Poster, Mark. "The Net as a Public Sphere?" *Wired* Nov. 1995: 135–36.

Pratt, Mary Louise. "Arts of the Contact Zone." *Profession 91* (1991): 33–40.

"Redoubling the Efforts at Teaching Geography." *New York Times.* 19 Nov. 1993: C, 11:1.

Rheingold, Howard. *The Virtual Community: Homesteading on the Electronic Frontier.* New York: Harper, 1993.

Rich, Adrienne. "Teaching Language in Open Admissions." *On Lies, Secrets, and Silence: Selected Prose 1966–1978.* NY: Norton, 1979. 51–68.

Rose, Gillian. *Feminism and Geography: The Limits of Geographical Knowledge.* Minneapolis: U of Minnesota P, 1993.

Rose, Mike. *Lives on the Boundary.* New York: Free P, 1989.

Schilb, John. "Articulating the Discourses of Postmodernism." Rhetoric Society of America, Norfolk, VA, May 1994.

Selfe, Cynthia and Richard J. Selfe, Jr. "The Politics of the Interface: Power and its Exercise in Electronic Contact Zones." *College Composition and Communication* 45 (1994): 480–504.

Shaughnessy, Mina. *Errors and Expectations.* New York: Oxford UP, 1977.

Slagle, Diane Buckles, and Shirley K. Rose, "Domesticating English Studies." *Journal of Teaching Writing* 13 (1994): 147–68.

Soja, Edward W. *Postmodern Geographies: The Reassertion of Space in Critical Social Theory.* New York: Verso, 1989.

Tannen, Deborah. "Gender Gap in Cyberspace." Vitanza 141–43.

"Teachers Lament Geography Scores." *New York Times.* 12 March, 1985: III, 11:1.

Tompkins, Jane. *West of Everything: The Inner Life of Westerns.* New York: Oxford UP, 1992.

Trimbur, John. "Consensus and Difference in Collaborative Learning." *College English* 51 (1989): 602–16.

Turner, Frederick Jackson. "The Significance of the Frontier in American History (1893)." *History, Frontier, and Section.* Albuquerque: U of New Mexico P, 1993. 59–91.

Vitanza, Victor, ed. *CyberReader.* Boston: Allyn, 1996.

Wiener, Harvey S. Rev. of *Errors and Expectations,* by Mina P. Shaughnessy. *College English* 38 (1977): 715–17.

Wilson, Elizabeth. "The Rhetoric of Urban Space." *New Left Review* 209 (1995): 146–60.

CHAPTER ELEVEN

Breaking Ground in Ecocomposition: Exploring Relationships between Discourse and Environment

SIDNEY I. DOBRIN AND CHRISTIAN R. WEISSER

> *By looking at writing ecologically we understand better how important writing is—and just how hard it is to teach.*
>
> MARILYN COOPER

> *Nothing goes by luck in composition. [. . .] Every sentence is the result of long probation.*
>
> HENRY DAVID THOREAU

In the last twenty-five years, theorists and researchers in the social sciences and humanities have embraced the systematic exploration of social relations and culture as integral to the study of the construction of knowledge. Likewise, in composition studies, the social dimensions of language have dominated scholarly conversations concerning the construction of knowledge. In the 1970s and 1980s many composition theorists and researchers began to focus on the social nature of writing and to suggest that the correlation between social experience and writing ability is palpable. This orientation had widespread implications for com-

From *College English* 64 (2002): 566–89.

position theory, and brought with it, for example, new ways of thinking about an individual's identity (very often, the student in a writing class) and how identity is manifested through writing and speaking. As Christian Weisser has suggested in "Ecocomposition and the Greening of Identity," social constructionist approaches to composition "expanded the way we thought of identity, asserting that it emerges not just from the internal processes of the individual, but also from a wider variety of influences: the social conventions we share with other human beings" (5).

Within the past decade, compositionists have focused much of their attention post-process toward the critical categories of race, gender, class, and culture. These beneficial inquiries have aided in continually redefining ways in which language affects human thought and identity. But within the past few years, some compositionists have begun to include place and environment as other critical categories in this inquiry, recognizing the importance of ecological approaches to composition. They have begun to assert that identity—and how it is manifested through discourse—is shaped by more than social conventions and is also influenced by our relationships with particular locations and environments. The inclusion of ecological and environmental perspectives in composition theory, we argue, is essential to the discipline's continued growth and development. Yet, with very limited exceptions, until the late 1990s compositionists have been wary of addressing issues of ecology, environment, place, location, and habitat. We hope to promote recognition of the importance of the intersections between discourse, place, and environment through theoretical examinations and pedagogical approaches and to explain how and why composition's roots do indeed tap into ecological sciences in their current incarnations, to show how the two massive cultural projects of composition studies and ecology might inform each other, and to identify how composition studies is very much an ecological inquiry. As we offer some preliminary definitions of the emerging subdiscipline of *ecocomposition*, we also issue a call to English studies to embrace this vital new field of inquiry. In the pages that follow, we not only offer some preliminary working definitions for ecocomposition, but we also examine the evolution of ecocomposition, distinguish between ecocomposition and ecocriticism, and offer some perspectives on ecocomposition pedagogy.

The Growth of the Field

At the 1999 convention of the Conference on College Composition and Communication in Chicago, a single roundtable specifically addressed issues of importance to ecocomposition (although a few others used the term "ecology" in their titles). "Ecology and Composition: Toward a Dialogics of Place" both initiated a public conversation directed toward ecocomposition and called for the formation of ASLE-CCCC, a special interest group supported by the Association for the Study of Literature and Environment. The following year, ASLE-CCCC held its first meeting, at which a large number of composition scholars and teachers voiced their enthusiasm for the development of ecocomposition. At the 2000 CCCC, more than half a dozen ecocomposition-related panels appeared on the program. In the course of this same three-year period, Utah State University Press, the State University of New York Press, and NCTE began to review and publish new books devoted to ecocomposition research and scholarship. The Association for Study of Literature and Environment also recognized the growing importance of ecocomposition in English studies, inviting two ecocomposition scholars (Sid Dobrin and Derek Owens) to serve as plenary speakers at their 2001 conference.

Although ecocomposition has only recently begun to gain widespread recognition and endorsement within English studies, its roots go much deeper. The mid-1980s saw composition move from examining individual writers' cognitive processes to inquiries regarding the interactions between writers and the social forces that acted upon them and upon which they had effect. Marilyn Cooper, in support of this move post-process, contended that pedagogies that address social issues of writing "signal a growing awareness that language and texts are not simply the means by which individuals discover and communicate information, but are essentially social activities, dependent upon social structures and processes not only in their interpretive but also in their constructive phases" (5). Cooper's essay, "The Ecology of Writing," was central to the post-process move; in it, she proposes an ecological model of writing, "whose fundamental tenet is that writing is an activity through which a person is continuously engaged with a variety of socially constituted systems" (6). Cooper suggests that writing not be examined as an individual process, but as an entity reliant upon environment and, in turn, a force on that very environment. Most important to ecocompositionists has been Cooper's suggestion that "in place of the static and limited categories of contextual models, the ecological model postulates dynamic interlocking systems that structure the social activity of writing" (7). Although Cooper does not use the term *environment*, she identifies *systems* that affect and are affected by writers.

What is critical about Cooper's ecological model for compositionists is that it introduces composition to the notion that writers interact with systems that affect their writing. As Erika Lindemann explains in "Three Views of English 101," "[t]he ecological model usefully complicates the learning and teaching of writing because it reminds us of the social context in which all writers work" (296). Writers, in essence, are organisms dependent upon their surroundings—surroundings that are dynamic, difficult to define, and susceptible to the forces imposed by writers. As Cooper notes, ecological models are not simply new ways of saying "contextual" (6); context suggests that potential effects of *all* local systems can be identified through heuristics in order to provide writers with accurate and complete information prior to writing.

Likewise, Richard M. Coe, in "Defining Rhetoric—and Us: A Meditation on Burke's Definitions," also began to question the relationships between writers and surrounding environment. In his examination of how Burke defines humans as human, Coe specifically addresses the nature-culture split in order to examine how rhetoric and language have been used to define the human species as separate from nature, yet functioning in relationship to it. He writes, "we are removed from nature" (43). For Coe this is a critical point, since his argument is that Burke's definitions of what makes us human offer important lessons for compositionists, particularly as they attempt to study the role of language and culture. Coe turns to Burke in order to begin to develop an ecological methodology for exploring the ways in which discourse helps shape the very relationship among humans, culture, and nature. Coe's work, like Cooper's, initiates ecocomposition by introducing concepts of human discursive participation in larger systems, including those often labeled as "natural."

Although many ecocompositionists see Cooper's and Coe's work as foundational to ecocomposition, an equal number look to *ecocriticism* as their gateway to ecocomposition. Although the term was coined by William Rueckert in "Literature and Ecology: An Experiment in Ecocriticism," most American literary scholars were introduced to ecocriticism by Cheryl Glotfelty. At the Western Literature Association (WLA) meeting in 1989, Glotfelty urged the adoption of the term as a critical approach to studying nature writing. By 1994, the term was widely used, although most were still unsure of its exact definition. Since that time, many have tried to come to agreement as to what ecocriticism is. In the 1996 collection *The Ecocriticism Reader*, Glotfelty and Harold Fromm posit that "ecocriticism is the study of the relationship between literature and the physical environment. Just as feminist criticism examines language and literature from a gender-conscious perspective, and Marxist criticism brings an awareness of modes of production and economic class to its readings of texts, ecocentrism takes an earth-centered approach to literary studies" (xviii). Glotfelty and Fromm note that ecocritics ask a range of questions, such as "How is nature represented in this sonnet? What role does the physical setting play in the plot of this novel? Are the values expressed in this play consistent with ecological wisdom? How do our metaphors of the land influence the way we treat it? How can we characterize nature writing as a genre?" (xix). More theoretically, ecocritics might also ask "Do men write about nature differently than women do? In what ways has literacy itself affected humankind's relationship to the natural world?" (xix). Most important, however, ecocriticism provides two critical components to ecocomposition: first, the inquiry as to whether "in addition to race, class, and gender, [. . .] place [should] become a new critical category" (xix), and second, the notion that "all ecological criticism shares the fundamental premise that human culture is connected to the physical world, affecting it and affected by it" (xi).

Ecocriticism's importance and recognition have grown rapidly over the past few years, thanks to work by scholars such as Lawrence Buell, whose landmark 1995 book, *The Environmental Imagination: Thoreau, Nature Writing, and the Formation of American Culture,* is one of the most cited ecocritical works. Similarly, ecocritic Scott Slovic, editor of ASLE's organizational journal, *ISLE: Interdisciplinary Studies of Literature and Environment*, has produced groundbreaking scholarship in ecocriticism, notably his articles "Ecocriticism: Storytelling, Values, Communication, Contact" and "Nature Writing and Environmental Psychology: The Interiority of Outdoor Experience" and his books *Literature and the Environment: A Reader on Nature and Culture* (coedited with Lorraine Anderson and John P. O'Grady) and *Getting Over the Color Green: Contemporary Environmental Literature of the Southwest.* Jonathan Bate's *The Song of the Earth* and *The Green Studies Reader: From Romanticism to Ecocriticism* have also had great impact.

At about the time that ecocriticism emerged within literary studies, an equally compelling investigation emerged within rhetorical studies: the investigation of *environmental rhetoric.* Two texts, in particular, have aided in the development of ecological/environmental rhetoric: M. Jimmie Killingsworth and Jacqueline S. Palmer's *Ecospeak: Rhetoric and Environmental Politics in America* (1992) and Carl G. Herndl and Stuart C. Brown's *Green Culture: Environmental Rhetoric in Contemporary America* (1996). Both of these texts critically analyze the discourse through which environmental issues have been conveyed by addressing contemporary issues in environmental politics through the lens of rhetoric. Foregrounded in *Ecospeak* is the notion that "the environmental dilemma is a problem generated by the way people think and act in cultural units" (2–3). Killingsworth and Palmer contend that "[s]ince human thought and conduct are rarely, if ever, unmediated by language and other kinds of signs, it is understandable—possibly inevitable—that rhetorical scholars enter the environmental discussion through the gate of humanism" (3). Ecocompositionists have embraced the notion that human thought and conduct are (most likely) always mediated through language, and they identify such mediation as the source for the construction of nature, place, environment, and the conduct and behavior directed at those locations.

Similarly, Herndl and Brown contend that "there is no objective environment in the phenomenal world, no environment separate from the words we use to represent it. We can define the environment and how it is affected by our actions only through the language we have developed to talk about these issues" (3). This assessment of the discursive construction of environment is the cornerstone of many ecocompositionists' understanding of environment. For Herndl and Brown, access to understanding this construction in its various incarnations is provided by rhetorical analysis of particular conversations and debates. As the authors suggest, rhetoricians "study the ways people use language to construct knowledge and to do things in the world" (vii). The essays in *Green Culture* take as their task the study of the ways in which language is used to construct various environmental debates.

Although these three conversations do not encapsulate ecocomposition's history, they do highlight some of the important work that precedes ecocomposition's emergence in the late 1990s. Many other critical schools, including cultural studies, postcolonialism, and ecofeminism, have contributed and continue to contribute to this growing discipline through their pointed investigations of discourse and environment. Indeed, at ecocomposition's core is its interdisciplinarity; it draws upon and melds many perspectives, methodologies, and investigations from disciplines across the academic spectrum. While these diverse origins provide much of ecocomposition's energy, they also account for some of the healthy disagreement evident about its issues.

Several composition scholars have begun to bring together these issues under the rubric of ecocomposition. Four books in particular address ecocomposition theories and pedagogies: Randall Roorda's *Dramas of Solitude: Narratives of Retreat in American Nature Writing*, Derek Owens's *Composition and Sustainability: Teaching for a Threatened Generation*, and our collections *Ecocomposition: Theoretical and Pedagogical Approaches* and *Natural Discourse: Toward Ecocomposition*. In "Nature/Writing: Literature, Ecology and Composition," Roorda points out that he is "a peripheral figure: a compositionist specializing in nature writing" (401). Roorda goes on to explore the role of nature writing in composition studies, examining "those two loaded terms, 'nature' and 'writing'" (401). Foretelling his book *Dramas of Solitude*, part of Roorda's linking between nature and writing and nature writing is composition's long-held interest in literary nonfiction. For Roorda, nature writing is "the sort of writing—the essay especially, personal or informational—that a great number of us teachers exhort our students to produce, and so it behooves us to comprehend its operations" (402). *Dramas of Solitude* is not, at an initial glance, a book of either composition theory or composition pedagogy *per se,* but a book about American nature writing, one that would seem more at home on the shelves of literary critics than on those of compositionists. But as Roorda notes early in the book, as nature writing becomes a predominant area of literary studies, it also begins to show signs of having the potential to initiate large-scale change in, as he quotes famed nature writer Barry Lopez, "a reorganization of American political thought" (1–2). Nature writing's interdisciplinarity, political charge, and potential for initiating change, Roorda claims, make "the genre an object of interest to rhetoric and composition as well as to literary studies within English studies proper" (2). For Roorda, narratives of solitude—what he terms "retreat narratives"—exemplify specifically the kinds of literary works that provide student writers with access to ecological literacies as well as models for texts they might produce on their own.

Derek Owens's *Composition and Sustainability: Teaching for a Threatened Generation* extends the discussion beyond the composition classroom in an effort to explore ecological thinking in a broader pedagogical location—the entire university curriculum. Owens argues for "reconceptualizing composition studies as a workplace wherein educators might imagine a new kind of curriculum through the metaphor of sustainability" (3). He also appeals to educators not directly affiliated with composition studies to entertain the prospect of composing their disciplinary objectives through what he refers to as a "reconstructive consciousness" (3). In doing so, Owens calls into question the "limitations of disciplinary thinking and the academy's compartmentalization of knowledge-making" (3). For Owens, being a compositionist entails more than just teaching writing; he argues that compositionists are interested in the art of composing, of putting things together, of "combining, arranging, mixing, and assembling: constructing with words or images or sounds (or all three) in virtual or physical space" (2). Likewise, our *Ecocomposition: Theoretical and Pedagogical Approaches* and *Natural Discourse: Toward Ecocomposition* specifically address the role of ecological thinking in composition studies. The former was the first book to treat ecocomposition as a school of thought; the latter explores ecocomposition and its relationship to composition studies.

Breaking Ground

In an effort to establish a working definition of what ecocomposition comprises, we provide the following as a conceptual framework, a ground from which more fruitful, complex studies might emerge:

> Ecocomposition is the study of the relationships between environments (and by that we mean natural, constructed, and even imagined places) and discourse (speaking, writing, and thinking). Ecocomposition draws from disciplines that study discourse (primarily composition, but also including literary studies, communication, cultural studies, linguistics, and philosophy) and merges their perspectives with work in disciplines that examine environment (these include ecology, environmental studies, sociobiology, and other "hard" sciences). As a result, ecocomposition attempts to provide a holistic, encompassing framework for studies of the relationship between discourse and environment.

Etymologically *ecocomposition* reflects *ecology*, a science that evolved specifically to study the relationships between organisms and their surrounding environments. Ernst Haeckel first defined "oecologie" in 1866 as "the total relations of the animal both to its organic and to its inorganic environment" and as "the study of all the complex interrelationships referred to by Darwin as the conditions of the struggle for existence" (qtd. in Ricklefs 1).

Haeckel may as well have offered these words as the definition for contemporary composition studies. After all, composition studies in its post-cognitive, post-process, post-expressivist incarnation is also a study of relationships: relationships between individual writers and their surrounding environments, writers and texts, texts and culture, ideology and discourse, and language and the world. Much of the recent work in ecocomposition highlights the impact of the spaces in which discourse occurs, suggesting that most inquiries into these relationships do not fully account for the degree to which discourse is affected by the locations in which it originates and terminates. And, as we now discuss it, understanding these relationships is crucial to survival. Oppressive hegemonies manifest themselves in discourse; racial, cultural, sexist, classist oppression recurs through discourse. How we transgress those oppressive constructs, how we survive in them, is a matter of discursive maneuvering. To paraphrase Haeckel, as Dobrin has explained in "Writing Takes Place," ecocomposition is "the investigation of the total relations of discourse both to its organic and inorganic environment and the study of all of the complex interrelationships between the human activity of writing and all of the conditions of the struggle for existence" (12).

Ecocompositionists inquire as to what effects discourse has in mapping, constructing, shaping, defining, and understanding nature, place, and environment; and, in turn, what effects nature, place, and environment have on discourse. This includes *all* environments: classroom, political, electronic, ideological, historical, economic, natural. Ecocomposition can be understood as the examination of not only the relationships between discourse and "nature," but the relationships between discourse and any site where discourse exists. As Arlene Plevin writes, borrowing from Norman McLean, ecocomposition

> is more than smuggling in an essay about trees—or even discussing the powerful pull of students' favorite places. It is arguably a more radical move, one capable of continuing a postmodern teacher's desire to diffuse his or her authority—in decentering the classroom. It is a move which is able to reduce, even critically disrupt, the archetypal binaries of culture/nature, male/female, and even human/non-human. (148)

That is not to say, however, that ecocomposition *excludes* investigations of nature and discourse. Far from it; some of the most important work in ecocomposition to date has focused on the relationships among humans, nature, and language or text. Much of the recent work in ecocomposition seeks to engender a critical awareness of how discourse "creates" natural places and how all environments affect written discourse. As ecocompositionists, we disagree with ecocritic Harry Crockett, who "resist[s] the idea that reality is socially constructed." All reality, including nature, is discursively constructed. The environment is an idea that is created through discourse. We argue not that mountains, rivers, oceans, and the like do not actually exist, but that our only access to such things is through discourse, and that it is through language that we give these things or places particular meanings. For example, the Florida State Park system has adopted the motto "the Real Florida" to identify natural Florida as opposed to developed Florida. The "Real Florida" is advertised on highway billboards and tourist brochures as the last bastions of natural Florida. The naming of certain fenced-off areas as "real" stands directly in opposition to all areas outside those fences which are "man-made." Large sections of the Everglades, for instance, have been designated as nature preserves, and as such they are accorded special significance, with particular rules regarding how and when humans may interact with them. However, within just a few miles of many of these preserves, the land is interpreted as a commodity, and it is there that huge sugarcane fields, complete with sugar-processing plants, have been developed. There is (or was) no real distinction between the land within the preserves and the land that is used for sugar farming other than the distinctions that have been discursively accorded to them by humans. As evidenced by the many recent debates on land use in Florida, sugar farmers and preservationists have radically different definitions of what the Florida Everglades is or should be. In a sense, then, there is no objective environment separate from the words we use to represent it. Like Herndl and Brown, we argue that "the environment is not a thing you could go out and find in the world. Rather, it is a concept and an associated set of cultural values that we have constructed through the way we use language" (3).

However, ecocomposition addresses the current environmental crisis as a potentially catastrophic biospheric event that demands our consideration and action, identifying the ecological relationships between humans and surrounding environments as dependent and symbiotic. It recognizes the decline of nature both discursively and materially. Like theorists Tom Jagtenberg and David McKie, as ecocompositionists we acknowledge the whole spectrum of our nonhuman physical environment as "so central to sustainable life that it undermines the very idea of space and the biophysical world as a context for human activity" (xii). While discourse does indeed shape our human conceptions of the world around us, discourse itself arises from a biosphere that sustains life; while discourse "creates" the world in the human mind, the biospheric physical environment is the origin of life (and consequently, the human mind) itself. The relationship between discourse and environment is reciprocal and dialogic. Similarly, the diversity and richness of language reflect the diversity of the world in which such language arises. So, in effect, preserving natural places, ecosystems, and their denizens is a move that preserves the fullness, depth, and precision of our discourse. In a sense, humans occupy two spaces: a biosphere, consisting of the earth and its atmosphere, which supports our physical existence, and a semiosphere, consisting of discourse, which shapes our existence and allows us to make sense of it. These two central spheres of human life—the biosphere and the semiosphere—are mutually dependent upon each other. Whereas a healthy biosphere is one that supports a variety of symbiotic life forms, a healthy semiosphere is one that enables differences to coexist and be articulated. In both a material and a discursive sense, differences are a critical measure of a system's health.

Ecocomposition's emphasis on relationships is a multifaceted area of study that draws on many other areas of inquiry, including rhetoric and composition, feminism and ecofeminism, cultural studies, ecology, literary criticism, and environmentalism. Ecocomposition thus fractures as those working inside of its loose borders direct their attentions toward subspecialties and disagree with one another over theory, method, and teaching, as illustrated in the following categories.

Composition as Ecology

Just as ecocriticism and environmental rhetoric have been crucial in the evolution of ecocomposition, so too has composition theory played a primary role. One of the key notions that composition theory provides ecocomposition is the idea that all discursive construction creates, maintains, defines, and reinscribes the ways in which we perceive nature. As Stan Tag writes, "When we study the relationships between language and landscape, text and terrain, or words and woods, we are not studying two separate things (as if we lived in some dualistic universe), but interdependencies, particular manifestations (even processes) of the thing we call life, each interconnected to the other, and both wholly dependent upon such basic natural elements for their survival as sunlight, water, and air." For ecocompositionists this interconnectedness is crucial. Composition's theoretical moves post-process contribute greatly to our understanding of these relationships.

When cognitivists in composition began examining the processes by which individual students compose written text, this inquiry was undertaken with little regard for the sites in which writing takes place. That is, cognitive process understanding of writing offers few means of considering the effect environment has on those very processes. As composition moved away from cognitive models of writing, compositionists began to consider the implications external forces might have for writers, and in turn what effect writers have on those same external forces: gender, culture, race, class, ideology. As Gail Hawisher, Paul LeBlanc, Charles Moran, and Cynthia Selfe explain, "During the period of 1983–1985, composition studies absorbed the changes brought about by the new emphasis upon process and began to chart the course it would follow postprocess, looking beyond the individual writer toward the larger systems of which the writer was a part" (65). In essence, composition began an ecological approach to understanding discourse, seeing writers as contributing members of larger systems. However, even in composition's move post-process there was little actual recognition of environment beyond theoretical understandings of ideology and other constructed critical categories. Even Cooper's article emphasizes human communicative systems to the exclusion of nonhuman physical locations in which such discourse exists; the actual places where writing develops and occurs were not considered. Ecocomposition continues the post-process move to understand relationships between writers and larger systems by taking into consideration the role of environment, place, nature, and location in those larger systems, examining the relationships between discourse and place.

The link, then, to connect ecological thinking with composition is simply to revisit composition studies in an ecological light. Writers (or users of discourse) are the fundamental units operating within these systems. Writers manipulate environments by writing and finding ways for their writing to fit within systems. Writers' structures and functions are determined, not by genetics, but by knowledge and ideology, which function much as DNA does; ideology and culture map (if not control) our thinking and actions much as does a genetic code. A writer can no more easily escape the discourse community in which he or she operates than an animal or plant can escape its own particular ecosphere. Certainly both can adapt, often quite successfully, but that adaptation nearly always comes with great difficulty. Writers are, as ecocompositionists and social constructionists argue, also influenced by environment and, in turn, influence that same environment. That is, while ideology and culture map our thinking, our environments shape the application of that thinking. Much like the finches and tortoises in Darwin's theory of evolution, writers enter into particular environments with a certain ideological code and then contend with their environments as best those codes allow. These environments have material, social, and ideological qualities. As writers shift from one environment to another, they readjust their discourses to match. Much as in genetic evolution, writers display certain characteristics in their writing that are determined by the environments in which they write. Just as a genotype offers a set of genetic instructions that are manifested through a phenotype, or an expression of those instructions, so too does an ideology offer a set of ideological instructions that are manifested in the use of discourse. Of course, as genetic evolution allows for organisms to develop new genotypes or characteristics over time in response to environmental conditions and express them phenotypically, so too do users of discourse react to environments and maintain the potential to alter ideologies. Discourse communities become ecological systems in which writers interact with and react to one another and their environments. And all writers are linked in a single discourse-sphere where we recognize that no discourse community exists free of other discourse communities.

Compositionists therefore can learn much about discourse and writing by turning to theories of ecology. After all, both disciplines share a common interest in communities and the ways in which their members work in accord with and in opposition to one another. Both look to the environments in which these interactions take place, whether they are biospheres, neighborhoods, classrooms, or texts. Both composition and ecology are concerned with the ways in which various groups and species compete for territory and resources within particular ecosystems. While compositionists speak of subaltern, marginalized groups and their struggles for the right to speak and act autonomously, ecologists speak of the struggles of particular plants and animals and the ways that they adapt to and often overcome environmental competition. Both disciplines recognize that environment is of great importance in the construction of identity; plants and animals react and adapt to their environments, while writers adopt identities that are shaped and molded by environmental factors. Even more basically and simply, both disciplines are relatively new arrivals on the larger intellectual horizon, but both deal with subjects that are as old as history itself: communities and communication.

Composition, Not Ecocriticism

Ecocomposition develops out of ecocriticism, yet ecocomposition is not an extension of ecocriticism. Several reviewers of our work have insisted that ecocomposition be treated as a subdiscipline of ecocriticism. It is not. Ecocomposition borrows from ecocriticism, but grows on its own. Ecocriticism is a literary criticism that looks toward textual interpretation; ecocomposition works from the same place, but is concerned with textual production and the environments that affect and are affected by the production of discourse. Ecocomposition should direct its focus not to literary criticism or even textual interpretation in the larger sense, but should evolve as its own inquiry into the relationship between the production of written discourse and environment.

The questions regarding nature's representation in texts are important to ecocomposition; however, as Glotfelty and Fromm's sample questions demonstrate, many of these questions are too confining and restrictive for ecocomposition. The critical goals of ecocriticism limit ecological understandings of writing to inquiries pertaining specifically to writing about nature and literary criticism. Ecocompositionists have begun to ask questions such as "What effects do local environments have on any kind of writing, any kind of writer?" This question must include asking about the political environments of classrooms, the technological environments of cyberspace, and the very metaphors by which we define writing spaces, not only natural places about which writers write. We must ask not just "Do men and women write about nature differently?" but "Do environments affect the difference between men and women writers?" Ecocomposition conforms with Glotfelty and Fromm's premise that "[i]f we agree with Barry Commoner's first law of ecology, 'Everything is connected to everything else,' we must conclude that literature does not float above the material world in some aesthetic ether, but, rather, plays a part in an immensely complex global system, in which energy, matter, and ideas interact" (xix). However, ecocompositionists are less likely to turn to the fields of literature and critical interpretation, but instead look toward text, toward discourse in more encompassing ways, and claim that language does not exist outside of nature. Ecocomposition's focus on discourse takes in more than just textual interpretation; it looks at discourse as the most powerful, indeed, perhaps the only, tool for social and political change. We agree with Barry Lopez when he argues that "this area of writing [environmental writing] will not only one day produce a major and lasting body of American literature, but [. . .] might also provide the foundation for a reorganization of American political thought" (297). Lopez is correct that the activity of writing, specifically the production of environmentally conscious writing, and not the critical analysis of that body of writing, can effect change. And despite claims by ecocritics such as Harry Crockett, Christopher Cokinos, and others that ecocriticism seeks to change environmental policy and "green" the world, the activity of literary criticism—à la Stanley Fish—does not effect change; activism effects change. As Raul Sanchez commented in an online conversation regarding the radical and political possibilities of interpretation/reading, "I'm always puzzled at the implicit and explicit faith some seem to have in the power of hermeneutics as if celebration or even proper postcolonial 'interrogation' of literary texts could represent anything remotely like radical political action." Sanchez later comments that he finds the "more useful" activity of teaching writing to lend itself to political action. Likewise, compositionist Susan Miller has noted quite accurately that textual interpretation (reading) is not writing, as she addresses the difference in power between interpretation and production (499). Encouraging students to be critical of the very environments in which they produce discourse and the effects those environments have upon their writing effects change. Teaching students to resist hegemonic discourses that create anti-environmental legislation effects change. Reading Edward Abbey does not. Hence, ecocomposition's split with ecocriticism comes from the will to examine and participate in the activity of textual production rather than to engage in textual interpretation. If ecocriticism looks toward textual interpretation, ecocomposition is interested in examining the *activity* and *locations* of textual production as well as all of the other environments that affect and are affected by the production of discourse.

We are particularly concerned with the pedagogical link between ecocriticism and ecocomposition as it has been manifest in recent discussions. Much of the current pedagogical work being generated in ecocomposition stresses the use of texts that can easily be categorized as "nature writing." Many of the textbooks currently on the market that intend to encourage students to think more ecologically and develop environmental awareness regard nature writing texts as ripe for literary criticism and analysis. Such an approach to composition offers no real insights into the activity of writing and does little to extend students' conceptions of how their discourse is already ecological. Many of the readers designed for composition classrooms, such as Scott H. Slovic and Terrell F. Dixon's *Being in the World: An Environmental Reader for Writers*, Richard Jenseth and Edward E. Lotto's *Construct-*

ing Nature: Readings from the American Experience, Carolyn Ross's *Writing Nature: An Ecological Reader for Writers*, and even Sidney I. Dobrin's forthcoming *Saving Place: An Ecoreader for the Composition Classroom,* are designed to provide readings for student writers. In these collections, environmental issues are presented as subjects that students read and write *about,* think *about,* talk *about,* rather than participate *in*. That is not to say that the editors of these collections or those writing about ecological pedagogies for the composition classroom do not take hands-on experience as a primary agenda in their pedagogies. However, ecocomposition should not address environment as merely another subject students may write about, but rather a critical instrument for understanding the very function and operation of writing. While examining nature writing certainly begins to forward the ecocomposition project, until students and teacher-scholars move beyond this limiting view of ecocomposition it will simply be another flashy subject about which teachers can assign writing but one that does not shed any light on the activity of writing. Ecocomposition is also about the environment of writing, and it must step beyond ecocriticism's agenda of textual interpretation.

Environmental Rhetoric

Like composition studies in general, ecocomposition is deeply enmeshed with rhetorical studies. If we are to claim that ecocomposition entails exploring the production of written discourse as it relates to environment and place and that ecocomposition grows from both ecological and environmental concerns, then part of ecocomposition's definition falls within the boundaries of rhetorical studies as well. Ecocomposition is concerned with rhetorical analysis of environmental/political issues, the effects of language on those issues, and the ways in which ongoing debates or conversations affect the ways in which writers write. Political debates, activism, and participation all rely on a rhetoric of the environment, which is of critical importance in ecocomposition. The environment, which has been at the forefront of many current public debates, has been defined through the words we use to represent it: it is the product of a variety of discourses and their intersections in the public sphere. Many ecocompositionists have begun to realize that studies in environmental discourse, for instance, are both important to us as human beings and valuable to us as rhetoricians.

Investigations into environmental rhetoric intersect with several important aspects of ecocomposition. First and foremost, they explore connections between discourse and environment, and as such they clearly serve an important task within the concentric environments of ecocomposition, composition, academia, and the world itself. They suggest that discourse is integral to mapping, shaping, and constructing the world, and in turn they see language as a powerful tool in eliciting social, political, and environmental action. In this sense, studies in environmental rhetoric align themselves with theories and pedagogies that assert the importance of student writing moving beyond the confines of academic discourse to address larger public issues and debates. Much of the recent work in environmental rhetoric emphasizes two principles at the core of ecocomposition: our interdependence with others and our interconnectedness with a larger biosphere. To this end, ecocompositionists might work toward theories and pedagogies that incorporate the interests of diverse members of our local and global ecosystems—including other intellectuals, other peoples, and even other organisms.

Studying environmental rhetoric is a powerful pedagogical approach that serves a number of purposes: it raises student awareness of the ways people use language to construct knowledge and accomplish things in the world; it allows students to see that language is a powerful tool that influences us and, in turn, can be used to influence others; it enables them to better recognize ways in which different discourse communities structure the contents, forms, and rhetorical appeals of their language to better communicate with their intended audiences; it gives them powerful discursive tools that they can use in larger public spheres; and last but certainly not least, environmental rhetoric informs students of global issues that are among the most important in the world today. As we and our students struggle to make sense of the deluge of information surrounding environmental issues, analyzing environmental rhetoric provides a means to organize and clarify much of this information.

Ecocomposition as Pedagogy

The project of knowledge making in composition is deeply implicated in how teaching practices are formed and argued for. Similarly, work in ecocomposition often returns to the kind of day-to-day practices that go on in college classrooms and departments under the rubric of reading and writing. In all ecocomposition courses, issues that directly assist students in becoming better producers of writing in a variety of writing environments should be the central focus, encouraging students to recognize their experiences in all environments as affecting and being affected by their writing. Students can become critical of how those places are mapped, defined, regulated, and managed through discourse so that they may identify for themselves how discourse affects and is affected by places they experience and find connection with. Nature and environment must be lived in, experienced, to see how the very discourses in which we live react to and with those environments. As Emerson wrote, "So lies all the life I have lived as my dictionary from which to extract the word which I want to dress the new perception of this moment. This is the way to learn Grammar. God never meant that we should learn Language by Colleges or Books. That only can we say which we have lived" (152).

An ecocomposition pedagogy thus encourages political activism, public writing, and service learning, and student writing can be directed beyond the limited scope of classroom assignments to address larger, public audiences. Students can be encouraged to become active; passive learning neither provides students with writing scenarios in which they encounter real audiences nor promotes ecological awareness and participation. Ecocomposition is a praxis; it engages and involves students. It employs Kenneth Bruffee's notion of the "conversation of mankind," encouraging students and teachers alike to participate in conversations about environment, place, and location, within and beyond the mapped places of classrooms. We see two primary branches of ecocomposition pedagogy. The first, and perhaps fastest-growing in American colleges and universities, is that which tends toward ecological literacy. Essentially, this pedagogy teaches environmental awareness in the writing classroom. The second form is what we call "discursive ecology." Much like social ecology, which examines the relationships within and among societies, discursive ecology examines the relationships of various acts and forms of discourse. This branch of pedagogy asks students to see writing as an ecological process, to explore writing and writing processes as systems of interaction, economy, and interconnectedness. Most ecocompositionists operate from one of the two perspectives, although some of the most productive and useful ecocomposition pedagogies are those that meld the two.

The Ecological Literacy Approach

The ecological literacy approach to ecocomposition has been the predominant way in which concepts of ecology have moved into composition studies. Most broadly, this approach to teaching ecocomposition regards the students' awareness of the importance of "place" as a central goal of the course. For the most part, these pedagogies have stressed a greater awareness of the "natural" world, the environmental crisis, and the role of human beings in the destruction of environments and in developing sustainable ways in which to continue to live on the planet. Such courses, it is argued, enable students to think more critically about the world they live in, and critical thinking is a necessary precursor to effective writing. Certainly, ecocomposition courses focusing on these topics could potentially cultivate critical thinking. However, these courses need not focus exclusively on "natural" places, nor should they present an environmental-activist approach as the only perspective. Ecocomposition courses could potentially, and occasionally do, focus on such topics as the ways in which city-dwellers develop certain patterns of behavior or how Internet chat rooms allow individuals to come together in "locations" that best suit their needs. People develop through their interactions in a variety of locations, and while there is much that we can teach and learn through the study of the natural world, this topic is by no means the only "place" worthy of examination. Compositionists in metropolitan areas are not unable to teach ecocomposition just because they cannot take students to pristine forests or beaches; the places their students come from and exist in are equally deserving of study, be they urban or rural.

In addition, ecocomposition pedagogies should expose students to positions and beliefs that often run counter to a "liberated" perspective. It is easy enough to force-feed students the sort of texts that we agree with, and it is equally easy to train students to say what we would like to hear. However, if critical awareness is a real goal, the best and perhaps only way to help students to become more critically aware of the world and their place in it is to expose them to the profusion of attitudes, ideas, ideologies, and perspectives that pertain to place or location. Interestingly, exploring "natural" environmental issues is one of the most effective ways of inquiring into that very profusion. Debates about environmental issues occur in a wide variety of institutional and cultural locations, and the actors in these debates range from the ultraconservative to the extreme liberal. By exposing students to this multitude of perspectives, we can hope to help them develop mature positions of their own.

In order for students to become familiar with the power of language and rhetoric and see that their words also have impact in discussions of environment and place, assignments and writing tasks can encourage students to write for audiences other than their teachers. As Paul Heilker writes, "Writing teachers need to relocate the *where* of composition instruction outside the academic classroom because the classroom does not and cannot offer students real rhetorical situations in which to understand writing as social action" (71). Assignments should encourage students to examine and participate in public debates in the places where they live and explore and write about those issues. These assignments should be context-driven and provide students with the room to direct their writing toward issues of both local and global concern.

One of the most compelling aspects of ecocomposition pedagogy is its links to Paulo Freire's dialogic methodology. Ecocomposition, like Freire's pedagogy, asks students to participate in conversations with both their environments and other members of their community or biosphere. When Freire offers his problem-posing approach to gaining hold of local discourses and local literacies, he is, in essence, asking members of a community to question the very roles of their environments and to engage those environments in dialogue. Dialogue places members of a community, such as writing students, *within* writing environments rather than asking them to merely write *about* those environments. Ecocomposition, like Freire, asks students to write in their environments, to be critical of those environments, and to consider what effect their own writing and literacies have on that very environment. If we ask students solely to write *about* environment, we situate both student writers and ourselves outside of environment, creating an oppositional position, one that might lend itself to dominance and oppression of those environments. But encouraging writers to be critically aware of their environments and to participate in them situates writers as participants both affected by and affecting those environments, rather than merely observers with minimal curiosity about those places. For example, an assignment about local cleanup efforts might read:

> It seems that cleaning up the places in which we live has become an agenda of almost all American communities. Most likely the community in which you currently live or where you grew up (should they be different places) is home to several organizations which orchestrate volunteer cleanups of local environments. Such efforts are extremely beneficial to local communities, but in order for them to be effective, volunteers must be reached and encouraged to participate. Volunteer work can be provided in many ways.
>
> One thing that you might consider is volunteering your skills as a writer to produce publicity material or fliers announcing upcoming events and encouraging new volunteers to participate.
>
> *Assignment*: choose a local organization whose agenda meets your own environmental goals. Design a flier which details the agenda and affiliations of the organization and invites volunteers to participate in an upcoming event.
>
> Remember that you will be writing for a very diverse audience, but an audience that will have some similarities in how they think about local environments (some one apathetic to cleaning up local rivers, for instance, is not likely to read a flier about a cleanup project), so you can make certain assumptions about your audience. You will need to be convincing, since motivating some concerned individuals to active participation may be difficult.

A second assignment might read:

> Quite frequently, readers come to learn about organizations which they did not previously know existed through reading what others have written about those organizations. When writers portray agendas of organizations, frequently those writings are the only access readers have to those organizations. Hence, a writer's words have real effect on readers' understandings of the political agendas of environmental organizations. Similarly, writers frequently provide the only access many readers have to understanding local environmental legislation. For instance, newspaper columnists often present editorialized articles which express their view of whether or not a piece of legislation is beneficial to a local community. These articles often sway readers' ways of thinking about that issue.
>
> There are countless forums through which to inform readers about local issues and organizations. One of the more effective ways is electronically: the Internet and the World Wide Web.
>
> *Assignment*: Select an organization or issue that is particularly interesting to you. Develop a Web page which explains, in detail, the organization's goals, the way to join the organization, the details of the legislation, and so on. Provide links to other similar pages so that your readers may access even more information about this subject.

Frequently the argument is made that students, particularly first-year composition students, do not possess the authority to publish their writing. But we academics too often think of public writing as published writing, and we tend to assign academic standards of value to how and what we evaluate and teach regarding public writing. However, as the assignments provided above exemplify, students can find public outlets for their writing; teachers can begin to explore broader definitions of publication so that they might direct their students to a variety of public places for their writing. Encouraging students to produce written work that reaches readers beyond their classrooms encourages students to value their own writing as part of larger, public conversations. Such encouragement helps students to better understand the power of rhetoric and writing while at the same time giving students real reasons to learn the "subject matter" of the issues they have chosen to address and support.

While we stand by our belief that the writing instructor's first duty is to teach writing, we also believe that students learn to write when they are writing to learn. Learning more about a particular subject—whether that subject is the natural environment, the political struggles involved in environmental debates, or any other subject of importance—is inseparable from learning to write effectively and well. Learning about our global, national, and local environments is perhaps the most important subject of study today.

The Discursive Ecology Approach

The second type of ecocomposition pedagogy—which we have called the discursive ecology approach—not only asks students to consider environmental issues as subjects about which to write and think, but also asks students and teachers to consider the very ecologies of writing. Ideally, such an approach to teaching writing might be combined with the ecological literacy approach in order to ask students to look more holistically at the relationships among written discourse, their own writing, and environments and environmental issues that affect their lives. While ecological literacy approaches may be developed devoid of the discursive ecology approach and vice versa, a more encompassing ecocomposition pedagogy involves both.

Discursive ecology pedagogy (and critical inquiry) is situated within the notion that words, language, and writing are themselves parts of ecosystems and that when writers write they affect and are affected by environment. Like the general definition that says ecology is the study of the relationship between organisms and their environments, this pedagogy examines the activity of writing and its relationship to surrounding environments. It asks that we, as teachers, conceptualize writing not as an individual activity, separating the author from the world, but as an activity of the world; that we step beyond examining the processes of individual writers to examining larger environmental forces on those writers; that in addition to the ideological, cultural contexts in which we have situated writers in recent times, we look to physical environments, textual relationships, and the locations from which language and discourse arises. It asks us to see writing as an activity of relationships.

A particularly good example of discursive ecology pedagogy are assignments that employ hypertextual writing, or "webbed writing." Whereas conventional methods of writing reinforce the idea of the single author writing in a hierarchical, linear style, writing on the World Wide Web allows for associations, connections, and junctures among words, ideas, texts, and authors. These connections are manifested through links, cyclical references, and paths of information that are not often found in traditional texts. A hypertext has no canonical order. In a sense, webbed writing projects often work like ecosystems. Ideas, words, and texts connect with one another, work relationally by referring to one another, and assume no intrinsically hierarchical order of importance. The use of hypermedia, such as digital images and sounds, adds another dimension to webbed writing, allowing for more diversity and variety—the attributes of a healthy ecosystem.

Webbed writing can indicate a hierarchy of topics, but its basic structure does not inherently categorize and codify information in the same linear structure as does a traditional printed book. Writing hypertextually reflects a mindset that more accurately corresponds to our current conceptions of ecology. Jay David Bolter writes eloquently on this subject:

> The electronic book reflects a different natural world, in which relationships are multiple and evolving: there is no great chain of being in an electronic world-book. For that very reason, an electronic book is a better analogy for contemporary views of nature, since nature is often not regarded as a hierarchy, but rather as a network of interdependent species and systems. We can expect contemporary scientists and scholars to come more and more to the conclusion that the book of nature is a hypertext, whose language is the computational mathematics of directed graphs. (258)

Students easily grasp the ecological nature of the webbed writing environment, and hypertextual writing assignments, when coupled with environmentalist discussions and texts, often seem to reinforce one another. The study of natural ecologies and the foregrounding of "ecological" types of discourse work together to underscore a central tenet of ecological thinking: that environments (whether they are natural, discursive, or otherwise) consist of interactions and relationships.

As a part of a recent WAC initiative, Christian Weisser taught an ecocomposition course that was linked with an environmental issues course. The students met with Weisser and their environmental issues professor at different times, but the courses shared several texts and discussed related and overlapping issues; students participated in joint activities with both professors and completed several shared assignments. For their final writing assignment, the students worked together in groups of three to develop group web projects focusing on environmental and ecological issues on campus. After composing a homepage for the project as a class, the students selected the following issues for group study: recycling on campus, energy use, flora and fauna on campus, water treatment and wastewater management, and waste disposal and hazardous waste management. The students quickly discovered that their university was inextricably linked with the city, the county, and the surrounding environments. In addition, the students quickly perceived connections among one another's web projects, and by including links and references to these the entire project became much more ecological.

By the project's completion, Weisser's students had created an ecosystem of texts and ideas, including links to local, national, and global environmental groups and organizations, references to one another's work, and graphics and digital images of the campus and its surroundings. In one group project, students initiated a cleanup of the campus park and gave special thanks to each of the other groups for participating. After numerous peer-evaluation workshops, the students presented their work to an interdisciplinary faculty panel. Nearly every group cited the others, and most came to see the entire web project as something in which they all owned equal shares. One student, during her group's presentation, stated that this Web project "allowed us [the students] to connect with each other much like plants and animals do in an ecosystem." Webbed writing assignments of this sort allow students to see bits of information, pages, links, and ideas relationally. Students recognize that knowledge depends upon its relationships with other knowledge, that facts, texts, and even selves depend upon shared resources, and that productivity can be group-generated and group-maintained.

Like ecological literacy pedagogy, discursive ecology pedagogy may indeed engage environmental texts and may ask students to write *about* environmental/ecological issues, yet it emphasizes writing and discourse as the subject. The first version of ecocomposition pedagogy closely mirrors what seems to have become the (unfortunately) conventional approach to teaching writing: the analysis of other texts or issues—which are often organized by either subject or genre; the teaching of writing conventions; and the writing of papers that address the texts or issues (or similar texts and issues) first analyzed. For many, ecological literacy pedagogy will be the most practical to approach, and it certainly has been the most widely used eco-pedagogy thus far. We do not mean to suggest this variety of pedagogy to be an inferior or secondary pedagogy. In fact, we encourage teachers to begin their first ventures into ecocomposition with this sort of pedagogy. It is familiar, and it asks students to engage ecological issues at the textual level. It urges students to think ecologically and asks them to write about ecological/environmental subjects, and many good textbooks have been produced that support this form of pedagogy (see Anderson and Runciman; Arnold; Jenseth and Lotto; Ross; Verburg; Finch and Elder; Walker; Halpern and Frank). However, what we must stress here again is that ecocomposition should emphasize the production of written discourse and ecocomposition pedagogy should foreground the student's writing, not the interpretation of others' work. The most progressive and dynamic forms of ecocomposition urge students to look at their own discursive acts as being inherently ecological. Writers operate in certain environments, write and speak differently when they enter new environments, and interact with other writers/speakers in various ways. The discursive-ecology model of ecocomposition pedagogy seeks to make these aspects of communication more obvious. The study of nature writing may help individuals to think more ecologically, but we must also help students to see communication, writing, and the production of knowledge as ecological endeavors. Teaching nature writing as a literary genre is an endeavor for the literature classroom, not the composition classroom. Ecocomposition must be about more than simply bringing nature writing texts to the writing classroom; it must be about the act of producing writing. Asking students to read nature writing is not *doing* ecocomposition.

Conclusion—A Journey Just Begun

We do not wish to suggest that an ecocompositionist approach to discourse and ecology offers a harmonious vision of relational existence. Rather, ecocompositionists look to understand how relationships to environments and other organisms might contend with oppressive hegemonies, and we offer not utopian promises, only critical gazes. As human beings, all of us are members of many different groups, ecosystems, and discourse communities, and the language we use at any given moment can never emerge from one exclusive location or environment. We come from multiple discursive ecosystems, and what we think and say is the product of all of these locations, despite their seeming dissimilarities. James Porter offers a useful discussion of this relationship between discourse and ecology:

> Discourse communities may operate a little like ecosystems. An ecosystem is a convenient ecological space defined by certain characteristics that set it off from abutting systems. But shift your perspective slightly and the borders of the original ecosystem break down, because ecosystems inevitably interact with systems abutting them. Discourse communities cannot be isolated any more than the writer can be isolated as an object of study from his social field. In other words, we need to remember that discourse communities overlap—and are flexible and locally constituted. They may cross academic and institutional boundaries, and they may exist only momentarily. (86)

What ecocomposition does and must continue to do is explore the co-constitutive relationships between discourses and environments. In order to do so, ecocompositionists should take as their primary agenda the study of the relationships among all environments and the production of written discourse; production, not interpretation, is the cornerstone of ecocomposition. We have argued that composition studies is already deeply vested in ecological inquiries—inquiries that question the relationships among writers, texts, knowledge, discourse, culture, race, gender, and a host of other categorical labels. Similarly, we have pointed out how composition might benefit from turning to methodologies employed by ecological sciences, and we have inquired as to what role all environments might play in writing and, in turn, what role writing might play in constructing environments. These are the very sorts of inquiries we hope to see ecocomposition move toward.

It is our hope that as composition studies continues to expand its focus on writing processes, the social conventions of writing, cultural issues of writing, and questions of disciplinary boundaries, compositionists will move toward ecocomposition and begin to explore the importance of the role of place, environment, space, site, location in ways that allow composition studies to both account for the importance of those places and understand their effect on written discourse. Ecocomposition has the potential to guide composition studies to exciting new sites of inquiry—assuming, of course, that we are willing to accept ecocomposition's link first to the natural world and then move beyond the limited scope of seeing ecocomposition as being about nature only. Composition cannot ignore the crucial role that environments play in the production of discourse, nor can critical studies of environments ignore the role of discourse in constructing them. Quite simply, discourse and environment cannot be separated.

Works Cited

Anderson, Chris, and Lex Runciman, eds. *A Forest of Voices: Reading and Writing the Environment*. Mountain View, CA: Mayfield, 1995.

Anderson, Lorraine, Scott Slovic, and John P. O'Grady, eds. *Literature and the Environment: A Reader on Nature and Culture*. New York: Longman, 1999.

Arnold, David. *The Problem of Nature: Environment, Culture, and European Expansion*. Cambridge, MA: Blackwell, 1996.

Bate, Jonathan. *The Green Studies Reader: From Romanticism to Ecocriticism*. New York: Routledge, 2000.

———. *The Song of the Earth*. Cambridge: Harvard UP, 2000.

Bolter, Jay David. *Writing Space: The Computer, Hypertext, and the History of Writing*. Hillsdale, NJ: Lawrence Erlbaum, 1991.

Buell, Lawrence. *The Environmental Imagination: Thoreau, Nature Writing, and the Formation of American Culture*. Cambridge: Harvard UP, 1995.

Coe, Richard M. "Defining Rhetoric—and Us: A Meditation on Burke's Definitions." *JAC* 10 (1990): 39–52.

Cokinos, Christopher. "What is Ecocriticism?" 23 Sept. 1997 <http://wsrv.clas.virginia.edu/~djp2n/conf/ WLA/cokinos.html>.

Cooper, Marilyn M. "The Ecology of Writing." *Writing as Social Action*. Ed. Marilyn Cooper and Michael Holzman. Portsmouth: Boynton, 1989. 1–13.

Crockett, Harry. "What is Ecocriticism?" 23 Sept. 1997 <http://wsrv.clas.virginia.edu/~djp2n/conf/WLA/ crockett.html>.

Dobrin, Sidney I. "Writing Takes Place." Weisser and Dobrin. 11–25.

Dobrin, Sidney I., and Christian R. Weisser. *Natural Discourse: Toward Ecocomposition*. Albany: SUNY P, 2002.

Emerson, Ralph Waldo. *The Journals of Ralph Waldo Emerson*. Boston: Houghton, 1909–14.

Finch, Robert, and John Elder. *The Norton Book of Nature Writing*. New York: Norton, 1990.

Glotfelty, Cheryl, and Harold Fromm. *The Ecocriticism Reader: Landmarks in Literary Ecology*. Athens: U of Georgia P, 1996.

Halpern, Danile, and Dan Frank, eds. *The Nature Reader*. Hopewell, NJ: Ecco, 1998.

Hawisher, Gail E., Paul LeBlanc, Charles Moran, and Cynthia L. Selfe. *Computers and the Teaching of Writing in American Higher Education, 1979–1994: A History*. Norwood: Ablex, 1996.

Heilker, Paul. "Rhetoric Made Real: Civic Discourse and Writing Beyond the Curriculum." *Writing the Community: Concepts and Models for Service-Learning in Composition*. Ed. Linda Adler-

Kassner, Robert Crooks, and Ann Watters. Urbana: NCTE and AAHE, 1997. 71–77.

Herndl, Carl G., and Stuart C. Brown, eds. *Green Culture: Environmental Rhetoric in Contemporary America*. Madison: U of Wisconsin P, 1996.

Jagtenberg, Tom, and David McKie. *Eco-Impacts and the Greening of Postmodernity: New Maps for Communication Studies, Cultural Studies, and Sociology*. Thousand Oaks: Sage, 1997.

Jenseth, Richard, and Edward Lotto, eds. *Constructing Nature: Readings from the American Experience*. Upper Saddle River, NJ: Prentice Hall, 1996.

Killingsworth, M. Jimmie, and Jacqueline S. Palmer. *Ecospeak: Rhetoric and Environmental Politics in America*. Carbondale: Southern Illinois UP, 1992.

Lindemann, Erika. "Three Views of English 101." *College English* 57 (1995): 287–302.

Lopez, Barry. "Barry Lopez." *On Nature: Nature, Landscape, and Natural History*. Ed. Daniel Halpern. San Francisco: North Point, 1987. 295–97.

Miller, Susan. "Technologies of Self?-Formation." *JAC: A Journal of Composition Theory* 17 (1997): 497–500.

Owens, Derek. *Composition and Sustainability: Teaching for a Threatened Generation*. Urbana: NCTE, 2001.

Plevin, Arlene. "The Liberatory Positioning of Place in Ecocomposition: Reconsidering Paulo Freire." Weisser and Dobrin. 147–62.

Porter, James. *Audience and Rhetoric*. Englewood Cliffs, NJ: Prentice Hall, 1992.

Ricklefs, Robert E. *The Economy of Nature*. 4th ed. New York: Freeman, 1997.

Roorda, Randall. *Dramas of Solitude: Narratives of Retreat in American Nature Writing*. Albany: SUNY P, 1998.

———. "Nature/Writing: Literature, Ecology, and Composition." *JAC* 17 (1997): 401–14.

Ross, Carolyn. *Writing Nature: An Ecological Reader for Writers*. New York: St. Martin's, 1995.

Rueckert, William. "Literature and Ecology: An Experiment in Ecocriticism." *Iowa Review* 9 (1998): 71–86.

Sanchez, Raul. Online conversation. 14 Sept. 1997 <postcolonial@jefferson.village.virginia.edu>.

Slovic, Scott. "Ecocriticism: Storytelling, Values, Communication, Contact." 8 Dec. 1998 <http://wsrv.clas. virginia.edu/~djp2n/conf/WLA/slovic.html>.

———. *Getting Over the Color Green: Contemporary Environmental Literature of the Southwest.* Tucson: U of Arizona P, 2001.

———. "Nature Writing and Environmental Psychology: The Interiority of Outdoor Experience." Glotfelty and Fromm 351–70.

Tag, Stan. "Four Ways of Looking at Ecocriticism." 8 Dec. 1998 <http://wsrv.clas.virginia.edu/~djp2n/ conf/WLA/tag.html>.

Verburg, Carol J. *The Environmental Predicament: Four Issues for Critical Analysis*. New York: Bedford, 1995.

Walker, Melissa, ed. *Reading the Environment*. New York: Norton, 1994.

Weisser, Christian R. "Ecocomposition and the Greening of Identity." Weisser and Dobrin. 81–95.

Weisser, Christian R., and Sidney I. Dobrin, eds. *Ecocomposition: Theoretical and Pedagogical Approaches*. Albany: SUNY P, 2001.

Chapter Twelve

Constructing Disciplinary Space: The Borders, Boundaries, and Zones of English

Daniel Mahala and Jody Swilky

It is early in the semester, and a teacher at a Midwestern urban university sits reading his first student essays in the waning hours. The window is closed, but his attention is broken by the sound of wind and sleet rushing through trees. The comforting background voices of the TV are interrupted by a beep, and a flashing light appears in the lower right corner of the screen, scrolling a warning of ice storms followed by a list of counties. He notices the news story now: an elderly black woman voicing anxiety over crime in the neighborhood, and expressing thanks to a charitable organization that delivers her groceries. One more essay. He rehearses the name on the paper, and calls to mind the face of an enthusiastic student whose name has been difficult to remember. The student announces himself in his opening lines as a Kuwaiti student whose experience as an international student on campus, and as a citizen in a country where there is a large population of foreigners, gives him a unique perspective on the theme of "cultural borders," a term introduced in the first course reading. The teacher is interested in what the student has to say, but now the light and TV are flickering, then suddenly extinguished. The teacher wonders if the drive to school in the morning will be treacherous, and is relieved to see that the telephone is working. He will be able to call in to the university answering system in the morning to get official word on whether or not class has been cancelled.

The scenario that introduces this essay offers a commonplace illustration of how geographic relationships constantly insinuate

From *JAC* 23 (2003): 765–97.

themselves into even the most private moments of our teaching. Understandably, we often ignore such fleeting, incongruous intersections of reality as appear in this scenario between the teacher, the elderly woman's image, and the international student's paper. And when we do reflect on such moments, it is not difficult to fit them into established frameworks that explain them in terms of globalization, time-space compression, our postmodern condition, and the like. New technologies of transportation, communication, and production have become so commonplace in industrialized countries over the last half-century that they have shrunk space and accelerated the motion of people, goods, and information both in local communities and across the globe. Among the frequently cited consequences of this compression of time and space are the internationalization of capital through lowered shipping costs and more flexible and mobile processes of production, the saturation of daily life with media representations, and the disruption of traditional ways of life as people negotiate new forms of cultural and economic contact often involving parties at great distances from one another.

There is little doubt that our work is profoundly affected by all this, whether we represent such changes as signs of a bright digital future or a bleak corporate takeover of public life. However, what we are troubled about is how our academic discussions of geography and space often obscure how individuals and groups are positioned differently in relation to the particular reconfigurations of time and space that present themselves in daily life. It is not unusual, for instance, to hear scholars talk about "contact zones," "border crossing," or even "our postmodern condition" as realities we all share. What often gets lost in such discussions is what the British geographer Doreen Massey calls the *power geometry* of time-space compression, a phrase she uses to explore the different ways in which groups and individuals are *inserted into* time and space, helped or hurt by the ways it is constantly being reconfigured. As Massey sees it, the issue is not only who moves and who doesn't but "about power in relation *to* the flows and the movement" (61). On one extreme, "jet-setters" hold international conference calls, send and receive faxes and e-mails, and move investments quickly between nations. On the other extreme, immigrants "from India, Pakistan, Bangladesh, and the Caribbean. . . come halfway around the world only to get held up in an interrogation room at Heathrow" (61–62).

Massey's concept of power geometry casts a different light on the issue of how we might be agents of change in our neighborhoods, institutions and classrooms. The problem is that reform discourse is often full of geographically-inflected language rallying us to negotiate the "contact zone," "redraw the boundaries," "cross borders," "break down the walls of the university." And yet, despite this, the issue of power geometry often remains unprobed. While spatial metaphors appear to address the material conditions of contact between individuals, groups, and forms of knowledge, we are struck by how such language screens out the full range of forces that constitute place as a material process. In perhaps the most obvious example, the "culture wars" metaphor maps the university in terms of warring camps of teachers or scholars occupying different critical territories against one another. This may seem a hardnosed, realistic view of our situations, but as we will show, it often works as a kind of utopian screen, diverting attention from the power geometries of our lived situations. Instead of attending to mundane realities such as institutional neglect, declining numbers of majors, displacement through outsourced programs, and so on, the culture wars maps an Adamic world where work has the meaning we give it through our teaching and writing. Materialist analysis drifts toward a method oriented study of ideology. Curricular content, classroom methods, and critical "approaches" to texts become focal points of reform debate. And as the focus narrows, the map of critical territories typically becomes more rarified and abstract, illustrating disciplinary work in terms of insider divisions between deconstruction, new historicism, gender criticism, and the like. What gets lost is how disciplinary knowledge functions in relation to built environments and the social and economic forces that assemble, delimit and circulate people in them. How do our institutions, neighborhoods, and classrooms embody different power geometries? How might we differently understand the metaphors of boundaries, zones, and borders so prominent in reform discourse if we considered them not as rallying cries, but rather as a challenge to understand how built environments actually mediate social interaction?

It is not enough merely to focus on representation because a built environment is always more than either its sensuous local character or its blueprint. That is, not only do built environments mean something; they also mediate the activity of people, patterning movement, connecting groups near and far, creating possibilities of visibility, social contact and privacy. Of course, no city, neighborhood, profession, or institution can be explained in terms of a single power geometry. A classroom, an office, a mall, and an urban street comer are all subject to overlapping and distinct social and economic forces, inviting us to recognize each place as unique and as constructed out of processes organized on a much larger scale. But this sort of mapping requires a broadly interdisciplinary view not only of interpretive approaches, policies, or curricula, but also how social desires, informal market behavior, and planning interact in different venues (education, architecture, housing policy, for example) to design the use of space in society. In this essay, we want to examine how life in urban universities and neighborhoods is shaped by different power geometries of time-space compression, and how this process of constructing space is typically elided by our commonplace geographical reform metaphors of border crossing, redrawing boundaries, and contact zones. In the next section of the essay, we examine some of the forces that have shaped the urban geography of the major midwestern city where one of us teaches, with particular attention to the struggle over a major thoroughfare recently completed about a mile to the east of the university. We also read the physical geography of the campus, a mid-sized, state university, and its relation to surrounding neighborhoods to illuminate how the campus has responded to similar social and economic forces in its own expansion and development. Through this comparative analysis, we will show more generally how universities pattern the movement of persons and commodities in society in ways that are both similar to and different from how the physical environment establishes zones of privacy, contact, exposure, and separation between groups and communities. In the third section of the essay, we turn our attention to geographical metaphors now common in our reform discourses, examining what they allow us to see about our environments, and what they obscure. Lastly, in the final section of the essay, we focus on the role of the English department in negotiating change, showing how commonplace metaphors of border-crossing and interdisciplinarity have reflected and shaped changes at the two midwestern universities where we teach, and how our departments have responded. In this section, we argue that our responses to troubling changes in the power geometries of four institutions have often been weakened by our lack of critical terms to describe geography. Hence, our aim is to highlight how we might usefully challenge the apparently transparent rhetoric of "a university without borders," a rhetoric of interdisciplinarity and openness that, as we will show, often masks shifts in power geometry that we ought to be directly engaging in our critical discourse.

Power Geometries of Public Space

Considering our opening scenario in terms of power geometry invites us to consider what the momentary convergence of student, television image, and teacher reveals about how each are inserted into processes of time-space compression. The Kuwaiti student can choose to attend a U.S. university because time-space compression has enabled the emergence of an international market for higher education, and because colleges have decided that international diversity in their student bodies is a good thing. The elderly woman can have her groceries delivered and become visible to the teacher on TV because of the mobility of charities and TV news crews. And almost everyone can get warning of an approaching storm if they are lucky enough to be tuned in. On the other hand, the elderly woman can plausibly be represented as being more trapped than liberated by these processes of time-space compression. If the lights go out, she will likely have to face more worrisome questions than whether the local university is closing its doors. After all, processes of time-space compression have likely been at least partly responsible for concentrating poverty and crime, and evacuating businesses like groceries, from her neighborhood. And although she appears on TV, far from having her say, her presence as an image is virtual, unidirectional, and fleeting, part of a standard news script for uplifting community stories. Similarly, the Kuwaiti student's choice to attend a U.S. school, and the particular forms of diversity produced by the sum of many such student choices, is only possible because her class position in a wealthy nation friendly to the U.S. positions her to take advantage of an internationalized market for higher education.

Examining this scenario in these terms suggests how time-space compression transforms social life not only by overcoming formerly insurmountable geographical limits, but also by establishing new boundaries, zones, and borders. Colleges rightfully celebrate on catalog covers and brochures how they have "opened doors" to new populations of students and faculty. But they seldom focus attention on the *assembled* character of this diversity, and how different groups are inserted into it. After all, it is clear that even in selective institutions that have strong records on diversity, minority students are likely to be from middle- or upper-class neighborhoods in the U.S., or from relatively affluent groups abroad. Since international students are not eligible for U.S. federal aid, more than eighty percent of foreign undergraduates, according to the Institute of International Education, depend primarily on the wealth of their families and home governments to provide access to the U.S. education market. Perhaps more important, large majorities of these students have had access to adequate or high quality primary and secondary education, and almost all (with the notable exception of some athletes in sports such as basketball and football) have avoided the prolonged stagnation, poverty and violence that have devastated primary and secondary schools for much of the underclass in the U.S. and third world countries. What this means is that the opening of doors accomplished through internationalized access to higher education may in some cases have further solidified class boundaries, enabling colleges to show their commitment to diversity even if they squeeze out local racial communities in favor of students of color abroad with more financial and educational resources.

Our point here is not to diminish the importance of recruiting international students, but to foster a *bifocal* view of how the practice helps construct place in higher education. Whenever we step into a classroom, we always find ourselves in a unique place, faced with a unique gathering of students. But at the same time, this uniqueness is always a function of social processes that are organized, often invisibly, on a much larger scale. The way a university, discipline, program, or department goes about "crafting a class," to quote the title of a recent book analyzing the subject, is not an accident but an act. This act, comprised of many smaller formal and informal acts, necessarily implicates our work within what architectural historian John Hancock has called the "ecology of social segmentation" in society. Hancock's analysis specifically focuses on housing, showing how public policy and informal market behavior have produced familiar patterns of neighborhood segregation in U.S. cities. For instance, Hancock notes how segregation of housing in the U.S. long predates the establishment of zoning laws in the 1880s, and how cities such as Houston, which have never adopted a formal zoning code or citywide planning, have nonetheless created "the same apparently rational segregation of people and activities" as exists in other cities (155).

Both Hancock's metaphor of ecology and Massey's metaphor of power geometry emphasize place as a network of relationships, which, however informal or unspoken, can nonetheless produce rigid economic and geographical divisions such as segregated neighborhoods. Both metaphors are bifocal, but while ecology emphasizes the cooperative relationality of local processes, geometry emphasizes their hierarchical qualities and large-scale geophysical form. Hence, in the remainder of the essay, we will continue to use both sets of terms: ecology to emphasize the intricate dance of social affinity, architecture, and policy that produce local places, and power geometry to emphasize the positioning of these processes in larger processes often occurring on a global scale.

Universities are part of both local ecologies of segmentation and larger-scale power geometries not only because they house people, but more importantly because they provide a crucial infrastructure for controlling access to privatized networks of people, goods, and information. An education from a premier institution is, as parents and students usually recognize, a promise of access to often highly exclusive pools of labor, as well as to hidden networks of alumni, employers, and public officials. In Derek Bok and William Bowen's extensive study of selective colleges, for example, the mean income of graduates of selective institutions correlates closely with the institution's degree of selectivity. Indeed, for some groups, such as blacks, twenty years after entering college, graduates of selective colleges studied enjoy *twice* the average income of black baccalaureate graduates nationally (257; see also 138–40). While it is typically argued that such institutions attract only the "best and brightest" students who should naturally be expected to succeed, Bok and Bowen's study dramatically illustrates the power of college selectivity as a variable in predicting students' long-term earning potential, dwarfing other variables such as SAT scores (133, 140).

The social networks to which different universities or programs provide access are often part of local and regional ecologies, linking regional or urban employers with nearby sources of prospective employees. But increasingly, regional ecologies of segmentation are tied into national or international power geometries, especially in the higher paying or more prestigious fields or professions. Over the last twenty-five years, these trends have produced an increasingly rootless professoriate, especially in doctoral-granting institutions where tenureable faculty are hired through national labor markets, which often require new faculty to relocate to communities where they have no prior experience or history (see Zencey; Owens 72–75). Ironically, it is part-time faculty who are most likely to be hired locally and rooted in the local communities in which they teach, even though our professional discourse typically represents them as in terms of rootlessness and marginality (part-timers as "gypsy scholars," "freeway flyers," or "temporary" labor).

In their internal structure, too, universities enact ecologies of segmentation, which have a complex relation to power geometrics in the larger society. Most obviously, universities segment and circulate students by offering them a smorgasbord of schools, programs, and majors to choose from. But this consumer freedom is more apparent than real, since even if students can pay, schools and programs always have the right to reject them. This gatekeeping function may be rationalized as a necessary means of quality control, but in fact, academic standards are often closely tied to the economic positioning of different schools and programs. Generally speaking, schools and programs with the strongest links to lucrative or high status professions (medicine, law, engineering) can typically count on attracting larger streams of interested and qualified students, and thus can afford to invoke more stringent standards than programs with links to lower-status or lower-paying professions (nursing or primary or secondary teaching, for example).

These differences in the character and function of programs and courses also help enact ecologies of segmentation among faculty. Faculty in disciplines or programs with strong ties to sought-after labor markets enjoy institutional prestige and gain leverage with administrations in the competition for faculty positions. Similarly, assignment to upper-division teaching typically marks status and privacy for the most senior or reputable members of a department. Such assignments promise smaller class sizes, an audience of students with stated interests in advertised subject matter, more professorial control over entry into the class, as well as freedom from the institutional supervision associated with large or multi-section lower-division courses.

The problem is that while faculty may compete for research support or choice teaching assignments, and while students may struggle for access to prestigious fields, programs, or job markets, our disciplinary discourse does not adequately consider the ways that social life inside the university can be understood by reference to the same desires for privacy and freedom from uncontrolled interaction that more obviously shape life outside the university. As Eve Sedgwick argues, it is difficult to come up with useful images of the "synecdochic relation of academic institutions to the larger world" because universities, as the very name suggests, aspire "to represent something huge in a disproportionately tiny space." The result of this drastic condensation is that the space of the university becomes "unreal or hyperreal." On the one hand, academic labor is "amazingly unrationalized" so that "the space of work for at least some in this industry can seem strikingly close to an idealized preindustrial workspace" where workers choose tasks based on desire, need, and aptitude. However, on the other hand, the construction of place as a material process—that is, the universities' constitutive relationships with labor, industry, government, and local economies—become hidden, or only visible through "repeated wrenching acts of re-recognition" (294–95).

Such acts of re-recognition become easier when we consider disciplinary work not only in relation to scholarly communities of discourse, but also in relation to the physical space of particular institutions and their borders with surrounding communities. Even the physical layout of a university, for instance, often bodies forth its relationships with surrounding development, revealing something of the niches the university occupies (or hopes to occupy) within local ecologies of segmentation. For instance, at the midwestern public university where one of us teaches, the marquis entrance to the university, recently refurbished, faces out onto a beautifully landscaped waterway to the north of the campus. The waterway was once an eyesore, a lowly polluted urban creek, but it has been rapidly transformed in the last few years, through a massive public and private infusion of capital. Following this flow of capital, the university has positioned its most public face alongside the luxury condominiums, conservation center, and private biomedical research center that have sprouted up along the creek. By contrast, the university has configured its physical border with the boulevard to the east, a road with a much rougher urban feel and widely considered the main racial dividing line in the city, by situating along this border parking lots, a purchasing office, service entrances, and the physical plant. Meanwhile, most of the university's recent building activity has been designed to create indoor and outdoor space for the university that insulates it from uncontrolled urban interaction.

These features of the university's layout and growth are largely coordinate with the current ecology of social segmentation in the city. Recent planning and building initiatives on the part of both the university and the city have devalued the possibilities of community integration that could be achieved by developing the urban boulevard to the east, which we will call, for the sake of brevity, the Boulevard. Indeed, the university's evolving architecture and growth activity has focused on presenting an attractive and aspiring face to the booming creek corridor, while creating interior spaces shielded from more mixed urban interactions. A copper-spired, stone-faced Science and Technology building forms the enclosing east side of a newly formed quadrangle, connected to other university buildings and to a new parking garage by elevated, glassed-in walkways. A block to the east, along the Boulevard, the university has spent much less money, renting out an aging, squat brick building, formerly home to the school of engineering, to a local charter school. These developments coordinate well with recent city planning, which is well illustrated by the opening of the urban highway passing about a mile east of the university. In many ways, this highway project represents a commonplace injustice in urban America, displacing and isolating the predominantly working class black community it traverses, while benefiting relatively affluent suburbanites in the south by simplifying travel to the downtown and midtown areas of the city (where the university is located). Meanwhile, it has absorbed resources that might have been used to develop roads that already are tied into the social fabric of the city, like the Boulevard, which also happens to provide an alternate route from the south.

In many ways, the Boulevard is a site rich in possibilities of social interaction across boundaries of race, class, and gender. Traffic is slowed by lights, intersections, and business activity, and the roadway is flanked on both sides with residential neighborhoods, often neighborhoods that are among the most racially integrated in the city. A range of different businesses line the roadway—from pawnshops, and rent-to-buy centers targeting the poor, to businesses such as a music store, garden center, funeral parlor, hardware stores, and pharmacies catering to mixed middle and working-class clienteles. However, in relation to the sort of cost/benefit analyses that typically drive urban as well as university planning, this heterogeneity of life along the Boulevard is exactly the problem.

Consider, for instance, how market logic often dictates the desirability of building urban freeways rather than developing multi-use urban roads such as the Boulevard. With the opening of the freeway, the drive to midtown is not only quicker for suburbanites, but also more private, involving only stopping at a light or two in zones where local inhabitants are mostly hidden behind fences, landscape greenery, and embankments. This privatization of space harmonizes the dream of suburban escape with the attractions of an enlarged job market and urban cultural amenities such as the university. And although city officials seldom admit that city planning gives priority to suburban desires and needs over those of urban residents, it makes economic sense that designers with an eye on market demographics will reflect the view of suburban shoppers, since they have more disposable income. If it can be shown that minimizing contact across borders of race and class can enhance flows of educated workers and shopping dollars downtown, then a project such as the freeway can be argued as making economic sense in spite of its social costs.[1] Further, a design that produces value by rigidifying race and class borders can also work to reinforce the desire for, and the economic value of, social insularity.[2]

The main criticism the project received in the local press was that it would establish an unwanted barrier in the heart of the city's working class black community, ripping "a tornadic ruin from the shadow of City Hall to the suburbs" in the words of a local editorial ("Time"). But as our former discussion suggests, the project is also part of larger power geometries in which both the city and university are embedded. After all, the project not only divides and obstructs, it also connects and compresses time and space, and different groups are positioned differently in relation to the new zones and borders. For the university and many local businesses, the roadway provides new streams of potential students, customers, and educated workers. On the other hand, for the five thousand residents who relocated, the roadway has meant a loss of trust and intensified racial segregation. Even personal relationships have been reshaped as the presence of the roadway cuts across neighborhoods, sometimes transforming a five-minute walk to a friend or relative to a noisy and dangerous half hour trek (see Spivak).

Of course, both the city and the university are tied into national and international ecologies as well as the local or regional ones we have been discussing. The plush development along the creek reflects a much broader competition among cities, states, and nations for niches in emerging biotech and information economies. Because these economies are organized on a global scale, the most lucrative job markets and professional cultures they support are often defined in terms of sumptuous mobility. This can be seen in the residential component of the boom along the creek, which is largely comprised of upscale condominiums and apartments sprouting up along the creek, as well as the university's recent attempts to develop large dormitories, even though historically most of the school's students have been urban commuters. Attracting top out-of-state scientists, researchers, and students requires facilities that can sustain a mobile professional class, or those who are aspiring to this class, at accustomed levels of comfort and safety.

Indeed, as we briefly considered earlier, the relation between universities' internal ecologies of segmentation and those on the outside is often deceptively complex. It is important not to underestimate the full range and complexity of positions that teachers and researchers occupy, even when we limit our view to one area, such as humanities disciplines. In research institutions with travel budgets, release time for research, and selective admissions, "star" faculty in the humanities are certainly in a position to take charge of opportunities afforded by mobility on a regular basis. However, in those same institutions, nontenure-track teachers or GTAs often have no travel support, or if they do, may find themselves one day at a conference hotel linked by glass tunnels to plush meeting rooms and restaurants, and the next day in an office cubicle sharing computers, phones, desks, and even desk drawers with co-workers. And with tenure requirements stiffening at many institutions, even tenureable faculty at prestigious universities may experience the opulence of conferences and research travel as only an ironic reminder of their own precarious situations.

Over the last decade, universities have cut labor costs in the humanities by expanding the use of part-time faculty, outsourcing programs, and putting a lid on hiring for tenureable positions. These changes have deepened the segmentation of the humanities as a labor force. At most institutions, huge gaps in pay, benefits, and institutional standing divide full- and part-time faculty. In addition, faculty at major research institutions have become increasingly isolated from the populations of general education students that make up the lion's share of enrollments of humanities departments at most institutions. In doctoral-granting English departments, for instance, the chances of an undergraduate encountering a tenure-line faculty in a first year writing course is now 1 in 20 (ADE 14–15). By contrast, tenure-line faculty in departments granting only bachelors degrees teach more than seventy percent of the undergraduate curriculum and staff forty-nine percent of first-year writing sections (15, 10). What this suggests is that different groups of humanities faculty, even limiting our consideration only to faculty at four year institutions, are coming to occupy increasingly divergent positions in the power geometry of higher education. And while the growing divisions between full-time and part-time faculty are much discussed in our professional discourse, even here the issue of how ecologies of segmentation internal to the university are related to those on the outside is often clouded by how we apply geographically inflected metaphors of race or class to explain the exploitation of faculty labor. Part-time faculty and GTAs may in some sense be, as our discourse often represents them, a "migrant" workforce or "academic underclass." But their exploitation is mainly an issue of wages, benefits, and institutional status, not of race or class boundaries.[3]

If we turn our attention from faculty to students, we also find that a complex convergence of economic, social, and legal factors threaten to increase the gap between the haves and the have-nots. Among these factors are the geographical enlargement of markets for higher education, the increasing influence of mass media college rankings (which often feature mean SAT scores as the mark of a good college), the more activist roles of state legislatures, trustees and prominent alumni in policy, the shift from need-based grants to merit scholarships and loans to finance college costs, and the erosion of the legal basis of affirmative action. While the effects of such changes are not entirely predictable, it is clear that the increasing sway of the "invisible hand" of the market over higher education policy over the last decade is eroding public discourse about how communities of higher education should be constituted, and privatizing decision-making about these issues. Indeed, while humanities faculty in all sort of institutions battle over multiculturalism and critical methods, the ground on which we stand is literally changing beneath our feet, and our standard ways of framing disciplinary issues and problems are ill-equipped to address the new conditions.

To briefly consider perhaps the most publicized issue on our list, affirmative action, consider how recent legal decisions have privatized decisions on the social and spatial character of the university, limiting not so much *what* can be said so much as *where* it can be said. Recent court decisions have increasingly instituted a policy of "color-blind constitutionalism" that limits how race can be considered in admissions and hiring decisions on campus.[4] What this means is that at the same time that race issues have gained visibility in humanities classrooms and scholarship, such issues are also increasingly regulated as topics of speech in institutional policy. At the moment that our disciplinary discourse visibly elevates "marginality as not just the stakes or subject but the privileged *site* of cultural critique" (Gates 315), many forms of difference are becoming legally *unmentionable* in precisely those venues (such as admissions and hiring decisions) that are most directly involved in the planning of space and community membership in higher education.[5] While on one part of campus a humanities class debates Toni Morrison's notion of blackness as an "excluded presence" in American literature, similar discussion risks legal sanction if it occurs on another part of campus where officials are "crafting a class." The effect of these legal actions is to privatize discourse about how university communities should be constituted, and to displace such discussions into a coded discourse of "merit" where race, class, gender, and sexuality are masked but continue to operate.[6]

Of course, the erosion of affirmative action is only one factor working to such an end, but disciplinary maps that separate the "imagined space" of knowledge from the material places where we live and work are also complicit in the process. While many who decry the erosion of affirmative action still might justify mapping disciplinary change independently, the content of disciplines has always been profoundly dependent on the design of physical and social space in universities, which is shaped not only by high-profile legal concerns such as affirmative action, but also by more mundane factors such as our ability to hire faculty, recruit majors, promise descent prospects of employment for graduates, and so on. Even though faculty have seldom exercised primary control over admissions—and hiring processes in the post-WWII development of universities, there is little doubt that the power geometry of higher education is now shifting in ways that further dilute faculty control over flows of student and faculty labor. And there is little doubt that the future content of humanities disciplines will depend profoundly on how faculty address these shifts.

Reform and the Imagined Space of the University

Like our own analogy between city and university, metaphors of boundaries, zones, and borders in humanities discourse aspire "to represent something huge in a tiny space," evoking images of the tense diversity of social life outside the university to account for the complexity of life inside it. However, as Sedgwick warns, such metaphors always run the danger of producing an "unreal or hyperreal" sense of the university, unless they recognize how universities and classrooms are built environments themselves. The image of curricula or classrooms as a microcosm of the larger world is just that—an image—accomplishing a kind of *representational* compression, but not necessarily addressing how material forces of time-space compression shape our programs, classrooms and identities.

In the early 1990s, for instance, Gerald Graff represented the university as an "academic citadel" transformed by the arrival of new groups, and suggested that his program of teaching the conflicts would help put the humanities at the center of the university's ongoing transformation from a cloistered, segregated space to a democratic forum. This optimism was not only uplifting; it also seemed a strategy to address the bleak economic circumstances of the humanities in an increasingly corporatized higher education environment. We can no longer imagine ourselves working in a "conflict-free ivory tower," warned Graff (6). With the end of the growth economy in higher education, peaceful coexistence, Graff warns, "is increasingly strained, since ideological challenges to curricula can no longer simply be accommodated," as in the past, "by painlessly expanding its frontiers" (7). Hence, Graff proposed making use of our conflicts in teaching and research as a way of legitimizing the humanities as a vital form of public discourse. In making this argument, Graff did not shy away from invoking synecdocal images of the university to represent its relation to the larger society. Teaching the conflicts promised to make the university more truly representative as an institution, turning the curriculum into "a prominent arena of cultural conflict[,] . . . a microcosm, as it should be, of the clash of cultures and values in America as a whole" (8).

Of course, Graff was right to marvel at the "mindboggling juxtaposition" in higher education of "corporate managers side by side with third world Marxists; free market economists with free-form sculptors; mandarin classical scholars with postmodern performance artists; football coaches with deconstructive feminists" (7–8). But by imagining these parties as potential partners in debate, Graff seems stricken with the same hyperreal sense of space that Sedgwick warned about, drastically condensing differences into an imaginary space that ignores the power geometries of the institution. After all, football coaches are often paid more than university presidents and will gain nothing from debating deconstructive feminists. Corporate managers and free market economists may enjoy an entertaining lecture from a third world Marxist, but they are not about to put economic policy, or even academic recommendations on economic policy, up for grabs.[7]

The hyperreality of the image of university as microcosm derives from its erasure of place, and specifically of the way places in higher education are constructed within an ecology of segmentation that directly shapes the rights of presence and movement of different groups. This erasure of place has become even more problematic in much of the reform discourse that has followed Graff, which has further developed his notions of disciplinary conflict through metaphors of boundaries and borders. One influential example of such disciplinary representation is *Redrawing the Boundaries: Transformation of English and American Studies,* a collection of essays published in 1992, the same year as Graff's *Beyond the Culture Wars*. In this collection, editors Stephen Greenblatt and Giles Gunn proposed to *map* changes in English studies over the last twenty five years, linking their discussion of boundaries to daily institutional life, and freely admitting that their map could have been drawn in other ways.

Overall, the contributors attempt to represent both traditional literary fields (medieval, eighteenth century studies) and newer arrivals (gender criticism, composition), mostly through the "new historical" critical perspective exemplified by Greenblatt's now well-known scholarship on Shakespeare. The collection itself tries to accomplish this by dividing English studies into twenty-four fields and enlisting well-known scholars to explain recent changes. However, despite this breadth, the metaphor of change as a redrawing of boundaries has been arguably more influential in shaping humanities reform than any of the individual essays published in the Greenblatt and Gunn collection.

Although Greenblatt and Gunn admit that "all talk of boundaries sits in a complex relation to a recognition of the larger whole within which most of the profession operates," their focus is on boundaries as a way of ordering the discipline's heterogeneous objects and methods of study (7). Greenblatt and Gunn often represent this heterogeneity in the most charged geopolitical terms, drawing on images of warfare, frontiers, and militarized zones (6–7). The problem with such analogies is, again, that they suggest a synecdocal equivalence of disparate places, occluding the politics of place. What virtually gets lost in this disciplinary mapping is any accounting of the relative importance of *different sorts* of boundaries in shaping the rights of presence and movement of different groups in higher education. Difference between ideological specialisms in English may pose menacing boundaries in some situations. But typically this is true only in a limited range of situations, most often involving internecine struggles between permanent English faculty (such as in tenure decisions). As soon as we place ourselves within a wider range of circumstances, we find our work valued differently—in terms of critical thinking, grammatical correctness, productivity, writing skills, high-brow taste, and so on. (For a more detailed discussion of how our work is valued as "abstract labor" rather than in terms of its specific content, see Watkins). Indeed, when humanists do work in interdisciplinary research and teaching programs, or when they sit on campus-wide committees with colleagues in the sciences and social sciences, they often find that the complex methodological and ideological underpinnings of their research matters much less than the fact that they are humanists. In such settings, it is not unusual for colleagues to turn to the lone English professor for the correct wording of a committee document, whether he or she is a Shakespearean or a feminist theorist, deconstructionist or formalist.

In our view, it is simply remiss to attribute vast changes in scholarly knowledge to the arrival of new groups in academia, to propose that volatile issues of nation, race, class, religion, and sexuality have driven and continue to drive such change, and at the same time, to reduce the "imagined space" of literary studies to the issue of drawing the boundaries of critical approaches or fields. The problem with this view is that it promotes the Adamic view of autonomy that we mentioned earlier, and it screens out how developments in the discipline are always being shaped by our positioning relative to flows of persons, goods, and information. It is one thing, for instance, to represent "African American Criticism" as a chapter in *Redrawing the Boundaries,* but it requires a much more complex set of changes to enable it to flourish as a field/space on a university campus. The ability of a department or campus to establish African American Criticism or Black Studies as a vital field is only partly a matter of ideological or methodological legitimacy. It is also related to regional demographics, the university's relationships with local black communities, minority student recruitment and retention policies, faculty salary considerations, and the reception of black faculty and students not only by other faculty but by the administration, staff personnel, and campus police.

In the last decade, a number of scholars have sought to move beyond the limits of "redrawing the boundaries," searching for metaphors besides chronology, periodicity, or essentialized categories of race, ethnicity, or gender to guide our work in English studies. For instance, Patricia Bizzell argues for (re)organizing English curricula in terms of Mary Louise Pratt's now famous metaphor of "contact zones." As Pratt defines the term, contact zones "refer to social spaces where cultures meet, clash, and grapple with each other, often in contexts of highly asymmetrical relations of power, such as colonialism, slavery, or their aftermaths as they are lived out in many parts of the world today" (qtd. in Bizzell 166). In her essay, "'Contact Zones' and English Studies," Bizzell advances contact zones as a new organizing principle for English studies:

> I am suggesting that we organize English studies not in terms of literary or chronological periods, nor essentialized racial or gender categories, but rather in terms of historically defined contact zones, moments when different groups within society contend for the power to interpret what is going on. (167)

The virtue of this approach, in Bizzell's view, is that it treats "multiculturalism as a defining feature" of English studies, and frees us from having to try to "squeeze new material into inappropriate old categories, where its importance could not be adequately appreciated." Instead of asking "prejudicial questions, such as whether Frederick Douglass was as 'good'. . . as Henry Thoreau," we would "look at the rhetorical effectiveness of each writer in dealing with the matter at hand, for example, the need to promote civil disobedience in the contact zone created by white and black efforts to define and motivate action in response to slavery in the antebellum U.S." (167–68). And, as Bizzell points out, since the focus here would be on historically contextualized rhetorical problems, "boundaries between 'content' (literature) and its traditional inferior, pedagogy (composition) are usefully blurred (168). Student writing, too, can be seen as contending in contact zones, since our students lives and words embody negotiations of difference no less than the writers we study.

Bizzell's approach provides a remarkably rich context for student reading and writing and is amply illustrated in her recent textbook *Negotiating Difference*, which includes casebooks of historical documents, narratives, and arguments, each centering on a particular contact zone in the past, such as "First Contacts between Puritans and Native Americans," and "The Debate over Slavery and the Declaration of Independence." Moreover, unlike Greenblatt and Gunn, Bizzell makes a serious effort to recognize students and the cultures they bring with them to the classroom as key to establishing the character of the classroom as a social space. However, despite such recognitions, Bizzell still conceives curricular reform in the traditional terms of content and method, offering new readings and new ways of organizing the intellectual work of English, but not analyzing how that work is institutionally embedded and constrained. If classrooms are contact zones no less than the spaces created by the abolitionist activists in Bizzell's textbook, in what ways are they similar or different? How do contact zones within academia or elsewhere function, regulating what architectural theorist Amos Rapaport calls "unwanted interaction" (285, 293, 297)?

The problem is that even the most provocative and inspiring theorists often shift freely between the multiple senses of terms such as contact zones and borderlands, often leaving those slippages of meaning unanalyzed. For instance, in her famous essay "Arts of the Contact Zone," Pratt uses the term contact zones to illustrate cultural interaction under conditions of colonial conquest in seventeenth-century Peru, Stanford general education classrooms, and her son's elementary school. To be sure, this imaginative range is one of the things that makes the concept of the contact zone provocative. But leaving these shifts unanalyzed also risks the same hyperreality as that created by Graff's use of the metaphor of university as microcosm. The danger is that the imaginative analogy between the contact zones of Peru, Stanford, and an elementary school will elide the materiality of each place in favor of an ideal of cultural negotiation (an ideal, incidently, not entirely dissimilar from Graff's ideal of "democratic debate").

Even the most provocative and inspiring theorists of the borderlands often make a shift similar to Pratt in envisioning borders as both a consequence of violence and oppression as well as a fertile space for social imagination and activism. Drawing on the work of Brazilian educator Paulo Freire, Chicana writer and activist Gloria Anzaldúa, and others, radical pedagogy has developed the idea of "borderlands" to describe how identity and space interact, both as a lived reality and as an ideal. For Anzaldúa, the borderlands of the U.S. and Mexico represent a real place "where the Third World grates up against the first and bleeds . . . the lifeblood of two worlds merging to form a third country—a border culture" (3). But it also represents a cultural project, the formation of "a new mestiza consciousness" (77).

Anzaldúa's *Borderlands* represents a hybrid of poetry, dream, history, and academic argument, and it addresses, at different points, specifically identified audiences of widely different educational levels, cultural orientations, and physical embodiments: Chicana workers, activists and intellectuals, lesbians, whites, heterosexual men, homeless people, and so forth. In its very form and imagined distribution, Anzaldúa's work anticipates networks of interaction and communication that go beyond those now integrated through the university as an institution. For Anzaldúa, the borderlands is a lived and imagined space that challenges the normative range of audiences, experiences, and knowledge found in the university and academic discourse. Despite or perhaps because of this transgressiveness, the idea of borderlands has become a widely influential figure in the discourses of multiculturalism and humanities reform. In its adaptation to the institutional settings of university teaching and research, the concept has been used to represent what Abdul JanMohamed defines as "deeply invested spaces for hegemonic and counterhegemonic contestation," where the "border intellectual" violates the "prescribed borders," in the interest of representing a revolt against the exclusiveness of academic knowledge and institutions (248). According to Henry Giroux, "border pedagogy" advocates "people moving in and out of borders constructed around coordinates of difference and power" and encourages students "to develop a relationship of non-identity with their own subject positions and the multiple cultural, political and social codes that constitute established boundaries of power, dependency and possibility" (qtd. in JanMohamed 246). JanMohamed contends that as teachers develop the mobility to cross cultural boundaries and identities, and thereby help students do the same in academic study and daily life, they develop knowledge of and the potential for "forming counterhegemonic organizations" (246).

We believe there is much possibility in the kind of teaching and research JanMohamed envisions, but there are dangers of romanticizing this role, especially in the designed spaces provided for us by U.S. universities. Most four-year universities, even those located along the U.S./Mexico border, have not yet come close to integrating the range of border tensions that Anzaldúa is exploring in her writing, or in her text's projected networks of contact and interaction. Indeed, the questions of power geometry that need to be emphasized here are implicit in Wendy Hesford's recent admonitions against romanticizing the fluidity of borders, since such borders also reflect "a deeply geographical and social history of exploitive migrant labor and forced movements" (49). As Hesford argues, we need to ask, "Who is crossing what borders? Who is in the position to create border identities? Are border crossers forced into such acts, or are such movements and crossings of their own choosing?" Hesford goes on to remind us that "the boundaries that define communities are freighted with radical inequalities and forms of domination" (52–53). While Hesford acknowledges that "it is possible to construct border identities as acts of solidarity with oppressed peoples," she is also quite wary of how white and middle-class cultures, and more specifically, professional and academic cultures, have historically exploited borders as sites for "cultural tourism" and for producing new credentials and careers, often in ways that benefit traditional constituencies of the higher education marketplace.

To avoid falling into such a trap, we need to be much more skeptical of commonplace assumptions that border-crossing is inherently progressive or good. Indeed, our assumption should be that programs that attempt to create new forms of knowledge and new forms of social contact between campus and community, whether interdisciplinary or not, are always embedded in larger ecologies of segmentation already at work in the campus and city as built environments. In addition, we might assume that border-crossing is a phenomenon driven not only by the choices of students, teachers, and researchers, but also by social and economic forces that are commonly understood as non-disciplinary or extra-disciplinary. To illustrate this more complicated view of border-crossing, we want to explore some recent attempts to cross borders and create new forms of social contact in programs at the universities where we teach. While we want to emphasize a sense of possibility in these attempts, we also want to highlight how these initiatives are embedded, and in some ways reenact, the larger divisions and boundaries already at work in the campus and city as built environments. Indeed, we argue that the hope of these initiatives depends on our vigilance about the power geometry of newly created spaces, and on our ability to counteract inevitable reassertions of older borders and identities. We also want to draw attention to how an increasingly commonplace, and generalized call to cross borders as well as to develop interdisciplinary programs often screens out exactly the sorts of developments we should be paying the most attention to.

Crossing Borders as Action and Effect

At the midwestern public university whose geography we have described above, the administration is now instituting the second phase of a "Blueprint for the Future" championed by the Chancellor, which has four major goals: building "academic excellence," "a community of learners," "a campus without borders," and "an environment that unleashes human potential." Faculty criticism of the blueprint process has focused intensely on its threat to academic freedom and faculty autonomy, and some have claimed that the "transformation workshops" sponsored by the Chancellor amount to heavy-handed propaganda or "corporate mind manipulations" (qtd. in Blackwood). The problem with such descriptions is that they picture the blueprint as a tightly coherent ideological project, rather than as a plurality of processes, each partly constituted by the actual place where the blueprint (or various oppositional appropriations of it) "happens." By focusing narrowly on the ideological content of the workshops, such criticism leaves unscrutinized how the blueprint process is also a response to specific social needs and market pressures that any project for change, progressive or otherwise, would have to engage.

In many ways, the blueprint is a response to a major shift in the power geometries of public and private universities that lack huge endowments to sustain the status quo. In such institutions, the goal of a campus without borders is, among other things, a response to a bleak economic environment for higher education that has pressured administrations to expand enrollments and contract the number of tenureable faculty, especially in English and other humanities or social science disciplines. The decision-makers know that competition for students is likely to intensify in the next decade and that there is little likelihood that budgets will increase proportionately. Administrations also know that the most reliable projections suggest that a majority of growth in student enrollments will likely have to come through expansion of minority student populations. For instance, a recent large-scale study published by the Educational Testing Service projects that over the next two decades the numbers of students attending college are likely to swell from seventeen to nineteen million students, with black, Hispanic, and Asian students accounting for eighty percent of the growth (Wilgoren 16). The study, however, also suggests that "while minority college enrollment is skyrocketing, it is not growing as fast as the black and Hispanic populations ages 18 to 24" (16). Hence, racial integration is likely to remain an elusive goal.

What this means is that campus diversity is not only a matter of social justice, but also the economic interests of universities. A "university without borders" promises more democratic access to education. But whether it achieves this aim or not, it is also an economic program articulated in an environment that demands "more with less." In such an environment, the "excellence" of a program may well depend not on the kinds of borders it crosses, but how it cuts costs (for instance, by lessening the university's dependence on tenureable faculty), and how it cultivates markets (for instance, by improving the university's relationship with local constituencies, eliciting further philanthropic or alumni support, and tapping into various growth sectors of the market for students).

Two programs with significant ties to the English department that are helping the university achieve these ends are the High School/College Dual Credit program (HSCP), and the Advanced Preparation Program (APP). Significantly, these programs primarily involve the English department on account of writing, which tenureable faculty seldom teach. Nevertheless, these programs are reshaping the power geometry of the institution in ways that warrant far more attention than faculty usually give them. The High School/College Program, for example, targets students in area high schools for introductory college courses that yield dual high school/college credit. From 1996–2001, enrollments in this program *increased by a factor of ten times*, climbing from a mere 300 students to roughly *twenty percent* of total college enrollments ("Credit"). While this growth is astonishing, what is even more so is that many faculty in the college are not even aware of the program. The HSCP first-year writing program, which is the largest segment of the overall program, has developed independently of the on-campus composition program, and, although it shares the same course number, the curriculum is built around different textbooks and assignments and has an independent program of teacher development run by college administrators.

The "excellence" of this program, then, has been operationally defined mainly in terms of the potential to open up new streams of students and revenue and to cut costs. In some sense, the first year of college is being subcontracted to local schools, where students are charged one-half tuition, and teachers are hired as university adjuncts even though they are paid by local school districts. With little cost for labor or space, and a new flow of tuition dollars, this is a lucrative operation for a cash-strapped college. It helps recruit students, and lessens tuition costs for students who can take advantage of it, and it provides an opening for some high school teachers to provide new challenges to students.

But how does such a major retrenchment redraw borders? By lowering costs, the HSCP may expand access to higher education for some students. But generally, these are students who are already academically well-prepared and college bound, students who local teachers, counselors and districts have already marked as qualified for, and worthy of being tracked to the program. Hence, although the program may enlarge the pool of local recruits, it also reenacts a class politics similar to that more widely enacted in traditional university admissions. Students who already possess the cultural capital and skills of the professional class are much more likely to be served by the program than those who do not. The program also redraws borders by allowing an increasing amount of instruction to be done off-campus. Although theoretically this change might seem to give humanities disciplines such as English a way to expand their sphere of contact and influence in the community, we would argue that the opposite is occurring. As more students take their general education requirements under programs like the HSCP, courses for underprepared students, first-year writing courses, and other general education courses are increasingly offered under the auspices of administrators and local school districts. If writing can be effectively taught by off-campus teachers with the limited involvement of English, or indeed of any campus faculty, then why hire more tenureable teachers on campus, or even risk the political tensions expanding the corps of adjunct teachers on campus? Without the oversight of campus faculty, the program can be expanded primarily with an eye on profits, and without developing adequate training, curricular focus, or opportunities for breaking down barriers between high school and college teachers. Indeed, in this program, despite its potential to open up dialogue between high school and college teachers, the barriers are formidable. College teachers are often hesitant to spend precious time in an academically marginal program, and high school teachers are often wary that colleagues in the university are less interested in dialogue than in dictating pedagogy and curriculum from above.

Another program attempting to cross borders and redraw boundaries on campus is the Advanced Preparation Program (APP). The program's stated aims echo the boilerplate blueprint rhetoric of "connecting to the greater community" and "celebrating a community of learners." But in this case the slogans sanction quite material changes, and in our view quite progressive changes, in the way the university "crafts a class." In particular, this program targets local public school graduates who are more than fifty percent African American and who have historically been drastically underrepresented in the student body, largely because of poor standardized test scores. As a recent program document describes them, these students are "a diverse group of students from local communities, who, though unable to meet the university's moderately selective admissions requirements, demonstrate potential to succeed academically." Almost forty percent of these one-hundred and nineteen "trial admits" in the first semester of the program were African American, and more than eighty-eight percent finished their first semester in good academic standing. In the second semester, the program has nearly doubled in size.

Like the HSCP, the APP program has received little attention in the English department, or the college, and has been initiated and developed primarily through administrative actions. In the program students typically receive academic advising not through disciplines, but through advisors specifically hired for this program. In certain subjects, these students take classes with the standard curricular designations but in special sections taught by instructors hired within the program. Interestingly, advertising of the APP program in academic disciplines has been quite discreet, and few faculty have shown much interest in trying to bring it under the auspices of disciplinary authority.

But why should faculty be concerned? One reason is because the APP and HSCP programs are one facet of the widescale development of "enrollment management" as a newly professionalized task in universities. Since the 1980s, universities have systemized and formalized the process of crafting a class. One result is that the political work of determining who will be part of academic discussions has been increasingly contained within a relatively insulated network of enrollment experts answerable primarily to the economic imperatives of university administrators. Faculty are becoming more distant from the process than ever, and seem content to be so, even though it is clear that by determining *who* may be part of dialogue, enrollment practices directly shape *what* is likely to become the content of those dialogues.

It is also important to consider that by opening the door for a new set of arrivals, the APP program has not only breached but has also *activated* new borders on campus. For instance, as the title of the Advanced Preparation Program suggests, teachers and students in the program must counteract the stigma that attends their association with the program, as well as persistent patterns of racism, sexism, and classism on campus. As students from the program circulate on campus—in non-APP courses, in shared spaces such as the writing center, and in dormitories and meeting places—they inevitably encounter borders that can be intensified by the expanded presence of underprepared or underrepresented students on campus. Indeed, administrative advocates of the APP program may have a progressive motive in mind for not circulating information about it among faculty, since to do so might arouse public resistance, either out of racist or classist attitudes about the new students admitted, or out of legitimate concerns about the lack of resources available to teach these often underprepared students.

By ignoring programs such as the APP and HSCP, English departments are ignoring how their work is embedded within a shifting power geometry that demands an analysis as close as the one we give to the texts our students read or write. Programs such as the APP and HSCP define a different domain of border negotiations that nonetheless are likely to have powerful effects, even on faculty whose research and classrooms are comfortably remote from such programs. When faculty encounter new populations of students in courses, offices, advising, informal interaction, faculty will inevitably have to make choices—preferably informed political choices—about how to accommodate the widened range of students' needs, levels of academic preparedness, and cultural expectations. However, because reform discourse has so often framed issues of border-crossing so abstractly or idealistically, we fear that faculty choices are now too likely to be made in isolation or by default, uninformed by a shared discourse that brings to the surface the political meanings and consequences of our decisions.

Reform discourse has typically invoked the rhetoric of borders and border-crossing to a much greater degree in addressing curricula, teaching, and self-governance than in engaging program innovations such as the APP or dual-credit programs. However, even in these matters, where faculty often do have more direct control, rhetorics of border-crossing have often been invoked in ways that romanticize the fluidity of borders, to use Hesford's phrase, and ignore how innovations in curricula and teaching also involve forced movement. Indeed, while reform often touts globalism, interdisciplinarity, and community-service as inherently positive terms, how these terms *function* in institutional change is often a far more complex matter.

For instance, one of us teaches at a private, midwestern, comprehensive university that is currently in the midst of implementing decisions derived from an extensive "Academic Program Review." Administrative statements explaining the review have been framed in a typically progressive language that emphasizes the familiar themes of campus and community partnership, globalism, and interdisciplinarity. Specifically, the "operational statement" (which announces itself as "decidedly an *internal* document") names goals such as "excellence," "external connections" (connections between "academic studies and the non-academic world" and between learning and "real-world tasks"), "internal connections" ("connections to other fields" through, for instance, "participation in multi-/interdisciplinary programs"), the "global nature of knowledge, of the workplace, and of human society," and "multiple access points to learning" through "community service," "experiential learning," as well as "technology-based learning" ("Vision" 2).

These may seem progressive and democratic goals, and in fact, the review, while strongly recommended by the university President, also received the faculty senate's endorsement. What soon emerged from the review was that these apparently progressive changes would require a redistribution of resources with some programs and academic units being enhanced and others eliminated. Each department would provide reports on their own currency, innovation, and essentiality to the mission of the university based on enrollment data, number of majors, faculty-student ratios, faculty credentials, and graduates' job success. Based on reports of this data to the Provost, programs would be slated for preservation, enhancement, or possible elimination. Moreover, only twenty percent of programs could be recommended for advancement, and at least twenty percent had to be recommended for further examination and possible "phasing out."

In essence, the rhetorics of globalism, interdisciplinarity, and border-crossing have proven decidedly double-voiced, functioning both to legitimize curricular innovation and to rationalize a thinly-veiled assault on faculty self-governance. The mandate from the Provost that has developed from this program review calls for reduction in the number of academic units in the college of arts and sciences from sixteen to seven or eight. Modern languages, sociology, and rhetoric have already lost status as independent departments, and many faculty have found themselves faced with either pressure to leave the university or find a new departmental home. Some of these faculty are now seeking to forge new interdisciplinary connections and they are crossing borders, but of course, it is often more out of a need to survive than a desire to explore. Interdisciplinary departments, such as the new Department for the Study of Culture and Society (SCS), have arisen, as displaced faculty consolidate around shared interests. The SCS department, for example, now is an umbrella for fields such as sociology, race and ethnic studies, rhetoric, and media studies, and has signed on faculty with such expertise from a number of eliminated or consolidated departments.

The emergence of the new department shows how easily interdisciplinarity and border crossing can be appropriated to serve the new power geometry of higher education. The new department allows a consolidation of resources by conserving space and supplies, streamlining the workforce (eliminating the need to maintain tenured or tenureable faculty, secretarial support, and so on, in many small departments) and enhancing executive control over faculty (submerging the diversity of faculty interests by forcing their representation in larger units). It also presents a major challenge to the English department, which maintained its departmental status despite being criticized in the review process for following its own course "without consultation with other units in the University." Many of the forms of study that are now central to SCS's mission—including multicultural studies, critical studies of media, and cultural studies—have historically had strong roots in English. What formerly existed dispersed across many disciplines, including English, now is grounded in its own physical space and curricular designations. These changes enhance the SCS's authority over the specialisms it has consolidated, and correspondingly, the English department's claim on them is weakened. For this reason, the English department is now under pressure to develop new narratives legitimating its claims to departmental status in the college.

Ironically, faculty in English have often represented writing as the disciplinary area most vulnerable to definition by 'outside' forces. However, in this case, we would argue that writing offers the English department one of the best strategies for maintaining its departmental status and autonomy. Indeed, developing a new interdisciplinary writing major, a process that has recently been begun, has the potential to address institutional concerns in ways that cannot be achieved through support of multicultural or cultural studies tracks housed in SCS. The writing major, which allows twelve hours outside English, highlights the English department as the center of the teaching of reading and writing. Hence, development of this program reinforces English's claims to departmental status by drawing on the general perception that English should be the central institutional space for developing writing programs and courses. This claim has been further strengthened by a recent national survey that suggests that the phasing out of the university's first-year writing requirement (Eng. 001) over the last few years, and its replacement by first-year seminars offered by departments across the college, has diminished the amount of practice first-year students get in writing and oral communication. For example, the survey showed that first-year students had received less experience developing class presentations, in speaking clearly and effectively, and in writing multiple draft assignments than first-year students from the four-hundred and sixty-six colleges also included in the sample (National Survey of Student Engagement).

However English departments handle their historically vexed relation with writing, there is no doubt that scarcity of resources demands that English *selectively* choose how to involve itself in interdisciplinary projects, rather than simply assume that interdisciplinarity and border-crossing are inherently good. Developing effective responses to the reorganization of the college is a key task for the English department, and the situation we have described likely represents circumstances that will become increasingly common in the future in many comprehensive and research universities. Our account of the situation emphasizes the degree to which border-crossing by faculty is perhaps more a matter of forced movement than choice.

However, we are aware that our use of border images to represent negotiations of disciplinarity and expertise among faculty is in many ways quite typical. There are a number of important issues that are left unaddressed by such a limited conception of border-crossing as the negotiation of difference and affiliation in our research or teaching, including demographic issues similar to those we discussed in relation to the APP and dual-credit programs. How will the reconfiguration of disciplinary borders affect the circulation of students within the power geometries of our institutions and the labor market? Will alteration of departmental boundaries change the way different forms of expertise such as cultural or multicultural studies link to the workplace?

Will the English and SCS departments attract enough students to warrant their survival? How employable will their students be?

Answers to these sorts of questions will have a role in determining the long-term viability of both the English department and new departments created by retrenchment. It is too early to answer them at this point in the reforms we have described. But we would note that the ethnic and racial composition of the university's student body has remained relatively constant over the last six years, with the entering class of minority students holding steady at eleven to fifteen percent, and with four to five percent of these students being international students. While many scholars have claimed that the shift toward cultural studies, multiculturalism, race and gender studies, and so on in the humanities has affirmed the cultural capital of underrepresented groups in ways that enhance such groups' access to college, we argue that it remains to be seen if programs like SCS, or the redesigned English department, will open up the university to students who have historically had limited access.

How far can curricular and organizational reform affect the development of new patterns of community membership in higher education? In an economic, political, and legal environment that is making equality of opportunity in higher education harder to achieve, and even the survival of English departments harder to ensure, this question is more important than ever. But we will never achieve even an adequate discussion of the issues unless we examine our teaching and research in relationship to larger ecologies of segmentation in the university and beyond. If we hope to sustain the possibility of critical democratic discourse and action in our classrooms and campuses, we will have to broaden our vision beyond romanticized ideals of border-crossing, contact zones and interdisciplinarity, and come to grips with the full range of factors that construct place in our universities and communities.[8]

Notes

1. For instance, the environmental impact statements used in the court battle over the freeway say little about social costs, prompting the Legal

Aid lawyer representing residents to comment that the "real issues of this case have never been litigated," even though the court struggle was then five years old (Nelson; see also Carroll).

2. For example, the most visible public spending for urban development has gone to projects such as Science City, a Jazz museum and Negro Leagues baseball museum, and inner-city shopping centers—all geared to attracting large flows of tourists and customers from the freeways into interior spaces, rather than interweaving their activities into local neighborhoods.

3. Indeed, labor exploitation in universities might arguably select in favor of faculty who already enjoy middle-class status. This issue has been little studied, but according to one study done by David Leslie, a professor of education at the College of William and Mary, only about ten percent of part-time faculty report household incomes under $25,000, while more than half report household incomes over $55,000 (qtd. in ADE 20).

4. For instance, in the case of *Hopwood v. Texas,* the Fifth Circuit court ruled that the University of Texas could not consider race in law school admissions, repudiating earlier Supreme court precedents. For a fuller account of this ruling, and of the broader legal underpinnings of "color-blind constitutionalism," see *Race and Representation: Affirmative Action,* particularly Reva B. Siegel's essay, "The Racial Rhetorics of Colorblind Constitutionalism: The Case of *Hopwood v. Texas.*"

5. Judith Butler argues this case in refuting statements by the California Board of Regents in 1995 that justified the banning of race as a consideration in university admissions in California. Butler argues that the regents shape disciplinary communities and conversations not so much by discouraging discourse about race, gender, and ethnicity so much as by "circumscribing the proper domain of their mentionability" (157).

6. For instance, the Board of Regents resolution stipulates in section 5 that "not less than fifty percent and not more than seventy-five percent of any entering class on any campus shall be admitted solely on the basis of academic achievement" (Post 400).

7. Of course, Graff's reform program proposes more realistic debates, but it still downplays the gap between curricular ideas and the social and economic forces that construct higher education as a material place. Reform alone can never turn the curriculum into "a microcosm . . . of America as a whole" without a corresponding revolution in the economic and social forces that determine who will be part of the debate, where it will be held, and on what terms.

8. The authors wish to thank the Drake University Center for the Humanities and the Missouri Research Board for providing funding in support of this research.

Works Cited

Academic Program Review, Report of the Provost, Drake University, October 2000.

ADE Ad Hoc Committee on Staffing. "Report of the ADE Ad Hoc Committee on Staffing." *ADE Bulletin.* 122 (Spring 1999): 7–26.

Anzaldúa, Gloria. *Borderlands: La Frontera.* San Francisco: Aunt Lute, 1987.

Bérubé, Michael. *The Employment of English: Theory, Jobs, and the Future of Literary Studies.* New York: New York UP, 1998.

Bérubé, M., and C. Nelson, eds. *Higher Education Under Fire: Politics, Economics, and the Crisis of the Humanities.* New York: Routledge, 1995.

Bird, J., ed. *Mapping the Futures: Local Cultures, Global Change.* New York: Routledge, 1993.

Bizzell, Patricia. "'Contact Zones' and English Studies." *College English* 56 (1994): 163–69.

Bizzell, Patricia, and Bruce Herzberg, eds. *Negotiating Difference: Cultural Case Studies for Composition.* Boston: Bedford, 1996.

Blackwood, Kendrick. "Brain Wash: Chancellor Martha Gilliland Takes UMKC On a Long, Strange Trip." *Pitch Weekly.* 20 Sept. 2001.

"Blueprint for the Future." 17 Mar. 2002. http://www.umkc.edu/blueprint/.

Bowen, William G., and Derek Bok. *The Shape of the River: Long-Term Consequences of Considering Race in College and University Admissions.* Princeton: Princeton UP, 1998.

Butler, Judith. "An Affirmative View." Post and Rogin 155–74.

"Credit Hour Production by Academic Unit Providing the Instruction, Winter 1996–Winter 2001." Office of Enrollment Management, University of Missouri-Kansas City, March 2002.

Carroll, Robert L. "Social Price Tag on Freeway." *Kansas City Times.* 12 Feb. 1976.

Duffy, Elizabeth, and Idana Goldberg. *Crafting a Class: College Admissions and Financial Aid, 1955–1994.* Princeton: Princeton UP, 1998.

Gates, Henry Louis Jr. "African American Criticism." Greenblatt and Gunn. 303–319.

Giroux, Henry A., and Peter McLaren, eds. *Between Borders: Pedagogy and the Politics of Cultural Studies.* New York, Routledge, 1994.

Graff, Gerald, and Gregory Jay. "A Critique of Critical Pedagogy." Bérubé and Nelson. 201–213.

Graff, Gerald. *Beyond the Culture Wars: How Teaching the Conflicts Can Revitalize American Education.* New York: Norton, 1992.

Greenblatt, Stephen, and Giles Gunn, eds. *Redrawing the Boundaries: the Transformation of English and American Literary Studies.* New York: MLA, 1992.

Hancock, John. "The Apartment House in America." King. 151–89.

Hesford, Wendy. *Framing Identities: Autobiography and the Politics of Pedagogy.* Minneapolis: U of Minnesota P, 1999.

Institute of International Education. "Open Doors: Source of Funds." 26 Sept. 2003. http://opendoors.iienetwork.org/?p=25183.

Internal memo from the SCS chair, Drake University, to the Interim Dean, 21 September 2001.

JanMohamed, Abdul R. "Some Implications of Paulo Freire's Border Pedagogy." Giroux and McLaren 242–52.

King, Anthony D., ed. *Buildings and Society: Essays on the Social Development of the Built Environment.* Boston: Routledge, 1980.

Kunstler, James Howard. *The Geography of Nowhere: The Rise and Decline of America's Man-made Landscape.* New York: Simon, 1994.

Massey, Doreen. "Power-Geometry and a Progressive Sense of Place." Bird 59–69.

Nelson, Robert T. "Freeway Lawsuit 'Rumble.'" *Kansas City Star.* 2 Mar. 1978: 6C: 1.

Owens, Derek. *Composition and Sustainability: Teaching For a Threatened Generation.* Urbana: NCTE, 2001.

Post, Robert, and Michael Rogin, eds. *Race and Representation: Affirmative Action.* New York: Zone, 1998.

Pratt, Mary Louise. "Arts of the Contact Zone." *Profession* 91. New York: MLA, 1991. 33–40.

Rapoport, Amos. "Vernacular Architecture and the Cultural Determinants of Form." King. 283–305.

Sedgwick, Eve. "Gender Criticism." Greenblatt and Gunn. 271–302.

Siegal, R.B. "The Racial Rhetorics of Colorblind Constitutionalism: The Case of *Hopwood v. Texas.*" Post and Rogin. 1998. 29–72.

Spellmeyer, Kurt. "'Too Little Care': Language, Politics, and Embodiment in the Life-World." *College English* 55.3 (1993): 265–83.

Spivak, Jeffrey. "Today's Road Opening Represents Progress, Pain." *Kansas City Star.* 27 July 1999: A1.

"Time to Update Freeway Views." *Kansas City Times.* 20 Feb. 1979: 6A:1.

Tornatzky, Louis, et al. "Who Will Stay and Who Will Leave?: Individual, Institutional and State-Level Predictors of State Retention of Recent Science and Engineering Graduates." Southern Growth Policies Board, 2000.

"UMKC's Advanced Preparation Program: Beyond Surviving to Thriving." 13 Mar. 2002. http://www.umkc.edu/stu-aff/enrollmentmgmt_experiencingumkc/app-bulletsummaryrevision.doc.

"Vision 2010." Draft Operational Statement, Drake University. Feb. 2000.

Watkins, Evan. *Work Time: English Departments and the Circulation of Cultural Value.* Stanford: Stanford UP, 1989.

Wilgoren, Jodi. "Swell of Minority Students Is Predicted at Colleges." *The New York Times.* 24 May 2000: A16.

CHAPTER THIRTEEN

Bodysigns: A Biorhetoric for Change

KRISTIE S. FLECKENSTEIN

As we move into the twenty-first century, Lillian Bridwell-Bowles writes, the most significant issue we face is ensuring that "our language and our writing should be adequate enough to make our dreams, our visions, our stories, our thinking, and our actions not just revolutionary but transformative" ("Freedom" 46). Our commitment as teachers is to "make our classrooms vital places where students learn not only the various conventions of academic writing, but also the power of communication to change things, to transform" (47). This dedication to transformation resonates to a similar agenda that permeates feminist studies and cuts across theoretical-philosophical-political lines.[1] Susan Jarratt notes that "both feminist inquiry and post-current-traditional composition studies . . . seek to transform styles of thinking, teaching, and learning rather than to reproduce stultifying traditions" (3). However, this commitment is fraught with difficulty because transformation—that is change radical enough to rewrite the rules supporting a particular arrangement of culture—is difficult to effect. Transformation presents us with three challenges: we must engage in a different way of seeing, one that allows us to recognize the constitution of the status quo through rules and through the enactment of those rules; we must evolve and deploy a different way of speaking, an alternative discourse that allows us to use language in ways that ex-

This essay has been excerpted from *JAC* 21 (2002): 761–90 with the permission of *JAC: Journal of Advanced Composition.*

ceed its representation; and, finally, we must live in different ways so that change is neither co-opted nor short-circuited.

A response to these challenges, as well as a tool for and a medium of change, lies with what I will call a "biorhetoric," or a discourse of bodysigns. In this essay, I explore the ways in which a biorhetoric offers the possibility of effecting radical change by positioning us within the ambiguous interplay of materiality and semiosis. "Materiality" refers to the fluid potentiality of physical reality. It includes bodies, places, and performances—"enactments" of reality in particular places at specific times. "Semiosis" refers to all that patterns or shapes the potential of physical reality. It includes any sign system, any rule-governed arrangement, including DNA, immune systems, art, ritual and language itself. "Bodysigns" emphasizes the inextricability of materiality and semiosis. Although language allows us to speak as if materiality and semiosis were separate, they are mutually entangled in a nonlinear weave of cause and effect. We can know them and live them only at the point where they blur. Positioned within the spin of bodysigns, a biorhetoric provides a double perspective from which to recognize the semiotic-material nature of the status quo and of change. Also, like the cyborg surrealism that Donna Haraway sees in Lynn Randoph's paintings, a biorhetoric offers us a double way to speak, one that can "embody and exceed its representations and blast its syntax" (Haraway, *How* 122). Finally, a biorhetoric provides a means to enact a double way of being, one in which we live within the blur of bodysigns.

I begin my examination of a biorhetoric as a tool for and a medium of change by exploring the facets of its double vision. Drawing on the work of feminist writing teachers, I demonstrate in the first section of this essay the desire for and the difficulties of a biorhetoric's double vision. Rather than defining reality as either a textual construct or an experiential one, a biorhetoric represents reality through a double lens of bodysigns. To borrow from Adrienne Rich, I suggest that the realm of a biorhetoric is the point at which the edges blur ("No. 29" 111). In my second section of this essay, I turn to Gregory Bateson's theory of meaning to reweave semiosis and materiality into a vocabulary of metaphor by which we can speak double. Bateson offers us double logics, that position us within a grammar, or a system of rules, while simultaneously offering us the means to disrupt that system. I illustrate the effects of double-speaking with an example of a paradigm shift in science, a discipline traditionally positioned outside the doubling of bodysigns. Finally, in my third section, I turn to the promise of a biorhetoric for a different way of living. A biorhetoric calls me to a double being, a mélange of what Haraway calls topos and tropos ("Promises" 296). I offer an enactment of that double living through a metalogue, a way of living writing that blurs the who, the what, and the how (see Bateson, *Steps* 1).

Double Vision: Seeing through Bodysigns

"May God us keep / From Single vision & Newton's sleep," William Blake wrote in a letter to Thomas Butts (qtd. in Bateson, *Sacred* 93), seeking in his "infernal process" a fusion of word and image that transforms representation. We also require the "partiality, irony, intimacy, and perversity" of a double vision (*Simians* 151). First, a double vision is needed so that we can recognize the ways in which we contribute to and are dependent on the status quo we wish to change. As participants in as well as creators of meaning, we automatically contribute to the constitution and the continuation of the contexts that give birth to us. Individual and institutional identity reveal as much. The very identity of women, Linda Alcoff reminds us, is constituted by women's position: "[S]he herself is part of the historicized, fluid movement, and she therefore actively contributes to the context within which her position can be delineated" (286). The paradoxical positioning of both composition studies and feminist inquiry also reflects this doubleness. "Despite the desire to reconfigure disciplinary boundaries," Jarratt perceptively points out, both feminism and composition studies "need to claim disciplinarity to achieve academic legitimacy and obtain resources (faculty members, courses, research support)" (3). To exist, composition studies and feminist inquiry organize themselves around two contradictory needs: the need to change institutional mandates and the need to honor those mandates in order to continue existing. To challenge the status quo, then, we have to see reality doubled, both our allegiance and our resistance to particular arrangements of culture.

Second, we need double sight to perceive the ways in which our discourse and our performances intertwine in systems of oppression and systems of privilege. Consider the swirl of bodysigns in the realities of nontraditional college students. In the academy, it is not institutional "edits"—or language alone—that conspire to limit our students' (and our) ability to succeed; it is institutional "edits" constituting and constituted by material conditions. Mary Soliday points to this double conspiracy of bodies and signs. She explains that the illogic of and inequities in many of our institutional practices can be traced to deliberate efforts to render material conditions meaningless. For instance, through their policies, institutions ignore the physical reality of working-class students' existence: the thirty- to forty-hour workweeks, the children, and the long hours commuting between home, school, and work. She ties institutional refusal to recognize such realities to the political resistance to remedial education in the City University of New York. But by dismissing the constraints of long work hours, by providing no flexible childcare, and by turning a blind eye to travel time, the institution renders those material factors an effective barrier to many students' education. It does so through language. Institutional mandates codify into a system the very differences the institution refuses to recognize. Language—an official language of rules and policies—is used to elide these material factors, and thus it is this language that makes these material factors significant in the academic lives of the students.

Recognizing and changing material inequities requires recognizing and changing the codification of those inequities through language. It requires seeing through bodysigns. We cannot gain for our students open scheduling, childcare support, and satellite classrooms if we do not tackle both the material contexts and the policies that render the need for change invisible. To ignore the power of the word to define what constitutes "reality" in a system is to divest us of any meaningful strategies for changing that pattern. To ignore the power of material contexts to impinge on the power of the word is to divest ourselves of any meaningful way of recognizing the tyranny of institutions. We can rage at inequitable material conditions, but we will remain in the grasp of dicta without the power to change them because we have split conditions and dicta into separate categories of meaning. By privileging either discourse or materiality, we rob ourselves of any way to alter the linguistic systems that, in a paradoxical move, evoke and reify material inequities by decreeing them nonexistent.

The desire for and the difficulty of maintaining a double vision are both evident in composition studies. The struggles over basic writing offers insight into these difficulties. The temptation in composition studies, a discipline that anchors itself in language arts, is to turn to discourse—to the writing and unwriting of institutional edits—as the means by which we can perceive the need for and enact change in material conditions. The rich work of David Bartholomae reflects the importance of conceptualizing meaning and identity as textual constructs. Dedicated to students, especially those traditionally marginalized by the academy, and to the transformation of social systems that limit students' potential, Bartholomae advocates a linguistic orientation that he hopes will open up opportunities for social change. Drawing on poststructuralist philosophies, Bartholomae argues that identity is a rhetorical construction that readers and writers configure within textual lacunae. Permeated by cultural and ideological discourses, identity does not exist prior to or outside of the discursive event. Thus, the writer outside the text is immaterial; it is the subject position, "the way the 'writer' is positioned within a discourse" that is important ("Reply" 123). And this subject position is in particular need of deconstruction if it is figured as first person singular: "a figure of the writer as a free agent, as independent, self-authorizing, a-historical, a-cultural" (123). Our pedagogical and scholarly energies should focus on deconstructing the writer's rhetorical manifestations, particularly those that are built on a "Jimmy Stewart/Joseph Andrews" or Marlboro Man kind of autonomy, Bartholomae argues (123).[2] As he explains, the aim of composition pedagogy predicated on a textual stance is to destabilize the traditional Western sense of identity as an independent construct outside language and to demonstrate the way in which identity is always lodged within language ("Writing"; "Tidy"). Such a linguistic orientation offers students the opportunity to disentangle the ways in which discourse writes them, constrains their identities, and limits their opportunities for growth. Simultaneously, this perspective offers them the means to rewrite those identities.

Without a doubt, this approach holds much promise for enabling members of our culture blessed with a sense of a stable identity to ascertain the degree to which linguistic privilege underwrites their sense of a stable self. By itself, however, it cannot address the doubling of semiosis and materiality in the status quo. First, a textual orientation is a problematic position for women and other marginalized minorities, who, as Celeste Schenck points out, have never achieved "the self-possession of post-Cartesian subjects" and thus do not have "the luxury of 'flirting with the escape from identity,' which the deconstructed subject may enjoy" (qtd. in Synder 25). Bracketing the material individual from the textual persona can be effective only if all writers share a similar material positioning and thus share access to the same textual identities. Such is not the case. For women, their identities are already fractured; their "I" is already dismissed.

A second problem unresolved by a solely textual approach to reality is the question of judgment: if we are caught within competing discourses of the real, how we do determine which discourse is "true," or as Susan Griffin asks, how do we call into question the lie that torture in Brazil never took place? We live tenuously positioned in a posthuman world, as Katherine Hayles warns us, a world that increasingly strips us of a sense of our materiality and translates us into pure discursive patterns, into exclusively semiotic beings. And within the womb of the word, we can so easily exist with no sense of what Cornel West calls "the ragged edges of necessity, of what it means to be impinged upon by structures of oppression" (277). By seeing bodies as signs, as lines of code, we can all too easily fall into the trap "of thinking that the state repression that scars human bodies can be understood in terms of linguistic models," which it cannot (271). As West points out, "Power operates very differently in nondiscursive than in discursive ways." He warns that a culture that denies "the knowledge that we cannot not know,"—the knowledge that people are starving and killing and dying, the knowledge that too many of our people live on the "ragged edges of necessity"—is a culture doomed (271).

Discourse is undeniably a primary means by which we constitute identities for ourselves and are constituted by others. But by conceiving meaning solely as a web of textual relationships, we bracket and ignore the material flow within the entire performance, especially the loop we call writing. Bodies in specific material sites write signs just as much as signs write bodies into specific material sites (see Fleckenstein, "Writing"). Jack Selzer points out, "Language and rhetoric have a persistent material aspect that demands acknowledgement, and material realities often (if not always) contains a rhetorical dimension that deserves attention: for language is not the only medium or material that speaks" (8). Likewise, Deborah Brandt articulates the need for a double vision in literacy studies:

> If we are going to understand better what literacy instruction represents to students in the future and how it sometimes, inexplicably, can go awry, it is especially important to know about the setting in which knowledge of reading and writing have come to them and the significance implied in those settings. We must understand better what is compelling literacy as it is lived. (477)

When bodies are conflated with signs, trapped in the single vision of the text, ethnographic studies cannot account for

> the complexities involved when a preschooler takes up writing to displace her mother's reading, or when a daughter decodes her father's burdens [budgets written in the margins of a newspaper] along with the nightly news or when a child's first attempt at *imitatio* [copying her mother's signature] begins with the guilt of theft. (460)

We cannot escape place, although we can deny it and redefine it; nor can we escape the paradoxes engendered by bodysigns, although we can deny and redefine them. What happens to the myelin on a nerve sheath directly implicates a writer's identity, essayist Nancy Mairs wryly reminds us. Who would she be if she did not have multiple sclerosis, Mairs muses? "Literally, no body." Who she is as a writer is directly tied to the demyelinated lesions in her central nervous system, to the fact that she, as someone bound to a wheelchair, is waist-high in the world. Mairs reflects,

"In all likelihood I would [have become a writer] . . . .But I could not conceivably have become the writer I am" (8–9).

An alluring solution to the single vision of the text is to turn to the vision of experience, to the performances of bodies in specific sites at specific moments. Breaking with the dominant textual orientation in composition studies, Kurt Spellmeyer laudably highlights in his concept of attunement the importance of experience, of being in the world ("After"; "Too"). Spellmeyer attempts to balance the overemphasis on discursivity in composition studies by emphasizing the necessary materiality in our constructions of self and other. "If the world is not a text," he points out, "then when we treat it as one we soon lose the capacity to differentiate between actions that can lead to meaningful change and those symbolic practices that substitute for action all too easily" ("After" 893–94). What gets lost in a "semiotic universe," Spellmeyer explains, "is the crucial distinction between 'codes' or 'signs,' which simply 'signify,' and the living words that foster a 'felt' resonance between ourselves and the world" (906). Spellmeyer insists on "attunement" with the world as a balance to the focus on textuality. Given a poststructuralist orientation in composition studies and a predisposition to honor the language in "language arts," it would be easy, temptingly so, to embrace Spellmeyer's attunement as a means of being in (and writing about) the world that bypasses the segmentation of semiosis.

Choosing attunement over rhetoric offers us an alluring perspective, but it is still a single vision, one that, like the linguistic turn, elides the inextricability of bodysigns and the ways they mesh to craft and to contest reality. Christine de Vinne highlights the inextricability of bodysigns in a visceral way through her examination of the confluence of both the cannibalism of the Donner Party trapped in the Sierras during the winter of 1846, the cannibalistic rhetoric of westward expansion, and the cannibalized narratives of the Donner Party survivors. While De Vinne's study emphasizes the tangle of bodysigns, Min-Zhan Lu and Bruce Horner warn of the danger of amputating bodies from signs and erasing signs from bodies. They argue that an exclusive focus on embodiment, such as Spellmeyer's emphasis on attunement, posits a "polarized, hierarchical relation between experience and discourse ('text'), valorizing experience as both prior to and greater than discursive understanding" (259). This stance imagines experience as beyond the "politics of representation," or beyond semiosis. Experience, however, can never be conceptualized outside of language. We have nothing so unproblematic as direct, unmediated access to the world. What is necessary, Lu and Horner urge, is finding a relationship "between experience and discourse [that] is not polar and hierarchical but dialectical," and that dialectical relationship is not easy to enact (259).

The need to attend to both semiosis and materiality vibrates throughout feminist approaches to writing and teaching writing. Concerned with women's historical erasure in rhetoric and with their literal silencing in the classroom, feminists in and out of composition studies have worked to validate women's experiences—the performances of their lives—as a source of knowledge. Jarratt points to the limitations of a strictly rhetorical agenda. "The maxim that everything is rhetoric," she explains, "a triumphant discovery for some, leaves unspecified what must be addressed by both composition and feminism: the specificity and materiality of difference" (9). A vision of writing as a vision of experience offers egress into difference, a process that Kathleen Dixon calls exposing the underside of the political subject (257). Mary Salibrici concurs: "We do not encourage our students to take their places within the broader academic community by asking them to erase themselves from their own singular material presence" (394). Instead, "we insist on experience, especially the representation of daily activity, as a source of feminist theory in composition and rhetoric" (Phelps and Emig 410). Feminists and composition pedagogy need to honor "individuals' eloquent stories as fundamental supplements to more abstract structural information and analysis as well as sources of theoretical concepts and insights in their own right" (410). Bridwell-Bowles explicitly centers her writing pedagogy on this experiential agenda, encouraging her students to compose, as she has gradually done, in "a more personal voice, an expanded use of metaphor, a less rigid methodological framework," in an effort to privilege more personal, nonlinear, and emotional forms and processes ("Discourse" 350). Our subjectivities, Salibrici ironically points out, "our ways of reading, may of course be fictions; but, fact or fiction, we have to start with them, if we are to learn how they may or may not be related to the world at large" (394).

Overlapping this effort to honor material experience is the simultaneous effort to honor rhetoric. Feminists in composition studies fear that an unalloyed emphasis on materiality will lead to an essentialized or polarized gender identity, erasing the differences that the emphasis was designed to illuminate. Gesa Kirsch and Joy Ritchie struggle with this problem in their discussion of research and the importance of "a politics of location," a phrase they borrow from Adrienne Rich. Committed to developing a more ethical approach to research, one that acknowledges the position of researcher and subject, Kirsch and Ritchie urge a problematized politics of location that is "unrelentingly self-reflective" (10). To avoid both the essentialism implicit within personal experience and the colonization implicit when the voice of a woman becomes the voice of women, Kirsch and Ritchie attempt to strike a balance between materiality and rhetoric, returning both to the web of "social relationships" and advocating an ethics of care in research practices. Jarratt seeks a similar dialectic. Fearing that experience, faceted through no other lens than itself, reenacts the tyranny of the autonomous subject, the autonomous experience, Jarratt argues for a materiality framed by the social/historical context within which it is born (4–9). Acknowledging the necessity and the limits of personal voice, Jarratt borrows from Spivak the concept of double rhetoric: "rhetoric understood as a dual process of representation—as both a figurative and political act—gives names to language that articulates difference while exposing the power relations at work in acts of naming" (9). Thus, voice is not only positioned materially, it is also positioned within the social and historical discourses that infuse it.

What continues to struggle for survival in this experiential/rhetorical doubling, however, is the nature of the experiential/rhetorical cusp. When grappling with life along the diagonal slash between experience and rhetoric, a line that is neither rhetorical nor material but both, the temptation is to hail the material into the realm of the rhetorical. Kirsch and Ritchie's "social relationships" are discursively crafted, shaped by language. What remains unclear is how social relationships—including bodies, places, and performances—shape language. Similarly, Jarratt's reliance on double rhetoric suggests that bodies are texts, but not that texts are bodies. As Jarratt explains:

> Examining rhetorical configurations keeps at bay any universal subject (man or woman), shifting the discursive grounds for authority. In other words, the "we" of my title cannot be known in any way distinct from the "were saying," and no claim of "as"—signifying either resemblance or simultaneity—will stand unchallenged by the continuing generation of other words. (10)

This leads Jarratt to focus on the "were saying." As she explains in the introduction to *Feminism and Composition Studies*, the goal of the collection of essays, as the subtitle indicates, is to "examine new strategies, 'other words,' for writing, teaching and learning at the productive spaces where the two fields meet and diverge," a process that might double rhetoric but still relegates materiality to the formative realm of the sign without choreographing what Michel de Certeau call the dance of "the word when it is spoken, that is, when it is caught in the ambiguity of an actualization" (Jarratt 4; de Certeau 117).

Without naming it as such, feminists' efforts in composition manifest a commitment to the bodysigns of a biorhetoric. But those efforts also reflect the difficulties of just such an agenda, for it requires a positioning where the edges between materiality and semiosis blur. Meaning is not material; it is not semiotic: it is both at the same time. Citing her Catholic upbringing as well as her training in molecular biology, Donna Haraway notes that "biochemistry and language just don't feel that different to me" (*How* 96). She explains, "The first thing I'd say is that words are intensely physical for me. I find words and language more closely related to flesh than to ideas" (85). Meaning relies on and implies the existence of material potential. But it also relies on and implies a semiotic marking or segmenting of that potential, for without that segmentation, potential remains unknowable. Without a doubt, we need Foucault's biopolitics, the insight that the material details of life—such as what we wear, how we sit, and where we eat—all conspire to maintain the dominance of a particular discursive arrangement of culture. As de Certeau observes, "There is no law that is not inscribed on bodies. Every law has a hold on the body. . . . It engraves itself on parchments made from the skin of its subjects. It articulates them in a juridical corpus. It makes its book out of them" (139–40). But we also need Antonio Gramsci's contradictory insight that material experiences—experience in and of the world—will always contend with the ideological apparatus implicit within a culture's dominant discourses (324–27). A biorhetoric offers a double lens that is neither the product of language nor the product of materiality but the confluence of both. . . .

* * * *

Double Being: Living through Bodysigns

Recognizing the need for change and evolving strategies of change require double vision and double tongues. But ensuring the continuance of change requires double living. Human societies and human lives possess amazing elasticity. Each can absorb an instrument of change and recast it so that it supports the system it was designed to undermine. To forestall co-optation, radical change requires of us a different way of being, as well as a different way of seeing and speaking. We have to "makes ourselves anew," bell hooks tells us, or our change will be preempted and rendered transient: "In that vacant space after one has resisted there is still the necessity to become—to make oneself anew" with "new, alternative habits of being" (17). A biorhetoric offers an invitation to a new kind of living, a kind of double being in which we precariously poise ourselves within the swirl of bodysigns. In that swirl, the edges between who, what, and how we exist blur. In this last section, I turn to my teaching as a site of that precarious double living.

To teach and write so that "the truth & the body / itself becomes a mouth" requires a reconfiguration of the web of meaning within which I am woven and a reconfiguration of who I am in that web. A flaw of critical pedagogy as manifested in cultural studies approaches to composition is the belief that students require transformation and that teacher as catalyst is outside the venue of that change (see Spellmeyer, "Out").[3] But lodged within the maelstrom of double speaking and weighed with double logics, it can never be students who change and teachers who elicit that change. Instead, it can only be the teacher-student-cum-classroom who changes. From the perspective of a biorhetoric, I cannot separate myself as writer or teacher from the meanings and the sites I create as they create me. I cannot separate myself from any radical change I hope to initiate. I, too, must be transformed. As a bodysign among bodysigns, I can no longer teach safe in the assumption that my identity stops at the end of a text or at the boundaries of my skin. A biorhetorical identity exceeds both bodies and sentences. As Haraway so wisely asks, "Why should our bodies end at the skin or include at best other beings encapsulated by skin?" (*Simians* 178).

My student Eileen and I offer an illustration of a biorhetoric that blurs the comfortable divisions among who, what, and how. I chose to focus the readings of a first-semester composition course on the problematics of gender. That topic also served as the starting point for students' writing. On the first day of class, Eileen, a poised 18-year-old, asked if she could select another topic because gender just did not interest her. When I refused her request, she acquiesced gracefully. The first draft of her first paper was built on her experiences babysitting children in two families. In both families, mother and father pursued active and demanding careers. Concerned about the welfare of the children, Eileen argued that the mothers in both situations needed to reorder their priorities because they were jeopardizing their "womanhood" in their efforts to prove their equality to men. My comments on her first draft focused on the need to balance her representation of family responsibilities; otherwise, I warned, she risked alienating the very audience she was addressing: career women. Eileen responded in a detailed email, concluding with a single paragraph set off from the rest of her response: "First, I don't want to write what you want to hear. My audience is not you. I'm not about to turn this into a totally feminist paper."

It would be easy (temptingly so) to interpret this conflict as a problem of rhetorical perspective: Eileen's problem, Eileen's perspective, Eileen's rhetoric. My role, then, would be heroic: to leap into the gaps created by the paradoxes rife in her message and use that position to leverage open—to transform—Eileen's thinking. I would rescue her from her own lack of critical sensitivity. This patriarchal figuration of teacher as heroic rescuer is the dominant stance, the dominant way of being, in composition studies. Kirk Branch claims that the central metaphor framing literacy efforts, including those predicated on narrow interpretations of Paulo Freire's work, is that of the hero. The literacy worker is cast in the role of one who "knows what students need, gives it to them, and thus enables their transformation," but the worker remains unaffected by that transformation (207). Quoting Lyotard, Beth Daniell calls this the "emancipation narrative" in which we assume the role of "heroes of liberty" (401). Within the context of the patriarchal hero narrative, the unit of power is that of the individual agent, bounded by discrete frontiers, interacting but not transacting. As a hero, I inhabit a site of power outside the process of the change that I demand of my students, serving as a catalyst rather than as a participant in their sea change. But in separating myself from my students, I see with a single vision and speak with a single voice, barring myself from the site of that transformation and thus barring myself and my students from any lasting change.

To believe that I am outside the transformation I wish to initiate in my writing and my teaching is to remain tied to a single way of seeing, a single way of speaking, and a single way of being. Eileen's choice of topic and perspective are not the product of "Eileen"; they are the product of "Eileen-and-me" joined into a complex web of mutually constituting relationships, including the physical weight of a technology-rich classroom with an avowed feminist teacher. "Her" paper is a contextual effort, the outgrowth of an overlap of bodysigns within which participants—me, Eileen, the children she cares for, my children whom I care for—struggle for identity. At work here is not merely a difference in philosophical or rhetorical perspective, a difference arising out of *as-if* logic. It is a difference ensuing from the contradictory and complementary loops of a biorhetoric. As Bateson explains, "[I]n the world of ideas, it takes a *relationship*, either between two parts or between one part at time one and the same part at time two to activate some third component which we may call the *receiver*" . . . (*Mind* 106). Neither Eileen nor I "exist" prior to those constituting relationships. The paper (the e-mail) written by Eileen-and-teacher is merely a linguistic manifestation of the looping web of logics permeating it. It is a statement about those logics. And as such it requires not that I rescue Eileen but that we rescue each other. . . . Eileen writes. I write. *Eileen is I.*

Here is the site of my double living. If I put Eileen outside of "me," if I set myself as authority and author of *her* transformation, if I claim all knowledge, insight, and enlightenment for myself and render Eileen clay to be molded—passive, ill-formed, inert—then she remains mine to exploit, mine to change, while I remain, like God, changeless. The patriarchal hero narrative that defines me as a transformer prevents me from achieving any lasting transformation. Under the threat of the grade, a student submits to "redemption"—for sixteen weeks, until another class and another round of messianic pedagogy. The old single way of thinking co-opts my strategies and makes them serve the system of oppression (and privilege) I wish to transform.

Spaces and gaps are not enough, as hooks reminds me. Alternative ways of being are required, and a biorhetoric—the swirl of double logics in which bodies and signs merge—provides a framework by means of which I can rethink transformation as an enactment of relationships, a performance of bodysigns. From the perspective of a biorhetoric, individuals exist only within the spirals of a particular network of logics joined at a particular moment. They live double: as a single loop but one that constitutes and is constituted by the intricate array of loops within which it is immanent. Transformative pedagogy and transformative writing must trace, not efface, the relevant pathways of logics swirling together. My individual identity exists lodged within the whorls comprising my body and in the convolutions of logics that destabilize the boundaries of my skin—ergo, Eileen is I. I cannot separate Eileen from me, nor can Eileen separate herself from me, without risking ethical disaster in which transformation is rendered coercion and change is absorbed back into the system. Bateson warns me that, if I set myself outside of my environment I will see the world around me as "mindless and therefore not entitled to moral or ethical considerations" (*Steps* 468).

In reducing my "survival unit" to that of the discrete individual, I make the world, my classrooms, and my students mine to exploit.

Rather than the hero's quest, a biorhetoric suggests for me a different narrative—the alchemist's fable—one that evokes a double way of being (see Keller). Hermetic wisdom is predicated on the double logics of a biorhetoric. Central to alchemy is the paradoxical notion that knowledge occurs via a union of subject and object: the identification of the self and the not self at the point of knowing yields the object to be known. Reality is innately contradictory to an alchemist, both real and metaphoric at the same time, a paradox that worked so powerfully for Galileo. Thus, the medieval alchemist could not engage in any transmutation of base metal into gold without simultaneously transmuting himself because self and base metal are the same. Material transformation and spiritual transformation must, therefore, be reciprocal processes. The alchemist can never stand outside of the process of radical change. Guided by the idea that metaphorical *is* the logic of the doctrine of correspondences, alchemy recasts individual as androgyne, a hermaphroditic figure that joins male and female into a composite of opposites. To alter one element of the androgyne requires altering the entire being because the two are fused in the one (see Serres xv–xvii).

Galileo challenged Aristotle's dictum that light bodies and heavy bodies fall at different rates by doubling the language of alchemy and the language of science. Perhaps the patriarchal hero in composition can be re-sited within an alchemy of pedagogy. I do not wish to disregard or lose the value of the hero, of individual agency for myself or my students. What I wish to do is move my sense of reality from one that relies on an individual unit of power to one that privileges the play of relationships. In Daniell's words, I want to shift from "the grand narrative where we all get to be heroes of an economic revolution [to] a grander narrative that calls us to be laborers in the vineyard" (403). Situated here, in the vineyard, any transformation I effect will affect me as well. I can never be outside of that transformation; therefore, I must take responsibility for that transformation. I want, in Haraway's words, to take "*pleasure* in the confusion of boundaries and *responsibility* for their construction" (*Simians* 150).

Transmutation for an alchemist is, after all, a material as well as a spiritual event. Daniell suggests a similar correspondence as a goal for composition pedagogy. She reminds me that Freire's critical pedagogy offers me two articles of faith: one, the difference between imparting knowledge and sharing knowledge; two, the reminder that "we teach out of relationship" (403). "What is missing in most North American accounts of Freire's methods is the intense *I-thou* relation he calls for between teacher and student," Daniell argues (402, author's emphasis). She explains that for Freire, education is an act of love, a view that grows out of his Catholicism as much as out of his Marxism, both providing a necessary "spiritual perspective on the teaching of literacy" (402). That intense I-thou relation is impossible for the hero, who is always separate from the humans he saves; but that I-thou relation is a constituent part of the alchemist's identity. Within an alchemical pedagogy, the crucial focus is on the constitutive loops of double logics, on the relationships among bodysigns on multiple levels. Teacher and student are merely reciprocal coils within the spirals of double logics out of which the identity of the system as a whole shapes and is shaped.

As an alchemical rather than a heroic quest, transformation is not something that happens to an "other," an "Eileen" who is defined as deficient in some way that "I" am not. Instead, transformation happens to an "us," happens by means of a biorhetoric inherent in that system called "us." Thus, if what I want to change (or understand) is Eileen's thinking and behavior, then the unit of consideration is not Eileen; it is the androgyne Eileen-and-I-in-the-classroom, an androgyne embedded within loops of mutually constituting androgynes. The relevant pathways include Eileen's visceral reactions, her intellectual aversion to the vision of feminist as the destroyer of family values, her habits of mind as well as her habits of body. Those pathways include the classroom where Eileen sits in front of a computer in the midst of her classmates. It includes her social activism with an on-campus Catholic youth group and her family history of civic participation. And I am a part of those transacting pathways as well: my visceral and intellectual aversion to the vision of my daughters trapped in the role of keeper of the family flame, my visceral and intellectual realization that I enact that role on a daily basis. The androgyne encompasses my position of power within the classroom beyond my students' computers, in front of the master computer that can both control and interrupt theirs, and it also encompasses the limits of that power. Changing Eileen requires that I join in that change because I am a part of what constitutes Eileen, a part of the system that gives her meaning at that moment. My identity and meaning are also embodied, also implanted within the classroom, also complicit with its technology, its chemistry, its space, its time. "The most important task today," Bateson warns, "is, perhaps, to think in [this] new way" (*Steps* 468).

The difficulties of teaching and writing from and with a biorhetoric are legion. Bateson himself admits that such a position is difficult to maintain for one trained in the dualistic thinking privileged in the West (*Steps* 469). But perhaps those difficulties are necessary. Here I sit, at sea within the bodysigns that constitute me. As I type *I*, I struggle to remember that *I* do not write, just as *I* do not teach. Rather, the *who-what-how* is comprised of keyboard, room, and child stretched out on the floor whispering over her collection of Pokémon cards, intermittently demanding my attention. It is comprised of the white, heterosexual, middle-class privilege that supports this warm, well-lit room serviced by the Internet that connects me to a wider network for intellectual work. It is comprised of the privilege of a tenure-line academic position that encourages/expects intellectual work, a position uneasily supported by the labor of part-time and contract faculty members. The androgyne—of which *I* am merely a single loop—writes. And I resist its chaos, for *I* fear the instability of a biorhetoric that shifts as the currents of double logics shift. But it is only by living within the midst of this chaos that I can begin to incorporate into this discursive loop "the reality *that one cannot not know* . . . .The ragged edges of the Real, of *Necessity*, not being able to eat, not having shelter, not having health care, all this is something that one cannot not know" (West 277). For Eileen-and-me, the reality "one cannot not know" includes the children she babysits, the children who write letters with their babysitter to their absent parents, the children she desires, the social inequities she actively seeks to address. It includes my daughters whom I passionately hope will define themselves according to something more than the cult of "true womanhood" which confuses *is* logic with *as-if* logic.

My own account of the Eileen-and-I web, then, is fraught with necessary contradictions that destabilize meaning as it creates it. As I write those words, I inevitably court the ambiguities and the pitfalls of mutually constitutive, mutually disruptive double lives because in writing Eileen, I write in the absence of Eileen. I do not write tangled in the intranet of my networked virtual classroom or even in the material classroom with Eileen murmuring in my ear, her fingers positioned over mine, guiding me as I simultaneously guide her. Instead, I configure and erode her presence here in my words twisted by her absence, her invisible corporeality and silent discursivity. Even if she had chosen to speak within this context, responded to my invitation and encouragement to do so, it would have been my invitation, my encouragement. The "she" therein evoked would have been shaped by this unfamiliar process, the uncertainty of her position within a system of meaning where she identifies herself as interloper, as one who lacks privilege. Metaphoric *is* logic breaks down, and I am left with the resounding "not" of language, the "not" of Eileen, the "not" of *I*. So I write, struggling *not* to reduce Eileen or my children to tropes. I write, struggling to configure an *I* that does *not* become another rhetorical flourish, but, instead, a biorhetorical enactment. What is at stake in that struggle is a meaning that consciously attends to the discursive and the nondiscursive, a meaning that is never outside its own system, but always and inevitably a part of it.

Drawing on Robert Frost, Louise Z. Smith argues that all metaphors break down, that that is the beauty of them. Within metaphors, we are required to leap between the words, girded in the *as-if* logic of classifications, and across the "is" that marks a linguistic structure as a metaphor rather than a "tamed down" simile. That "is" negates the *as-if* logic of its own identity, trapping us in a feedback loop between the "is" and the "is not." Linguistic metaphors tie us to the contradictions of is and is not, and in so doing they break down. However, Smith points out that this breakdown is not a tragedy of failed meaning. Instead, it is an enigma that opens up to us the possibility of new meaning. The cracking of a linguistic metaphor is the site of its writability, the site of new insight. Thus, within the metaphoric writing of Eileen, daughters, and *I*, I break down—as well I should, for in writing I must shuttle between the contradictions in my own system, the contradictions of bodysigns. Therein lies a biorhetoric that might rescue me, even as it endangers me, for it requires that I remain always poised uncertainly in the moment when corporeality and rhetoricality blur. It requires that I write to the paradox, in the paradox, for in writing Eileen, I also write myself, my daughters, and a world for us to live in. This is the knowledge that I cannot *not* know as teacher, as mother, as writer. Living within the swirl of bodysigns is the double living required if I wish to write and teach for transformation. Rich writes,

> remember: the body's pain and the pain in the streets
> are not the same   but you can learn
> from the edges that blur   O you who love clear edges
> more than anything watch the edges that blur ("No. 29" 9–12)

Here is the site of bodysigns, of a biorhetoric for change.[4]

Notes

1. Because of the constraints of space, I present transformation as an unproblematic goal. However, transformation is always value-laden, never ethically neutral. What might be seen as a desirable move by one segment of the population (or the classroom) need not be seen as desirable by another. The boundary between transformation voluntarily pursued and transformation imposed is a narrow and vitally important line.

2. See Fleckenstein "Resistance, Women, and Dismissing the 'I'" for an analysis of the androcentric bias in Bartholomae's approach to subjectivity.

3. Spellmeyer, in a scathing review of *Left Margins: Cultural Studies and Composition Pedagogy,* an anthology of essays on teaching composition as cultural studies, highlights the problem of separating teachers from the changes they hope to effect in their students and their classrooms. Spellmeyer claims that the authors in the anthology represent and share a major characteristic of the "strong" cultural studies position: "a scarcely veiled contempt for their own students, whom they represent as deeply 'atomized' and 'mystified'"("Out" 427). These scholar-teachers inhabit the moral and ethical high ground of their own

critical enlightenment; their mission is to rescue their students from the morass of their uncritical thinking. In response, France, a co-editor of the anthology, contends that Spellmeyer "writes from a position largely incurious about its own cultural and historical formation, from what might be called an autobiographical position" (284).

4. I would like to thank Nancy Myers and Sue Hum for their patience, tolerance, and detailed responses to multiple drafts of this essay. Such collaboration highlights the richness and the intimacy of a biorhetoric.

Works Cited

Alcoff, Linda. "Cultural Feminism versus Post-Structuralism: The Identity Crisis in Feminist Theory." *Reconstructing the Academy: Women's Education and Women's Studies*. Ed. Elizabeth Minnich, Jean O'Barr, and Rachel Rosenfeld. Chicago: U of Chicago, 1988. 257–88.

Bartholomae, David. "A Reply to Stephen North." *Pre/Text* 11 (1990): 121–30.

———. "A Tidy House: Basic Writing in the American Curriculum." *Journal of Basic Writing* 12 (1993): 4–21.

———. "Writing with Teachers: A Conversation with Peter Elbow." *College Composition and Communication* 46 (1995): 62–71. 84–86.

Bateson, Gregory. *Mind and Nature: A Necessary Unity*. Toronto: Bantam Books, 1980.

———. *A Sacred Unity. Further Steps to an Ecology of the Mind*. Ed. Rodney E. Donaldson. New York: HarperCollins, 1991.

———. *Steps to an Ecology of the Mind: Collected Essays in Anthropology, Psychiatry, Evolution, and Epistemology*. Northvale, NJ: Jason Aronson, 1972/1987.

Battersby, Christine. *The Phenomenal Woman: Feminist Metaphysics and the Patterns of Identity*. New York: Routledge, 1998.

Branch, Kirk. "From the Margins at the Center: Literacy, Authority, and the Great Divide." *College Composition and Communication* 50 (1998): 206–31.

Brandt, Deborah. "Remembering Writing, Remembering Reading." *College Composition and Communication* 45 (1994): 459–79.

Bridwell-Bowles, Lillian. "Discourse and Diversity: Experimental Writing in the Academy." *College Composition and Communication* 43 (1992): 349–68.

———. "Freedom, Form, Function: Varieties of Academic Discourse." *College Composition and Communication* 46 (1995): 46–61.

de Certeau, Michel. *The Practice of Everyday Life*. Trans. Steven F. Rendall. Berkeley: U of California P, 1984.

Daniell, Beth. "Narratives of Literacy: Connecting Composition to Culture." *College Composition and Communication* 50 (1999): 393–410.

Dixon, Kathleen. "Gendering the 'Personal.'" *College Composition and Communication* 46 (1995): 255–75.

Fleckenstein, Kristie S. "Resistance, Women, and Dismissing the 'I.'" *Rhetoric Review* 17 (1998): 107–25.

Foucault, Michel. *The Archeology of Knowledge and The Discourse on Language*. Trans. A. M. Sheridan Smith. New York: Pantheon, 1972.

France, Alan W. "Theory Cop: Kurt Spellmeyer and the Boundaries of Composition." *College Composition and Communication* 48 (1997): 284–87.

Gramsci, Antonio. *Selections from the Prison Notebooks*. Ed. and Trans. Quintin Hoare and Geoffrey Nowell Smith. New York: International Publishers, 1971.

Griffin, Susan. "Red Shoes." *The Eros of Everyday Life*. New York: Doubleday, 1995. 161–76.

Haraway, Donna J. *How Like a Leaf: An Interview with Thyrza Nichols Goodeve*. New York: Routledge, 2000.

———. "The Promises of Monsters: A Regenerative Politics for Inapproprate/d Others." *Cultural Studies*. Ed Lawrence Grossber, Cary Nelson, and Paula A. Treichler. New Youk: Routledge, 1992. 295–337.

———. *Simians, Cyborgs, and Women: The Reinvention of Nature*. New York: Routledge, 1991.

Hayles, N. Katherine. *How We Became Posthuman: Virtual Bodies in Cybernetics, Literature, and Informatics*. Chicago: U of Chicago P, 1999.

hooks, bell. *Yearning: Race, Gender, and Cultural Politics*. Boston: South End, 1990.

Jarratt, Susan C. "Introduction: As We Were Saying. . ." *Feminism and Composition Studies: In Other Words*. Ed. Susan C. Jarratt and Lynn Worsham. New York, MLA, 1998. 1–18.

Keller, Evelyn Fox. *Reflections on Gender and Science*. New Haven, CT: Yale UP, 1985.

Kirsch, Gesa E., and Joy S. Ritchie. "Beyond the Personal: Theorizing a Politics of Location in Composition Research." *College Composition and Communication* 46 (1995): 7-29.

Lu, Min-Zhan, and Bruce Horner. "The Problematic of Experience." *College English* 60 (1998): 257–77.

Mairs, Nancy. *Waist-High in the World: A Life Among the Nondisabled*. Boston, Beacon, 1996.

Phelps, Louise Wetherbee, and Janet Emig. "Editors' Reflections: Vision and Interpretation." *Feminine Principles and Women's Experience in American Composition and Rhetoric*. Ed. Louise Wetherbee Phelps and Janet Emig. Pittsburgh: U of Pittsburgh P, 407–26.

Quinn, Naomi. "The Cultural Basis of Metaphor." *Beyond Metaphor*. Ed. J. W. Fernandez. Stanford, CA: Stanford UP, 1991. 56–93.

Rich, Adrienne. "No. 29" of "Contradictions: Tracking Poems." *Your Native Land, Your Life*. New York: Norton, 1986. 111.

Rorty, Richard. "The Contingency of Language." *Rhetoric in an Antifoundational World: Language, Culture and Pedaogy*. Ed. Michael Bernard-Donals and Richard R. Glejzer. New Haven: Yale UP, 1998. 65–85.

Salibrici, Mary M. "Reality Check at the Crossroads." *Feminine Principles and Women's Experience in American Composition and Rhetoric*. Ed. Louise Wetherbee Phelps and Janet Emig. Pittsburgh: U of Pittsburgh P, 1995. 393–406.

Selzer, Jack. "Habeas Corpus: An Introduction." *Rhetorical Bodies*. Ed. Jack Selzer and Sharon Crowley. Madison: U of Wisconsin P, 1999. 3–15.

Serres, Michel. *The Troubadour of Knowledge*. Trans. Sheila Faria Glaser with William Paulson. Ann Arbor: U of Michigan P, 1997.

Smith, Louise Z. "Enigma Variations: Reading and Writing Through Metaphor." *Only Connect: Uniting Reading and Writing*. Ed. Thomas Newkirk. Upper Montclair, NJ: Boynton/Cook, 1989. 158–73.

Soliday, Mary. "Class Dismissed." *College English* 61(1999): 731–41.

Spellmeyer, Kurt. "After Theory: From Textuality to Attunement with the World." *College English* 58 (1996): 893–913.

———. "Out of the Fashion Industry: From Cultural Studies to the Anthropology of Knowledge." *College Composition and Communication* 47 (1996): 424–36.

———. "'Too Little Care': Language, Politics, and Embodiment in the Life-World." *Rhetoric in an Antifoundational World: Language, Culture, and Pedagogy*. Ed. Michael Bernard-Donals and Richard R Glejzer. New Haven, CT: Yale UP, 1998. 254–91.

de Vinne, Christine. "Conspicuous Consumption: Cannibal Bodies and the Rhetoric of the American West." *Rhetorical Bodies*. Ed. Jack Selzer and Sharon Crowley. Madison: U of Wisconsin P, 1999. 75–97.

West, Cornel. "Interview with Anders Stephanson." *Universal Abandon? The Politics of Postmodernism*. Ed. Andrew Ross. Minneapolis, MN: U of Minnesota P, 1997. 269–86.

West, Thomas G. *In the Mind's Eye*. Amherst, NY: Prometheus, 1997.

Yaeger, Patricia. *Honey-Mad Women: Emancipatory Strategies in Women's Writing*. New York: Columbia UP, 1988.

A Place in Which to Stand

Claude Hurlbert
Indiana University of Pennsylvania

1.

I have not adopted a textbook for an undergraduate composition class in over a decade: no handbooks, no readers, and no rhetorics. Textbooks are just not responsive to my students and the locations in which they write.

Textbooks offer a no-geography. A no-place set out to take the place of place. A no-place that pretends to the status of everywhere. No-place everywhere? Yes. Their glitzy covers suggest that they contain subjects of interest to everyone everywhere: culture or multicultures, ecology or America, gender or class, process or argument, or one of a myriad of other important topics. The textbook companies advertise how adaptable their materials are, how they can be used in any college, how our concerns are, generally, the same. But their gross generalities about process and instruction mystify and keep us from grappling with the complexities of composing, our students' needs and lives. Composition textbooks are a distraction from the realities of the places in which we live. Or better, they are a dream. They are a professor's dream of the perfect student performing the perfect writing process and producing the perfect essay. In the dream, certainty and excellence come with standardization. All students have to do is follow how their professor presents the textbook writer's or editor's take on culture, meaning, or writing. If students only would, or could, they would make A's.

But, of course, writing and studying are not that easy. Our students are living particular lives in specific places, and they carry the places of their pasts with them, even as they worry about the places they will inhabit in the future.

2.

I ask the students in my composition classes to write short books about what they are burning to tell the world. Later in the semester, I ask them to exchange their manuscripts so that another student may write a foreword for them. Beyond the length of the books, twenty single-spaced, typed pages for midterm manuscripts, and usually longer for finished books, the project entails attention to difficult matters such as coherence, structure, and style. Writing these books also demands abstract rhetorical thinking, such as defining the world, what students are burning to tell it, and what it is burning, or not, to hear; in other words, defining their places within the world (Blitz and Hurlbert).

Many of the books I receive are about hometowns: the streets the students ran, the ones they cried on, laughed on, and danced on, the parents who loved them, died, or ran off, the gangs there, the murders, the guns, the boys and the girls and the beatings. Or, sometimes, the fields and mist rushing by as they scream through the night on motorcycles and pain from which they cannot escape, rusted out cars, drinks they stole from their parents' liquor cabinets, the glow of neon lights of bars in the black hollows of hills or factories.

One semester, a student wrote the story of his western Pennsylvania hometown:

> I come from the small town of R______. If you ever have the chance to visit, don't. To me it's a fucking wasteland of empty dope bags and lost lives . . . Downtown is just one main street with a few stores and lots of cigarette butts. You'll walk past a group of people sitting on a bench at 5:00 p.m., and if you walk past again at 10:00, you'll see the same group in the same spot, some of them still there because there's nothing else to do, some of them because they're just too fucked up to stand. My town is infested with heroin. . . It's a horrible experience to walk past someone who was one of your best friends a few years earlier

> and not even be able to look in their eyes because of how far into the abyss they have fallen. You don't even see a soul anymore...

Sometimes we, our students and ourselves, write to escape a place, or not. This student's hometown looms as the locus of his anger and disappointment at the center of his work. Later, he even chronicles his failed attempts at extricating himself from his past. It could seem hopeless. Still, the student sees his town, and he can name one of the ways a person loses a soul. With time, perhaps, his critical vision might become a measurement of distances traveled, the meaning of movement, and, perhaps, distance still ahead.

Another student started a history of her small western Pennsylvania mining town. What she discovered was her real topic: the presence of the Ku Klux Klan there. Her book became a reevaluation of the graffiti on the town bridge, once she understood it as Klan tagging. The book became a road leading away from a place, behind which the Klan met at night. The book stands, today, as a coming to terms with one's childhood origins, one's home place, a reading of a public text in order to learn, and maybe to burn a bridge.

Another student researched the history of his family's farm, tracing its ownership through county records and colonial era tombstones. He researched the Native Americans who originally lived there. And in his book he tells the story of the farmhouse, and how, while still owned by his grandmother, it was gutted by fire. He relates how his father and he restored the house. It is a story of stewardship, of family bonding, and of accepting the responsibility of history. It is about learning to understand the future as well as the past because "maybe someone a hundred and fifty years from now will be doing what I am doing, only this time they'll be writing about my father and me, who will be the next two owners of this beloved house and the land on which it sits." It is writing inspired by place that teaches others about love of place. This student did not need a textbook to do this work. He needed individualized guidance from a qualified writing teacher. He needed options: for how to design a project, for relevant readings, for research and writing strategies, for how to edit grammar, and for desktop publishing.

Another student, who took my class while studying in the United States, wrote a book about his grandfather who died shortly before the student left Ghana. One night, the grandfather, worried that this modern teenager was forgetting his heritage, started a story that he felt his grandson should know. The tale was about a young man and woman who, in the past, had been captured from their village, shackled, and taken to the coast for sale in the slave trade. Tragically, the grandfather died before finishing the story and before the student left Ghana. For class, the student chose to research the middle passage and finish his grandfather's story because he felt that his grandfather's "rest would not be sound until I completed the work that he had started." This student did not need a multicultural reader to understand the meaning and significance of this project, its truth, and neither did his classmates.

Yet another student wrote of how he and his family left Vietnam by boat:

> The ship held about one hundred escapees trying to get out of the country . . . With all the checkpoints, we had to be down below deck for more than five hours. When people got up to the deck, they started to throw up. Some got sick from the lack of oxygen . . . we were at sea for more then a week, and . . . the food was running out.

This student writes of death, of his family's survival, of the beatings at a refugee camp in the Philippines, and of fighting in the streets of his adopted country. He, too, did not need a textbook to do his work. It would have just been in the way.

The students in my classes are writing to locate themselves, to plot directions. They will not all research and write the same things in the same ways at the same time. They will not, necessarily, even learn the same things at the same times. And so, as I construct my composition pedagogy, I try to create space for students to write locations in which to stand, to see, and from which to move.

3.

Every day, everywhere, it is a struggle to develop teaching that is responsive to the contexts in which we work. Teaching assistants and adjuncts are, many times, simply told which textbooks to use. When this occurs, each must read the contingencies of their location and decide what action is best. Some may follow the textbook carefully. Some may have freedom to use the books creatively. Some may see programmatic recourses. But without inspired writing program administration or collective action, there may be little to do, sad to say, but adapt. These can be lonely decisions. Still, all composition teachers remain united in our search for meaningful interpretations for figuring what and how to teach. Maybe there is some hope in that fact.

And maybe there is hope in the changes we may see in the coming years. Attending to the particularities of context calls for a rhetoric of location. This rhetoric challenges traditional curricula and pieties about composition as a service course. It questions our authority and the need for textbooks to teach writing. In this way, it reconstitutes our classroom roles. It even calls on us to rethink what an academic institution is, including how it locates itself in relation to the world. If taken seriously, location invokes a stewardship that challenges the consumerism that fuels textbook-driven composition curricula. In turn, stewardship resists the ideology of individualism by calling on us to take up our social and collective responsibilities. This is a stewardship of our homes, lands, and minds, and also our students' real touching and real feeling—their real work.

Work Cited

Blitz, Michael, and C. Mark Hurlbert. *Letters for the Living: Teaching Writing in a Violent Age.* Urbana, IL: National Council of Teachers of English, 1998.

Location and (Dis)placement in Composition Pedagogy

Ellen Cushman
University of Michigan

First-year students, returning students, and graduate students to some degree may share an understanding of displacement when they enter the classroom. Very few places in society act, feel, and sound like universities. Bartholomae pointed to the foreignness of the university's discourse in an a frequently anthologized essay "Inventing the University." In this essay, he looks at students' entrance essays written to place them into or out of a section of first-year composition. The essays have in common an apparent struggle with the discourse, an incomplete approximation of the ways students believe that university professors want them to sound. Jim Gee, a sociolinguist who describes the power of institutional discourses, might call this a kind of mushfake, where students are trying to create an identity kit that includes the intellectual and rhetorical moves that they believe approximate university discourses. Bartholomae argued that if we give students a fairly deep immersion in the discourses of various fields, students might be in a better position to adapt. In fact, *Ways of Reading*, which he edited with Anthony Petrosky, is often assigned in first-year writing classes. Some would trace the entire Writing Across the Disciplines movement to Bartholomae's single essay.

To acknowledge the foreignness of the university is to equip students with further metadiscourse and learning strategies. I am with Lisa Delpit on this point (she goes after Jim Gee for not allowing that secondary, powerful discourses can and should be explicitly taught and learned): yes, the language of the university is a powerful discourse, so acknowledge it as such and try to create for first-year students a legitimate way of engaging it. Therefore, I ask first-year students to understand how the language and place and layout of the university relate to making knowledge. I ask them to locate themselves within this place, trying to demystify the structures (e.g., disciplines, schools, colleges, departments, fields), understand epistemological and rhetorical structures, read this world through its words (Freire). In other words, with the first-year students I teach, critical pedagogy and writing across the disciplines are wed.

This might seem an odd choice in curricula for someone who has written about the need for university knowledge-making and teaching to be bridged with communities (Cushman, "Sustainable," "Service," *The Struggle*, Special Issue, "The Public," and "Rhetorician"). Critical pedagogy, for me, is about opening the university to communities, making knowledge with people in communities, honoring students' home literacies in our classrooms. As Kirsch and Ritchie find, understanding a politics of location in our research is absolutely critical to creating socially just knowledge. Institutional critique (Porter et al.) and understanding the university's politics of space (Reynolds) are absolutely central to a civically minded research trajectory. Research, teaching, and service should be done with community members, addressing problems they find pressing or needs that they have. So, why would someone who has made these claims create a first-year curriculum that looks like indoctrination into foreign and powerful discourse? What gives?

Recognizing that many first-year students experience dislocation when they enter the university, I try to create assignments that build upon their primary discourses while demystifying the secondary discourses of academe. In one assignment, first-year students apply sociological theories of culture shock to their first-year experiences at the university, an assignment adapted from Malcolm Kiniry and Mike Rose's *Critical Strategies for Academic Thinking and Writing*. What kinds of language use are they accustomed to? How is what they are hearing in their classes, or reading in their textbooks, or seeing in scholarly journals different from their primary discourses? How is knowledge made in their communities? How is this process similar to or different from knowledge making here? In their writing, they walk through the phases of culture shock, illustrating these ideas with discussions of their experiences; they describe their initial excitement about coming to college, their increasing disenchantment and ill ease that can sometimes last for months, their finding a resolution to this problem, and finally coming to some comfortable place within the university. This assignment typically stems from an assignment about students' own identities and how these identities grow and change when new learning situations are engaged. Taken together, students begin to see how place, language and literacy, agency and power, and identity are mutually sustaining.

An assignment like this is quite challenging for professors to teach and for students to write. To begin with, this is a writing-to-learn assignment, and so the audiences for it include the student(s) and myself. Students are initially motivated by the assignment because they are vested in figuring out what makes their professors tick, understanding the language and gaining a feel for the classes, trying on some rhetorical and intellectual moves. They like the way it asks them to compare a lecture in communication to a lab in physics to a discussion in philosophy (they choose the classes). They talk about why and how formats of classes impact learning; when and to what degree students and professors hold the floor; and what kinds of texts, media, and requirements the classes have. They like comparing what they already know to what is happening in these courses, but at times, they would come away feeling overwhelmed by how much they did not know—this was especially true at the University of California Berkeley (UCB).

Students in the writing intensive classes at UCB were enrolled in what used to be known as "subject A," the very classes and types of students Mike Rose wrote about in *Lives on the Boundary*. These students had tremendous knowledge and skills from their home communities, often spoke two languages, and were at the top of their classes in their high schools. Building on their abilities, they would still experience dishearteningly difficult language, esoteric knowledge, and writing that even in its organization and style made little sense. One math major from mainland China decided to explore the applied math curricula there and looked into a scholarly journal article on the topic. Using the format of the article, the student replaced the content with her own findings about the intellectual and rhetoric skills she saw reflected in each particular section of the essay. In the end, she could articulate what she did not know and began to understand how applied math differed from theoretical math, a difference that she noted had an influence on the types of prestige professors from each area accrued. Following up with interviews with professors, her speculations were confirmed, and the professors were quite open about the ways in which their positions differed according to their areas: the applied math professor taught the undergraduates, was paid less, and was a lecturer. The student's understandings were smart and hard won, despite the initially daunting nature of the task she set for herself.

You have probably noticed at this point that the word *place* is woven throughout this essay. If we agree with Bourdieu that the habitus writes our dispositions to act in particular ways, then place is written into the body's location. When we are displaced, i.e., going through culture shock or moving into a contact zone, we need to learn new dispositions to act and speak in various ways. Our bodies are rewritten both in theory and practice with every essay, every assignment, every learning activity. Writing teachers are in a position to, at the very least, explain to students how they are being written through this displacement, and at the very best, they are in a position to facilitate students' revisions of themselves in this place. Understanding that first-year students have already left their comfort zone by coming to our classrooms is a place to start.

Works Cited

Bartholomae, David. "Inventing the University." *When a Writer Can't Write: Studies in Writer's Block and Other Composing-Process Problems*. Ed. Mike Rose. New York: Guilford, 1985. 134–65.

Bartholomae, David, and Anthony Petrosky, eds. *Ways of Reading*. 6th ed. New York: Bedford/St. Martins, 2002.

Bourdieu, Pierre. *The Logic of Practice*. Cambridge, UK: Polity, 1990.

Cushman, Ellen. "Sustainable Service Learning Programs." *College Composition and Communication*. 64.1 (2002): 40–65.

———. "Service Learning as the New English Studies." *Beyond English Inc.* Ed. David Downing, Claude Mark Hurlbert, and Paula J. Mathieu. Portsmouth, NH: Heinemann, 2002. 204–18.

———. *The Struggle and The Tools: Oral and Literate Strategies in an Inner City Community.* Albany: State University of New York P, 1998.

———. (Guest editor). Special Issue on Service Learning. "Letter from the Guest Editor." *Language and Learning Across the Disciplines.* 14.3 (October 2000). 1–5.

———. "The Public Intellectual, Service Learning, and Activist Research." *College English* 61.3 (1999): 328–36.

———. "Rhetorician as an Agent of Social Change." *College Composition and Communication* 47.1 (1996): 7–28.

Cushman, Ellen, and Chalon Emmons. "Contact Zones Made Real." *School's Out*. Ed. Glynda Hull and Katherine Shultz. New York: Teachers College Press, 2002. 203–31.

Delpit, Lisa. "The Politics of Teaching Literate Discourse." *Other People's Children: Cultural Conflict in the Classroom*. New York: New Press, 1995. 152–66.

Freire, Paolo, and Donaldo Macedo. *Literacy: Reading the Word and the World*. South Hadley, MA: Bergin and Garvey Publishers, 1987.

Gee, James Paul. "What is Literacy?" *Teaching and Learning* 2 (1987): 3–11.

Kiniry, Malcolm, and Mike Rose. *Critical Strategies for Academic Thinking and Writing: A Text and Reader*. 2nd ed. Boston: Bedford Books of St. Martin's Press, 1993.

Kirsch, Gesa E., and Joy S. Ritchie. "Beyond the Personal: Theorizing a Politics of Location in Composition Research." *College Composition and Communication* 46.1 (1995): 7–29.

Porter, James E., Patricia Sullivan, Stuart Blythe, Jeffrey T. Grabill, and Libby Miles. "Institutional Critique: A Rhetorical Methodology for Change." *College Composition and Communication* 51 (2000): 610–42.

Reynolds, Nedra. "Composition's Imagined Geographies: The Politics of Space in the Frontier, City, and Cyberspace." *College Composition and Communication* 50 (1998): 12–35.

Rose, Mike. *Lives on the Boundary: The Struggles and Achievements of America's Underprepared*. New York: Free Press, 1989.

Teaching In Situ

Derek Owens
St. John's University

Let's begin with where you are. You are probably a teaching assistant (TA) or an adjunct; most composition instructors are. This means your office, if you're lucky enough to have one, might well resemble my first adjunct hole, a closet under the stairs, tucked away in the basement. If so, maybe your students are often late for appointments because your office is so hard to find, and when they finally arrive maybe they make offhand references to films like *The People Under the Stairs*, or remark how it is almost quaint in a Dickensian kind of way, like Harry Potter's room in the Dursley house. Or maybe your office is like my current one, a cubicle in a long row of other beige, flimsy boxes of equal size and dimension. But because you are a TA or an adjunct and not nearly as high up on the academic food chain as I am, you must share your cubicle with an extended family of fellow TAs and adjuncts, which is not so bad so long as your schedules are staggered—although you do grow tired of the microturf battles: who gets which drawer, who is selfishly using up more than his or her two feet of allotted bookshelf space, who has been swiping your teabags. You and your colleagues tack up the obligatory Dilbert and *New Yorker* cartoons with their references to cubicle humiliation as you quote lines from *Office Space*, one of your favorite movies because you can so relate to it. Nor does it help when a student, like the basketball player in one of my first-year composition courses, who has since turned professional, sits in your cube for the first time, looks around and sniffs, "you *work* here?" Maybe if you're like me you dress up your cube as best you can, decorating it with all manner of esoteric ephemera to help you forget that it's a cube. Maybe you're like my colleague down the hall who built up the cubicle, adding makeshift extensions to the ceiling to gain a semblance of privacy. Maybe you think, A few more of those and this hall could look like a shanty town, and the idea pleases you: a hall of ramshackle hobbit holes, reflecting their instructors' personalities. Or, maybe you are like thousands of composition faculty and have no office at all—or rather, your "office" is the bus or your car or, when you have to meet with students, a bench on the quad or a cafeteria table. Which is to say that in terms of professional real estate you are, for all intents and purposes, homeless, which is perhaps apropos given your part-time wages, the lack of benefits, the nonexistent job security.

And the classrooms you teach in? They are bland, spare, institutional. *Functional*. Nothing too terrible certainly, but surely not places anyone would want to hang out in for any length of time. Classrooms are not designed to make you want to stay there; they are temporary holding tanks, largely absent of aesthetic design. As you move from room to room to teach your classes, you notice how they blur together, interchangeable sites of both presence and absence: throughout the day scores of bodies pass through these rooms, and yet they leave barely any residue, save for some gum under a desk, a name half-heartedly inked into the seat, some soda spilled on the floor. And when you are not teaching you are walking through the halls of the building, looking through the windows in the doors at other classes: at the faculty standing in front of students seated in rows, students who are kind of listening, kind of not, as the instructor talks, and points, and talks, lobbing sixty minutes of words over the heads of those students, and an image pops into your head, of how in boot camp soldiers crawl on their bellies as superiors fire ammunition over their heads.

And where do you and your students go when you're done with the campus (or the campus is done with you)? Do you bridge and tunnel your way home, like many of my urban students do, spending easily ninety minutes commuting from Queens to Brooklyn? Do you inch your way home on congested expressways and parkways? Does your commute take you into dense suburbs, or farther out into some new exurban development? Or are you lucky enough to walk home, living near campus, and thus cars for you are not a daily necessity? Maybe you have money—maybe you married well, and your partner has access to a swell house in a "desirable" neighborhood (in which case this adjunct business might not be all that bad, a professional hobby of sorts). Or maybe you're fortunate enough to live in or near a vibrant, eclectic urban community. Or are nestled in some tranquil corner of rural America somewhere. Wherever you live, to what degree do these landscapes, burbscapes, and cityscapes imprint themselves in subtle, even subliminal ways across your consciousness? Through them do you see your local worlds as invigorating? Blasé? Threatening? Indistinct? "Okay"? And how do these impressions translate back to your own sense of identity: do you see yourself as a vibrant person living in a dull landscape? Or are you conditioned against your will to conform to the blandness, or busyness, or sameness, or variation embodied in the local sites you call home? How do you negotiate between the various sites you need to pass through en route to work and home? Are you connected to these places? Disconnected? How do the spaces direct you, shape you, make assumptions for you?

And to what degree do these landscapes influence the writings our students compose on a daily basis, as they adapt to the discursive blueprints they have inherited from us, blueprints we have inherited from our peer review journals, our colleagues, our mentors? Think of the billions of student papers designed over the decades. If one could spread them out across the country, might not a considerable percentage resemble a sprawl of rhetorical Levittowns, a sea of prefab forms? How complicit have we been in contributing to this terrain, we who have been conscripted, conditioned, and determined in part by the obligatory prose forms assumed within our institutions and professions? (Every semester—*every* semester—I have undergraduate and even graduate students asking me, "so, you really *want* our opinions in these papers?" How astoundingly successful our academic institutions have been at convincing students that their ideas are irrelevant, that one must first receive permission to think.) Is it any wonder that so often what we get is a safe, middle-of-the-road prose where students have taken "ownership" of their discourse but only *up to a point*, while never losing sight of the explicit rhetorical hierarchies to which they are expected to conform, and mold themselves accordingly? It is the equivalent of so many suburban ranch homes stretching along dead end cul-de-sacs. Hints of individuality here and there, but from an aerial perspective, the lot of them blur together. Functional. Forgettable.

Along with these questions of cultural geography and architecture, the subtle ways they affect our patterns of thinking and communication, we must inevitably consider a host of ecological and environmental considerations directly affecting where we live and work. And this is where English and composition studies I think is at its worst, embarrassingly out of touch and overwhelmingly uninterested in the severity of the sundry ecological crises so widely documented in the fields of architecture, ecological economics, environmental education, environmental studies, future studies, planning, and risk analysis. If this sounds overstated, one need only consider how all of our major anthologies of literary theory and criticism parade the canons of body criticism, ethnic and race studies, gender and sexuality, and class concerns, and yet are virtually silent when it comes to addressing matters of ecology and environment. (The bad news is nothing if not extensively documented—see Bossel, Bowers, Brown, Buell, Diamond, Dowie, Greider, and O'Sullivan for possible entry points into this discussion.) If we take the time to reflect upon these contemporary environmental crises, we start to contemplate how much our local arenas are at risk, and thus to what degree we ourselves are at risk. What is the status of one's local watershed, one's local economy, the health of one's immediate neighborhood? How might we gauge the indirect effects of diminishing arable soil, overflowing sinks, large-particle air pollution, climate change, and mass extinctions on our work as scholars and practitioners—or are we willing to argue that there is no correlation? Weakened immune systems, rising levels of toxicity, the body burden, rising infectious diseases, and global social crises brought on by escalating environmental injustices—how do these realities impact our work as educators? Why are these matters so absent in English and composition studies, whereas our work has been so radically transformed and enhanced by our willingness to explore race, class, and gender? To what do we owe this inexcusable lapse?

I have arrived at the point where I always want to bring the classroom home. Root our activities in the immediate local environs of our students and where they call "home"—not so much their residence halls but where they return to when they are on break, where they drive or bus or tunnel to when they are commuting. How are these places woven into their psyches? Are they good places? Bad? Boring? Tiresome? Nondescript? Do they fulfill students' needs and wants? Are they just placeholders, sites students long to leave some day? Do they want to live and die right where they are? To what degree are these sites at risk? Or thriving? And what will they be like in five, ten, twenty-five years?

I try to make room in my writing courses for such conversations. Students construct place portraits, researched photo essays of their local neighborhoods where they document the status of their homes: not their residence halls or the campus, but their legal addresses, where their families live—which means when they return home on break they shoot photos and make videos of their neighborhoods that they later incorporate into their "neighborhood portfolios." Some students (they select their assignments from a handful of options) write oral histories of family members or neighbors, the older the better. In addition to these accounts being full of discoveries and surprises ("I've lived with my grandmother all my life but never knew what she went through during the war!"), these are exercises in preservation, of sustaining memories and histories that might otherwise have been lost. Or they fashion portraits of cultures or subcultures they belong to or have access to. Other students write commentaries on their work environments, or where their parents work, documenting the conditions of those environments, weighing in on what makes them desirable or miserable (generally the latter). Some assemble critiques of their educational histories; some put together plans for better neighborhoods, "eutopias" (*good* places, as opposed to the idealized perfection of utopia). Everyone puts together a future portrait of how they see the world in several decades. All of these assignments are tied together with readings I throw at students by environmental educators, regional planners, cultural geographers, sustainable designers, architects, ecologists, urban and environmental historians, and futurists, all of which, in my eyes anyway, directly or indirectly address matters of preservation, risk, environmental crises. Through it all, I keep returning to the metaphor of sustainability as a mechanism for framing the course, my need to imagine something like a sustainable pedagogical ethic, something I've discussed in more detail elsewhere (Owens). I admit that such gestures are tentative, speculative, and humble; getting students to take photos of their blocks, read essays by Lester Brown, and imagine their worlds in twenty-five years hardly translates into transformative change. I am loathe to call what I do liberatory, and I suspect it falls far short of what many people strive for within their own brands of critical pedagogy. What I am doing is struggling to fashion a temporary environment where students, through written (and visual) expression and research, might give voice to matters I consider to be of utmost importance to them (and me): the welfare and survival of their local communities, families, aspirations, and future generations. The question I keep asking myself is: If in a writing course I am able to lead students to write and think about virtually anything—if our collective subject matter always remains to be written—what are the most supremely important issues and ideas that we can write about? What most warrants our focused attention?

If we're in the business of getting students to critically and creatively explore what matters to them, and if we recognize, as Gregory Bateson did, the necessity in understanding mind as inseparably connected to environment—mind/environment, two sides of the same coin—then not to consider the local is to severely misrepresent the self. It is not just a matter of writing about one's neighborhood, or lack thereof, but exploring all local environments: the workplace, the campus, the dream house one has imprinted inside one's head, the bioregion, the watershed, the town or village one left long ago but which still lingers in one's memory. These sites run deep throughout our psyches. More importantly, these local arenas (and I speak of the local more than the global, not to reject the abstraction of "global" thinking, but to emphasize the benefits of thinking locally, acting locally—and of course, "local" is, on some level, wherever you happen to be) are under duress, threatened, and in trouble. Real trouble. It is more than weird that we do not acknowledge this; it is downright creepy. If you were teaching a class full of students who had suddenly discovered that they all had cancer, but did not want to address this fact and instead chose to write about T. S. Eliot or abortion, you would be freaked out by the Twilight Zone atmosphere. But this is the situation we find ourselves in today: we are all of us living in and around states of cancer. The ecological and environmental crises of the early twenty-first century are today's primary master narratives, and the narrative for the most part goes unread and ignored. There is perhaps no way to say this without sounding sensational. But not to say it is inexcusable.

What I continue to wrestle with is how out of whack our work is, given the desperate conditions of our local worlds. How do I continually remind myself and my students of the seriousness of our current condition? How do I do this without turning into some obnoxious missionary, co-opting the classroom with my own agenda, pushing my students' noses into the information I consider to be of crucial importance? And how do I provide spaces for them to compose on their own terms and yet get better at talking the talk and walking the walk expected of them by other faculty—discourses that they themselves seek to emulate, and for good reason? In struggling to resolve these tensions, I start and often end with the material conditions of their local, lived environments: to come to grips with the degree to which our places shape us and we shape them—the commensalism, and often parasitism, that comprises our relationships with our lived, local environs. These territories, these spatial flows and interruptions, these physical and psychical realms and zones, material and rhetorical, these cube walls and parkways and virtual distractions and threatened watersheds, down to the very toxic bodies we are housed in—all of these interspatial zones of construction, these sites of determination, impact us in a thousand different ways: how we read, why we read, what we write and where, and why. How writing grows out of the architectures and mappings that comprise our psychotopological orientations, and how as writers we choose to contribute to, or resist, or alter, those very forces—these are matters I cannot let go of, and which continually shape my conception of the writing course.[1]

Note

1. I am in the process of putting together an interactive website where faculty and students can upload photos and commentaries of their neighborhoods. My goal is to eventually have several thousand such student essays archived online, resulting in an ever-growing virtual map of the world as seen through students' eyes. In addition to serving as a site for students to share their insights with the public, I am hoping such information might eventually be made accessible to professionals working in community revitalization, urban planning, and environmental studies. If interested in participating or hearing more about the project, e-mail me at owensd@stjohns.edu.

Works Cited

Bateson, Gregory. *Mind and Nature: A Necessary Unity.* New York: Dutton, 1979.

Bossel, Hartmut. *Earth at a Crossroads: Paths to a Sustainable Future.* Cambridge: Cambridge UP, 1998.

Bowers, C. A. *Educating for an Ecologically Sustainable Culture: Rethinking Moral Education, Creativity, Intelligence, and Other Modern Orthodoxies.* Albany: State University of New York P, 1995.

Brown, Lester R. *Plan B: Rescuing a Planet Under Stress and a Civilization in Trouble.* New York: Norton, 2003.

Buell, Frederic. *From Apocalypse to Way of Life: Environmental Crisis in the American Century.* New York: Routledge, 2003.

Diamond, Jared. *Collapse: How Societies Choose to Fail or Succeed.* New York: Viking, 2005.

Dowie, Mark. *Losing Ground: American Environmentalism at the Close of the Twentieth Century.* Cambridge: Massachusetts Institute of Technology P, 1997.

Greider, William. *One World, Ready or Not: The Manic Logic of Global Capitalism.* New York: Touchstone, 1997.

O'Sullivan, Edmund. *Transformative Learning: Educational Vision for the 21st Century.* London: Zed Books, 1999.

Owens, Derek. *Composition and Sustainability: Teaching for a Threatened Generation.* Urbana: National Council of Teachers of English, 2001.

III

Theories of Position

In the preface to *An Introduction to Composition Studies*, published in 1991, Erika Lindemann and Gary Tate differentiate our discipline from others by defining "its central concern" as "the act of writing" (v). While their book, on the whole, is less constrictive than this definition would suggest, Lindemann and Tate tend to reinforce here the warrant driving much process-based writing theory and pedagogy: if our central concern is the act of writing, by implication our primary focus ought to be on the actor. A range of assumptions is entailed by this thinking, including the idea that the individual writer can be usefully conceived of as a self-motivated, originating agent of the text he or she produces. As we have seen in the prior two sections, however, focusing exclusively on the writer when thinking about writing tends to obscure a great many influences on what actually gets written. As Anis Bawarshi puts it, to figure the writer as "the prime agent is to ignore the agency that is already at work on the writer as he or she makes decisions, shapes meaning, and reformulates it" (68). This section of *Relations, Locations, and Positions* examines the possibility of overturning the individual writer as the subject *of* composition studies, and instead considers the individual writer as subject *to* the social and linguistic conditions that "position" him or her in varied ways within varied writing contexts.

As composition scholars recognize that concepts such as *genre*, *literacy*, *discourse*, and *discourse community* are situated and intersubjective, and may be sites of transformation and power struggle, they also recognize that those who inhabit these discursive spaces occupy specific *positions*. These positions affect the ways both teachers and students inhabit classrooms as readers and writers. The 1970s gave rise to the idea that categories of race, gender, and class contribute to and influence the *positions* we take and the *positions* we are written into by others. By *positionality*, we mean how one is situated *in terms of* gender, race, class, ableness, sexual orientation, and other categories of experience. According to Gregory Jay in "The Subject of Pedagogy," one becomes a subject through language, and a subject "comes into being through the assumption of positions offered to it by cultural discourses" (790). How one is situated is not solely a product of one's own intention or manipulation because one's positionality is never immutable. Rather, through our objectives or those of others, we simultaneously occupy different *subject positions*—those particular ways of being, knowing, and moving in the world that influence what we may say, what we can know and write, and how and what we learn. In this way, the positions we inhabit in and out of the writing classroom shape how classroom dynamics unfold, how knowledge is constructed, and how students relate to teachers, each other, and course content.

Varied positionalities—reflective of both tangible and linguistic diversity—indicate critical differences within a community, differences that define a social hierarchy in which some are marginalized while others enjoy advantages. Many argue that there exists an implicit institutional authority that continues to work against the disabled, the nonwhite, and others who vary from historically privileged norms. This persistent and deeply embedded legacy of discrimination is often rooted in conceptions of the material—biology and geography, for example. Theories of positionality, however, depend on uncoupling matters of difference from such categories, as Sue Hum argues in "Articulating Authentic Chineseness" (included in this anthology). Race, and by extension, subject position, is never genetically or geographically determined. Rather, a writer, or "writing subject," is "a social construct that emerges through the linguistically-circumscribed interaction of the individual, the community, and the material world" (Berlin 489). Critical differences are not a result of fixed, stable, and essential characteristics, but are produced as contingent, momentary, and situated. Such claims give rise to theories of *performativity*, which contend that the positions we inhabit, "like performative speech acts, bring into existence that which they name, and, through their repetition, come to constitute the identities they are purported to be" (Kopelson, "Dis/

Integrating" 17). Rather than endorsing biological determinations of difference, performativity helps redefine our understanding of identity politics. In "Of Ambiguity and Erasure: The Perils of Performative Pedagogy" (included in this volume), Karen Kopelson describes the contradictory tensions between her subjectivity as a lesbian and her performance of a teacher persona that is neutral and ambiguous. Kopelson argues that feigning disinterest and objectivity allows her to advance a progressive political agenda. In short, how Kopelson positions herself in the classroom impacts not only her ethos, but also the positions her students take and how they engage each other. Performative positionality takes into consideration the ways in which knowledge and learning are influenced by the situated demands of literacy events, and how they are mediated by place, culture, and time.

The recognition that *truth*, *knowledge*, and *value* can no longer be begun with capital letters—representing a universal, easily generalizable, and even homogeneous way of knowing and being—brings about an awareness of multiple, shifting, and often contradictory subject positions, as well as an awareness of the importance of, and impossibility of ignoring, difference. Many visible and invisible factors contribute to and influence the *positions* we occupy, whether in pedagogy, curriculum, and/or within an institution. They also mediate our ways of being, knowing, and moving in the world; they shape what we may say, what we can know and write, and what and how we learn. In addition, these factors represent a socially agreed upon system of distinction, so that some groups become dominant while others are marginalized. To be a *subject* means that one is often only *momentarily situated* while moving within discursive spaces; the structures of authority, power, and privilege that we are bound up with affect the positions from which we speak and write, but positionality is fluid and heavily contextual.

Scholars have recently proposed that "identity is not, in fact, individual but is embedded in a community of discourse" (Maher and Thompson 204), and that each factor of our positioned experience—race, class, gender, and so on—contextualizes and specifies the others (225). Catherine Prendergast relies on critical race theory to underscore the ways in which students are "*already* socialized into discourses of race and power relations" (49). She demonstrates how a rhetoric of double consciousness helps position some minorities as insiders while acknowledging the limitations of that "insider" status (51). Who we are, then, is an ongoing process stimulated by social convention and discursive practices; to "communicate from somewhere" is to realize that education is fundamentally engaged in articulating, altering, and re-creating positionality.

Recognizing a need for a more diverse representation of positionality in composition scholarship, writing theorists in the 1970s and 1980s engaged in projects of inclusion, embracing voices, perspectives, and events that were shaped by the politics of gender, race, class, and disability. One example is the formation of the College Language Association in 1949, a response by a group of African American scholars to exclusion from the Modern Language Association (Williams 37). More recent scholarly attention to positionality and power continues to herald the contributions of marginalized minorities, addressing silences and erasures within the status quo. Inclusion projects comprise scholarship with autobiographical details (such as works by Mike Rose, Keith Gilyard, and Min Zhan Lu), scholarship that highlights how race and gender influence literacy (such as Cameron McCarthy's *The Uses of Culture* and Elizabeth Flynn's "Composing as a Woman"), and qualitative research on marginalized and/or diverse populations (such as Lisa Delpit's *Other People's Children*, Margaret Finders's *Just Girls*, and Danling Fu's *My Trouble Is My English*).

In acknowledging positionality through projects of inclusion, we recover excluded "subaltern counterpublics"—the source of narratives of difference, publics that were never "*the* public," collectives that contest the norms of who may speak, who may be heard, and to what end (Fraser 61). Frequently, such scholarship involves meticulous archival work, such as Jacqueline Jones Royster and Jean Williams's investigation (included in this anthology) of the challenges African American educators leveled against the existing power structures of an exclusionary, Eurocentric educational institution. Their essay illustrates how racism and violence are enacted in the classroom, which represents a microcosm of the larger society.

Although early scholarship informed by theories of position foregrounded the contributions of people from diverse, frequently excluded backgrounds, more recent work reverses the gaze, investigating popular stereotypes, institutional commitments, and persistent dominant histories from diverse subject positions. In "Becoming Visible: Lessons in Disability" (included in this anthology), Brenda Jo Brueggemann et al. describe the "paradox of visibility" that surrounds the disabled. Scholarly work like theirs argues for competing and contradictory positions; it diversifies the activity of knowledge making and expands the range of acceptable discourse conventions. Similarly, by pointing to the institutional barriers faced by working-class students, Mary Soliday's "Class Dismissed" (included in this volume) explains that working-class students who struggle for access to "cultural means of production create educational life narratives that sharply differentiate them from their bourgeois counterparts" (734). By highlighting issues of diversity, such texts model new ways to define the writer's role while they unsettle exclusionary patterns of speaking, writing, and educating. These authors write against normative white, male, middle-class academic discourse conventions.

Not infrequently, however, both scholarly and pedagogical efforts to create space for diverse subject positions end up encouraging superficial tolerance and cultural relativism, and erasing critical differences that could be capable of effecting social and institutional change. Peter Vandenberg, in "Taming Multiculturalism: The Will to Literacy in Composition Studies" (included in this anthology), examines the relationship between multiculturalism and writing instruction, concluding that the transformative potential of difference is often undermined by Western literacy education, which seems designed to homogenize students. The site of education, where differences are often eliminated, can be reimagined as the place where varied subject positions emerge through the self-conscious negotiation of home, school, and work cultures. A resulting "hybrid" or "mestiza" consciousness, characterized by ambivalence and contradiction—a "deliberate emphasis on and strategic exploitation of the 'in-between' moments of social and linguistic translation" (West 25)—can lead to a strategy by which "existing borders formed in domination can be challenged and redefined" (Giroux 28).

Theories of position, then, disrupt the possibility that any set of norms can be justified by reference to something outside language and culture. In composition studies, as in other contemporary fields informed by theories that account for both the linguistic and the material, the interrogation of *hegemony*—the domination of one group over another—is often called the study of whiteness. While *whiteness* need not signify skin color, the term reflects the fact that privilege in the United States has most often accrued to whites. Central to the study of whiteness is the observation that the habits, routines, and customs of the privileged, over time, become imperceptible to those who manifest them. The noun *whiteness* refers to the cultured misperception of a privileged but socially constructed, middle-class subject position as "common sense" or "reality." Joe Kincheloe explains that whiteness represents "orderliness, rationality, self-control," while nonwhiteness is cast as the alternative, representing "chaos, irrationality, violence, and the breakdown of self-regulation" (164). These norms of whiteness are examined as discursive, positioned, and rhetorical formations in Amy E. Winans's "Local Pedagogies and Race" (included in this anthology). The persistent invisibility of whiteness and the white subject position can be countered—by both examining the rhetorical construct of whiteness, as well as telling difficult stories about personal and systemic oppression.

Positionality impacts the work of writing, learning, and teaching; possibilities for agency depend on the ways in which writers mediate and acknowledge the very real struggle of educational and social transformation. Composition studies is changing through scholarship that includes voices of diversity and reconceptualizes our understanding of difference. Such transformations reflect the changing landscape of education in America; there has been a nearly twenty percent increase of minority students in higher education over the last twenty years, and the number of faculty of color has risen to more than eighty-two thousand (American Council).

Scholars and researchers who embrace theories of positionality necessarily produce situated research and value knowledge claims that are bound up with context (*Relations*) and materiality (*Locations*). We see the *positions* that are represented here in this series of essays as a reflection of this process of transformation, yet by each included narrative, we also recognize the voices that become absent. Our purpose is not to suggest a binary between "universal" and "native" voices, or to suggest that certain positions, say of race or gender, must be dutifully covered for a "well-rounded" section on positionality. We see each essay, as we hope you do, in dialogic engagement with the other essays here, as well as essays that you will read elsewhere that represent the continuum of possible positions. We suggest that, as Malea Powell does in "Learning (Teaching) to Teach (Learn)" (included in this volume), these positions are not "'topics' to be introduced"; rather, they are materially, historically, and discursively lived realities that are produced and reproduced through power relationships, discourse communities, and specific places and times. Scholarship that honors "othered" voices provides access to the navigation of borderlands and public space, and demands rhetorical engagement that goes beyond the status quo into the realm of social struggle and transformation, ensuring that our uses of English nurture a better world.

Works Cited

American Council on Education, 1995–2004. "Minority College Enrollment Surges over the Past Two Decades; Students of Color Still Lag Behind Whites in College Participation." ACE News Press Release. 8 October 2003. <http://www.acenet.edu/AM/Template.cfm?Section=Search&template=/CM/HTMLDisplay.cfm&ContentID=3719>

Bawarshi, Anis. *Genre and the Invention of the Writer: Reconsidering the Place of Invention in Composition.* Logan: Utah State UP, 2003.

Berlin, James. "Rhetoric and Ideology in the Writing Classroom." *College English* 50 (1988): 477–94.

Brueggemann, Brenda Jo, Linda Feldmeier White, Patricia A. Dunn, Barbara A. Heifferon, and Johnson Cheu. "Becoming Visible: Lessons in Disability." *College Composition and Communication* 52.3 (February 2001): 368–98.

Clifford, John. "The Subject in Discourse." *Contending with Words:*

Composition and Rhetoric in a Postmodern Age. New York: MLA, 1991. 38–51.

Delpit, Lisa D. *Other People's Children: Cultural Conflict in the Classroom*. New York: New Press, 1995.

Finders, Margaret. *Just Girls: Hidden Literacies and Life in Junior High*. New York: Teachers College P, 1997.

Flynn, Elizabeth. "Composing as a Woman." *College Composition and Communication* 39 (December 1988): 423–35.

Fraser, Nancy. "Rethinking the Public Sphere: A Contribution to the Critique of Actually Existing Democracy." *Habermas and the Public Sphere*. Ed. Craig Calhoun. Cambridge: MIT Press, 1992. 56–80.

Fu, Danling. *My Trouble Is My English: Asian Students and the American Dream*. Portsmouth, NH: Boynton/Cook, 1995.

Gilyard, Keith. *Voices of the Self: A Study of Language Competence*. Detroit: Wayne State UP, 1991.

Giroux, Henry A. *Border Crossings: Cultural Workers and the Politics of Education*. New York: Routledge, 1992.

Haraway, Donna. *Modest_Witness@Second_Millennium.FemaleMan ©_Meets_OncoMouse™: Feminism and Technoscience*. New York: Routledge, 1997.

Hum, Sue. "Articulating Authentic Chineseness: The Politics of Reading Race and Ethnicity Aesthetically." *Readerly/Writerly Texts* 9.1–2 (Spring/Summer & Fall/Winter 2001): 61–82.

———. "Yes, We Eat Dog Back Home: Contrasting Disciplinary Discourse and Praxis on Diversity." *JAC: Journal of Advanced Composition* 19.4 (1999): 367–87.

Jarratt, Susan. "Teaching across and within Differences." *College Composition and Communication* 43.3 (1992): 315–18.

Jay, Gregory S. "The Subject of Pedagogy: Lessons in Psychoanalysis and Politics." *College English* 49 (1987): 785–800.

Kincheloe, Joe L. "The Struggle to Define and Reinvent Whiteness: A Pedagogical Analysis." *College Literature* 26.3 (1999): 162–94.

Kopelson, Karen. "Dis/Integrating the Gay/Queer Binary: 'Reconstructed Identity Politics' for a Performative Pedagogy." *College English* 65.1 (2002): 17–36.

Lindemann, Erika, and Gary Tate, eds. *Introduction to Composition Studies*. New York: Oxford UP, 1991.

Lu, Min Zhan. "From Silence to Words: Writing as Struggle." *College English* 49.4 (1987): 43–48.

Maher, Frances A., and Mary Kay Thompson Tetreault. *The Feminist Classroom: Dynamics of Gender, Race, and Privilege*. Lanham, MD: Rowman & Littlefield, 2001.

McCarthy, Cameron. *The Uses of Culture: Education and the Limits of Ethnic Affiliation*. New York: Routledge, 1998.

Miller, Susan. *Rescuing the Subject: A Critical Introduction to Rhetoric and the Writer*. Carbondale: Southern Illinois UP, 1989.

Mossman, Mark. "Visible Disability in the College Classroom." *College English* 64.6 (2002): 645–59.

Prendergast, Catherine. "Race: the Absent Presence in Composition Studies." *College Composition and Communication* 50.1 (1998): 36–53.

Rose, Mike. *Lives on the Boundary: The Struggles and Achievements of America's Underprepared*. New York: Free Press, 1989.

Royster, Jacqueline Jones, and Jean C. Williams. "History in the Spaces Left: African American Presence and Narratives of Composition Studies." *College Composition and Communication* 50.4 (1999): 563–84.

Soliday, Mary. "Class Dismissed." *College English* 61.6 (1999): 731–41.

Vandenberg, Peter. "Taming Multiculturalism: The Will to Literacy in Composition Studies." *JAC: Journal of Advanced Composition* 19.4 (1999): 547–568.

West, Thomas. *Signs of Struggle: The Rhetorical Politics of Cultural Difference*. Albany: State U of New York P, 2002.

Williams, John A. "Through the Glass Looking." *Power, Race, and Gender in Academe: Strangers in the Tower?* Ed. Shirley Geok-Lin Lim and Maria Herrera-Sobek. New York: MLA, 2000.

Winans, Amy E. "Local Pedagogies and Race: Interrogating White Safety in the Rural College Classroom." *College English* 67.3 (2005): 253–57.

CHAPTER FOURTEEN

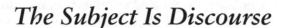

The Subject Is Discourse

JOHN CLIFFORD

The most basic inquiries are often the most perplexing: What do we teachers of composition hope to accomplish? Are we intent on developing in our students the literacy skills and attitudes necessary to succeed in college and beyond, or do we hope to empower them with critical habits of mind, with a skeptical intelligence, with an awareness of themselves as potential actors in a sociopolitical context? Or, more pointedly, do we want to fulfill our contractual obligations to the university and the state by focusing primarily on rhetorical competence, syntactic clarity, and other communicative conventions highly valued in business, industry, and government; or do we dare to encourage oppositional thinkers, social activists, and resistant readers and writers? Are these two goals incompatible? Must we choose, or could we or should we do a little of both? Can we be politically responsible in traditional institutions? With whom do we want to be aligned? The implications are significant, as Kenneth Burke chillingly implies in his not so enigmatic analogy: "The shepherd, *qua* shepherd, acts for the good of the sheep, to protect them from discomfiture and harm. But he may be 'identified' with a project that is raising the sheep for market" (*Rhetoric* 27).

Somehow, for writing theorists and instructors this burden of political responsibility seems more acute. Perhaps the Romantic suspicion of rhetoric for the "palpable designs" it has on us is still an anxious influence in the profession. The Marxist critics Mas'ud Zavarzadeh and Donald Morton recently characterized the increasing demand for writing courses as nothing but "career

---

From *Contending with Words*. Ed. Patricia Harkin and John Schilb. New York: MLA, 1991. 38–51.

and vocational training" (12). But even among more traditional humanists, composition is usually the minor term in the literature-rhetoric polarity, disparaged as utilitarian, marginalized as an editorial service to other departments. It would not be too difficult to deconstruct these false oppositions, to demonstrate how reading literature in certain formalist ways can also be seen as training for careers in the establishment and, conversely, how recent essays by, say, Alice Walker or Adrienne Rich challenge dominant ideas. But I want to take a different and somewhat paradoxical tact: I want to think hard about the plausibility of the charge that in educational institutions writing is, in quite subtle ways, a servant to the dominant ideology. I do not, however, want to suggest that writing instruction is somehow more politically complicit than literature is or that literature in general is in any way more subversive or more filled with liberating possibilities than rhetoric is. Even if, as Julia Kristeva and other radical feminists contend, avant-garde texts disturb the patriarchal order, it matters little within the constraints of educational institutions and all their pedagogical apparatuses whether the class reads Percy Shelley or Denise Levertov or writes a descriptive essay. Differences are incidental to the larger function of education in contemporary American culture. This is the theme I want to explore, that the teaching of writing is inevitably an ideological act and thereby one part of any culture's attempt to reproduce itself, both intellectually and economically, by creating accommodating students who are eager to fill designated positions of influence within various institutional landscapes.

One way to put into focus the perhaps insoluble contradictions facing politically conscious instructors is to consider the struggle over the meaning and status of the writer, or the writing subject, in English studies, especially in rhetoric and composition. For the traditional humanist, the writer has always been seen as a creative individual, the locus of significance, the originator of meaning, an autonomous being, aware of ends and means, of authorial intentions and motivations. In other intellectual contexts, the unconscious or the political is certainly admitted, but rarely is the writer thought of as the site of contradiction, as being written by social or psychological forces that might diminish the clarity of consciousness or the singularity of individual intentions. Traditional and expressive rhetorical theory, in fact, unproblematically assumes that the individual writer is free, beyond the contingencies of history and language, to be an authentic and unique consciousness. Since the theory boom of the sixties, however, the centuries-old tradition affirming the power of the unfettered individual writer has come under increasing pressure, first from structuralists and later from Marxists, feminists, poststructuralists, and motley social constructionists.

The structuralist projects of Claude Levi-Strauss and Roland Barthes cast doubt on the autonomy of the freely choosing individual positing instead a subject created or written by linguistic, sociological, and anthropological codes. Writers do not simply express themselves or reflect unique social realities, the structuralists asserted, but rather mirror a general and systematic pattern of oppositions common to all narratives, myths, or languages. Writing does not directly express an individual's ideas; it transmits universal codes. The poststructural (re)vision, however, was more historically aware of the specificity of the contingencies of power and struggle; consequently, this movement was and still is skeptical of general transhistorical systems of meaning. Discourse, for example, is now thought to achieve meaning only in "the concrete forms of different social and institutional practices" (Macdonell 12). Meaning is thereby made situational and relational. Everything depends on the specific institution where the discourse takes place; in varying contexts the same words are radically transformed to mean one thing and then another. Poststructuralism, then, decenters writing as well as the self, seeing both not only as the effect of language patterns but as the result of multiple discourses already in place, already overdetermined by historical and social meanings in constant internal struggle. In the writings of Jacques Lacan, Michel Foucault, and Jacques Derrida, as well as of the neo-Marxist philosophers Louis Althusser and Antonio Gramsci, the stability of writing and the fixity and coherence of the writer have been relentlessly challenged.

Lacan, for example, develops a materialist theory of the speaker, or the speaking subject, where the "I" that enunciates differs from the ego that employs the "I." The "I" is split between the imaginary and the symbolic, between desire and the social order, between the signifier and the signified. The subject position one enters through language never fully reveals itself since the unconscious always displaces and condenses through such linguistic masks as metaphor and metonymy. The subject thus becomes positioned through language. Derrida similarly displaces the subject from the center, for example, in his notion of *differance* where attempts to define linguistic signifiers create an endless postponement of presence, an endless play of signification. For Derrida, one signifier gives way to another so that meaning is always relational, always changing. From another perspective, Foucault asserts similar decentering ideas, denying the possibility of objective knowledge by claiming that only discourses exist, some more powerful than others. Our knowledge of the subtle rules of these specific discourses lies beyond our consciousness, beyond our ability to know accurately why we write and think as we do. As a result, the independent and private consciousness formerly endowed with plenitude and presence, with a timeless and transcultural essence, becomes in postmodern thought a decentered subject constantly being called on to inhabit overdetermined positions, the implications of which can be only dimly grasped by a consciousness written by multiple, shifting codes.

These postmodern themes—especially the decentering insights that subjects who write are also written, that all discursive signs are unstable and institutionally specific, that the truth is negotiated only within the conventions of various disciplinary discourses at specific historical moments—are all developed in Althusser's 1971 essay, "Ideology and Ideological State Apparatuses." Althusser makes an important contribution to our understanding of ideology and discourse by revising the negative connotations of traditional Marxian notions of ideology as pure illusion. Marx, like other humanists, believed that insight into the exploitative class struggle would eventually allow individuals to locate the real through the distorting fog of ideology. Althusser, however, destigmatizes ideology as natural and inevitable, as ineluctably woven into everything we do; consequently, it cannot simply be expunged. The dominant ideas, assumptions, expectations, and behaviors of this ubiquitous ideology are transmitted from a centerless web of educational, legal and cultural institutions where, in Richard Ohmann's Gramscian terms, "domination filters through a thousand capillaries of transmission, a million habitual meanings" (*Politics* xii).

Critics often see Althusser's rather rigid structuralist approach as antihumanist because he so relentlessly downplays the subject's power of cognition in favor of the constraining force our disciplinary subject positions carve out for us in institutions. Although his system does not leave room for much resistance to dominant ideas, Althusser is not antihuman, nor is he content to accept the status quo. His work is insightful and useful, and his later work hints that he might reconsider his gloomy Foucauldian perception about the seamless efficiency of the ideological state apparatuses. He might have eventually seen, like contemporary theorists Raymond Williams and Edward Said, that inevitable contradictions within subject positions can be a catalyst for resistance and counterhegemonic thinking. Nevertheless, as it stands, Althusser's conception of the ideological state apparatuses offers a powerful heuristic for looking at the ways composition and the political intersect.

Althusser begins his influential essay with what is now a post-Marxian commonplace: that schools, families, the arts, sports, and churches are more subtle but more powerful conveyors of ruling-class ideas than are the agents of state power—the police, army, courts, and penal institutions. Control is maintained not by brute force but through an internalized ideology embedded in practical knowledge, such as law or writing. Two levels of ideology exist, then: general and local, with the general level embedded in all language and the more local variety situated in specific disciplines. Although diversity thrives among university discourses, they are unified "beneath the ruling ideology, which is the ideology of the ruling class" ("Ideology" 146). Since these discourses are not formally connected except through language in their unified replicative goal, the crucial ground of ideological socialization and resistance is, as Frank Lentricchia reminds us, "the specific institutional site" where we find ourselves, "in (our) specific, detailed, everyday functioning" (*Criticism* 6, 7). Local and specific resistance and not global struggle makes the best sense in Althusser's conception, since each discourse has the same teleological aim: to "construct subjects for a particular social formation" (P. Smith, *Discerning* 14). Althusser's distinction between ideology and ideologies dramatically raises the importance of the apparently trivial conventions and rituals of teaching composition, for these same disciplinary behaviors help to install us as subjects within society.

Playing off Freud's notion of the eternal unconscious, Althusser asserts that these ideologies last forever. Although his conception differs sharply from the false consciousness traditional Marxists hope to dissolve, Althusser still insists that ideology represents "the imaginary relationship of individuals to their real conditions of existence." Within disciplines, for example, rhetoricians, literary theorists, and sociologists all have "world outlooks" that Althusser judges to be "largely imaginary, i.e., [that] do not correspond to reality" ("Ideology" 162). In responding to the obvious question of why, say, composition instructors would represent reality to themselves in an imaginary form, Althusser first dismisses conspiracy and alienation as possibilities: "Cynical men who base their domination and exploitation of the people on a falsified representation of the world" have not enslaved the unwary. He also dismisses Ludwig Feuerbach's answer: "The material alienation which reigns in the conditions of existence" (163, 164). Unlike many traditional Marxists, however, Althusser does not really talk about how accurately the factual world is being represented. He is mostly concerned with the illusionary relation we have to social and political reality; or, to cite a more specifically Marxist idiom, disciplinary ideologies distort the actual relation we have to the conditions of production and reproduction. Since in Marxian economic theory the superstructure allows the base to reproduce class distinctions and asymmetrical distributions of wealth, Althusser suggests a provocative analogy between economic reproduction and the ways knowledge gets reproduced through academic discourse.

Dismissing the paranoid notion that a devious clique of ideologues have obfuscated our real political situation, Althusser claims that ideology always has a material existence in whatever discourses we use, "assured by their subjection to the ruling ideology" (166). But the writing subjects usually feel that they can adopt a range of discourse options. For instance, in writing across the curriculum they might decide whether to write feminist history, Marxist economics, ecological biology, or existentialist philosophy. The internal range of options depends on the degree of hegemony within each discipline. In the fifties, for example, compositionists and literary critics were largely univocal; in the nineties we appear to have more alternatives. According to Althusser, however, these choices matter little; more germane, the subjects believe that these are the only reasonable choices, that these norms are already firmly in place, that the personas, values, and expectations saturating the discourse and classroom behavior reflect the allowable parameters of disciplinary reality. Hundreds of minor and arbitrary truths are taken for granted, unchallenged, accepted as inevitable. Thus the governing conventions, rules, and rituals of a particular discipline become naturalized and institutionalized.

The "good" subject who comes to internalize the ideology of academic success, individual achievement, and rhetorical competence "decides," because it is the normal course, to write appropriately and to have appropriate attitudes about the discipline of work, about evidence, syntax, form, and so on. Althusser, however, claims that these positions have already been constructed to create just this seductive illusion of choice. Conventions about form, for example, "still appear in our rhetorics and handbooks as merely a problem in organizing our thinking" (Clifford 35). But form is also an attitude toward reality, it is rhetorical power, a way to shape experience, and as such it constructs subjects who assume that knowledge can be demonstrated merely by asserting a strong thesis and supporting it with three concrete points. But rarely is knowledge or truth the issue. Writing subjects learn that the panoply of discourse conventions are, in fact, the sine qua non, that adherence to ritual is the real ideological drama being enacted. This lesson serves them well in other institutional and public spheres. The myriad ways in which writing subjects can make the world intelligible have already been carefully proscribed so that the dutiful subject, true to ideals already internalized, believes it is possible to "inscribe his own ideas as a free subject in the action of his material practice. If he does not do so, 'that is wicked'" (168).

Writing subjects are, for instance, allowed to feel that the rhetorical stance they are encouraged to take is the only credible one, really the only possible one. In *English in America*, a critique of our profession, Ohmann cites numerous writing textbooks that almost universally affirm the need for a balanced, judicious, and authoritatively informed persona for the writer to argue effectively. That position still holds in the recent, best-selling *St. Martin's Guide to Writing* (Axelrod and Cooper), perhaps the most well received of the new process rhetorics. Ohmann expresses disappointment that the rhetorics from the seventies privileged the middle way while denigrating strong positions, conflict, and a committed sociopolitical agenda. In "How to Argue in Liberal" (182), a section of *English in America*, Ohmann claims that these seemingly progressive rhetorics blur and distance the flesh-and-blood writer, offering instead a restrained mask of moderation. A decade later little has changed.

The St. Martin's Guide claims that arguing "means presenting a carefully reasoned, well-supported argument . . . in a thoughtful and convincing way" (494). In this view, writers base their positions on reasons (also facts, statistics, authorities, and textual evidence), which can be "thought of as the main points supporting a claim" (498). The primary purpose of "argumentative writing is to influence readers. Therefore, careful writers seek to influence their readers with each choice of a word, each choice of a sentence" (509). Although *St. Martin's* does mention that a writer might want to build "a bridge of shared concerns" (509), it makes no attempt to put writers or readers in a concrete social situation, considers none of the overdetermined complexity governing the motivations of a writer trying to persuade, and pays no attention at all to how race, class, gender, sexuality, religion, nationality, or material interests might prevent readers from objectively following a logical sequence of facts and reasons. I can just imagine my students using cogent reasons and cold facts to persuade Jesse Helms to support abortion rights or funding for AIDS patients, or perhaps students could use logic and statistics to persuade their professors to give up tenure or to convince the tobacco industry to make the ethical gesture of switching its crops to bean sprouts. Like almost all contemporary rhetorics, *St. Martin's* creates the illusion that we can transcend ideology with three well-developed paragraphs of evidence, that we can somehow change the minds of others in a rhetorical vacuum freed from the pollutants of prior social alignments. This thinking is more than naive; it denies identity, represses class conflict, negates the way ideas originate in specific social configurations. It asks writers to believe that by adopting and carefully orchestrating an objective, rational argument, they can win the day and bring Jesse Helms to his senses.

The subject position constructed for the student writer in this seemingly pluralistic rhetoric leaves out resistance, excluding radical feminism, Marxism, and other committed political agendas. Masked as reasonable pragmatism, it seeks to ignore and therefore disparage dissent, discontinuity, and confrontational discourse. Our felt experiences, our various subjectivities, and our specific social situatedness as readers and writers are obviated under the guise of disinterestedness, as if race, class, and gender were messy accidents. Wayne Booth, for instance, in an apparent attempt to exclude these same irrelevant, confounding subjectivities, asserts that foregrounding them is "reductive vilification" (259). Obviously he feels that something important is being threatened. Ellen Rooney suggests that Booth wants to vindicate the hegemony of a pluralist polemic, which she sees as inescapably partisan (14).

Although the kind of pluralist rhetoric that *St. Martin's* exemplifies asserts an "ethic of tolerance and intellectual openness" (21), Rooney holds that such a discourse is interested in domination. It claims to be antitheoretical and nonideological, but its exclusion of writers considered antipluralist suggests its hegemonic intentions. Rooney notes that "the subject of pluralism assumes an infinitely persuadable audience" (53), one that is willing to enter a dialogue, one that is open to reason, all the while ignoring the social contingencies, forgetting the intricate web of ideology. Rooney believes that what these rhetorics leave out is not random; gender, race, and class are not simply overlooked. They are, in Althusser and Etienne Balibar's terms, pluralism's "invisible . . . forbidden vision" (26). An analysis of the ideological stance of contemporary rhetorics that focuses on the outside, on what is excluded, reveals as much as an examination of actual content. In Althusser's symptomatic reading, absence is as revealing as presence. He refuses innocent readings that take the immediate transparency of the text at face value, holding instead that Marx created a radically new mode of reading, opposed to "the myth of the voice (the Logos) speaking" (*Reading* 17). From this perspective, what *St. Martin's* does not say validates what Ohmann asserted in 1976, "that the educational system will support the tacit ideas of the dominant groups in the society" *(English* 159). A critique of writing theory and practice can only be fully understood when it is situated in a sociopolitical context. Teachers who ask students to rehearse particular composing rituals in the classroom impose an ideological agenda, admitted or not.

By constantly enacting these discursive rituals, the subject imperceptibly begins to identify with an appealing image reflected in a particular position. Individuals, enthralled by this image, soon subject themselves to it (Eagleton 172). Althusser thus uses the Pascalian dialectic—that belief follows from the ritual of kneeling down in church and moving one's lips—to conflate and dissolve our traditional notions of how ideology is created: "Ideology interpellates individuals as subjects" ("Ideology" 170); that is, ideology exists only by subjects and for subjects, constituting their subjectivity in language imbued with ideological overtones. Without a strong commitment from subjects to fulfill the tasks of their positions, an ideology would not be easily replicated. Tasks must, therefore, seem unavoidably obvious. "Yes," we must say, "this is what needs to be done; this is the only way." Teachers must recognize the need to punish the unwilling and reward the dutiful, eventually coming to see themselves in subject positions of unquestionable authority because others constantly refer to them as occupying such positions. This phenomenon, known as the recognition function, is exemplified by the familiar answer "It's me" to the question "Who's there!" Even though we are "always already subjects," already fathers or daughters, managers or workers, humanists in an English department or executives at IBM, we are constantly required to rehearse such rituals of ideological recognition. Teachers, for example, always call on specific students, require them to sign their names, and grade essays that guarantee that they are indeed "concrete, individual, distinguishable and (naturally) irreplaceable subjects" ("Ideology" 172–73).

Encouraging writers to develop prose styles that reflect their individuality, for example, is one technique among hundreds that ensures our positions as teachers and grade givers, the writer's position as student and supplicant, and both as unequal subjects in a constructed hierarchy. At the same time, such rituals foster the illusion of individuality and choice, as if the student writers created the possible styles of a given discursive genre. The pellucid naturalness of heading an essay with one's own unique name; the endless routines of assignments written to exacting specifications; the quizzes, grades, and discussions, and all the disappointments and failures, successes and rewards of school life become absolutely recognizable through repetition, not logic. As we successfully find our place, our position in the hierarchy of "merit," we also learn not to wonder if this rather particular and arbitrary way of teaching people to write is the only way. And, of course, since ideology thrives on anonymity, we think of our appointed tasks as commonsensical, not ideological.

Because we so thoroughly inhabit academic discourse, we often reify its arbitrary and contradictory conventions into inevitable organizational patterns that seem to have evolved through judicious, apolitical consensus. This tendency is especially true for students, many of whom lack both a historical perspective on rhetoric and a skeptical turn of mind, particularly when they are eager to become willing participants in the university's discursive mystifications. Gramsci's idea of struggling working-class students' giving "spontaneous consent" to values that are inimical to their best interests certainly applies to the almost blissfully naive attitude with which composition instructors and their students approach their assigned roles, as if the whole point of becoming a writer could be limited to the learning of certain skills and the acquisition of abstract rhetorical principles.

Students want to become writers not because they have mastered syntax but because they are convinced they have something to say and, more important, somebody to say it to. They want an audience they can trust, one that encourages (even expects) them to interrogate dominant values as part of their composing process, to look carefully at the social contingencies of family, religion, gender and class that have shaped their unique histories. Writers do not want to rehash what is already known; they are propelled forward by the quest to clarify their identities, order their existence, and understand their values and world's. Instructors can help students become inquisitive writers by avoiding rigid rules, constant evaluation, and an obsession with socializing students into the conventions of "normal" academic writing. They can, instead, develop interactive writing workshops imbued with a sense of the writing process as multifaceted, evolving and exploratory. Readings that foreground the ideological and cultural also encourage the critical consciousness necessary for committed writing.

Since writing is always much more than a technique, students need to understand explicitly that defying normative discourse, attempting to stretch the parameters of traditional thought, and not agreeing with all our purposes and procedures will not put them at a disadvantage. A climate conducive to good writing often strikes a delicate balance between acceptance and support and the pressure to produce. Although such an environment is not easy to create or sustain, it is possible and, in our present institutional context, necessary for psychological and political survival. Those who know the pleasures and excitement of discovering and writing a truth not in concert with institutional norms are difficult to silence or mystify. Perhaps more than other students, writers seem better poised to understand their intellectual and psychological possibilities in institutions. Writing, when studied and practiced in a rich sociopolitical context, can open spaces for the kind of informed resistance that can actually affect hegemonic structures. Although most students decide not to inhabit these oppositional spaces, dissonance and conflict stimulate the complex mix of contending forces out of which all discourse evolves. Without the awareness of ideological struggle that comes from trying to intervene into academic conversations, students remain confused about the purpose of composition studies.

In graduate school I can remember being perplexed by the negligible effect early composition research had on classroom practice. In 1929, a review of empirical studies compiled by Rollo Lyman overwhelmingly demonstrated that direct instruction in grammar did not have a significant effect on the student's actual writing. Needless to say, this research was not acted on in the schools and colleges. But I was looking in the wrong direction. Grammar was taught not because it was effective but because it was good discipline. It was rigorous and arcane, and it privileged upper- and middle-class language conventions against those of the working class and the poor. Teaching grammar, like teaching math or science, clearly installs the instructor as the Subject who knows against those subjects who clearly cannot know, unless they apply themselves diligently and, of course, without wondering why. As a metonymy for a host of other disciplines, grammar successfully interpellates subject into clear relations of power and authority. Students submit, teachers dominate. Ironically, students have very little to show for their great effort. One might argue that such submissiveness should have a payoff in mastery of some kind, but as Paul Diederich used to say, grammar instruction is probably harmful to writing since it takes the place of direct writing instruction. Although traditional grammar instruction functions as an almost pure ritual of control and domination, it also serves as an effective sorting mechanism for race and class discrimination, with poorer students always already speaking and writing incorrectly—a blunt reminder that school life often seems alien and hostile and offers no stairway upward for those on the wrong end of the class struggle.

Of the many other methods used to make students occupy submissive subject positions, perhaps the most familiar—and the one most adults remember about their writing instruction—is the way teachers seem overly concerned with error, misspellings, syntactic lapses, and usage distinctions of the most subtle dimensions. If we include rhetorical shortcomings in structure, development, focus, and logic, the stage is set for an elaborate drama in which the Subject cannot be challenged and in which subjects must always be wanting, must always be in fear of offending conventions and codes beyond counting. The good student who can negotiate this minefield intuitively knows that little depends on the ideas in the essay, that the discursive shell matters more than the ideation inside. As a result, the status of the "I" that "writes" the essay is so decentered, so alienated from actual experience that many students have as much emotional identification with their school writing as they do with geometry. That identification is absent because students sense that only their submission to a task is required. Those who enthusiastically embrace the positions typically available in the composition classroom are accepting the inevitability and strength of the dominant ideology. If they fail, they often blame themselves, seeing their deficiencies as personal rather than systemic. They are learning how academic discourse and institutional reality proceed: one is assigned tasks to be completed on time and according to the Subject's wishes; those who comply succeed, those who don't deserve to be excluded.

It seems to matter little if these tasks are modified by pedagogical innovations. The process approach to writing, for example, is easily appropriated by the ideological state apparatuses. An instructor down the hall from me has turned composing into such a labyrinthine sequence of prewriting heuristics, drafts, revisions, and peer-editing sessions that she has probably truncated years of bureaucratic socialization into three months. With dozens of discrete steps and scores of self-interrogating, self-purifying questions about coherence devices and structuring techniques that M. A. K. Halliday and Rugaiya Hasan would be proud of, she has validated the darkest epiphanies of Foucault and Althusser. Quite naturally she has been praised and rewarded for her commitment to improving her students' writing. And her supporters are right: she has forged a truly constructed subject, committed primarily to reinscribing the obvious and the known in hypercorrect and bloodless prose. However perverse she might be professionally, she is emblematic of the ways dominant ideologies resist change and replicate inequality through rituals of ideological interpellation.

Although many specific and obvious correlations exist between subject positions and educational institutions, Althusser holds that the structure of ideology changes little from one institution to another: a voice of authority addresses individuals, assigning them tasks to be completed according to indisputable criteria. Take, for example, religion—specifically Catholicism: a God (another Subject with a capital letter) speaks through a pope to the faithful, requiring them, if they are to be saved, to reproduce the model of the virtuous subject adherence to numerous rituals and commandments, thereby becoming "his mirrors, his reflections" ("Ideology" 179). Only thus can they be interpellated as Catholic subjects. Similarly, traditional writing instructors speak and judge from a position of authority, bolstered by the sacred rules of handbooks and rhetorics whose precepts are repeatedly reproduced in essays carefully orchestrated to instill respect for academic writing as it is now and will be hereafter. And because most good subjects are believers, excessive punishment is not needed to compel obedience. Schools and churches do use "suitable methods of punishment and expulsion," but the good subject wants to do what is required; thus, ironically, this "individual is interpellated as a (free) subject in order that he shall submit freely to the commandments of the Subject, i.e., in order that he shall (freely) accept his subjection, i.e., in order that he shall make the gestures and actions of his subjection all by himself" (Althusser, "Ideology" 145, 182).

The guarantee of salvation, academic success, or worldly advancement given by the Subject to his or her subjects precludes the appropriate mirror recognition, a power that ultimately allows the relations of production and reproduction of knowledge to be replicated. When subjects eventually complete their training and receive their new posts in society, the internalized mechanism of ideology begins once again in a new institutional situation. And so it goes.

Althusser, however, wants to remind us that ideological state apparatuses entail more than this technical, mutual recognition of Subjects and subjects. Relations of production within the class struggles of advanced capitalism typically involve exploitation. It follows, then, that these struggles between the dominant and the exploited are inevitably reenacted within the ideological conflicts of educational institutions. This confrontation has two dimensions: one struggle is directed against the former ruling class, as for example in the expressive revolt against the dominance of traditional handbooks in the sixties; the other struggle is against the exploited class itself, as in the conservative backlash in the seventies against nonstandard dialects. The discursive conflicts in composition classrooms, then, derive their form and function from the specific conditions of existence that govern class conflicts beyond the educational institution. The ideologies of the state apparatuses we find enmeshed in our discourse are internalized versions of those ongoing confrontations between the dominant and the other. As instructors we can never fully transcend these struggles or our role in them as Subjects of hegemony. We must learn to live with this contradiction if we work in institutions. We are Subjects who do the sorting work of an unequal society. And although we may also hope to be oppositional agents, we cannot fully escape the institutional interpellation.

The implications of this crucial Althusserian insight need to be developed. If we can accurately speak of a "source" of ideology, we usually try to locate it in the consciousness of a particular group, as in Marx's famous dictum from *The German Ideology* that the ruling ideas of a given time are ruling class ideas. But Althusser situates ideology's origin instead in the continuous struggle between antagonistic classes, in the "simultaneity of these relations within a particular context" (Dowling 67). Ideology is not simply a mirror of the values of the dominant class but rather those ideas modified through bitter, contentious struggles with one another, a compromise, a trade-off, a melding of opposing discourses. So too does the struggle for dominance within English departments, between historians and deconstructionists or empiricists and cultural critics, determine the shape of the ideas that survive. As a result, no pure ideas or conventions develop in an ahistorical, apolitical vacuum. As Diane Macdonell notes, "No ideology takes shape outside a struggle with some opposing ideology" (33). Of course, although opposing discourses such as epistemic and expressive rhetorics exhibit many differences, they still operate beneath a powerful ideology with its inevitable dialectic of domination and resistance. Yet, even the most carceral Foucauldian discourse, which college rhetorics clearly are not, always has room for dissent, for resistance. For oppositional critics, the parameters of this opposition must then become the contestatory sites of political possibility as ideas are relationally reshaped, never fully constructed, always marked by that which they oppose, always carrying traces of that which they would flee, always brimming with contradictions, constraints, and openings. The discursive subject positions available to students and indeed to all of us within these ideologies are also constructed by conflicting, partial, interesting codes, not by the coherent and stable consciousness posited by traditional humanists or by the completely decentered subject of poststructuralism. Terry Eagleton notes that he does not feel he is "a mere function of a social structure" (172). Part of that belief, of course, comes from ideology's ability to disguise itself, but we are so written by contradictory discourses that we think there is space for "dialectical self-consciousness" (Goleman 113). When we finally perceive how hegemonic rituals construct us in ways we would like to oppose, we want to be agents instead of subjects. This self-consciousness can assist us in the academy with the "project of respeaking both our own subjectivity and the symbolic order" (Silverman 283). Paradoxically, this undertaking seems both trivial and ambitious. It is trivial because much of the work would have to be carried out on a local level in our classrooms, in conversations with colleagues, in committee and departmental meetings, and in journals and texts and at conferences, where we profess a more sociopolitically aware rhetoric to a wider audience. Gramsci believes that only through such a "minute, molecular process" (194) can a transformational collective be born. The results probably seem modest indeed. But we seem to have no other plausible strategy. True, our work with students can often be exciting and rewarding, but no matter how effective we are in raising their consciousness about the ideological dimensions of rhetoric, we receive little positive reinforcement from an essentially conservative academic culture. Gramsci and others certainly recognize this dilemma. Their alternative to professional paralysis is quite simple: since power is also decentered in our culture, finding its energy in properly socialized subjects, the most ambitious undertaking is not to storm the hegemonic barricades. Instead we should do the intellectual work we know best: helping students to read and write and think in ways that both resist domination and exploitation and encourage self-consciousness about who they are and can be in the social world. This is where our hope lies; even if, as James A. Berlin suggests, we are "lodged within a hermeneutic circle" ("Rhetoric and Ideology" 489), we can still change ourselves and others. When we achieve a distance from the inherited ideas of traditional rhetoric, multiple possibilities of "revising, synthesizing, or transforming ideas that had been merely passively accepted before" (Cocks 68) are opened for our intervention.

Our beliefs about rhetoric, finally, do not originate in an authentic, voiced consciousness; do not exist primarily in enlightened cognition; and are certainly not the cumulative result of consensual, transcendent scholarship, research, and intellectual will. For perhaps obvious political reasons, the discourse of rhetoric as conventionally constructed has ignored or repressed the ideological dimension developed in the work of neo-Marxist thinkers like Althusser. A critique of our rhetorical ideology, however, suggests that the struggles in our disciplinary discourses are not esoteric, ivory-tower theories without social impact; they just may be the primary areas where hegemony and democracy are contested, where subject positions are constructed, where power and resistance are enacted, where hope for a just society depends on our committed intervention.

Works Cited

Althusser, Louis. "Ideology and Ideological State Apparatuses." *Lenin and Philosophy and Other Essays*. Trans. Ben Brewster. New York: Monthly Review, 1971.

Althusser, Louis, and Etienne Balibar. *Reading Capital*. Trans. Ben Brewster. London: NLB, 1970.

Axelrod, Rise B., and Charles Cooper. *The St. Martin's Guide to Writing*. 2nd ed. New York: St. Martin's, 1988.

Berlin, James A. "Rhetoric and Ideology in the Writing Class." *College English* 50 (1988): 477–94.

Booth, Wayne. *Critical Understanding: The Powers and Limits of Pluralism*. Chicago: U of Chicago P, 1979.

Burke, Kenneth. *A Rhetoric of Motives*. Berkeley: U of California P, 1969.

Clifford, John. "Burke and the Tradition of Democratic Schooling." L. Z. Smith 29–40.

Cocks, Joan. *The Oppositional Imagination: Feminism, Critique, and Political Theory*. New York: Routledge, 1989.

Dowling, William C. *Jameson, Althusser, Marx: An Introduction to the Political Unconscious*. Ithaca: Cornell UP, 1984.

Eagleton, Terry. *Literary Theory: An Introduction.* Minneapolis: U of Minnesota P, 1983.

Goleman, Judith. "Reading, Writing, and the Dialectic since Marx." L. Z. Smith 107–121.

Gramsci, Antonio. *An Antonio Gramsci Reader: Selected Writings, 1916–1935.* Trans. Quintin Hoare, Geoffrey Nowell-Smith, John Matthews, and William Boelhower. Ed. David Forgacs. New York: Schocken, 1988.

Lentricchia, Frank. *Criticism and Social Change.* Chicago: U of Chicago P, 1983.

Macdonell, Diane. *Theories of Discourse.* New York: Blackwell, 1986.

Ohmann, Richard. *English in America.* New York: Oxford UP, 1976.

———. *Politics of Letters.* Middletown: Wesleyan UP, 1987.

Rooney, Ellen Frances. *Seductive Reasoning: Pluralism as the Problematic of Contemporary Literary Theory.* Ithaca: Cornell UP, 1989.

Silverman, Kaja. *The Subject of Semiotics.* New York: Oxford UP, 1983.

Smith, Louise Z., ed. *Audits of Meaning.* Portsmouth: Boynton, 1988.

Smith, Paul. *Discerning the Subject.* Minneapolis: U of Minnesota P, 1988.

Zavarzadeh, Mas'ud, and Donald Morton. "Theory, Pedagogy, Politics: The Crisis of 'The Subject' in the Humanities." *Boundary 2* 15.1–2 (1986–87): 1–22.

CHAPTER FIFTEEN

Class Dismissed

MARY SOLIDAY

In the academy at large, in English departments, and—my particular concern—in writing programs, what is at stake in a culturalist framework is how students make meaning, not how they or their parents make a living. Discussions of diversity typically foreground racial and ethnic difference, all but dismissing social class; at the same time, a concern with identity conflicts is rooted in a discursive conception of cultural difference. But within this discursive framework, cultural politics have obscured the material realities of social class, with grim consequences for working-class students and their prospects of attaining four-year degrees.

Progressive academics tend to locate their resistance to dominant academic culture in a critique of the discourses used in classrooms or in scholarship. In English studies, literary specialists advocate diversity by debating the canon, recovering literary traditions, or studying popular cultures. Compositionists critique assimilationist discourses, recover lost rhetorical traditions, and develop pedagogies that respect students' nonacademic languages. These activities are enormously productive, but they have overshadowed the material struggles that preoccupy many working-class students. I want here to investigate how social class affects the educational narratives of working-class students—both their initial access to four-year institutions and their ability to persevere until they obtain bachelor's degrees—and to argue that a genuine concern with diversity should lead us to question the

From *College English* 61 (1999): 731–41.

selective functions of the academy and the role of composition in maintaining them.

Challenging these selective functions is of primary importance most obviously because social class and a four-year degree are so closely related. Statistically speaking, the BA degree determines whether individuals will perform physical or mental labor, and it also determines the amount of autonomy they will have over their work. According to David Lavin and David Hyllegard, researchers agree that "educational attainment is the single most important influence on occupational success, overshadowing by far the direct effects of family background" (21). As important for my analysis, a broad wage differential exists between the AA and the BA degrees over a lifetime (see, e.g., Lavin and Hyllegard), while a BA provides greater status and class mobility for Blacks than it does for Whites (Weis). However, achieving class mobility through a four-year education is becoming increasingly difficult for large numbers of students. The numbers of middle- and upper-income college students have increased dramatically since the 1970s, but the number of low-income students is actually decreasing in the 1990s (*The Condition of Education*).

The sector which traditionally provides a BA degree to working-class students is public higher education. However, as Paul Lauter argues, public higher education is being privatized in the 1990s: funding is being shifted from the state and federal levels onto the shoulders of individual students and their parents. Astoundingly sharp income gaps now appear to distinguish students attending public two-year colleges, public four-year colleges and universities, private liberal arts colleges, and elite private universities. According to the Council for Aid to Education, "The United States must overhaul its system of funding higher education or face growing stratification along class lines. . . . continuation of these trends will lead to intensified clustering of rich students in more expensive institutions and poor students in vocational and community colleges" (Dembner). Furthermore, in many states downsizing involves tightening admissions standards at public institutions, which reflects "a national trend of public colleges and universities toughening their standards, bringing them closer to those of private institutions" (Thomson A:1). Post-secondary education is being increasingly differentiated by social class because institutions are narrowing access. A contradiction arises, for, as Alice Roy argues, "Systems of higher education, in the throes of downsizing, cannot at the same time enable policies of inclusion and diversity" (193). Thus we must examine not only what Roy calls the rhetoric of inclusion at our institutions, but also what we mean by cultural diversity in our professional discourses.

Most culturalist writing in composition, including my own, is chiefly concerned with how students enter the academy without losing their pre-academic sense of self. The differences between academic and nonacademic life are defined mostly in terms of a struggle over ways of making meaning—with language practices, rhetorical traditions, worldviews, and ideologies. Compositionists work not just to help students develop acceptable academic discourse but also to persuade the academy to change in response to the students, translating insights about difference into an institutionally transformative pedagogy.

This institutional transformation begins in the classroom through the language we use and teach. For instance, in several important essays, Min-Zhan Lu has developed the concept of "repositioning," which "asks students to consider the relationships between their academic and nonacademic experiences" ("Writing as Repositioning" 18). According to Lu, students' access to discourse is accomplished mainly in the classroom, where their intellectual struggle to redefine their relationships to different discourses takes place: "I would argue that students' access to these competing discourses, and their experience of the friction points between these discourses, can have a positive effect. Rather than impeding their learning, it can motivate students to change as well as reproduce the academic discourse taught in the classroom" (18). Lu defines resistance to dominant academic culture as resistance to conventional ways of experiencing, interpreting, and knowing the world through language.

If cultural difference is defined chiefly as a struggle over making meaning, then the conflicts that we know many nontraditional students experience within the academy will revolve primarily around students' ability to position themselves in ways that don't violate their own cultural integrity. Gail Okawa describes the threat of higher education:

> When student writers bring with them different languages, discourses, cultures, and world views, the culture of the academy would leech out their cultural uniqueness, absorb them, assimilate them, graduate them uniform in their uniforms. Admittance requires conformity and the attendant cultural loss. (98)

It is not surprising that students "often refuse that absorption, overtly or covertly" (99). Okawa is discussing students from "nonwhite minority backgrounds," but studies like Howard London's show that working-class whites also resist, drop out, and fail primarily because they "refuse . . . absorption." From this perspective, it is students' ambivalence about their identities that causes poor retention rates, unless, with teachers' help, they reposition themselves by imagining "the possibility of cultural coexistence" (Okawa 99).

Lu's and Okawa's accounts are persuasive, and they help us to translate insights about cultural difference into pedagogy and scholarship. However, in our emphasis upon culture as a mode of making meaning, we have not adequately recognized that material conflicts are central to the experiences of many working-class students. The one factor that is consistently linked with college students' retention rates—across ethnic, race, and gender lines—is the number of hours worked at an outside job while attending school (Astin). The few working-class students, many of them Black, Latino, and Asian American, who do attend four-year schools don't graduate in four years because they experience higher education intermittently. In Richard Richardson and Elizabeth Skinner's interviews with first-generation students, working-class and minority, they found that balancing work with school schedules created major conflicts for students and that "many spent relatively little continuous time as students" (35). Here is how one African American interviewee described her typical day: "'Getting up at 6:30 to prepare and go to school, taking my son to day care, going to school from 8:00 to 12:30, working on one job from 1:00 to 4:30. Going home . . . Then I would leave at night going to my night job'" (35).

This student's struggle does not necessarily involve an identity confusion. Moreover, as teachers, our response to this student's predicament cannot be particularly affirmative if we think about her problems in a discursive context. As John Guillory puts the case,

> a culturalist politics, though it glances worriedly at the phenomenon of class, has in practice never devised a politics that would arise from a class "identity." For while it is easy enough to conceive of a self-affirmative racial or sexual identity, it makes very little sense to posit an affirmative lower-class identity, as such an identity would have to be grounded in the experience of deprivation per se. . . . The incommensurability of the category of class with that of race or gender (class cannot be constructed as a social identity in the *same way* as race or gender because it is not, in the current affirmative sense, a "social identity" at all), does not, on the other hand, disenable a description of the relation between these social modalities. (13)

In other words, we don't affirm a student's inability to buy a computer or textbooks in the same way that we affirm that student's street slang as a creative, oppositional use of language. Martha Marinara, responding to her adult students' essays about their physical labor, observes that "Unlike narratives of race and gender, class status works against difference; the lower classes cannot afford not to be mainstreamed" (8). We may see abandoning one's first language as assimilationist, but we don't say that buying books or a computer involves assimilation into dominant cultures. Though these material gains may also represent cultural dislocations, because we have assumed that language, ethnic tradition, and ideology are the primary features of cultural difference, we don't discuss the points at which students can't afford *not* to assimilate.

If we include social class as a significant feature of cultural experience, then students may not achieve access to academic discourse through reflection and critique in the classroom alone; nor will their experience of college be determined purely by their willingness to lose their cultural identities. As Guillory points out: "An 'institutional' fact such as literacy has everything to do with the relation of 'exclusion' to social identity; but exclusion should be defined not as exclusion from representation but from access to the *means of cultural production* . . . literacy [can thus be defined] . . . *as the systematic regulation of reading and writ-*

ing" (18). From my perspective as a teacher of working-class students, purchasing expensive books for a college course and having uninterrupted time to revise an essay on a personal computer also represent significant forms of access to the cultural capital of the academy.

Working-class students' struggles to gain and sustain access to the "cultural means of production" create educational life narratives that sharply differentiate them from their bourgeois counterparts. The number of hours worked and various family responsibilities are correlated strongly with both the type of institution that these students attend and their retention rates. Remedial courses and other institutional hurdles also contribute to two broadly different stories of educational progress associated with different class backgrounds.

In *Fear of Falling,* Barbara Ehrenreich proposes that the professional middle class can be distinguished from the working class below and the elite above primarily through a liberal arts education, an education that, for about 20 percent of the population, constitutes a defining life experience. One hallmark of this cultural experience, Ehrenreich notes, is the "guildlike quality" associated with a long period of intense study and apprenticeship "essential to the social cohesion of the middle class" (13). Most bourgeois students live a relatively uninterrupted narrative, typically proceeding from high school to four or five years of liberal arts study to professional jobs; in the 1990s, the narrative often extends to several years of graduate school and the mid-life raising of children by two-career couples. Unsurprisingly, the sooner a student makes the transition from high school to college, the more likely he or she is to earn a BA degree (*The Condition of Education*).

Education is likely to be far more discontinuous for working-class college students, chiefly because most low-income students attend two-year colleges, work while they are in school, and take part-time loads (Otuya and Mitchell). In addition, these students may "stop out" to raise children or care for family members (Sternglass). Working-class students sometimes begin college later in life and take remedial coursework before actually beginning college classes; they often withdraw from or repeat courses; and they tend to commute to school (see, e.g., Brint and

Karabel). One consequence of the intermittent relationship such students have to institutions, of course, is diminished personal contact with faculty and with peers, both factors strongly correlated with the guildlike quality of the experience of their middle-class peers (Astin).

Obviously, working-class students take longer to complete their degrees—and some never do graduate. Well over half of one CUNY open admissions cohort David Lavin and David Hyllegard examined took more than four years to complete a degree, while a quarter needed more than five and 16 percent more than seven years to do so (57). Similarly, in his study of working-class Asian-American students enrolled at a public university, Peter Kiang notes that fewer than 14 percent graduated in five years. Longitudinal research provides a lens through which to examine the effects of social class upon students' educational progress as they struggle to finance their educations and to move through institutions over time. In her remarkable book, *Time to Know Them,* Marilyn Sternglass follows nine students at the City College of New York (CCNY) for six years, from their initial writing courses through courses across the curriculum and into graduation. Some of these students were poorly prepared for college and some struggled to negotiate the institution's demands for identity changes, but what most negatively affected their academic achievement was outside work and the related stress of commuting and sustaining a meaningful family life.

Consider Delores: in 1991 she lived during the week in the Bronx in order to qualify for in-state tuition but commuted seventy-five minutes each way to New Jersey to work in a restaurant on Fridays, Saturdays, and Sundays; on weeknights, she worked at the library at the City College campus in Manhattan. Chandra, another student, told Sternglass, "I want to do quality work, but juggling two jobs and school becomes confusing—what do I do today? My first concern is how to get money to continue next semester" (105). To be sure, students like Delores and Chandra benefited from multicultural curricula and learned to question dominant ideologies. But these intellectual struggles were empowering—unlike students' long-term struggles to pay tuition and rent, care for family members, and commute across the city.

Sternglass focuses particularly upon the experience of Ricardo, whose case "encapsulates the feelings and frustrations of many of his classmates." Depressed by increases in tuition and cutbacks in financial aid, Ricardo said his academic commitment was diminishing: "I've been on the honor roll for three years, but if I can't pay the rent and eat, who cares about grades?" (105). When he dropped courses at one point, it was not because he didn't see the possibility of cultural coexistence—it was because he had increased his working hours outside school. Ricardo persisted and garnered high grades in advanced math and science courses, but, given his financial obligations and the exhaustion of his protracted economic struggles, he finally abandoned his dream of becoming a doctor and instead completed the physician's assistant program.

Many of the students in Sternglass's study also spent several semesters completing noncredit coursework in reading and writing in order to prepare for required liberal arts courses or to pass exit exams, the most difficult of which was the CUNY Writing Assessment Test, the WAT. Though he earned high grades on all his essays, Ricardo took the WAT eight times before he passed it. As Barbara Gleason documents, the CUNY WAT constitutes a chief institutional barrier to students' progress toward a BA, in part because students had to enroll in various remedial courses and non-credit workshops in order to pass it by the time they had accrued sixty credits. The WAT is an example of one way in which composition regulates students' access to the liberal arts even after they have been admitted to a college.

Tests like the WAT, mandatory remediation, extensive testing and counseling, penalties for withdrawing from courses, and course sequencing function as barriers; they are a less visible means of selection within many open admissions institutions. Colleges use such internal barriers to resolve a fundamental paradox in American society: how to fulfill students' aspirations for class mobility through education without relinquishing the academy's traditional selective functions? In response to such tensions, Burton Clark proposes that public institutions will do one of two things: either establish a series of internal barriers to "cool out" working-class students, or create less selective colleges that siphon off students who will not fulfill traditional educational narratives. In their case histories of public higher education, Steven Brint and Jerome Karabel further document how the leadership of selective state institutions consciously encouraged the growth of less selective institutions in order to protect the selectivity of their own. From this perspective, then, the use of internal barriers and the differentiation of public higher education institutionalize our historical ambivalence toward the uses of education to achieve class mobility. As Clark suggests, the unselective institution exists *in order to* maintain selectivity within a democratic society.

In the 1970s, open admissions at the City University of New York was a conscious effort to contest the differentiation of higher education by social class and ethnicity. To study whether open admissions achieved this goal, Lavin and Hyllegard compared the educational progress of two cohorts of CUNY students: the 1970 group enrolled before tuition was phased in and before remediation was centralized through skills testing; the 1980 cohort attended after severe budget cuts forced the university to establish tuition and to enact a series of policy modifications or internal barriers. Lavin and Hyllegard's longitudinal research thus compares the effects that open access and restricted access may have had upon the long-term progress of working-class students. They conclude that the 1980 cohort "achieved considerably less academic success" (238), which they attribute largely to "the changed academic context created by policy modifications" (239)—such as charging tuition to students who, in both cohorts, were primarily working-class, stricter admission standards for initial access into senior colleges, and mandatory remediation (210–12). I would add that, as is true nationally, CUNY's ideological and budgetary commitment to remedial education diminished in these years.

The brief experiment in open admissions did not erase decades of socioeconomic inequality in New York City, but even so, widening access to the BA degree did foster class mobility for thousands of Black, White, and Latino students. Lavin and Hyllegard argue persuasively for the success of the early phase of open admissions in that thousands of working-class students received BA degrees which they used to find and keep white collar jobs, to obtain post-graduate degrees, and to contribute to the overall growth of an educated urban class. However, the 1970 policy was not sustained in terms of economic and institutional support: with the charging of tuition, more students had to work more hours so that socioeconomic backgrounds, which had had a negligible impact upon the fates of the 1970 cohort, became a determining factor in the ability of working-class students in the 1980 cohort to stay in school. With the addition of repeated testing and gateway courses, CUNY students' progress toward the BA degree was slowed down, and the slower the progress toward a degree, the less likely a student is to persist beyond the first year. In addition, of course, higher tuition and stiffer admissions requirements probably cooled out the aspirations of working-class students who turned to vocational programs in two-year colleges. And though an AA degree does represent a significant form of social mobility for millions of students, it does not fulfill the aspirations of individuals like Delores, Chandra, or Ricardo.

My analysis does not result in a pedagogy, but instead suggests that, if we are serious about sustaining diversity, then we must examine and challenge the barriers the academy places in the way of working-class students. Because such contestation is both institutionally specific and collaborative, I want to conclude by sketching out some of the work that I and my CUNY colleagues have been engaged in since 1991.

Remediation and assessment may foster students' progress at some institutions, but Barbara Gleason and I had evidence that both acted as internal barriers by slowing students' progress toward a BA at CCNY. While tuition was soaring and the poverty level of minorities was increasing in New York City, our students could neither use their financial aid to pay for remedial courses nor enroll in required core curriculum courses while simultaneously completing remedial requirements. We felt that the remedial program was not receiving adequate funding or intellectual attention from the institution commensurate to its functions, and we had collected evidence that the CUNY WAT did not accurately predict who would succeed in a college writing course. We thus proposed a two-semester writing course that mainstreamed basic writers with freshman students and that offered specific educational support to basic writers while also supporting teachers' efforts to develop a multicultural curriculum.

In addition, we obtained temporary permission for our pilot project students to take core courses they wouldn't normally be eligible for and to garner college credit for their writing courses regardless of their placement scores on the WAT. Between 1993 and 1996, the remedial students who elected to take this course passed it, along with one other core literature course that we studied, at rates equal to those of regular freshmen. In addition, one representative group produced portfolios that were judged by outside readers to be roughly equal to those portfolios written by students who earlier passed the WAT. At the same time, hundreds of remedial students took fewer remedial writing courses and more core courses than they would have normally (Gleason and Soliday; Soliday and Gleason).

In part, our project was not institutionalized because we developed it during a period of intense political attack upon CUNY's commitment to open admissions. While Gleason and I argued against using skills tests for traditional placement purposes, a vocal neoliberal/conservative coalition—of journalists, politicians, think tank intellectuals, and political appointees to the CUNY Board of Trustees—argued that skills tests such as the WAT should be used for admissions purposes. This argument gained force when local newspapers lambasted some bilingual students at Hostos Community College who had failed the WAT. The resulting blistering attack on students' literacy helped to justify tuition hikes, a decrease in financial aid, tougher rules on college students' use of welfare, an increase in faculty teaching loads, and sweeping budget cuts to public higher education; the critique of CUNY's standards (including specific attacks upon our project) legitimated the abolition of remedial courses in four-year colleges and the mandatory use of skills tests for initial admission to these colleges.

The overt politicizing of literacy within this local context not only shows how composition can be used to restrict access to a liberal arts degree; it also urges us to resist rather than to comply with composition's insitutionalized roles. As institutional agents who administer writing programs (see Gunner), or as scholars who study institutional relationships, compositionists can use whatever authority and knowledge we have to contest the traditional selective functions that our programs may perform. Beyond these traditional roles, we can also work with others outside composition to contest the local politics that maintain selective functions and to build relationships with progressive groups outside the academy.

In our case at CUNY, progressive faculty responded by organizing an insurgent faculty union, the New Caucus, to sponsor opposition activities of students and faculty and to foster alliances with labor organizations in the city. New Caucus members also helped students to organize, for example by linking them together with the New York Public Interest Research Group (NYPIRG). Over the years faculty visited Albany and encouraged students to do likewise; with NYPIRG's help, they persuaded students to register to vote and to vote for politicians who support public higher education and financial assistance. Progressive groups like the CUNY Coalition of Concerned Faculty and Staff sued New York State for unequal funding of public institutions serving different student populations, and, more recently, purchased airtime on the radio for CUNY students to testify to the value of remedial education. Along with staging rallies, marches, and teach-ins, faculty organized letter writing campaigns, wrote editorials, prepared working papers, and spoke on radio and television. Others used their institutional research to question conservative assumptions about retention rates or students' literacy. As I write now, one of my colleagues at CCNY has, through a lawsuit, temporarily blocked the CUNY Board of Trustees from implementing a plan that requires students to pass three skills tests (including the WAT) in order to be admitted to a senior college.

This conception of resistance is not incompatible with critiques of academic discourse; we might think of ways to bring the discursive turn to bear upon transforming activist work into scholarship and scholarship into activist work. But we must go beyond a critique of discourse because I know of no strong evidence that changing the way we use language transforms the academy's essential selective functions. Challenging these functions is crucial because public higher education is one of the few potential avenues into the middle class in a society increasingly stratified by education itself. To begin to address growing divisions between the urban working class and the suburban middle class, between immigrants and the native-born, between the rich and the poor, we must question more vigorously than we have what we mean by cultural diversity at our own institutions. And as we work to expand access to higher education for the twenty-first century, we cannot afford to dismiss social class.

Works Cited

Astin, Alexander. *What Matters in College*? San Francisco: Jossey-Bass, 1993.

Brint, Steven, and Jerome Karabel. *The Diverted Dream*. New York: Oxford UP, 1989.

Clark, Burton. *The Open-Door College*. New York: McGraw-Hill, 1960.

The Condition of Education, 1997. The National Center for Education Statistics. <http://nces.ed.gov/pubs/ce/index.html>

Dembner, Alice. "Overhaul of College Funding is Urged." *Boston Globe* 6 Jan. 1995: 4.

Ehrenreich, Barbara. *Fear of Falling*. New York: Harper Collins, 1989.

Gleason, Barbara. "When the Writing Test Fails: Assessing Assessment at an Urban College." Severino, Guerra, and Butler 307–24.

Gleason, Barbara, and Mary Soliday. *The City College Writing Program: An Enrichment Approach to Language and Literacy (1993–1996)*. Final Report to the Fund for Improvement in Post-Secondary Education, 1997.

Guillory, John. *Cultural Capital*. Chicago: Chicago UP, 1993.

Gunner, Jeanne. "Among the Composition People: The WPA as English Department Agent." *JAC* 18 (1998): 153–64.

Kiang, Peter Nien-chu. "Issues of Curriculum and Community for First-Generation Asian Americans in College." Zwerling and London 97–112.

Lavin, David, and David Hyllegard. *Changing the Odds*. New Haven: Yale UP, 1996.

Lauter, Paul. " 'Political Correctness' and the Attack on American Colleges." *Higher Education Under Fire*. Ed. Michael Bérubé and Cary Nelson. New York: Routledge, 1995. 73–90.

London, Howard. *The Culture of a Community College.* New York: Praeger, 1978.

Lu, Min-Zhan. "Conflict and Struggle: The Enemies or Preconditions of Basic Writing?" *College English* 54 (1992): 887–913.

———. "Writing as Repositioning." "Writing Within and Against the Academy: What Do We Really Want Our Students to Do? A Symposium." *Journal of Education* 172.1 (1990): 8–21.

Marinara, Martha. "When Working Class Students 'Do' the Academy: How We Negotiate with Alternative Literacies." *Journal of Basic Writing* (Fall 1997): 3–16.

Okawa, Gail Y. "Cross-Talk: Talking Cross-Difference." Severino, Guerra, and Butler 94–102.

Otuya, Ebo, and Alice Mitchell. "Today's College Students: Varied Characteristics by Sector." *Research Briefs* Vol. 5. Washington, D.C.: American Council on Education, 1994.

Richardson, Richard, and Elizabeth Skinner. "Helping First-Generation Minority Students Achieve Degrees." Zwerling and London 24–45.

Roy, Alice. "The Grammar and Rhetoric of Inclusion." *College English* 57 (Feb. 1995): 182–95.

Severino, Carol, Juan Guerra, and Johnnella Butler, eds. *Writing in Multicultural Settings.* New York: MLA, 1997.

Soliday, Mary, and Barbara Gleason. "From Remediation to Enrichment: Evaluating a Mainstreaming Project." *Journal of Basic Writing* 16 (Spring 1997): 64–78.

Sternglass, Marilyn. *Time to Know Them.* Mahwah, NJ: Lawrence Erlbaum, 1997.

Thomson, Susan C. "UM Proposes Harder Prep Course Load." *Saint-Louis Post Dispatch* 2 May 1992: A1.

Weis, Lois. *Between Two Worlds.* London: Routledge, 1985.

Zwerling, L. Steven, and Howard B. London, eds. *First-Generation Students: Confronting the Cultural Issues.* San Francisco: Jossey-Bass, 1992.

CHAPTER SIXTEEN

History in the Spaces Left: African American Presence and Narratives of Composition Studies

JACQUELINE JONES ROYSTER AND JEAN C. WILLIAMS

This essay begins with a statement that is fast becoming, if it is not already so, an aphorism: History is important, not just in terms of who writes it and what gets included or excluded, but also because history, by the very nature of its inscription as history, has social, political, and cultural *consequences*.

A Short Review of Histories of Composition

In the last twelve years several scholars have produced historical accounts of composition studies, seeking to define a field which is still, in many ways, in its infancy. Both James Berlin's *Rhetoric and Reality: Writing Instruction in American Colleges, 1900–1985* and Stephen North's *The Making of Knowledge in Composition: Portrait of an Emerging Field* were published in 1987, just one year short of 25 years from the 1963 date they propose as the birth of composition as a discipline. In 1990 Albert Kitzhaber's often copied 1953 dissertation, *Rhetoric in American Colleges, 1850–1900* was published in book form. In 1991, Susan Miller joined the discussion with *Textual Carnivals: The Politics of Composition,* and since then several other accounts, such as John Brereton's, *The Origins of Composition Studies in the American College, 1875–1925* (1995) and Sheryl Fontaine

From *College Composition and Communication* 50 (1999): 563–84.

and Susan Hunter's edited volume, *Writing Ourselves into the Story: Unheard Voices from Composition Studies* (1993), have continued to enrich our views and participate in establishing national parameters for the field.

Each of these texts has a different focus and contributes positively, along with others not cited here, to knowledge and understanding. They offer perspectives on the emergence of rhetoric and composition as an academic field; discuss ways in which knowledge has been and continues to be made, applied, disseminated, and interpreted in the field; and address some of the broader trends and issues pertinent to the historical and ideological trajectories of the field. None, however, can be described as comprehensive, definitive, or all inclusive. Each sustains a point of view and occupies an ideological and/or cultural location. In fact, setting aside Kitzhaber for the moment as a scholar who in 1953 was a precursor of the field, neither Berlin nor North as two of the earliest historical accounts make claims to universality. Quite the contrary, Berlin actually warns us that "there are no definitive histories" and that "each history endorses an ideology, a conception of economic, social, political, and cultural arrangements that is privileged in its interpretation" ("Octalog" 8).

The challenge suggested by this comment is twofold. On one hand, researchers who produce discipline narratives are called upon to contextualize historical work so that gaps and limitations in the purview of their work are clearer and so that their interpretive claims do not exceed their reach and thereby serve to disregard, exclude, or misrepresent other viewpoints. On the other hand, and perhaps more importantly, those of us who use the narratives would better serve the discipline if we were required by common practice to re-articulate those gaps and limitations in our own uses of the narratives, rather than drifting in our valorization of them toward the assigning of primacy and the assumption of universality, even by default. The latter challenge is for all of us to have a critical perspective of the extent to which images and valorized viewpoints shape interpretive visions and thereby create consequences, given the interpretive frameworks that grow out of these visions, in terms of knowledge making, policymaking, and day to day operations.

Examples that demonstrate the need for caution are evident in each of the studies cited above. Kitzhaber, the earliest written narrative and, again, a precursor in the field, has certainly achieved a status of high regard. His effort was to look at the nineteenth century from 1850 to 1900 as the backdrop for establishing a shift in English studies and the teaching of rhetoric that made modern composition studies possible. One event, for example, that Kitzhaber identifies as important is the rise of land grant institutions. He says:

> These new state institutions, founded squarely on the notion that it was the responsibility of American colleges to offer a wider selection of courses than had been commonly available before, were very influential in breaking up the older pattern and in supplying a new one for the next century. (12)

Nowhere in his analysis, however, does Kitzhaber consider what this statement suggests regarding the seventeen historically African American colleges and universities that constitute what is popularly known in African American academic circles as the "1890 institutions," a label referring to the second round of land grants that permitted federal monies to be used in establishing separate land grant institutions for African Americans in states (primarily in the South) where they could not attend the white land grant institutions established thirty years earlier.

The point to be emphasized for this analysis is that neither Kitzhaber nor the numbers of researchers who have since used his work as a building block have been pushed to specify, not just the groundbreaking strengths of this seminal work, but also the limitations of it in terms of the ideological location of the scholar who has produced it: where he sets the gaze, the particular historical experiences on which he draws, and the intersecting experiences of others whom he does not notice but who could, nevertheless, be written into the story.

Further, while both Berlin and North acknowledge that they do not intend their narratives to be definitive, in a manner similar to Kitzhaber, they also do not permit their own group identity or the politics of location to have visibility or consequence inside their narratives. In essence, though, they do not violate common practice in the field. Historically, the viewpoint of these narratives has not had to be articulated. These scholars operate within the dominant field of vision. In centralizing their historical viewpoints within mainstream experiences, without having to specify their locations as researchers in a more diversified landscape, their narratives become naturalized within this very mainstream, as other such narratives are habitually naturalized, as universal and thereby as transparent. Neither Berlin nor North was compelled at the time of publication by good practice in the field to make clearer the extent to which their narratives represent the dominant perspective. In effect, they may have acknowledged that other viewpoints are possible, but in this type of dynamic the other viewpoints are inevitably positioned in non-universal space and peripheralized, and the exclusion of suppressed groups, whether they intend it or not, is silently, systemically reaffirmed.

By 1991 with the publication of *Textual Carnivals: The Politics of Composition,* Susan Miller holds this dynamic up for interrogation. She says:

> Without "good" stories to rely on, no minority or marginalized majority has a chance to change its status, or, more importantly, to identify and question the "bad" tales that create it. In this case, the required new narrative portrays teachers and students of writing in American higher education, who have for some time been the subjects of a marginalizing and negative—but nonetheless widely believed—myth. I hope to substitute a new narrative for that denigrating tale by rereading this myth. (1)

She makes a case for seeing the legitimacy of composition and for taking into account the engendering of composition teaching and the implications of other power relationships. She casts a different narrative light, but her story is not all inclusive either and cannot be expected to be given how wide the range of marginalized participants can be. Miller acknowledges the existence of other viewpoints, but does not craft a space, for example, for the voices of people of color.

The same holds true in a different way in John Brereton's *The Origins of Composition Studies in the American College, 1875–1925.* In his preface, Brereton does indeed identify rather specific intersections between his work and other narrative viewpoints. Focusing on major trends in composition studies occurring in major institutions, he notes that his research is limited to the public record, a record that he acknowledges does not present the whole story. He states that "the most widely circulated professional documents of the time ignore important trends in writing instruction by women. . . . And a great deal of what we would now regard as postsecondary writing was done by immigrants in settlement houses, by men and women in Bible colleges and normal schools, and at historically black institutions" (xv–xvi).

Brereton also mentions the absence of the voices of African American educators in the general discourse about writing instruction in the fifty years that he covers, but posits that "most black colleges seem to have taught writing in strict accord with the standards of white America" (21). In addition, he creates space for historically African American institutions (HBCUs) and those associated with them by inference, e.g., when he mentions that "very traditional approaches [old-fashioned rhetoric with text books by Blair, Campbell, or Whately] survived at colleges, not universities, in the East and South" (14) into the twentieth century. Since most HBCUs are located in the South, we can infer that the pedagogical practices of HBCUs are included, referentially, in this statement. Further, as a note to the abilities of black students at the time, Brereton also adds that W. E. B. DuBois, a graduate of Fisk University, elected to take Barrett Wendell's writing course while pursuing graduate studies at Harvard (21). In other words, Brereton does indeed create a space for others, including African Americans, but he does not actually fill the space, or substantially credit African American viewpoints of it, or permit it to enrich, refine, or redefine what he is suggesting is the "larger," publicly documentable story.

Sheryl Fontaine and Susan Hunter, editors of *Writing Ourselves into the Story: Unheard Voices from Composition Studies,* also endeavored to be more inclusive than preceding composition narratives. The purpose of their collection, as the title indicates, was to add voices to the story that are not normally heard. Their intent was to define or extend the parameters of the disciplinary discussion. The contributors include a number of part-time, untenured instructors, primarily women, who carry not only their voices into the text but also the varied voices of their students. As Fontaine and Hunter review the contributors who responded to their call, however, they note their regret that submissions from ethnic minorities were "conspicuously absent" (11) despite their attempts to have the call for submissions broadly advertised and circulated.

In discussing their concerns about the absence of minorities, Fontaine and Hunter state:

> Still, since there are many voices we expected to hear that we did not, we find ourselves wondering why more two-year college faculty did not respond, why ethnic voices are so conspicuously absent. One potential contributor, an ethnic minority, told us that she didn't have much to say about basic writers; instead, she wanted to get back to more empowering concerns about African American writers and multicultural curricula. (11)

Fontaine and Hunter go on to dismiss a reviewer's comment that suggested a lack of professional interest or "savvy" on the part of ethnic minorities in participating in scholarly publication and to put forth their suspicion that "the powerlessness that comes with continually being unheard and uninvited has left them [meaning ethnic minorities] untrusting of our invitation or of their own voices" (12).

While either of these readings of the potential contributor's response may indeed have merit, we wonder whether Fontaine and Hunter were able to see any connection between the place where they were inviting the potential contributor to stand and her refusal, not to participate perhaps, but to speak to the particular issue that they had identified for her? Is it possible that they were conflating ethnicity in higher education with powerlessness and basic writing and assuming that her viewpoint, her place for writing herself into the story as an ethnic minority would be the same as the one that they imagined for her? Did they credit her response that her work, and perhaps her students, did not conform to their images for the collection? Perhaps neither she nor her students, despite the inescapable existence of systemic suppression, saw themselves either historically or currently in these terms. Did Fontaine and Hunter hear that perhaps she did not see her work as marginalized in the same way that they were seeing it, saying it, and drawing the lines of possibility for it? Was, perhaps, her reluctance to "trust" the invitation a resistance to circumscription, even in a project that otherwise sought to celebrate "multivocality, heteroglossia, and nonhierarchical relationships" (9)?

The concerns of Fontaine and Hunter about the participation of ethnic minorities in scholarly projects raise questions about the metaphors and interpretive frames that editors use to solicit contributors from suppressed groups, about what a choice to remain silent portends from various points of view, and about the extent to which editors themselves, given their authority to set the parameters of submission, should assume some responsibility for the ways in which their choices passively and aggressively exclude and circumscribe participation.

What seems consistently clear across these narratives is the point with which we began this section. Those of us who write composition narratives and those of us who use them need to be critically disposed to see the negative effects of primacy, the simultaneous existence of multiple viewpoints, and the need to articulate those viewpoints and to merge them in the interest of the larger project of knowledge making in the discipline.

Representations of Students

As indicated by the preceding section, many of the narratives in composition studies are not directly student centered. The focus is more on conceptions of the field and on pedagogical practices and processes. Recent texts, however, such as Marguerite Helmers' *Writing Students: Composition Testimonials and Representations of Students,* and Harriet Malinowitz's *Textual Orientations: Lesbian and Gay Students and the Making of Discourse Communities,* and Valerie Balester's *Cultural Divide: A Study of African American College-Level Writers* have turned to look at students and how they are depicted or represented in our field. In *Writing Students,* Helmers draws on the lore of the field using the CCC's "Staffroom Exchange" column and discusses the stock figure of "*the student,* . . . a character whose inability to perform well in school is the defining feature" (4). She reports that students, as a whole, "have been the subject of despair, ridicule, rhetorical distancing, and fear for centuries" (5). Helmers' description affirms that the good or successful students are not often mentioned in our lore, our practice, or our scholarship. However, we know they are there because they represent the standard by which those *other* students are judged. For Helmers, *the student* is also a generalized term "absent of a specific ethnic or gendered referent" (11). While this seemingly neutral approach could be thought of as placing all students on an equal level, the neutrality often erases the presence of students of color with the resultant assumption that, in not being marked as present, they in fact were not there.

Students who are not generic and also not recognized as present in the field literature become the focus for Malinowitz's study of lesbian and gay student writers. Focusing on student writing, Malinowitz directly confronts prejudice and bias as she questions how "homophobia in society, and as it is reproduced in the writing class, constitute[s] a basic form of interference in lesbian and gay students' . . . writing processes and performances" (xvii). Her issues become not only how teachers construct lesbian and gay students but how the students, in their writing, work toward constructing themselves. Malinowitz's study takes place in an urban multiracial college, and students of color were present in her classrooms. While her text does not contain extended discussions focusing on students of color, her work is noticeably cognizant of issues involving sex, gender, race, and class.

Balester, to her credit, reports that although work has been done on underprepared African American college level students, "we have paid scant attention to the average or superior college student. . . . [and] we can learn a great deal by attending to the texts of *successful* African-American college-level writers" (2). Her actual focus, however, is on Black English Vernacular (BEV), and she describes her students (despite one student's objection to the description) as speakers of BEV who are "attempting to construct a scholarly identity which, as novices, they had not yet fully assumed, and to address audiences of whom they as yet had little knowledge" (2–3). Even though Balester acknowledges the success of these students, she still positions them as non-universal outsiders, as aliens to the traditions to which other students lay claim, and essentially as "basic writers." This narrative furthers this inscription in the Foreword written by M. Jimmie Killingsworth whose opening line reads:

> One of the strongest threads of research and criticism in composition studies reveals the inherent consistency, the rhetorical integrity, even the brilliant folkways that emerge among students whom we have labeled "basic writers" (often as a way of predicting their failure) (vii).

Only toward the end of the page, do we learn that Balester's work has an "interesting twist" because she has decided to study African American students who have "made it" across "the cultural divide between life in a second-dialect minority and the life in the educated classes represented by the American university" (vii–viii). This Foreword assigns monolithically "second-dialect" status to all of the students in the study, without recognizing class stratification in the African American community and the class distinctions, therefore, of this particular group of African American students. The Foreword also assigns this group a place outside of "the educated classes represented by the *American* [our emphasis] university," ignoring the longstanding presence of African Americans in arenas of higher education and the possibility that successful students who are African American could be insiders in *American* universities, whether these particular students were insiders or not.

Throughout the text itself, Balester works to fit the African American students into her framework and to identify them with BEV, even when they resist that categorization. She describes her students in the same way most basic writers are described, i.e., as students seeking a way into an academic culture to which they presumably have no traditional moorings.

Balester's study illustrates that the connections that we have made in the field in conflating ethnicity, otherness, and basic writing are strong and remain compelling, despite the extent to which these connections are not automatic.

The Conflation of Race and Basic Writing

Among the touchstones of student-centered research, Mina Shaughnessy's *Errors and Expectations: A Guide for the Teacher of Basic Writing* occupies a well-respected space, and many scholars have turned to this text for a description of the basic writer. Despite the popular perception, however, that Shaughnessy's text contributes to the conflation of students of color and basic writing, the basic writers in *Errors and Expectations* are actually broadly constructed. Shaughnessy indicates that because of the protests taking place in the late 1960s, many four-year colleges began admitting students who may not have been considered ready for college. While subsequent researchers tend to focus on the 60s as a "decade of protest" in terms primarily of the civil rights protests staged by African Americans, there were also protests against the Vietnam War and the treatment of veterans, for women's rights, for workers' rights, and for the overthrow of what was seen as an elitist, capitalistic system in order to create a more egalitarian system providing for the basic needs of all people. Looking, therefore, at this broader conception of who actually came into the university during this era of protest, Shaughnessy focuses more on economic characteristics than she does on racial ones. She states that the students admitted were:

> academic winners and losers from the best and worst high schools in the country, the children of the lettered and the illiterate, the blue-collared, the white collared, and the unemployed, some who could barely afford the subway fare to school and a few who came in the new cars their parents had given them as a reward for staying in New York to go to college; in short, the sons and daughters of New Yorkers, reflecting that city's intense, troubled version of America. (2)

Shaughnessy does not negate the presence of race in the students admitted. She makes clear that most of the students were from "one of New York's ethnic or racial enclaves . . . had spoken other languages or dialects at home and never reconciled the worlds of home and school" (3). Race, however, never becomes a focal point for her analysis. Even her discussions of BEV are used as points of comparison and example for other racial and ethnic groups as she points out that the syntactic structures of BEV are present in non-black American-born students such as Jewish students who are influenced by Yiddish, Irish Americans, and Chinese Americans (91). Speaking a language or variety of English other than standard English appears to be much more a contributing factor to Shaughnessy's characterization of basic writers than does race. Where Shaughnessy emphasizes race, though, is in pointing out that the absorption of negative views of language makes learning formal uses of English a more contentious process, and she does say that the "black student has probably felt the bite of this prejudice more persistently and deeply" (158).

Shaughnessy's connection between the politics of racial location and the perception of writing performance is insightful, but this insight suggests more about the impact of persistent oppression than the centrality of a direct association between race and poor writing performance as a predictable consequence. Nevertheless, since the publication of this study, there has been a deepening sense that African Americans entered the university during the 60s era and that, as students of color, they entered quite predictably as basic writers and only as basic writers. The conflation of basic writers with students of color has become deeply embedded in the literature, despite lengthy histories that demonstrate other realities.

Setting aside African American experiences, however, remedial writing programs existed for "traditional" students in historically white colleges and universities well before 1960s protests movements and the establishing of open admissions policies and well before Shaughnessy popularized the term "basic writing" and set in motion processes by which this area became a legitimate area for scholarly study. When we take this alternate point of view and look in the shadows of composition history for a different space for underprepared students, we find that *CCC* is a good resource. Basic writing was actually one of the primary topics addressed during CCCC conferences and in *CCC* articles during the 1950s, the first decade of the organization. Surveys taken during the period and reported in *CCC* relate that the percentage of underprepared freshman students enrolled in what at that point were labeled remedial composition classes often reached ten to twenty percent and sometimes more than thirty percent of the entering class. What we take note of in these reports is that these articles were not talking about African American students (or even people of color more generally) since, indeed, this group did not command ten to twenty percent of the general college population in the United States in the 1950s.

A number of colleges and universities also reported that they had offered remedial composition courses since the 1920s—the era of progressive education which focused on the democratization of education and which clearly had consequence, as continues to be the case, in composition teaching as a critical point of acculturation for the university itself. In looking from these viewpoints, the point to be emphasized is that controversies about underprepared students did not start in the 1960s and were not historically connected with people of color. Historically, we could look for narratives of underpreparedness at several places other than the 1960s: in the late nineteenth century when Harvard instituted its written entrance examination; at the rise during the progressive era of standardized testing; at the moment in 1956 when the University of Illinois decided to drop its remedial classes. In this latter case, while many institutions followed suit, many others remained committed to having classes that would serve a wider range of students, including those who were inexperienced in college environments and in writing. All of these moments are before the 1960s and the perception that people of color, and particularly African Americans, came into colleges and universities and created "the basic writer."

A Historical View of African Americans in Higher Education

If, then, African American students as active participants in higher education, are not substantially yoked to the open admissions processes of the 1960s and to basic writing programs, where can we set the gaze to get a fuller understanding of their historical presence in academic arenas, and thereby in composition studies? We find that looking at the 19th century rather than the 20th century is a good place to begin.

According to Carter G. Woodson (1919; 1991), the first organized efforts in the United States to offer higher education to African Americans began in 1817 when advocates of the American Colonization Movement, i.e., the movement to send people of African descent, especially free ones, back to Africa, opened a school in Parsippany, New Jersey. In political contrast with this effort, many African Americans and white abolitionists who disagreed with this movement were determined to establish colleges that supported the making of a life at "home," i.e., in the United States. This latter strategy led to the incorporation of Avery College in Allegheny City, Pennsylvania, in 1849. Moreover, an ongoing strategy was also to open the doors of white institutions to African Americans, an effort that resulted in:

- John B. Russwurm (who would become the co-editor of the first African American newspaper in the United States, *Freedom's Journal*) becoming the first college graduate when he completed studies at Bowdoin in 1828.
- Oberlin College opening its doors to African Americans (and to women and other racial minorities) in 1833.
- A small but steady stream of African American men and women during the nineteenth century who enrolled, successfully matriculated, and consistently graduated from *American* colleges and universities.

In addition, there were two other historical moments that add light to the participation of African Americans in higher education. The earlier of these moments came before the Civil War in 1856 when Wilberforce University in Ohio and Lincoln University in Pennsylvania were established as institutions focused specifically on the education of African Americans. After the Civil War, with support from the African American community, the Freedmen's Bureau, the American Missionary Society, and other philanthropic groups, these two institutions were joined in the endeavor to educate African Americans by a collective of other private institutions, mostly in the South, who one hundred years later constitute the thirty-nine colleges and universities associated with the United Negro College Fund.

The dominant educational philosophy of these institutions is captured by a statement made by Mary McLeod Bethune, President of Bethune-Cookman College (an HBCU in Daytona Beach, Florida), in 1932 at the celebration of the twenty-fifth anniversary of Henry Lawrence McCrorey as President of Johnson C. Smith University (an HBCU in Charlotte, North Carolina). Bethune was one of several prestigious speakers who gathered during the anniversary celebration for critical dialogue on higher education among African Americans, past, present, and future. Bethune spoke for the future in an address entitled, "What Should Be the Program for the Higher Education of Negroes for the Next Twenty-five Years?" She said:

> This age increasingly demands that the Negro youth, along with the youth of every other race, know the truth about the world in which he lives. While facing facts, he must prepare himself to function successfully in that world as a happy individual. He must develop power of independent thought and effective expression. Within large areas he will discover that he must make compromises and adjustments to the religion, ethics, and economic principles of the dominant group that surround him. To make these adjustments adequately, he must be capable of formulating for himself a philosophy that will sustain his courage and his self-respect. The future college for the higher education of Negroes must bear the tremendous responsibility of guiding this youth in his search for truth, of developing his innate capacities, and of unfolding to him a philosophy of life that will encourage him ever to keep his face toward the sun. (Mckinney 59)

As implied by the attention to effective expression and the development of critical thought in Bethune's address, this network of institutions was indeed committed, not only to a strong liberal arts focus, but to the specific development of literate abilities, including writing abilities. Moreover, the student populations in these institutions varied widely in terms of students who were well prepared for college experience and students who were variously underprepared, such that the popular sentiment among these institutions was that their tradition was to take students from wherever they were in terms of knowledge and performance and to educate them, a view that demonstrates a general commitment to a student-centered approach and to educational progress.

The second historical moment occurred on July 2, 1862, when Representative Justin S. Morrill of Vermont succeeded in getting the Morrill Act inscribed in law. This Act authorized the establishment of one land grant institution per state, providing federal funding through the sale of public lands for education in practical professions, such as agriculture, mechanical arts, and home economics. As indicated earlier in this article, thirty years later with the Second Morrill Act in 1890, seventeen historically African American institutions were incorporated into this system, creating a core group for what we now recognize as the network of historically African American publicly supported colleges and universities.

To be noted in rendering a narrative about African American presence in higher education is Howard University. This institution, established in 1867 in Washington D.C., stands separately from both sets of the institutions cited above as a university intended primarily, but not exclusively, for African Americans. While private donations were also its primary source of funding, what marks one distinction for this university is that for many decades, it was semi-supported by appropriations from Congress, semi-monitored by the United States Office of Education, more stable in its base of funding than most of the other colleges in the private network, but not tied to the practical professions as other publicly funded African American institutions of this era.

To be highlighted, then, is that Howard University shared in the dominant educational philosophy of historically African American institutions generally, and it also held its own secure place as a premier institution in the liberal arts tradition. Among the collective of historically African American institutions, Howard helped to set the pace, along with Atlanta University, Fisk University, Talledega College, Tougaloo College, Hampton University, Tuskegee University and others throughout the network, in scholarly production and in the creation of academic spaces for intellectual development and leadership in the African American community. Historically African American colleges and universities served as beacons of light for academic excellence and for the nurturing of talents and abilities across a full range of academic experience and potential.

The Recovery of Contributions

The recovery of contributions to composition history by African American teachers and scholars is a complex enterprise also. Given the historical place of African Americans as a suppressed group in the United States, the work of these professionals has not been historically celebrated in arenas of the dominant academic culture, and it has not typically been visible in prime documentary sources of the dominant community. Evidence of this work does exist, however, and the rendering of it within the context of other stories of the profession creates a provocative view of what we have come to know historically as the study and teaching of rhetoric and composition. If we take just three cases in point, we can see how these exemplars contributed to the field distinctively in terms of the general ways in which we value excellence in theory, practice, and professional activity, and we can also see how they do so in ways that are distinguishable from each other. In other words, neither they nor their contributions are one dimensional. They cover a spectrum of the types of achievements that we *normally* honor in the field. We have chosen to highlight:

- *Alain Locke,* for his work as a cultural theorist, literary and arts critic, and educational philosopher.
- *Hallie Quinn Brown,* for her expertise in developing literate abilities through her pedagogy and textbook production, and also for her own expertise as an orator.
- *Hugh M. Gloster,* for his role as a literary critic, as the editor of an anthology of African American writers, and also for his pioneering leadership in the development of English professional organizations.

Alain Locke

Alain Locke was the son of educated parents who had professional careers in teaching and government. He received a BA degree with honors (Phi Beta Kappa, magna cum laude, winner of the Bowdoin Prize for an essay in English) from Harvard University in 1907. He was the first African American to be awarded the prestigious Rhodes Scholarship, attending Hertford College of Oxford University (after being denied admissions by five other Oxford colleges) where he studied philosophy, Greek, and literature from 1907 to 1910. From 1910 to 1911, he attended the University of Berlin, and in 1918, he received the Ph.D. from Harvard.

While at Oxford, Locke was a founder and the secretary of the African Union Society, a group established with other men of African descent to nurture leaders, to encourage broad interests in matters of race as a global concept, and to establish a global network among leaders. Returning to the United States in 1912, Locke was appointed to the faculty of the Teachers College at Howard University as assistant professor of English, where he remained throughout his career, with various periods in between devoted to an incredible range of intellectual and sociopolitical activities, from participating in 1924 in the re-opening of the tomb of Tutankamen in Luxor, to a stint with the League of Nations to study the development of African education since World War II, to a well-funded project to evaluate adult education programs in Atlanta and Harlem which led to the establishing in 1935 of the Associates in Negro Folk Education.

In light of this wide array of experiences and achievements, Locke is nationally recognized as a pioneer in comparative ethnic studies who made contributions in several areas, including education, literary and arts criticism, philosophy, and cultural studies. He published extensively, but is perhaps best known for his edited collection, *The New Negro* (1925), a demonstration of the cultural and social progress of African Americans in creative writing and literary scholarship. What may be more critical for this analysis is that Locke, in collaboration with other intellectual leaders at Howard University (including the President, Mordecai Johnson, and his fellow faculty members: Sterling A. Brown, Kelly Miller, Margaret Just Butcher and several others) conceptualized a culturally rich liberal arts curriculum that included the teaching of writing and the development of what we now call critical literacies.

Hallie Quinn Brown

Hallie Quinn Brown, the daughter of freed slaves, was born c. 1845. She received a bachelor's degree from Wilberforce University in 1873, began her teaching career in the public schools of Mississippi, South Carolina, and Ohio, and took the opportunity while teaching in Dayton, Ohio, for further training in the art of speech and oratory by attending in the summers the Boston School of Oratory. From 1885 to 1887, Brown administered a night school for adults in South Carolina and served as Dean at Allen University (an HBCU in Columbia). From 1892 to 1893, she served as Dean of Women at Tuskegee Institute (an HBCU in Alabama), and in 1893, she accepted an appointment as professor of elocution at Wilberforce University, where she remained until her death in 1949.

During these years, Brown was simultaneously building a sterling record as a charismatic speaker who was actively involved as a member of the Black Clubwomen's Movement, various women's temperance associations, and the Woman's Missionary Society of the African Methodist Episcopal Church. She lectured nationally and internationally in the interest of a variety of social concerns; she founded the Neighborhood Club in Wilberforce; she was active in the formation of the National Association of Colored Women, of which she was president from 1920 to 1924; she was president of the Ohio Federation of Colored Women's Clubs; she was vice president of the Ohio Council of Republican Women and in 1924, she spoke at the Republican National Convention in Cleveland (Hine). Her appointment as professor of elocution at Wilberforce, therefore, is not, in hindsight, a surprise.

For the purposes of this article, what stands out most distinctively about her professional activities in light of composition history is that as professor of elocution at Wilberforce University from 1893 to 1923, Brown produced pedagogical materials, as documented most recently by Susan Kates, that innovatively enriched the learning experiences of her students. As Kates says:

> She raised questions about the relationship between schooling and social responsibility, using and transforming mainstream elocution theory in order to address these issues. The goal of Brown's pedagogy was an "embodied rhetoric," that is to say, a rhetoric located within, and generated for, the African-American community. (59)

In essence, Hallie Quinn Brown embraced a student-centered approach to the development of literate abilities, centralized, as we do today, the notion that there should be some relationship established by curriculum and pedagogy between home knowledge and academic knowledge, and fashioned both a theoretical perspective as well as practical classroom activities that permitted her students to do as Bethune suggested, to lift their faces toward the sun with courage and self-respect and to enhance their expressive abilities.

Hugh M. Gloster

Hugh M. Gloster received a bachelor's degree from Morehouse College (an HBCU in Atlanta) in 1931, a master's degree from Atlanta University, and the Ph.D. in English from New York University in 1943. Gloster taught in English departments, directed communication programs, and served in administrative positions in colleges and universities in the United States, Africa, Asia, Europe, and the Caribbean. He authored *Negro Voices in American Fiction* (1965) and co-edited with Nathaniel P. Tillman, *My Life, My Country, My World: College Readings for Modern Living* (1952). In 1967, he was appointed President of Morehouse College and retired from this position in 1988 (See Jones 1967).

Given the focus of this current analysis, what is most informing about Gloster's work is that in 1937, as a professor of English at Lemoyne College (an HBCU in Memphis, Tennessee), he sent out a call to teachers of English in historically African American colleges to gather in dialogue, and on April 23, 1937, the participants became charter members of the Association of Teachers of English in Negro Colleges (ATENC). In his letter of invitation, Gloster had stated:

> Believing that the main burden of the educational task rests on correct language usage and that a college should at least require a knowledge of the language skills, many institutions of higher education have undertaken a critical evaluation of current curricular practices for the purpose of raising standards of proficiency in the use of the English language. As a result of this investigation, many constructive changes have been made. The fact still remains nevertheless, that there is need for further improvement in oral and written expression, and that a valuable and mutually beneficial program might be developed by those who are in daily contact with the problem. (Fowler 3)

This concern was a central one for ATENC, but as a professional organization in English Studies, this group had other concerns as well, including the teaching of literature, the ongoing production of creative works, and research and scholarship on African American culture. They sustained an agenda to encourage publishers to include African American writers in anthologies, and they recognized the need to have a space in which African American scholars could flourish, despite the chilly reception that they received in other professional organizations, such as the Modern Language Association (MLA). To be noted, as suggested by this latter concern, is that members of ATENC were certainly active in ATENC, but they were also members of other national organizations and active in them to the extent that the particular organizations permitted.

In 1949 at the ATENC in New Orleans, the Committee on Resolutions recommended and the members approved a change in the name of the ATENC. It became the College Language Association (CLA), an organization that remains viable and active among contemporary professional organizations in English Studies. One further connection also emerged in 1949 with the founding of the Conference on College Composition and Communication (CCCC) of the National Council of Teachers of English (NCTE). As an organization interested in the development of oral and written language abilities, CCCC also drew members from CLA as they had previously been drawn to NCTE and MLA. In fact, the formation of the Black Caucus of NCTE/CCCC in 1970 was very much informed by the multiple alliances of many of the African American members who were also members of CLA, as demonstrated by the CLA documents that were shared with the new group and thereby helped to shape their ideology.

Over the years, CLA has sustained its own vitality as an organization dedicated to excellence in scholarship, teaching, and professional development; to the preservation of African American culture; and to ongoing cultural production. Beyond this mission, however, CLA has also carried these interests into other organizations, influencing these groups variously, as CLA members through their multiple alliances have been actively involved in MLA, NCTE, CCCC, and other professional organizations. This process was originally enabled by the vision and collaboration of Hugh M. Gloster with colleagues across the network of African American scholars in English studies, such that from one point of view, without attempting to be totalizing in scope, one might say that the ripple effects of the vision of Hugh Gloster and the other charter members of ATENC have been considerable.

Implications

This essay has focused on history in the spaces left and has sought to bring light to the effects (i.e., the social, political, and cultural consequences) of officialized narratives. Our specific goal has been to adjust the historical lens by shifting the gaze to the experiences of African Americans. Our intent has been to counter mythologies about African American presence in composition studies in two ways: 1) by acknowledging that in officialized narratives, the viewpoints of African Americans are typically invisible, or misrepresented, or dealt with either prescriptively, referentially, or by other techniques that in effect circumscribe their participation and achievements; and 2) by identifying more instructive ways of looking at African American experiences that support a different view of presence, in terms of:

- an historical view of African Americans in higher education that begins in the nineteenth century, not the twentieth century.
- representations of students that are not keyed by the metaphor, "basic writer."

- a recovery of specific contributions that suggest a history of scholarship and a tradition of professional engagement.

In choosing the title of the essay, we have based the central image "history in the spaces left" on an image used by William Cook in his 1992 CCCC Chair's address, "Writing in the Spaces Left." In that address, Cook asserted that historically our "official" national narratives have excluded from metaphors of universality groups that have been systemically suppressed by sociopolitical constructions of power. Inside these narratives, such groups are typically unacknowledged and rendered invisible, or positioned as non-universal or "other," or inscribed in ways that circumscribe and often misrepresent them. Cook asserted, however, that the members of these groups have persistently resisted this treatment and taken the authority to write themselves in more animated ways onto the narrative landscape, as we have ventured to do in this essay.

Cook cites Olaudah Equiano, Frederick Douglass, Richard Wright, Ralph Ellison, Ann Petry, Toni Morrison, and Maya Angelou as writers who, by their insistent narrative presence, have reconfigured the story. He demonstrates that even though their perspectives and experiences have not been authenticated historically by "official" narratives, these writers and others have, nevertheless, tampered with "the word," inserting themselves boldly into the spaces left, and they have literally changed the page—that is, the historical narrative that might be rendered instead. In like manner, we have claimed an insistent presence for African Americans that, if acknowledged, could also reconfigure the story of composition.

The problem, as Cook suggested and as mirrored in this essay, is not simply that, given our national history of sociopolitical suppression, opportunities for remarkable exclusions exist and need correction. The problem is that these official narratives have social, political, and cultural consequences, a situation that is exacerbated by the ways in which the officializing process itself grants the privilege of primacy to texts. The privilege of primacy—that is, the status of being the official viewpoint, sets in motion a struggle between these "prime" narratives and other narrative views (that for whatever reasons the official narratives exclude) for agency and authenticity and, most of all, for the rights of interpretive authority. "Official" narratives set the agenda for how and whether other narratives can operate with consequence, and they also set the measures of universality—that is, the terms by which we assign generality, validity, reliability, credibility, significance, authority, and so forth.

As illustrated by this analysis, such a struggle shows itself vibrantly in composition studies as we examine *our* own national narratives and the metaphors that we use to talk about or not talk about members of historically suppressed groups. As in other officializing processes, as existing histories of composition acquire an "official" status, they participate in the making of metaphors and the symbolic systems of reality by which we draw the lines of the discipline and authenticate what is "real" and not, significant enough to notice and not, or valuable and not. These constructions set the default boundaries, and, in effect, determine the range of what can be rendered in composition history in "mainstream" or "traditional" terms, and what is consistently rendered in the terms of exception or "other."

In wanting field narratives to be more inclusive of historically suppressed groups, our view is that we need to take a critical stance in composition studies against the negative effects of primacy. The imperative is to emphasize the need for historicizing practices that both contextualize the historical view, as composition narratives typically do, but that also go beyond contextualizing to treat that view as ideologically determined and articulated. This imperative indicates that, while we recognize that narratives of composition have been successful in increasing our understanding of long-range views of the field, we recognize also that these same narratives have simultaneously directed our analytical gaze selectively, casting, therefore, both light and shadow across the historical terrain. In acknowledging areas of both light and shadow, we suggest that there is a clear and present need to pay more attention to the shadows and to how unnoticed dimensions of composition history might interact with officialized narratives to tell a reconfigured, more fully textured story than we now understand.

When we render stories of composition from points of view other than dominant academic perspectives, we have the opportunity to see the historical page in ways that subvert the negative effects of primacy. Instead of always measuring progress and achievement by the tape of mainstream experiences (Du Bois 1903), and discounting viewpoints that do not match them, we have the opportunity to set the terms of historical engagement with a more critical view, to shift locations, and to raise questions, previously unasked, that might more fully animate knowledge and understanding.

The basic commitment in such shifting is to ground both our assumptions and our experiences with the intent of clarifying the purview of our gaze. In this way, claims and assertions do not seek so easily or immediately for universal status. We can ask, instead, basic questions, such as: For whom is this claim true? For whom is it not true? What else is happening? What are the operational conditions? In the interest of the larger enterprises of knowledge making and public policy making, we are encouraged by such strategies to resist primacy and to operate in a more generative and less offensive manner.

As suggested by the preceding pages, this type of paradigmatic shift is consistently demonstrated by the case of African Americans as one historically suppressed group. Consider, for example, the data reported in *Souls of Black Folk* by William E. B. Du Bois who noted that by the turn of the century, 35 years after the end of chattel slavery, approximately 2000 African Americans had received college degrees from 34 historically African American colleges. He noted also an additional 400 African Americans who received bachelor's degrees from historically white northern colleges and universities such as Harvard, Yale, and Oberlin. These data were for the turn of the century—that is, sixty plus years before the era of open admissions and the emergence of people of color as substantive entities in mainstream composition narratives. Even without the preceding interrogation of composition histories, we might well imagine, if we were inclined to do so, the tradition of academic achievement generated by this cadre of graduates and others since them. These data alone suggest that the prevailing view of the participation of African Americans in composition histories is, at the very least, a specific case of an inadequate representation. Composition histories show that when we consistently ignore, peripheralize, or reference rather than address non-officialized experiences, inadequate images continue to prevail and actually become increasingly resilient in supporting the mythologies and negative consequences for African American students and faculty, and also for their culturally defined scholarly interests, which in their own turn must inevitably push also against prime narratives.

Ultimately, then, our goal in presenting this viewpoint is to raise a call for both a clearer understanding of the past and better practices in the present and future. In composition studies, we suggest:

A systematic commitment to resist the primacy of "officialized" narratives.

We might begin this process with a basic framework for resistance: The writers of composition histories can obligate themselves to contextualize the historical view and to specify their own ideological position. The users of composition histories can remind themselves to systematically re-articulate the limitations of that viewpoint and the accompanying ideological position. In other words, the imperative is for both historians and users of history to acknowledge both areas of light and areas of shadow.

A search for better interpretive frames that are capable of accounting more richly for the participation and achievements of the many rather than just the few.

In other words, when we resist primacy, traditional paradigms for seeing and valuing participation, even in composition studies, are inadequate. They obviously miss the experiences and achievements of many, and they privilege by this process the viewpoints and the interpretations of the officialized few, whether they are acknowledged as prime or not. The challenge then is to broaden the research base, the inquiry base, the knowledge base from which interpretive frameworks can be drawn, not simply to say that we know that we don't know but to do the work of finding out. We need methodologies for seeing the gaps in our knowledge and for generating the research that can help us to fill those gaps.

A renewed interest in using the knowledge and understanding acquired through suggestions one and two in order to help a broader range of students to perform at higher levels of achievement.

In other words, what has constituted progress and achievement in the past and what might be meaningfully used to nurture progress and achievement in the present and future seems better tied to knowledge making processes that are recursive, ones that allow us to re-see and re-think.

This list of suggestions indicates that at the fiftieth anniversary of *CCC*, we can benefit greatly from an interrogation of the relationships of "suppressed" experiences in the field to our considerably anointed ones. Our sense of the landscape is that a more positive and productive future in composition studies actually depends, and rightly so, on finding less exclusive ways to envision our horizons, whether we are setting the gaze in the past, the present, or the future. The cautionary tale, then, is the statement with which we started. History is important, not just in terms of who writes it and what gets included or excluded, but also because history, by the very nature of its inscription as history, has consequences—social, political, cultural. As instruments of ideological processes, histories of composition, like our other national narratives, have participated in the generating of a record of misdeeds—exclusions, misrepresentations, negative stereotyping, and non-hearings. Our view is that we would be well advised to acknowledge this record and its systemic modes of operation in our research, scholarship, and pedagogy, but that we would be even better advised, especially at this moment of critical reflection, to build into our work systematic practices of both acknowledgement and resistance.

Works Cited

Balester, Valerie M. *Cultural Divide: A Study of African-American College-Level Writers*. Portsmouth: Boynton, 1993.

Berlin, James A. *Rhetoric and Reality: Writing Instruction in American Colleges, 1900–1985*. Carbondale: Southern Illinois UP, 1987.

Brereton, John, ed. *The Origins of Composition Studies in the American College, 1875–1925.* Pittsburgh: U of Pittsburgh P, 1995.

Charmaine, Sylvia. "Land-Grant Colleges and Universities: 100 Years of Excellence." *About . . . Time* (Nov. 1990): 12–15.

Cook, William. "Writing in the Spaces Left." *CCC* 44 (1993): 9–25.

DuBois, W. E. B. *The Souls of Black Folk.* (1903) Greenwich: Fawcett, 1961.

Fontaine, Sheryl, and Susan Hunter, eds. *Writing Ourselves into the Story: Unheard Voices from Composition Studies.* Carbondale: Southern Illinois UP, 1993.

Fowler, Carolyn. *The College Language Association: A Social History.* Ann Arbor: UMI, 1988.

Gloster, Hugh M. *Negro Voices in American Fiction.* New York: Russell, 1965.

Gloster, Hugh M., and Nathaniel P. Tillman, eds. *My Life, My Country, My World: College Readings for Modern Living.* New York: Prentice, 1952.

Helmers, Marguerite H. *Writing Students: Composition Testimonials and Representations of Students.* Albany: State U of New York P, 1994.

Hine, Darlene Clark, ed. *Black Women in America: An Historical Encyclopedia.* Brooklyn: Carlson, 1993.

Jones, Edward A. *A Candle in the Dark: A History of Morehouse College.* Valley Forge: Judson, 1967.

Kates, Susan. "The Embodied Rhetoric of Hallie Quinn Brown." *College English* 59 (1997): 59–71.

Kitzhaber, Albert R. *Rhetoric in American Colleges. 1850–1900.* Dallas: Southern Methodist UP, 1990.

LaPati, Americo D. *Education and the Federal Government: A Historical Record.* New York: Mason/Charter, 1975.

Locke, Alain, ed. *The New Negro: An Interpretation.* New York: Boni, 1925.

Logan, Rayford W., and Michael R. Winston, eds. *Dictionary of American Negro Biography.* New York: Norton, 1982.

Malinowitz, Harriet. *Textual Orientations: Lesbian and Gay Students and the Making of Discourse.* Portsmouth: Boynton, 1995.

McKinney, Theophilus Elisha, ed. *Higher Education among Negroes.* Charlotte: Johnson C. Smith U, 1932.

Miller, Susan. *Textual Carnivals: The Politics of Composition.* Carbondale: Southern Illinois UP, 1991.

North, Stephen M. *The Making of Knowledge in Composition: Portrait of an Emerging Field.* Upper Montclair: Boynton, 1987.

"Octalog: The Politics of Historiography." *Rhetoric Review* 7 (1988): 5–49.

Shaughnessy, Mina P. *Errors and Expectations: A Guide for the Teacher of Basic Writing.* New York: Oxford UP, 1977.

Woodson, Carter G. *The Education of the Negro Prior to 1861.* 1919. Salem: Ayer, 1991.

CHAPTER SEVENTEEN

Articulating Authentic Chineseness: The Politics of Reading Race and Ethnicity Aesthetically

SUE HUM

The minute our train leaves the Hong Kong border and enters Shenzhen, China, I feel different. I can feel the skin on my forehead tingling, my blood rushing through a new course, my bones aching with a familiar old pain. And I think, My mother was right. I am becoming Chinese.

***

"Someday you will see," said my mother. "It is in your blood, waiting to be let go." And when she said this, I saw myself transforming like a werewolf, a mutant tag of DNA suddenly triggered, replicating itself insidiously into a syndrome, *a cluster of telltale Chinese behaviors . . . But today I realize I've never really known what it means to be Chinese.*

AMY TAN, "A Pair of Tickets," *The Joy Luck Club*, 306–7

"When you go to China," I told her, "you don't even need to open your mouth. They already know you are an outsider."

***

My daughter did not look pleased when I told her that she didn't look Chinese. . . . How can she think she can

---

From *Readerly/Writerly Texts* 9 (2001): 61–82.

blend in? Only her skin and her hair are Chinese. Inside—she is all American made.

AMY TAN, "Double Face," *The Joy Luck Club*, 288–9

What does it mean to be Chinese? Is one born Chinese, as Jing-Mei Woo comes to believe in "A Pair of Tickets?" Is genetics the primary way for identifying Chineseness? Must one come-of-age in China in order to grow up Chinese, as Lindo Jong decides in "Double Face"? Both epigraphs depict the tensions of Chinese identity politics, highlighting the confusing, ambiguous, and sedimented categories that are mapped on physiologically marked bodies. Both epigraphs underscore Chineseness in binary terms, as either material or semiotic constructions. However, Chineseness cannot be delineated neatly within biological origins or geographical borders.

Adding to the complexity of Chinese identity politics is the diaspora. If one's body displays the overt phenotypical markers of Chinese identity—slanted eyes, sallow yellow complexion, and coarse black hair—is one automatically considered Chinese? Are those who grow up outside mainland China, like American-born daughters Jing-Mei and Waverly, considered legitimately Chinese? Jing-Mei identifies her mother's embarrassing habits of "haggling with store owners, pecking her mouth with a toothpick in public" as "telltale Chinese behaviors" (307). Are there behaviors that can be identified as intelligibly Chinese? What other material performances highlight a person's identity as Chinese, of feeling and thinking Chinese, of maintaining a Chinese face?

In this essay, I use Chineseness as an avenue for exploring the disjunctures, complications, and contextual embodiments of people who bear the visible markers of difference. I contend that there is a broadly shared tendency to read diversity through an aesthetic lens, thus maintaining a superficial and static conception of racial and ethnic authenticity. As a result of this aesthetic perspective, racial and ethnic performances are reduced to exotic, consumable, surface characteristics, like those portrayed at Disney's Epcot Center. Predicated on fixed, erroneous notions of difference, aestheticism, which relies on biology and geography as central definitional criteria, cannot adequately explain and predict how race and ethnicity operate in everyday life. Therefore, what is required for challenging aestheticism is a materialist approach that pays attention to two integral factors: daily material-semiotic performances and the process of normalization that creates systematic, institutional inequalities. To that end, I open with a critique of the two dominant modes for conceptualizing difference—biology and geography—pointing to the limitations of such popular, vernacular principles for determining cultural legitimacy. Drawing on a personal anecdote, I illustrate how individuals from mainland and overseas Chinese communities practice aestheticism when they judge other Chinese as authentic or inauthentic. By prioritizing authenticity, we ignore temporal and spatial contingencies, accentuating transhistorical essences.

Next, I turn to the work of N. Katherine Hayles, whose differentiation between body and embodiment, offers a necessary first step out of the straightjacket of biology and geography. Using Hayles' theoretical framework, I begin by examining embodiment, critiquing aestheticism for its tendency to (i) treat individual embodied practices as stable, accurate articulations of culture and (ii) interpret visibly marked bodies as normative and naturalized. I situate racial and ethnic identity within the fluid interplay of body and embodiment, highlighting the precarious, dispersed, constructed, and enfleshed nature of Chinese subjectivity. By delineating how embodied enactments of Chineseness shift according to locale and are received differently by natives of that locale, I underscore both the fragile, fluid nature of authenticity and challenge the tendency to read changes in embodiment as inauthentic.

Then, I examine the reciprocity of the processes of normalization in American and Chinese cultures, demonstrating that authenticity is no longer a useful concept. On the stage of Western normative culture, performances of difference are not only taxonomized according to hierarchies of value and relevance, but they are also regulated and policed according to the stringent, orthodoxed habits and conventional rituals, as is the case with the "model minority" myth. In addition, some native and immigrant Chinese also participate actively in normalization by altering their own faces through cosmetic surgery to approximate more

Western European features. In the final section, I illustrate how, despite their increased inclusion of multicultural texts, teachers fail to inculcate a robust, reflexive, critical view of inter- and cross-cultural struggles over identity politics. Localism and universalism, two primary aesthetic reading strategies that contain diversity, cannot adequately highlight the contested nature of race and ethnicity to a student audience unfamiliar with the deep, contextual, embodied flux of difference.

Searching for Authenticity in Origins

Contemporary theories of race and ethnicity offer a quick resolution to the debate on whether Jing-Mei and Waverly are Chinese or not-Chinese. Race theories highlight visible physical appearances, biological inheritances, and common cultural ancestry for understanding "certain fundamental, biologically heritable, moral and intellectual characteristics" (Appiah 274–76). Using the yardstick of biological essences and ancestral descent, Jing-Mei and Waverly would certainly be considered Chinese. Racial tags, such as "X is Chinese," serve as a semantic, conceptual shorthand, encouraging a homogenizing, unreflective understanding of race. "Chinese" is imprecise, restrictive, and obfuscative, reducing difference to fixed, measurable characteristics. By working out of a perspective that material bodies and their innate essences exist prior to discourse, race theories neither adequately explain nor predict identity formation and behavior beyond the limits of nature.

While race theory highlights biological essences, ethnicity theory underscores nationalism and nativism within geographical boundaries (Sollors 288). Like the category "Asian" on U.S. census forms, such vernacular identifications of ethnicity are inescapably functional. However, such categories tend to limit cultural identity to geographical origin so that ethnic identity is inseparable from national identity. Because ethnicity theory uses citizenship as the primary criteria for directing and explaining the actions of its members, Jing-Mei's and Waverly's affiliations are less than evident since they are American-born. Jing-Mei's and Waverly's visibly marked bodies may represent Chineseness to Americans but, to many Chinese, racial heritage and ethnic affiliation are not the inevitable by-products of genetics. The underlying assumption is that, in essence, one can identify a "true" and "authentic" Chinese, legitimized by intrinsic and transcendental essences of biology and geography. However, race and ethnicity are not a result of some predetermined, intrinsic, and fixed attributes. Both race and ethnicity theories valorize origins, assuming a stable homogeneity, oversimplifying difference in an ahistorical, depoliticized manner. Race theory—limited to biological factors—and ethnicity theory—limited to nation and citizenship—represent easy yet limited ways of understanding the material-semiotic performances of identity politics; neither effectively elucidate the hyphenated vicissitudes of Chineseness.

Race and ethnicity theories cannot adequately account for the slippery illusiveness of Chinese identity, a definitional conundrum further exacerbated by the diaspora. The following anecdote illustrates how questions of origin complicate rather than illuminate, highlighting the reductive nature of authenticity. In 1991, a graduate school friend from Beijing pronounced emphatically that I was "not Chinese." Rather, she considered me "American." When this disagreement occurred, I had lived in the United States for only four years, having just begun work on a doctorate in English. My Chinese friend's judgment was at best troubling and disconcerting. As an "authentic" mainland Chinese, my friend enjoys an unquestionable epistemological privilege. She called into question a concrete, taken-for-granted, undebatable part of my identity—my racial descent and ethnic affiliation. My friend's assessment demonstrates how racial identity can be conflated into a single, resounding verdict—not Chinese! In other words, I am not authentic, not legitimate, no-body.

Both my friend and I read identity aesthetically, using authenticity to valorize biological and geographical origins for competing purposes and conflicting conclusions. What we failed to understand then is that "racial categories obviously do not exist outside cultural and spatial context, but are thoroughly framed by and within it" (Ang, "On" 550). I am a Malaysian-born Chinese. My parents and their parents are Chinese and continue to celebrate their racial heritage. My paternal great-grandparents immigrated from China to Malaysia for economic reasons, making me a third generation Malaysian. While my racial lineage is Chinese, I lack a direct, physical connection with mainland China, a country I could not visit until recently due to government-imposed travel restrictions. In addition, I do not speak Mandarin, the language spoken by *all* "real" Chinese, a primary yardstick for measuring legitimacy. However, I am tri-lingual, speaking English and an oral Chinese dialect, Hokkien, at home; in school, the language of instruction is Malay. While the slant of my eyes announce my racial heritage, my Malaysian nationality is less tangible, heard only in my pronunciation that I have worked systematically to Americanize by erasing those tell-tale cultural inflections and rhythmic markers. My ethnic world-view is influenced by post-colonial Malaysia's democratic political processes, open market economy, and multi-racial communities. My adult identity, then, is shaped by my obvious physiological markers, my upbringing, and the more invisible influences of growing up in Malaysia and immigrating to America.

Within the cultural and spatial context of Malaysia, I *am* considered Chinese. Growing up Chinese in Malaysia means growing up without privilege or power, with limited social, economic, and political options. The federal preferential policies developed to correct economic and racial inequalities resulting from British colonialism extend to higher education institutions. University applicants are organized according to racial origins, thereby ensuring the hegemony of a single ethnic group, the Malays (Basham 64–67). The racial quotas and the attendant material consequences play a crucial part in my identity and life story. The principal reason for pursuing higher education in America is race-related, rooted in my Chinese descent, resulting in painful personal consequences. At nineteen, I had to leave my family and travel to America to further my education. Thus, my friend's judgment of "not Chinese" invoked within me a jarring dissonance. By not interrogating the essentializing discursive regimes of authenticity, my friend and I reiterate the aesthetic notions of race and ethnicity as closed, self-perpetuating, regulating systems.

My Beijing friend interprets my physical enactments as "non-Chinese" because they do not communicate timid politeness, humble consideration, rigid discipline, and continuous self-deprecation. Involving the interplay of cultural discourse and materiality, racial and ethnic identity—Chineseness—acquires intelligibility through precise, highly complex physical movements, body posture, and especially, ways of speaking. In order to be authentically Chinese, one must behave in identifiably, if not stereotypically, Chinese ways. The materialization of Chineseness "takes place (or fails to take place) through certain highly regulated practices" (Butler, *Bodies* 1). Any deviation from accepted material enactments, as distinguished by my Chinese friend, labels the embodied, performative aspects of my body, its contours, and its movements as "not Chinese." "'Chineseness' is a homogenizing label whose meanings are not fixed or pre-given, but constantly renegotiated and rearticulated, both inside and outside China," explains Ien Ang, a well-published cultural critic and Cultural Studies professor of Chinese descent, who was born in Indonesia, emigrated to Netherlands, and currently teaches in Australia ("On" 545). Ang's examination of Chineseness reveals both the "*precariousness* of identity" (544, author's emphasis) and the "porousness of [geographical] borders" (541). Instead of a static, reliable category, Chineseness oscillates in relation to multiple levels: in the context of other Chinese communities both within and without the borders of mainland China, and in relationship to Western civilization, particularly the ideological, socio-political alignments of America.

The visibly marked Chinese body is not a constant amidst flux. Rather, the body and its instantiated embodiments are the epitome and indicator of that flux. Thus, our bodies are mutating surfaces that respond concretely and organically to environmental change. Just as "body" is a historical and cultural discursive construct, bodies and their embodied instantiations are the real, situated, individual enactments that cannot be understood outside the discourses of "body." Although biology and geography are commonplace, predictable ways of understanding racial and ethnic "authenticity," the disagreement between my Beijing friend and I highlights how visibly marked Chinese bodies are not static, anthropological documents that illuminate the particulars of an exotic, distant culture. Chinese bodies, simultaneously biological entities and culturally constructed phenomena, should not be treated synecdochally, parts that stand for the whole cultural identity. Chinese bodies are not guarantors of reliable, precise cultural knowledge, whether in American or Chinese communities. Rather, Chinese bodies are unstable, opaque signifiers, sedimented with multiple definitions and meanings. Chinese bodies and identities have accrued a social and symbolic significance, traversing beyond the horizons of familial genealogy and ethnic nationalism. By valorizing authenticity, contemporary theories are unable to delineate effectively the mutable, ever-changing instantiations of subjectivity, framed in the interplay of material-semiotic factors.

Instantiated and Constructed Embodiments of Race and Ethnicity

In 1997, during a visit home to Penang, Malaysia, my mother began introducing me as her daughter, "visiting from the United States." This introduction, with its implication that I am American, was inaccurate, even though I had lived in America for ten years. Despite my protests, my mother remained unmoved, justifying that "everyone knows you are not from here. All they have to do is look at you." Although my adult identity was formed in Malaysia, no amount of discussion, argument, or cajoling would convince my parents that I was not from "the United States." My parents and locals no longer consider me a bona fide Chinese-Malaysian for three reasons. The first is physiological—I no longer look Malaysian. My complexion, which betrays my foreignness, is too "unnaturally" fair, resulting from long winter months with little exposure to the sun. The second is cultural—I enact Western embodied practices. After over a decade in America, my erect body posture, bold gaze, quick movements, and "forward" disposition contribute to a non-Malaysian materiality, a simulacrum of stereotypical Western physical enactments. According to my parents, my physicality, my posture, and my behavior are too American, too informal, too assertive, and too big. It contradicts the Chinese-Malaysian concept of the feminine body in space, imprinted with politeness, passivity, and restraint. And the third is semiotic—I speak as an American. Although my pronunciation, rhythms, and inflections revert to

Malaysian English when I speak to my parents on the telephone or return home—my parents' friends praise me for not sounding American despite the many years away—my rhetorical style is too up-front, neither dancing around conflict, working to save face, nor feigning rigorous self-criticism as proof of proper humility, three fundamental Asian discursive strategies of courtesy. Paradoxically, my body, which carries the visible markers of my race, no longer exhibits the physiological, material, and semiotic enactments of Malaysian-Chinese ethnicity. These changes are identified as inauthentic and illegitimate.

The different interpretations of and responses to my instantiated, embodied enactments are situated within historically positioned, homogenizing assumptions, whether American, Malaysian, or Chinese. In effect, my visibly marked body and its attendant embodiments are sites of contest and resistance that cannot be explicated adequately by race and ethnicity theories. As my own situation illustrates, the question of authenticity demands both a racially marked body and accepted physical enactments within a culture. N. Katherine Hayles, doyenne of cybernetics and materiality, explains the differences between body and embodiment: the body is a cultural and discursive construct, "always normative relative to some set of criteria" (196); embodiment is always contextual and "inherently performative" (156), representing the experiences that "individual people within a culture feel and articulate" (193). In other words, embodiment is "enmeshed within the specifics of place, time, physiology and culture that together compose enactment" (196). Therefore, embodiment, or actual bodily practices, "can never be fully assimilated into discourse" (195). Yet, in order to understand and analyze embodiment, we must do so discursively and as soon as we do, these unstable, syncretic, instantiated behaviors become reified and idealized, embedded in essentialist racial and ethnic configurations. The very process of describing and naming through language—for cxample, stating that Asians postures tend to be more formal while Americans are more forward—renders these behaviors as typical, thus producing a yardstick to measure authenticity. Questions such as "how do true Chinese behave" and "how authentic is she" ignore the inchoate conflicts between body and embodiment. By focusing on materiality, particularly the ephemeral dimension of embodiment, we can develop a more robust, reflexive understanding of the hybrid, contingent, operations of race and ethnicity in daily life.

Although embodied performances are not accurate representations of culture, it is commonplace to assume that actual bodies provide tangible information about cultural identity. My parents' and my Beijing friend's reactions to my embodied enactments highlight how the perception of bodies is socially constructed, how culture writes itself on the body even though ways of walking, talking, gesturing, and moving vary from context to context, culture to culture: "Experiences of embodiment, far from existing apart from culture, are always already imbricated within it" (Hayles 197). Embodiment epitomizes the deep, contextual, bodily flux while in "continual interaction with constructions of the body" (197). Just as boys and girls learn different, gendered ways of carrying their bodies, physiologically marked bodies exhibit posture and movement that are environment specific. Similarly, Chinese materiality and culture simultaneously collaborate yet conflict as they construct racial and ethnic identities, binding culture with biology, semiotics with materiality, body with embodiment. American-born Chinese, Phoebe Eng describes her hyphenated identity as she moves to Hong Kong, assuming her Chinese origins would afford her some advantage not gained from years of living in America:

> My American [speech] would earn me the dubious label of *jook-sing*, a foreign-born, literally a bamboo hollow brain (which, by the way, is *not* a Chinese compliment). With a faltering, American tongue that tried in vain to sound truly Chinese, and a western swagger that hardly fit within the rules of how a good Chinese woman ought to walk, I fell through the crack of an East-West divide. (4)

Here, Eng's visibly marked body is read in relation to other marked (Hong Kong) bodies so that her embodied performances are "not Chinese *enough*." Yet, in comparison with unmarked or white bodies, Eng is "*too* Chinese." Although Eng's body serves as a natural and autonomous referent, the questions of authenticity flatten out deep-seated tensions, histories, and discontinuities.

Chineseness is not a natural, static condition, connected to a visibly marked Chinese body. The reciprocal relationship between body and embodiment is emphasized in the importance of physically occupying a small space. For example, standing akimbo with one's hands on hips, that is, taking up a large physical space, is seen in Malaysia as a fighting, rebellious stance. To show proper respect to representatives of institutional authority—police officers, high school principals, judges, etc.—Malaysians assume a humble, deferential stance, making their bodies inhabit a small space. It is not unusual to find Malaysians unconsciously bending at the knee and hunching their shoulders, thus making themselves shorter to demonstrate physical obeisance. A similar expression of embodiment is taught to first grade Chinese students. My Beijing friend recounts how her daughter is taught to sit straight, knees together, chest out, shoulders back, and hands clasped, resting lightly on the lower back. Through prolonged reiteration, these Beijing first graders learn the proper way of sitting. The lesson is reinforced every day for two weeks, with ten-minute intervals after fifty minutes of assuming this "courteous" posture, which also discourages children from fidgeting. The Chinese body, materialized through "forcible" reiterations of embodiment, is reflected in the popular Chinese dictum, "stand straight as a pine tree, sit steady as a bell, and lie taut as a bow." These two examples indicate the ways in which embodiment is, in part, a social construct, culturally specific articulations of material practices that then become fixed, naturalized physical expressions of identity. Thus, Chineseness is an imagined, idealized construct that is "forcibly materialized through time . . . a process whereby regulatory norms materialize 'sex' [read race and ethnicity] and achieve this materialization through a forcible reiteration of those norms" (Butler, *Bodies* 1-2). Visibly marked bodies are disciplined to perform bodily behaviors and actions that represent the naturalized, normative, reified criteria within a given culture. Rather than represent authentic articulations of a person's culture of origin, these changing embodied enactments highlight the importance of context and the interpellation of hegemonic discourses on the body.

This aspect of "forcible reiteration" is observed in Dorinne Kondo's experiences of living and researching in Japan. Even though Chinese and Japanese cultures are vastly different and are not synonymous, Kondo's experiences are apropos to illustrating the contextual constructedness of embodiment constantly negotiating with dominant definitions of the body. A Japanese American anthropologist, Kondo returned to Japan only to find herself a "living oxymoron, someone who was both Japanese and not Japanese" (523). Because of Kondo's lack of Japanese cultural competence and facility with the proper etiquette and correct social behavior, the people who met her were forced to confront "the chaos of meaninglessness" (525). In order to "resolve their crises of meaning and to confirm their assumptions about their own identities," Kondo's informants contained her in ready-made, familiar cultural roles, such as "daughter, guest, young woman, student, prodigal Japanese who had finally seen the light and come home" (527). The more diligently Kondo performed within those accepted behavioral conventions, the more legitimate she became in the eyes of her factory-worker informants and her surrogate family. Being Japanese, in Kondo's case, resulted from a "complex collaboration" between herself as the ethnographer and her informants, rendering her "genuinely" Japanese (529).

However, the more legitimate a Japanese identity Kondo created, the more conflict, dissonance, and fragmentation of self she experienced (529). As Kondo's body is read against other Japanese identities and established social roles, Kondo's sense of self as a unified being who is fundamentally the same is challenged. She recounts a moment of shock when she realizes that the typical Japanese housewife, "walking with a characteristically Japanese bend to the knees and a sliding of the feet," is her own reflection (529). The processes of constructing subjectivity, both Kondo's and mine, are a result of often contradictory, complex, instantiated enactments dancing with dominant linguistic codes and accepted socio-cultural practices. As Judith Butler explains, performativity is "not a singular 'act,' for it is always a reiteration of a norm or set of norms, and to the extent that it acquires an act-like status in the present, it conceals or dissimulates the conventions of which it is a repetition" (12). The Japanese conventional norms that regulate Kondo's body smooth over the differences in individual embodiment. These norms offer familiar habits for interacting with each other in a community, while simultaneously maintaining the romanticized yet illusory possibility of unfettered self-representation. However, Kondo's (mis)-recognition highlights how racial and ethnic identity and their attendant embodied performances are never merely the culmination of a person's own voluntary, self-determined choices. Whether Chinese or Japanese, cultural discourses emphasizing normative authenticity ignore the messy, polysemic nature of individual embodiment that entails processes of articulation and rearticulation, coding and recoding, disclosure and concealment. These performances, shifting according to time and place, are simply interpreted as signals of inauthenticity.

Within the negotiations between body and embodiment, it is possible for a person to be too Chinese or Japanese in one context and not Chinese or Japanese enough in another. This (mis)reading of identity results from the constant interplay between body and embodiment, enabled by processes of normalization. In Kondo's case, living in Japan means abiding by those "ready-made" cultural roles so that her material performances make sense to the Japanese community, even though they no longer reflect her sense of self and world-view. In my case, the Chinese diaspora has led to times of pain, confusion, and a loss of belongingness. The disjunctures in identity Kondo and I endure are a result of the restrictive codes that discourage variation, rigid conventions that present a deceptive harmony. In order to be part of a community, one must negotiate those established racial and ethnic codes that simultaneously guide and constrain how we carry our bodies and what responses we anticipate from others. At the same time, such context-dependent material-semiotic performances may also prevent individuals from entering a community, from finding sustenance and connection while developing networks of support within that community. In short, these intricate articulations and precise bodily modulations may become the basis for communal solidarity or for individual isolation.

By locating authenticity in biological and/or geographical origins, we cannot sufficiently clarify under what conditions actual, physiologically marked Chinese bodies come into being, acquiring meaning and asserting legitimacy. The essentializing forces of aestheticism, while ignoring the normalizing influences of culture and discourse, seldom account for the constructed, syncretic nature of materiality. For example, at the end of "Double Face," Lindo Jong considers the difference between an American and Chinese face, concluding that "[i]f you show one, you must always sacrifice the other" (304). Jong recounts her experiences of alienation and dislocation when she returns to China after living forty years in America: "I had taken off my fancy jewelry. I did not wear loud colors. I used their local money. But still, they knew. They knew my face was not one hundred percent Chinese. They still charged me high foreign prices" (304–5). Bodies and their attendant embodiments resist stability, allowing for subtle yet tangible ambiguities and contextually influenced permutations that then are considered inauthentic. Like Lindo Jong's body, my visibly marked body remains an uninterrogated yet colonized space. In three worlds—one I lived in until I was nineteen, one I have settled in for fourteen years, and one I visited briefly for a week in summer 2000—my body contains the contradictions of being less than, apart from.

Hayles maintains that "[f]ocusing on embodiment would help to clarify the mechanisms of change, for it links a changing technological landscape with the instantiated enactments that create feedback loops between materiality and discourse" (154). Physiologically marked bodies and their attendant embodiments challenge our sense of order and continuity—new images, words, and objects are integrated from the periphery into the dominant discourse and hegemonic master narratives:

> Fissuring along lines of class, gender, race, and privilege, embodied practices create heterogeneous spaces even when the discursive formations describing those practices seem uniformly dispersed throughout the society. The assimilation of embodiment into discourse has the additional disadvantage of making it difficult to understand exactly how certain practices spread through a society. (Hayles 154)

By paying attention to the dynamic interplay between body and embodiment, we focus on a more mutable, liminal space that takes into account how visibly marked bodies perform race and ethnicity in everyday life. By so doing, we begin challenging the aesthetic tendency to focus on superficial, exotic enactments, while drawing attention away from the processes of normalization that naturalize the individual instantiated enactments according to dominant discursive regimes, whether American or Chinese. Without examining the processes of normalization, we are limited in how we address the structural nature of racism, the methodical regimes of heteronormativity, or the systematic, unequal distribution of power and wealth in institutions.

Bodies and the Processes of Normalization

Just as the body becomes "naturalized within a culture," Hayles explains, "embodiment becomes naturalized only secondarily through its interactions with concepts of the body" (198). Both body and embodiment, two interconnected modalities, teach us "naturalized" ways of being in the world, ways mediated by language. Although Hayles describes the process of normalization, I extend her theories by delineating in more detail how difference at the level of physiology and materiality are absorbed and neutralized in inter- and cross-cultural communities. In this case, processes of normalization are analogous to orientalization, a notion popularized by Palestinian writer Edward Said. According to Said, the Orient emerged as an imagined geography, a mirror and differentiator to the West and Western values of rationality, peace, logic, and humanism (49). Visibly marked bodies—Chinese bodies—are not natural and autonomous, but are subject to normalization by Orientalist discourses. At the same time that Chinese bodies are circumscribed by Western whiteness, white bodies acquire meaningfulness in relation to Chinese bodies. An accepted norm, whiteness represents "orderliness, rationality, self-control," while the alternative, non-whiteness, embodies "chaos, irrationality, violence, and the breakdown of self-regulation" (Kincheloe 164). In this section, I illustrate through two examples—the model minority myth and cosmetic surgery—the reciprocity of normalization in American and Asian cultures.

Through the model minority myth, Chinese bodies and identities are curtailed by Western norms and imagination, a notion explicated in *Orientalism*. Within the utopian myth of an immigrant's Americanization, visibly marked Chinese bodies are produced and regulated, judged by the universalizing, regulatory cultural expectations of "proper ways to behave." Correct, compliant behaviors, performed by these desirable minorities, may be rewarded by white approval and social advancement, a shining testimony to successful Americanization. Sapna Cheryan and Gale V. Bodenhausen examine the popular stereotype that Asians—most intellectually exceptional and mathematically accomplished—have an enviable work ethic; model minorities exemplify successful assimilation. Accordingly, the Chinese are favored as industrious, disciplined, uncomplaining, acquiescent, and loyal. The myth assumes that all Asians (note the slippage from Chinese to Asians) quickly achieve financial and personal success, making them a benefit and a welcomed addition to *any* community. Thus, the label "model minority" has dual connotations of "role model" and "model citizen."

The processes that naturalize both connotations also render their pervasive effects invisible. While many Asians and Asian Americans do conquer their cultural differences in order to fit in and succeed, others are negatively impaired by these "normalizing" expectations. Disputing the belief that positive stereotypes have beneficial effects, Cheryan and Bodenhausen demonstrate that "when a positive performance is anticipated by an external audience, an individual may experience apprehension about meeting those high expectations, and such feelings can lead to the phenomenon known as 'choking under pressure'" (399); they conclude that "positive" stereotypes can and do impair individual performance (401; see also Magner). The "model minority" stereotype is constructed and maintained against a seamless backdrop of white value systems. Echoing Butler, Kondo maintains that "performative citations are thus never merely the voluntary choices of a humanist subject; rather, they are the product of constitutive constraints that create identities, creative performances elicited under duress" ("Politics" 7). In this case, visibly marked bodies interact with and are rendered intelligible through networks of texts, including formal laws and informal rituals, and institutional forms of organization (Lowe 33). Thus, interactions with and reactions to minorities cannot be separated from the white imagination: "how we theorize, live, and contest race, nation, and other collective identities in a world where these boundaries are being continuously transgressed, problematized, yet reasserted for complicated political ends" (Kondo, "Politics" 5).

In an age of globalization and diaspora, it is not enough to discuss how Chinese/Asian immigrants might be constructed by Orientalist discourses. To recognize the consequences of normalization, we must examine how mainland and overseas Chinese simultaneously define themselves through Western norms, identifying with an idealized, authentic white body. Once existing outside dominant definitions of Western beauty, visibly marked bodies are now challenging those genetically determined, once impregnable boundaries, underscoring the constructed, malleable nature of physiology. For example, many Asian women, cursed with vanishing eyelids, are having their eyes surgically altered, thus not only bringing them closer to Western ideals of beauty, but also creating a multi-million dollar industry in Asia. Cosmetic surgery can correct the "defects" of ancestry, creating visible eyelids so that Asian eyes can look "large, rounded, doe-like." *Changing Face*, produced by the Department of Anthropology at the University of California-Berkeley, documents how many Asian-Americans choose cosmetic eyelid surgery in order to achieve a more Caucasian look. Even in Asian countries, Occidental features have currency as the *Korean Journal* and *Free China Journal* report. Female Chinese and Japanese job seekers are aspiring to American standards of beauty through cosmetic surgery, including eyelid creation, nose ridge heightening, and silicon injections to make the chin and jaw line more pronounced. During the recession of the 1990s, Japanese women began securing their jobs through the prestige and currency of a "foreign look." Karen Ogulnik, an American teacher who lived in Japan, laments, "[s]alient images of beauty promoted by Hollywood have been responsible for countless cases of cosmetic surgery among Japanese models and actresses, who have had their eyes enlarged, noses heightened, and skin whitened" (14). These surgical procedures not only demonstrate the constructedness of physiology and the instability of those accepted anatomical boundaries, but also how individual experiences of actual bodies are modulated by and in constant (re)negotiations with dominant idealized notions of the body.

Hayles reminds us that "[e]xperiences of embodiment, far from existing apart from culture, are always already imbricated within it. Yet because embodiment is individually articulated, there is also at least an incipient tension between it and hegemonic cultural constructs" (197). In this case, whiteness assumes a sacrosanct position, surveilling, regulating, and policing the kinds of material-semiotic performances that take place and how they are perceived. Racial and ethnic bodies are not just different, because difference is both "relational and value-laden"; they are judged as *different from* white bodies.[1]

Through the lens of white normative discourse, physiology becomes a neon sign of difference. As Clifford Geertz points out: "Foreignness does not start at the water's edge but at the skin's" (112). A natural boundary that contains and announces difference, a signpost to alien cultures and ancient traditions, skin conveys undesirability and disorder. Native Chinese and Japanese who choose cosmetic surgery are expressing the belief that the idealized white body can be replicated. The features of the white homogeneous body, especially the eyes and nose, are normed in relation to and against the exotic Chinese body.

The reciprocity between American and Chinese processes of normalization underscores the fluidity of authenticity and the belief systems that undergird it. In America, an aesthetic reading of difference emphasizes how minorities are a mirror and a differentiator for white bodies and values. In addition, expressions of race and ethnicity are reduced to cuisine, clothing, and traditions, all of which represent a narrow, cursory understanding of culture. White definitions of race and ethnicity limit difference to surface, aesthetic features, whether physical or social. An example of this aesthetic perspective is the neon pink flyer in my campus mailbox, extending an alluring invitation to "Celebrate Diversity Day." "Come experience the authentic costumes, dances, and foods of Indian, Chinese, Vietnamese, and Arabic cultures," the flyer clarifies, reducing material enactments of race and ethnicity to spectacles that can be circulated and consumed, a superficial aesthetic distributed by ideological discourses. Usually a simulacrum, the exotic costumes, surreal dances, and strangely flavored foods represent tangible, digestible elements of difference, sources of objectified pleasure that consumers can easily devour. For example, the fortune cookie is an American creation, produced and circulated within an Orientalist discourse that envisions Chinese wisdom as impenetrable and thus must be dispensed in bite-sized tidbits—ancient Chinese knowledge becomes "fortune cookie wisdom."

At the same time, Chinese who undertake cosmetic surgery participate in those same Orientalist discourses, reducing white bodies to essential, homogeneous parts. The voyeuristic scopic regime that undergirds aestheticism trades on the legitimacy of essences, a semiotic framed by processes of normalization. Race and ethnicity can neither be limited to visceral experiences nor separated from the significant political and socio-economic consequences of the imposition of cultural values and beliefs on visibly marked bodies. Nor can difference be separated from the asymmetrical, web-like network of power relations that keep in place a complex system of class privilege and oppression. Issues of exoticism and homogeneity that arise in reading bodies also occur in aesthetic interpretations of multicultural texts. In the following section, I conclude by offering an illustration of two reading approaches grounded in an aesthetic understanding of difference: localism and universalism.[2]

I close with criteria for developing strategies that encourage interpretations of race and ethnicity that are neither essentialist nor aesthetic, but processual and constructed in nature.

On Reading Race and Ethnicity Aesthetically

> But the worst was when Rich criticized my mother's cooking, and he didn't even know what he had done. As is the Chinese cook's custom, my mother always made disparaging remarks about her own cooking. That night she chose to direct it toward her famous steamed pork and preserved vegetable dish, which she always served with special pride.
>
> "Ai! This dish not salty enough, no flavor," she complained, after tasting a small bite. "It is too bad to eat."

> This was our family's cue to eat some and proclaim it the best she had ever made. But before we could do so, Rich said, "You know, all it needs is a little soy sauce." And he proceeded to pour a riverful of the salty black stuff on the platter, right before my mother's horrified eyes.
>
> Amy Tan, "Four Directions," *The Joy Luck Club*, 197

In "Four Directions," the Jong family is meeting Waverly's new fiancé for the first time. Waverly recognizes the conflicts between American and Chinese cultures as she recounts how Rich, through his eagerness to please and his ignorance of proper Chinese etiquette, inadvertently insults his hosts, the very people he works diligently to impress. Rich brings the Jongs a bottle of French wine, a gift Waverly's parents cannot appreciate, and then drinks too much, not noticing the small, polite sips of the others. Next, Rich offends by inconsiderately filling his plate with a large portion of shrimp and snow peas rather than waiting until everyone at the table has taken his or her share. In declining an expensive delicacy of greens, Rich does not "give face" to Waverly's mother, a time-honored Chinese strategy where guests feign enjoyment of the food served. His refusal leads Waverly's daughter, Shoshana, to follow suit, rejecting the greens. Instead of following his host's cue and helping himself to seconds in order to compliment the chef's outstanding cooking, Rich declines to demonstrate his polite thoughtfulness, inadvertently offending Waverly's mother yet again. Such unintended rudeness is the prelude to Rich's largest blunder, salting Lindo Jong's carefully prepared dish because he interprets her ritual criticism of her own cooking literally. Rich's action also reveals his erroneous assumption that soy sauce is the only condiment for salting Chinese food. This catalogue of offenses that Waverly narrates not only highlights the differences that divide American and Chinese cultures, but also the despair and anguish American-born Chinese feel as they mediate between the two.

The situation, portrayed above, demonstrates how differing cultural expectations and beliefs clash in the contact zone of everyday life. By assigning texts that portray such clashes, teachers assume that students can develop more sensitivity to other cultures and their differences and an awareness of the historical con-

exigencies of identity politics. Certainly, that is my goal when I assign texts written by minorities about minorities. I hope to encourage a deeper, more reflexive understanding of race and ethnicity, including whiteness. However, without careful pedagogical attention to strategies of reading, such attempts do backfire. Once a young, male graduate student of Spanish descent, in response to my general inquiry to a class, responded, "I'm not sure what I'm supposed to get out of the reading. I couldn't relate to it because I'm not Chinese." As an afterthought, he added, probably in response to my frozen expression, "And I'm not a woman." Situated in this student's statement is an epistemology grounded in biological and geographical essentialism, a Janus-faced way of reading the world that can be characterized in two contradictory, aesthetic approaches to reading: localism and universalism.

Reed Way Dasenbrock defines localism as reading that is focused on the particular, contextual, difference-centered details of a text; by contrast, universalism is reading that is focused on the commonalities we all share as members of the human race. Both these modes of reading bracket off difference selectively, by either reifying or denying race and ethnicity. Further, both approaches treat subjectivity as natural, stable, and convenient categories, while purposefully ignoring the normalizing effects of Orientalist discourses. Emphasizing embodiment is a way of countering aesthetic reading, a way that "subversively undercuts essentialism rather than reinforces it" (201).

The first aspect, a localist reading of Tan's excerpt, focuses on the features that are considered inherently Chinese, in this case dinner guest and host etiquette. Readers may also highlight the contrary expectations and differences in courteous behavior. Through careful exegesis and close reading, readers may extrapolate the true nature of Chineseness, including the superstitions, traditions, and customs that constitute a civilization, accentuating the alienness of that civilization. Through Waverly, Tan becomes a cultural interpreter, a provider of authoritative knowledge about nations and cultures *different from* the white American norm. Through a localist reading, difference manifests itself as a hermetically sealed, self-contained essence, tied to no particular place and free from the intractability of time. Cultural knowledge is treated as referentially absolute in its authenticity. In addition, many inexperienced readers, invested in culture's stability, nurture an uncritical acceptance of Chineseness (and whiteness) as portrayed in this text.

The above excerpt may also encourage a localist interpretation because the text itself is framed in localist terms, foregrounding the problem of cultural difference. Ironically, because their texts may encourage localist interpretations, writers who emphasize race and ethnicity, including Arundhati Roy, Frank McCourt, and Maxine Hong Kingston, are also strategically relegated to the prison-house of multicultural aestheticism. Their creative endeavors, inseparable from their status as geographical jailbirds, are read through an Orientalist lens that glamorizes strangeness. The prescriptive goal of aestheticism, which elides historical contingencies, is the integration of eclectic cultural experiences that accentuate individual uniqueness, fetishizing the exotic nature of difference while simultaneously affirming the value of a liberal approach to knowledge. However, the emphasis on foreignness as a prerequisite for authenticity may blind some readers to the political and cultural exploitation that occurs.

The second aspect of aesthetic reading is universalism, a mode that emphasizes collectively shared themes and experiences. By examining the cultural clashes in order to ascertain how people, despite their many differences and permutations, share a common humanity, such texts broaden our horizons, providing avenues for a harmonious coexistence. By overlooking the particular, local, and culturally derived differences, universalists see Waverly as just another young woman who desires her parents' approval. At the beginning of the chapter, Lindo comments on the profuseness of Rich's freckles, an observation Waverly interprets as criticism and disapproval. Linguist Deborah Tannen uses this situation as an example of the "complexities of communication between mothers and daughters" (215). According to Tannen, Tan poignantly "dramatizes the power of mothers over daughters—power created in part by daughters wanting their mothers' approval so badly" (216).

Tannen's approach to reading underscores universalism, a helpful approach for students, who may not relate to the text because they are not Chinese. These students are persuaded instead to uncover the similarities within a text, for example enduring the stings of parental judgment. In addition, this excerpt may be an occasion for exploring generational differences, developing an adult identity, and finding one's own voice. Students may be encouraged to write about their own experiences of alienation and discomfort as an avenue for helping them "relate" to a text, for recognizing the ways in which their own responses are mediated by their background information, cognitive schema, and cultural maps. Teachers, who use similarity to illustrate how acts of reading are acts of negotiation, may unwittingly undermine the crucial details of highly local knowledge and cultural struggle. By underscoring universalism, teachers and students may in fact be advocating assimilation and acculturation; differences become superficial, located only on the skin.

This uninterrogated sameness has three consequences. First, it surreptitiously denies the systematic, structural, and institutional asymmetries that many minorities encounter. Christine Sleeter describes how white teachers purposefully cultivate a colorblindness, developing a pedagogy that treats race as a matter of "individual choice." Sleeter admits, "my own color [whiteness] gives me a degree of comfort, privilege, and insulation that serves me in ways I continue to take for granted" (168). Second, Min-Zhan Lu warns against conflating histories of oppression, explaining how "institutions have not targeted 'blacks' and 'Asian immigrants' in the same way in US history" ("Politics" 178). She highlights her "own tendency to conflate the history of all racially oppressed groups" ("Politics" 185). She also recognizes her own "privileged class and ethnic ranking within the Asian immigrant community" ("Politics" 190) as well as the white American academic community. In other words, having experienced antagonism on the basis of one's skin color does not necessarily encourage a united front against all white institutions of domination. Lu insightfully observes, "[O]ur chances of changing the particular system most immediately oppressive to each of us will remain limited until we learn to confront our own *complicity* with various systems of oppression" ("Politics" 176, my emphasis; see also "Vitality" 335). Third, failure to acknowledge the all-too-real material differences of class struggle, systematic inequalities, and institutional barriers—a result of political and economic oppression—perpetuates the status quo. Teresa Ebert argues for a systematic critique of the material inequalities of the distributions of wealth, power, and privilege, all necessary catalysts for emancipation ("For" 796; "Ludic" 18). Ebert reminds us that materiality, particularly that which is considered genuine or legitimate, is the product of class antagonisms, produced by labor divisions ("For" 807; "Untimely" 138).

Neither localism nor universalism can accurately configure race and ethnicity as messy, noisy, protean, and inconsistent. To understand better the instability of racial and ethnic subjectivity, we need to develop ways of reading that highlight disjuncture and instability. We must begin by taking embodiment into account. Embodiment simultaneously colludes with and resists the cultural, discursive definitions of the body at the more mundane, micro-level of everyday practices, choices, and rituals. A focus on embodiment counters the tendency to conceptualize Chineseness and whiteness as decorative, stereotypical differences that reside in the flesh. Second, we must realize that by naming and abstracting these embodied enactments, we engage in the processes of normalization. Building on Pierre Bourdieu's concept of habitus, Hayles acknowledges that by "reducing some area of embodied knowledge to analytical categories and explicit procedures, one has in the process changed the kind of knowledge it is, for the fluid, contextual interconnections that define the open horizons of embodied interactions would have solidified into discrete entities and sequential instructions [. . .]. Abstraction thus not only affects how one describes learning but also changes the account of what is learned" (202). This failure to produce new theories of representation results from the cooptation through aesthetic reading habits. Third, we must avoid the uncritical celebration of Epcot Center-ness that merely (dis)plays racial and ethnic goods, laying them out in ever more enticing configurations for easy consumption.

While a direct translation and application of reflexive reading habits into pedagogy is beyond the scope of this essay, I conclude with three key criteria for developing a materialist way of reading. Both localism and universalism offer a valid first step in reading race and ethnicity, providing useful taxonomies for novice readers. However, teachers must remember that these categories are artificial, abstract, and stable. Situated within a restricted, homogeneous conceptualization of Chineseness is an unawareness of the negotiated intricacies and dialectical plurality of ways of belonging. If the goal of assigning multicultural texts is to nurture greater awareness and sensitivity, then we cannot stop at the frameworks offered by localism and universalism. Instead, we must focus on the struggles of Waverly and Jing-Mei as they continually construct who they are: "what it means to be Chinese varies from place to place, moulded [sic] by the local circumstances in which peoples of Chinese ancestry gave settled and constructed new ways of living" (Ang, "Differential" 73). In investigating the politics of Chineseness, Ang calls for a creative, productive tension between the questions "where are you from" (emphasizing origins) and "where are you at" (emphasizing local and temporal contexts). She emphasizes that "the diasporic subject can never return to her/his 'origins', but also, more importantly, that the cultural context of 'where you're at' always informs and articulates the meaning of 'where you are from'" ("On" 558).

Second, because the very processes of reading are always already circumscribed by the politics of normalization, such abstraction stabilizes the embodied enactments described in these multicultural texts. Acts of reading are acts of negotiation; each act of reading changes the terms out of which we read. A politics of materialist reading requires that each of us ask how we participate in essentializing discourses that stress cultural homogeneity, that naturalizes the apparent transparency of meaning. We must also recognize the taken-for-granted-ness in our attitudes, particularly these reductive, normalizing tendencies. Thus, we must interrogate and destabilize the terms we privilege. For example, why are we invested in discerning "authenticity"? How does "authenticity" then regulate our reading, directing us in certain directions while ignoring others? When we do not find authenticity, what powerful vested interests are at stake in the text, in ourselves, and in the institutions?

Third, we must develop a politics of materialist reading that accommodates the indeterminacy that results from this interrogation of difference. Difference is the result of a two-fold process, wherein language and materiality simultaneously constrain and enable each other. Because difference lies in the dialectic between body and embodiment, public and private, community and individual, expressions of diversity are simultaneously improvisational and contextual. Our inability to locate or clearly identify authenticity is especially important. Thus, materialist reading must be prepared to confront such indeterminate fissures, ones that cannot be filled, explained, or ignored. We must foster the ambivalences, multiplicities, and elusiveness of identity politics. Otherwise, multicultural texts are curtailed by habits of reading that remain intact, unconscious, and unexposed. Rather than assimilate or colonize difference as exotic, we must envision situations of profound contradiction and dislocation. After all, struggles over interpretation are also struggles of epistemology, disputes about the ways in which we view and construct the world.

The meanings of race and ethnicity are not rooted in biology or geography, but are blurred, ambiguous, transitory, and dependent on temporal and spatial contingencies. The mutable nature of Chineseness dances with whiteness. The material-semiotic performances of race and ethnicity are always complex, shifting, and only partially revealed: "To study race, identity, or culture, and to intervene in their fields of effects, one must be prepared to live with extraordinary complexity and variability of meaning" (McCarthy 6). Materialist reading, grounded in hermeneutic openness, asks all of us, regardless of our race and ethnicity, to read both against the vision of identity that is culturally favored and against the familiar practices that may even be propounded by many multicultural texts. The concern for authenticity seems to be reinforced and, at the same time, challenged by many multicultural writers. The characters in Tan's novel, my parents, my Beijing friend, and I struggle with definitions and expressions of authenticity; student readers also recapitulate that same struggle. A politics of materialist reading travels against the grain of the ideological forces situated in a text, especially its construction of its own implied readers. A politics of materialist reading foregrounds cultural ambiguity, transience, and hybridity, whether embodied by Tan's characters or by visibly marked bodies. A politics of materialist reading emerges in the interplay among reader, text, and community.

Notes

1. I build on Ann Ducille's insightfully eloquent analysis of black Barbie and the politics of representing blackness authentically (126). Ducille argues that cultural authenticity and difference, generally caricatures of a white imagination, cannot be reduced to physiological markers or even ethnic attire as Mattel sought to accomplish: "Just as Barbie reigns ubiquitously white, blonde, and blue eyed over a rainbow coalition of colored optical illusions, human social relations remain in hierarchical bondage, one to the other, the dominant to the different" (126).

2. I am indebted to Reed Way Dasenbrock for the critical framework, terminology, and definitions of these two approaches to reading. While Dasenbrock uses these concepts to discuss the meaningfulness of multicultural works, I build on his framework, using it to highlight the limitations of aesthetic habits of reading.

Works Cited

Ang, Ien. "On Not Speaking Chinese: Postmodern Ethnicity and the Politics of Diaspora." *Feminism and Cultural Studies*. Ed. Morag Shiach. New York: Oxford UP, 1999. 540–64.

———. "The Differential Politics of Chineseness." *Southeast Asian Journal of Social Science* 22 (1994): 72–79.

Appiah, Kwame Anthony. "Race." *Critical Terms for Literary Study*. Ed. Frank Lentricchia and Thomas McLaughlin. Chicago: U of Chicago P, 1990. 274–87.

Basham, Richard. "National Racial Policies and University Education in Malaysia." *Culture, Ethnicity, and Identity: Current Issues in Research*. Ed. William C. McCready. New York: Academic P, 1983. 57–77.

Butler, Judith. "Revisiting Bodies and Pleasures." *Theory, Culture and Society* 16.2 (1999): 11–20.

———. *Bodies That Matter: On the Discursive Limits of "Sex."* New York: Routledge, 1993.

Changing Face: Cosmetic Surgery on the Asian Eyelid. Dir. Clarence Ting et al. Videocassette. U of California-Berkeley, 1995.

Cheryan, Sapna, and Galen V. Bodenhausen. "When Positive Stereotypes Threaten Intellectual Performance: The Psychological Hazards of 'Model Minority' Status." *American Psychological Society* 11.5 (2000): 399–402.

Dasenbrock, Reed Way. "Intelligibility and Meaningfulness in Multicultural Literature in English." *PMLA* 102.1 (1987): 10–19.

Ducille, Ann. "Black Barbie and the Deep Play of Difference." *Feminism and Cultural Studies*. Ed. Morag Shiach. New York: Oxford UP, 1999. 106–32.

Ebert, Teresa L. "For a Red Pedagogy: Feminism, Desire, and Need." *College English* 58.7 (1996): 795–819.

———. "Ludic Feminism, the Body, Performance, and Labor: Bringing Materialism Back into Feminist Cultural Studies." *Cultural Critique* (Winter 1992–93): 5–50.

———. "(Untimely) Critiques for a Red Feminism." *Transformation* 1 (1995): 113–48.

Eng, Phoebe. *Warrior Lessons: An Asian American Woman's Journey into Power*. New York: Pocket, 1999.

Geertz, Clifford. "The Uses of Diversity." *Michigan Quarterly Review* 25 (1986): 105–23.

Hayles, N. Katherine. "The Materiality of Informatics." *How We Became Posthuman: Virtual Bodies in Cybernetics, Literature, and Informatics*. Chicago: U of Chicago P, 1999. 192–221.

Kincheloe, Joe L. "The Struggle to Define and Reinvent Whiteness: A Pedagogical Analysis." *College Literature* 26.3 (1999): 162–94.

Kondo, Dorinne K. "On Being a Conceptual Anomaly." *Signs of Life in the USA*. 2nd. ed. Ed. Sonia Maasik and J. Fisher Solomon. New York: St. Martin's, 1997. 523–30.

———. "The Politics of Pleasure." *About Face: Performing Race in Fashion and Theater*. New York: Routledge, 1997. 3–28.

Lowe, Lisa. "Heterogeneity, Hybridity, Multiplicity: Marking Asian American Differences." *Diaspora* 1.1 (1991): 24–44.

Lu, Min-Zhan. "The Politics of Critical Affirmation." *College Composition and Communication* 51.2 (1999): 172–94.

———. "The Vitality of the Ungrateful Receiver: Making Giving Mutual between Composition and Postcolonial Studies." *Journal of Advanced Composition* 19 (1999): 335–57.

Magner, Denise. "College's Asian Enrollment Defies Stereotype." *Chronicle of Higher Education* 10 Feb. 1993: A34.

McCarthy, Cameron. *The Uses of Culture: Education and the Limits of Ethnic Affiliation*. New York: Routledge, 1998.

Ogulnick, Karen. *Onna Rashiku (Like a Woman): The Diary of a Language Learner in Japan*. Albany: State U of New York P, 1998.

Said, Edward. *Orientalism*. New York: Vintage, 1978.

Sleeter, Christine E. "How White Teachers Construct Race." *Race, Identity, and Representation in Education*. Ed. Cameron McCarthy and Warren Crichlow. New York: Routledge, 1993. 157–71.

Sollors, Werner. "Ethnicity." *Critical Terms for Literary Study*. Ed. Frank Lentricchia and Thomas McLaughlin. Chicago: U of Chicago P, 1990. 288–305.

Tan, Amy. *The Joy Luck Club*. New York: Ivy, 1989.

Tannen, Deborah. *I Only Say This Because I Love You: How the Way We Talk Can Make or Break Family Relationships Throughout Our Lives*. New York: Random, 2001.

Wong, Sau-ling Cynthia. "'Sugar Sisterhood': Situating the Amy Tan Phenomenon." *The Ethnic Canon: Histories, Institutions, and Interventions*. Ed. David Palumbo-Liu. Minneapolis: U of Minnesota P, 1995. 174–210.

Chapter Eighteen

Local Pedagogies and Race: Interrogating White Safety in the Rural College Classroom

Amy E. Winans

On May 4, 2001, the *New York Times* published a front-page article entitled "As Diversity Sweeps Nation, a Placid Town Is Unchanged" (Barry). Susquehanna University, the Lutheran-affiliated liberal arts college where I teach, is located in that "placid town": Selinsgrove, a town of 5,383 people, in a rural county of central Pennsylvania. As the article noted, although national demographics are shifting significantly in ways that suggest that non-Hispanic whites will become a minority in the United States by 2050, these population shifts are scarcely evident in Selinsgrove and in similar towns where the overall population and the percentage of people of color—approximately 7 percent—have stayed virtually constant over the last decade. Most people of color in Selinsgrove live on campus or in public housing across the street from the main campus. The student body is composed of 1,865 students, approximately 7 percent of whom are identified as students of color.[1] Although most students who attend Susquehanna did not grow up in the local area, 61 percent of them do come from Pennsylvania, many from rural areas whose population, like Selinsgrove's, is overwhelmingly white. Racial difference has not been apparent in the daily lives of many of my students. As one white student wrote, "I was never allowed to watch MTV, which is how most teenagers in my town became familiar with blacks."[2] It is not unusual for

From *College English* 67 (2005): 253–73.

white students to explain that they have never had a personal relationship with a person of color before arriving at college. Students who have grown up in more racially and culturally diverse areas—typically suburbs—often have had little experience thinking critically about race and their own racial identities, in part because their home and school lives have been marked by residential and social segregation (see Rothenberg, for example, for a discussion about suburbs that are racially and culturally diverse demographically, yet remain socially, residentially, and academically segregated). The racial homogeneity of Selinsgrove, the campus, and many of my students' hometown experiences would seem to render race a difficult or even a peripheral topic to explore in the classroom.

Although the racial and cultural diversity of our campus is comparatively limited, nonetheless, it is significant for many students, particularly those who have grown up in areas that are even more racially and culturally homogenous. As one white student commented in her essay, "The diversity in this school is not even immense, but it is still a big step from my town." Indeed, as Cameron McCarthy has suggested, "[e]ducation is indeed a critical site in which struggles over the organization and concentration of emotional and political investment and moral affiliation are taking place" (333). During their first year in college, many students are unconsciously and consciously confronting unexplored questions about affiliation and race. Students who grew up in areas more diverse than Selinsgrove are often struck and puzzled by the demographic differences they notice upon their arrival to campus, yet like students from predominantly white areas they frequently lack the tools to explore the impact of those differences and to understand how their race and their experiences with racial difference influence their beliefs and assumptions about the world.

Exploring race helps students learn to think and write critically. A growing body of scholarly literature establishes a positive correlation between diversity experiences (including, among other things, courses that directly address diversity) and improved critical thinking. Indeed, a recent study conducted by Ernest T. Pascarella and his colleagues at the University of Iowa found that the critical-thinking skills of white students benefited most greatly from diversity work (270). A fundamental aspect of critical thinking and effective writing entails recognizing, as Richard Paul and Linda Elder note, that "all reasoning is done from some point of view" (178). Making diversity central to my teaching helps students recognize that all ideas and writing emerge from a specific subject position, a position or point of view shaped and reshaped by one's lived experiences of race, class, sexual orientation, gender, religion, region, and ability. Any stance or position that might appear to be neutral or objective, or simply to constitute "common sense," is in fact one whose power and positionality have been naturalized. Although this challenging work can be undertaken in numerous classes, I have found that a useful starting point is the first-year writing course required of all students. My students are often profoundly affected by reading and writing assignments focused on race, in part because the assignments challenge a fundamental, unquestioned assumption that almost all white students share: that is, that the only people who have a racial identity and who are affected by race are people of color.

White students' perception that "race has nothing to do with me" is common at rural, predominantly white institutions like mine. When students express this belief, they seem to mean both that racism and their own race play no role in their lives. "I don't see race," they often say, explaining, "I treat everyone the same." As one white student wrote, "[W]hen everyone else around you is white, denial of the importance of race is inevitable. It almost becomes a mental shortcut just to think, 'Race doesn't matter because it doesn't affect me.'" My students have gathered significant amounts of information about race throughout their lives, yet, like the students Pamela Perry describes in her study of white students at a predominantly white high school in California, they seldom recognize the impact this information has had on them, in part because their limited direct interaction with people of color has made immediate questions regarding racial differences appear less pressing. Interestingly, many of the students who have relationships that they describe as close with people of color note that they have seldom or never discussed race within the relationship. White students' common assumption that race plays no role in their lives supports a key assertion of many critics who explore whiteness in contemporary U.S. society: whiteness achieves power because it generates norms so effectively that the constructed nature of those norms remains invisible to many, particularly to white people themselves. Yet I believe that exploring how those norms function and how whiteness operates is important work that can be pursued effectively in settings where racial and cultural diversity is not readily apparent. Especially on a rural, predominantly white campus in the North, exploring race in a way that is accessible for white students and that allows them to understand their own positionality means directly addressing whiteness and the strategies that white students use to approach race. Doing so helps white students develop a personal investment in their work that serves as a basis for their thinking more critically about how race affects the lives of all people and how it structures the world in which they live.[3]

Ruth Frankenburg argues that "[w]hiteness needs to be delimited and 'localized'" if it is to be understood and if its power is to be challenged (qtd. in Rodriguez, "Emptying" 32). As she adds in a recent essay, "[W]hiteness's meanings are complexly layered and variable locally and translocally" (76). Proposals like Frankenburg's to localize the study of whiteness have led to a number of important studies of whiteness for specific populations in particular areas of the United States. John Hartigan, Jr., for example, has explored the experiences of working-class whites living in predominantly black areas of Detroit, and, more recently, Perry has compared white students' understandings of whiteness in two California high schools, one that is predominantly white and one that is racially and culturally heterogeneous. Despite important projects like these, much scholarship still seems to essentialize whiteness, often presenting it as something that is interchangeable with white privilege. Scholars such as Charles A. Gallagher and even Frankenburg herself, a key figure in whiteness studies, have offered broad generalizations about how white Americans have come to understand whiteness over the last decade. Yet as Joe L. Kincheloe and Shirley Steinberg remind us, "[W]hiteness scholarship to this point has sometimes failed to recognize that its greatest problem is the lapse into essentialism" (182). To use Perry's terms, scholars addressing the "invisible pernicious ways that white cultural and political domination permeates people's lives [. . .] have tended to reify it into a monolithic 'fact' that affects all whites more or less consistently" (3). Ian Marshall and Wendy Ryden offer a related critique, asserting that "[a]ll students need to be enabled with a critical rhetoric of whiteness, but it is not a one-size-fits-all proposition" (249).

The essentializing or oversimplifying of whiteness, suggests Jennifer Seibel Trainor, has created problems within critical pedagogy because it "contribute[s] to static stereotypic pictures of white, middle class students and their values and beliefs" (632). Indeed, many of the current approaches to whiteness and white students create obstacles to developing effective pedagogies, ones that allow students to explore the complex, often contradictory experiences that are obscured by the broad narratives that they are frequently encouraged to adopt when they do talk about race in their lives. The difficulty that emerges in recent scholarship on whiteness and pedagogies of whiteness is not unlike that encountered by many white students in or from predominantly white areas: similar narratives are repeated, yet they efface the complexities of race in people's lived experiences and the role that emotions play in one's understanding of those experiences. Just as white students often assert that race is irrelevant in their lives and that they are colorblind, many scholars addressing whiteness repeat arguments that equate whiteness with a uniform white privilege and construct a generic, middle-class white student who needs to learn about his or her own racism, but who is unable or unwilling to do so. In so doing, they ignore the suggestions of scholars such as Richard E. Miller, who cautions instructors about the pitfalls of approaching their "students as makers of error who need to be corrected, or as believers in immoral or improper ideology" (qtd. in Skorczewski 232).

My goal is to illustrate how race, particularly whiteness, can be usefully addressed in a predominantly white classroom by developing a local pedagogy, one that respects and addresses the complexities of students' often contradictory experiences of race. In crafting a local pedagogy, my approach is influenced by Kincheloe's argument about the importance of studying "the social, historical, rhetorical, and discursive context of whiteness, mapping the ways it makes itself visible and invisible, manifests its power, and shapes larger socio-political structures in relation to the micro-dynamics of everyday life" (169). Designing a local pedagogy entails considering the roles that the campus location, the campus demographics, the demographics of students' hometowns, and students' experiences within their families and communities play in shaping what is happening in the classroom. Although my focus is on illustrating how I have crafted a local pedagogy for teaching race and critical thinking at a small private liberal arts college with a predominantly white population, I believe that this type of work can and should be done in classrooms in all academic settings.

Interrogating White Safety

The rural, predominantly white setting of the town, campus, and classroom in which I teach creates a false sense of security for many white students, one that seems to extend the presumably racially "safe" atmosphere of many of their hometowns. In the case of the campus and classroom settings, the white safety many white students experience depends upon seeing the campus as a sort of innocent space, one that appears to remain apart from crime. In part, this notion of white safety emerges from white parents' and students' perceptions of the campus as a physically safe place because it is rural and predominantly white. As bell hooks has commented in a discussion of white socialization, many white people "are socialized to believe the fantasy, that whiteness represents goodness and all that is benign and non-threatening" (340). Although whiteness and the racial homogeneity of the campus do not have a stable, uniform meaning, its rural, predominantly white character is often read by whites as "benign and non-threatening." The perception of white physical safety on campus sets up an expectation for another sort of white safety within the classroom: social safety. In particular, white students seek to remain safe from the threat of being perceived as racist, a safety that is facilitated but not guaranteed by the predominantly white setting of the classroom and campus.

Retaining this white social safety, a sort of innocence, means relying upon narratives, generalizations, and definitions that students have consciously and unconsciously adopted in order to mediate their experiences of race and to help ensure that, at least in the atmosphere of the classroom, they are not perceived as racist. Most white students perceive being racist as socially unacceptable in the middle-class environment of the campus, particularly within the classroom. For some students, often but not only those from working-class backgrounds, the middle-class culture of campus becomes a place where the openly racist speech they might have heard growing up seems to have no place. The self-censoring becomes clear when students struggle to recount their experiences in class, as in the following student anecdote: "At church one evening, my grandparents argued about who did more work around the house. My grandmother knows that she does more, due to my grandfather's handicap, and she replied, 'Why don't you just paint me black and call me a nigger?'" The anecdote was told differently in class—the word "nigger" wasn't used as it was in the student's paper—and had to be repeated several times so that it was audible to most in the classroom.

My local pedagogy interrogates types of white safety by focusing particularly on the narratives and colorblind stance that many white students use to establish social safety and thus to preserve their innocence. White students often assume that racial identity is fixed within and across time and that people of color are the only ones who have racial identities and who are affected by race. They tend not to consider the ways race is created in the context of social relations and how it can be experienced differently by people from moment to moment as a social interaction unfolds. The perception of safety and innocence and the narratives that support this perception become easier to explore when we directly address students' own positionality, especially racially and historically. Where and when do white students often feel most comfortable or safe and why? What and whom do they perceive as sources of discomfort or danger? In what sense is safety itself always an illusion? What happens when white students' sense of innocence and safety is disrupted? My goal in exploring such questions is not to help students craft new narratives of whiteness but to teach them ways to question their own narratives, the standpoints from which they craft those narratives, and the consequences of those narratives. If, as Frankenburg has asserted, "[w]hiteness is a 'standpoint,' a location from which to see selves, others, and national and global orders" (76), then a key aspect of my work is helping white students to explore the narratives they use to remain "safe" by effacing their own positionalities or, in Frankenburg's terms, their "standpoints." Thus I discuss how notions of white safety shape the classroom setting and students' experiences, thinking, and writing about race, and I describe how students begin to deconstruct their own narratives about race. Specifically, I argue for the usefulness of encouraging students to explore contradictions in their experiences of race, contradictions that often inform narratives of colorblindness; in particular, it is important to challenge essentialized notions of identity that are often caught in the dichotomy of innocence and guilt. Further, I assert the importance of taking the ethical aims of students' narratives seriously, even when the narratives themselves are problematic. As I discuss the development of a local pedagogy, I use examples of student writing that are drawn from one assignment from my first-year writing course.

Unexamined assumptions about white physical safety are linked to the rural setting of my school in ways that are clearly racialized. The description of the town from the *New York Times* article itself is virtually pastoral: "Rabbits hop across the well-kept lawns of well-kept houses" in the blocks that surround the "idyllic campus of small Susquehanna University." Selinsgrove itself is described as the "center of Snyder County, a pretty patchwork of farms and small towns that comes to a stop at the western banks of the Susquehanna River." The attractive, rural campus receives significant attention from visitors to campus as well as from those who live and work there, and it is frequently mentioned as a key factor in students' decisions to attend Susquehanna. (In some cases students are struck to learn that their parents' notions of safety and comfort are directly tied to race. One white student noted in her paper that she was shocked to learn that the reason that her father was happy about her decision to attend Susquehanna rather than another school was not its strong academics but the fact that "it has a very low minority rate.") The clean, well-cared-for campus, distant and apart from urban areas, connotes safety for many white students and parents. In my first-year students' essays, white students mention their own and their parents' fears about cities, fears that are often expressed in racialized terms. Such fears exist in stark contrast to the feelings of safety linked to familiar rural settings, like that of our campus. As one white female student from rural Pennsylvania commented in her essay, "I always felt safe with them [her parents] and anywhere I went in my town or area of my state." The rural areas of Pennsylvania that appear safe to many white students are, according to the Southern Poverty Law Center, home to the fifth-highest number of hate groups of any state in the nation. The essay of one white male student from a farming community about thirty miles from our campus explored how whiteness worked in his community, arguing that it functioned "as a term for domination," one often associated with threats of violence. Ezra explains in part,

> Day in and day out my best friends would sit and [. . .] talk about doing harm to black kids, but it never happened. They just made the comments because they thought it was cool because of something they saw on television or heard from relatives. The kids from my area saw hate crimes and thought that the violence was cool.

The perceptions of white physical safety that frame white students' experiences on campus encourage them to overlook race, and set up the expectation of a certain level of comfort and social safety within the classroom. Preserving social safety for white students in the middle-class classroom means protecting themselves from charges of racism. Overt racism is socially unacceptable, and it functions as a potential threat to students' acceptance in a white, middle-class world that has developed coded ways for talking about race and that, as Jane Lazarre has argued, often seeks to disguise beliefs about or discomfort with racial difference (34). Further, Hartigan suggests, "[w]hites in the upper and middle classes craft forms of decorum that keep race from being raised in 'polite' conversation" ("White Devils"161). As my students note, this coded language can emerge when people seek to discourage an interracial romantic relationship. Describing the reaction she received to the interracial relationship she began after arriving at college, one white female student explained, "The parents that found out he was black made mostly negative comments. My friends who had told their parents would say things like, 'My Mom was thinking that maybe you shouldn't have gotten into a relationship that quickly,' or, 'My parents don't want me to date anyone that's different from us.'" The student noted in her essay, "[M]y parents are more than ready to deny their views so they can seem open-minded."

Significantly, despite and perhaps because of the strong negative connotations of the term "racist," its meaning is broad and unclear for most who use it. Students' uncertainty about the meaning of the term "racist" only increases its power. It is an epithet, but also one "with distinct classed inscriptions"; Hartigan argues, "[t]here is a long tradition of this intraracial positioning of working-class whites as the 'real' bearers and promoters of racist sentiment" ("White Devils" 165). Remaining silent on issues of race allows white students of all class backgrounds to preserve middle-class social safety. Explaining her silence in class during many of our discussions of race, one white female student wrote apologetically, "I would rather be known for having no opinion than [for] having a bad one."

White students' motivations for not wanting to be perceived as racist are multiple and interwoven. Clearly social acceptance in the middle-class world of the classroom is immensely important to students. Yet so too is their sense of ethics: they believe that racism is morally wrong and that it doesn't accurately represent their country's values or their own moral and religious beliefs. They view racism as morally abhorrent and thus fear acting or speaking in ways that might be understood as racist, both because such an interpretation challenges their understanding of their own identities and because they worry they could speak or act in such a way unintentionally. White students' fears are also often grounded in their own confusion about what racial identity and racism are. For many white students, race and racism are virtually interchangeable, and although their definitions may be unclear, their connotations are inescapably negative. Indeed, the opening line of one student's paper illustrates this point quite clearly. Writing in response to an assignment asking students to write an essay "that reflects critically on the role that race plays in your life," one white student read "race" as "racism." She explains, "[W]hen given the paper assignment to write about racism in our life, I immediately went on the defensive." Knowing that many white students in my classes may assume a defensive stance when asked to think critically about race, and that a range of interrelated motivations affect their desire for white social safety, has proven immensely helpful as I craft a local pedagogy, in part by seeking to understand students' comments about race in the context in which they are made and as they are informed by students' upbringing.

My race contributes to white students' feelings of safety in the classroom as well. When we talk about how the racially homogenous classroom affects our discussions, white students often mention that the homogeneity makes it easier for them to talk openly about race. They are less concerned about saying something that might be, or might be understood as, racist in front of a white professor and in front of a class they assume, sometimes inaccurately, to be exclusively white, than they would be in a more racially diverse setting. Indeed, as Ann E. Green has argued, "finding ways to talk about race and class is in some ways more difficult when students are confronted with lived race and class differences than when facing race and class differences as represented in textbooks and readings" (18). In some cases, the class includes one or two students of color and sixteen or seventeen students who identify themselves as white. One white female student compared what it was like to address race in an all-white high school classroom to discussions in our classroom, which that semester was made up of one African American student and sixteen white students: "Without a minority present, it was easier to speak my mind without thinking that anyone was judging me or saying that I was racist because we all felt a little the same due to non-exposure."

Understanding Colorblindness

In an exclusively or predominantly white class, white students may engage in what Alice McIntyre refers to as "white talk," a practice that entails "colluding with each other in creating a 'culture of niceness' that [makes] it difficult to 'read the white world'" (46). Designed to preserve white social safety by asserting innocence of racism, the "white talk" used most frequently in my classrooms is colorblindness. A colorblind stance asserts that one doesn't see or care about color or race. Matt's comment at the opening of his paper is representative: "I had never thought much of race before. To me it is not a big deal, you can be white, black, red, yellow, or purple, you're still the same to me." Many white students' colorblind stance emerges from the belief that noticing or mentioning race means that one is racist and that the way to avoid being racist is to ignore race. As one white male student explained, "I realized I've been brought up to believe that everyone is the same—and thought if I recognized race I'd be racist." For this student, believing that "everyone is the same" and that he does not see race connotes innocence. He continues, explaining that colorblindness "makes you believe that since you aren't confronting race, you can't be racially offensive." The colorblind approaches of many white students reflect the assumption that a white person who notices the race of a person of color might well do so because he or she has stereotypes about others, simply based upon what they look like. As one white female student explains, "My parents taught me to treat everyone equal. I was raised to see each person for who they are rather than the color of their skin." She explains further, "There is nothing different in a person whether they are black, white, Chinese, or Hispanic. It is simply color and has nothing to do with the inner person [. . .] the outer covering does not determine what is inside." Her references to "the inner person" and "what is inside" are echoed by many students in their references to "the true beauty that lies within." Although it may be tempting for instructors to write these statements off as clichés, clichés themselves, as Dawn Skorczewski has suggested, may in fact engage with issues that are the very ones we need to address more fully. Further, engaging with these issues is central to developing an effective local pedagogy.

Students' narratives of colorblindness typically rest upon unstated assumptions about racism and identity. The strategy of colorblindness would seem to have the potential to work quite effectively if racism is understood as simply "individual acts of meanness" in a world in which the individual is "an independent moral actor," separate from the influences of the culture in which he or she lives (McIntosh 126). This perspective is captured quite well in a memoir we sometimes analyze in class in which Jane Lazarre refers to a time when she "still believed that claiming a blindness to color could make you blind, that if people only treated each other as equals, centuries of history could be dismissed, even erased" (30). The strategy of colorblindness is one that sidesteps institutional and structural racism, something of which most white students have limited understanding.

In exploring students' narratives of colorblindness it can be tempting to focus on the difficulties with these narratives. Much scholarship does just that. For example, Nelson M. Rodriguez argues that "colorblindness enables whites to erase from consciousness [. . .] the history of racism and how that history plays itself out economically, politically, socially, and culturally in the present" ("Projects" 9). Frances V. Rains suggests that colorblindness "works to deny and, therefore, erase the identity of the subject(s) of the response. It denies persons of color their right to have their own identities as well as the values, histories, contributions, language and richness of such identities" (93). Many scholars use critiques of colorblindness and other strategies meant to preserve white safety as the basis for a criticism of white people's failure to challenge racism effectively. Stephanie M. Wildman and Adrienne D. Davis assert that "[w]hite people know they do not want to be labeled racist; they become concerned about how to avoid the labels, rather than worrying about systematic racism and how to change it" (91). Such critiques often shed important light on the consequences of colorblindness. Yet students are already so worried about saying the wrong thing that they often say nothing at all, which moves them no closer to understanding how antiracism might function in their lives. Although we do need to help students explore the implications of colorblindness critically, we also need to listen carefully to what they are struggling to express given the contexts in which they grew up and the local contexts in which they are speaking and writing. Following Susan Welsh's urging, we might seek to cultivate "positioned listening" (570), something I believe is crucial for any effective local pedagogy.

My concern is that focusing primarily on the limitations of colorblindness can distract us from realizing that for many people, colorblindness functions, as one student explained, as a sort of cover for "hesitant and confused feelings concerning race." When considering how and why white students so often use colorblindness, it is important not to place so much emphasis on the antiracist work that students are not doing that we obscure the implications of the strategies they have developed for making sense of race. Developing a local pedagogy that helps students understand how narratives like colorblindness work and where they come from is more effective than employing what Rodriguez terms "guilt-tripping pedagogies" ("Emptying" 34).

Colorblindness is motivated by at least two things: a desire to protect the self (social safety) by seeking to demonstrate that one is not racist, and a desire to protect others and to act ethically. The difficulty is that these two motivations are interwoven, as is clear from the frequent references to equality in statements of colorblindness. One white student's reflections on the reasons for her reticence during class discussion clearly illustrate this. Initially, the student explained her concern about the consequences of her actions and their potentially hurting the feelings of the only African American student in the room. As she questioned her own motivations further, however, she wondered, "Was I really afraid of hurting the only black person's feelings or was I afraid of being perceived a racist?" I believe we need to attend to both of these motivations—self-protection/social safety and ethics—as well as the emotions linked to each, rather than privileging one, if we are to work effectively and to help students move beyond a dualistic, innocent-versus-guilty framework, a framework analogous to what Elizabeth Ellsworth terms the "double binds of whiteness." Preserving innocence is one aspect of colorblindness, yet another aspect emerges from a desire to act ethically toward others, to affect the lives of others in positive ways. Employing an effective local pedagogy in a predominantly white classroom entails taking students' ethical beliefs and goals seriously rather than seeing them as misguided assumptions to be worked through. Furthermore, we need to explore the limits of colorblindness and the meanings of students' silences in ways that take into account strong, often unstated emotions. This can pave the way for further understanding and, if a student chooses, action, rather than leaving students stuck and silenced.

Moving Beyond Safety

One of the most effective local strategies that I have found to prepare students to deconstruct their own narratives about race is to demonstrate this process by analyzing autobiographical narratives that reflect the tensions present in other people's lived experiences of race. Because many students are so cautious about unknowingly making racist comments (or, as one student wrote in her paper, saying something that "could be twisted to be racist"), it is useful to begin with analysis of other people's experiences. Examining concrete examples of how racial identity is learned and how it can change is particularly helpful, because, as Kincheloe notes, students often see racial identity "as an absolute, fixed essence" (189). As Perry has suggested, it is valuable to explore race and identity operating as "social processes that are created and recreated by people in their daily lives and social interactions" (30). Analyzing other people's experiences and recognizing the complexity of racial identity—that it is learned and socially created, that it can shift, that people can make choices about how to respond to race, and that it can be experienced differently—open up discussions of race that address its messiness and complexity, rather than leaving students bound within an oppositional framework that seems to offer only two options for white people: innocence or guilt.

The challenge lies in helping students recognize the relationships between race and power and in helping them understand how race and racial identity can change not only from minute to minute, but also historically across time. We can move beyond conversations that seem to repeat points, often in the interest of preemptive defensive posturing ("I'm not racist, but . . .") by considering the shifting meanings of race in a memoir such as James McBride's *The Color of Water: A Black Man's Tribute to His White Mother* with questions like these: How does Ruth McBride's whiteness function inside and outside the house? How do her biracial children respond to their race differently from each other? How do their responses change over time? In what ways are the family members' approaches to race and ethnicity affected by conversations occurring inside and outside the household during the civil rights movement? Students explore Ruth McBride's statements of colorblindness and her son James McBride's discussion about the contradictions that shaped his mother's life as a means of practicing the sort of analysis many will subsequently employ when they analyze their own narratives.

Reflecting on the experience of growing up in a house with a white mother who did not acknowledge her whiteness and eleven brothers and sisters who understood their biracial background in different ways, James McBride explains:

> Mommy's contradictions crashed and slammed against one another like bumper cars at Coney Island. White folks, she felt, were implicitly evil toward blacks, yet she forced us to go to white schools to get the best education. Blacks could be trusted more, but anything involving blacks was probably slightly substandard. (29)

Considering the relationship between Ruth McBride's statements of colorblindness and her conscious and unconscious beliefs about race helps students explore the complexity beneath seemingly simple narratives and belief systems that many white people use to order and understand their worlds. Students respond sympathetically to the character of James, in part because of the value he places on family bonds and the devotion he expresses toward his strong, loving mother. They also frequently identify with Ruth and admire her not only because of her hard work and devotion to her children, but also because she offers a model of a sympathetic though clearly imperfect white person. Students often approach identity and hence whiteness in essentialized terms, equating whiteness with being the oppressor. One challenge lies in helping white students understand that whiteness is not interchangeable with "white person." Ruth offers students a concrete illustration of the important distinction "between whiteness, with its power to signify, and white people" (Kincheloe and Steinberg 182). Although in some ways Ruth might function as a positive role model for students, her stance of colorblindness (echoed in the memoir's title) is presented critically. Critiquing Ruth McBride, one student wrote

> Envisioning and acting out what the present should be like does not pull the dream of the future any closer to reality. Her twelve children deserved to know the origin of the stares, rumors, and questions. They sensed they were different, needing only to look at their mother for firm proof. She had the opportunity of their impressionable minds to teach them acceptance, but denied, in essence, that race even exists. In their confusion, they searched elsewhere for answers.

Analyzing Ruth's impact on her children allows students to consider the multiple ways in which race is consciously and unconsciously taught and learned and to reflect on the rift that can emerge between one's good intentions and the outcome of one's actions.

Some students notice direct links between Ruth McBride's approach to racial difference and their own. One white student whose sister was adopted from Colombia explained that because of her love for her sister (and because of her limited experiences with racial and cultural difference) she initially paid no attention to her sister's race and cultural background. Yet when she brought her baby sister to meet the students in her all-white classroom in Vermont, she was greeted by questions that focused exclusively on what was different about her sister: Where did they get her? Did she speak Spanish? Why was she brown? Why didn't her mother just have another baby of her own? The student explains, "I discovered, so did Ruth in some ways, that making race 'invisible' causes more problems than one would think. This goal is problematic because by making race 'invisible' you are ignoring reality." The student's colorblindness tested, she increasingly began to notice how her sister was treated, realizing that her sister's racial and cultural background had a significant impact on many people and that how it was read differed, depending, for example, on whether she was in a predominantly white classroom, on vacation in Mexico, or in the home of her adoptive grandparents, who made critical comments about Latinos but not specifically about their Colombian granddaughter. As the student noticed how meanings of race were contextual and established via social relations, she also considered her own race and its shifting meaning in Vermont and Mexico. Exploring questions of racial and cultural difference led her to consider issues of power and culture and to learn Spanish to prepare her to travel with her sister to South America; she concludes, "An individual needs to be willing to cross boundaries."

Students with more limited first-hand experience with interracial interactions also find themselves juggling signs that race does matter and that they and others they respect do notice it. Frankenburg's comments on colorblindness are useful: "This discursive repertoire [of colorblindness] is organized around evading difference or acknowledging it selectively, rather than literally not 'seeing' differences of race, culture, and color" (qtd. in Rains 92). In some instances students don't know where to begin; all available speech seems to threaten to trap them and expose them as racist. Describing how the racism of her grandmother's speech only became clear to her over time, one student described remaining guarded in her speech so that she herself didn't unknowingly say something racist. Students often are apologetic and describe feeling guilty, especially because for many, being guilty of racism seems to be the only alternative to being innocent. Indeed, as Rains notes, guilt can "become an immobilizer" (90). Discomfort stemming from questioning one's sense of innocence and safety occurs as white students address issues that are deeply interwoven with their identities and their senses of personal and familial history.

Another facet of my local pedagogy entails asking students how they learned about race, something that temporarily shifts some attention away from the specific beliefs they currently hold. Many students thus feel more open to exploring their ideas and experiences without assuming a defensive stance. They don't necessarily feel responsible for the messages they have received about race from others (though they do feel responsible for what they do with those messages), so they are more willing to describe their experiences, which offer the groundwork for future analysis. Ann's explanation of how she learned about race shows how the double binds of whiteness were constructed within her family.

> My grandfather had taught me that I had a reason to watch out for black people, and that they were 'under us.' My mother taught me that everyone was equal in the world, no matter what color

> they were. Naturally, I spent a good amount of time trying to understand what was right and wrong in regards to racism [. . .]. My grandfather's strong opinion about the black race and my mother's reluctance to discuss with me exactly why her father's opinions were not correct left me at a very confused stage when the time came for me to make my own decision.

Ann seems drawn to her mother's assertions of equality, in part because of a close friendship she has with an African American girl. Yet this stance conflicts with her experience within her own family because the grandfather she also loves and respects repeatedly asserts that race does matter and that white people are superior to and more trustworthy than black people like Ann's close friend. Ann's attention to her mother's silences points to a common experience of many students: what is said is inaccurate, and neither her mother's assertion (which initially seemed to offer a path to innocence, neutrality, and safety) nor her grandfather's being "guilty" of overt racism fit Ann's experience. As Welsh argues, "The places where contradiction lives are places where the encounter with difference is already nascent—where it is troubling yet most revealing of difference precisely because valued affiliations constrain the knower and constrain the rush to theorize others" (562). Exploring the sources of her discomfort allows Ann to take a step back from what functions as the double binds of whiteness, though it does not offer her a "solution" or "correct" answer, in part because she is torn between what seems logical and morally appealing to her and the emotions and memories that continue to affect her. On one hand, she explains, "I believe that people have a choice in whether or not to respond to the way in which they were raised." In the following paragraph, though, she concludes, "[M]y grandfather's views have stuck in the back of my head. No matter how hard people try to develop their own ideas, sometimes the things they learn in childhood will stick with them, even if it is just in their subconscious." Ann's essay engages what Welsh (drawing on Ellsworth's work) terms a pedagogy of the unknowable; that is, Ann begins to "accep[t] the impasse of understanding, the intransigence of some contradictions, and the productivity of efforts to make them visible" (570).

When white students write critically and analytically about race, they are being asked to decenter themselves by exploring their positions, thereby challenging the perception of their own neutrality and innocence. As one white student explains, "Every individual is different, but seems to think that they are the 'normal being' and going about life as if there were nothing different." When innocence is challenged, being guilty of racism might seem the only white identity available, and so some students respond with frustration, asserting that they are being treated unfairly. Within a framework of colorblindness in which all people are the same (and privilege and power are erased), white students' sense of being victims emerges in the context of references to affirmative action, especially in college admissions (which they sometimes term reverse discrimination); in the context of perceived restrictions on their speech ("Why is it OK for African Americans to use the term 'nigger' if it's not OK for white people to use?" they ask); and occasionally in references to organizations that they believe—usually incorrectly—are exclusively for people of color (what would happen if I wanted to form a group for whites, they ask, how do you think that would look?). Although some white students express vague sympathy for affirmative action, those who are most vocal about this policy, usually white men, assert that even if it made sense at one time, because "things have changed now" it is no longer needed and thus is unfair to whites. When I hear references to white people as victims, I am tempted to get on my moral high horse: can't they see any irony in expressing worries that people of color are taking all "their" jobs and "their" spots in college as we sit in a predominantly white classroom on a predominantly white campus? Yet I realize that to do so would both efface the details of their varied experiences, thereby essentializing them, and construct a hierarchy in which knowledge is stable and flows only in one direction. Many factors influence students' perception of white victimhood: an uncertain economy, media that frequently equate affirmative action with quotas, limited background regarding the impact of inequalities on the present day, and a feeling of disorientation as attention is drawn to whiteness. A mix of accurate and inaccurate information, both public and private; strong emotions, often anger, confusion, and frustration; and appeals to fairness and rights all have an impact on their verbal and written responses. One white student writes,

> How can this be true, that whites have such a great advantage over everyone, when we constantly have to censor ourselves when around people of a different ethnic background? Isn't it actually a form of oppression that we are perpetually forced to apologize for wrongs that white people (who have nothing to do with me) have done to minorities in the past?

Discussions of affirmative action[4] and white privilege are challenging because they tend to tap into three of my white students' most deeply held beliefs: that the United States is a meritocracy that rewards all individuals' hard work; that their identity is individual and can be chosen and shaped by them alone; and that they are not affected by history or racism.

Engaging with these issues seems to work best when we examine specific examples of individuals' experiences, as opposed to more overtly theoretical articles. In addition to drawing on memoirs such as McBride's and Lazarre's, I turn to essays in *How Race Is Lived in America,* a collection that is especially helpful because it uses current examples yet frames them historically and, to a lesser extent, theoretically. Amy Harmon's essay, "A Limited Partnership," for example, explores the collaboration of a black man and a white man on a start-up Internet company in Atlanta. She addresses the impact of race on the partners' business and interactions, especially when they seek financing for the new company or decide which partner will be named CEO. Concrete examples like this illuminate the complexities of white privilege and offer students the chance to consider both the possibilities and challenges of interrupting it. It is useful for students both to consider what a white person—in this case the white partner in the firm—might do to challenge racism and white privilege and to consider the limits of what can be accomplished on an individual level. After discussing an essay like Harmon's, students are more willing to explore Peggy McIntosh's well-known essay on white privilege, "White Privilege: Unpacking the Invisible Knapsack."

Some students quickly identify experiences with white privilege in their own lives, sometimes noting how the rhetoric of colorblindness has obscured white privilege and has made it seem natural or neutral. Jane writes in part,

> In a way I wish that my mother had been more open with me about the issue of race from the start and not just tell me that everyone was the same no matter what [. . .]. I found it hard, later in life, to accept the fact that people are not always the same and that they do not all have the same values and outlook to life that I do. Even though I was taught that I was no different than anyone else, there was still an understanding, especially in my community, that I was the average and ideal. I graduated in a class of ninety-one, and in my class there were only two people from different races. At times I could see these two people being treated inferior to the rest of us in class. My paper could be late and no repercussions would follow, but if their papers were late there was no grace for them. Though the idea of white privilege was never verbally said directly to me, it was just understood that I had white privilege.

Other students react with frustration and anger when we discuss white privilege, arguing that it oversimplifies the experiences of white people in this country, particularly those of the working poor. One white student whose family had emigrated from Ireland (where they worked as farmers) offered this response to McIntosh's article on white privilege: "Although I can understand white privilege to some extent, I also feel like I know what it's like on the other side of the fence, for those who do not get those supposed 'privileges.' I have also experienced both receiving 'white privilege' and what it's like to see that privilege given to somebody else because of their social status." Rob's comments highlight the fact that no category of identity is experienced in isolation and that class is often overlooked. He offers a useful reminder that whiteness and white privilege are not interchangeable concepts, and his essay encourages us to think more about "the changing meaning of whiteness for young, working-class Whites" (Kincheloe and Steinberg 184). Drawing on texts such as Noel Ignatiev's *How the Irish Became White* or Matthew Frye Jacobson's *Whiteness of a Different Color: European Immigrants and the Alchemy of Race* can offer an important historical perspective to the questions of class and white privilege raised by students.

Beneath the frustration and disorientation that emerge for some white students as they talk and write about race lies a real concern regarding their identities, a concern that is especially pressing for traditionally college-aged students. Those who try to break out of the innocent/guilty double bind often feel trapped by lack of information and opportunity. As one white student wrote, "As a teenager trying to find an identity of some kind, I wrestled with my own heritage and how that impacted my daily life. But being white in a school with almost no diversity meant being like everybody else." To some extent, students' statements that they prefer not to identity themselves as white but rather as German or German American can be seen as sidestepping the issue of race; yet some students adopt this approach, at least in part, in order to consider how their identities are more than simply white, a category they see associated only with oppression. I sometimes draw on Mary Waters's essay "Optional Ethnicities: For Whites Only?" to explore similarities and differences that emerge in the experiences of white students and students of color during adolescence as questions of identity and discrimination grow more pressing.

Although white students begin by reflecting on their experiences with people of color, in so doing they are exploring their own identities. Many white students who describe interracial friendships haven't thought much about how race affects their friends or themselves. One white student describes an African American friend, one of three students of color at the high school, in this way:

> I never thought of her as different from anyone else in the school, even though she was the only black girl in our class. She talked the same, acted the same, and dressed the same way anyone else did [. . .]. Because our school was almost all-white, we presumed that almost all black people grew up in a broken home in poor neighborhoods, and used slang when they talked, listened to rap, and dressed a certain way. Of course this was not the case with the few black people that went to our school because their upbringing was just like ours. They were just like us. They wore preppy clothes, came from nice neighborhoods, talked proper English, and listened to various types of music.

In other cases, reactions to interracial relationships do challenge a white student's identity. One student began his essay by asking what it might mean to "understand being white without being racist." He seemed frustrated that the perimeters of his world were narrowed by his stereotypes of people of color. Growing up in a predominantly white community in New Jersey, he had limited contact with people of color, although that changed when he moved to a more racially diverse environment in high school. He explained that before he met Jon, his first close African American friend, "I would have been hesitant to be myself around people who didn't look like me because I was afraid of ridicule. I was worried that people would only see me as sheltered and narrow-minded white person. Basically, I was afraid that people of different races would stereotype me the way I did them." The change brought about by means of his relationship with Jon meant reconsidering his own racial identity, a process that entailed moving away from safety and familiarity:

> From my interactions with Jon I lost all preconceptions of my own white identity and started over. I interrupted the racial connection I had with my community, friends, and family and learned to identify with morality. I was never lacking good morals or etiquette, but I knew there was more that I could exemplify, more than just the color of my skin, the way I talked or the way I dressed. The white privileges that I had taken for granted for so long were now more apparent to me.

Recognizing how privilege works in his life does not mean that this student equates a white person with being racist or simply being the beneficiary of white privilege. As he concludes his paper, he still seems to be exploring the something "more" his identity might represent.

Conclusion

Local pedagogies are based upon respect for students, their experiences, and their creativity. They emerge via experimentation based upon a critical engagement with place and a careful listening that recognizes that all knowledge is partial, and that, as Ann's essay suggested, silences require as much attention as disclosures, which are themselves always partial, to employ a term that Welsh and Ellsworth (in her essay "Why Doesn't This Feel Empowering?") use to describe a pedagogy of the unknowable. A local pedagogy of the sort I have outlined above helps students to explore what Welsh terms the "places of lived contradiction," rather than encouraging them to arrive at unitary resolutions (562). At its root, this work engages with ethical questions to which both students and instructors might be tempted to seek conclusive answers. Yet, as noted previously, discursive frameworks based upon dichotomies such as innocence and guilt offer false resolutions that misrepresent the complexities of students' experiences and their multiple strategies for understanding and responding to those experiences, and they efface the multiple contexts of shifting knowledge.

If we approach morality and ethics by seeking to understand the consequences of our actions and responding accordingly, then we are freed to explore students' narratives of those experiences rather than facing, confronting, and rediscovering "correct" conclusions. And this, I believe, is ultimately the most effective way to approach the teaching of race, critical thinking, and writing. As Catherine Fox argues, "adopting the pragmatic insistence that 'meaning resides in consequences' [Ronald and Roskelly 614], we might begin by positing critical thinking as what examines the consequences of our choices and the locations from which we make them, not what suggests the relative correctness of choices and locations" (204). An effective local pedagogy for teaching race, critical thinking, and writing asks both instructors and students to confront their own positions at the same time that they recognize that the consequences that emerge from the local are themselves always shifting. This approach challenges instructors and students to think more critically as they reflect carefully on their positions and on the consequences of their assumptions, actions, and inaction.[5]

Notes

1. According to the registrar's office, 7.7 percent of students are minority Americans: 2.5 percent are African American, 1.9 percent are Asian American, 2.0 percent are Hispanic American, .4 percent are Native American, and .9 percent are other minority Americans. For the 2002–3 academic year, tuition and fees are $28,500.

2. All students quoted in this essay have given me written permission to quote from their writing. All names are pseudonyms.

3. With few exceptions, the students in the writing classes I have taught at Susquehanna have identified themselves as white. Our readings and class discussions, of course, do not focus exclusively on whiteness, although that work is the focus of my analysis in this essay.

4. Patrick Bruch and Richard Marback argue that the rhetoric that has historically framed discussions of affirmative action has tended to ignore how the country has been and continues to be structured according to white privilege. Rights rhetoric, they assert, has "simultaneously advocated for inclusion and resisted confronting the conditions and legacies of exclusion" (656). Both "civil rights and affirmative action rhetorics [have] defined the meaning of racial equality [. . .] in terms of realizing the universal potential of human ability, rather than in terms of dismantling the racist dynamics of American society" (657).

5. I wish to thank Susan Naomi Bernstein, University of Cincinnati; James Black, Susquehanna University; and Ann Green, Saint Joseph's University, for their encouragement and feedback on earlier drafts of this essay. I am also grateful for the revision suggestions I received from Tom Fox and anonymous *College English* reviewers.

Works Cited

Barry, Dan. "As Diversity Sweeps Nation, a Placid Town Is Unchanged." *New York Times* 4 May 2001: A1+.

Bruch, Patrick, and Richard Marback. "Race, Literacy, and the Value of Rights Rhetoric in Composition Studies." *College Composition and Communication* 53 (2002): 651–74.

Carter, Robert T. "Is White a Race? Expressions of White Racial Identity." Fine et al. 198–209.

Ellsworth, Elizabeth. "Double Binds of Whiteness." Fine et al. 259–69.

———. "Why Doesn't This Feel Empowering? Working through the Repressive Myths of Critical Pedagogy." *The Education Feminist Reader.* New York: Routledge, 1994. 300–27.

Fine, Michelle, Lois Weis, Linda C. Powell, and L. Mun Wong, eds. *Off-White: Readings on Race, Power, and Society.* New York: Routledge, 1996.

Fox, Catherine. "The Race to Truth: Disarticulating Critical Thinking from Whiteliness." *Pedagogy* 2 (2002): 197–212.

Frankenburg, Ruth. "The Mirage of Unmarked Whiteness." Rasmussen et al. 72–96.

Gallagher, Charles A. "Redefining Racial Privilege in the United States." *Transformations* 8 (1997): 28–39.

Green, Ann E. "'But You Aren't White': Racial Perceptions and Service-Learning." *Michigan Journal of Community Service Learning* 8 (2001): 18–26.

Harmon, Amy. "A Limited Partnership." *How Race Is Lived in America: Pulling Together, Pulling Apart.* Ed. Joseph Lelyveld. New York: Times, 2001. 79–95.

Hartigan, John, Jr. *Racial Situations: Class Predicaments of Whiteness in Detroit.* Princeton: Princeton UP, 1999.

———. "'White Devils' Talk Back: What Antiracists Can Learn from Whites in Detroit." Rasmussen et al. 138–66.

hooks, bell. "Representing Whiteness in the Black Imagination." *Cultural Studies.* Ed. Lawrence Grossberg, Cary Nelson, and Paula Treichler. New York: Routledge, 1992. 338–46.

Ignatiev, Noel. *How the Irish Became White.* New York: Routledge, 1995.

Jacobson, Matthew Frye. *Whiteness of a Different Color: European Immigrants and the Alchemy of Race.* Cambridge, MA: Harvard UP, 1998.

Kincheloe, Joe L. "The Struggle to Define and Reinvent Whiteness: A Pedagogical Analysis." *College Literature* 26 (1999): 162–94.

Kincheloe, Joe L., and Shirley Steinberg. "Constructing a Pedagogy of Whiteness for Angry White Students." *Dismantling White Privi-*

lege: Pedagogy, Politics, and Whiteness. Ed. Nelson M. Rodriguez and Leila E. Villaverde. New York: Peter Lang, 2000. 178–97.

Kincheloe, Joe L., Shirley R. Steinberg, Nelson M. Rodriguez, and Ronald E. Chennault, eds. *White Reign: Deploying Whiteness in America*. New York: St. Martin's, 1998.

Lazarre, Jane. *Beyond the Whiteness of Whiteness: Memoir of a White Mother of Black Sons*. Durham, NC: Duke UP, 1996.

Marshall, Ian, and Wendy Ryden. "Interrogating the Monologue: Making Whiteness Visible." *College Composition and Communication* 52 (2000): 240–59.

McBride, James. *The Color of Water: A Black Man's Tribute to His White Mother.* New York: Riverhead, 1996.

McCarthy, Cameron. "Living with Anxiety: Race and the Renarration of Public Life." Kincheloe et al. 328–41.

McIntosh, Peggy. "White Privilege: Unpacking the Invisible Knapsack." *Race: An Anthology in the First Person*. Ed. Bart Schneider. New York: Three Rivers, 1997. 120–26.

McIntyre, Alice. *Making Meaning of Whiteness: Exploring Racial Identity with White Teachers*. Albany: SUNY P, 1997.

Pascarella, Ernest T., Betsy Palmer, Melinda Moye, and Christopher T. Piersen. "Do Diversity Experiences Influence the Development of Critical Thinking?" *Journal of College Student Development* 42 (2001): 257–71.

Paul, Richard, and Linda Elder. "The Elements of Critical Thinking (Helping Students Assess Their Thinking)." *Teaching Developmental Writing: Background Readings*. Ed. Susan Naomi Bernstein. Boston: Bedford, 2001. 177–80.

Perry, Pamela. *Shades of Whiteness: White Kids and Racial Identity in High School*. Durham, NC: Duke UP, 2002.

Rains, Frances V. "Is the Benign Really Harmless? Deconstructing Some 'Benign' Manifestations of Operationalized White Privilege." Kincheloe et al. 77–107.

Rasmussen, Birgit Brander, Eric Klinenberg, Irene J. Nexica, and Matt Wray, eds. *The Making and Unmaking of Whiteness*. Durham, NC: Duke UP, 2001.

Rodriguez, Nelson M. "Emptying the Content of Whiteness: Toward an Understanding of the Relation between Whiteness and Pedagogy." Kincheloe et al. 31–62.

———. "Projects of Whiteness in a Critical Pedagogy." *Dismantling White Privilege: Pedagogy, Politics, and Whiteness*. Ed. Nelson M. Rodriguez and Leila E. Villaverde. New York: Peter Lang, 2000. 1–24.

Ronald, Kate, and Hephzibah Roskelly. "Untested Feasibility: Imagining the Pragmatic Possibility of Paulo Freire." *College English* 63 (2001): 612–32.

Rothenberg, Paula. *Invisible Privilege: A Memoir about Race, Class, and Gender*. Lawrence: UP of Kansas, 2000.

Skorczewski, Dawn. "'Everybody Has Their Own Ideas': Responding to Cliché in Student Writing." *College Composition and Communication* 52 (2000): 220–35.

Tatum, Beverly Daniel. *"Why Are All the Black Kids Sitting Together in the Cafeteria?" and Other Conversations about Race*. New York: Basic, 1999.

Trainor, Jennifer Seibel. "Critical Pedagogy's 'Other': Constructions of Whiteness in Education for Social Change." *College Composition and Communication* 53 (2002): 631–50.

Waters, Mary C. "Optional Ethnicities: For Whites Only?" *Rereading America: Cultural Contexts for Critical Thinking and Writing*. Ed. Gary Colombo, Robert Cullen, and Bonnie Lisle. 5th ed. Boston: Bedford, 2001. 642–52.

Welsh, Susan. "Resistance Theory and Illegitimate Reproduction." *College Composition and Communication* 52 (2001): 553–73.

Wildman, Stephanie M., with Adrienne D. Davis. "Making Systems of Privilege Visible." *White Privilege: Essential Readings on the Other Side of Racism*. Ed. Paula S. Rothenberg. New York: Worth, 2002. 89–95.

Chapter Nineteen

Becoming Visible: Lessons in Disability

Brenda Jo Brueggemann, Linda Feldmeier White, Patricia A. Dunn, Barbara A. Heifferon, and Johnson Cheu

We have been puzzled by how hard it has been to get to this "visible" moment. This struggle to get over, around, and through the multiple intellectual and physical barriers we felt were still strongly in place around our profession became the subject of passionate discussion at the 1999 "Teaching about/with Disability SIG" held during the Atlanta CCCC Convention, the theme of which was "Visible Students, Visible Teachers." Late on a Thursday evening, some forty people—double and then quadruple the numbers that had attended the 1997 and 1998 SIGs respectively—filled the room.[1] All were deeply concerned about the "visibility" of disability at CCCC.

Disability studies activists and scholars talk and write a lot about "visibility." It concerns them because even at the dawn of this brave new millennium disabled people still aren't very visible in our culture. There are, according to one recent estimate, 56 million Americans with a disability, a stunning one-half of whom are underemployed or unemployed (and this in a currently thriving employment environment).[2] But as one student in my freshman composition class last spring finally asked me, point-blank—"You've said that several times now—that there are about 56 million Americans with disabilities. Then why don't we ever *see* any of them?" If you want to cast a quick glance around any meeting room at a CCCC Convention—or just your own class-

From *College Composition and Communication* 52 (2001): 368–98.

rooms at your own institutions—you'll quickly understand why he would ask this question; you'll *see* what is meant by the *invisibility of disability.*

But then again, you won't. This is the paradox of visibility, another of disability culture's great concerns: *now you see us; now you don't.* Many of us "pass" for able-bodied—we appear before you unclearly marked, fuzzily apparent, our disabilities *not* hanging out all over the place. We are sitting next to you. No, we *are* you. As the saying goes in disability circles these days: "If we all live long enough, we'll all be disabled. We are all TABs—temporarily able-bodied." We are as invisible as we are visible. And it is only in often having to claim the rights that are due to us, to gain the access we are equal to, to enter the public space we are guaranteed, that we uncloak ourselves, turn "passing" into "outing," turn discreditability into discredit (in Erving Goffman's terms for the assignation of *stigma*); it is in no less than a civil rights frame that we become fully visible.

Another concern lies in the metaphor of visibility to begin with—in the very ways that the language we and our students use is laden with metaphors of ability. Not that we would want to police the propriety of sight equaling insight; the political power gained with "visibility" in our culture; the importance of "hearing others' voices"; the meaning of "throwing our own voices," "turning deaf ears," or coming up with "lame ideas." To do so would pretty much have emptied out the 1999 CCCC's program book, which was overladen with these very metaphors. But disability studies does invite us all to at least consider the able-bodied agenda lurking in the way we make meaning through so many crippling metaphors, in the way we compose and communicate that disables even as it might be attempting to "enable."

In such an honest enabling move, CCCC has recently and significantly begun to attend to the elements of access and accommodations for disabled students and teachers who want to fully, equally, meaningfully participate in its annual convention. It is only rather recently that CCCC teachers and scholars have begun to imagine richly the ways that an awareness of and attendance to disability furthers much about and in our field and our own classrooms. It is only recently that CCCC members have gathered to seriously consider the presence (and absence) of disabled students and teachers in our midst. Past CCCC Chair Cindy Selfe's response to a 1997 Sense of the House motion at the CCCC Business Meeting that asked the organization to begin including disability within its other "diversity" considerations was to put in place the Disability Issues Task Force (DITF). In addition, the 1999 Program Chair, Keith Gilyard, and his assistant, Debi Saldo, did so much to work toward an accessible convention, and they also had the insight to imagine the promise of inviting Simi Linton to take a featured place in the program. Linton's presence—her visibility, as it were—was one major mark of CCCC's recent attendance to and imagination in the realm of disability. After the publication of her book, *Claiming Disability: Knowledge and Identity,* Linton resigned her academic position as associate professor at Hunter College (in counseling and sociology) to take up full-time the work that she was increasingly being called to do anyway: that of "disability ambassador"—an activist and educator at large. Educationally, she seeks no less than a transformation of curriculum, particularly at postsecondary institutions, that would include a "disability studies perspective." This perspective, she tells us in *Claiming Disability,*

> adds a critical dimension to thinking about issues such as autonomy, competence, wholeness, independence/dependence, health, physical appearance, aesthetics, community, and notions of progress and perfection—issues that pervade every aspect of the civic and pedagogic culture. They appear as themes in literature, as variables in social and biological science, as dimensions of historical analysis, and as criteria for social policy and practice. (118)

These same issues and their appearances also, we believe, occupy a central place in our writing classrooms, in our entire college curriculums, and certainly, as we've known it in at least the last decade, in the interests of each CCCC Convention. As Simi Linton suggested during the "Teaching about/with Disability SIG" during the 1999 CCCC Convention, we are "becoming visible" by organizing here some of our presentations from the 1999 CCCC program. Our goal in this article is to move toward "enabling composition," both in our collective field and in our individual classrooms. In the four sections that follow, we argue that not only will the enabling of our pedagogy and curriculum for the college writing classroom make disabilities and people with disabilities (both students and teachers) visible, but that it will also make visible the continuum that links "abled" (or TABs, those who are "temporarily able-bodied") with "disabled" (or PWDs, "persons with disabilities").[3] With such a continuum, the us/them dichotomy that is often in place for designating and dividing disability and disabled persons disappears.

Why should these things—the attention to disability and the disappearance of such entirely unclear distinctions in the first place—matter? Issues of disability matter in composition studies and classrooms, first, because we have a long, proud history of making the invisible visible and of examining how language both reflects and supports notions of Other. We should be receptive to disability studies' powerful exposure of the dehumanizing societal constructions of disability and difference. Second, we also rightly pride ourselves on our attention to practice—and on our refusal to separate it from the theoretical assumptions that explicitly or implicitly inform it. Disability and the presence of disabled students in our writing classrooms return us squarely to issues of practice that both interrogate and enrich our theories about literacy and empowerment. Third, connected to the first two reasons, because we already challenge the binaries of theory/practice, writing/thinking, and self/other, we should be well equipped—even eager—to embrace the critique of the (false) abled/disabled binary that is articulated by disability scholars such as Simi Linton, Lennard Davis, Rosemarie Garland-Thomson, David Mitchell, and Sharon Snyder.

We can disrupt these binaries in the ways articulated by the sections that follow this opening section. As Linda White suggests, we can disrupt the "handicapped" (and handicapping) construction of "learning disability." We can also disrupt the "special privilege" myths of the learning disability backlash, as Patricia Dunn argues, at the same time we supplement writing-as-a-mode-of-learning with challenging, multi-model representations. Tapping into these multiple intellectual pathways and using what I have called "alternative formats" for teaching, learning, thinking, writing, and being in literacy, we can reach beyond the letter of the "accommodation" laws and invigorate praxis for all of us, nd TABs alike, leading us all to "disability as insight." ctment of "disability as insight," as Barbara Heifferon illustrates, using texts like Nancy Mairs's *Carnal Acts,* can disrupt societal taboos about what is or is not an acceptable coping strategy and can also resist conventional binaries regarding perfect/imperfect bodies. Exposing these constructions of "disability," by extension, disrupts other disabling myths about gender, race, class, sexual orientation, and age that limit us all. And as Johnson Cheu demonstrates, teaching a class in disability studies (within the frame of a second-level writing course) can bring us "from silence to visibility to consciousness" in ways that surprise us as well as our students. In sum, these five pieces added together make visible how reconceptualizing "disability" uncovers harmful constructions of "normal/normalcy" and has everything to do with issues of confidence, power, and identity—issues we already know affect how we write, or are written by, the world.[4]

Constructing Learning Disability

Before I had read much about learning disabilities or worked with many LD students, I would have argued for excluding them from the legal protection guaranteed students by the Americans with Disabilities Act.

I thought that LD was different from other disabilities. It was easy to see that not being able to walk could, but need not, prevent anyone from doing the work of a college student, as long as reasonable accommodations were provided. But I couldn't see what might constitute reasonable accommodation for a student with LD, since learning is the work that college students do. From my current perspective, this argument depends on a too-narrow definition of learning and intelligence, one that Patricia Dunn critiques in the next section. It is always easy to forget that tests are made, and that they are often made (constructed, manipulated, revised) to produce the "normal" distribution of the bell-shaped curve. Reasonable accommodation for LD means questioning our definitions of intelligence and questioning how integral certain teaching and testing methods truly are to higher education.

Becoming aware of the work being done in disability studies has also changed my perspective on LD. Our culture sees disability as handicap—something wrong with an individual. Disability studies makes a distinction between *impairment* and *disability*. Impairment is a physical difference—a difference in hearing, vision, mobility, brain function. Disability is more than impairment; disability is what society makes of that impairment in constructing "disability" as the opposite of something thereby recognized as "normality," part of a structure that privileges some and oppresses others (Linton 138–41).

An important insight of disability studies is that members of the helping professions have a stake in maintaining disability. As Harlan Lane comments, "the troubled-person professions serve not only their clientele but also themselves, and are actively involved in perpetuating and expanding their activities" (156). As objects of study in medical discourse, people with disabilities have been disempowered; their interests are not the same as those of the (usually nondisabled) professionals who participate in disciplinary discourse. The field of learning disability provides particularly salient examples of how attempts to "help" seem to reproduce rather than disrupt the political structures that place the disabled in subordinate positions. Since its popularization in the mid-1960s, the field of learning disability has flourished. The individuals it studies have not, despite more than thirty years of research and federal laws designed to protect them from discrimination (Gerber and Reiff 3–13).[5]

A commitment to social justice demands that we examine the way learning disability is constructed. No disability is determined by its physical components. As Linton explains, disability is a category of oppression, a political status, not a condition for an individual to overcome. She argues not for passing or overcoming, but for *claiming* disability, a move that will necessarily "disrupt the social order," as disabled people come out (from "the institutions that have confined us, the attics and basements that sheltered our family's shame, the 'special' schools and classrooms designed to solve the problems we are thought to represent") to demand an inclusive society: "We are, as Crosby, Stills, and Nash told their Woodstock audience, letting our 'freak flag fly.' And we are not only the high-toned wheelchair athletes seen in recent television ads but the gangly, pudgy, lumpy, and bumpy of us, declaring that shame will no longer structure our wardrobe or our discourse" (3–4).

Being shamed is a prominent feature in the autobiographical essays written by people with LD, whose stories provide vivid accounts of the way impairments become disabilities. Children suffer when they find out in school that they belong at the bottom of the scale, a discovery cogently described by Thomas West in *LD Online:*

> It is hard to remember any details of my earliest years—except a pervasive sense of confusion and personal failure. . . . I seemed to be at the bottom of the class or near the bottom of the class in nearly everything. In reading, writing and arithmetic I seemed to have no ability at all. I could not spell, write clearly or remember my multiplication tables. . . . I could not learn to read at all until the fourth year of primary school. . . . I always wanted to catch up with the others.[6]

When people with LD describe their experiences in school, they describe abuse and humiliation. Someone who learns to read in the fourth grade is a slow learner, not someone who learned to read in the fourth grade. Someone who cannot spell is stupid, because spelling is a basic skill, universally acquired in elementary school—even though it quite evidently is not. Children are routinely told that they will "never amount to anybody," that they are limited, stupid, hopeless—in a word, "retarded" (Westall).

The LD movement argues against this construction by establishing an identity different from mental retardation. The learning disabled have specific dysfunctions, not the pervasive cognitive impairment thought to be characteristic of mental retardation.[7] "[S]ignificant difficulties in the acquisition and use of listening, speaking, reading, writing, reasoning, or mathematical abilities," according to the National Joint Committee for Learning Disabilities definition, might "occur concomitantly with other handicapping conditions (for example, sensory impairment, mental retardation, serious emotional disturbance)" but are not the same (qtd. in Torgesen 4). LD autobiographies testify to the positive impact of this identity. Being diagnosed with LD is described as epiphany, the turning point of the story. Diagnosis initiates a transformation because when someone finds out that he has LD, he realizes that he is not stupid, limited, or lazy and thus is capable of learning, as Dirk Funk describes in this passage from the *LD Resources* web site:

> As the reality of what Dr. Williams had told me [that tests revealed dyslexia] set in it was like one of those aha experiences. The lights went back on. . . . Finally, I had an answer and a lifeline I could hold on to. It was a new direction for me. I became hyper-dedicated to succeeding at school. . . . By the time the Fall semester of the following year was over, my grade point average jumped to 3.2. I wasn't failing anymore.

To some extent, the LD movement has helped students who learn differently. By emphasizing that dysfunctions are specific, "LD" reveals abilities obscured by more pejorative constructions. Paul Orfalea, the entrepreneur who founded Kinko's, tells the story of a college professor who at first fails Orfalea for making so many spelling errors on a test. Finding out that Orfalea has LD has a dramatic effect on his assessment of Orfalea's ability: "When [the professor] found out I had LD, he announced to the class that I was 'on the brink of brilliancy' because he looked at my ideas instead of the spelling" (Orfalea).

And yet, because of the political status of disability, because the LD identity does not disrupt the basic premise that some fixed, unitary quality called "intelligence" is distributed unequally at birth, people with LD remain vulnerable. They are vulnerable to those who want to help, as long as help is provided by professionals unaware that they participate in "ableist" culture. One adult with LD remembers an experience in remedial education so abusive that it might have been invented to parody the way professions create dependency. As a junior high student, he was instructed to practice crawling as part of attempts to improve his "hand-eye coordination." He comments that he didn't mind doing the crawling exercises in the doctor's office, but that he disliked being forced to do them at home, since his brothers and their friends would see him: "They would bring their girl friends and all of them would see me doing that. . . . It was like I had to go back, I guess I felt like I was failed back to childhood" (Gerber and Reiff 191).

Learning-disabled students will remain vulnerable as long as schools are organized less to educate than to sort, a function that requires the convenient fictions of standardized testing in order to make some children Others. If schools were more inclusive, less hierarchical places, we might see reading and writing as abilities acquired at different rates and in different ways. Instead, schools pathologize difference; differences in performance are ranked, and identities assigned, so that some of us become "retarded" and "learning disabled." The boundary between "normal" and "retarded" is of great cultural importance and constantly policed. Thus, the existence of LD remains controversial and "learning disabled" is still an identity less "real" than "retarded." Even those who would dispute his views are as much aware as Massachusetts Board of Education Chair John Silber that "some of the things that pass for learning disabilities used to be called stupidity" (qtd. in Shapiro 31). As a composition teacher reading from the perspective of disability studies, I argue against such scorn for learning-disabled students, and I read their work with the ability to see myself constructing a stupid person, from marks that could have other meanings and different weight.

Analyzing the Rhetoric of the Learning Disability Backlash

The story of Somnolent Samantha is familiar to anyone who has followed the public discussion regarding disability legislation. In 1995, when Jon Westling was provost of Boston University, he gave a speech bemoaning what he saw as outrageous accommodations given to learning disabled college students: a quiet room in which to take tests; a seat in the front row; lecture notes; and—for one student who might fall asleep in class because of her disability—more time from a professor to update her on what she missed during her classroom naps. According to the *New York Times*, Westling repeated this story of a sleepy LD student he called "Somnolent Samantha" in other speeches and referred to her in a 1996 interview with that newspaper. However, in papers filed during a 1997 lawsuit brought by students against Boston University, Westling admitted that the dozing young woman he called "Somnolent Samantha" did not exist. He had made up this extreme example to make a point about college LD accommodations.

The rhetorical strategy of finding, or, if necessary, inventing, an extreme example of LD students' "demands" has become routine practice in a growing learning disability backlash. Since the passage of the Rehabilitation Act of 1973, the testing and accommodating of students with learning and other disabilities have been governed by federal law. However, it was the 1990 ADA that put physical and learning disabilities in the foreground for some Americans who never had to think about them before, including compositionists.

Of the many learning disabilities now being debated (mathematical, spatial, attention-deficit, etc.), I am focusing here on language-related ones because they cause the most anguish for students in word-loving humanities divisions, English departments, and especially composition classes. For example, college students I interviewed with language-related learning disabilities have told me that they are often made to feel stupid, lazy, or even morally degenerate because of the kinds of errors they make in their writing. However, few people in composition studies (or even disability studies, for that matter) pay much attention to learning disabilities. Or if we do pay attention, it is mostly to dismiss the whole idea or field of learning disabilities.

One reason for the near invisibility, or dismissal, of LD in composition is the highly controversial nature of LD-related research, testing, and treatment. The entire LD field has been critiqued by Gerald Coles, Barry Franklin, James Carrier, and Kenneth Kavale and Steven Forness, who argue cogently that LD research is flawed and testing for LD is inconsistent. They also critique the LD label, saying it locates "dysfunction" in a person, which blames the victim and allows the present ineffectual education system to continue.[8] Saying physical cause is unproven, and research exploring it is flawed, however, does nothing to address problems some people seem to have with writing—difficulties not fully explained by social, historical, or economic factors, or by controversial research on intelligence.[9]

A second reason for the hostility toward or dismissal of LD, and the one I examine here, is a rhetoric of difference that has shaped public attitudes toward LD students and toward nontraditional approaches used to accommodate them. Questionable rhetorical strategies, of course, can be found on both sides of the debate, but the widespread, negative reaction to disability legislation successfully employs metaphors and false dichotomies that are particularly divisive.

In their essay on environmental rhetoric, Michael Bruner and Max Oelschlaeger maintain that if an argument is to actually change people's minds or move them to act, it must "evoke sentiment" (215). In other words, the audience must feel something. Citing Richard McKeon, Bruner and Oelschlaeger also argue that if public policy is to be altered, there must be a strong, controlling metaphor or image that defines the debate. McKeon calls this transformative rhetoric "architectonic," an art so powerful it can change the structure and shape of public discussion (2).

In Jon Westling's made-up anecdote, Somnolent Samantha functioned as a powerful architectonic rhetorical device. The image of one student dozing through a lecture, only to be given a private catch-up session with the professor when she finally awoke, was designed to infuriate other students, themselves struggling to stay awake through long lectures, let alone have office-hour access to the professor. Somnolent Samantha also shifted the public's focus from controversial policies at Boston University onto one (invented) student's outrageous (albeit fictional) request. This story, with its construction of "special treatment," played to notions of "fairness" and delivered a rhetorical double punch. Setting up a false dichotomy, it positioned students against each other rather than against banking-model teaching. It also absolved professors who rely exclusively on word-based pedagogies from having to rethink their epistemological assumptions, philosophical goals, or classroom practices.

This rhetorical double punch is also seen in Mark Kelman and Gillian Lester's book, *Jumping the Queue: An Inquiry into the Legal Treatment of Students with Learning Disabilities*. They ultimately promote a teaching environment that includes all students, a recommendation with which I agree. However, their book's controlling metaphor—"jumping the queue"—is an image that depicts the LD student as somehow stealing public money for "special treatment" while so-called normal students are ignored. This metaphor also constructs "special treatment" in a way that works with cultural commonplaces that one should wait one's turn and take only one's fair share. The metaphor functions as an effective architectonic rhetorical strategy and disturbingly false dichotomy. It implies that LD students are jumping the queue, cutting the line, pushing patient, suffering, "average kids" out of the way and into the shadows while they, waving their LD label, rush to the front to grab an oversized piece of a shrinking pie. "Special treatment" is being successfully posited in this controversy as "unfair" advantage for one group of people: those labeled LD. In a review of the Kelman and Lester book in the March 1998 *Lingua Franca,* S. D. Metcalf accepts without question the "special treatment" construction in the "jumping the queue" metaphor. He sympathizes with "beleaguered public school administrators" who reportedly complain of "children willfully malingering to land special perks" (64).[10]

In the 6 August 1999 issue of the *Chronicle of Higher Education,*Wendy M. Williams and Stephen J. Ceci argue that accommodations for learning-disabled students are "unfair advantages" that "shortchange other students" (B4–5). This opinion piece triggered 75 responses in the *Chronicle's* online Colloquy, one of which said, "This talk of learning disability is all smoke and mirrors" (Wolf). Responding to the same article were seven lengthy letters to the editor in the September 24 issue of the *Chronicle.* Emotions ran high on both sides, with one letter writer using the phrase "special privileges" as a synonym for accommodations, calling them "a scam, a breach of academic integrity, and a fraud" (Katz B5).

Variations on this theme can also be found in popular magazines. In a September 1998 *Time* magazine feature article entitled "Lost in the Middle," so-called average students are depicted as "pay[ing] the price" for special education programs. One mother is quoted as saying, "If I could give him a label, I know there would be all sorts of extra help for him" (Ratnesar 60). Not mentioned in this parent's lament nor anywhere else in the four-page *Time* article is an alternative view of what "special assistance" and "extra help" often mean in a system where difference is not celebrated but condemned, and where not-so-coveted labels accompany the LD label. Even in this *Time* article, for example, the terms "slow learners" and "misbehaving problem children" were routinely used as synonyms for learning-disabled students.[11]

Why does all this matter to compositionists? Those who criticize the LD field are right that the problems LD students experience are partly the result of how society constructs "disability" and "difference." And the LD label may be implicated in causing that which it problematically names.

However, "disability" is also a result of the way in which most intellectual tasks in composition classes are pursued. Different academic fields, of course, construct intelligence in different ways, valuing whatever talents are most useful in their particular disciplines. Science and technology schools may privilege mathematical or logical ways of knowing, and the arts may stress a visual or kinesthetic ability. But in English departments and composition classes, what counts is a facility for reading and writing texts.

Granted, a writing class must be about writing. But composition professionals may, unwittingly, be privileging a way of knowing with which we ourselves are most comfortable, perhaps not realizing that our students have other talents we might use even as we teach writing. We may, unwittingly, play a part in disabling some of our best thinkers by overusing one pathway—writing—in the many intellectual tasks leading up to a finished piece: written journals, written peer responses, freewriting, written proposals or outlines, written e-mail discussions, and so on.

Very few of us compositionists are language "learning disabled." We chose this field for its intrinsic, if not financial, reward of what we probably do very well. But many of our students would gladly avoid composition classes because they fear any difficulties they have with writing will (once again) be interpreted as intellectual or moral flaws. If people who do not write in technically correct prose were not so thoroughly humiliated in so many implicit and explicit ways in the first place, there would be less need for LD-related legislation that, though problematic, was intended to address some of these issues.

Now, however, composition professionals are in a unique position to take advantage of multiple talents and ways of knowing. For decades we have spoken about "writing" as learning. We know that writing is about complex intellectual processes. We know that writing is intimately connected with issues of authority, identity, power, and confidence, and that if students are to become more sophisticated thinkers and writers, they should be both challenged and taken seriously. The rhetoric of the learning disability backlash interferes with this critical dynamic between writer and reader, between student and teacher, by introducing stereotype into the equation.

Michael Bérubé, in describing how people sometimes cannot conceive of a Down syndrome child as an individual, uses Wittgenstein's concept of "seeing *as*" as opposed to "seeing." "'Seeing-as' is not a part of perception. And for this reason it is *like* seeing, and then again *not* like" (xii). In *Life As We Know It,* Bérubé uses this concept in describing how people do not see the individual child who has Down syndrome; they see only the child as a Down syndrome child, as a stereotype. They do not *see.* They *see as.*

Similarly, the prevailing metaphors about LD students work by preventing us from seeing individuals. These false analogies force us to see these students only as lazy learners, line jumpers, and pie gobblers. The emotions evoked here are righteousness, anger, and fear— rhetorical enzymes strong enough to force people to act. In this case, this architectonic rhetoric functions as an attempt to change public policy back to thinking LD students are, after all, just lazy and stupid. This is ironic, of course, since the general public never really stopped thinking of them in any ways other than negative.

My purpose here is not to defend the LD label, or tests for LD, or LD research—though all three have implications for composition studies that too many of us are rejecting out of hand because the methodological or epistemological assumptions supporting them conflict with our own. As Linda White explained in the previous section, every issue in the LD controversy is a complex one, fraught with constructed assumptions of difference. Yes, tests for LD are not clear-cut, and anecdotal abuses of this legislation are not difficult to find (or invent). And yes, there are substantial educational resources at stake in schools and universities.

But dehumanizing metaphors and false analogies eventually harm everyone by supporting a business-as-usual pedagogy that legitimates only one way of knowing in writing classes—that makes learning too frustrating for some and too easy for others. We need to supplement writing-centered instruction, even in our writing classes, not only because people do make knowledge in different ways, but also because everyone can benefit from occasionally using nonwriting strategies to alter perspectives and create the intellectual distance needed for sophisticated revising. The system needs to change not because some people are labeled LD but in spite of it. Those called "normal" also learn along a continuum of difference and would be better challenged if classrooms became more interactive, student-centered, multimodal, and collaborative.

"Learning disability" matters in composition because of the critical questions it raises about *our* preferred mode of learning—writing—as an effective intellectual pathway for everyone. "Learning disability" also matters in composition because of the questions it raises about constructions of difference in society, and constructions of difference in our composition theories. I propose a shift in theoretical assumptions about "writing" and an exploration of classroom practices that challenge received (but usually unspoken) assumptions in composition regarding intelligence and writing ability. Expectations, assignments, and assessments will re-emerge after teacher-researchers reflect seriously on that theoretical shift.

Here are just a few examples. If a course requires reading logs or dialogue journals, every student might be asked to produce both oral and written ones—perhaps alternating the format throughout the semester. Good writers who might have difficulty organizing their thoughts orally, without first writing them down, would be challenged to do so. Those dynamic students who contribute much to the quality of class discussions—but who sometimes are not the best writers—would be recognized for their verbal contributions. If written proposals, outlines, or early drafts are required for inquiry-based papers, students might also experiment with drawing, sculpting, or dramatizing the plan. Being asked to conceptualize a project from a different perspective can trigger new insights for all writers, helping us generate connections we might not have made in word-locked prose.

When we ask all students to tap into multiple pathways to generate and rethink their ideas, we disrupt constructions of "normal," we broaden notions of "writing," and we bracket off some of the petty, hateful aspects of the disability debate—both sides of it. When we expect all students—and ourselves—to think in oral, visual, and kinesthetic arenas, in addition to the ones that privilege written words, we learn from those who were previously excluded. What is more, when we disrupt our own comfort with writing as a way of knowing, we problematize our assumptions, tilt our perspectives, and recast our metaphors. This discomfiture will invigorate the teaching, learning, and writing in our classrooms and in our lives.

In a field that rightly prides itself on its self-reflective praxis, we in composition should become especially aware of cultural biases supporting limited definitions of "writing" in composition. With our analytic skills in language, we should problematize limited constructions of "special treatment," "disability," and other key phrases in the LD controversy. Analyzing the rhetoric of language and learning used in public debates (or perhaps in our own syllabus) can help us to learn about—and challenge—harmful metaphors, false dichotomies, and stifling cultural assumptions about writers and writing.

Making Disability Visible to Students

As composition professionals we are in a unique position to challenge pervasive and misguided assumptions about disability. I argue here that introducing disability texts into the classroom not only makes disability visible but also empowers students to see that "writing is intimately connected with issues of authority, identity, power, and confidence," as Patricia Dunn indicates in the previous section. She goes on to state that "if students are to become more sophisticated thinkers and writers, they should be both challenged and taken seriously." In this section I show how introducing a text written by a differently abled writer challenged students in exactly the way Dunn advocates. Although the text centers on physical disability rather than learning disabilities, what students experienced writing in response to the text clearly demonstrates this intimate connection writing has "with issues of authority, identity, power, and confidence."

One way to move past the disabling and disenfranchising labels examined above as well as the invisibility of differently abled persons is to debunk concepts of "normalcy" and "ideal bodies" in the classroom. Traditional students are most prone to such constructions of people and bodies, given their developmental stage of late adolescence. In this section I examine a particular case of introducing a disability text into the composition classroom. The description constitutes a reflection on what happened in a particular classroom, relying both on memory and the final essay exams written in the class. However, preliminary observation could suggest future questions for researchers, such as the following: (1) Does introducing disability texts into the classroom raise awareness and increase visibility of differently abled people? (2) Do disability texts in particular challenge students' conceptions of "authority, identity, power, and confidence"? and (3) Are there gender differences in reactions to disability texts?

Again to situate this classroom description, we can point to the increasing acceptance of teacher research within our discipline. Teacher research "is not designed to investigate cause and effect; instead it aims to describe, as fully as possible, what happened in one teaching situation" (MacNealy 243). This definition also frames what I do here, giving a limited description of the teaching situation within our page limitations. To summarize the situation, in the fall semester of 1996 the University of Arizona composition program gave a common final for all 130 sections of its first-semester, first-year composition classes. All of us teaching sections of 101 were to give our students a copy of Nancy Mairs's essay "Carnal Acts" to read and discuss before the final.

In "Carnal Acts," Tucson writer Nancy Mairs responds to a request from a student at a small liberal arts college at which she has a speaking engagement to discuss "how you cope with your MS disability, and also how you discovered your voice as a writer" (81). Mairs reviews the intimate details of how multiple sclerosis has affected her body and her sense of self, and she concludes that she cannot remain politely silent on such details if she is to write as a woman who has experienced birth, love, and disease. The intimate writing that she shares with her readers is what she ironically calls a "carnal act." Drawing on her own experiences, Mairs raises basic questions about living and writing; she uses research and her knowledge of feminist writers to develop her perceptions. As a woman who is physically challenged, Mairs confronts issues such as disability labels, stereotyping, and cultural biases toward the differently abled body.

In the essay, Mairs goes into explicit detail, especially after her failed suicide attempt from which her husband, George, rescues her. Her descriptions of her body and her honesty about being unable at times to cope with her disease are about as graphic as any text you can read. She doesn't make it pretty (and this is one of the milder passages) as she talks about a body "which trips you even when you're watching where you're going, knocks glassware out of your hand, squeezes the urine out of your bladder before you reach the bathroom, and weighs your whole body with a weariness no amount of rest can relieve" (83).

When the director of composition announced this text as a final, I wondered if this work would demand too much maturity from our students, most of whom were eighteen years old, from Southern California, and often attracted to University of Arizona's reputation as an affordable party school with beautiful coeds. (This description is not the official one in *Peterson's,* but it can be found in some of the more student-centered guides.)

But I trusted our director's judgment and looked forward to the days of discussion just prior to the final. I had expected emotional responses to Mairs's work, but was surprised at certain phenomena I observed. In the often heated and vehement student-led discussion about this work, I saw clear gender splits. The young women in the class were clearly moved by Mairs's words and were sympathetic and empathetic, and young male students were outraged, not just "grossed out" by descriptions of body functions and other things that go awry in MS, but angry, furious, livid in the classroom. One young male exclaimed in his final essay, "[This is] everything you don't want to hear." Other young men said that they were "uncomfortable" reading the text and wondered if she wrote it in order to "shock the reader."

Our composition curriculum calls for a hands-off approach to this classroom discussion prior to the final, so that we are not in effect "teaching the final." But in this case, I felt some direction might be necessary. I followed my instincts to intervene when the voices in the classroom became overwhelming to the degree that students could no longer hear each other because everyone was talking at once. I suggested to my students that we rhetorically analyze the phenomenon we saw happening before us and make use of this teachable moment. What was it about disability issues in general, whether LD or physical disability, and Mairs's MS in particular that caused young women to react with such empathy and young men (for the most part) to react with such anger? Well, that question certainly shut down discussion for a few minutes. I then backed up and said I was not blaming men for reacting this way—I just wanted to understand why. I suggested that they take their anger into the finals, citing passages that repulsed them and arguing in a rhetorical analysis or writing personally in a reader response why Mairs did not reach her audience. Anger, any emotion in fact, is an excellent catalyst for writing well because students are engaged and motivated. As Dunn points out, Bruner and Oelschlaeger suggest that cogent arguments must also "evoke sentiment" in order to change minds (215). On the final exams, male students wrote about their initial reactions to Mairs's text with such terms and comments as: "lurid," "not easy to read," "offensive," "anger," "mad," and "reading those words infuriated me."

I tried to put myself into the shoes/often sandals in Arizona of the young men in my class. One of the issues I discovered by looking at their verbal and written reactions was that they were outraged at the schism between the idealized body image of women they see projected in the culture and the body image Mairs wrote about. Their reactions then generated another question for future research: Do male reactions hinge on the idealization of women's bodies? They were equally outraged by her admission of self-doubt, weakness, and disability. These young men are barely out of puberty at eighteen, still in it in many cases, just achieving sexual maturity or striving to. One male student writes:

"At [this] point in my life, I [am] entering the transition state of moving from boyhood to manhood." Another male student writes, "This [separation between the mind and body] is largely due to social views of what the ideal person should be: able in both mind and body. . . . [P]eople in our society are expected to be both mentally and physically desirable." Their fantasies are based on women projected by our popular media, a media that offers no alternatives to the Barbie doll ideal, a totalizing gesture that wipes difference from our cultural map, rendering it invisible. As Susan Bordo documents in *Unbearable Weight: Feminism, Western Culture, and the Body,* "the vulnerability of men and boys to popular imagery, the contribution of their desires and anxieties, the pressures thus brought to bear on girls and women" are the fallout from the constructs our culture has created around youth and ideal bodies (46).

Mairs articulates the pressures on her as a female in this culture: "I was never a beautiful woman, and for that reason I've spent most of my life (together with probably at least 95 percent of the female population of the United States) suffering from the shame of falling short of an unattainable standard" (87). When Mairs makes the invisible visible, she creates an emotional as well as intellectual dissonance for these young men. They see women as idealized sexual objects, while Mairs presents a real woman, one who bleeds, one who drops things and struggles to cope on a day-to-day basis. Many young male students form identities based on their own strong, healthy bodies, and because they are young and abled, their initial response to a disabled woman's body is an angry one.

The author challenged us to *see* ourselves beyond the packaged images that our culture sells us. As Bordo also articulates, "in our present culture of mystification—a culture which continually pulls us away from systemic understanding and inclines us toward constructions that emphasize individual freedom, choice, power, ability—simply becoming *more conscious* is a tremendous achievement" (30; emphasis in original). Mairs's essay succeeded in making such constructions more conscious and in increasing awareness.

In the finals, I thought I would get the same angry male responses as in class discussion. I told students in advance that I would not penalize them for writing against the grain as well as reading against the grain. Instead, their responses surprised me. I realized the young men had processed their dismay and gotten underneath and beyond it after the initial shock. The class discussion seemed to help them process the initial anger and move them from outrage to more awareness of and acceptance of difference. Not only did Mairs succeed in coming to voice herself in her essay, but she also succeeded in enabling young men who are still discouraged from expressing feelings to do so in response. Those feelings shifted dramatically, and that change was reflected in the final essays.

To illustrate the most articulate change in a male student's perception, here is part of one young man's final essay in which he wrote about his father's death: "When Mairs spoke of coping with her illness in the beginning of the essay, she said, 'In these terms, I have to confess, I don't feel like much of a coper' (82). Reading those words infuriated me!" This student initially responds angrily to Mairs's text and must challenge his assumptions of an idealized picture of strength and the ability to cope. Later in his essay, this same student identified with Mairs when she admitted she did in fact cope and did so "by speaking about it" (91). Mairs helped this student find his own voice by speaking the unspeakable.

> For me speaking about my father's passing would be too traumatic right now. Until this semester I'd never even written about it, but now I'm glad that I finally did. I found solace in writing about my dad, and when I was through writing about his death, I felt as though a weight had been lifted off of my shoulders.

This student, like Mairs, found that bringing the unspeakable to the foreground helped him to understand that he did not need to embrace the idealized model of masculinity (strong, silent type) along with the idealized model of femininity. Instead, the disability text opened up an opportunity for him to express his own grief and loss. The introduction of her honest text and the chance to write in response to that honesty reinforce our notions that writing is closely linked to how we form our identities. Having to confront the toughest issues through writing empowers students and increases their confidence, because they find that they can meet the emotional challenges that will confront them as they move from a teen's perspective to an adult's perspective.

Texts on disability, honest, real, open texts such as Mairs's essay, have a valuable place in the writing classroom, particularly in a culture that continually blasts the able-bodied, idealized, and commodified body into our eyes and ears, and in a culture that often denies men the right to express their innermost feelings. I doubt a tamer text or a text that did not confront such stereotypes could have moved students so far from the previously unquestioned assumptions they carried with them, invisible and silent assumptions that render those with disabilities invisible and silent. Thus we moved from dismay to discussion past dissonance to the discovery of a place where disability texts in the classroom help students confront issues of authority and power. Students' ability to grapple with such texts that challenge the views they take for granted increases their confidence and enables identification with persons different from themselves.

Building Bridges between Students and Disability

Brenda Jo Brueggemann, Linda White, Patricia Dunn, and Barbara Heifferon have all commented on the idea of invisibility as related to disabilities such as LD and on students' assumptions about disability—previously unquestioned assumptions that, as Heifferon notes in the preceding section, were "invisible and silent assumptions that render those with disabilities invisible and silent." My students, like Heifferon's, had "assumptions" about disability; but for me, as a wheelchair user, as someone whose disability is visibly marked, *disability*—and the assumptions therein—was never really invisible to me. Disability, to me, had been, and often still is, present, couched in stares, whispers, pointing fingers, in the function, often dysfunction, of my own body. Thus, upon teaching my first class in disability, I admit, the "silence and invisibility" of disability—mine and others'—surprised me, indeed surprised all of us, my students and myself. In this section, I examine the teaching of a class in what some humanities scholars are calling "the new disability studies"—one approaching disability from a cultural rather than medical paradigm. Like Heifferon's section, this does not constitute a case study but is instead a reflexive recounting. Still, there are issues here that call for further research: (1) What are students' preconceptions about disability, and how should their literacies regarding disability influence pedagogy and curriculum? (2) How does a teacher validate students' "uneasy" feelings and experiences surrounding disability yet assist them in finding their own way of engaging with the subject matter?[12]

During the quarter that a national colloquium on disability, "Enabling the Humanities: Disability Studies in Higher Education," was being hosted by The Ohio State University, I decided to design my class around issues of disability and to entitle the class "Cultures and Literatures of Disability." I'd been teaching English 367—an intermediate-level writing class and a "diversity" class in one—for almost three weeks when one day I encountered a silence that was a bit unnerving, but not surprising. We'd seen *Storm Reading,* a video of vignettes by disabled performance artist Neil Marcus. We had traversed through Lennard Davis's chapter "Constructing Normalcy," where most students at least grasped the idea that "normalcy" is something society defines; and we had waded through most of Kenny Fries's autobiography *Body, Remember* about being disabled, gay, Jewish, and human. Students had also written their first critical response paper, so I knew they all had thought about *something* related to disability. Because this is a required course, and it's also required that we talk about race, class, gender/sexuality (that "diversity triad"), students are often silent. Afraid to say the wrong thing, they persist in saying nothing, especially when they're there "just to fulfill the requirement." That day there we were, in a silent room, attempting to discuss some aspect of Fries's *Body, Remember,* when a student ventured to break the silence by saying that he, and by extension *they,* staring straight at me, were silent because "I don't know *anyone* with a disability."

I had never felt so invisible.

Only four students out of twenty snickered. To the rest, my disability status seemed invisible. As I discovered, this was one of the three main reasons they found themselves silent: not being disabled or not knowing anyone disabled, never having been asked to consider disability, and disability being a "personal issue" no one talked about. As Jack writes:

> I have had some experience with disabled people because I have a mentally handicapped older cousin and I guess growing up that my other cousins and I alienated him from our activities. Whether the activity was watching TV or playing a game of basketball, he was never a part of the group. Was it right to not do any activities with him? Probably not, but we were little and didn't know any better at the time.

As Michael Oliver notes, "reduc[ing] the problems that disabled people face to their own personal inadequacies or functional limitations . . . [organizations] do not see disability as arising from social causes" (6–7). Such categorizing of disability as a "personal problem" is one of the major barriers to understanding disability as a societal construction.

Students also revealed that they were never asked to consider disability in other contexts, not even, as a women's studies major pointed out upon reading Hubbard's "Abortion and Disability," in four years as a women's studies major. And, because they were not themselves "disabled," they felt they had no authority to speak, write, or say anything about disability. It was the classic us/them binary at work. Tom writes:

> I was brought up on the east side of Cincinnati into a school system that had always segregated the disabled. In junior high they had special classes that they took nearly all day long so I never had any contact with disabled people unless it was the ones which were able to perform in the band. In high school the disabled people were sent off to an entirely different school which over there they were even segregated from the undisabled. Needless to say that I haven't been around disabled people long. In the last year of high school they were trying to make it more accessible for disabled people but yet there was only about a handful that came back to my school.
>
> I was never engaged in any activities with disabled people and that is a reason that I would never know if they need help when you see them having problems doing something. I never talked about anyone's disability to them before, this doesn't mean that I am not interested in it, it just means that I don't have the

> know how to carry on an intelligent conversation with them. I was always taught not to stare and that meant for me that I couldn't look without staring so I felt that it might be rude to ask if they needed help. It is never because I don't want to help them but because I wouldn't know how a disabled person would feel. Sure I'll help them if they ask me to but I had never had anyone ask for my help. I just never gained the knowledge about disabled people to see how they feel. Do they want my help or don't they?

Tom's experience was typical of many. Here, however, the effects of isolation, of invisibility, are felt not only by the disabled, the bearers of "negative stigma" (as Erving Goffman names it), but also by the nondisabled student as well. Most of the questions students had at the beginning were about access. "Do we or do we not hold the door open?" Having answered that question personally since before I can even remember, *I* hadn't even considered that to be a part of this class. I wanted to talk about literature, about theory, about hot-button issues such as Dr. Kevorkian. But clearly, I had to begin someplace else. I had assumed, wrongly, that everyone who had had some experience in hospitals could relate to Fries. They could, but I had to start where they were, and that meant talking about opening doors. And although this perhaps, unwittingly, set me up as some "paragon of disability," it also, I think, created a common vocabulary and validated their experiences and discomfort. It created for us a place to speak.

Then, they could write about the literature. Cindy, who "came out" as disabled by clinical depression, wrote passionately about how she could "relate to Anne Finger's experiences in her memoir *Past Due: A Story of Disability, Pregnancy, and Birth* on the basis of common experiences of womanhood." Similarly, after reading Donovan's poem, "For a Paralyzed Woman Raped and Murdered While Alone in Her Own Apartment," students talked about powerlessness and control. They were beginning to make connections between disability and larger cultural issues. They were talking now. And by far, one of the better experiences of the class was, again, letting their experiences guide me.

They loved movies, and we spent a whole class talking about *Star Wars* and whether Darth Vader is disabled. Or would we consider Luke Skywalker disabled after he acquires a mechanical hand? We discussed Donna Haraway's "Cyborg" theory then. We spent a good hour talking about Disney films, Quasimodo's *Hunchback,* the Beast's transformation, the Little Mermaid as a "freak," and on and on. In the beginning of the class, the students were silent because "they were not themselves disabled." By beginning to view disability in larger cultural contexts, however, they were gaining some authority, some comfort. Cole said to me, "you never notice it [disability] in the movies, but once you're trained to look for it, it's everywhere."

Having students run the class, in many ways, often meant that I had to concede my own political and personal goals for the class. Beginning where students were meant that I had to allow them to go where they needed to with the subject matter. When nearly half of them wrote their final research papers on medical discourse, I had to relinquish my desire to have them all become social and cultural critics, displacing the medical paradigm. After all, it would be perfectly natural for Monica to want to do research on cystic fibrosis because "my niece has it" and she had never been allowed to think or talk about it before. It had been a "personal family problem." So she did her medical research paper, but we also had a nice talk about family dynamics, parental expectations, and other such cultural issues.

Today, I am still mulling over what, in actuality, I taught them about disability as a cultural issue, or how to combat more effectively the pigeonholing of myself as the sole disabled member of the classroom, or about the best ways to go about breaking down the "us/them" binary. Those are big questions, and even loftier pedagogical goals. But we were an active and interactive classroom. Some time after the class was over, one of the students stopped me as I was rolling on campus. He was one of the students interested in Darth Vader's "disability status," and he wanted to discuss the Website for *Episode 1: The Phantom Menace,* something I hadn't yet downloaded. He'll be looking for disability, he informed me. I laughed, thinking somehow we got from silence to visibility to consciousness, even if it wasn't always the consciousness I wanted. But, in retrospect, building that bridge was as much about *my* changing my notions and expectations about disability as it was about students' coming to their own voices and views. Disability, invisible and unspeakable, became not only visible but also speakable (and writeable)—indeed, knowable in the context of the classroom and in our culture, changing, as Michael Bérubé notes, "life as we know it."

Enabling Conclusions

In this essay, we five composition teachers have joined our voices in a chorus—a chorus to break the silence. We have attempted, in various ways, to make the invisible visible to those who, like us, also want to learn to "see" and "speak" differently. Seeing and speaking are often not taken for granted among the people we attempt to represent here. Even such an attempted representation is in itself problematic, we know. Like Michael Bérubé ending his account of "a father, a family, and an exceptional child" in *Life as We Know It,* we hope for a future that offers better options for such representations. "My job, for now, is to represent my son, to set his place at our collective table," Bérubé writes in conclusion as he inconclusively muses on the difficulties of representing people with disabilities, his son included: "But I know I am merely trying my best to prepare for the day he sets his own place. For I have no sweeter dream than to imagine—aesthetically and ethically and parentally—that Jamie will someday be his own advocate, his own author, his own best representative" (264).

Aesthetically and ethically and pedagogically, we aim here for the kind of "enabling conclusion" that will make it more possible in the future for students with disabilities in our writing classrooms (and for us, too, as teachers with disabilities in those classrooms) to be their own best advocates, their own authors, and their own best representatives. Disability advocates often say, "Nothing about us without us" (Charlton). Some of us here are both visibly and invisibly disabled, some of us are currently TABs (temporarily able-bodied), and some of us are already PWDs (persons with disabilities). But all of us have joined together here to disrupt certain assumptions about both physical and learning disabilities, and none of us wants to continue to take "abilities" for granted.

We believe that even as our own limitations disrupt certain portions of our lives, like Foucauldian "ruptures" and Kuhnian "revolutions," these disruptions provide rich veins to work and grist for our mills. These disruptions bring us—as they do other teachers—opportunities to enrich learning for those in our classrooms. We see differences in *abilities* (not in *disabilities*)—like other differences of gender, race, ethnic backgrounds, and class—as generative in their place within writing classrooms. Yet, even in their generative potential, we know that the most initially disruptive difference to composition teachers is likely to be the differing abilities of learners. These differences call into question the very notion of composition itself. For but one example, people without hands who, at an earlier time, could not "write" in the conventional senses can now write with technological assistive devices. Likewise and by extension, we suggest that when teaching learning-disabled students, sometimes all of us, teachers and students alike, must learn to "compose" without words—visually, graphically, orally, using new strategies that perhaps seriously challenge all our traditional pedagogical practices and our strongly held beliefs about literacy and writing as empowerment.

Earlier in our recent history, composition studies stumbled over poststructuralism and deconstruction. When the author disappeared, many of us in the field were afraid we would also be subject to a disappearing act and be rendered invisible. But many of us learned in, through, or perhaps even in spite of these challenging theories to find a place within a different world—a world more open, flexible, and playful. We not only survived but enriched our theoretical bases, our discourses, and our practices. Now we face a new and different challenge as disabilities move away from their position on the margin. The five of us seek to push toward the center and disrupt some previous patterns and positionings in our fields about the inherent ability *of* writing and the inherent ability (power) *in* writing.

The five of us, presenting different perspectives throughout this piece but now "speaking" in unison, believe that all of us in composition studies and college writing classrooms—whether at the teacher's desk or in the student's seat—are capable of meeting challenges, are willing to embrace, as we have formerly embraced, other "Others." We are humble in our approaches here.

We don't have all the answers, but we have a powerful lot of questions, as Huck Finn might say. Embrace these hard questions with us—questions about the visibility of disability in the academy generally, about accommodations for disabled students (and teachers) in writing classrooms particularly, and about the not-so-binary distinctions (call it a continuum) between "abled" and "disabled," between TABs and PWDs, between "normalcy" and "disability." And in such an embrace, we all can learn how to meet the transitions most of us will need to make in the future. In the meantime, too, the composing of our lives and teaching will become richer as a result, enabling conclusions about abilities that we might once have barely imagined.

Acknowledgments

We wish to thank some very important people for helping make this work truly "visible": *CCC* editor Marilyn Cooper, for her support and vision concerning the emerging themes that she helped us identify in our first draft; Roberta Kirby-Werner and Joanne Buckley, for their readings and reviews, which helped us work through the thornier parts, particularly in building a more cohesive opening and closing and in "walking" around and through the contentious learning disabilities issues more "surefootedly"; and finally, Maureen Stanton and Melissa Goldthwaite, our own excellent readers, copyeditors, and compilers of multiple versions into this final piece.

Notes

1. If you are interested in a fuller, four-page history of "the disability movement" within CCCC, contact Brenda Brueggemann, brueggemann.1@osu.edu.

2. This figure comes from the Smithsonian's National Museum of American History current exhibit on "Disability Rights and American Culture" (see <americanhistory.si.edu/disabilityrights>). Thanks to Neela Thapar for the 1990 census statistics from the U.S. Department of Commerce, Economics and Statistics Administration, Bureau of Census, 1996, for other relevant figures on disability among the workforce population (ages 16–64). Also thanks to Linda M. Long for referring me to the

NIDRR's 1998 *Chartbook on Work and Disability* and to Kathryn Maher for several government sites quoting similar figures.

3. These terms—PWD for "person with a disability" and TAB for "temporarily able-bodied" (meaning all those who aren't currently PWDs)—are common parlance in disability scholarship and activist circles.

4. For samples of college course syllabi that either incorporate disability as an issue or even center on that subject in the humanities classrooms (especially in language, literature, and composition), we suggest the Disability in the Humanities (DS-HUM) Website, listserv, and syllabus bank: <http://www.georgetown.edu/crossroads/interests/ds-hum/index.html>. In addition, two of us have sample syllabi from courses we have taught in these areas: <http://people.english.ohio-state.edu/Brueggemann.1> and <http://people.english.ohio-state.edu/cheu.1>.

5. Gerber and Reiff review studies that attempt to determine the long-term effectiveness of LD interventions; they find that LD students educated after legislation required schools to provide services for them have not achieved greater levels of success than those educated before services were required. Kelman and Lester report similar findings in their review of longitudinal studies (147–52). In pointing to the different fortunes of those who study LD and those who have LD, I am not singling out the field of learning disability as especially culpable. My intent is to explore a mechanism at work in many fields, to understand the ways disciplinary discourse works to perpetuate inequities. David Bartholomae, Bruce Horner, and Min-Zhan Lu have made similar points in critiquing the field of basic writing, as does Trinh T. Minh-ha in describing the way anthropologists write about the native peoples they study. As Linda Alcoff argues in "The Problem of Speaking for Others," having the authority to speak is a position of power, both a privileged and a limiting position. We are learning to be critical of our attempts to represent those who do not share our authority.

6. My analysis of LD autobiographies is based on essays published at the Internet sites of *LD Online* and *LD Resources,* including those I cite here: Dirk Funk's "Finding Out," Paul Orfalea's "Succeeding with LD," Thomas West's "Left Behind at the Very Beginning of the Race," and Sandra Westall's "I Made It." My other sources are Paul Ziminsky's autobiography, *In a Rising Wind,* and Gerber and Reiff's *Speaking for Themselves,* a 1991 collection of interviews with nine learning-disabled adults. I am grateful to learning-disabled writers for telling their stories. The stories they tell most often and most enthusiastically have heroes who overcame their disabilities to achieve normalcy; most LD authors support hierarchies I would challenge. But it was reading what they

wrote that enabled me to see connections between LD and mental retardation and to understand that LD is not a sham or an excuse.

7. Michael Bérubé's *Life as We Know It: A Father, a Family, and an Exceptional Child* challenges the myth that people with mental retardation are unintelligent.

8. However, the sociological research Gerald Coles cites to support his attack on LD research also has methodological flaws, which he does not mention, as well as its own share of un-self-reflective researchers whose pre-existing assumptions impact their "findings" (i.e., that mothers are primarily responsible for their children's linguistic development). For a fuller critique of Cole's assumptions, see chapter 1 in my book *Learning Re-Abled: The Learning Disability Controversy and Composition Studies.*

9. For discussions regarding controversial aspects of intelligence, see Coles, Gardner, Siegel, and Stanovich.

10. The idea that there are armies of children "willfully malingering to land special perks" is as widespread as it is preposterous. Adolescents, who more than anything else want only to be perceived as "normal," are not lining up for admittance to a special education class so that they'll have a few extra minutes on exams. Only the most desperate children in our educational system would risk enduring the stigma revealed in comments from ignorant classmates, parents, or, worse, their own teachers, who think, as do most of the general public, that "LD" is simply PC for "lazy" or "stupid." And if educators privately think that poor writers are really not too bright, they may unconsciously lower expectations for these students—the worst thing they could possibly do.

11. In spite of the 1973 and 1990 legislation, the general public continues to think of LD as a euphemism for more insulting terms, which is why, as Linda White explains in the previous section, those with an LD label have tried to distinguish themselves from the "retarded." While this distancing is not admirable, it is perhaps understandable. Examples of insults regarding intelligence come from schoolchildren at the nearest bus stop as well as from administrators at major universities.

12. I should note that although I ascribe to the difference between *impairment* and *disability,* as my colleagues have noted, I did not make that distinction for my students; therefore, my use of the term *disability* in this article encompasses both medical impairment and cultural constructionism.

Works Cited

Alcoff, Linda. "The Problem of Speaking for Others." *Cultural Critique* 20 (1991): 5–32. Rpt. in *Who Can Speak? Authority and Critical Identity.* Ed. Judith Roof and Robyn Wiegman. Urbana: U of Illinois P, 1995. 97–119.

Bartholomae, David. "The Tidy House: Basic Writing in the American Curriculum." *Journal of Basic Writing* 12 (1993): 4–21.

Bérubé, Michael. *Life as We Know It: A Father, a Family, and an Exceptional Child.* New York: Vintage-Random, 1998.

Bordo, Susan. *Unbearable Weight: Feminism, Western Culture, and the Body.* Berkeley: U of California P, 1993.

Bruner, Michael, and Max Oelschlaeger. "Rhetoric, Environmentalism, and Environmental Ethics." *Landmark Essays on Rhetoric and the Environment.* Ed. Craig Waddell. Mahwah, NJ: Lawrence Erlbaum Associates, 1998. 209–25.

Carrier, James G. *Learning Disability: Social Class and the Construction of Inequality in American Education.* New York: Greenwood P, 1986.

Charlton, James I. *Nothing about Us without Us: Disability Oppression and Empowerment.*Berkeley: U of California P, 1998.

Coles, Gerald. *The Learning Mystique: A Critical Look at "Learning Disabilities."* New York: Pantheon, 1987.

Davis, Lennard. *Enforcing Normalcy: Disability, Deafness, and the Body.* New York: Verso, 1995.

Donovan, Leslie A. "For a Paralyzed Woman Raped and Murdered While Alone in Her Own Apartment." *With Wings: An Anthology of Literature by and about Women with Disabilities.* Ed. Marsha Saxton and Florence Howe. New York: Feminist P, 1987. 31–32.

Dunn, Patricia A. *Learning Re-abled: The Learning Disability Controversy and Composition Studies.* Portsmouth, NH: Heinemann-Boynton/Cook, 1995.

Finger, Anne. *Past Due: A Story of Disability, Pregnancy, and Birth.* Seattle: Seal, 1990.

Franklin, Barry M., ed. *Learning Disability: Dissenting Essays.* London: Falmer P, 1987.

Fries, Kenny. *Body, Remember: A Memoir.* New York: Dutton, 1997.

Funk, Dirk. "Finding Out." *LD Resources*. Ed. Richard Wanderman. <www.ldresources.com/articles/findingout.html>. 9 Aug.1998.

Gardner, Howard. *Frames of Mind: The Theory of Multiple Intelligences.* 2nd ed. New York: Basic Books, 1985.

Gerber, Paul J., and Henry B. Reiff. *Speaking for Themselves: Ethnographic Interviews with Adults with Learning Disabilities.* Ann Arbor: U of Michigan P, 1991.

Horner, Bruce. "Discoursing Basic Writing." *College Composition and Communication* 47 (1996): 199–222.

Hubbard, Ruth. "Abortion and Disability." *The Disability Studies Reader.* Ed. Lennard J. Davis. New York: Routledge, 1997. 187–202.

Katz, Jonathan I. Letter to the Editor. *Chronicle of Higher Education* 46.5 (24 Sept. 1999): B4 and B11.

Kavale, Kenneth, and Steven Forness. *The Science of Learning Disabilities.* San Diego: College Hill P, 1985.

Kelman, Mark, and Gillian Lester. *Jumping the Queue: An Inquiry into the Legal Treatment of Students with Learning Disabilities.* Cambridge: Harvard UP, 1998.

Lane, Harlan. "Constructions of Deafness." *The Disability Studies Reader.* Ed. Lennard J. Davis. New York: Routledge, 1997. 153–69.

Lewin, Tamar. "Apocryphal Student in Front Row as the Learning-Disabled Battle a College." *New York Times* 8 April 1997: B9.

Linton, Simi. *Claiming Disability: Knowledge and Identity.* New York: New York UP, 1998.

Longo, Judith. "The Learning Disabled: Challenge to Postsecondary Institutions." *Journal of Developmental Education* 11 (1988): 10–14.

Lu, Min-Zhan. "Conflict and Struggle: The Enemies or Preconditions of Basic Writing." *College English* 54 (1992): 887–913.

MacNealy, Mary Sue. *Strategies for Empirical Research in Writing.* Boston: Allyn and Bacon, 1998.

Mairs, Nancy. “Carnal Acts.” *Carnal Acts*. New York: HarperCollins, 1990. 81–96.

McKeon, Richard. *Rhetoric: Essays in Invention and Discovery*. Woodbridge, CT: Oxbow P, 1987.

Metcalf, S. D. “Attention Deficits: Does Special Education Leave Many Poor Learners Behind?” *Lingua Franca* 8 (March 1998): 60–64.

Minh-ha, Trinh T. *Woman, Native, Other: Writing Postcoloniality and Feminism*. Bloomington: Indiana UP, 1989.

Oliver, Michael. *The Politics of Disablement: A Sociological Approach*. New York: St. Martin’s P, 1990.

Orfalea, Paul. “Succeeding with LD.” *LD Online*. Ed. Noel Gunther. WETA, Washington, D.C. <www.ldonline.org/first_person/orfalea.html>. 27 April 1998.

Ratnesar, Romesh. “Lost in the Middle.” *Time* 14 Sept. 1998: 60–62.

Shapiro, Joseph P. “The Strange Case of Somnolent Samantha: Do the Learning Disabled Get Too Much Help?” *U.S. News & World Report* 14 April 1997: 31.

Siegel, Linda S. “An Evaluation of the Discrepancy Definition of Dyslexia.” *Journal of Learning Disabilities* 25 (1992): 618–29.

Stanovich, Keith E. “Has the Learning Disabilities Field Lost Its Intelligence?” *Journal of Learning Disabilities* 22 (1989): 487–92.

Storm Reading. Dir. Neil Marcus. Storm Reading Video Production, 1996.

Torgesen, Joseph. “Learning Disabilities Theory: Issues and Advances.” *Research Issues in Learning Disabilities: Theory, Methodology, Assessment, and Ethics*. Ed. Sharon Vaughn and Candace Bos. New York: Springer-Verlag, 1994. 3–21.

West, Thomas G. “Left Behind at the Very Beginning of the Race.” *LD Online*. Ed. Noel Gunther. WETA, Washington, D.C. <www.ldonline.org/first_person/west.html>. 27 April 1998.

Westall, Sandra. “I Made It.” *LD Online*. Ed. Noel Gunther. WETA, Washington, D.C. <www.ldonline.org/ first_person/westall.html>. 31 Dec. 1998.

Williams, Wendy M., and Stephen J. Ceci. “Accommodating Learning Disabilities Can Bestow Unfair Advantages.” *Chronicle of Higher Education* 6 Aug. 1999: B4–5.

Wittgenstein, Ludwig. *Philosophical Investigations.* 2nd ed. Trans. G.E.M. Anscombe. New York: Macmillan, 1958.

Wolf, Robert. Online Colloquy. *Chronicle of Higher Education.* <http://www.chronicle.merit.edu/colloquy/99/disabled/64/htm>. 10 Aug. 1999.

Ziminsky, Paul C. *In a Rising Wind: A Personal Journey through Dyslexia.* Lanham, MD: UP of America, 1993.

Taming Multiculturalism: The Will to Literacy in Composition Studies

PETER VANDENBERG

Out of the woods two hulking tramps
(From sleeping God knows where last night,
But nor long since in the lumber camps).
They thought all chopping was theirs of right.
Men of the woods and lumberjacks,
They judged me by their appropriate tool.
Except as a fellow handled an ax,
They had no way of knowing a fool.

Robert Frost

I certainly don't want us to get close to the culture of the undergraduate students at [the University of Virginia]. I take our function to be to confuse them by presenting them with a culture they have never seen before. We don't want to assimilate to theirs, we want to attempt to assimilate them to ours.

Richard Rorty

If we think of knowledge as socially justified belief, then to teach . . . seems to involve creating contexts where students undergo a sort of cultural change.

Kenneth Bruffee

From *JAC* 19 (1999): 547–68.

Cultivating a deep-level allegiance to the evolving discursive values of dominant-culture institutions has historically been central to the work of composition teachers. "Language loyalty," what Judit Kadar-Fulop identifies as a primary societal function of literacy education, is also "a form of cultural loyalty," a consequence of the systematic reduction of "language distance" through a trained habituation to a language's written form (32–36). When we teach writing, in other words, we are also teaching a commitment to a social system that frames social issues and negotiates conflict in particular ways.

What gives takes away, of course, and at least since the NCTE began drafting a resolution on dialect diversity in the early 1970s, writing teachers have struggled mightily with composition's legacy of reducing "language distance" by eradicating linguistic difference. The affirmation of "students' right to their own patterns and varieties of language," the critical relationship between "identity and style," and the call to "respect diversity" embodied by the 1974 resolution on Students' Right to Their Own Language have been in many ways central to the development of contemporary composition studies. Nonetheless, these matters have not completely altered the importance, for example, of the traditional writing handbook as a model of correctness and a textbook-industry standard. In a field rife with ironies the tension between composition's heritage of dominant-culture assimilation and its more recent inquiry into linguistic difference looms large.

As a writing teacher, I find myself constantly trying to elude the ideology of literacy, the fearsome complicity of *writing*—and all its epistemic promises—with social restriction. I want to imagine the potentiality of a culture not divided by writing. I want to embrace the possibilities of a culture not divided by writing. I want to embrace the possibilities of a reconstructionist multiculturalism, what Carol Severino calls "multicultural literacy." *Literacy*, however, regardless of the adjective one places in front of that term, reflects the circumstances of definition—for those of us teaching in American higher education, the needs, aspirations, and technologies of the social and economic cultural center. Literacy manufactures a difference of its own, and it is by this difference—in relation to other critical differences—that we are socially arranged. Representations of multiculturalism have not disrupted the role of writing teachers in sorting students along a literacy standard that serves already-dominant cultural institutions. Literacy legitimates, as J. Elspeth Stuckey has it. And that awareness situates writing teachers out along a cultural perimeter, perhaps reluctant to use the habitual to push back or absorb the unfamiliar but institutionally constructed in a primary sense to sort diverse language users rather than validate them. My intention here is to suggest, by exploring composition textbooks and composition's professional discourse, that the transformative potential of multiculturalism is often ironically subordinated to the task of reducing "cultural distance," and that acquiring what we've come to call "multicultural literacy" may demand a long, deep, and compliant congruity with dominant-culture literacy education.

From Standard Edited English to Multiculturalism

Readers of the professional discourse of contemporary composition studies know well the field's prevailing histories. The dominant view of undergraduate composition as the distaff partner of literary studies in English departments throughout most of the twentieth century (Connors, Berlin) has been written into all corners of the published discourse, and it continues to serve as the springboard for much of the scholarship produced today. These histories typically enact a rhetoric of emergence in which the contemporary discipline of composition studies is shown to have cast off the truncated epistemology of skills-based writing instruction—often labeled "current-traditional rhetoric." As James Berlin has it, the privilege of literature in English departments helped to compose its opposite, expository writing, as primarily a set of skills which, when used "correctly," could lend clarity to the results of method, "to reproduce in the mind of the reader the particular experience as it took place in the mind of the writer" (25–31). According to Berlin, the "scientistic" assumptions about knowledge that linked literary studies and rhetoric/writing early on created a hierarchical relationship between them, freezing the latter within the preparatory framework of the undergraduate college and giving writing, as a school subject, the appearance of a preliminary enterprise, a discursive boot camp where effective prose and its composers were either shaped up or shipped out.

Institutionalized as basic-skills instruction, composition as Berlin defines it constructed writing as a kind of cultural gate in the American university of the early 1900s. What later came to be known as Standard Edited English was understood as something of a "managerial art" (Berlin 42) consistent with the university's new role as a certifying agency of an emerging meritocracy. If non-literary writing was little more than transcription of a truth external to language, then adequate teaching must focus on avoiding "distortion" at all costs. Enlightenment ideals such as Clarity, Coherence, and Unity were understood as the route to the overarching axiology for written discourse, precision. And precision could be guaranteed only through rigorous adherence to standardized usage criteria. Standard Edited English (SEE) came to be understood as a dominant "skill" or "tool," and already by the early 1900s its acquisition had been firmly linked to the probability of success in mainstream American culture. The hardening of SEE helped define "error-free prose [as] the mark of an educated person" (Crowley 11).

SEE was framed as both the barrier before and the ticket to mainstream success, and the writing classroom served implicitly as a turnstile. While writing was understood to manage knowledge, the teaching of writing helped to manage a privileged American mono-culture by enforcing a norm by which all variations came to be judged. During most of this century, in most American colleges, writing instruction focused largely on indexing social class according to the surface features of Standard Edited English. Freshman English, once described as "the students' first introduction to the world of the mind and the serious discussion of ideas" (Moyer 169), served for the better part of the last one hundred years as a ritual of certification at the front end of the college or university experience.

The ideological confluence of SEE and America's meritocratic elite is starkly evident in what was perhaps the most influential Freshman English textbook between the end of World War II and the Reagan administration. "Non-standard English," according to James McCrimmon, in the 1950 edition of *Writing With a Purpose*, "is the language of the farm, the factory, the mine, the lumber camp, the railroad, and, in general, of those occupations which do not require what we call 'higher education.'" Standard Edited English, on the other hand, represents

> the speech habits of those who enjoy a favored economic and social status in our society, and since this class may be roughly described as the educated class, we may say that standard English is the way that educated people speak and write. It is, therefore, the kind of English written and spoken by business executives, lawyers, doctors, ministers, teachers, writers, editors, artists, engineers, and other professional people, and, of course, by their wives. (229; qtd. in Faigley 152)

As Robert Frost's lines show in my epigraph, criteria for exclusion obtain in the lumber camp as well. But Frost underscores McCrimmon's point; for it is Frost, after all, who has "written the book."

McCrimmon's textbook remained influential and substantially unchanged long after its patriarchal assumptions had been revised away. And while many writing programs continue to expect conformity to Standard Edited English either explicitly or implicitly, McCrimmon's legacy is nearly impossible to find anywhere in composition's professional literature or textbooks—except the conventional handbooks. The powerfully persuasive critique of "current-traditional rhetoric" advanced by composition scholars in the late 1970s and early 1980s has bankrupt the warrants for college-level writing instruction represented by texts like McCrimmon's. A focus on correctness gave way to the process movement and widened the field's attention from text to context, and the list of what students were understood to lack became longer and more complex than McCrimmon might have imagined in 1950. As SEE gave way to *academic discourse*, however, little changed about the relationship between writing instruction and cultural assimilation.

In 1979, Mina Shaughnessy deployed *academic discourse* in her extraordinarily influential *Errors and Expectations* as a collective noun for the cognitive abilities non-mainstream or "basic" writers were said to lack (Mahala and Swilky), the shared discourse practices of the academic community: "way[s] of knowing, selecting, evaluating, reporting, concluding, and arguing"

(Bartholomae 135). These conventions would no longer be implicit in college teachers' expectations for student writing. Together these practices and conceptual strategies defined a specialized discourse and means for its production that students would appropriate—or be appropriated by—if they were to expect what the dominant-culture institutions reserve for college graduates.

When Kenneth Bruffee linked social epistemology to a classroom pedagogy he called "collaborative learning," he worked to adjust the writing teacher's points of evaluation from surface correctness to other socially determined norms. Arguing that "there is no fixed and certain point of reference, no Arnoldian 'touchstone' against which we can measure truth," Bruffee was among the first to elaborate a social epistemology for composition: "[T]he generation of knowledge, what we call 'creativity,' must also be a social process" (405–407). Drawing on the American pragmatist philosopher Richard Rorty, who makes his own cultural work explicit in the epigraph above, Bruffee argued for the cardinal importance of adherence to "normal discourse," a socially derived "'set of conventions about what counts as a relevant contribution, what counts as a question, what counts as having a good argument.'" (Rorty qtd. in Bruffee 401). According to Bruffee, "Much of what we teach today—or should be teaching—is the normal discourse of most academic, professional, and business communities. . . . [N]ot to have mastered the normal discourse," Bruffee contends, "is not to be knowledgeable" (402). The normalizing desires of Bruffee's pedagogy are evident as well in one of the field's best-known essays, David Bartholomae's "Inventing the University." As Bartholomae has it, "Every time a student sits down to write for us, he has to invent the university for the occasion . . . The student has to learn to speak our language, . . . to try on the peculiar ways of knowing, . . . reporting, . . . and arguing that define the discourse of our community" (134).

From our vantage point a couple of decades hence, the assimilative potential of these early claims are both conspicuous and well noted.[1] Taking notice of the latter's inattention to the roles of institutionalized power in delimiting the infrastructure, upon which the new is constructed, contemporary social *episte-*

mologists move to distance themselves from these early social *constructionists*: "Social-epistemic rhetoric challenges the status quo," William Thelin argues, "while social-constructionist[s] capitulate to it." Nonetheless, what often goes missing from such taxonomies are assumptions about the value of writing, or literacy itself that continue to link those Thelin differentiates. The perceived value of high literacy training is a stable axiological substructure upon which the field's theoretical positions float and collide like tectonic plates. Whether one imagines the writing class as the locus of cooptation or liberation, or defines writing as a set of jobs-based skills or a "post-biological evolutionary step" (Kaplan 12), literacy training appears to promise a world impossible without it.

McCrimmon's textbook implies SEE as an economic and social marker; contemporary writing theorists, however, are far more likely to identify *writing itself* as the necessary catalyst for meaningful social and institutional involvement. As Mary Kalantzis and Bill Cope have it, the workings of western society can only be "conceived and acted upon through historically specific, abstract, sociolinguistic skills," which are crucial if one is to "achieve adequate levels of social participation" and "actively conceptualize and negotiate one's social roles and social relations" (17). Effective participation in—or resistance to—dominant cultural institutions is often understood to be dependent on synthetic, critical, and analytical operations, "metacognitive strategies and . . . conceptual negotiations" that are expressly related to reading and writing—what Miles Myers, immediate former executive director of the National Council of Teachers of English, has called "translational/critical literacy" (122).

Never in the history of writing instruction has teaching writing been so crucially important in the eyes of its practitioners. As former Modern Language Association president Catharine Stimpson's apocalyptic 1990 address has it, "If the erosion of soil would concern an agronomist, if the flickering out of all the stars would concern an astronomer, so we must care acutely about the fate of literacy" (406). With that care comes a profound conviction in the implications of literacy training. Writing teachers such as Joseph Comprone contend that "what we are teaching when we teach literacy are new forms of consciousness, new ways of seeing and constructing reality" (8). Bruce Edwards argues that, through writing, "we come to know things and come to know ourselves in differing ways" (4). If the product of normal discourse is "the sort of statement that can be agreed to be true by all participants whom the other participants count as rational" (Rorty qtd. in Bruffee 401), no instance of discourse in rhetoric and composition could be more "normal" than a claim for the transformative potential of advanced literacy training.

Teaching writing changes people, but how so and along what standard? Helen Fox, in *Listening to the World: Cultural Issues in Academic Writing*, describes "academic discourse," the consequence of a peculiarly American high-literacy training, like this:

> In short, it is at once a writing style, a method of investigation, and a world view that has been part of western cultural heritage for hundreds of years and that is learned through a process of both formal and informal socialization that begins in early childhood, especially by those who come from "educated families," go to "good schools," and aspire to positions of influence and power in the dominant culture. (xviii)

As Fox states explicitly, and as Bruffee, Comprone, Edwards and others imply, the acquisition of academic discourse is not simply the development of discursive strategies and techniques, it is a reorientation in values—a cultural conversion that Rorty, in my epigraph, acknowledges straightforwardly. Chief among these values are the preconditions of civil-society discourse Patricia Bizzell has identified as "ethical qualities": "'formal courtesy,' 'shrewd assessments of what constitutes adequate proof'" (355), and the sanctity of "intellectual property"; the assumption that reasoned debate "cannot resolve controversial problems" (354). As Thomas West suggests, criteria for civil-society discourse are fully imbricated with the effective manipulation of argumentative elements: "Learning how to receive direct and critical speech, how not to take such criticism personally, to *think* it and not simply *feel* it is as important as learning how to craft critical arguments" (14). Discourse becomes civil, regularized, and institutionally managed, West shows, only when parties agree to abide by and develop commitment to its operations.

In *Education as Cultural Imperialism*, Martin Carnoy argues that Western schooling as a whole transmits "the social and economic structure from generation to generation through pupil selection, defining culture and rules, and teaching certain cognitive skills" (qtd. in Willinsky 107). Chief among what Carnoy calls "cognitive skills" are those Myers bundles under the rubric, "translational/critical literacy"—text-based mental operations that, as D. R. Olson points out, privilege and sustain activities valued by dominant-culture institutions. Writing teachers can promote awareness of the way evolving conceptions of literacy are used to index social class, and they can lead their students in resistance to dominant-culture institutions through writing pedagogies. Ironically, however, the extent to which such projects are "successful" may suggest the extent to which students have become incorporated or legitimized by the very structures they are encouraged to resist. Even oppositional, liberatory, and critical pedagogies, by reflecting the deeply embedded civil-society values of their agents and the sorting function of the institution in which they are allowed to appear, inevitably necessitate that students learn resistance through patterns of conformity. Translational/critical literacy, thoroughly imbricated with the values that promote its acquisition, cannot easily be disconnected from a commitment to the sites, habits, and rituals—the culture—associated with it. And it is within this paradox that the discourse of multiculturalism has emerged in composition studies.

To write or speak of multiculturalism is to first invite a reverberation of meaning and then attempt to squelch it. In *Keywords*, a study of terms whose "meanings are inextricably bound up with the problems [they are] used to discuss" (15), Raymond Williams identifies the word *culture* as one of the three or four most problematic in the language. To attach the prefix *multi-* is to open up an already contested term to a broad range of social and discursive concepts and practices; to add the suffix *-ism* reflects a desire to reduce this range "to a formal singularity" (Goldberg), ironically, to exclude differences in service of definition. However, as one moves away from the speculative theorizations represented by David Goldberg's *Multiculturalism: A Reader* toward discussions of curricular development and writing instruction, however, one sees a rather surprising degree of convergence among definitions. For, here, multiculturalism is seen in transformative, pluralist terms; it is typically a "reconstructionist" procedure driven by a relatively uniform axiological consensus—value is placed on how to elaborate, investigate, and tolerate *difference*:

> Multicultural education . . . . seeks to promote the valuing of diversity and equal opportunity for all people through understanding of the contributions and perspectives of people of differing race, ethnicity, culture, language, religion, gender, sexual orientation, and physical abilities and disabilities. (Kitano 12)

> We define multiculturalism as the effort in the latter half of the twentieth century to encourage citizens in the United States to embrace the racial, ethnic, class, gender, religious, age, and physical-ability differences in our population; multiculturalism is an approach to living that respects, incorporates, and mediates the differences and similarities of our population. (Severino, Guerra, and Butler 1)

Almost invariably, in this context the possibility of conceptualizing difference and diversity is contingent on some conception of high literacy—critical, analytical, metacognitive abilities understood to emerge through the extended familiarity with "text-to-text relationships in an area of knowledge" (Myers 122). As Morey and Kitano have it, multiculturalism is dependent upon "more accurate and comprehensive disciplinary knowledge" that will emerge "through enhancement of students' academic achievement and critical thinking applied to social problems" (12). Carol Severino defines "multicultural literacy" as "the knowledge of the beliefs, practices, and roots of the cultures in one's environment and the ability to communicate such knowledge in . . . written discourse" (106). Effective writing instruction, then, holds the promise of a multicultural society. Yet such conceptions can place difference and diversity in front of students without explicitly disrupting the rather conservative sorting function that writing instruction continues to play in American higher education. What it means to be literate has always been tied to the needs, aspirations, and technologies of dominant sociopolitical institutions; and at least since the development of Freshman English in the 1880s, some conception of literacy has functioned as an indicator of success within those institutions while its absence has been associated with criminality and social abnormality.

As I'll go on to show, however, a pedagogy linking a reconstructionist multiculturalism with some conception of high literacy, by placing the former in a dependent relationship to the latter, may reinscribe the same assimilationist desires and exclusionary effects of its earlier, "current-traditional" counterpart. That is, expressly promoting literacy as a conceptual tool kit necessary for the awareness of critical difference and cultural change begins with literacy, rather than any other possibility, as the most crucial determinant of difference. It is, then, *by and through* conceptions of literacy that difference is constructed and coordinated—writing remains the ticket inside, and its ideological sorting function remains effectively obscured.

The Thematic Reader

Multiculturalism's dominant presence in composition textbooks comes in the shape of the "thematic reader," perhaps the most painful reminder of the field's arhetorical, "current-traditional" past. Lacking a self-reflexive attention to questions of cognitive alteration and assimilative potential, such textbooks tend to present a conception of "good writing" that goes largely unexamined. When they link writing instruction with multiculturalism, these textbooks almost invariably subordinate reconstructionist intentions to a monocultural conception of literacy—one supposedly free of bias because it is pure bias. Little more than anthologies of essays and excerpts, thematic readers provide representations or models of preferred or idealized forms, typically the narrative essay. They also are repositories of "content," decontextualized fodder that students discuss and then repackage into representations of the ideal. As this explanation from *Writing About Diversity* reveals, a reader's "content" is determined primarily to serve the goals of the course in which it is deployed:

> *The topic of cultural diversity was selected because* it is not only complex and controversial, but timely and relevant. Indeed, diversity has been referred to as the most significant issue of the 1990s and, as such, has been accorded widespread media attention and generated considerable controversy on college campuses. Aside from the "trendiness" of the topic, though, I believe that students should become aware of the conflicts associated with diversity in order to function effectively in an increasingly complex, multiethnic world. (Clark ix, emphasis mine)

This introductory statement appears to offer the axiology of reconstructionist multiculturalism—an attention to difference; what it does better, however, is frame multiculturalism as a trend composed of "conflicts" and "issues" that must be managed in order to "function effectively." Difference, here, is a contested category to be explored first in order to be later administered. This implicit managerial approach to diversity and the subordination of difference to enculturation through conventional forms and practices is expressly evident in *Connections: A Multicultural Reader for Writers*:

> *Connections* does much more than simply provide a collection of readings that represent various cultures. The introductory section demonstrates critical-reading and -thinking skills and suggests that these skills become particularly important when readers encounter unfamiliar circumstances and ideas. . . . The readings are divided into three sections, each of which offers selections exemplifying one aim of writing: expressive, explanatory, and persuasive. (Stanford v)

The notable feature of most multicultural readers, such as *Writing About Diversity* and *Connections,* is their startling uniformity. Anthologized writers appear to consider difference in remarkably similar fashion. In a very brief 1988 conference talk, Bonnie Lisle offered an example of how "multicultural" texts in thematic readers are made to appear "thoroughly assimilated—no different from the other 'great works' they rub shoulders with." Lisle points to the headnote (or introduction) to Martin Luther King's "Letter from Birmingham Jail" in *The World of Ideas*. Lisle explained that the book's editor

> locates King's politics in the white pacifist tradition of Thoreau, while it neglects his place in the black activist tradition of Sojourner Truth, Frederick Douglas, Ida B. Wells, and W.E.B. DuBois. The same introduction devotes a full page to explaining King's indebtedness to the rhetorical tradition of European Christianity. (157)

Lisle goes on to catalog works of scholarship locating King in African-American rhetorical traditions that might have been included in the headnote but were not.

A decade later, such examples continue to leap off the shelf. James D. Lester's *Diverse Identities: Classic Multicultural Essays* is one book in a series of NTC's "Library of Classic Essays." The tension between the book's multicultural "content" and its inclusion in a series of "classic" essay collections is perhaps its greatest irony—*Diverse Identities* demonstrates the potential to safely define and circumscribe "multiculturalism," and make room for it between *Plato's Heirs: Classic Essays* and *Classic Essays by Women*. Lester's collection begins with the same Preface that graces each volume in the series, which lays claim to "some of the finest essays ever written." This preface locates the origin of the essay with Plato and Aristotle, celebrates its flowering at the hand of Montaigne, and its continuance through "the American Ralph Waldo Emerson and the British George Eliot" (ix). The "multicultural essay" here is "classic" precisely in terms of its capacity for assimilation. Through a formalist pedagogy the multicultural "content" can be emptied out to display the perceived power and potential of the "classic" narrative essay, as you like it: either a privileged, knowledge-producing heuristic or an elegant container for the West's finest literary achievements.

The consolidation of multicultural "content" with the supposed ameliorative potential of literacy is often completed with a group of "multicultural" texts that praise the critical importance of literacy in the preferred form represented by the book. In Lester's reader, this section is titled "Classical Multicultural Essays about the Importance of Language," yet five of the seven texts are narratives specifically about the acquisition of literacy. In thematic readers, works such as Carlos Fuentes' "How I Started to Write," or Gloria Anzaldúa's "The Path of the Red and Black

Ink," are flattened and homogenized to represent not difference, but similarity. Longer works are segmented or edited to represent the preferred form. Painful narratives of cultural assimilation, such as Michelle Cliff's or Richard Rodriguez', are bundled together apparently to demonstrate that, like Platonic truth, literacy is painful to come by but worth the effort.

While *Classic Multicultural Essays* is perhaps the most obvious example, thematic readers with a "multicultural content" reflect a paradigm of assimilation. The "multicultural" essays in these textbooks, implicitly pressed into service as models for student writing and having survived the powerful legitimizing process of publication, are intended to represent literate Western school culture through formal features—the dominant criteria for their inclusion; their "content" might well have been about handgun control, the legalization of recreational drugs, or doctor-assisted suicide. While the professional discourse of composition studies reflects an attention to rhetorical concerns, composition textbooks continue to privilege a narrow range of empty forms and stock strategies, and it is within these structures that all possibilities are incorporated; only when knowledge produced outside dominant-culture conceptions of literacy—myth; folktales; the "signifying" rhetoric of African American orality—is reproduced in preferred forms that it becomes legitimate. What justifies the presence of authors in these books is their ability to conceptualize their cultural experiences—or the editors' ability to shape them—in a way that implies a thoroughly assimilated standard-English speaker as audience. Implicit, at least, for students is the message that other forms of knowledge creation are not worthy of notice (Vandenberg, "Accounting").

The "Benetton Effect" in Composition Studies

In exploring the adaptation of a "multicultural logic" to the standard operational procedures of corporate and nonacademic entities, the Chicago Cultural Studies Group finds institutionalized *multiculturalism* too often reduced to slogan, what it calls "the

Benetton effect" (115). Lacking critical content, "multiculturalism" can implicitly frame difference as something to manage or administer rather than as something to investigate. Writing textbooks that harness multiculturalism to conventional pedagogies without an exploration of difference enact the Benetton effect. The result can be a disturbingly monocultural or homogeneous impression of what constitutes "good writing." Consider, for example, Tracey Baker and Barbara Kennedy's *Writing and Synthesis: A Multicultural Approach to Writing*.[2] The Preface identifies this textbook as a "process-approach rhetoric" with a "multicultural aspect" or "dimension." Theoretically informed by "an information-processing perspective," the book is ordered according to two foundational assumptions: that "repetition of the writing process is important," and that "an awareness of ideas that both differ from, and are similar to, [students'] own"—what the authors call a "multicultural understanding"—is "essential" in a "world that is growing smaller" (xiii–xv). The assimilative ambitions of the book are apparent already here in the reduction of producing text to "*the* writing process," something that is achieved through repetition. While the authors assert the "essential" significance of difference, they will go on to demonstrate that difference has little if any impact on their pedagogy.

Writing and Synthesis is broken into eight chapters in which timely, uniquely Western constructions (Medical Ethics, The Environment) or widely-drawn categories (Religion, Humor, Education) are linked with the concept "Culture" for the purpose of providing "topics on which students are required to write" (xiv). Each of the chapters is intended to result in a processed essay, and each is divided by the same subheadings—Planning, Organizing, Drafting, Revising, and Editing. Each also contains several short, professional "essays," which are often excerpts of longer works, on the chapter's theme.

The authors situate the textbook in the "service course" tradition of composition immediately in the introduction. In positing that the majority of texts students will go on to write will be based on sources, Baker and Kennedy constrict the possibilities for writing to "academic" texts. According to the authors, the capable production of academic writing is dependent on exercises that "focus . . . on developing the higher levels of cognitive processes—comprehension, application, analysis, synthesis, and evaluation" (xiv). Chief among these is synthesis, and each chapter leads students toward the goal of synthesizing elements of the professional essays with their own responses to them. Teachers who have grown suspect of formulaic or prescriptive approaches to process have some reason to be encouraged by *Writing and Synthesis*. To the book's credit, the "Reading and Synthesizing" section of each chapter does not always appear at the same point. Sometimes the essays follow other invention strategies; sometimes the reading functions as an invention technique, either before or after students are asked to construct a rough draft.

Unfortunately, innovative thinking about process or the integration of texts and invention does not extend much further. Students are asked in the Introduction to recognize the controlling interrelationship of purpose and audience in planning an essay; decisions about both, they are told, "take the form of one sentence—the *thesis statement*" (17). Through repetition, it becomes apparent that a student's overriding purpose should be to construct a thesis, and the book's "Planning" sections seem to assume that discussion questions or invention strategies like "looping" or freewriting unproblematically culminate in a sentence that will control an essay. When they don't—or even if they do—students are encouraged to think of audience to help define purpose. What *audience* is and how it should be considered, however, is much less than clear in *Writing and Synthesis*. Baker and Kennedy move among radically different theoretical conceptions of audience—as "real" readers who act passively as "targets," and as the results of writers' inventive strategies that help define intentions—without acknowledging or exploring this complexity. Most problematic is the conception of audience that goes unexplained and perhaps unconsidered. The authors suggest that decisions about purpose and audience "[u]ltimately . . . take the form of one sentence, the *thesis statement*." When "the thesis statement" is figured as an indispensable element of *any* essay as it is here, *audience* becomes (or is limited to), in part at least, a discursive feature—"good writing" is wholly consistent with the formal features of an approved discourse.

Rather astonishingly, given their stated attention to respecting diversity, Baker and Kennedy's normalizing intentions are finally explicit in their desire that students develop a non-reflexive, habitual, and uniform relationship with preferred ways of knowing. According to the authors, learning to write is accomplished through repetition of "mental processes [that] are most beneficial once they become automatic. . . . [A]utomatization of these processes does not take the work out of writing, but it does simplify some of the problems" (xiii). Rather ironically, the problems that are solved through Baker and Kennedy's prescriptions all seem to involve *erasing* the possibilities of difference. In a section called "Understanding Writing" the authors announce that "writing well is not magical; it is a matter of learning and practicing skills. . . . [A]lmost everyone can learn to craft effective, clear essays that readers can understand" (16). Student writers, Baker and Kennedy assert, are all "in the same position" (24). Because *Writing and Synthesis* is "based on an information-processing model of an efficient and productive way for people to learn," student writers "Joel Dixon, Muhammad Ahmadin, Michele Hites, and Jing-zhang Zhao" can all sit down together and search each other's papers for information that "seems to 'stray' from the topic and thesis" (249). All this comes after the disturbingly elemental—yet effectively clear—Introduction on "Culture," which sums up with the observation that "[o]ne way to understand the word *culture*, then, is to acknowledge that people of different nationalities perceive, and react to situations differently" (4).

No one associated with this project seems to have noticed that the authors' theoretical frame and the pedagogy it supports do not at all mesh with what they call a "multicultural perspective." Indeed, they directly contradict each other. While the readings in the book are ostensibly about understanding cultural difference and negotiating it with respect, their prescriptions for student writers both depend on and promote an alarming conceptual uniformity—one expected, no less, to become automatic. Baker and Kennedy are considerably more accurate, as well as ironic, in claiming that "this textbook aims to give an equal voice to all" (xv). The serious problem with this textbook is not the authors' definition of *multiculturalism*, nor even their rather uninspired articulation of process pedagogy, it is the yawning gap between the two that students and teachers are apparently expected to ignore. Lacking a considered articulation of their informing sources, information processing and multiculturalism, their book buckles with one of the central tenets of Baker and Kennedy's pedagogy—synthesis. *Writing and Synthesis* will strike some as what the historian Gary Nash has called "the powdered sugar approach"; multicultural content sprinkled over "the same old cake" (qtd. in Landers 686).

"Translation" or Assimilation?

In a genre analysis of 212 texts found in three different multicultural readers published during the late 1980s, Nancy Shapiro determined that well over 90 percent could be described as personal narratives—stories of maturation fully realized in the telos of Western literacy standards. Its "classical" essayistic implications aside, however, the personal narrative has been reframed in many composition pedagogies as a foundational writing exercise. On the assumption that narrative is easier, less intimidating, the personal essay is typically a tune-up leading to persuasion or "transactional" writing—writing with sources in support of an argumentative thesis. Such sequential writing pedagogies concentrate on weaning students off narration and on text-based activities that mean business in dominant-culture institutions: "to write to inform or persuade; to work with subject matter that is outside of personal experience; to gather and organize raw materials, shaping them into discourse that accomplishes something" (Farr and Daniels 56–57). Writing instruction, then, is figured as a sort of cultural negotiation in which students and teacher become aware of differences while swapping narratives; multicultural course content is proposed as a "bridge between home and academic cultures" (Buffington and Cai 160). "[T]eachers need to structure learning experiences," Terry Dean suggests, "that both help students write their way into the university and help teachers learn their way into student cultures" (23). No doubt more explicitly than some teachers would like, Dean others student "cultures" against the one represented by the university. The bridge metaphor works, of course, only if one is willing to first accept a gulf of separation. And of critical importance here is that teachers appear to only read and listen while students must "write their way" across the bridge and "into the University."

It is in this sequencing or bridge building that the assimilative potential of high literacy training is most contestable. Students are expressly taught to abstract, analyze, reconstruct, and reconceive their pre-college "cultural" experiences, yet those who propose such pedagogies sometimes deny the capacity of higher-order cognitive processes to disrupt or conceptually alter "primary-culture" orientations. It is in these pedagogies that two powerful axiologies, or theories of value, collide. Writing teachers who employ such pedagogies deeply value the possibilities of a culture attentive to multiple manifestations of difference; however, they also are deeply committed to transformative critical processes that well may abstract and assimilate differences into a public space where they risk neutralization or absorption within business-as-usual. Given that the critical mental operations are understood to be anterior to the promise of a multicultural society, the student is initially and unavoidably subject to the diagnostic gaze of the teacher who will mediate her capacity to contribute to cultural change.

Deborah Dixon's *Writing Your Heritage: A Sequence of Thinking, Reading, and Writing Assignments* is just such a pedagogy, one that on reflection produces considerable slippage between its aims for respecting and promoting cultural diversity and the homogenizing effects of its writing pedagogy. This short text promotes a complete course outline, a sequence of assignments that, according to the author, "expands the students' cognitive powers and prepares them to think through and write about difficult problems when they are asked to do so in other academic courses" (36). Although students begin by writing free-style descriptions of their families' oral histories, the stated goal of the course is "[t]o help the students cross over from personal writing to cognitive writing" (2). Citing James Moffett, Dixon suggests that "reportage and research represent an important bridge between personal writing and transpersonal writing" (2).

In an invention assignment that precedes the first formal essay, students are asked, "tell what characteristic habit or feature of your personality seems to have come most directly from your ethnic, national, or familial origins" (9). Yet while the students are being asked to consider heritage, the assignment sequence makes it clear that such experience is appropriately understood and communicated through the "rhetorical modes"—description, narration, exposition, and persuasion. Already by the second formal assignment students are told that heritage can be packaged and disseminated in a fashion alien to personal experience. Even narration, the mode most often assumed to characterize student's communicative capacity, becomes something foreign, an act requiring displacement; they are required to abstract themselves as narrators necessarily attentive to conventions of genre. Heritage, the concrete or tangible experiences called for in the early invention writing, is transmuted into an abstract, mental construct—historiography on a "topic":

> [W]hat you are attempting to do is . . . create a narrative history—not a story, but a telling of an historical event from a subjective point of view . . . . Students put away all notes and books, and using only a brief outline, write everything they know now about their *topic* in fifty minutes. This difficult, even painful, process helps students to clarify what they know. (21)

It is not insignificant that this process is described as painful; students are asked to accept as clarification a retrofitting of their stories. By the time students reach the final assignment in the sequence, their lived experience and family histories are subsumed to the task of advancing a position on the generalized category of heritage itself.

Like Baker and Kennedy, Dixon doesn't consider the disjunction between her intention to allow students to "express their individual identities . . . through the exploration of a subject that belongs to [them]" (49) and the pedagogical goal of "building the academic skills and self-confidence they need to progress from academic 'outsiders' to privileged 'insiders' of the university community" (51). While it would be suspect to say that a student somehow "owned" her heritage either before or after this sequence, one can safely say that if Dixon's goal for each assignment is achieved—"to enlarge the student's powers of thinking, organizing, and expressing ideas"—any sense of that pre-literate heritage has been unmistakably altered.

Dixon begins her text with an epigraph taken from My Le:

> Heritage is not some little trinkets that one gets from one's great-grandmother. Nor is it material possessions that one gets from a will. Heritage is physical traits, mannerisms, attitudes, tastes, and customs that people inherit from past generations.

Ironically, she doesn't consider that her own heritage and its will to high literacy appropriates the attitudes, tastes, and customs of her students, recasting them in its own image. Dixon's short textbook reads like a detailed explication of the claim Richard Rodriguez makes about Alex Haley's *Roots*: "That book tells us more about [Haley's] difference from his illiterate tribal ancestors than it does about his link to them. . . . The child who learns to read about his nonliterate ancestors necessarily separates himself from their way of life" (227).

I invoke Rodriguez here because he figures prominently in Mary Soliday's *College English* article, "Translating Self and Difference Through Literacy Narratives." Soliday offers a pedagogy that revolves around autobiographical storytellings "that foreground issues of language acquisition and literacy" (513). Soliday differs markedly from Dixon, and Baker and Kennedy, in one important respect. She defines the successful literacy narrative as a "deliberately constructed rendering of experience" that necessitates a "dynamic sense of the autobiographical self" (512), a "narrative agency" that allows writers to "articulate the meanings and the consequences of their passages between language worlds" (511); however, drawing on the literacy narrative of one of her students, Soliday wants to insist that the process of abstracting a "new sense of self" (518) from a writing pedagogy does not infect one's relationship to a primary discursive order. Soliday's argument emerges through liberal quotations from the writing of one of her students, Alisha. Yet there is considerable ontological discord between Soliday's description of Alisha's "negotiated self" (518) and Alisha's own description of a unified, solitary consciousness. Alisha reduces to simple mimicry and imitation Rodriguez' complicity in his assimilation, his desire to, as he puts it, "*be* like my teachers, to possess their knowledge, to assume their authority" (55). Despite Soliday's stated awareness that Alisha's "I" is multiple and constructed, Alisha essentializes herself and Rodriguez as unified, self-motivated subjects: "I totally disagree with [Rodriguez'] motives to imitate others. When you imitate others, you're a stranger to yourself, because you do not possess your own ideas" (519).

It is unclear to what extent Alisha's experience as an African American woman attending college in the early 1990s is comparable to Rodriguez' experiences as a bilingual child born to Mexican immigrants in the late 1940s. It is clear, however, that Alisha emerges from Soliday's class with a strong ideological orientation to dominant-culture institutions. Ultimately, Soliday's pedagogy is subsumed under the trope of *negotiation*; "[Alisha] concludes that she has begun to develop a new sense of self that allows her to negotiate the complex demands of her cultural situation in mature ways" (518). As Thomas West points out, though, negotiation always implies congruity with dominant power structures, those that invariably delimit the strategies, protocol, and procedures of negotiation. In this case, Alisha emerges "mature" in that she possesses a strong social orientation, a vigorous belief in a unitary self and personal responsibility, and an unflagging desire to deny the constructive potential of her educational experience. "Whenever I learn something new," Alisha writes, "I process the information for my own benefit" (qtd. in Soliday 518). Despite Soliday's protests, it is difficult to imagine a more thoroughly assimilated college student than Alisha. Soliday presents, celebrates, and defends the transformative potential of translational/critical literacy, and then chooses not to find its effects. She claims to give her students the tools to build a bridge between cultures, and then wants to make the tools disappear.

A Conclusion

The postcolonial heritage of Western education—to adjust those outside the cultural mainstream to dominant conceptions of productivity and preferred economic and social relationships—appears to be tremendously resilient. For many, the "American University" continues to sustain a legacy of systematic oppression, functioning as a mechanism of homogenization, a site where non-dominant others are pulled into negotiation and, therefore, conceptual alignment with dominant-culture institutions; a place where differences are called out into the open and absorbed, where alternate ways of knowing, of seeing the world, are erased or neutralized.

Surely, however, no *particular* field of study appears to its practitioners as such a cold and involuntary ideological apparatus. And this is likely why, as John Willinsky points out, the residual colonizing functions of specific educational domains await a fuller accounting. As I have shown, the institution of college writing instruction has routinely hierarchized the student population according to whatever conception of textual literacy is dominant; however, the evolving definition of *literacy* is always accompanied by a deep-seated belief in its ameliorative guarantee. We tend to see a less benevolent disciplinary face only in the rearview mirror. The early Harvard writing program of Berlin's critique and the 1950 edition of McCrimmon's *Writing With a Purpose* look bad in retrospect, but our own intense idealism about literacy masks its assimilative function in the present. Even the promotion of "powerful literacy," control of a "meta-discourse to critique . . . dominant discourses" (Gee 8), can be seen as a simple demonstration of the pliability of dominant discourses. An evolving definition of *literacy* functions in composition studies like a trustworthy set of disciplinary high-beams—lighting a path determined by institutional momentum, blinding us to the shadows created by our own pattern of illumination. This is surely what Stuckey calls the ideology of literacy, an instrument of awesome consequence, one so powerful it legitimates itself. Trying to dampen its glow only strengthens it. When we're thinking about our own high literacy we're using it. When we're not thinking about it we're still using it in some thoroughly integrated sense, like the map in the glove box we never unfold because we know so well the narrow roads we travel.

Whether one defines *literacy* as a simple ability to decode a preferred religious text according to convention, or as a complex set of metacognitive operations such as those identified by Miles Myers, it will unavoidably mean *what it takes*, or *what it should take*, to function within dominant-culture institutions. Whatever else we also do as writing teachers and theorists, we reproduce privilege. Even oppositional, liberatory, and critical pedagogies, by reflecting the deeply embedded civil-society values of their agents and the sorting function of the institution in which they are allowed to appear, necessitate that even resistance is learned through patterns of conformity to dominant culture values. Definitions of literacy have always been synchronized with the technologies, knowledge, and ideals of dominant-culture institutions; it is this that makes them valuable, desirable. In linking *multiculturalism* with *literacy*, composition's textbooks and scholarship implicitly make the promises of the former (whatever they are said to be) crucially dependent on the latter. Thus, literacy constitutes a mechanism of composition and a yardstick for preferred competencies—whether those competencies are, say, critical analysis or a tolerance for difference. When yoked to the sorting process by which one does or does not acquire writing, a primary means of cultural production, the transformative potential of multiculturalism is fully tamed.

Despite composition's growing interest in the normalizing influences of institutional power, its scholarship reflects a tendency to further delimit categories of literacy rather than investigate the enculturating function of mass literacy training. Its teaching tools tend to misunderstand preferred literacies as somehow divorced from the problems they are meant to address. We ought never become comfortable and complacent at the cultural center or about the consolidating function we serve there, but we must be careful not to imagine ourselves somewhere else, serving wholly different ends. As academic authors, compositionists might continue to explore the ideology of literacy at work in our own scholarly machinery—particularly the role writing serves in indexing writing faculty (Vandenberg, "Composing"). As teachers, we might help students more critically examine any claims, including those of multiculturalism, that propose cultural rehabilitation through dominant literacies.

Notes

1. See, for example, Trimbur; Myers; Vandenberg and Morrow.

2. Parts of this section were first published as a book review; see Vandenberg, Rev. of *Writing and Synthesis*.

Works Cited

Baker, Tracey, and Barbara Kennedy. *Writing and Synthesis: A Multicultural Approach to Writing*. New York: HarperCollins, 1993.

Baumlin, James S., and Jim W. Corder. "Jackleg Carpentry and the Fall from Freedom to Authority in Writing." *Freshman English News* 18 (1990): 18–20.

Bartholomae, David. "Inventing the University." *When a Writer Can't Write: Studies in Writer's Block and Other Composing Process Problems*. Ed. Mike Rose. New York: Guilford, 1985. 134–165.

Berlin, James A. "Rhetoric and Ideology in the Writing Class." *College English* 50 (1988): 477–494.

Bizzell, Patricia. "The Ethos of Academic Discourse." *College Composition and Communication* 29 (1978): 351–355.

Bruffee, Kenneth. "Collaborative Learning and the Conversation of Mankind." *College English* 46.7 (1984): 635–52.

Buffington, Nancy, and Guanjun Cai. "Multiculturalism." Heilker and Vandenberg, 159–162.

Chicago Cultural Studies Group. "Critical Multiculturalism." Goldberg 114–139.

Comprone, Joseph. "The Meaning of Literacy in a Culture of Writing and Reading." College Conference on Composition and Communication. 13 March 1986. New Orleans, LA. ED 270 785.

Connors. Robert. "Historical Inquiry in Composition Studies." *The Writing Instructor* 3 (1984): 157–167.

Crowley, Sharon. "The Perilous Life and Times of Freshman English." *Freshman English News* 14.3 (1986): 11–16.

Dean, Terry. "Multicultural Classrooms, Monocultural Teachers." *College Composition and Communication* 40 (1989): 23–37.

Dixon, Deborah. *Writing Your Heritage: A Sequence of Thinking, Reading, and Writing Assignments*. Berkeley: National Writing Project, 1993.

Edwards, Bruce. "The Politics of Non-literacy Logocentrism in the Classroom." National Council of Teachers of English. 16 November 1984. Detroit, MI. ED 252 863.

Faigley, Lester. *Fragments of Rationality*. Pittsburgh: Pittsburgh UP, 1992.

Farr, Marcia, and Harvey Daniels. *Language Diversity and Writing Instruction*. ERIC Clearinghouse on Urban Education. Urbana: NCTE, 1986.

Fox, Helen. *Listening to the World*. Urbana, IL: NCTE, 1994.

Frost, Robert. "Two Tramps in Mudtime." *Selected Poems of Robert Frost*. New York: Holt, 1963.

Gee, James Paul. "What is Literacy?" *Rewriting Literacy: Culture and the Discourse of the Other*. Eds.Candace Mitchell and Kathleen Weiler. New York: Bergin, 1991. 3–11.

Goldberg, David Theo, ed. *Multiculturalism: A Critical Reader*. Cambridge: Blackwell, 1994.

Heilker, Paul, and Peter Vandenberg, eds. *Keywords in Composition Studies*. Portsmouth, NH: Boynton/Cook, 1996.

Inside UVA. "A 'Curmudgeon's' View of the Condition of Universities." 11 March 1994. URL: gopher://minerva.acc.Virginia.EDU:70/ORO-3965-/pubs/InsideUVa/94-03-11/5.

Kadar-Fulop, Judit. *Writing Across Languages and Cultures: Issues in Contrastive Rhetoric*. Ed. Allan C. Purves. Newbury Park, CA: Sage, 1988. 25–50.

Kalantzis, Mary, and Bill Cope. "Pluralism and Equitability: Multicultural Curriculum Strategies for Schools." NACCHE Commissioned Research Paper #3. 1986. 1–45. ED 300 171.

Kaplan, Robert B. "Cultural Thought Patterns Revisited." *Writing Across Languages*. Ed. Ulla Connor and Robert B. Kaplan. Reading, MA: Addison-Wesley, 1987. 9–21.

Kitano, Marie K. "A Rationale and Framework for Course Change." *Multicultural Course Transformation in Higher Education*. Ed. Ann Intili Morey and Margie K. Kitano. Needham Heights, MA: Allyn & Bacon, 1997. 1–17.

Landers, Robert K. "Conflict over Multicultural Education." *Editorial Research Reports* 1 (30 November 1990): 682–94.

Lester, James D. *Diverse Identities: Classic Multicultural Essays.* Lincolnwood, IL: NTC, 1996.

Lisle, Bonnie. "Culture and Academic Literacy." *Academic Literacies in Multicultural Higher Education.* Ed. Thomas Hilgers, Marie Wunsch, and Virgie Chattergy. Manoa, HI: Center for Studies of Multicultural Higher Education, 1992.

Lisle, Bonnie, and Sandra Mano. "Embracing a Multicultural Rhetoric." *Writing In Multicultural Settings.* Ed. Carol Severino, Juan C. Guerra, and Johnnella E. Butler. New York: MLA, 1997. 12–26.

Mahala, Daniel, and Jody Swilky. "Academic Discourse." Heilker and Vandenberg, 9–13.

Mandel, Barrett J. "Losing One's Mind: Learning to Write and Edit." *College Composition and Communication* 29 (1978): 362–368.

McCrimmon, James M. *Writing With a Purpose.* 1st Edition. Boston: Houghton, 1950.

Moyer, Charles R. "Why I Gave Up Teaching Freshman English." *College English* 31 (1969): 169–173.

Myers, Greg. "Reality, Consensus, and Reform in the Rhetoric of Composition Teaching." *College English* 48.2 (1986): 154–74.

Myers, Miles. *Changing Our Minds: Negotiating English and Literacy.* Urbana, IL: NCTE, 1996.

Olson, David R. "The Languages of Instruction: The Literate Bias of Schooling." *Schooling and the Acquisition of Knowledge.* Eds. R. C. Anderson, R. J. Siro, and W. E. Montague. Hillsdale, NJ: Erlbaum, 1977.

Rodriguez, Richard. *Hunger of Memory.* Boston: Penguin, 1982.

Severino, Carol. "Two Approaches to 'Cultural Text': Toward Multicultural Literacy." Severino, et al. 106–117.

Severino, Carol, Juan C. Guerra, and Johnnella E. Butler, Eds. *Writing In Multicultural Settings.* New York: MLA, 1997.

Shapiro, Nancy. "Rereading Multicultural Readers: What Definition of Multicultural are We Buying?" *Academic Literacies in Multicultural Higher Education.* Ed. Thomas Hilgers. Marie Wunsch, and Virgie Chattergy. Manoa, HI: Center for Studies of Multicultural Higher Education, 1992.

Shaughnessy, Mina. *Errors and Expectations*. New York: Oxford, 1979.

Soliday, Mary. "Translating Self and Difference Through Literacy Narratives." *College English* 56.5 (1994): 511–526.

Stanford, Judith A. *Connections: A Multicultural Reader for Writers*. Mountain View, CA: Mayfield, 1993.

Stimpson, Catharine R. "Modern Language Association 1990 Presidential Address." 28 December 1990. Chicago, IL.

Stuckey, J. Elspeth. *The Violence of Literacy*. Portsmouth, NH: Boynton/Cook, 1991.

"Students' Right to Their Own Language." Conference on College Composition and Communication Position Statement. http://www.ncte.org/ccc/12/sub/state1.html.

Thelin, William Howard. "Terms We Use." 2 June 1998. Online Posting. WCS-L (Working Class Studies Listserv).

Trimbur John. "Consensus and Difference in Collaborative Learning." *College English* 51.6 (1989): 602–616.

Vandenberg, Peter. "Accounting for Institutional Blindspots: The Search for a Multicultural Textbook." *Diversity* 2 (1994): 97–104.

———. "Composing Composition Studies: Scholarly Publication and the Practice of Discipline." *Under Construction: Working at the Intersection of Composition Theory, Research, and Practice*. Ed. Christine Farris and Chris M. Anson. Logan, UT: Utah State UP, 1998. 19–29.

———. Rev. of *Writing and Synthesis: A Multicultural Approach to Writing*, by Tracey Baker and Barbara Kennedy. *Focuses* 7.2 (1994): 105–107.

Vandenberg Peter, and Colette Morrow. "*Inter*textuality or *Intra*textuality? Rethinking Discourse Community Pedagogy." *The Writing Instructor* 14.1 (1994): 17–24.

West, Thomas. "Differencing Negotiation." *Composition Studies* 25.2 (1997): 7–18.

Williams, Raymond. *Keywords*. Revised Edition. New York: Oxford, 1983.

Of Ambiguity and Erasure: The Perils of Performative Pedagogy

KAREN KOPELSON
University of Louisville

As much as it pains me to admit it, I am pretty much a walking stereotype. I look like a dyke (and I am): cropped hair, little black glasses, clunky shoes. I never wear makeup, can't remember the last time I wore a dress, and, as my mother has been fond of telling me since I *can* remember, I dress "like a man." One evening last summer I found myself standing behind another of my "clan" in the grocery store; we looked at each other, gave the usual insider nod of recognition, and I thought, "What is this, a *uniform*?" We looked like twins whose parents had put us in little matching outfits—and then pierced our noses (on the same side) for good measure. Yep, I am an easy read.

Because I am an easy read, I have spent much time and energy carefully constructing a pedagogy that works within and against what I consider to be my identity's glaringly evident markers. In other words, in order to forestall potential student resistance to identities (my own and others') or issues of difference, I have tended to perform, as much as is possible, a certain amount of ambiguity with regard to my sexual self—I never really "come out" in the classroom, but I don't make concerted efforts to "stay in" either—and a certain amount of "neutrality" with respect to my "professorial intentions," by which I mean that I perform (again, as much as is possible) "an absence of an overtly politicized pedagogical agenda" (see Talburt, "On Not" 69). While advocates of visibility, inclusion, and other hallmarks of identity politics see these moves as those of retreat, hiding, "selling out" even, I see them, as I have argued elsewhere,[1] as rhetorically savvy responses to many contemporary classroom and university contexts, and to a larger (multi)cultural moment, wherein "reticence, misperception, and distrust" are so prevalent, they may serve to structure the entire pedagogical exchange (Caughie 136). I see these moves, that is, as the effective rhetorical and performative *strategies* of a marked teacher-subject struggling to keep students receptive to the political issues I *do* raise in my courses. And I am not alone in considering such strategies both smart and necessary. As Homa Hoodfar has written, "[c]learly visible minority teachers are faced with questions and dilemmas which are fundamentally different" from those faced by teachers who are not so readily marked (225). We know, for example, that advocating particular political positions in the classroom becomes much more highly charged and fraught with risk when we are going to be read as occupying somehow "corresponding" identity positions, and thus as advancing political/pedagogical "agendas" based on or arising from those identity positions. The question then, the dilemma, is how to advocate those political positions to which we are committed anyway.

Proponents of what is coming to be known as *performative pedagogy* suggest that we might do just what I have described above: work to rescript the scripting of our body-texts and the expectations—and political suspicions—they inevitably call forth. Carol Davis (pseudonym), for example, a participant in Susan Talburt's ethnographic study of lesbian academics, *Subject to Identity*, explains that she performs her sexuality as "ambiguous," "lets" students think that "perhaps [she is] straight," because she does not want them "to think the only reason [she raises sexuality issues in her courses] is that [she is] queer and [has] some sort of axe to grind" (96). Judith Butler similarly warns that "out" teachers risk having whatever they say in the classroom read as some sort of "overt or subtle manifestation" of an "essential homosexuality" (*Psychic* 93), and another participant in Talburt's study (who happens also to be a renowned queer theorist) describes how she interferes with such likely readings by "perform[ing] herself as tabula rasa"—both with respect to her sexual identity *and* with respect to having *any* preconceived agendas for student learning whatsoever ("On Not" 69). These teachers strive, in other words, as do I, to anticipate and avert unproductive student resistance, ultimately to prevent students from shutting out critical sociocultural issues they would likely interpret as "merely" personal. Moreover, and crucially, proponents of performative pedagogies tend to see ourselves *not* as committing sacrificial acts of "voluntary self-erasure" in these efforts to counteract student resistance (Shankar 199), but as constructing *productively indeterminate* teacher-identities that exceed, confuse—queer, if you will—our always-already-read queerness/difference itself.

For the most part, I have found that such performances of ambiguity and neutrality work: While my political commitments occasionally leak through to sully the slate, if you will—that is, while I do occasionally receive the student's teaching evaluation that accuses me of being "too much of a feminist," or, most recently, of "beating the dead white male thing to death" (as if I personally killed them all?)—I far more typically receive glowing evaluations wherein students praise me, in particular, for creating such a "comfortable" and "respectful" classroom environment, and for my "openness" to "all points of view." Wow, I think, time and again, semester after semester, because this little production of mine is an encore performance, this ambiguity/neutrality show sure goes over big; they like me; they *really like me!* And, more importantly, much more importantly, I come away from my courses with the sense that students have been open to, and opened up by, what I have been teaching them—to the political issues that I have determinedly "snuck in" to class discussions and assignments—precisely because I have performatively prevented them from discerning and resisting the political agenda that I do have, the axe that I *am* grinding.

Flash backward: Last day of classes, a few years ago, at the institution where I did my graduate work. A few of my teaching assistant colleagues and I (including my girlfriend at the time) are celebrating the semester's end at a local watering hole. Because watering holes are scarce in small midwestern university towns, I run into several of my former and current students. After talking to a couple of these students for a while (two young men who had been among my "favorite" students that very semester, and with whom I'd had a particularly relaxed and amicable relationship), I say, "Come on over here, I want you to meet my girlfriend." Screeching halt to jovial bar banter. Two boys with wide eyes and open mouths, and finally: "You mean your girl*friend*, or your girlfriend-girlfriend?" from one of them. "My girlfriend," I answer. "You know, my partner." (I honestly thought these kids knew; they *had* to know. *Who didn't? How could they not?*) "You mean . . . you're a *lesbian*?" the other asks. "Yes. Of course," I answer back, and attempt again to start the procession over to where my girlfriend is sitting. "Wait," he stops me again: "an *actual* lesbian?"

I wasn't sure then and I'm not sure now what separates an "actual" from a—what?—"virtual" lesbian? But I was sure at the time, and am increasingly sure today, that something was wrong with this picture. I meant to perform my "savvy" neutrality—especially in this particular writing course, which had been focused on gender and sexuality issues. I did not, however, mean to *disappear.*

Flash forward: Different university, where I have my grown-up job. A student who has just taken my Writing about Literature course comes to chat with me in my office. He is young, male, a self-identified "jock," and he wants to do an independent study with . . . *me* (?!)—something related to masculinity and textual representation. As we are discussing possibilities for his project, he tells me he "hates feminists." I am wearing a woman's symbol pendant around my neck. I still look like a dyke. In the Writing about Literature course we have just completed together, I taught Octavia Butler's *Kindred*, and Margaret Atwood's feminist *über*text, *The Handmaid's Tale*. I tell him that I'm a feminist, remind him that he seems to get along with me just fine. "You *are*?" he asks. "Yes, of course," I reply. The student is not the only one who is stunned here, and there is something very wrong with this picture indeed.

Those who have argued against performative pedagogies have repeatedly expressed concern that enactments of ambiguity and neutrality ultimately amount to "just more self-effacement"(Elliott 700), a dangerous return to invisibility for the queer/different teacher-subject, and have suggested that visibility—even if "mired in identity politics" (Elliott 699)—is "too precious a concept," and too crucial a strategy, "to sacrifice to the ostensibly greater good" of identity's deconstruction (Malinowitz 75). I, on the other hand, have found myself firmly opposed to this critique, and resolutely committed to (what I have viewed as) performative pedagogies' many greater goods: I have believed, to invoke Talburt once more, that "a rejection of 'neutral' teaching" is neither the only "desirable strategy" nor the only way to be political in the classroom. I have believed, in fact, that ambiguity may prove far more effective than "visibility, or overt personal mediation" in "combat[ing] heterosexism and homophobia" and other forms of resistance to and fear of difference (Talburt, *Subject* 96–97). I have held firmly as well to the idea that performances of ambiguity/neutrality can infuse academia with unanticipated, productively confusing, *indeterminate* modes of subjectivity, and, perhaps most important, I have believed that the dreaded return-to-invisibility phenomenon was not even a real risk in the first place—because of the differences that would (obviously and always) remain on the teacher's body to queer the performance of neutrality or ambiguity before it even begins.

However, as even the most vociferous proponents of performative pedagogies have acknowledged, "[t]he teacher's performance is never in full possession of itself" (Ellsworth 164), and the will to normalization is omnipresent, and (sometimes literally) *unimaginably* strong. To put this another way, glaringly evident identity markers only glare in the eyes of the beholder, and performance is only ever actualized in its reception. As Butler has written, all acts, utterances, and selves "continue to signify in spite of their authors, and sometimes against their authors' most precious intentions" (241). And sometimes, as my own experiences should make disturbingly clear, acts/selves simply fail to signify at all.

As my experiences should also suggest, I am now quite ambivalent, straddling a theory/practice divide even, with regard to the issues and dilemmas raised in this essay. I still do believe that pedagogical performances of ambiguity and neutrality can introduce new modes of subjectivity in the classroom, and can mitigate student resistance to politically progressive pedagogies, thus ultimately helping to *advance* progressive political goals or even "agendas." And yet I also believe that it is politically *re*gressive, and, well, just sad, when students spend sixteen weeks with their queer teacher and can leave that course still thinking they have never *had* a queer teacher. Over the last few decades, many teacher-scholars in Rhetoric and Composition and English studies more generally have offered advice for how to, and even mandates that we must, come out in the classroom: As early as 1974, for example (certainly a less politically supportive time for gays and lesbians in educational institutions and beyond), Louie Crew stated unequivocally in a *College English* essay that coming out in the educational setting was an "academic responsibility" for teachers, and that to refuse to do so was to deprive gay and lesbian students of role models and support, and to perpetuate the cycles of "self-loathing, ignorance, and fear" afflicting gays in the university and society at large (288). Twenty years later, literature professor George Haggerty echoed Crew, reminding us that, in addition to whatever else queer teachers are teaching our students, we are also responsible for teaching our gay and lesbian students "to be gay and lesbian," for teaching them "that it is possible to flourish as lesbians and gay men in a culture that does everything it can to silence and oppress us" (12). Somewhat less didactically and with more attention to rhetorical nuances, Mary Elliott recommends coming out at what she calls the "golden moment"—that is, when class discussions "provide a relevant context for self-disclosure" (704–5). And, of course, other teacher-scholars, such as those I have cited in the earlier portions of this essay, have argued that coming out in the classroom is unproductive and unnecessary at best, counterproductive at worst, to course goals.

I'm afraid I cannot offer one-size-fits-all advice for what gay/lesbian teachers should do, for how they should "be queer" in the classroom, or for how queer they should be. Coming or being out in the classroom seems to me to be an intensely personal choice, precisely because it is such an intensely public and political act, one that reverberates far beyond its moment—golden or otherwise. But I think Elliott is onto something here, in her hint of a suggestion that coming out it is also a *rhetorical act*, one dependent on context, intention, and audience reception.

What I do know: I would not have taught with a woman's symbol pendant around my neck a few years ago. I might not even have taught *Handmaid's Tale*—too political, too incendiary, too *anything but neutral*. Over the last few years I have been increasingly "out" to my classes (or at least I think I have been). I must be getting braver in my old age, I think to myself, or braver as the gap between my age and my students' age gets wider and wider. Or maybe it's those three letters after my name, granting me a personal and pedagogical confidence and authority that I feel is much less likely to be challenged than when I was a teaching assistant. Or maybe I'm just getting tired of "voluntary self-erasure," and the more pernicious erasure of otherness/difference that it risks translating into. Maybe I am tired of being misread—*unread*. Identity politics may be passé, a big, glaring pomo no-no for the oh-so-pedagogically and politically sophisticated among us. But, certainly, invisibility is a bit behind the times itself, and closets are, after all, still for (all my dykey) clothes.

Note

1. See my "Rhetoric on the Edge of Cunning; Or, The Performance of Neutrality (Re)Considered As a Composition Pedagogy for Student Resistance." *College Composition and Communication* 55 (2002): 115–46.

Works Cited

Butler, Judith. *Bodies That Matter: On the Discursive Limits of "Sex."* New York: Routledge, 1993.

———. *The Psychic Life of Power: Theories in Subjection.* Stanford: Stanford UP, 1997.

Caughie, Pamela. *Passing and Pedagogy: The Dynamics of Responsibility.* Chicago: U of Illinois P, 1999.

Crew, Louie. "The Homophobic Imagination." *College English* 36 (1974): 272–90.

Elliott, Mary. "Coming Out in the Classroom: A Return to the Hard Place." *College English* 58 (1996): 693–708.

Ellsworth, Elizabeth. *Teaching Positions: Difference, Pedagogy, and the Power of Address.* New York: Teachers College Press, 1997.

Haggerty, George E. "'Promoting Homosexuality' in the Classroom." *Professions of Desire: Gay and Lesbian Studies in Literature.* Ed. George Haggerty and Bonnie Zimmerman. New York: MLA, 1995. 11–18.

Hoodfar, Homa. "Feminist Anthropology and Critical Pedagogy: The Anthropology of Classrooms' Excluded Voices." *Radical In(ter)ventions: Identity, Politics, and Difference/s in Educational Praxis.* Ed. Suzanne De Castell and Mary Bryson. New York: State University of New York P, 1997. 211–32.

Malinowitz, Harriet. *Textual Orientations: Lesbian and Gay Students and the Making of Discourse Communities.* Portsmouth, NH: Boynton/Cook, 1995.

Shankar, Lavina Dhingra. "Pro/(Con)fessing Otherness: Trans(cending) National Identities in the English Classroom." *Teaching What You're Not: Identity Politics in Higher Education.* Ed. Katherine J. Mayberry. New York: New York UP, 1996. 195–227.

Talburt, Susan. "On Not Coming Out: or, Reimagining Limits." *Lesbian and Gay Studies and the Teaching of English: Positions, Pedagogies, and Cultural Politics.* Ed. William J. Spurlin. Urbana, IL: National Council of Teachers of English, 2000. 54–78.

———. *Subject to Identity: Knowledge, Sexuality, and Academic Practices in Higher Education.* Albany, NY: State University of New York P, 2000.

Learning (Teaching) to Teach (Learn)

MALEA POWELL
University of Michigan

This is a story.

Some of you have heard some of this story before.

So, I'm sitting at a table with the Oklahoma Miami woman who has taught me most of what I know about beadwork. I am struggling with the awkwardness of my first piece of medallion-work, struggling with the beads and the thread and the light and the chair and the table and the piece of buckram upon which I am trying to bead. She moves in and places her hands over mine and rearranges the way I am holding everything—she reorients my body to the beads and thread and buckram, but also reorients the combined whole of "us" to the room, the light, the table, the chair. This is how I learned to do beadwork.

Years later, I'm sitting at another table with an Oklahoma Cherokee woman who I am teaching to do medallion-work. She is struggling with the same awkwardness, and I see in her face the same sense of failing self that I myself felt. I move in to teach her how to reorient herself, how to do this beadwork. I recognize the cycle here—both when I was involved in this event and now, as I revisit it as an event. As much as I would like to wax poetic about this moment of returning the gift of reorientation, to infuse it with articulated scholarly meaning, I also recognize that both of these events are already infused with meaning as the very center of the mundane, the displaced "real" of the lived everyday experiences of folks like me *and* of folks who have never heard the word *pedagogy*. In the practice of lived experience, this "return" is simply "what you do," is "the right way to behave," is "the way to be."

Because of the mundane context in which I have been a teacher/learner, I do not intend to bore you with more deep and significant evocations about pedagogy, nor with sly or sinuous criticisms that lead you away from ever wanting to talk publicly about teaching; instead, I will do what we claim to tell our students to do every day—write what I know, say what I want to say.

One of the things I know about my own graduate school experience of being "trained" pedagogically is that I was extremely fortunate to have mentors and colleagues who felt that the business of teaching writing was a worthwhile intellectual enterprise. I'm grateful to them for that, and for the kind of passionate care that they invested into their own teaching. I know that I was a difficult student. It has taken me years to work through my own discontent—with graduate school, with the academy, with the business of scholarship, with teaching as a function of the institution's desire, and many, many other things that are beyond the scope of this text. One thing that has become clear to me, though, at least in terms of my own pedagogical education, is that even the most radical, critical pedagogical instruction and training I received still theorized students (especially students in composition classrooms) as *individuals* engaged in the business of producing, and negotiating, meaning. Yeah, yeah, yeah—we were certainly encouraged to think of these students as highly complex, socially positioned individuals who should be allowed to operate within their own systems of linguistic and cultural signification in order to produce this meaning—but they were still individuals. The goal of writing instruction was still—is still—individual mastery, the measure of the teacher still determined by individual students who we have "helped" achieve that mastery—whose writing/thinking "got better" during the semester. I really never had an academic model that theorized students in composition classrooms in the ways that my own scholarly work encourages members of the discipline to theorize themselves and their practices—as a collective of connected humans, a community allied for a common purpose. So my goal for the next few pages is to try to clear a path through the European American obsession with the individual, and instead present a reorientation that might help us establish a theory of writers/students that sees the act of writing as an event that expresses/represents/produces our collectivity, not our individual mastery (or lack thereof).

So, what's the difference between those two theoretical visions—the individual and the communal? Basically, one is arranged for the benefit of the goals of the institutions in which we work—to train students to be "better" thinkers, writers, scientists, citizens, etc. The other is, I believe, arranged for the benefit of all who reside within whatever imagined community is operational within the particular collective space where the "teaching" is being enacted.

Yikes, that just won't do. I need about a million conditional clauses and clarifying phrases up there, and I don't want the texture of traditional academic language to lead me by the nose. Let me see if I can make this clearer since my own writing is also getting crowded by the collection of voices speaking through, and jostled by the struggle to negotiate the needs of the many communities in which I participate. So, let me just think out loud in alphabetic-print form as a substitute for a full-blown, citation-ridden pedagogical theory. Okay.

What is "the difference"?

1. A communally focused pedagogy sacrifices the needs of the individual for the needs of the whole, whereas an individually focused pedagogy attends to the needs of the individual at the expense of the whole.

2. A communally focused pedagogy requires that teachers act as guides and elders, subsuming their own needs for the needs of the whole; an individually focused pedagogy pretends to community by claiming that the teacher has "given up" his or her authority in the classroom but, in making that claim, instantiates his or her authority even more firmly, operating within the same tired definition of power relations that race politics in the United States have relied on for decades—the belief that it is possible for folks in power to simply relinquish that power through the expression of individual will.

3. A communally focused pedagogy is rooted in place in such a way that discussions of race, ethnicity, culture, gender, orientation, ableness, etc. will always already be part of the

community's understandings of itself and of what it means to attend to the good of the whole; an individually focused pedagogy denies place by positioning *difference* as its own special category of *need*—forcing us into a fragmented and tokenized understanding of difference which pits "us" against "them" and defines "the good of the whole" as "to the advantage of the majority."

This is the point at which someone always asks, What about what composition classrooms are supposed to *do*—teach writing?!

My response: This is a question used to silence those of us who believe that writing is not a nice, neutral tool that we can use as easily as, say, a screwdriver, safe in the belief that it is essentially innocent and can only turn into a weapon through the bad intentions of the user—users whose interior lives are only "our business" to the degree which they interrupt our sense of appropriate behavior by being disruptive, resistant, or by jamming the screwdriver ungratefully into our skull.

Okay, okay, so, what about *writing*?

Well, I teach writing. All the time. Every day. Here is a list of some of the significant writing instruction I've done so far this week (it's Friday):

1. Wrote several e-mails to faculty and graduate students in the graduate program here inviting them to visit the two graduate seminars I'm teaching this semester—885, a year-long professionalization colloquium for first-year PhD students, and 848, a course that examines theories and methodologies used in American Cultural Rhetorics scholarship

2. Wrote a long e-mail to the editorial board of the journal for which I am the editor— included was a draft of our updated "procedures" manual, a report on the status of current editorial projects, and a request for assistance with some of those current projects

3. Wrote an e-mail in which I requested feedback on a revision of our graduate program mission statement—attached to the e-mail was a draft of that revision document

4. Wrote several e-mails to arrange meetings

5. Responded to the first chapter of an American Indian Studies graduate student's thesis;
6. Responded to two chapters of a Rhetoric/Critical Race Theory graduate student's dissertation
7. Spent several hours in a graduate committee meeting in which we made decisions about who to admit to our PhD program for the coming academic year (these admissions include teaching assistant funding for four years)
8. Taught the first class meeting of the above-mentioned 848 seminar—went over the syllabus
9. Responded to questions, pursued discussion of the three essays we had read for that day
10. Attended the Native American Literature community reading group, of which I am the facilitator, at the local Native cultural center
11. Wrote three letters of recommendation—one for a scholar in Chicana rhetorics for a Ford Foundation fellowship; one on the behalf of an American Indian student for admission to an American Studies PhD program; and one for a PhD recruit for a university fellowship
12. Met with two students—an American Indian student earning a PhD in anthropology who wants to do an independent study on Native writing and rhetoric, and a white, working-class student to arrange for him to finish an incomplete in the course I taught last semester (Rhetoric in American Culture)
13. Taught the first class meeting of the other above-mentioned course, 885—went over syllabus, responded to questions, facilitated student drafting of new "goals" statements for the semester
14. Sent out an e-mail reminding participants in the local craft circle that our monthly meeting is this Sunday at my house
15. Talked to three colleagues concerning my anxieties about this essay, about its exigency, its situatedness, and its looming deadline—this included reading them a draft out loud

It's probably clear how each of these items are *writing*. It's also probably clear how each of these events are *teaching*. So, you tell me, how are these activities *teaching writing*? This is the point in class where I would say, Do you want to break into groups and generate responses to share with the class or would you rather tackle this in a big group discussion? So, this is a place where you should probably take a minute and talk to your peers. (Yes, this means that I assume that you are not alone in your writer's garret reading, drinking coffee, and rubbing your frozen fingertips together—if, in fact, you are alone, call/e-mail/find someone to talk to now.)

Wait, wait, wait—one more thing—keep in mind the way in which the editors of this collection have framed *writing* as more than just a process. Writing is "a constitutive, invariably social activity." Writing is "inevitably situated, shaped by material places and intellectual spaces." Writing "embodies contingent markers of identity—beliefs and values—which we develop and alter through symbolic activity."

Okay, now talk amongst yourselves.

No fair. This isn't helpful.

Okay, you want instructions. Specific instructions. Okay. Here we go.

1. Go read bell hooks's *Teaching to Transgress*. Yes, really, go to the library, your own bookshelf, your friend's bookshelf, your teacher's bookshelf, the local independently owned bookstore, an online clearinghouse for independent bookstores, wherever and read this book—the whole thing preferably, but at least Chapter 1, "Engaged Pedagogy," Chapter 13, "Eros, Eroticism, and the Pedagogical Process," and Chapter 14, "Ecstasy." No, really, go read hooks. Yes, in the middle of this essay. Really. And when you read this book, don't roll your eyes or argue back or submit to your desire to "critique"; conversely, don't nod your head off your shoulders or underline entire chapters or fall into the comfort of hooks's prose—just listen. Listen. Read and listen. Write about what you heard. Cool. I'll wait.

2. Okay, you should also read Julie Lindquist's "Class Affects, Classroom Affectations: Working through the Paradoxes of Strategic Empathy." It is available online through the National Council of Teachers of English (NCTE) Web site, and

I'm sure your library has a copy if you're not an NCTE member/subscriber. (And if you don't belong to NCTE, we should probably talk about why not—I mean, why do you want to hear me tell you how to do the things in your classroom that my scholarly work theorizes about if you're not interested in being a member of a community of folks who have made teaching and theorizing about writing and rhetoric the central focus of their lives? Really. Yeah, yeah, I know all about the lack of diversity in our discipline and the hegemony of professionalization, but you can't change a community unless you are a part of it—Audre Lorde's "master's tools" argument aside—and you can't learn from a community unless you are a part of it. Period.) So, read Lindquist's essay. Again, stomp on the same urges detailed above. Listen. Write. I'll wait.

3. Yes, you are going back to the library (or to the bookshelf or online) for two things. First, Patricia J. Williams's *The Alchemy of Race and Rights: Diary of a Law Professor*—again, the whole book is stunning but at least read Section IV, "The Incorruptible Simplicity of Being: A String of Crystalline Parables," which contains the famous essay "On Being the Object of Property"—under no circumstances should you just read this one famous essay and ignore the larger frame in which it is situated. Second, find LeAnne Howe's "The Story of American: A Tribalography" (available in *Clearing a Path: Theorizing the Past in Native American Studies*). If you can't find a copy of this book, send me an e-mail. I'll put you in touch with this essay. Really. (It's totally easy to find me using a Web search engine.) Listen. Write. I'll wait—I have some writing of my own to do.

Okay, while I would like to keep this whole "read X" thing going, you might be losing patience with it by now and wanting to talk about what hooks and Lindquist and Williams and Howe and I are trying to say. (Not to mention how irritated the publishers are that I am directing you *outside* of the boundaries of this collection in which they have invested much labor and money in order for you to hold it in your hands. Or how disrespectful to the collection editors it is for me to ask you to step *outside* the text they crafted so carefully—sorry.) And you might be a little irritated with me for having to go *outside* this text and maybe even spend more money just to read a single essay *within* the text—how is that subsuming my desires for the good of the whole? And you're probably thinking how inappropriate it is for me to be so bossy, so authoritarian, so directive as a teacher—how is that student-centered? How is that community-centered? Can't I even practice what I preach?!

Here's the deal, at least as I see it. Teaching is a responsibility, not an opportunity for me to show you how cool I am by pretending to waive the authority that the institution grants me as one of its more privileged minions, not an opportunity for me to pretend not to have the experiences that led the editors of this volume to ask me to compose this piece of alphabetic text, and not an opportunity for me to pretend to a wisdom that I don't believe that I have. The process of teaching is a conversation that takes place at the intersection of a web of communities in which we are situated. You and I share some of those communities, so my goal in the last few paragraphs has been to *show you* how I situate my own teaching, my own understanding of the responsibilities of being a teacher, within a larger community of scholars. This is *use* in its most productive sense—engagement with the alphabetic-print artifacts produced by others in my community in order to produce my own artifact, all of it circumscribed by mutual beliefs and practices that *mean* something and that have the potential to produce more meaning when taken into other communities where other beliefs and practices have currency and value.

Further, teaching is, like reading the writing of others in our community, an opportunity to listen and hear, to enter the conversation that is "pedagogy in our discipline," to answer the call and then respond. To hear the call. To respond. With your peers, your colleagues, talk. Hear the call. Respond. Talk about what you heard in hooks, in Lindquist, in Williams, in Howe, in my essay collected in this volume, in all of the essays collected in this volume, in your students' papers, in your classrooms, in your communities. Think about the confluence of voices. Hear that confluence. Enter it. Engage in it. Participate in it fully.

Remember, too, that race, gender, ethnicity, class, orientation, ableness, etc. are not "topics" to be introduced into the classroom, or "issues" that "come up" in the classroom—they are lived realities that are always already present in the lives of the students who sit in classrooms, in the lives of teachers who teach in those classrooms, in the lives of administrators who make decisions about which students to admit and which teachers to hire, even in the fact that there are classrooms in universities—classrooms built and maintained by laboring bodies, erected on lands gained through the blood of colonization, of slavery, of oppression, of empire.

The buildings that you teach and live and learn in are sunk into a place, a landscape with a history. Honor that history and the people whose lives created it. The students that you teach are people who come from communities that have a history, that have a place. Honor those histories. Even when they intersect in ways that are painful and uncomfortable. Especially then, because learning happens there in those intersections laden with discomfort. *Of course*, each of you and I will create different ways to negotiate the situatedness of our students, and the material consequences of our surroundings. *Of course* we will have different personal stakes and investments in infusing those negotiations with meaning, and in learning to help the community of students in any given classroom negotiate, manage, situate meanings. But that is, after all, the work of rhetoric, of critical engagement, of learning to analyze and manipulate discourse in ways that articulate our selves, our worlds, our lives in relation to one another. (Notice I did not say "others"—a community is made through the relations of people to one another.)

And whatever you may finally say about me, this essay, this class, this textbook, know that I believe rhetorical education to be the work of writing teachers. And I believe that our lives, and the lives of our students, are composed through stories of who we are, who we come from, where we came from, how we came through the mundane and everyday legacies of colonization, settlement, slavery, imperialism, and oppression. And, in the end, I believe all of our accomplishments here in academe do not mean much if our relations do not believe that we were decent and caring and humane to those around us.

How to teach writing? Listen to the people around you, to the places in which you live. Be willing to reorient yourself in relation to each and every one of them. Give them the attention and care that you would want to receive. Honor their histories. Honor their stories. Listen. Think. Learn. Live in the care you give and receive. Teach.

Works Cited

hooks, bell. *Teaching to Transgress: Education as the Practice of Freedom*. New York: Routledge, 1994.

Howe, LeAnne. "The Story of American: a Tribalography." *Clearing a Path: Theorizing the Past in Native American Studies*. Ed. Nancy Shoemaker. New York: Routledge, 2002. 29–50.

Lindquist, Julie. "Class Affects, Classroom Affectations: Working through the Paradoxes of Strategic Empathy." *College English* 67.2 (Nov 2004): 187–209.

Williams, Patricia J. *The Alchemy of Race and Rights: Diary of a Law Professor*. Cambridge: Harvard UP, 1991.

INDEX

Editors

Peter Vandenberg is professor of English and a member of the graduate faculty at DePaul University in Chicago. A former editor of rhetoric and composition's oldest independent journal, *Composition Studies*, he is coeditor, with Paul Heilker, of *Keywords in Composition Studies* (1996). He has published in *College English*, *JAC: Journal of Advanced Composition*, *The Writing Center Journal*, *Writing on the Edge*, and various other journals and edited collections.

Sue Hum is assistant professor of English and a member of the graduate faculty at University of Texas at San Antonio, where she teaches graduate and undergraduate courses in writing. Her research and teaching interests include composition theory and pedagogy, modern rhetorical theory, multicultural and contrastive rhetoric, cultural studies and popular culture, and postcolonial gender theories. Drawing on her experiences as a Malaysian Chinese teaching in American institutions, Hum's recent publications focus on the intersections among identity politics, materiality, and composition theory, appearing in *JAC: Journal of Advanced Composition* and *Readerly/Writerly Texts*. With Kristie Fleckenstein and Linda Calendrillo, Hum is currently coediting an anthology of original essays, titled *Ways of Seeing, Ways of Speaking: The Integration of Rhetoric and Vision in Constructing the Real*, that explores the nexus of imagery and discourse in four areas of material rhetorics: race/ethnicity, gender, science, and technology. Since 1994, Hum has taught many graduate and undergraduate courses that explore alternative rhetorics, including Cultural Studies, Language and Its Use, Popular Culture: Writing about Race and Gender, and Communication Theories.

Jennifer Clary-Lemon holds a master's degree in writing from DePaul University and is currently a PhD candidate and teaching associate at Arizona State University. She is assistant editor of the journal *Writing Program Administration*, coeditor of *Electronic Guides to Composition: A Guide for Teaching Argument*, and coauthor of an essay in the *Handbook of Writing Research*. Her scholarly interests include writing and positionality, theories of identity, rhetorical activism, and disciplinarity.

Pedagogical Insights Contributors

Ellen Cushman is associate professor at Michigan State University currently researching Western Cherokee language and identity as these unfold at the intersection of new media, critical pedagogy, and community literacies. She has recently published shockwave essays in *Computers and Composition Online* and *Kairos*, and print essays in edited collections (*The Realm of Rhetoric, Beyond English, Inc*, and *Composition Studies in the New Millennium*). She teaches community literacy-based multimedia writing and English education courses, as well as graduate courses for the Critical Studies in Language and Pedagogy Program and Rhetoric and Writing Program.

Claude Hurlbert is professor of English at Indiana University of Pennsylvania, where he teaches in the Graduate Program in Composition and Teachers of English to Speakers of Other Languages. He has cowritten *Letters for the Living: Teaching Writing in a Violent Age* and coedited *Composition and Resistance* with Michael Blitz. He has also coedited *Beyond English, Inc.: Curricular Reform for a Global Economy* and *Social Issues in the English Classroom*. In addition, he has written or cowritten articles for *Stories from the Center*, *Changing Classroom Practices*, *Cultural Studies in the English Classroom*, *Practicing Theory*, *Sharing Pedagogies*, *Works and Days*, *Pre/Text*, *Writing on the Edge*, *Composition Studies*, *Composition Forum*, *English Leadership Quarterly*, and *The Writing Instructor*.

Karen Kopelson is assistant professor of English at the University of Louisville, where she teaches undergraduate courses in writing, literature, and critical theory and graduate courses in composition theory, critical theories, and the teaching of writing. She has published in *College English*, *College Composition and Communication*, and *JAC*.

Nancy Myers is associate professor of English at the University of North Carolina at Greensboro (UNCG) where she teaches composition, linguistics, and the history of rhetoric. She received the UNCG Alumni Teaching Excellence Award in 2002. Along with Gary Tate and Edward P. J. Corbett, she is an editor of the third and fourth editions of *The Writing Teacher's Sourcebook*. In addition to her other articles, she most recently published "Cicero's (S)Trumpet: Roman Women and the Second Philippic" in *Rhetoric Review* (2003) and has an essay forthcoming in *The Locations of Composition*.

Derek Owens is the author of *Resisting Writings (and the Boundaries of Composition)* and *Composition and Sustainability: Teaching for a Threatened Generation*. Associate professor and director of the Writing Center at St. John's University in Queens, New York, he lives with his wife Teresa and son Ryan on Long Island.

Malea Powell is a mixed-blood of Indiana Miami, Eastern Shawnee, and European American ancestry. She is associate professor of writing, rhetoric, and American culture at Michigan State University where she is a faculty member in the Writing & Rhetoric program and the American Indian Studies program. Her current research focuses on the relationship between the rhetorics of survivance used by nineteenth-century American Indian intellectuals and contemporary indigenous material cultural production, and she has published essays in *College Composition and Communication*, *Paradoxa*, *Race, Rhetoric & Composition*, *AltDis*, and other essay collections. She is currently editor of *SAIL: Studies in American Indian Literatures*, a quarterly journal devoted to the study of American Indian writing, and is editor of the forthcoming *Of Color: Native American Literatures*.

Mary Jo Reiff is associate professor of English and the director of composition at the University of Tennessee, where she teaches courses in rhetoric, writing, and composition theory and pedagogy. She has published in the areas of audience, including an article in *JAC* and a recently published book, *Approaches to Audience: An Overview of the Major Perspectives* (2004), and in rhetorical genre theory, with a forthcoming reference guide (edited by Charles Bazerman) titled *Genre: A Historical, Theoretical, and Pedagogical Introduction* (with Anis Bawarshi) and a textbook (with Amy Devitt and Anis Bawarshi) titled *Scenes of Writing: Strategies for Composing with Genres* (2004). Her scholarly interviews and work on audience, genre, critical ethnography, and writing in the disciplines has appeared in journals such as *College English, Issues in Writing, The WAC Journal, Composition Forum,* and *Writing on the Edge*. She is currently at work on a project on the rhetoric of public petitions.

This book was typeset in Sabon by Electronic Imaging.
Typefaces used on the cover were Champion HTF Lightweight
and ITC Officina Serif.
The book was printed on 50-lb. Williamsburg Smooth Offset paper
by Versa Press, Inc.